Playing Games
in
School

Video Games and Simulations for
Primary and Secondary Education

Edited by **Atsusi "2c" Hirumi**

International Society for Technology in Education
EUGENE, OREGON • WASHINGTON, DC

Playing Games in School

Video Games and Simulations for Primary and Secondary Education

Edited by Atsusi "2c" Hirumi

© 2010 International Society for Technology in Education

Director of Book Publishing: *Courtney Burkholder*
Acquisitions Editor: *Jeff V. Bolkan*
Production Editors: *Lynda Gansel, Tina Wells*
Production Coordinator: *Rachel Williams*
Graphic Designer: *Signe Landin*
Copy Editors: *Kathy Hamman, Beth Ina*
Proofreader: *Nancy Olson*
Indexer: *Seth Maislin, Potomac Indexing*
Cover Design: *Signe Landin*
Book Design and Production: *Kim McGovern*

Library of Congress Cataloging-in-Publication Data

Playing games in schools : video games and simulations for primary and secondary classroom instruction / edited by Atsusi Hirumi. — 1st ed.
    p. cm.
 Includes bibliographical references and index.
 ISBN 978-1-56484-271-8 (pbk.)
 1. Simulation games in education. 2. Video games and children. 3. Video games and teenagers. 4. Computer-assisted instruction. I. Hirumi, Atsusi.
 LB1029.S53P53 2010
 371.39'7—dc22

2010035216

First Edition
ISBN: 978-1-56484-271-8
Printed in the United States of America

Cover image: ©istockphoto.com/Aleksandar Velasevic
ISTE® is a registered trademark of the International Society for Technology in Education.

About ISTE

The International Society for Technology in Education (ISTE) is the trusted source for professional development, knowledge generation, advocacy, and leadership for innovation. ISTE is the premier membership association for educators and education leaders engaged in improving teaching and learning by advancing the effective use of technology in PK–12 and teacher education.

Home of the National Educational Technology Standards (NETS) and ISTE's annual conference and exposition (formerly known as NECC), ISTE represents more than 100,000 professionals worldwide. We support our members with information, networking opportunities, and guidance as they face the challenge of transforming education. To find out more about these and other ISTE initiatives, visit our website at www.iste.org.

As part of our mission, ISTE Book Publishing works with experienced educators to develop and produce practical resources for classroom teachers, teacher educators, and technology leaders. Every manuscript we select for publication is carefully peer-reviewed and professionally edited. We value your feedback on this book and other ISTE products. E-mail us at books@iste.org.

Contact Us

Washington, DC, Office:
1710 Rhode Island Ave. NW, Suite 900, Washington, DC 20036-3132
Eugene, Oregon, Office:
180 West 8th Ave., Suite 300, Eugene, OR 97401-2916

Order Desk: 1.800.336.5191
Order Fax: 1.541.302.3778
Customer Service: orders@iste.org
Book Publishing: books@iste.org
Book Sales and Marketing: booksmarketing@iste.org
Web: www.iste.org

About the Editor and Authors

Editor and contributor **Atsusi "2c" Hirumi** is an associate professor and co-chair of the Instructional Technology program at the University of Central Florida (UCF), Orlando. Born in New York, Hirumi spent most of his formative years in Nairobi, Kenya. He earned a bachelor's degree in science education at Purdue University, a master's degree in educational technology at San Diego State University, and a doctorate in instructional systems at Florida State University. He earned tenure and promotion to associate professor at the University of Houston–Clear Lake (UHCL) before moving to the University of Central Florida in 2003. Since 1995, Hirumi has centered his teaching, research, and service on the design of alternative e-learning environments. At UHCL and UCF, he led efforts to transform entire certificate and master's degree programs in instructional technology for totally online and hybrid course delivery and has worked with more than 10 universities, community colleges, school districts, and medical centers across the U.S. and in Mexico to establish online training programs, courses, and degree programs.

For the past four years, Hirumi has focused his research on story and game-based approaches to teaching and learning as an extension of his research agenda. He is examining the neurobiological foundations of human learning and conducting research to guide the design of instructional games and help explain game-based learning. Hirumi has published many refereed journal articles and seven book chapters and has made more than 100 presentations at international, national, and state conferences on topics related to his research. He is working on two forthcoming books, one on the use of games for learning and one on the design of alternative e-learning environments. Recent awards include the Texas Distance Learning Association (TxDLA) award for Commitment to Excellence and Innovation, the WebCT Exemplary Online Course Award, the University of Houston–Clear Lake Star Faculty Award, the Phi Delta Kappa Outstanding Practitioner Award, the Enron Award for Innovation, and an award for excellence for an electronic performance support system designed to help faculty develop and deliver interactive television courses.

Chapter Authors

Tom Atkinson has a PhD in educational leadership and research from Louisiana State University, Baton Rouge. With more than 30 years in higher education, he specializes in designing, producing, delivering, and evaluating interactive instruction. Atkinson teaches Instructional Technology at the University of Central Florida, where his research focuses on game design, virtual worlds, and mobile learning.

Michael Barbour is an assistant professor of Instructional Technology at Wayne State University in Michigan. He received his PhD from the University of Georgia, and prior to his doctoral studies was a secondary social studies teacher in Newfoundland and Labrador, Canada. His research interest focuses on the use of online learning at the K–12 level as a way to provide equitable opportunities to rural students.

Anthony K. Betrus is associate professor and chair of the Department of Information and Communication Technology at the State University of New York at Potsdam. He teaches classes in educational technology, media development, and simulations and games. He has been teaching at the collegiate level since 1995, when he taught his first class on game development at Indiana University. Betrus has taught at least one Simulations and Games class each year since then. His primary research interest is the intersection of educational technology and simulations and games, specifically, finding better ways to use simulations and games to enhance and improve learning.

J.V. (Jeff) Bolkan is acquisitions editor for ISTE's book publishing group. For the past decade, he has been deeply involved with the organization's flagship magazine, *Learning & Leading with Technology (L&L)*, formerly as a senior editor and now as a product reviewer. He has written about technology for more than 20 years, and hundreds of his articles have been published in magazines, journals, and books on the topics of education, computer gaming, digital video, geospatial systems, and computer-aided drafting. He lives in Springfield, Oregon, when he isn't visiting his favorite online role-playing environments.

Luca Botturi holds a PhD in communication sciences and instructional design from the Università della Svizzera italiana in Lugano, Switzerland. He has worked as a researcher and practitioner in Italy, Switzerland, Canada, Spain, and the United States. He is an instructional designer and researcher in Lugano and online instructor at the Universitat Oberta de Catalunya, Spain. Botturi's research interests focus on design and games. He is the founder of seed, a nonprofit organization that promotes the development of a culture of educational technologies for international development and nonprofit education. He is also a freelance game designer.

Joe W. Burden Jr. is assistant professor in the Sports and Fitness Program of the Department of Child, Family, and Community Sciences in the College of Education at the University of Central Florida. Burden has a PhD in pedagogy from Louisiana State University. His research interests focus on the social, psychological, and physiological dimensions of race and ethnicity and its implications for teaching and learning in sports and physical education. He is also interested in research on understanding how instructional technologies facilitate aspects of human movement. He may be reached at jburden@mail.ucf.edu.

Edward Dieterle, EdD, is an education researcher in SRI International's Center for Technology in Learning, where he studies the psychosocial and policy aspects of learning and teaching with current and emerging technologies, using quantitative and qualitative methods. He studies media-based learning styles made possible by virtual worlds and augmented realities and investigates the roles of science, technology, engineering, and mathematics in secondary school reform. He has worked as a high school science teacher in Prince George's County, Maryland; as an instructor at Johns Hopkins University and Trinity College; and as a researcher on Harvard University's River City Project. Dieterle served on the National Academy of Sciences Committee on Improving Learning with Information Technology and as an advisory board member of Microsoft's Partners in Learning National Projects. He holds a doctorate in learning and teaching from Harvard University, a master's degree in technology for educators from Johns Hopkins University, and a bachelor's degree in chemistry from Virginia Polytechnic and State University. Dieterle, his wife Jenny, and their two sons reside in Washington, D.C.

Peter J. Fadde is associate professor of instructional design and instructional technology in the College of Education and Human Services at Southern Illinois University, Carbondale. He is co-coordinator, with Sebastian Loh, of the Collaboratory for Interactive Learning Research. Fadde teaches graduate courses in Instructional Games and Simulations, Learning Models for Instruction, eLearning, Multimedia for Learning, Advanced Instructional Design, and Instructional Video. His research interests include training of expertise and expert performance, simulation-based training, and video in education and training. In an earlier life, Fadde was an album rock DJ and video coordinator for a major college football team. He may be reached through his website, http://web.coehs.siu.edu/units/ci/faculty/pfadde/.

James Gentry is assistant professor in the Department of Curriculum and Instruction of the College of Education at Tarleton State University in Stephenville, Texas. Prior to teaching at the university level, he served as a special education teacher of students in Grades 2–8, social studies middle school teacher, middle school technology instructor, and assistant principal of middle school curriculum and instruction in diverse public schools in East Texas. Gentry's research has focused on assistive technology's impacts on students with limited English proficiency, learning disabilities, and/or autism. Additionally, he has conducted several studies that involved college students' attitudes toward reading and the effects of their attitudes on reading comprehension and vocabulary development. He can be reached at gentry@tarleton.edu.

Ingrid Graves is assistant professor in the Department of Curriculum and Instruction in the College of Education at Tarleton State University. Prior to teaching elementary literacy and assessment courses at the university level, she taught third through fifth grade reading in public schools. Graves conducts her research primarily in the elementary setting to study nontraditional assessment measures, student marginalization, collaborative learning, differentiated instruction, and effective instructional practices for teachers' professional development. She can be reached at graves@tarleton.edu.

Rick Hall is a 15-year veteran of the gaming industry with experience as a producer, studio head, programmer, and game designer. He has worked on role-playing games, adventure games, real-time strategy games, fighting games; and flight, sports, and fishing simulations. He has worked on the following platforms: online, personal computer, PlayStation, PlayStation2 (PS2), Nintendo's third home game video console (N64), Nintendo DS (Nintendo's dual-screen handheld game console), and Sony PSP (Sony's PlayStation Portable handheld game console). Hall started his career at Paragon Software, a studio that eventually became the core development group for Take 2's initial 1994 startup. After leaving Take 2, he joined EA's Origin studio in Austin, Texas, where for five years he served as a live producer on Ultima Online and later as executive producer on Ultima X Odyssey. Hall joined EA's Tiburon studio in Orlando, Florida, where he was a senior producer on the Madden Football handheld products. In 2006, he joined the faculty at the University of Central Florida, where he teaches game design in the Florida Interactive Entertainment Academy master's degree program. Hall is also the creative director at 360Ed, a company that specializes in creating educational games.

Robert T. Hays received a PhD in general experimental psychology from Virginia Commonwealth University. He serves as adjunct professor in the Education, Research, Technology and Leadership Department of the University of Central Florida. For more than 30 years, Hays worked for the federal government as a research psychologist. He conducted research and development in many areas of instruction and training, including advanced distributed training, electronic classrooms, virtual reality, intelligent pedagogical agents, instructional gaming, and simulation-based training. Hays has written more than 40 journal articles, technical reports, books, and book chapters. His latest books are *The Science of Learning: A Systems Theory Perspective* (2006) and *Quality Instruction: Building and Evaluating Computer-Delivered Courseware* (2008).

Michael C. Hynes is professor emeritus in the College of Education at the University of Central Florida and was named a Pegasus Professor in 2005, an award that recognizes outstanding teaching, research, and service. During his tenure as a faculty member, he was founding director of the Lockheed Martin/UCF Academy for Mathematics and Science. He now serves as chair of the Department of Teaching and Learning Principles and has been named co-director of the new University of Central Florida School of Teaching, Learning and Leadership. His areas of research and development involve mathematics education, the use of technology in teacher education, and the use of mixed reality simulation in teacher education.

Jeffrey Kaplan is associate professor in the Department of Teaching and Learning Principles of the College of Education at the University of Central Florida, Orlando. He has written extensively on adolescent literacy and reflective practice, serving as general editor of the volume *Using Literature to Help Troubled Teenagers Cope with Identity Issues* (1999) and as editor of the series *Teen Life Around the World* (2004). He has published numerous refereed articles on teaching and learning in journals that include *Theory into Practice, Studying Teacher Education, English Journal*, and *ALAN Review*. He holds bachelor's and master's degrees in theatre from the State University of New York and a doctorate in curriculum and instruction from the University of Florida.

Mansureh Kebritchi is a faculty member at the Richard W. Riley College of Education and Leadership, Walden University, an online university based in Minneapolis. She holds a master's degree in curriculum, teaching, and learning from the University of Toronto and a PhD in instructional technology from the University of Central Florida. She is interested in studying innovative ways of teaching and learning in electronic environments. Kebritchi has conducted research on educational computer games, including examining the pedagogical foundations of games, the factors affecting adoption of games in school settings, and the effect of mathematics games on learners' achievement and motivation levels. The results of her research have been published in international journals and as conference papers.

Matthew Laurence is obsessed with games of all kinds. His career is in the video gaming industry, where he is lead designer at 360Ed, an educational game company based in Orlando, Florida. To prepare himself for this path, he acquired a master's degree in interactive entertainment from the Florida Interactive Entertainment Academy at the University of Central Florida. Laurence earned a bachelor of arts degree in psychology from New College of Florida and has found this area of expertise to be surprisingly useful for game design. He doesn't have a website for you to avoid visiting or a blog you'll never read, but if you have further questions for him, feel free to send an e-mail to mlaurence@360ed.com and he'd be happy to answer them.

Marc Prensky is an internationally acclaimed thought leader, speaker, writer, consultant, and game designer in the critical areas of education and learning. He is the author of *Digital Game-Based Learning* (2001) and *Don't Bother Me Mom—I'm Learning* (2006), and more than 50 essays on learning. Prensky is the founder and chief executive officer of Games2train, a game-based learning company, whose clients include IBM, Bank of America, Pfizer, the U.S. Department of Defense, and the LA and Florida Virtual Schools. He holds a master's degree in business administration from Harvard University and a master's degree in teaching from Yale University. More of his writings can be found at www.marcprensky.com/writing. Prensky can be contacted at marc@games2train.com.

Dawn Rauscher is an instructor at Flathead Valley Community College in Kalispell, Montana. She has an MEd in Instructional Technology from the University of Georgia. Currently, she teaches undergraduate courses in instructional technology and web design. The most fulfilling part of her job is challenging her students to find new ways to incorporate technology into the classroom.

Lloyd Rieber is professor and program coordinator of instructional design and development in the Department of Educational Psychology and Instructional Technology of the College of Education at the University of Georgia. He has a PhD in curriculum and instruction from The Pennsylvania State University and is a former classroom teacher. His most recent research is about the integration of computer-based microworlds, simulations, and games into instruction, using play theory as the theoretical framework.

Melinda Stevison is an educator whose career has spanned the K–12 and military arenas. A former public high school world history and television production teacher, Stevison's research interests have included the use of digital video games within adolescent education, teaching presence among K–12 educators enrolled in online professional development, digital archiving among primary school gifted students, and quality of statistical reporting in doctoral dissertations. She is an instructional systems specialist for the U.S. Department of Defense, designing and procuring training systems for various branches of the military. Stevison holds a master's degree in curriculum and instruction and a PhD in instructional technology from the University of Central Florida. She and her husband, Jack, reside in Central Florida.

Gretchen Thomas is a former middle school science teacher who teaches undergraduate courses in instructional technology at the University of Georgia. She has an EdS in Instructional Technology from the University of Georgia. While her work focuses on enhancing learning environments through technology, her real interest lies in the resources, people, and places that help people learn.

William R. Watson is assistant professor in the Educational Technology Program in the Department of Curriculum and Instruction at Purdue University and the director of the Purdue Center for Serious Games and Learning in Virtual Environments. He has a PhD in education from Indiana University. Watson's research interests focus on advanced technologies for information-age instruction, including the design, implementation, and evaluation of educational video games. He may be reached at brwatson@purdue.edu.

Yadi Ziaeehezarjeribi is a researcher in the Department of Instructional Systems Technology of the School of Education at Indiana University and a co-researcher in IU's Virtual Xperience Lab. He is also an instructional designer at Educational Outreach at Black Hills State University, South Dakota. While his research is mainly conducted in laboratory environments, he has also provided technology consultation for business and industrial training for over 15 years. His research interests lie with the effective integration of technology into K–16 classrooms. He may be reached at yadi@indiana.edu.

Contents

Section III
Planning to Play Games

Introduction

Atsusi "2c" Hirumi

The last time you asked a kid, "How was school today?" what was his or her response? More often than not when I asked my kids that question, I would get a groan or a blank stare, or if they were feeling particularly articulate that day, they would say, "BOOORRRING" or "It S*CK*D!" What was wrong? Was something wrong with me? Was I an overbearing parent who did not understand how to communicate with his own children? Was something wrong with my kids? Were they bad students who didn't care about getting an education? Were they rebelling against the establishment? Was it the fault of the particular school they were attending or just a few poor teachers? At times, I probably overreacted to their negative remarks, or my children may not have been trying hard enough, or particular teachers were mediocre. However, for the most part, I'm afraid many students' petulant, turned-off feelings about school are more the norm than the exception.

In many ways, my children, Shane and Savannah, inspired this book. Far too often, they would come home from school grumpy, unhappy, and totally unmotivated to do their homework. Rarely did they come home excited about what they were learning or what they had done at school. As a parent and an educator, I was concerned about their negative feelings toward school. My kids were associating school with boredom, and because they were supposed to learn in school, they associated learning with boredom. That scared me. I believe that one of the fundamental purposes of schools should be to nurture a love of learning within students.

Having been a high school biology teacher and now a university professor, I know how hard it can be to inspire today's youth. With limited time and resources, how can we compete with Hollywood, reality TV, Nintendo, and YouTube for our students' time and attention? While I'm sure many educators have figured out ways to inspire students and motivate them to learn, I'm afraid just as many or even more have not. To add to my concern, I've met many educators over the past five years as I've been studying game-based learning, who believe that learning is "serious business" and should not necessarily be fun. Entertainment is frivolous, they say, and should not be a part of school. While I agree that training and education should be taken seriously, I wonder what happened to these serious people when they were children and teenagers. As an educator, I take my work and my students' learning very seriously, yet we also have fun. So, what can educators do to engage learners and foster a love of learning? One possible answer … play games in school!

Why Read This Book?

I requested chapters from various experts and edited this book with three basic purposes in mind. First, I wanted to help educators, including teachers, administrators, and other educational policy makers, make informed decisions about when to play games in school and to create a vision of how games may be played in schools to facilitate learning. For many, playing video games in school may be a foreign concept. Thus, I felt it important to help educators paint their own pictures of how games may be played to help students learn in school. Second, I wanted to help educators plan for and take concrete steps toward achieving their vision by helping them locate, select, and integrate games into class work in meaningful, effective ways. And third, I wanted to help educators develop a deep and a broad understanding of some of the nuances associated with playing games in school and game-based learning in general.

How Is This Book Organized?

To achieve these three purposes, I divided the book into four sections. Section I addresses the fundamental question, "Why Play Games?" For those who may not have formed opinions on whether to play games in school, I tried to answer the fundamental question from four different perspectives. In Chapter 1, Marc Prensky answers the question based on his own observations and his interpretation of key societal trends and issues, focusing on how today's youth differ significantly from prior generations. In Chapter 2, Anthony Betrus and Luca Botturi answer the question from a historical and a psychological perspective, describing how games have been played over time for educational purposes and relating fundamental attributes of games to key principles and theories of human learning. In Chapter 3, I worked with Tom Atkinson to examine recent advances in neuroscience to answer the basic question "why play games?" from a physiological perspective. In Chapter 4, Jeff Bolkan notes educational reasons for playing games, describing how gameplay can meet the National Educational Technology Standards for Students (NETS•S) and for Teachers (NETS•T).

Section II concentrates on the use and availability of games in the four core subject areas (math, science, language arts, and social studies) and in physical education. In Chapter 5, Edward Dieterle provides recommendations, best practices, and examples of high-quality science video games. He also presents an interesting, insightful case study that illustrates how gameplay can bring about positive changes in curricular content, relationships among students and teachers, and assessment practices and can enhance the knowledge and skills of teachers. In Chapter 6, Mansureh Kebritchi and Michael Hynes examine past and present trends in math education and discuss how gameplay addresses current trends. They review games on the market for use in math education, note barriers to gameplay, and suggest ways to overcome the barriers. For Chapter 7, Melinda Stevison and Jeff Kaplan examine how games may be played in schools to ease the move from teacher-directed to learner-centered instructional methods in language arts education. They also review a number of games for language arts and discuss how they may be played to develop literacy. For Chapter 8, William Watson presents a persuasive argument for focusing on citizenship in social studies education. He identifies available games and ties them to national standards for social studies and citizenship education. In Chapter 9, Joe Burden explores the emerging use of exergames for health and fitness. He examines a variety of exergames, reviews related research, and relates their use to national standards for high-quality K–12 physical education.

In Section III on planning and playing games, chapters from multiple perspectives focus on how to select and integrate games into schools to facilitate student learning. Section III begins with my own views on how to integrate games into classroom instruction. In Chapter 10, I relate the structure and function of courses to the structure and function of games and suggest the use of instructional strategies that are rooted in theories on human learning and instructional design. In Chapter 11, Robert Hays reviews empirical studies on the effectiveness of video games in education and presents guidelines for selecting, planning, playing, and evaluating gameplay in schools based on the research. For Chapter 12, Yadi Ziaeehezarjeribi, Ingrid Graves, and James Gentry note that research on the effectiveness of games in education is limited. They examine several case studies on the use of games in schools to establish criteria for selecting and repurposing commercial off-the-shelf (COTS) games for use in schools to enhance learning. In Chapter 13, Peter Fadde examines a small, yet important subset of gameplay in schools that combines the proven instructional strategy of drill-and-practice with arcade-style gameplay to expedite learning. He helps teachers locate appropriate drill-and-practice games, evaluate them in terms of drill structure and gameplay, and integrate them into regular classroom activities.

Section IV captures alternative perspectives on games and playing games in school that are not directly addressed in Sections I–III. In Chapter 14, Michael Barbour, Gretchen Thomas, Dawn Rauscher, and Lloyd Rieber remind us of the barriers that prevent educators from encouraging students to play video games in schools, ranging from cost and infrastructure, to perceived violence, to the current political climate. The authors show us how we can engage students and reap the benefits of game-based learning by creating simple Microsoft PowerPoint games. Botturi takes the idea of enhancing learning without actually playing video games one step further in Chapter 15. He discusses how we can motivate learners by applying the "nuts and bolts" of games to incorporate game-based learning into classrooms without computers. In Chapter 16, Rick Hall distinguishes three types of online games—basic, multiplayer, and massively multiplayer—and talks about how online gameplay can improve the benefits of games in terms of student engagement, collaboration, teacher interaction, and a variety of logistical advantages. In Chapter 17, Atkinson presents yet another perspective, characterizing the use of virtual worlds and illustrating how a simple, online, immersive environment may be much more than just another video game. Finally, in Chapter 18, Matthew Laurence discusses the current state and potential future of the video game industry in education.

Are Games *the* Answer?

As you read this book, it's important to keep in mind that games are not *the* answer for overcoming the challenges facing education. In fact, I believe video games, like many other educational interventions, are a fad that will come and go within a relatively short period of time. I know a number of high-level game developers who are tired of producing first person shooter and fighting games and are already thinking about and creating the next generation of entertainment. Who really knows what the next 5–10 years will bring, particularly in terms of technology?

However, I do believe that the principles of interactive entertainment will transcend time and are essential keys to motivating and enhancing learning now and in the future. We must learn from our counterparts in entertainment and the video game industry to figure out what makes their creations so fun and entertaining that millions of people around the world spend hundreds and even thousands of dollars and many, many hours of their free time fully engaged with their methods and materials. In fact, the importance of interactive entertainment is why I want to remind readers that it is not necessarily video games that matter, but the principles of interactive entertainment that can make game-based learning—as well as conventional, distance, and blended learning—fun and engaging. Isn't the quality of learning what really matters?

Section I
Why Play Games?

1

Educating the Millennial Generation

Marc Prensky

All games are educational.

—Will Wright

THIS CHAPTER OFFERS A RATIONALE for why computer and video games can be helpful tools for educating 21st-century students. The pervasive use of digital technology, resulting changes in students, and the enormous progress that games have made over the last 30 years have renewed interest in the use of video games to enhance learning in K–12 settings. This chapter examines the rapid changes in our environment and in our children, compares them to the relatively slow changes in our schools, and illustrates how complex games, employing specific rules of engagement, have emerged as powerful tools for changing schools and reaching and teaching students.

Playing video and other electronic games to learn—especially to learn well and deeply—is not an obvious academic approach. Therefore, some background may be required to understand why games may, in fact, be used as appropriate ways to help educate our children at the beginning of the 21st century.

While many agree that our ability to prepare our children well for the future has been declining, there is no consensus on the reason or reasons for this. Teachers complain that their students pay less and less attention; students complain that their teachers are boring them. Critics blame the testing, the administration, the curriculum, and the teaching methods. Solutions are proposed ranging from vouchers, to smaller schools, to charter schools, to more qualified teachers, to more technology; yet again, there is no consensus.

The problem is most acute for our middle students: those neither in the top 10%, who will almost certainly do well in spite of what we do or don't do, nor at the bottom, where special education cares for their needs individually. We really have little idea of *what* and especially *how* to reach and teach this middle group, and this is not just an American phenomenon. Students around the world, in every developed country that tries, as America does, to educate all its children are complaining and struggling.

Video Games as a Solution?

Educational computer and video games have recently emerged as a potential solution. The first book on this subject, my own *Digital Games-Based Learning*, was published in 2001. Since then, numerous books have been published, and a serious games movement has emerged, which is daily gaining advocates. In 2001, I was able to cite roughly 50 games for learning in a variety of areas and subjects. By 2005, it was possible to find more than 500 games. At the rate these games are now being created, I would guess that one will be able to find several thousand of them by 2010. This book will discuss a number of these games and the reasons for their success.

Games alone, of course, certainly will not solve all our current education problems. But can they help? Can they be used as teaching tools to help reach and teach the currently unreached and untaught? Almost certainly.

Making the Case

To make the case for why video and other electronic games can and should be used as teaching tools in our schools—and elsewhere, such as in home schooling and in the myriad forms of after-school learning activities—we need to examine four evolving and interrelated trends:

1. The incredibly rapid technological changes that are taking place in all our lives—and especially in our children's lives—as we begin the 21st century and the expectations of where these changes will lead

2. The changes that are taking place in our students, especially in their intellectual readiness, their technical fluency, and their attitudes (which are, to a large extent, a result of number 1 in this list)

3. The way our schools have reacted to these changes, including what schools have done to accommodate 21st-century learners—actually very little—and what needs to be done in order to help our kids learn what they need to succeed in the future

4. The enormous evolution that has taken place over the last 30 years—largely unremarked until recently by educators and other adults—in the phenomenon known as "games"

As these four strands come together, they define the opportunities that electronic games hold for our kids' education. We will examine each one in turn and then discuss the opportunities that games offer to educators.

Our Changing Technological Environment

Perhaps the hallmark of the developed world in the early 21st century is extremely rapid technological change. Already, in the first years of this fledgling century, a great many people in developed countries have radically changed the way they phone, bank, shop, make political contributions, take photos, plan trips, and do many other daily tasks. You have likely experienced many of these changes, perhaps without even stopping to notice them.

Incredibly Rapid Technological Change …

The younger generation, however, is the age group most affected by these changes. They have experienced from birth, with the first flash of the digital camera or video and possibly even earlier (with digital ultrasound, monitors, and other digital medical devices), the power of digital technology. Many of these kids grow up totally surrounded in their homes by these technologies ("I never lived in a house without a computer," says one). While many adults experience the technologies in a more limited or secondhand way, today's youth are "digital kids." Unlike many of their parents and teachers, they are cognizant of the myriad digital technologies around them—technologies they can control and customize to fit their own lives and styles. They all use whatever they can, coveting and waiting for the rest. Digital music players are ubiquitous among young people in most developed countries; most of them have also played some form of digital games. Most have, at some point, been on the Internet, and a great many have their own cell phones. In some inchoate and typically unexpressed way, these "millennials"—or, as I prefer to call them, "Digital Natives"—understand that this technology is their birthright as the first generation to grow up in the digital world.

… Leads to Changes in Attitudes …

These young people are different in numerous important ways from their parents and teachers—ways I will discuss in more detail later in this chapter. To start, it is important to remember this: What distinguishes these "Digital Natives" from their "Digital Immigrant" elders is not so much what they know about computers and things digital. Although most know more than their parents or teachers, the amount of specific knowledge varies greatly among them. Rather, the common and distinguishing factor is their attitude and comfort level: they see digital technology as a friend and a support—an integral part of their lives. Technology is a concept they don't have to struggle with but take for granted. From their perspective, if you have a cell phone, why wouldn't you use it wherever you can, especially in school?

… And a Growing Number of New Capabilities: Facebook and YouTube and More—Oh My!

As the Internet has quickly matured, many adults have been taken by surprise by the incredibly fast growth of socially created sites like Wikipedia, by the speed of students' adoption of social networking sites like Facebook, and especially by the exponential growth of YouTube, despite what some adults see as its cheap, unprofessional, user-created videos.

All of these new capabilities and more, including virtual worlds like Second Life, have ushered in a new era of online connectivity and collaboration. While still in its infancy, this creative, connected gameplay of virtual worlds is becoming more and more sophisticated, not just every year but every month and almost every day!

What's Coming

In the very near future because of digital technology, we will all—youth and adults alike—see many more life-altering changes from technological advances. These will almost certainly include such developments as our cell phones taking the place of cash and credit cards, diseases being diagnosed and cured inside our bodies by nanobots, materials changing their properties and color on demand, machines responding directly to our thoughts, personal virtual worlds viewable through our contact lenses, and a great many other technologies. Most of these are already here and being tested in labs.

In fact, if technology continues to develop at its current pace of doubling in power every year—and most scientists see nothing to prevent this—our students of today will be living with and using, in the middle of their working lives, that is, within 40 years, technology over 1 trillion times more powerful than what we have today. Most scientists agree that as a result of a combination of Moore's law, storage gains, and throughput gains, technology is currently doubling in power every year, on average—although some, like Ray Kurzweil, think it is going even faster, at a rate of 2^{30} per year, which equals approximately one billion. And we are already working at the atomic level!

Today's tremendous, exponentially increasing rate of change—and especially its implications in terms of changing beliefs and behaviors—is often very hard to accept for adults who, despite the changes noted earlier, grew up living their entire lives in roughly the same way: living in the same houses, driving similar cars, and working in pretty much the same workplaces and environments.

In contrast, the increased speed of change is being eagerly greeted by our children, who have been "born to the idea of rapid change" (Griffith, 1995, p. 137). What seems today like far-off science fiction will soon become our kids' reality, just as today we routinely use things, such as flying machines, that seemed impossible to our forebears. The difference is that these new, immense changes will come much more quickly for our children than they did for us—in times measured in months, and years, rather than in decades, scores of years, or centuries.

How can we prepare our children for such a different, fast changing world? As we will see in this book, electronic games can—and almost certainly will—provide an important piece of this answer.

Our Changing Children and Students

Now let us look more closely at our 21st century children. Obviously, young people haven't changed in *all* ways. Although they have evolved somewhat with better medicine and nutrition, kids' physical and psychological development probably remains relatively close to what most of us remember. But our young peoples' experiences and intellectual development have changed radically.

Digital Natives

Today's young people grow up immersed in a digital world. They are, metaphorically, "Digital Natives"—native speakers of the digital tongue (Prensky, 2001, online). This, I think, is true for all our kids, even those who may have less access to the technology through personal ownership. They all are aware of the technology, and, with few exceptions, want more and more of it. They are good at sharing it and teaching each other about it. As I pointed out earlier, they are "natives" not in the sense of having it all or of magically knowing how everything works at birth, but rather, in their attitudes toward technology: wanting to get their hands on the latest and greatest and to use it with the confidence that they can always figure it out.

An Emerging Online Life

And, quickly, the Digital Natives have evolved and continue to evolve. They live parallel "online lives" with behavior that is very different from and often puzzling or frightening to the generations that came before. They communicate via texting and instant messaging (IM), and "E-mail," they say, "is for old people." They share via blogs, Facebook, MySpace, and wikis. They exchange music and other things with peer-to-peer software, such as Bit Torrent. They buy and sell on eBay and Craigslist. They learn from Wikipedia and YouTube. They meet in online places, such as multiplayer games, and multiuser virtual environments, such as Second Life. They coordinate, collect, evaluate, create, search, analyze, report, program, socialize, transgress, and a large part of the time basically grow up online.

And one of their biggest pastimes is electronic gaming. According to a 2008 Pew report, "Fully 97% of [U. S.] teens ages 12–17 play computer, web, portable, or console [electronic] games" (Lenhart et al., 2008, p. i). In fact, by the time the average American boy or girl is 21, he or she will have played 5,000–10,000 hours of games versus a maximum of 5,000 hours of reading. That our kids like to do this to such a degree is one important factor that leads us to think about games in learning. As we shall soon see, it is far from the only factor.

"New" Students

Things have changed so much for our kids along the "intellectual and knowledge" dimension, that we have, I think, reached the point where our students are no longer the ones that our systems were designed for and that our teachers were trained to teach. Unlike in the past, our students are no longer "little us's," whom we can teach the same ways we, ourselves, were taught. Because of the pervasive technologies of cable television, the Internet, cell phones, and so on, young people's knowledge and connections to the world far outstrip those of the past.

It is this state of affairs—that our kids know and can do so much more while remaining, in many ways, young people needing adult guidance for true understanding and making their way in the world—that lies at the root of many of today's educational problems.

Interactivity

One of the great differences from the past that has been written about frequently is interactivity. At the same age when young people in the past only read books or watched television, experiencing stories they could not control or change except in their imaginations, today's kids now experience games and other interactive entertainments within which they can physically control what happens and participate much more actively in the story, using not only their imaginations, but their ability to make choices that affect the outcome of the stories they see. This is a change from which there is no return. Not that pre-built stories lose their meaning, but it has become more and more difficult for traditional fiction to hold kids' attention unless it is extremely engaging, such as the Harry Potter series. And even then, the kids demand the interactive version (i.e., the game) as well.

One great result of interactivity is that "telling" as a way of presenting information has declined rapidly in importance and effectiveness, especially in its longer forms. Kids dislike teachers that just "talk and talk and talk" and students go to sleep or otherwise tune out these teachers after only a few seconds.

Beyond Interactivity to Creation

It is important to understand that interactivity is only a small part of what digital technology has brought these kids. Much more important is creation—the ability to make new things and to use readily available new tools to express themselves. This has happened everywhere, from Facebook, to Wikipedia, to YouTube, to blogs, to mash-ups, to machinima. "User-created content" has become a web mantra. Professor Henry Jenkins, formerly of the Massachusetts Institute of Technology and now of the University of Southern California, refers to this as the "participatory culture."

User-created content has especially "happened" in games, where so-called player-created aspects of content (characters, furniture, clothing, teams, weapons, designs, logos, and so on) have become more than half of the content that gets used in these games, much to the game makers' delight (because if the players create the content, the companies do not have to spend time and money doing so). New and better tools to facilitate this creation arrive daily—often available for free. Some of these player creations are sold inside the games and on eBay for real money in substantial amounts.

YouTube is a great example of users creating content. As of this writing, YouTube has more videos online than the combined U.S. television broadcast networks have created in their entire history. Most of these videos were created by Digital Natives—our kids—using the tools now built into almost every new laptop and cell phone.

Recently, my grade-school nephew was given the traditional Thanksgiving task of making pilgrim costumes by pasting cut-out bits of leather, cloth, felt, and other materials onto colored paper. He found the task so ridiculous—compared with the enormously complex and nuanced costumes he had created for the characters in his many games—that he refused to do the project. Sadly, rather than confront the school, his mother just did it for him.

Beyond The Classroom—Affecting the World

The Digital Natives go still further with their digital tools—out into the world itself to affect and change it. "I want to put my mark on things," says one student. "I want to change the world," says another. And, with modern-day digital tools, they can—even in elementary school. Kids are using their cell phones, Internet connections, and, increasingly, their gaming tools to reach out to, connect with, and help their peers around the world.

Our Slowly Changing Schools

Although digitally related changes are evident at home and in schools, some educators still choose to ignore them. Some argue that "kids are still kids," and that the ways and means of the past are still sufficient and adequate to do the job. Unfortunately, this attitude only gets us deeper into trouble.

Obviously, kids still do need to learn about the world—young people, by virtue of their short time spent on this planet, still have a limited understanding of things, an understanding that needs to be refined and shaped as they grow. This has traditionally been the job of parents and teachers.

But the conclusion that today's kids can (or worse, should) be taught in the same ways as in the past misses an essential change. Up until recently, all our kids' developmental processes, both psychological and intellectual, proceeded in a way we all understood fairly well, thanks to researchers such as Piaget, and were prepared for. So we could accurately classify kids' learning activities and content by their age appropriateness. Content and style that were appropriate for 10-year-olds were not appropriate for most 5-year-olds. Large segments of current educational curricula are based on this.

But today, due to early and frequent interactions with technology of all kinds, our kids' intellectual abilities and skills at early ages have changed rapidly. Today, exercises that were used in recent memory in colleges and graduate schools are perfectly appropriate for and usable by fourth graders. For example, I particularly recall a National Aeronautics and Space Administration (NASA) simulation of a crisis on the moon that I used in business school that would be perfectly appropriate for elementary and junior high school kids.

As a result, our concepts of age appropriateness in education need to be reexamined in ways that have, up till now, hardly even been discussed. In the opinion of many, including at least one of Piaget's former students, it is time to rethink Piaget's conclusions completely. Former Piaget student Edith Ackermann asks, "In what areas in a child's cognitive and emotional life do we witness a true 'anthropologic mutation' that scatters developmentalists' views, like Piaget's and others? I tend to think that kids don't just 'get' to the stages earlier, but that they are onto another path" (personal communication, 2008). We need to recognize that our children and students are capable of using and understanding much more sophisticated tools than have ever been used in the past—tools that are sometimes beyond the ken of our educators.

Games are one important place—although only one of many—where this change in age-appropriate content has happened: kids confront ideas, goals, decisions, and ethics in their complex games that were almost never confronted by kids that young in the past. This happens partially, of course, with choices about violence. But is also happens, to a much greater extent, with other, nonviolent strategies and choices. Encouragingly, more and more violent games offer players nonviolent alternative strategies, such as stealth, making the ethical choices even clearer.

Most of the choices today's kids are making daily in their game playing are important, nonviolent ones. Kids today are deciding how to build their theme parks and other businesses so that they thrive, making money by keeping their customers happy; they are creating and building winning sports franchises; they are engaging in scientific quests and exploring the universe; and they are doing many other extremely complex tasks in the games they play beginning at very early ages, often when they are only four or five years old.

What Is School Really Like? Bo-ring …

What is today's school actually like for most of our kids at the turn of the 21st century? Let's leave aside for the moment our students in the top 10%, who often do well in school, like it, and even thrive on it, although increasing numbers of these students are falling into the patterns I am about to describe.

If there is one word cited almost universally by kids today to describe their school experience, it is "boring." I regularly hear this from the students around the world that I interview. (See my article, "Young Minds, Fast Times: The Twenty-First-Century Digital Learner—How tech-obsessed iKids would improve our schools," 2008). Typical kids' comments are "I'm bored at least 50 percent of the time"; "I'm bored in five out of my seven classes." For elementary school students, the boredom numbers often approach 100 percent.

And sadly—despite their teachers' best efforts and intentions—the fact that our students are often bored at school makes perfect sense.

Outside of school, the world continuously competes for our students' attention with multimillion-dollar multimedia efforts in movies, music, games, television, and elsewhere. A single song on their iPods may have cost $1 million to produce. In many ways, they have become very sophisticated consumers of media. Companies have learned that they can't just tell these kids what to consume; instead, companies spend millions observing and analyzing kids' behaviors.

Our students are not yet sophisticated consumers of ideas, but they need to learn to be. Unfortunately, though, educators don't spend enough of their time and resources trying to understand today's kids and trying to reach each of them in as many ways possible. Rather, to a great extent, our educators still try to educate our students with the tools of the 18th century—talking and lectures, writing boards—which are much the same to the kids, whether black, white, or electronic—and textbooks. "My teachers just talk and talk and talk," say the kids over and over again. Teachers often repeat in class the exact material in the textbook, afraid that the kids didn't read it. They're probably right.

Despite the oft-heard, false, and self-serving claims of many adults, young people today don't have "short attention spans" for everything. Today's kids often pay close attention for extended periods to their movies, games, music, or anything that truly interests them. The "short attention span" claims are self-serving because they are frequently used as an excuse for lack of teaching success. But in the words of one teacher, "Kids have short attention spans for the old ways of learning."

Anyone who has ever taken the trouble to "shadow" kids (follow them throughout their school day, sitting in on all their classes) knows that school is generally not very exciting. Despite the fact that most kids recognize and like their good teachers, when students are being honest, they consistently say that they are engaged with their schoolwork in only a small percentage of their courses. I have heard this from kids who attend our so-called "best" schools, as traditionally measured.

Why Yesterday's Education No Longer Works

It's not that yesterday's methods never worked. They did, in another world, for most students. Despite all the changes that have occurred in the late 20th and early 21st centuries and despite educators' good intentions, we have reached a point where our curriculums and our methods are totally out of touch with our students' present and future lives. Our schools give out useful credentials, such as a diploma and transcript, but the actual material they offer students is almost entirely from and about the past. Fewer and fewer of them—especially outside of that top 10%—see its relevance. And for the most part, the kids are right. If all parents and teachers were made to take the SATs, they would see just how little of what kids are supposed to learn and know is relevant to an adult life, particularly today and in the future.

So our kids find much of their schoolwork uninteresting, and we increasingly have to push it on them, forcing them to achieve even what we now call "minimum yearly progress." According to America's Promise Alliance, kids drop out of American high schools at the rate of one student every 26 seconds.

What We Teach and How We Teach Must Change

Yet, even though updating what we teach should be made a huge priority, our current K–12 curriculum, until we change it, could be presented to students in other, different ways—ways that out students could relate to and learn from. This is another important reason for using games as tools in our schools.

Just because students drop out of school—either physically or mentally—doesn't mean they stop learning or preparing for their 21st-century lives. The 21st century provides our kids with another key learning component in addition to school—one that they often prefer.

The New School Competition: "After School"

Although up until now many have ignored it as part of the educational context, much of the future-directed education students are getting comes when school is over. It comes from a combination of their time on the Internet, their robotics and programming clubs, their exchanges with peers around the world, and, increasingly, their games. I have written an entire book about how games are preparing our kids for 21st-century success, a book that has been translated into several languages, *Don't Bother Me Mom—I'm Learning* (2005).

I label this entire combination of additional learning activities "After School." The MacArthur Foundation refers to it as "another node" in our kids' learning system. Some after-school learning is formal, but much of it is not. More and more kids are just following their interests and passions rather than a pre-set curriculum. Jim Groom calls this learning on kids' own "edupunk." Whether kids will adopt the term "edupunk" as their own remains to be seen.

Learning without School?

And how do the kids learn in this after-school environment? They teach themselves and each other, sometimes but not always with the guidance of an adult, using all the digital tools of the 21st century—many of which are electronic video games. "What do video games teach, besides violence?" you may ask. The answer is a surprising but nonetheless true, "Everything we want our kids to know." I will show why and how later in this chapter, and you will see it in much more detail, subject by subject, in the remainder of this book.

One important thing to consider about after-school learning is that it involves using digital tools—tools kids enjoy using. Using tools in education is, of course, not new. We have been using books and abacuses, for example, for centuries. Even the classroom teacher is a learning tool— one that largely replaced an earlier tool, the tutor.

Yet for some reason there is a lot of resistance from adults, especially adults who are educators, to their students' using contemporary, digital tools to learn—especially as these new tools become capable of replacing some of or some parts of the old ones.

Darkness or Light?

A metaphor I often use about our schools is this: Until not that long ago, kids used to grow up "in the dark" intellectually, in the sense that they didn't travel much or know much about the world. Then they came to school, where gradually their teachers opened up their window on the world, with all its knowledge and wonders. Educators were, justifiably, very proud of what they did, because they were the people who "showed kids the light."

However, in the 21st century, our kids grow up flooded by the light of information and knowledge. They are connected to the world and what is happening in it by television, Internet, messaging, and much more, long before their formal schooling begins. That doesn't mean they have more wisdom, but they are certainly better informed than children were in the past.

We could, of course, use their knowledge and their connections as our educational starting points, knowing they are full of misunderstandings to correct, while admitting we no longer need to tell our students everything—they either know or can find out a lot. But far too often, in a knee-jerk reaction to disruptive changes, educators limit students' connections to the world by banning the tools that provide them. And, in so doing, educators may unwittingly force our kids back into darkness.

While educators in the 21st century would like to be the people who show kids the light and often think of themselves in this way, the danger is that—with the very best of intentions—they wind up doing precisely the opposite.

How do educators justify their resistance to the use of 21st-century tools and the new educational methods they enable? Some claim that the old methods are sufficient to produce an educated mind and person; after all, they have been doing so for hundreds of years. Others complain they are not being given enough money and training to use innovative methods, especially those that involve technology. Finally, as their "big guns," they generally bring out the argument that they are "required to follow the prescribed curriculum" and, therefore, essentially must teach to the test.

The Other Side of the Story

But there is another side to this story. First, the methods that indeed worked for the last hundred years prepared our kids for an industrial world—a world that no longer exists in the developed nations. Those methods prepared students for a relatively slowly changing world, in which lessons from the past could be applied easily to the present and future.

Second, while many tasks we still require in education are the same, the tools we use to accomplish them have changed or are changing. No one argues that being able to express one's ideas skillfully in a clear context is no longer important—the ability to communicate effectively is becoming even more important. However, expressing oneself by using a pen on paper is fast becoming a thing of the past, just as perfecting fine cursive handwriting and calculating algorithms on paper are nearly obsolete. Machines such as computers and calculators now complete these tasks more efficiently, though students still need to master the writing and math skills necessary to use the machines effectively.

Opponents of change almost always cite lack of funds, but it's not lack of money that prevents educators from using and learning about 21st-century tools—it's most often educators' inability or unwillingness to communicate with and learn from their students. Increasingly large numbers of our students bring computers to school on their own, in the forms of notebooks and increasingly powerful cell phones. We could be using these. We could unblock important 21st-century learning tools, such as YouTube and Wikipedia, and give our students the responsibility of doing what they should with them. If a 21st-century hospital were to do what many of our schools do, using only the equipment and training of the 18th or 19th centuries, how many patients would show up? In most fields, people trained in another era are expected to update their skills on their own. And today, this is easier and easier to do if one wants to. Students and our smartest educators are already using YouTube, for example, to teach and learn from each other.

It is terribly important that today's educators accept that there are so many more ways than "telling" to help students learn. Far too many educators feel that they have not done their jobs unless every word they want the students to learn has, literally, come out of the teachers' mouths. But today's kids hate being talked at and lectured to. They know there are other, better ways available—such as researching, doing, presenting, and discussing—for them to learn the same material, and they'd much rather be learning that way.

The "one lesson fits all," or "broadcasting" part of the teachers' job is rapidly becoming obsolete, as a new "Partnering" pedagogy of "kids teaching themselves with their teachers' guidance" replaces the old pedagogy of the "sage on the stage" (Prensky, 2010). Medical schools around the United States and the world, for example, are quickly abandoning their traditional lectures for case-based and simulation-based methods. Teachers and schools, from K–12 to universities, are adopting problem-based, inquiry-based, student-centered approaches. And games, which seem out of place in a lecture-based pedagogy, are an important building block for what most education is moving toward.

How Rapid Technological Change Affects Education

Although many educators today don't yet see or admit it, the nature of education—both what it means and how to do it—is changing rapidly as a result of technology. And it will only change faster in the years to come. Consider the following:

▶ The primary source of knowledge for our students, which used to be their teachers, their textbooks, and the books in the library, is now the Internet.

▶ The more or less predetermined jobs and careers for which we formerly prepared our students have become uncertain ones with the required preparation unclear.

▶ The learning tools and learning methods considered fundamental to teach in the past—from long division, to library research methods, to not using outside sources on tests, to not asking a fellow student for an answer you don't know—no longer meet our 21st-century needs. We have to invent new tools and methods to meet current needs.

While educators' desire to preserve what is valuable from the past is important and commendable, it is equally if not more important for educators to orient our kids' education toward the future that they will be living in. "My passion is my future," one high school student told a convocation of his teachers recently. And well it should be.

Future-Oriented Education

At least two important areas must be addressed as we orient our students' education to the future: what we teach and how we teach. What we teach is our current curriculum. It is, on all levels, from kindergarten through high school, hopelessly outdated for the 21st century and desperately needs to be completely re-thought. We need to add many subjects that didn't exist in the past and many future-oriented skills that are currently not being taught. And, as our curricula are not only full but overloaded, in order to make room to teach new skills, we must drop others that are no longer needed—many of which are near and dear to educators' hearts.

Ask yourself the following: what should we eliminate to make room for nanotechnology, bioethics, biomimickry, programming, genomics, and proteomics? How do we make room in our teaching for the desperately needed skills of ethical behavior, critical thinking, decision making, and problem solving? Where can we fit our teaching of goal setting, planning, self-direction, and self-evaluation? Of communicating and interacting with individuals and groups using technology? Of communicating with our evermore powerful machines (e.g., programming)? Of communicating with a world audience? Where should we put our teaching of creative thinking, designing, playing, and helping kids to find their own voices? Where do we teach our students to be proactive; to take prudent risks; and to think long-term, laterally, and strategically?

Thirty years from now, will today's kids be better off with a solid knowledge of the long division algorithm, which today's educators try desperately and often unsuccessfully to give them, or with a solid foundation in problem solving, which most of today's schooling does not provide? Will they be better off writing neat cursive letters or writing computer code?

Fortunately, because of the rise of "after school," a large number of today's students are already learning many of these skills for the future through their video and computer games.

Changing Our Pedagogy

This book is not concerned with how the curriculum needs to change, important as that is. It is focused, rather, on *how we teach*—in other words, our pedagogy. And this, too, is, in the main, hopelessly out of date. To quote a middle school student, "There is so much difference between how [today's] kids learn and how [today's] teachers teach."

Most of our educators learned through content being delivered to them via presenting and telling, linearly, one thing at a time, with the same information or explanations being presented to everyone in the same fashion at a relatively slow pace. Teachers delivered content face to face, or students read books.

But today's students, for the most part, learn best through an entirely different set of activities. They learn from becoming engaged, from doing and gameplay, from random access to information, from exploring multiple options, from multitasking, from being given and making lots of choices, and from seeing what they do directly relate to and affect the world they live in. They are accustomed to learning online, and they prefer for information to arrive and be updated at a much quicker pace than traditional educational methods are capable of delivering.

Despite what some may think, this new way does not necessarily mean today's students learn less. In fact, it almost certainly leads to the opposite—*more* learning. Understanding this is particularly important in the face of declining (or not sufficiently increasing) test scores. Even if your only goal is to improve test scores, better teaching methods than lecturing and assigned readings are available to use with today's kids.

No More Telling: Active Learning

When dealing with today's young people, telling or lecturing is no longer a useful skill, not because it never worked but because it *no longer works* with the vast majority of today's students. They want and need to be active in their learning, to find their own information and answers to questions, to share their opinions with their peers around the world, and to make a real difference to others, even while they learn.

Although it is sometimes referred to as new pedagogy or a new teaching paradigm because it is, in more and more classrooms, replacing most of what educators typically do now, student-centered learning (also called problem-based learning, case-based learning, learning by doing, and progressive education) has a long and honorable history in education. It was championed by John Dewey, among others. Although many experts consider it a better way to teach, it was driven out as our main pedagogy in favor of "telling," principally because of the rise in importance of comparing our students to each other, mainly through testing and evaluation. The idea of students learning on their own with our guidance was also hampered by a lack of appropriate resources—the textbooks, the library, and bits of the teacher's time were just not enough. The great boon of technology is that it allows these better methods of teaching to make a comeback—and to be much more effective than they were before.

Today's kids have had far more experience in finding their own information actively and interactively than they ever did in the past. Preschoolers, for example, are voracious learners, typically full of questions and wanting to explore. The digital technology that they've grown up with from birth allows them to indulge this need at a tremendous pace. Kids now, at younger and younger ages, increasingly have their own digital phones, digital cameras, video cameras, digital music players, Internet connections, IM accounts, accounts on multiple websites, and so on. Educators who deride youngsters' "trial and error," "push every button" learning would be wise to consider seeing this as the true scientific inquiry that most of it is.

The Rise of the Complex Electronic Game

The evolution of today's complex video games is a story not generally known to most educators, but it has enormous implications for what they do and how they will do it in the future. The first commercial video game, Pong (see Figure 1.1), was launched in 1978.

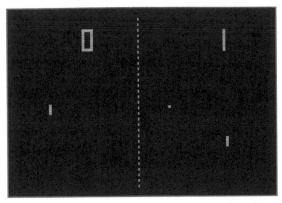

FIGURE 1.1 ▶ Pong, the first video game

Pong was a limited affair. It was a time-passer, albeit a new and captivating one, much like the card games or board games that most of today's adults grew up with. Because they grew up thinking of games as these trivial types of activities, it makes sense that many adults still see games of any type as trivial and not useful for deep, complex learning.

However, electronic games quickly began to evolve in a variety of complex directions. Some games made the graphics more realistic, creating the simple characters of the early Nintendo games. Other games created adventures, puzzles of exploration for players to solve. Still others used simulations, letting players take on roles in a virtual world.

One issue that most of these early games shared, however, was that because the technical issues of networking were not yet worked out, most electronic games of this era were stand-alone (except in arcades). Many adults who watched kids grow up during the late 1970s through the 1980s retain the now totally outmoded view that game players are "loners," who hunch over their computers with no live person at the other end of the conversation. The truth is that this has changed 180 degrees, with the solo player now the exception rather than the rule. Most computer and video games are played with others over an increasingly sophisticated set of networks.

Games and Learning

Despite all the limitations of the early electronic games, some pioneers saw great promise in them and began creating "educational" versions, which later became known collectively as "edutainment." Despite some notable exceptions—such as Oregon Trail—these were for the most part drills for review and reinforcement, dressed up with game-like graphics.

Although some parents may have been fooled into buying them, neither kids nor teachers were. Despite the word "educational" on the box, these electronic games were hardly considered serious learning tools or a serious way to teach. They were certainly not considered interesting games by the kids (with the exception of preschoolers, for whom they were still engaging). Parents had to force older kids to use them, and most of the copies ended up being dumped into the trash. The "entertainment generation" of educational gaming died an ugly and embarrassing death, with the Learning Company being bought by Mattel for $3 billion and then sold by them, only a short time later, for under $300 million.

Complex Games

While most educators derided or ignored electronic learning games, the commercial games industry was rapidly progressing and evolving. Companies like Nintendo, Sega, and Electronic Arts began to grow quickly, and kids lapped up what they were offering. Every five years or so an entirely new, much more powerful generation of game consoles (that is, playing machines that plugged in to televisions) was introduced, to greater and greater sales (see Figure 1.2).

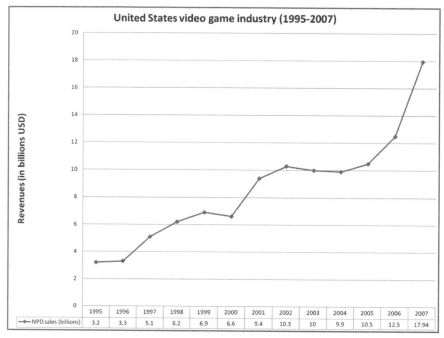

United States video game industry (1995-2007)

	1995	1996	1997	1998	1999	2000	2001	2002	2003	2004	2005	2006	2007
◆ NPD sales (billions)	3.2	3.3	5.1	6.2	6.9	6.6	9.4	10.3	10	9.9	10.5	12.5	17.94

FIGURE 1.2 ▶ Growth of video game industry in terms of revenue over time
(Source: http://vgsales.wikia.com/wiki/File:Us_revenues_1995-2007.png)

Watching the market for electronic games grow, powerful giants like Sony and Microsoft moved into the business, expanding it even further. And as the game hardware became more and more powerful (and PCs and Macs jumped into the action), the games themselves went through some radical transformations.

Sports simulations became a major piece of the market, growing from offering game players the opportunity simply to play the game, to enabling them to manage players' careers, manage teams, and buy and sell franchises. Action and adventure games became more and more sophisticated in their storylines, their characters, and the moral and ethical choices they posed to the players. Simulations became technologically good enough to use to learn to fly real airplanes and drive high performance cars.

In only 30 years, we have gone from the trivial behavior of Pong and quiz games to incredibly powerful game experiences, such as The Sims 3, where young players control an entire family of individuals; World of Warcraft, where they have action-packed adventures with other people from around the globe; and Spore, where players help an organism evolve from a single cell to a creature that can form a civilization and can explore and survive in a multiplayer-created universe.

As electronic games have become enormously complex, they have evolved into incredible teaching and learning tools. Because of this, we find ourselves on the cusp of an enormous change in how our children learn.

Violence?

Many educators and parents worry about violence in video games, and its effects on our children. Clearly, violence is a component of some (actually a relatively small percentage) entertainment games, just as violence occurs in much great literature. Some of these games may not be appropriate for young people. But for *educational* games to be both engaging and effective, there doesn't have to be any violence at all. By focusing solely on the violence, worriers about games often miss most of what is really going on in computer and video games in terms of learning.

What is really taking place in the minds of the young people who play almost all computer and video games is *exactly what we are all looking for: learning with engagement.* More about how this happens in a moment.

We now have a wide variety of shapes and sizes of learning games, ranging from games that teach one skill or bit of knowledge in a couple of minutes, to complex games that teach multiple behaviors, objectives, and skills over the course of more than a semester. And with all the major new capabilities being added to the already complex video and computer games by developments such as cell phones, cameras, video, GPS, voice control, and other devices, both learning and engagement are becoming even greater.

The Opportunity

So our enormous opportunity—to be ignored only at our own and our students' peril—is to realize the potential of games, which kids love and are even willing to spend their own money for, to facilitate learning with engagement and to teach our children what we think they should know to survive and thrive in the world. And, of course, we need to do this without killing the kids' natural curiosity and desire to learn.

More about Complex Games

Why do I keep using the term "complex" games? Aren't all games the same? Not at all. They vary in their complexity as much as a fairy tale differs from a great novel. The main objection we hear to using games in school is that "games are trivial"—and some are. But those are only a fraction of the games that our kids play today. When many of today's adults grew up, games were mostly trivial—card and board games that we played on rainy days. The few exceptions were chess, Go, bridge, and, later, Dungeons and Dragons. While most of the small games still exist—and are played mostly online—we call them "casual games" or, if you are an academic, "frame-games."

Over the last 30 years, though, another type of game has developed: the "complex" game. Complex games are what the game stores sell and what most of our game-playing kids play. Unlike casual games that often take less than an hour (or only a few minutes in some cases) to complete, complex games can take days, weeks, months, or even years to finish to the end. The time players spend mastering these "complex" games is often far longer than the traditional, 40-hour Carnegie course unit. These complex games have multiple goals and multiple levels and require a great deal of skill and learning to master.

What do kids learn from these complex games that we can consider important and not trivial? Without even thinking about the curriculum—which can, of course, be included as well—kids learn a great many things from playing complex games, including:

- To cooperate, collaborate, and work in teams—to work effectively with others
- To make effective decisions under stress
- To take prudent risks in pursuit of objectives
- To make ethical and moral decisions
- To employ scientific deduction
- To master and apply new skills and information quickly
- To think laterally and strategically
- To persist and solve difficult problems
- To understand and deal with foreign environments and cultures
- To manage business and people

Most would agree that we want all our children to learn these skills and acquire the knowledge included in the above list. But most of the items in the list are not part of our traditional school curriculum, except perhaps peripherally. In games, however, they are central.

Dedicated, custom-designed complex games that *combine the above skills with the required curriculum* are now beginning to appear in the market, and many are, or soon will be, available to educators—as you will learn in the remainder of this book.

Rules of Engagement

What do complex games do, and have, that engages our kids so effectively?

Often, to the surprise of those who don't play games, very little of the long-term engagement kids have with games comes from the games' graphics or violence (if any) or what happens on the surface that can be casually observed without actually playing. Most of the engagement comes from what I call the "deeper" levels. Not the "how" (to do whatever the game is about) level, but rather, the "what" (the rules, which need to be figured out) level; the "why" (the strategy, which needs to be successfully worked out) level; the "where" (the game's context) level; and the "when or whether" (the ethical and moral choices in the game) level.

I have distilled 10 "rules of engagement" from video and computer games. These are the things game designers do, often unconsciously, that lead to a game's success and to their players' engagement. These rules apply not only to the longer games, but also to shorter "complex" games. In fact, they don't apply only to games but to any activity done with students, even to a classroom lesson. The 10 rules of engagement are the following:

1. Focus on engagement.
2. Establish "be a hero" goals.
3. Add frequent decision making.
4. Don't suck the fun out.
5. Emphasize gameplay over eye candy.
6. Provide a strong emotional connection.
7. Level up for evaluation.
8. Balance cooperation and competition.
9. Personalize and adapt content and skill levels.
10. Iterate to please users.

Let me illustrate each of these:

Focus on engagement. When game makers design a game, their prime directive is to keep players engaged. At any moment in the game, the answer to "Are my players having fun?" must be a "Yes," or they'll stop playing the game. The game designer figures out how to adjust the game's content, often on the fly, to keep the players engaged.

This is different from a teacher designing a lesson, with its prime focus typically on content. The teacher asks, "Am I covering everything I need to so that my students do well on the achievement test?" Keeping all the kids engaged at every moment in the lesson is secondary and is often sacrificed because we have taught teachers that their prime directive is to cover all the content.

Games provide more engagement than lessons *because that is the designer's focus*. And even though teachers must teach a prescribed curriculum (unlike game designers), teachers are more successful, I think, when they are not slaves to the content but are fierce partisans of keeping their students engaged and interested in going further—even if a few items of the curriculum are left out. For example, using a game such as Making History or Age of Empires might not teach every important fact and concept about a particular period of history, but the game is likely to motivate students to learn more about that era. Engaged students are much more likely to discover missing content on their own than bored students are apt to remember any content that was covered in an uninteresting way, no matter how completely. Games engage students' imaginations and are likely to be remembered. Thus, a good way to help students learn and retain content is to use a game.

Establish "be a hero" goals. The one universal goal for complex games is some form of being a hero. Save the world. Help your friends. Do something you weren't sure you could accomplish. There are, to be sure, short- and medium-term goals along the way. Always in the best games, these goals are clear and related to the "be a hero" part. Players buy into these goals, accept them as their own, and strive to achieve them.

What goals do we usually give our kids in school? Learn the material? Pass the test? Understand? These are not particularly motivating goals next to being a hero. If a teacher were to answer the question, "Why should I learn algebra?" (or anything else) with "To save the world," he or she just might get the unexpected answer: "Oh, OK, I'll do it."

Add frequent decision making. Many educators may not be aware that making decisions is a major part of the fun of game playing. One well-known game maker defines a game as "a series of interesting decisions that lead to a satisfying conclusion." The fun is in making all those decisions—several a minute in many games—and getting immediate feedback on just how good those decisions were. Sometimes combinations of decisions have longer-range consequences, so the feedback comes later, but it always comes.

Interestingly, decisions and feedback are also the basic "stuff" of learning. David Kolb (1983) has illustrated this with his well-known learning loop of "Decision > Action > Feedback > Reflection," performed over and over again. Somehow we have left decision making out of most of our curricula, letting students slide by with volunteering decisions (i.e., raising their hands) only when they feel like it, which studies show most students rarely or never do. We tend to leave the required decision making to the test, where it comes with no feedback at all or until generally too late to be useful for learning.

This is why even casual games like *Jeopardy* have such power in the classroom—students love to make decisions and find out if they are right. Simple trivia games can work, but complex games make these decisions and feedback much more powerful learning tools. Playing Civilization IV can mean making 50–100 decisions per turn about everything from politics to the economy to religion.

Don't suck the fun out. "Whenever you add an instructional designer [to a game-making team]," said a game designer at a discussion I once moderated, "the first thing they do is suck the fun out." Because every game is about learning *something*, game designers are also, in a sense, learning designers. But their approach to learning is different from that of educators and academics. Game designers' approach to learning is purely practical; they know from sales results that learning and fun must not be separated.

Games are one good way to allow educators who would like to add more "fun" to their teaching to do so. Interestingly, not all fun has to be of the "ha-ha" type. Much of the fun in games is decision making, problem solving, and struggling-to-be-a-hero-type fun.

Emphasize gameplay over eye candy. Although today's complex game players are used to a great deal of graphic sophistication in their games and other online entertainments, they know that it is *not* the graphics that make a game fun and worth playing. Rather, it is the gameplay, the combination of goals, decisions, pacing, balance, and other elements that make what you do from moment to moment enjoyable and worth continuing.

While every game needs a minimally acceptable "professional" quality of graphics, many games that are older or were not made with the largest budgets (most of which, ironically, goes to the graphics) can still be more than acceptable as learning tools. As one student said about the older electronic games, "I don't compare these to the games I play on my Xbox 360—I compare them to the regular stuff we get in school. Compared to that, even a simple game rocks."

Provide a strong emotional connection. The emotion in complex games, coming in more and more sophisticated ways, already approaches and surpasses that of many movies and books. Game designers employ a variety of techniques, from what advertisers call SiSoMo (sight, sound, and motion) to story, character, interactivity, sound, and music to produce emotion. They also spend much of their design time thinking about the emotional effects of their game on players.

From a learning perspective, the advantage of having an emotional connection with whatever one is learning is increased memory and retention. That alone is a pretty strong argument for using games in class—kids will probably remember them.

Level up for evaluation. In a good complex game, all players know exactly where they stand, what skills they have or do not have, what material they have mastered, and on what fields they can compete. Yet games, as you've probably noticed, don't have tests. So how do they provide all of this feedback? Games use the ingeniously effective evaluation method of "leveling up."

The idea is simple: every skill necessary to be learned and mastered in order to achieve the game's goals is broken down into tiny steps. As players demonstrate repeatedly that they can perform a step, they move up a numerical level in that skill. When certain combinations of individual levels have been reached, players move up to more "global" levels. Each succeeding level is harder to reach, but it brings with it better rewards, such as treasure, new abilities, and new places to explore. This makes moving up within the game a desired experience in itself—not to mention that it advances you toward your ultimate goal, which you can only achieve at the highest level.

What is extraordinary about this evaluation system, compared with the way things are done in schools, is that no additional testing of any kind is needed. If one is a level 10, or 20, or 60, or 80 in a particular game, it means something specific—a player wouldn't be at that level if he or she weren't ready. This is something that players know and can share with anyone. (It's a kind of résumé among players.) By making the work to level-up difficult and often repetitive (e.g., "Heal 1000 wounds"), while making the rewards very attractive, the leveling-up process elicits enormous amounts of skills practice from players—time and effort far beyond what could ever be accomplished with homework—mostly without complaint.

Balance cooperation and competition. Complex games also do an excellent job of balancing two elements that are important in learning: competition and cooperation. A frequent misrepresentation of games is that they are *only* about competition. But, just like with sports, what makes a good game work is actually a careful balancing of the competitive (inter-team) and the cooperative (intra-team) elements.

In any good game, this balance is thought about and designed in from the very beginning, and much time is spent on getting it right. As previously noted, these days very few complex games are designed to be played by one person working against the computer. Although games may contain a mode to play solo, almost all are based on multiplayer participation of one sort or another: one-on-one, small teams or large guilds, or synchronous or asynchronous.

Because every game accomplishes this difficult balancing act of competition and cooperation somewhat differently, players and teachers need to experiment to find the best games and the best modes and roles within games for their own situations.

Personalize and adapt content and skill levels. One of the great benefits of electronic games is that they can easily do precisely what it is hardest for a teacher to do with a class of 20 to 40 students—personalize and adapt to each player individually. This is accomplished through various forms of what is known in game programming as artificial intelligence. The game "watches" every move that players make and from these observations attempts to figure out the players' preferences—what they like to see, in what order, how they like their information presented, and what their preferred interfaces might be. Most important, the program knows whether or not the player is doing well at the game and whether or not he or she is succeeding in mastering the skills, mounting the levels, and reaching the intermediate goals on the way to the final "be a hero" goal.

A well-designed game takes this information and uses it to make the game a better experience for the player—continually and on the fly. If a player is doing well, the game will increase the challenge level by inserting extra barriers, enemies, or hazards in the player's way or by making it harder to find things that are needed. If a player is struggling, the game will give assistance by inserting extra clues or providing more supplies or even inserting a computer-controlled "buddy" to help the player.

As a result, any well-designed game feels like it was designed just for each player—because it was. It is continually challenging all players in different ways enough to make them want to struggle to continue but never so hard or so easy that they want to stop—keeping each player in his or her "flow zone." Mihály Csíkszentmihályi coined this term in his book *Flow: The Psychology of Optimal Experience* (1991).

Iterate to please users. Serious game designers do not believe they can design a good game just by sitting down and thinking about it. Designers must know how to iterate, that is, to make changes based on feedback from players. This is the universally accepted game development process. Game designers know they will need to create prototypes, put them before players, get honest feedback, and then adapt them, producing new and better iterations of the game to test. Designers will do this over and over again, tens or even hundreds of times, until they have made most players happy.

Of all the things that game designers do, iteration is by far the most important, because it creates and cements a strong connection between what the game designers are trying to do and the needs and preferences of the players. Curiously, iteration is also, perhaps, the furthest from the way educators typically design curricula and lessons, which tend to be designed on a one-and-done-forever basis by one or more experts, with almost no student feedback.

So the last, and possibly the most important reason to integrate games into teaching is that they have been tested, over and over—*by kids*—and revised—*until kids really want to use them!*

Integrating Electronic Games into the Curriculum

Even though they may understand and accept all these reasons and benefits for using games, a big question often remains on educators' minds: "How do I/we integrate games *into the curriculum*?" This is, of course, a very important question, and it is what this book is about.

Although *not* our topic here, it should be noted that the process of integrating the curriculum itself into new custom-designed educational games about math, science, language arts, and social studies (or other school subjects) is also an important issue for game designers. This is a very difficult task because they have to create "be a hero" goals, add decisions, and follow the other rules of engagement while incorporating the material to be learned. They need to proceed very carefully, with much adaptation, to make sure that they don't suck the fun out. It is important to understand that such educational games (at least the good ones that teach subject matter and that kids want to play) cannot be pumped out by following a recipe; they require a great deal of creativity, plus countless adaptations of many iterations. That is why not enough of them have been created. Still, numerous examples in all disciplines show it can be done.

However, the topic of this book is how to integrate games that already exist—both commercial games and games designed for education—into daily teaching. And this, too, requires work. Unfortunately, for those looking for an easy way, at this point in the evolution of games and teaching, there are no "mindless pre-built" solutions to choose from. No list of all games coordinated to the daily breakdown of subjects teachers teach exists. There is little connection between the standards to be taught and what various entertainment games might offer for teaching students those standards (the few that are available have been developed mainly in the United Kingdom). The list of available games changes almost every day as new ones are added.

Thus, teachers who want the benefits of games for their students must be inventive. Like explorers, they must search the Internet to find relevant games. They must find sites devoted to making games available to teachers. Fortunately, such sites are becoming more popular, and teachers are sharing information about how to incorporate games into classes. Teachers must be willing to ask their students for help along the way, rather than confront students with a "game accompli," which they might not want. Teachers must say to themselves: "That won't work in my situation or my classroom, but this will." And finally, whatever they try, they must be willing not to judge success or failure by the first try, but to adapt and iterate, again and again, with confidence that good results will come sooner or later.

The Need for Mutual Respect

Because the successful use of games involves a partnership between teachers and students (instead of doing yet another thing *to* students), it is important that we play whatever games we use in schools (as we should do in life) in an atmosphere of mutual respect.

All educators think—correctly—that their students should respect them, and most, if not all, would say that they respect their students. But the truth is some educators may not give their students enough credit, especially when it comes to modern technology. One example is the "short attention span fallacy" discussed earlier, where students' lack of attention is not true in general, but only for what the educators offer.

Nowhere is this lack of credit more evident than with the kids' video and computer games, and in this area it often verges on disrespect. "Your games are a waste of time, money, and brain cells," said the parent of one young man who called me in tears after having found my book on the Internet. Educators often say similar things to kids. Any attempt at game-based education will not work in such environments. Teachers must accept the truth that games, far from being a waste of the kids' time, provide exactly what we are searching for—learning with engagement. That is the principal reason for using them in our schools.

Some teachers may know very little about modern video games, which makes them effectively "illiterate" in that domain. This lack may, in turn, be disrespected by the students because relatively few teachers show even the interest to learn more about games in a nonjudgmental way. When was the last time you heard a teacher or a parent say to a kid: "I know you spend a lot of time with those games, so they must bring you something you think is really valuable and worth your time. I'm genuinely interested in finding out what that is."

For learning to happen, it is crucial that each party respect what the other finds valuable. Students will be much more likely to listen to their teachers if they feel that the teachers respect their ideas and games.

Final Thoughts

Using electronic games to facilitate learning is something that we already see in some of our schools, and, for all the reasons discussed in this chapter, I believe we will see an increased use of games in the future. Nevertheless, using games as effective learning tools is not going to be a piece of cake for many teachers, any more than using any other complex, unfamiliar tool will be. Particularly in this early-stage environment, incorporating gameplay into classroom instruction will certainly involve a good deal of hard work on the part of teachers. That work includes conferring with students, choosing the right games for the students and the subject, figuring out an effective process for using the games in and out of class that works for the particular situation, evaluating the results, and, of course, a great deal of adaptation to students' individual proficiency levels—both in the subject area's content and skills and in gameplay.

Is all this work worth it? How important is it to bring more engagement to the learning process and, in multiple senses, to make learning more fun? I've heard some educators argue that true learning is *not* fun but hard work. And maybe for them that is true. However, it is emphatically *not* the case for the current generation of learners. From their "Sesame Street" days onward, these kids have received—and prefer to receive—their challenges in a fun manner, even if it is "hard fun" (a term from MIT educator Seymour Papert and the MIT Media Lab cited in Nicholas Negroponte's book *Being Digital* (1995)). In the video game world, fun certainly involves solving some very hard problems. I have heard Will Wright, one of the most creative game designers, often point out that "all complex games really are just difficult problems," problems that kids pay game companies for the opportunity to solve.

It is very important to keep in mind that using electronic games to educate students is a newly emerging field and skill. This means that there are no "best practices" to follow. Instead, at this point, there are only "good" practices; practices that can (and should) be shared, along with successful experiments that someone—probably an educator like you—has thought up and tried.

To increase your expertise and ability to add to these good practices, I recommend that you read the following chapters of this book carefully and that you read other books as well. In the References list for this chapter you'll find the articles and books I've mentioned and many useful resources can be found in other chapters. And, as books typically take a long time to get published, it is important to search YouTube, TeacherTube, Google, and other online places often for examples of educators in your subject who have successfully used games with their students.

Finally, before you actually try any games in your classes, I recommend having a serious conversation with your students. Let them know that you are thinking about using some electronic games as part of your teaching and are trying to figure out the best ways to do it. Ask them whether they think this is a good idea and why. Inquire about the games they play, what they like about those games, and what they dislike. Don't expect unanimity in the answers, but listen carefully for commonality and consensus. Ask your students where, in their learning, they think games would be useful and how they would want to use those games. Request that they be your advisors, and that they give you their honest feedback, which you, in exchange, agree to listen to carefully and act upon. And remember that students don't have all the answers either. But they do know what they find "lame."

As you get started, I recommend you try a number of different games and a number of different ways of using them, such as in class, out of class, set up in advance, on the fly, and other ways. Use different students as your advisors to get a variety of ideas and to see what you and your students are most comfortable with.

After every trial, be sure to ask, in classroom-friendly language, the key question: "What aspect of this game was so bad that it would make you never want to play it again?" (In the game world, the technical form of this question is "What sucks?") We are always searching hard, in the game world, for harsh feedback like this, because if players intensely dislike a certain element as a general consensus, we want to remove it immediately and for all time from our game. That's how games get better.

And, once again, remember that the final and most important rule of engagement is to iterate. The more you do this, removing with each successive iteration the unpopular elements from your games and your teaching and replacing them with more interesting and dynamic elements, the more likely you will be to succeed in engaging your students and helping them learn.

Let the games and your journey begin!

References

Csíkszentmihályi, M. (1991). *Flow: The psychology of optimal experience.* New York, NY: Harper Perennial.

Griffith, N. (1995). *Slow river.* New York, NY: Ballantine/Del Ray.

Kolb, D. A. (1983). *Experiental learning: Experience as the source of learning and development.* Upper Saddle River, NJ: Prentice Hall.

Lenhart, A., Kahne, J., Middaugh, E., Macgill, A. R., Evans, C., & Vitak, J. (Sept. 16, 2008). Teens, video games, and civics. Pew Internet & American Life Project report. Available at www.pewinternet.org/Reports/2008/Teens-Video-Games-and-Civics.aspx

Negroponte, N. (1995). *Being digital.* New York, NY: Alfred A. Knopf.

Prensky, M. (2001). *Digital games-based learning.* New York, NY: McGraw-Hill.

Prensky, M. (2001). Digital natives, digital immigrants: A new way to look at our kids. *On the Horizon 9*: 5 (Part I, MCB University Press, Oct. 2001); Digital natives, digital immigrants: Do they really *think* differently? *On the Horizon 9*: 6 (Part II, MCB University Press, Dec. 2001). Both parts are available under the link titled "The Classics" at www.marcprensky.com/writing/

Prensky, M. (2005). *Don't bother me Mom—I'm learning!* St. Paul, MN: Paragon House.

Prensky, M. (2008). "Young minds, fast times: The twenty-first-century digital learner—How tech-obsessed iKids would improve our schools." *Edutopia*, June. Available at www.edutopia.org/ikid-digital-learner-technology-2008

Prensky, M. (2010). *Teaching digital natives: Partnering for real learning.* Thousand Oaks, CA: Corwin Press.

2

Principles of Playing Games for Learning

Anthony K. Betrus and Luca Botturi

THIS CHAPTER PROVIDES READERS with sound reasons for integrating video games and game-based activities into K–12 classrooms. To achieve both depth and applicability, we first offer historical insights into the use of games for teaching and learning. These insights form the basis for a discussion of the benefits and drawbacks of using games in education; these points are then used to present applied principles, in the form of structured advice to teachers who would like to use games in their classrooms to enhance student learning.

The word *playing* has many facets. It can describe an extremely pleasant experience, such as, "I'm playing golf," or a terrible one, such as, "She's just playing with me." Playing can refer to games, music, theatre, relationships, and even mechanics, as in "too much play [looseness] between the cogs." Whatever the context, we tend to feel that this word should somehow be distant from schools and formal education—the older the students, the more distant play is from their classes, an activity reserved for sports and games played after school hours and on weekends.

At its core, playing is our word for describing a child's activity of exploring the world. As soon as newborns achieve control of their sight and of their hands, they start staring at all new objects, touching and grasping everything they find—often putting these things into their mouths as acts of intense learning and appropriation. For babies and young children, it seems natural to associate playing with learning and learning with the pleasure of making new discoveries.

Principles of Playing Games for Learning

Games are specific forms of playing that often develop out of human beings' natural tendency to play. Games are a set of rigid structures—namely, rules and rules embodied by toys—that define a limited action space. Playing a game means willingly entering a rigid structure and animating it with free movement (Salen & Zimmermann, 2003, p. 304). An example could be a basketball player's ability to perform graceful, effective movements on the court, such as scoring a basket after perfect dribbling. Just as the basketball player derives a refined form of pleasure from his or her achievement, players of instructional games in K–12 classrooms can gain new insights into subject matter while enjoying the excitement of the game.

In this chapter, we provide historical insights into the use of games for teaching and learning. These insights prepare the way for a discussion of the relative benefits and drawbacks of using games in education. These benefits and limitations, in turn, lead to a set of applied principles and prescriptions: structured advice to teachers who would like to use games in their classrooms.

Insights into the History of Games in Education

In this section, we explore the past use of simulations and games in education. This would be a good subject for a huge book, but we will limit our scope in two respects. We will consider only the history of Western culture, and we will do it through the eyes and words of two educators and authors who identified a common theme across the centuries: Quintilian, who lived in Rome in the first century AD, taught rhetoric, wrote a multivolume work on oratory, and worked as a pleader (similar to a defense attorney), and Maria Montessori (1870–1952), an innovative Italian educator whose strategies for teaching young children, *The Montessori Method* (1912), continue to be influential today.

Quintilian: Games and Education in Ancient Rome

The Roman Empire embraced almost all the known world of ancient times, from Africa to England and from Spain to the near East. Rome was a busy and lively city, overflowing with people from all races and traditions, and public and private life was filled with games. We are aware of a number of dice, marbles, and board games from Roman times that blended different traditions and were built with precious materials. An example is Tabula, a military version of modern backgammon, whose roots can be traced back to Egypt. Some exemplars of this game were carved in marble or precious wood; Emperor Claudius purportedly had one built into his imperial carriage. At a public and institutional level, the year was structured around religious and public feasts, when games and shows—such as sports competitions, gladiator fights, and/or theater productions and musical performances—were high points of annual celebrations.

The Latin words for "game" and "playing" were *ludus* and *ludere*, so that gladiators fought in *ludi gladiatori*, and theater shows were acted in *ludi scaenici*. Ludus indicated any activity that was not related to working and earning money for living and was, therefore, part of the *otium* (leisure) that only free and rich people could enjoy (Botturi & Loh, 2008). Leisure activities included sports, music, arts, fighting, public speaking, reading and writing literature, and learning mathematics and science. Indeed, these activities included all that the Romans understood to be part of the education of the sons of their best families. In short, the early Romans' leisure activities included what we now call "school," even if it took a rather different form.

The word *ludus* also indicated the place where people trained for sports or other games, such as the outside-of-city location of a *lanista*, the owner and trainer of gladiators. When public schools were founded, they, too, used the name *ludus*, so that the very word used for "game" was also used for "school." From our modern perspective of regarding fun as being opposed to work and viewing studying as work, using the same word for game and school can be counterintuitive. Yet, when we begin to see that teaching and learning, the education of children, and games have a great deal in common, we are reminded of the roots of Western culture. Games actually have a large potential as teaching and learning tools that we can learn to exploit in the 21st century.

What was the role of games in Roman formal education? Parents carried out the education of their children until the later age of the Empire, when public schools and eventually fee-based schools were opened. While we do not have many documents about the teaching methods of ancient Rome, we can rely on the words of Quintilian (1856/2006), a Hispanicus Roman citizen. He opened the first public rhetoric school, funded by the state treasury around AD 70. In the *Institutio Oratoria* (*Institutes of Oratory*, comprising 12 books or volumes), Quintilian recorded the school's method for the fundamental education of an orator. In Rome at that time, before a man could participate fully in the civil life of the Empire, he had to be an excellent orator. Although specific in terms of subject matter, Quintilian's work is regarded as the highest summary of Roman education.

In the first book of *Institutes of Oratory*, Quintilian emphasizes the connection between amusement and learning, saying that children need to enjoy (not dislike) instruction so that they will be motivated to continue to learn as they grow older:

> For it will be necessary, above all things, to take care lest the child should conceive a dislike to the application which he cannot yet love, and continue to dread the bitterness which he has once tasted, even beyond the years of infancy. Let his instruction be an amusement to him. (1856/2006, book 1, chapter 1, paragraph 20)

Amusement is paramount, "because application to learning depends on the will, which cannot be forced" (Quintilian, 1856/2006, book 1, chapter 3, paragraph 8), just like in games, where no one can be forced to play (Botturi & Loh, 2008). How can teaching and learning become amusing and enjoyable?

> … let him be questioned and praised; let him never feel pleased that he does not know a thing; and sometimes, if he is unwilling to learn, let another be taught before him, of whom he may be envious. Let him strive for victory now and then, and generally suppose that he gains it; and let his powers be called forth by rewards such as that age prizes. (Quintilian, 1856/2006, book 1, chapter 1, paragraph 20)

If we were asked to rewrite this last quotation with modern terminology, we would use words such as feedback (be praised/never feel pleased); competition (let another be taught before him/ strive for victory); and rewards. Interestingly, these words belong to the domain of games. Games, and video games among them, offer tools, design concepts, and new yet traditional perspectives for education.

Another reason for integrating games into teaching and learning is that boys and girls naturally like to play. Quintilian offers an even more convincing argument for making games part of instruction: when we observe their gameplay, we see students' natural vivacity:

> Nor will play in boys displease me; it is also a sign of vivacity, and I cannot expect that he who is always dull and spiritless will be of an eager disposition in his studies, when he is indifferent even to that excitement which is natural to his age. (1856/2006, book 1, chapter 3, paragraph 10)

Yet Quintilian moves a step further, noting that when students enter a game, their individual personalities become more evident: "In their plays, also, their moral dispositions show themselves more plainly … " (1856/2006, book 1, chapter 3, paragraph 12). A game is indeed a safe space, delimited and at the same time protected by its rules, where the players' personalities can more freely emerge. Indeed, this is an important point for teachers to remember as they try to develop empathy with their students.

But what exactly are the games to which Quintilian refers? The Roman public speaker was experienced enough to understand that not all games have positive impacts on learning:

> There must, however, be bounds set to [play], lest the refusal of it beget an aversion to study, or too much indulgence in it a habit of idleness. There are some kinds of amusement, too, not unserviceable for sharpening the wits of boys, as when they contend with each other by proposing all sorts of questions in turn. (1856/2006, book 1, chapter 3, paragraph 10)

While playing remains a natural mode of learning, structured play, i.e., through games, is a way to control this mode and to make it purposeful. We will discuss the notion of play more in the next section, as we discuss the writings of Montessori. The importance of play structured by rules is also the reason why the next section of this chapter and parts of other chapters in this book provide basic notions of game design. The definitions of goals, rules, feedback structures, and other game elements are what can turn students' natural attitude toward playing into a constructive force for learning, even in formal settings. Teachers may find that their goals are to leverage games "not unserviceable for sharpening the wits" of students and to propose new ones. Additionally, as the authors of Chapter 14 in this book advocate, educators will be amazed to observe that when students design their own educational games, they learn content at deep, analytical levels.

Maria Montessori: School and Games in the Early 1900s

Two thousand years ago, experienced teachers such as Quintilian recognized the value of playing and games in education. The notion of play to enhance or otherwise facilitate learning has moved on through the history of education and educational theory until today, when the explosive growth of the video game industry and the diffusion of digital technologies have brought renewed attention to games. Before we discuss current educational practices, let's examine some insights from Maria Montessori (1912), an Italian educator who proposed her own pedagogical method for the early education of children. This method, presented in her book *The Montessori Method*, was implemented in the first Children's House in Rome. She moved to Spain and later lived in Sri Lanka and India and established Children's Houses in each country. As more educators heard about the effectiveness of this new method, Montessori schools were established throughout Europe, North America, and eventually worldwide. Many preschools and elementary schools around the world today base their pedagogy on Montessori's methodology.

The main idea supporting the Montessori method is that children and human beings in general are natural learners, curious and with a thirst for knowledge. The main goal of formal education is not to spoil intrinsic motivation but to nurture it, according to each child's character. Montessori's method emphasizes self-paced and self-initiated learning, promoting hands-on and sensory education that fosters experimentation and hypothesis testing, in which the naturally "absorbent mind" of children can find new knowledge. Value is also placed on the community of learners as a stimulus to personal development.

For our purposes, Montessori's idea of discipline, which does not mean sitting still and listening but being active in an ordered way, is insightful. In Montessori's words:

> The pedagogical method of observation has for its base the liberty of the child;
> and liberty is activity. … We call an individual disciplined when he is master of
> himself, and can, therefore, regulate his own conduct when it shall be neces-
> sary to follow some rule of life. Such a concept of active discipline is not easy to
> comprehend or to apply. (1912, p. 86)

Now, liberty in children is expressed through playing. Of course, Montessori was aware that some forms of playing are destructive and must be avoided. But she maintains that educating means stimulating the development of the good nature of children, without constraining their natural drive to learn by imposing rigid forms, helping them grow to their full potential. By allowing free movement within a structured environment—which actually echoes the very idea of gameplay as presented at the opening of this chapter—the teacher can properly observe his or her pupils, because "from the child itself he will learn how to perfect himself as an educator" (p. 13).

> We must, therefore, check in the child whatever offends or annoys others, or whatever tends toward rough or ill-bred acts. But all the rest—every manifestation having a useful scope—whatever it be, and under whatever form it expresses itself, must not only be permitted, but must be observed by the teacher. (Montessori, 1912, p. 87)

The very backbone of the Montessori method shares so much with the ways that playing and designing educational games can enhance learning. Actually, an analysis of Montessori's text reveals that the words "game/games" appear as often as "example/examples" (93 and 95 times, respectively), and more often than "experiment/experiments" (only 28 times).

Montessori cautions that teachers must be careful to select materials that convey useful information, not games or stories with frivolous content. And teachers must take care not to obscure the distinct roles of teacher and students by acting like children themselves; instead, they need to appeal to children's need to understand worthwhile content that will help them function well as adults.

> (…) those who teach little children too often have the idea that they are educating babies and seek to place themselves on the child's level by approaching him with games, and often with foolish stories. Instead of all this, we must know how to call to the man which lies dormant within the soul of the child. (1912, p. 37)

So what is the point in using games, or even thinking of education as something that has to do with playing? How does this work in practice? We mentioned that the observation of children during free play is the first way teachers can help their students learn. At the same time, directed and purposeful play through educational games with rules is one of the primary tools of the Montessori Children's Houses. Providing a direction that makes playing ordered toward a definite end is what distinguishes natural play from playing educational games, making the teacher's guiding role paramount:

> We speak, it is true, of games in education, but it must be made clear that we understand by this term a free activity, ordered to a definite end; not disorderly noise, which distracts the attention. (Montessori, 1912, p. 181)

Montessori promotes the idea of nurturing children's inner lives with freedom to follow activities that provide motivation in and of themselves. While teachers and game designers often try to find a prize, a reward, or a punishment that will motivate learners and/or players, Montessori claims that true motivation arises from within, as individuals are given the freedom to pursue activities from which they gain a feeling of power or mastery:

Man, disciplined through liberty, begins to desire the true and only prize which will never belittle or disappoint him—the birth of human power and liberty within that inner life of his from which his activities must spring. (1912, p. 101)

There is a truth of game design: performing well in a good game is enough to make it worth playing. As we learn to be better players, there is no need for external prizes or motivators. For game designers, this means that players will play only good games. Teachers, in turn, should understand that students will engage only with content and activities that they perceive to be relevant and through which they understand they will learn. Once that happens and they feel engaged, this will be enough to sustain intense, rewarding work.

We hope that these brief insights into the Montessori method shed more light on the connections among games, learning, and education. Indeed, a major game developer, Will Wright, father of SimCity and The Sims and a former Montessori school student, testifies to the power of the Montessori method:

> [The] Montessori [method] taught me the joy of discovery. … It showed you can become interested in pretty complex theories, like Pythagorean theory, say, by playing with blocks. It's all about learning on your terms, rather than a teacher explaining stuff to you. SimCity comes right out of Montessori—if you give people this model for building cities, they will abstract from it principles of urban design. (Will Wright, quoted in Seabrook, 2006)

Wright gave a video presentation in 2007 in which he credits the Montessori school he attended in Atlanta up to sixth grade for engendering his fascination with learning (www.ted.com/talks/will_wright_makes_toys_that_make_worlds.html). Before he demonstrates aspects of the game, Spore, which he was developing at that time, he talks about learning by playing with toys designed by Montessori:

> And she would design these toys, where kids in playing with the toys would actually come to understand these deep principles of life and nature through play. And since they discovered those things, it really stuck with them so much more, and also they would experience their own failures; there was a failure-based aspect to learning there. It was very important. (Wright, 2007)

Games and Video Games, Yesterday and Today

Through the words of Quintilian and Montessori, our speedy journey across the centuries offered a number of convincing reasons to integrate games and game-based activities into formal education. Indeed, these types of activities seem to be a part of the Western educational tradition in their own right.

Why is it, then, that many educators feel games are so distant from school? Peters (2008) argues that distance education is the most industrialized form of education and that "undoubtedly, distance education is … a result of the historical development of teaching and learning" (p. 140). The last two centuries have achieved the great goal of opening education to all citizens and children, a movement that is ongoing under the heading of "lifelong learning." While lifelong learning is an extremely valuable achievement, public schools have had to cope with large numbers of students, bringing about the standardization of education, or, as Peters (2008) puts it, "mass production." Technology, and digital technology in particular, has played a special role in this transformation of education. On one hand, technology supports and reinforces the mass production and wide availability of education, specifically in the forms of distance and online education (Peters, 2008). On the other hand, recent advances in technology have pulled educators' attention back to more human, individual concerns. Digital art, social software, Web 2.0, and instructional video games are so integrated into educational, training, and assessment practices in the business world and in nearly every field, including education, that technology itself is no longer in the foreground. What generates high value is how individual teachers and students (as well as industrial and personnel trainers, bank managers, and many others) choose to use these technologies. The emergence of pervasive technologies coincides with a movement advocating the rediscovery of integrated, meaningful learning in schools, fueled by a recent emphasis on constructivism, as opposed to traditional, teacher-centered instruction.

Younger teachers have grown up in this different, more advanced technological environment; thus, they belong to the first generation of "digital natives" (Prensky, 2001). Moreover, today's children are fully digital natives because they are growing up with technologies that they do not even perceive as being unusual; personal computers, cell phones, iPods, and more are normal parts of their lives. Herein lies one more important reason for and benefit of using games in education: many students are already familiar with them, so why not use video games as our allies and as catalysts for learning?

Components of Interactive Entertainment

The first step for integrating a new technology into teaching is to become familiar with the technology itself, not only as a user but also as a reflective user. Teachers need to play games themselves to understand how to integrate them into their curricula and classroom practices most effectively and to use them as additional tools to encourage students' creativity. Playing games is not enough—or all gamers would be great teachers! Teachers need a reflective experience (i.e., to understand the technology while they use it) to perceive the inner workings of the game, understand how it was constructed, and grasp the logic behind the interface.

To this purpose, we offer a short primer on the basic elements of interactive entertainment. Having the right vocabulary enhances observation, as it allows us to focus on specific elements. The challenge is blending terminology from instructional design and game design in a sensible and useful way.

Story, Game, Play

Due to the variety of games and playing experiences, it is difficult to find an agreed-upon, crystal-clear definition of game or entertainment. However, we can identify three major components that occur in all gameplay: play, game, and story (Hirumi & Stapleton, 2008). We know that playing is a spontaneous mode of experience for human children, as it apparently is for other animal species. Natural play develops as children explore their surroundings, playing with toys and with other children in make-believe situations, with games, and in competitions. Playing takes a more specific place in the life of individuals as they grow up and is restricted to limited time spans and situations. When play takes the form of games, gameplay is structured by a set of rules and goals. Additionally, most games are set in a fictional environment and develop based on a story, with characters, locations, and events.

These three elements, play, game, and story, are closely interrelated and commonly referenced in entertainment design, including game and video game design (Hirumi & Stapleton, 2008). In the next few paragraphs we provide working definitions and examples for each of them.

As Hirumi and Stapleton (2008) note, story is concerned with the question, "Why should players care about the game?" A good story is a compelling medium that hooks readers' or players' attention and interest because it says something that relates to them, for example, "That world is like my world"; "I feel like that character"; "What happens to him could happen to me." What we, as readers, audience, or players, demand from a story is that it affects our emotions, including feelings of empathy. Good stories do so through conflicts, sometimes external, such as hero vs. villain, and sometimes internal, such as marry her or not? (McKee, 1997).

The elements that make a story are characters, worlds, and plot events (Hirumi & Stapleton, 2008). As different from linear storytelling, video games and simulation games use interactive storytelling; the main character is the player who can influence the storyline with her/his actions. It is therefore paramount that players can easily identify with the main character and experience the game from the character's point of view: "Who am I in the game? What are my goals and drivers (motivations)? Who are my friends and enemies? What world do I live in?"

Successful video games almost always rely on a strong story. Some borrow it from other entertainment products, such as the video games that retell narratives from popular cultural fixtures, such as *Lord of the Rings*, *Dora the Explorer*, and Barbie. Other games create an original story based on existing characters or worlds, for example, Enter the Matrix and Star Wars: Knights of the Old Republic. The majority of entertainment games, however, create completely new narratives, as in World of Warcraft, Half-Life, and Grand Theft Auto.

Creating an interactive instructional game with a compelling narrative and believable characters in a consistent world requires talent and experience. As nonprofessional storytellers, we can rely on old stories or on archetypal figures that have appeal because they awake cultural memories. For example, we could design a game for children that re-invents *The Three Little Pigs*, maybe giving them magic abilities. Or, we could build on archetypal patterns, such as hero versus villain, catastrophe versus rescuer, or outcast versus hero. Watching movies—especially the movies that students enjoy—would offer a wealth of ideas.

Once the player has entered the fictional world of the story, through a narration or animation, gameplay is concerned with the questions: "What do I do? How do I act in the game?" (Hirumi & Stapleton, 2008). Interactive entertainment is not as much about multimedia, 3-D graphics, and high-definition music as it is about actions and decision making. The whole point in a game is that players can lose or win depending on their choices and moves.

Within a digital or nondigital game, play can be described by causes that prompt players to act (e.g., avoid a blow, defeat enemies, explore a place), responses or actions taken (e.g., jump, combat, talk), and consequences or results in terms of a new state of the game (e.g., points, feedback, new challenges to be taken). Each action in the game should be related to the game itself; it's disappointing to play a game only to realize that one's decisions make no difference. Good games do not need to have many actions allowed during play, but they must have the right ones, actions that actually allow players to act and to influence how the game turns out. Is the game about exploring and finding objects? Then players should be able to move, observe, and collect things, such as in Zelda. Is it about trades? Then players should be able to buy and sell properties and make money, such as in Monopoly.

The most important point when designing a game is finding the right pillars (Lipo, 2008), that is, the core actions in the game, and to invest in making them appealing to players. To be appealing, the actions should be easy to initiate, possibly spectacular in their application/s, and designed to give fast, clear feedback.

"Game" includes the procedural aspect of playing a game, its mechanics or inner functioning, and the structure that constrains the free movement of playing—making it an enjoyable challenge. A game is a potential play experience, like a toy that is not in motion until a child turns it on or holds it and moves it.

A game is basically a set of constraints described by (1) the goal/s it assigns to players (e.g., earn the most points, fulfill your destiny, destroy the red army); (2) the rules the players have to follow; and (3) the tools they have to help them achieve the goal (Hirumi & Stapleton, 2008). Some of the rules and possible moves are supported or represented by the setting or instruments/toys used to play the game, such as a board, the pieces, or a set of computational rules programmed into a video game's code.

Once again, less is more: good and playable games have a limited set of rules, resulting in a soft learning curve. This leaves space for learning to master the game and winning by developing good strategies. The best examples of limited sets of rules are chess or Go; it can take half an hour to learn the basic moves, yet it can take a lifetime to become a good player. In video games, car racing games and the Wii are good examples of limited rules. The focus is on playing rather than on learning to play, or, as we could say in instructional terms, the focus is on participating in the activity and absorbing the content rather than on memorizing the assignment text.

Goals, rules, tools, and toys are the necessary ingredients for generating a meaningful play experience. Combining these ingredients effectively requires specific expertise, so that a good strategy for comprehending how games work is to observe common games and to try to understand them from the design point of view. This involves experimenting with or examining known sets of rules for developing games with new content.

Games as Experience

Talking about different elements of interactive entertainment design should not lead readers to suppose that any entertainment product can be divided into discrete parts. Of course, the design idea can start from any point: an intriguing world or a beloved character; an interesting game mechanism that simulates a thinking process for students to experience and learn; or a set of actions that generate meaningful interactions, and so on. But actually, such elements are the colors with which a skillful painter can produce a consistent, unified work of art.

The key to designing a game or learning experience is to think of it as an experience arc (Stapleton & Hirumi, in press) that supports a memorable and intense experience. An experience arc means an experience that stays together as a good story does: it has a beginning that motivates the learner/player to act; a middle during which the story develops through challenges, wins, and losses; and an end that resolves conflicts, rewards players for skillful play, and mentions the possibility of another new adventure (Parrish, 2008).

The whole point of using any technology in education is to lift instruction from knowledge transmission to an experience students find meaningful, that is, to set the stage for moments in life when people—learners and teachers—are living in the present moment and engaged with the activity. The expectation or goal is that everyone involved will become a different and maybe even a better person.

Terminology Throughout This Book

The triad of story, play, and game can be used to describe different products in interactive entertainment. In Chapter 15 of this volume, Botturi proposes the same distinction through a metaphor, in which games are described as structures and the play dynamic as a force animating the structure.

Of course, story, play, and game are intimately related: play actions must be supported by adequate sets of goals and rules and should be consistent with the narrative setting. Actually, game design is not about conceiving an idea for the three elements and then stapling them together; rather, it is to let the ideas grow harmoniously from the same core idea.

Adding an educational dimension to the mixture is the challenge tackled throughout this book. How can instructional goals be integrated into the game flow without disrupting it? How can assessment take place within a game? The core idea, which is useful both to small-scale and large-scale development, is that tacking education onto the back of entertainment or vice-versa will only spoil the original product, resulting in fancy-colored, dull instruction or in poor edutainment. Designing an instructional game means designing the game while designing the instruction, blending the two together, leveraging the power of two very different but compatible approaches to tackle the same problem: making an experience memorable (for more details see Hirumi & Stapleton, 2008).

Benefits for and Challenges to Learning

An abundance of games, and not just video games, are available to teachers. They include not only games designed for learning but edutainment titles and commercial, off-the-shelf (COTS) games. Making their own games is an option for teachers as well. While not all teachers have the computer software skills or programming knowledge necessary to make a complex video game, they certainly have the ability to make non-computer-based games using conventional class-room supplies. They may choose to create a game using accessible tools, such as PowerPoint (see Barbour et al., Chapter 14, for further details), or in some cases they can modify existing commercial games, such as Neverwinter Nights. With all of the options available to teachers, finding or creating the right game to motivate their learners has become an achievable task.

Like any instructional method or tool, the most important thing for teachers is to match their goals and objectives with the appropriate means to achieve them. In some cases a game may be an appropriate choice. As we have discussed, both Quintilian and Montessori emphasized that games should be used appropriately and with specific educational purposes. It is not always easy to determine whether a game and which type of game will be the most effective means of instruction. The following section outlines the advantages and the disadvantages associated with using games for learning.

Advantages of Playing Games

Games for learning have many advantages that scholars and teachers have proposed in this book and in many other publications as well, most of which have merit. This chapter does not propose to include all of those; instead, it focuses on what we consider to be the most critical points for teachers to understand. The list below summarizes the advantages that we will cover in detail in the following paragraphs.

- ▶ **Increased Motivation.** Students who are having fun and are engaged tend to find the learning experience meaningful and memorable.

- ▶ **Complex Understanding.** Complex processes, especially relationships among systems and system components, can be well reflected in games.

- ▶ **Reflective Learning.** Learners are given the chance to experiment within a safe play space and to reflect upon the outcomes of the decisions they make.

- ▶ **Feedback and Self-Regulation.** Through experimentation and feedback, players learn to refine their choices and to control their actions within the game space.

Increased Motivation. People enjoy playing games. They can be fun and are often highly engaging—these are the reasons why we play games. While it may seem obvious, this point cannot be overstated: learners who are having fun and are engaged tend to be successful. Games are surely not the only method to motivate learners, but they are certainly one of the best. Games often intrinsically motivate learners because the rewards built into the game increase content knowledge and thereby improve game performance.

While games are powerful in fostering motivation, their application is not that straightforward. Some people like playing, some do not, and different players—by gender, age, expertise, and temperament—like different games. Finding the right game can fire up your classroom, but remember that this will require some observation. Students will not enjoy playing a game they find too easy or unimaginative. We will come back to the key role of observation in the next section, devoted to principles.

Complex Understanding. Complex processes, especially relationships among systems and system components, can be well reflected in games.

A game comprises a finely balanced system of rules that should work together to create a meaningful, interesting experience for players (Salen & Zimmermann, 2003). Indeed, simulation games can be an extremely useful tool, especially to teach complex systems. The power of games, on which many of Montessori's games leverage their appeal, is that players do not need to dismantle the system analytically to understand it, but they can interact with it through the game directly, leaving analysis to grow on the more solid basis of direct experience.

Take for instance the video game Civilization. Squire and his colleagues investigated the acquisition of complex knowledge structures and understandings among students who played this game. Squire, Giovanetto, Devane, and Durga (2005) found that students tend to acquire a fundamental understanding of the workings of society, including politics, the military, and civilian life, along with the sub-components of each of these (e.g., diplomacy, research and development, food supply, entertainment, population safety, etc.). In ways that a teacher using didactic instruction would have a difficult time conveying, these complex, interrelated concepts make sense to students who played this game (Squire et al., 2005).

Recently, there has been an interest in games that place students in the roles of adults interacting as professionals would in real-life situations. Otherwise abstract and apparently out-of-reach concepts can be effectively taught through a game, especially a game that simulates the real world, called a simulation game. In an NPR radio interview, Becky, a 15-year-old Urban Science simulation game player, reflected on a neighborhood she had visited during gameplay: "They also need to pay attention to green space, because if you place green space in the wrong place, it attracts more crime instead of what its purpose is" (Lichtenstein, 2008). Not only was she reflecting about the gamer and her actions in the game, but she also was extending her reflection to the real world, a lesson that mainstream education should find noteworthy.

A tangible side benefit of this complex understanding of system components is the ease of assessing learners' knowledge. Specifically, knowledge is demonstrated by successfully playing the simulation game itself. In other words, without an understanding of complex system components and their relationships, the student could not play the game or could not play very well. The game, in this case, doubles as the means of instruction and the assessment tool. However, this does not imply that learning happens by itself. Squire used teachers and moderators to conduct frequent debriefings, asking students to see themselves in action and then to reflect on their experiences. By analyzing their gameplay, they learn from the game and from each other, improving with each iteration. This reflective process is what Montessori referred to as learning about oneself.

Reflective Learning. Learners are given the chance to experiment within a safe play space and to reflect upon the outcomes of the decisions they make.

Reflective learning is the fundamental commonality instructional games have with the Montessori method, constructivism, and active learning in general. The ability of learners to have some level of control over their learning is fundamental. With improved control comes improved playing of the game, and as students become more proficient players, they increase and enhance their knowledge. As learners become more and more aware of their own learning, they gain confidence in their abilities and in themselves. Quintilian referred to learners' personalities emerging as they play games, also a central point in Montessori's method, which focuses on the individual child (1912, p. 104). Games have helped teachers and students to rekindle this old flame, one that may have once seemed lost to standardized education in the 20th century.

Feedback and Self-Regulation. Through experimentation and feedback, players learn to refine their choices and learn self-regulation within the game space.

Games often provide more feedback to learners than traditional forms of instruction. The game rules and mechanics demand action from players and provide feedback to them based on their actions. This happens frequently when playing a game. A feedback loop, whereby players make choices, deal with the consequences, and refine those choices, is created. Montessori (1912) referred to this type of experimentation when she emphasized the importance of children seeing and understanding their errors to learn self-regulation. Throughout her method, Montessori also emphasized careful note taking and observation of learners during activities to help students reflect upon their own actions. The teacher may choose to point out specific events to reflect on either during the game or in the debriefing following play. Stolovitch and Thiagarajan (1980), when giving advice for promoting self-regulation by players, make a further suggestion that the teacher "Stop and ask brief questions of players as they wait their turns. How appropriately do they reply?" (p. 90).

Disadvantages of Using Games

As with any choice of instructional method, a good teacher wisely anticipates learners' various possible reactions. The following section outlines some of the ways that learners can react to a game that could work against the intended learning outcomes. A knowledgeable teacher can avoid each of these. The Principles and Prescriptions section that follows will explain how to avoid these potential pitfalls.

▶ **Subversion of Rules.** In competitive situations, players may employ strategies that ignore the learning outcomes in favor of winning tactics.

▶ **Games Take Time.** The increased time associated with preparing and delivering a game may not seem to be an option for some teachers.

▶ **Loss of Teacher Control.** Teachers may not always have complete control over which parts of the game the students find meaningful and memorable.

▶ **Traditional Learning May Now Seem Dull.** Traditional learning, during which students receive less feedback and have fewer choices, may be more difficult for them after playing a game.

▶ **Learners May Be Accustomed to Professional Game Media.** With modest budgets, expertise, and tools, teachers may not be able to provide games of the same quality that learners are used to playing at home.

Subversion of Rules. In competitive situations, players may employ strategies that ignore the learning outcomes in favor of winning tactics.

Most teachers who have used games in their classrooms can report instances when some clever students figured out a "flaw" or "loophole" in the game rules that allowed them to perform exceptionally well and win often. This behavior is to be expected from learners who are comfortable manipulating, bending, shaping, and modifying games. Terms such as "hacks," "mods," "cheats," and "trainers" are familiar to these digital natives. It is not surprising that they would apply such tactics to games in the classroom. Unfortunately, these behaviors, while arguably useful in learning technology skills generally, can have detrimental effects during the game on their learning and on the other players, as these subversive, inappropriately competitive tactics can create a negative game experience for everyone. Students who are less adept at video gaming will be likely to regard such behavior as unfair and may not want to associate themselves with further gameplay.

Rather than completely subverting the innate, lateral thinking processes that the students are using to find the right hack or cheat, consider this a chance for students to understand that sometimes certain behavior is acceptable, and sometimes it is not. This is in and of itself a level of complex understanding and a meta-skill worth developing in the students. Indeed, in the appropriate circumstances discovering the right "trick" can be a goal in itself, just like finding the alternative and shorter way to solve an apparently complex geometry problem.

Games Take Time. The increased time associated with preparing and delivering a game may not seem to be an option for some teachers.

This is, perhaps, the section of the chapter that some veteran teachers may skip to and read first. In an era of standardization of instruction along with an ever-increasing amount of content to be covered, concern over time is understandable. For teachers experiencing this squeeze, if a game takes too long, it may not seem an option, regardless of the potential positive learning outcomes. The increased time associated with playing a game may be due to the perception (often correct) that a game requires an increase in either the teacher's preparation time before playing or in the class time needed to play the game or both.

A limited length of time to cover certain material is by no means a simple obstacle to overcome. Teachers often have no choice in the matter; they must cover a certain amount of material within a given length of time. For the teachers who skipped to this section to see how this significant problem can be overcome, we apologize. You will have to look ahead to the Prescriptions section of the chapter for specific advice on how to tackle this problem. For now, suffice it to say that this is a significant issue to be dealt with and that just as when playing a game choices have to be made, sometimes there may have to be a trade-off between positive learning outcomes and the increased time it may take to achieve them.

Loss of Teacher Control. Teachers may not always have complete control over which parts of the game the students find meaningful and memorable.

In an era of standards, goals, and objectives, control over the instructional environment is extremely important to teachers if they are to "get through" everything they need to. In some cases, learners may gain profound understandings or insights through a game, yet they may not be related to the intended goals or objectives. In other cases, a learner may achieve the teacher's intended understanding, yet the teacher may find it difficult to interpret that understanding, especially if the teacher is inexperienced at debriefing learners after the game. On the whole, the game may be of great benefit to the learner, but the teacher may still feel obligated to re-teach the content through more traditional forms to ensure that the intended goals and objectives of the instruction are met.

Traditional Learning May Now Seem Dull. Traditional classroom learning, during which students may receive less feedback and be given fewer choices, may be more difficult for students after playing a game.

Just as games can be fun and engaging, traditional learning may not be. The contrast between the two may be significant for some students, and they may seem to disengage during traditional instruction. As Stolovitch and Thiagarajan (1980) caution, "Once wound up, a group is hard to wind down. Games are so motivating that they may stir up hornets' nests with unpleasant consequences. Who wants to listen to a boring lecture after an exciting game? And when can we play again?" (p. 89).

However, the opposite also holds: once energy is spent in mastering a game that hooked the students' interest, they might be willing to sit for a while and be helped to understand the actual point of the activity clearly from the teacher. The real challenge is to strike a healthy balance between games and other media or forms of teaching, so that each one plays its role and is reinforced by the others.

Learners May Be Accustomed to Professional Game Media. With modest budgets, expertise, and tools, teachers may not be able to provide games of the same quality that learners are used to playing at home.

There is a stereotype in popular culture in the United States of over-stimulated, impressed by nothing, apathetic youth. These students are so used to popular movies, prime-time television, and knock-your-socks-off, high-tech games that any effort by a teacher to motivate them falls on deaf ears. While this is indeed an exaggerated portrait, as with any stereotype, there is a core of truth to it. Efforts by the teacher to provide an exciting and stimulating learning environment, including the use of games, may not have the intended motivational outcome, as these students may see the school game as inferior to the out-of-school entertainment media. To these jaded students, the classroom game may seem not worth even trying.

Principles and Prescriptions for Educators on Integrating Games into Instruction

This next section wraps up this chapter by outlining eight key principles and prescriptions that can guide teachers who are trying to integrate games or game-based instruction into their classes. Within the guidelines, we use the following terms:

▶ A *principle* states a relationship between/among some game elements or variables. These stem from the advantages and disadvantages presented above and are based on existing research or theory.

▶ A *prescription* uses the principle to give advice or to provide a strategy for improving student learning and the teaching/learning environment.

▶ The *rationale* provides information about how the principle and prescription were derived.

Principle 1: Briefing and debriefing are critical to learning from a game.

Prescription 1.1. Always conduct a briefing before playing. Briefing should not constrain the game within a compulsory learning setting, but should stimulate the following questions:

▶ What is the goal of this game?

▶ What are the rules of this game?

▶ Why are we going to play this game?

▶ What should I observe during the game (my own playing, how teams behave, etc.)?

Rationale: The briefing before the game is played establishes rules, expectations, and intended learning outcomes. Unless you are attempting to have your students discover the point of the game, it is important to explain the appropriate structure during the briefing.

Prescription 1.2. Always conduct a debriefing after playing. Debriefings should ask learners to respond to the following questions:

▶ How do you feel?

▶ What happened?

▶ What did you learn?

▶ How can you extend and apply this knowledge beyond the game?

Rationale: Without a debriefing, learning outcomes are unpredictable. Even with a debriefing, outcomes may be erratic. A good debriefing is based on a solid briefing, well-designed game-play (including careful observations by the teacher, see below), and appropriately allocated time to conduct the debriefing. The debriefing sets aside time for students to reflect on their complete experience while playing the game. Without a debriefing, students' perceptions of what they learned from the game can be extremely biased or distorted. It is also important to move through each of the questions in order, without skipping to "what did you learn?" Many students' emotions will be high, and some students may dwell on negative interactions with other students or feelings of frustration from not being able to play the game well or as well as others. Allowing them to express their negative as well as positive feelings honestly prepares for the reflection that is to come. During this part of the debriefing, the teacher models how to understand and accept emotions and to analyze how our feelings affect our ability to think and to learn.

Principle 2: Prior knowledge required for gameplay is best achieved through different instructional methods.

Prescription 2.1. Make sure players have an appropriate level of content knowledge before they play the game.

> *Rationale:* Students who lack proper content knowledge may be quickly overwhelmed, which will hinder their learning during the game and in the future when they encounter the same subject area.

Principle 3: The teacher must be aware of the players' actions during the game.

Prescription 3.1. Observe your learners while they play; take notes and ask them probing questions during down time.

> *Rationale:* The majority of students' learning will take place as they reflect on their experiences. The more aware of their actions you are, the better you will be able to help them reflect and learn from the game.

Principle 4: The teacher should be not only a content expert but also a game expert.

Prescription 4.1. The teacher should like games or learn to like them before attempting to integrate them into instruction.

> *Rationale:* If you do not like to play games in general, consider not using them. Students may have difficulty enjoying something you obviously do not like. You can learn to like them, though, by starting to play them and trying to appreciate their designs, graphic effects, and/ or narratives. The best way to learn to appreciate games is to play with those who really like games—maybe your students! If you do not enjoy competition, you might find simulation games to be engaging. And if you have never played games online, try playing the ones designed for elementary students—you may be surprised at how much fun they can be.

Prescription 4.2. Pick games that you or your students enjoy.

> *Rationale:* If you are going to use a game, choose one that you enjoy. Your enthusiasm for a game will be contagious, and your students will start with positive expectations. Also, there might be games that you do not like but that most of your students enjoy. If you are willing to relinquish complete control for a while and support your students while they do their own learning, those games could become powerful learning tools in your classes. Another possibility if your students are hooked on a particular game you do not like, perhaps because you think it is too violent or superficial, would be to ask them to remodel or supplement the favored game's design or rules so that its goal is to teach one of your class or course learning objectives. This would be a great challenge for students who are accomplished game players. Alternatively, you could ask students to create a PowerPoint game (see Chapter 14 in this volume) and model it on their favorite video game's best qualities. They could design it to

teach one or more of your class's learning objectives that you find difficult to teach in a traditional way or that students in the past have found tedious.

Prescription 4.3. Play the game—a lot.

Rationale: In order to keep control over the activity, you should be part of the game. So, become a player; play the game yourself a number of times before you propose that students play it. Try not to use a game you have not played before. If you do not have a full understanding of the game yet want your students to play it in your class, someone should be present to help. Perhaps this would be a teaching assistant, a student teacher, or the students themselves. While this possibility might be feasible in a pinch, ultimately, you should learn to understand the game yourself so that you can conduct an adequate debriefing after gameplay.

Principle 5: Competition is a double-edged sword; it can yield different results depending on the players involved.

Prescription 5.1. Be careful not to overemphasize "winners" and "losers."

Rationale: Keep in mind that losers may leave with a negative perception of their experience, which could easily be transferred to the content when students conclude, "It's not interesting." Or if they fear the game is designed above their ability to succeed, they may say, "It's not for me." If the game is managed well, losers may actually learn more from their failures than self-satisfied winners. Keep in mind what game developer Wright said about how highly he valued his Montessori elementary school's educational toys: he learned from his failures.

Prescription 5.2. Consider cooperative gameplay.

Rationale: The moderator of the simulation or game should account for varying types of competition and not always use the typical winning team/losing team scenario. Consider having the cumulative score of all teams be measured against a standard. In this case, the teams work cooperatively to achieve a desired outcome rather than working against each other. Gredler (1997) offers another good example of well-conceived cooperative gameplay in her outline of the teams-games-tournaments (TGT) cooperative task structure. In this structure, the more advanced students would be grouped with the less advanced, or more experienced game players would be grouped with those who have less game experience, with three to four students per group. The TGT point structure is designed so that the less experienced or less advanced students score more points, and the more advanced students score fewer points. This requires the advanced students to tutor their less advanced peers. Thus, the gameplay rewards cooperation and collaboration rather than competition. Students' reactions to TGT showed that they perceived a decrease in classroom competitiveness and course difficulty. Gredler (1997) claims that competition is the essence of any game and that students' dependence on each other reinforces cooperation, an important characteristic of a positive classroom environment. Even if you choose not to use Gredler's approach, try to adopt an approach whereby every player can leave the game with a significant feeling of achievement and confidence.

Principle 6: The type of game should be appropriate for the content and objectives.

Prescription 6.1. When learning objectives are known and the content domain is structured, the amount of learner control can be decreased.

> *Rationale:* The teacher should use the known objectives and structured content to form a structured environment for the simulation or game. Efficiency is a real component of instruction, and a structured environment during gameplay yields more teacher control and greater efficiency. It also typically reduces the instructional time needed to complete the game. Structured environments are especially appropriate for lower levels tasks, such as discriminating or matching. While motivation may seem to be an issue, keep in mind that entertainment games incorporate rigid structures, in which players have little or no impact on the structure of the environment, yet they manage to maintain high levels of motivation. The movie industry has been successful, for example, and members of the audience exercise zero control over what is presented in a particular film. Just as a good story captures the audience's imagination, a well-designed game engages students' attention and serves as an efficient learning tool.

Prescription 6.2. When learning objectives are unknown and the content domain is unstructured, the amount of learner control can be increased.

> *Rationale:* In the case of a less-structured domain, providing learner control is effective in providing intrinsic motivation without dramatically increasing the instructional time otherwise needed. The designer should match the environment of the game to the less structured content domain. The structure of the game itself, including the rules, can be modified and objectives created at a later time, based on the experiences of the learners and/or negotiation with the instructor. For example, the players could interact and play in a space, without playing a game. Then they could create the game and the rules that would transform the play space into a game.

Principle 7: Small-scale games are extremely useful tools.

Prescription 7.1. Don't be afraid of small-scale games. Games smaller in scale, especially frame-games (Stolovitch & Thiagarajan, 1980, p. 5), are simple and familiar, and content can be interchanged easily from topic to topic.

> *Rationale:* For some, the use of complex games, such as Civilization, as powerful a learning tool as it is, may not, due to time and logistical constraints, be feasible. Often, smaller scale frame-games and drill-games, because they are simple to prepare and to play, can make efficient use of time and be effective learning tools. These are much smaller in scale and have interchangeable content. The teacher will not need to spend significant time discussing the rules, as the structure of the game is familiar to students. The time it takes to play the game is reasonable, and the teacher can often conduct mini-debriefings as each question is asked or as each aspect of content is brought up. There is no shame in using these small-scale, manageable games. If you, like many teachers, are worried about the time constraints that more complex games present, frame-games may be elegant solutions for you. Games such as bingo, or games based on shows like *Jeopardy!* and *Who Wants to Be a Millionaire* are a few

examples of some frame-games, and there are thousands of others (see Fadde's Chapter 13 in this volume for further details on drill-games). Remember to conduct a proper briefing and debriefing even when using these small-scale games.

Principle 8: Engaged game players march to the beat of a different drummer.

Prescription 8.1. Be aware that when students are playing good games, time flies, as it does during any activity when people are highly engaged.

> *Rationale:* Highly engaged learners reflect good teaching and planning. When students are playing a game as a learning activity, teachers need to be very careful in managing time. Keep in mind that even highly engaged learners might not learn the targeted skills and content if they do not reflect on their actions properly—so take time for debriefings and reflection.

Prescription 8.2. Test how long it takes to play the game ahead of time.

> *Rationale:* To present untested instruction to learners is something new teachers do nearly every day and what experienced teachers do when trying out an innovative method or presenting new research for the first time. However, presenting an untested game to students is, to put it mildly, not a sensible teaching practice. All sorts of things can arise, such as having to stop gameplay early due to malfunctioning or inadequate equipment, not allowing time for a debriefing, not being able to clarify the rules when students become confused, ad infinitum. Proper testing of the game before using it in class will prevent most of these setbacks. As you plan, a good rule of thumb is for every 15 minutes of gameplay, allow 5 minutes for briefing and 10 minutes for debriefing.

Conclusions

Our goal in this chapter is to provide sound reasoning for the integration of instructional video games and game-based activities into K–12 education. To provide depth and applicability, we revisited insights from the history of education through the eyes of Quintilian and Montessori, and then we provided a set of potential advantages and disadvantages of using games as instructional tools.

We then condensed practical guidelines for the use of computer games in the classroom into eight principles, each accompanied by a set of prescriptions and explained by a rationale. We believe that, by their very nature, games and video games can be powerful learning tools in many educational settings. For example, Chapters 5–9 in Section II detail games that may be played to facilitate learning in math, science, language arts, social studies, and physical education.

As with any instructional approach, method, or device, games entail some risks and require a minimal level of expertise. Every time a game is used as an instructional tool, teachers need to understand (1) how to play the game, (2) the rules of the game, (3) how the game will convey particular content to students, and (4) how to allow sufficient time for a briefing before and a debriefing after gameplay. And, perhaps most important, teachers need to enjoy playing the game themselves. While there are certainly pitfalls to avoid, learners can gain significant levels of understanding through well-placed, well-managed games in the curriculum. Of course, as games are not always the best instructional solution, teachers need to select the right times for using games. Expert teachers also determine the most appropriate games that will accommodate their students' needs and interests, the curriculum's content, and the school district's constraints.

We hope that our advice will help you, as a professional educator, to use games effectively to enhance students' learning. We also hope that our encouragement will help you to reexamine and understand anew the educational process and to think about teaching and learning from a fresh point of view.

References

Botturi, L., & Loh, C. S. (2008). Once upon a game: Rediscovering the roots of games in education. In C. T. Miller (Ed.), *Games: Their purpose and potential in education* (pp. 1–22). New York, NY: Springer Publishing.

Gredler, M. E. (1997). *Learning and instruction: Theory into practice* (2nd ed.). Upper Saddle River, NJ: Prentice Hall.

Hirumi, A., & Stapleton, C. (2008). Integrating fundamental ID tasks with game development processes to optimize game-based learning. In C. T. Miller (Ed.), *Games: Their purpose and potential in education* (pp. 127–162). New York, NY: Springer Publishing.

Lichtenstein, B. (Senior Executive Producer). (2008, August 18). Taking games seriously. *The infinite mind* [National Public Radio (NPR) broadcast]. Cambridge, MA: LCMedia. Available at www.lcmedia.com/mindprgm.htm

Lipo, P. (2008, July). Battling the curse of "more": Focusing your game on what's important. A presentation at the Games+Learning+Society (GLS) Conference 2008, Madison, WI. Summary retrieved August 6, 2008, from www.patricklipo.com/2008/06/09/pillars-and-razors/

McKee, R. (1997). *Story: Substance, structure, style and the principles of screenwriting*. New York, NY: HarperCollins.

Montessori, M. (1912). *The Montessori method* (A. E. George, Trans.). New York, NY: Frederick A. Stokes Company. Full text available online at http://digital.library.upenn.edu/women/montessori/method/method.html

Parrish, P. (2008). Plotting a learning experience. In L. Botturi & T. Stubbs (Eds.), *Handbook of visual languages in instructional design: Theories and practices* (pp. 91–111). Hershey, PA: IGI Global Information Science Reference.

Peters, O. (2008). *Distance education: Current issues, pedagogical considerations*. Hagen, Germany: FernUniversität Hagen.

Prensky, M. (2001). Digital natives, digital immigrants, part I. *On the Horizon, 9*(5), 1–6. Bradford, UK: MCB University Press.

Quintilian. (2006). *Institutes of oratory* (L. Honeycutt, Ed., & J. S. Watson, Trans.). (Original work, *Institutio Oratoria*, written ca. AD 90; English translation 1856.) Retrieved July 20, 2008, from http://honeyl.public.iastate.edu/quintilian/

Salen, K., & Zimmerman, E. (2003). *Rules of play: Game design fundamentals.* Cambridge, MA: MIT Press.

Seabrook, J. (2006, November 6). Game master. (Profiles: Will Wright). *The New Yorker.* Available at www.newyorker.com/archive/2006/11/06/061106fa_fact?currentPage=all

Squire, K., Giovanetto, L., Devane, B., & Durga, S. (2005). Building a self-organizing game-based learning environment. *TechTrends, 49*(5), 34–42.

Stapleton, C., & Hirumi, A. (in press). Interplay instructional strategy: Engaging learners with interactive entertainment conventions. In M. F. Shaughnessy & S. W. Veronikas (Eds.), *Pedagogical implications for online instruction.*

Stolovitch, H. D., & Thiagarajan, S. (1980). *Frame games.* Englewood Cliffs, NJ: Educational Technology Publications.

Wright, Will. (2007, July). Technology, entertainment, design (TED): Ideas worth spreading. TEDTalks video, filmed in March 2007 and posted in July 2007. New York, NY: Ted Conference LLC. Available at www.ted.com/talks/will_wright_makes_toys_that_make_worlds.html

3

The Game Brain

Tom Atkinson and Atsusi "2c" Hirumi

Successful gamers must focus, have patience,
develop a willingness to delay gratification, and
prioritize scarce resources. In other words, they think.

—Ron Nagy (2008, p. 1)

THE BRAIN HAS LONG BEEN A SUBJECT of study and fascination. Although many discoveries in the 1800s and early 1900s advanced interest about the brain and its functions, the word "neuroscience" as the study of the central nervous system, including the brain, did not appear until the 1960s. Traditionally, neuroscience represents a branch of the biological sciences. Recently, however, a surge of interest from many disciplines, including psychology, computer science, statistics, physics, philosophy, and medicine has broadened the scope to include any investigation of the central and peripheral nervous system. Neuroscience studies range from analyses of nerve cells to perceptual and motor tasks in the brain. With new imaging techniques, cognitive neuroscience describes how human cognition and emotion are mapped to specific neural circuits in the brain. While many forms of instruction may benefit from discoveries of the complex processes that occur when we think, learn, and play, game-based learning (GBL) may have the potential to benefit the most. This chapter describes processes that occur in the brain when learning and suggests how playing games, particularly video games, may support those processes.

Rapid advances in neuroimaging technology and neuroscience research have revolutionized our understanding of the human brain. Not long ago, scientists thought we were born with a finite number of brain cells and that the brain developed primarily during infancy and childhood. By the time we reached adulthood, brain structure was thought to be relatively complete. New information could be added to memory, but the overall structure was basically fixed. Scientists believed brain cells could not be regenerated and cautioned us against drinking and taking drugs because such behavior would kill whatever limited number of cells we had. It was also commonly assumed that particular regions of the brain were responsible for specific types of processing (e.g., right hemisphere—emotions, versus left hemisphere—logic). Before scientists understood the intricate network of communications that occur when individuals perform particular tasks, people were tagged as "right brained" if they could draw and "left brained" if they were analytical.

As technology continues to advance, so does our capacity for measuring brain activity and correlating it with human cognition and behavior. Sophisticated, high-density electroencephalography (EEG) arrays and advanced brain mapping tools, such as functional magnetic resonance imaging (fMRI) and diffusion tensor imaging (DTI) technologies, enable us to understand more comprehensively how the brain works in "real" time and how complex networks are connected across both hemispheres of the brain. For example, scientists now know that the brain generates new neurons and constantly "rewires" connections between existing ones. Recent research also indicates that the brain is organized in much more complex and interconnected ways than previously thought. Vast networks that connect regions of the brain are responsible for processing information, storing memories, and producing consciousness. Demystifying the brain brings us closer to understanding how and why people learn. This knowledge, in turn, enables us as educators and educational researchers to formulate better, more effective ways of stimulating and facilitating learning among our students.

In Chapters 1 and 2, Prensky, Betrus, and Botturi present a number of poignant, pragmatic, and psychological reasons for playing video games in schools. In Chapter 4, Bolkan advances educational reasons for including games in the curricula by relating gameplay to ISTE's National Educational Technology Standards for Students (NETS•S) and Teachers (NETS•T). In this chapter, we explore the physical and chemical neurological processes that support game-based learning (GBL). We begin by describing basic brain structure and function as a foundation for discussing physiological reasons for playing games in schools. We then describe neurological processes that support several components of GBL. To provide a balanced perspective, we then review cautions for interpreting neuroscience research and relating human behavior and educational practices to molecular and cellular studies of human physiology.

Basic Brain Structure and Function

With the consistency of tofu, the human brain weighs about 3 lbs. and floats in fluid, mostly water, that is replenished daily. Through sensory inputs, the brain records our experiences and responds to threats or pleasure by releasing chemicals and sending electrical impulses throughout the body. Although survival is foremost in the brain, adapting and responding to life's many challenges is a formidable task that requires learning. To help follow our physiological rationale for playing video games in schools as presented in the next section, we begin by summarizing our latest understanding of three fundamental aspects of the brain's structure and function—the cerebral cortex, plasticity, and neurotransmitters.

Cerebral Cortex

Surrounded by one trillion glia cells that nourish the brain, neurons form the cerebral cortex, the largest part of the human brain associated with higher functions, such as thought and action. The cerebral cortex is nearly symmetric in shape, with left and right hemispheres. As illustrated in Figure 3.1, each hemisphere is further divided into four lobes. While it is now recognized that the brain works together as a whole, the four lobes are associated with certain functions: (a) frontal—reasoning, planning, parts of speech, movement, emotions, and problem solving; (b) parietal—movement, orientation, recognition, and perception of stimuli; (c) occipital—visual processing; and (d) temporal—perception and recognition of auditory stimuli, memory, and speech (Bear, Connors, & Paradiso, 2007).

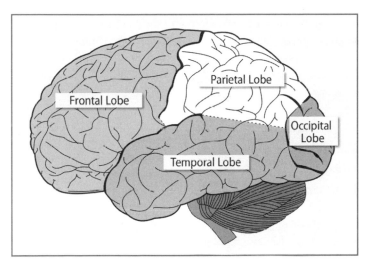

FIGURE 3.1 ▶ Each hemisphere of the cerebral cortex is divided into four lobes *(Hemisphere, 2009).*

Even though each lobe's functions appear to be highly localized (see Figure 3.1), the more we understand about how intricately the two hemispheres are linked, the clearer it is that the four lobes function interdependently. The corpus callosum, located in the center of the brain beneath the cerebral cortex, is made up of 200 million bundled fibers that bridge communications between the two hemispheres and among the four lobes to link billions of neurons throughout the brain. Although the corpus callosum is reportedly larger in musicians than non-musicians (Levitin, 2006) and slightly larger in left-handed people than right-handed people (Driesen & Naftali, 1995), there is little research that correlates such structural differences with functional differences. Our discussion of how video gameplay may facilitate learning from a physiological perspective is based on the assumption that with normal brain function, no one is actually "left-brained" or "right-brained," as discussed by Goswami (2006), who points out that teachers are still being misled by materials that perpetuate these outdated designations.

Plasticity

Early anatomists considered the nervous system fixed and incapable of regeneration. Only recently has it been recognized that neurogenesis (the creation of new brain cells) occurs in adult brains and plays a role in learning and memory (Eriksson et al., 1998; Gould et al., 1999). In fact, depending upon the area of a brain injury, function can sometimes be restored by another region, even in the opposite hemisphere. Current studies indicate that new neurons may also increase memory capacity, reduce interference among memories, and add information about time to existing memories (Becker, 2005). Increased levels of neurogenesis, in turn, are linked to stress-relieving activities, such as novel learning experiences, voluntary exercise, exposure to nonthreatening situations; in contrast, aging, lack of sleep, stress, or depression appear to diminish the creation of new brain cells and inhibit emotions (Castrén, 2005; Mirescu, Peters, Noiman, & Gould, 2006).

While the old adage "use it or lose it" generally applies to physical exercise, it appears equally important for mental processes. One of the most remarkable aspects of human behavior is the ability to modify that behavior by learning. The brain is far more adaptable than scientists formerly believed. Neuroplasticity, or simply plasticity, refers to the brain's ability to adapt as we learn new things. From a physiological perspective, learning can be viewed as changes to the structure and actions of neurons to retain information (McGowan, 2009).

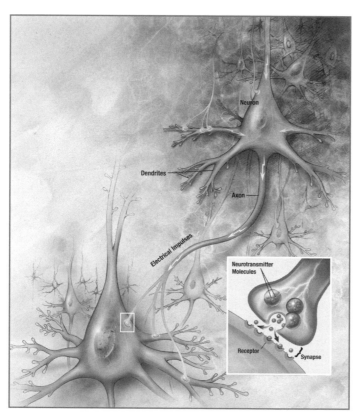

FIGURE 3.2 ▶ Neurons consist of a nucleus, dendrites, synapses and receptors, and an axon *(Neuron, 2009)*.

Although glial cells outnumber all other brain cells, neurons are the major focus of most neuroscience research. Neurons are nerve cells that receive and send information encoded as patterns of electrical and chemical activity. Extending from the neurons like the short branches on a tree, dendrites receive signals from many other cells, integrate these signals over time, and pass this information on to the axon. Insulated in a myelin sheath, axons allow this information to be encoded in an electrical signal called an "action potential," which propagates down the length of the axon. Axons continue the transfer process with the dendrites of many other neurons (illustrated in Figure 3.2).

The point of contact between dendrites and axons, known as a synapse, is changed or "modulated" as signals are passed on from one cell's dendrites across the miniscule gap of the synapse to the dendrites of the next cell. Synaptic modulation is thought to be the basis for memory. Once an impulse reaches a synapse, it stimulates tiny sacs that release chemicals, called neurotransmitters, across the small gap, and these chemicals bind with receptors on the dendrite, which then creates an electric charge (Bear, Connors, & Paradiso, 2007). This signaling process has gained attention among researchers as they try to explain changes that occur in memory as we learn.

Neurotransmitters

Neurotransmitters play a critical role in how the brain responds to sensory input by activating a receptor to transfer as well as change signals between a neuron and another cell. By attaching to specific receptors, neurotransmitters can increase (excite) or decrease (inhibit) activity in neurons by permitting the flow of chloride and potassium ions into the cell. The positive or negative charges of the ions that enter the cell either excite or inhibit the neuron. A neuron's activity depends on the balance between the number of excitatory and inhibitory processes affecting it, which can occur simultaneously (Bear, Connors, & Paradiso, 2007).

For example, the chemical acetylcholine (ACh) was one of the first neurotransmitters shown to increase synaptic strength following long-term activity in many regions of the brain connected with learning and short-term memory. It appears that ACh has a variety of effects upon plasticity, arousal, and reward, such as enhancing sensory perceptions when we wake up and sustaining attention on specific events and activities throughout the day. Norepinephrine (INN) is another important neurotransmitter that affects parts of the brain controlling attention and focus. Along with dopamine and epinephrine, INN underlies the fight-or-flight response, directly increasing heart rate, triggering the release of glucose for energy, and increasing blood flow to skeletal muscle. Release of INN increases the level of excitatory activity within regions of the brain that affect attention and arousal. Depletion of INN causes a decrease in drive and motivation and may be linked to depression (Casey, Giedd, & Thomas, 2000). Noradrenaline, serotonin, and dopamine also work together to control many of our mental states, sometimes acting alone and at other times together (see Figure 3.3).

These same three chemicals—noradrenaline, serotonin, and dopamine—are released when individuals play or watch games. When people watch their favorite sports teams win or lose, they experience feelings of euphoria or disappointment as these chemicals are released in the brain. Understanding the basic structure and function of the brain establishes a foundation for understanding how playing video games can facilitate learning. Many components of GBL support the same brain processes that enhance memory through repetition, attention, and emotion. Although we describe them separately, all of these brain processes work in harmony.

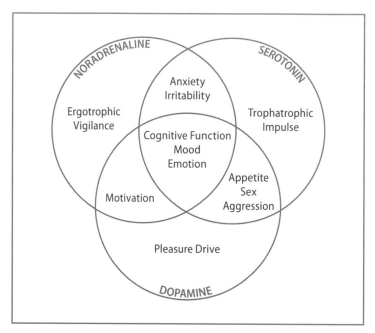

FIGURE 3.3 ▶ Neurotransmitters work cooperatively and independently to control mental states. The chemicals noradrenaline, serotonin, and dopamine are neurotransmitters released during game playing.

Neuroscience of Game-Based Learning

An important first step in understanding the learning process in general and how video games may facilitate specific types of learning is to identify how information is stored. Psychologist Donald Hebb's explanation of how neurons function has been paraphrased frequently: "Neurons that fire together, wire together" (1949). Although the process is considerably more complex, research has shown that Hebb was right: Memories can reside in synaptic alterations. Although non-synaptic changes may account for some types of memory, research leaves little doubt that the synapse is an important site for information storage. Studies point to lasting alterations in the effectiveness of synapses in the brain as a basis for memory.

When a baby is born, parents and others provide cultural information that affects how the child behaves. Adults do this principally through language and the mirror neuron system. Consider this familiar expression: "Imitation is the sincerest [form of] flattery" (Colton, 1820). When it comes to learning, imitation is not simply flattery. Mirror neurons in the motor cortex of the frontal lobes initiate and regulate movement (such as the sequential actions involved in grasping an object), based on observations of others performing the same or similar actions. A mental model of movements is created by simulating and then often imitating what is observed (Rizzolatti & Sinigaglia, 2008). Just as this "mirroring" process forms the foundation for learning, people respond to various stimuli when playing games.

Playing is one of the first ways that children learn. When a parent or older child demonstrates to a young child how to play with a toy (i.e., holding a doll, stacking blocks, rolling a toy car), the child imitates the actions and stores them in mirror neurons and sends the actions to motor neurons for playback when those new actions are needed. Rehearsal of this process improves the actions by adjusting the signals to the motor neurons. While most athletes and musicians are familiar with the phrase "practice makes perfect," in reality, "practice makes permanent" because most actions are imperfect. Forming connections between neurons defines learning, and the use of repetition to strengthen and expand such connections remains an important feature of GBL, particularly in "drill" games like those discussed in Chapter 13.

Repetition

Repetition is a time-honored strategy for teaching reading, writing, and math skills. When scientists examine brain processes, they observe that repetition clearly promotes learning by strengthening connections in the synapses of motor neurons (Squire & Kandel, 2000). So it comes as no surprise that GBL uses frequent repetition as a tactic for promoting learning and memory.

Repetition in GBL typically takes two forms. First, simple motor processes often occur over and over as players repeat short sequences (i.e., linking parts or typing words or numbers). Second, procedures are usually embedded within the game at various points that involve learning a motor response or procedural response in reaction to a sensory input by mirroring that action. This type of learning in a video game is similar to what happens when we observe someone yawn; the brain's yawning motor response is activated. Even thinking about yawning activates mirror neurons to respond. If someone sticks out his tongue at an infant who is only a few hours old, the infant will likely reciprocate, even though the infant never did this before. Mirror neurons help explain how we learn to speak, how empathy develops, why observing others engaged in sports and artistic performance is so appealing, and the effects of role modeling and electronic media on behavior. In the same ways, GBL triggers mirror neurons to stimulate learning through play that refines motor behaviors and visuomotor skills.

For example, studies of video game players demonstrate that they have decreased reaction times, increased hand-eye coordination, and augmented manual dexterity. Further, studies show improved spatial skills among game players, such as mental rotation, spatial visualization, and the ability to think and perform in three dimensions. In a study of laparoscopic surgeons, the ones who played games to improve professional techniques performed with 37% fewer errors than their non-gaming peers. The performance gain was attributed to improved hand-eye coordination and depth perception from the motor sensory training (Rosser, Lynch, Cuddihy, Gentile, Klonsky, & Merrell, 2007).

Another aspect of GBL that contributes to repetition is challenge. To encourage repetition, gameplay should be challenging enough to require effort for success but not too challenging to discourage continued play. Repetition is inhibited when users stop playing games that are too easy or too difficult. Cognitive psychologists call this the "regime of competence" principle. Neuroscience research adds further support for the principle and the use of video games. As games progress, puzzles become more complex, underlying patterns become subtler, and there are often more challengers to conquer who also become swifter and more skilled. In fact, most games delay progress until players reach a certain level of expertise (Gee, 2007). The level of challenge or degree of difficulty, however, should not be confused with failure. Most game players expect or even thrive on periodic failure. As long as skill improvement or progress to other levels seems possible, players appear unable to stop playing.

Scholars are the first to admit that games can be addictive, and part of their research explores how games connect to the reward circuits of the human brain by releasing dopamine, which the brain interprets as pleasurable. They now also recognize other cognitive benefits of playing video games, such as pattern recognition, system thinking, and even patience. Lurking in this research is the idea that gaming can exercise the mind through repetition the way physical activity exercises the body.

Another aspect of challenge and repetition that video games encourage is competition—players try to outperform others or themselves. While competition against others is common to most games, in video games, players can often compete against the game itself or against themselves by improving scores in subsequent play. In a recent study that examined climate change, ecological demands, and social competition to explain the evolutionary increase in the size of the human brain, researchers concluded that social competition is most likely the major cause of increased cranial capacity (Bailey & Geary, 2009).

Attention

Teachers have always known that learning is compromised when the students are not paying attention. In GBL, the term "engagement" refers to involvement in the game when attention is focused on play. Attention is a prerequisite for engagement in most activities. GBL engages learners by drawing attention to specific details. Players demonstrate several aspects of enhanced visual attention, including the ability to divide and switch attention, the temporal and spatial resolution of visual attention, and the number of objects that can be attended. In fact, games are so successful in grabbing attention that players often block out all other stimuli, including their temporal judgment. Many gamers become so absorbed in the activity that time seems unimportant except as it relates to the game. In a study that examined the brain activity of game players, researchers were surprised by the behavior of the players, who remained focused on the game for an hour, despite the distractions created by the researchers (Johnson, 2007).

The executive control system, a network located mainly in the front of the brain, exerts a top-down influence on conscious and unconscious thought, directing the brain's activity toward important goals. Other regions of the brain belong to a default network that is more active when individuals sit idly compared with when they are asked to perform particular tasks. The default network also becomes active during certain kinds of self-referential thinking, such as reflecting on personal experiences or picturing oneself in the future.

The fact that the executive control and default networks may become active at the same time suggests that mind wandering is not necessarily useless. Instead, it allows the brain to work through some important tasks. Our brains process information to reach goals, but some of those goals are immediate while others are distant. Somehow we have evolved a way to switch between handling the here and now and contemplating long-term objectives. It may be no coincidence that many of the thoughts that people have as their minds wander have to do with the future. While the brain processes what we hear in a conversation, it anticipates what will be said. Sometimes during conversations, people pause and respond with "huh" while their brains finish processing what they just heard. From the perspective of GBL, such pauses may include applying game strategies by thinking ahead while continuing to play. Even more telling is the discovery that zoning out may be the most fruitful type of mind wandering. In an fMRI study, researchers found that the default network and executive control systems are even more active when individuals are completely "zoned out" compared with times when the same individuals' minds wander with some awareness. When we are no longer even aware that our minds are wandering, we may be able to think most deeply about the big picture (Zimmer, 2009).

Zoning out by simply letting attention drift induces daydreaming. In contrast, many athletes report that intense focus can lead to smoother and more accurate performance, sometimes described as being "in the zone" or "in flow state." This phenomenon has been associated with decreased brain activity in cortical regions of the brain. People in a state of flow report conditions that are consistent with decreased prefrontal function, such as the disappearance of self-consciousness, no worry of failure, a sense of timelessness, and no distractions when actions and awareness merge (Dietrich, 2004). GBL provides many of the same conditions associated with zoning and inducing a flow state. When playing video games, players are observed to experience or report the following conditions:

▶ Goals are clear.

▶ Feedback is received immediately.

▶ Balance between challenges and skills.

▶ Action and awareness merge.

▶ Distractions are excluded.

▶ The possibility of failure is not a worry.

▶ Self-consciousness disappears.

▶ Sense of time is distorted.

▶ Activity becomes autotelic (done for its own sake).

Another example of redirecting attention to maximize our resources may occur when talking on a cell phone when driving. Processing language may take precedence over analyzing visual information, as the driver misses a turn or fails to see an obstruction in the road. Similarly, a driver may stop conversing with a passenger when visual information floods the senses, such as when the driver needs to read signs or change lanes in busy traffic. GBL provides an effective means for helping learners manage their experiences, as the games are designed to respond to players' performances by continually adjusting the pace, sequencing, and cognitive load of the instructional content to fit each learner's skills and abilities. Thus, when children play video games, each child's progress or learning curve is monitored carefully and constantly; the learning experiences in game playing could be compared to receiving the full attention of a one-on-one teacher or tutor. The game, however, never gets tired, focuses its entire attention on the individual's progress and needs, and gives consistent, positive feedback for every correct move and wise decision at each achievement level.

Another phenomenon of focusing attention during GBL is novelty. This involves newness either in terms of completely different information perceived as interesting or old information presented in new ways. When confronted with novel situations, the brain must quickly decide if a solution already exists in memory from prior experience. The right hemisphere of the brain processes novel challenges and develops creative solutions, as the left hemisphere processes familiar problems and executes established routines. The brain reacts by releasing chemicals that create more synaptic connections to accommodate the new information. Recent studies of memory suggest that such changes in the synaptic structure from our experience may define a fundamental mechanism by which memory is encoded and stored to long-term memory. As we gain experience and novelty fades, viewing life through the eyes of a child becomes more difficult, and we often respond in prescribed ways. In other words, we become set in our ways and follow established patterns of behavior. GBL often uses the element of surprise to perpetuate novelty and maintain attention.

Emotion

As William James (1890) wrote in *The Principles of Psychology*, "An impression may be so exciting emotionally as almost to leave a scar upon the cerebral tissues" (p. 670). This phrase highlights the commonly held belief that emotion enhances episodic memory. Research on the cognitive neuroscience of emotion and memory has specified a range of statistical means by which emotion can change the formation and recollection of episodic memory. It has been suggested that emotion, primarily from the influence of the amygdala, can alter three components of episodic memory: encoding, consolidation, and the subjective sense of remembering. Although episodic memory critically depends on other brain regions, most notably in the hippocampal complex, the amygdala may be important for modulating the neural circuitry of memory (Phelps, 2006).

Emotional experiences trigger a release of dopamine that stimulates amygdala activity in the limbic system and frontal lobe activity associated with reasoning, planning, parts of speech, movement, and problem solving. Using neuroimaging, researchers measured a significant increase in the amount of dopamine released in the brain during video gameplay, especially in areas thought to control reward and learning. The level of increase was comparable to that observed when amphetamines are injected intravenously but without the detrimental effects induced by drugs. Dopamine is one of many chemicals in the brain called neurotransmitters that allow the modulation of information as it passes through the brain. Dopamine is of particular interest because it is thought to play a role in a wide range of human behavior including pleasure, engagement, and learning. Many aspects of GBL, such as challenge, competition, and novelty can evoke emotional responses that release dopamine. Emotion and attention are the brain's activation systems, in that the brain mainly responds to emotionally arousing phenomena. It must then frame and focus on the salient elements that led to the arousal. Emotion, thus, drives attention, and attention drives responsive decisions and behaviors that lead to effective engagement (Giedd et al., 1996).

Because games involve a series of responses and feedback, learners frequently attach their emotions to winning the game through a series of reward structures. Rewards in GBL often include several performance measures, such as high scores, pleasant sounds or images, and additional playtime. Most games have specific rules that must be observed when playing. Players usually assume that following these rules leads to some form of reward. Rewards may be extrinsic, in the form of social recognition, or intrinsic, through feelings of accomplishment for reaching the next level in the game.

At the most basic level, the human brain is wired for survival, and we are intrinsically motivated by physical rewards that extend or improve life. As a result, most cultures condition children with three primary rewards for successful learning: food, approval, and perceived social status. All other complex experiences, such as learning how to use money, perform one's physical and intellectual work, and follow rules are conditioned with these same primary rewards. Rewarding experiences release dopamine and trigger activity in the amygdala and frontal lobe. The amygdala calculates the emotional intensity of an experience to determine the degree of negative or positive emotion resulting in the release of dopamine. The frontal lobe records the reward values of the experience and activates behaviors leading to the greatest rewarded outcome. Games take advantage of this rewards system by stimulating the emotion state of players (Cahill, Gorski, & Le, 2003; LeDoux, 2002).

Several studies provide evidence that when games include "pro-social" content—situations in which characters help each other in nonviolent ways—they increase "pro-social" conduct outside of gameplay. In short, students played one of several violent games, neutral games, or pro-social games, in which helpful behavior was required. After playing the game, they completed a task in which they could either help or hurt another student. Those who had played the violent games demonstrated more hurtful behaviors to other students while performing the task, whereas those who had played the pro-social games exhibited more helpful behaviors (Gentile, Anderson, Yukawa, Ihori, Saleem, & Lim, 2009). The types of rewards a game offers as well as a game's content may desensitize or change the perceptions of the player. Our understanding of how emotions are processed in the brain supports the observed data that playing video games can affect players' behaviors in positive and negative ways.

While the amygdala and hippocampus provide emotion-related functions, they influence our decisions and behavior through cognitive processing in the prefrontal cortex (PFC). Recent anatomical evidence suggests the existence of fiber loops that integrate our emotions with cognition. For example, amygdala signals broadcast widely to regions known to be important for the control of attention. Although cognition and emotion appear to exist in separate areas of the brain anatomically, new insights suggest these areas have a remarkable potential for integrating data. Regions that traditionally were thought to be purely affective, that is, processing only feelings and attitudes, might function as hubs for connecting emotion and cognition (Pessoa, 2008). One example of a brain function that requires cognitive-emotional integration is the evaluation of sensory information. Here, the interaction between cognition and emotion addresses the question: given your present sensory information and internal state, how should you act? This process is often described as the "fight or flight" dilemma. While cognitive psychology seeks to understand this process from a functional perspective, recent information from neuroscience may explain the actual processes that occur in the brain when faced with such dilemmas.

For instance, neurons in the PFC encode the probability of reward; at the same time, these neurons make decisions about the costs of making particular efforts. Areas of the PFC evaluate whether the benefits are worth the cost of taking action. While the PFC maintains and manipulates information, it also integrates this information with affective concerns, which include motivational information. The PFC might, therefore, act as a control hub in which multiple types of information converge and are integrated. Critically, the convergence of both cognitive and affective/motivational information enables the PFC to weigh multiple types of information dynamically as it guides action. As cognitive decision-making processes, affected by emotional states that motivate behaviors as well as by facts and logical reasoning, are integral to our learning and to our survival, games provide numerous effective ways of simulating realistic situations or conditions. Thus, game players rehearse and develop control of varying levels of the cognitive and affective processes involved in decision making.

Learning in school can often seem abstract and without real-world application. As a result, learners may not see how information fits into a larger context (Atkinson, 2008). However, simulations in GBL allow learners to place information or actions within a realistic environment that can be motivated by the students' emotional states. For example, instead of asking students to solve math problems on a piece of paper, a game might require players to solve a puzzle to complete a task or to advance to a higher level.

Neuroimaging studies show that remembering and imagining an event mobilize many of the same brain circuits. When a person is instructed to imagine personal events that might happen in the future and then to remember actual events from the past, an extensive and very striking overlap in areas of brain activity occurs (Kensinger & Schacter, 2007). The way gamers explore simulated environments mirrors the way the brain processes multiple, but interconnected streams of information in the real world. How we think is through running perceptual simulations in our heads that prepare us for the actions we're going to take. By modeling those simulations, video games externalize how the mind works (Gee, 2007).

Cautions and Criticisms

The use of neuroscience research to support and to guide the design and delivery of educational programs, including content-based video games, comes with cautions and criticisms. In an effort to present a balanced perspective, the major arguments are summarized against the use of neuroscience for explaining student learning, informing classroom practices, and providing physiological reasons for playing games in schools.

Designated by the U.S. government as the "The Decade of the Brain," the 1990s saw prominent groups, such as the Carnegie Task Force, the Education Commission of the States, and the U.S. Department of Education, publish reports that referenced neuroscience research to highlight early childhood as a critical period for child development (Jones & Mendell, 1999). Discoveries, such as rapid increases in synaptic connections in the brain during early infancy, critical periods of experience-dependent sensory and motor development, and new neurological formations resulting from exposure to enriched environments, prompted educators and educational policy makers to support and fund a number of early childhood programs.

However, in an early appraisal of efforts to connect neuroscience with education, Bruer (1997), a cognitive scientist, argued that researchers were inflating neuroscience findings and falling victim to "neuromyths." For instance, he noted that it is the pattern of synaptic connections that affects brain functions, not simply the number of connections. "Our current understanding of synaptogenesis (the rapid increases in synapses during early infancy) can tell educators little, if anything, about what kinds of early childhood, pre-school, or learning experiences might enhance children's cognitive capacities or their educational outcomes," he stated (p. 7). Bruer also noted that synaptogenesis has been found to occur early in the development of the visual cortex, which affects vision and motor skills, but synaptic density in the frontal cortex, which is responsible for planning, the coding of information, and the executive control of cognitive functions, does not stabilize until mid- to late adolescence. Given these findings, Bruer concludes that what neuroscientists know about synaptogenesis does not support calls by educators and researchers to focus on the ages of birth through 3 years as a critical period for human learning.

TABLE 3.1 ► Summary of concerns and opportunities associated with the educational applications of research in neuroscience

SPECIFIC TOPICS	OPPORTUNITY	CONCERN
Scientific Area		
Method	Innovative research designs can allow neuroscientists to study variables of interest in education, such as context.	Clinical studies do not take into crucial learning variables such as context and thus cannot be generalized to education.
Data	Neuroscience relates structure to function at a concrete level necessary to explain human behavior.	Data from a cellular (synaptic) level cannot be used to guide classroom practice at a behavioral level.
Theory	Reducing complex phenomenon (such as learning) to its component parts is appropriate as long as our common-sense understanding of the mind is not wrong.	Reducing complex phenomenon (such as learning) to its component parts is not appropriate.
Philosophy	Neuroscience may help resolve issues in education previously thought to be incapable of being judged, measured, or considered comparatively.	Neuroscience and education are incommensurable; they lack a common unit of measurement on which they can be compared.
Pragmatic Area		
Cost	Neuroscience may attract additional research funding for education.	Neuroscience research techniques are cost prohibitive for education.
Timing	Examples of how neuroscience research findings have improved teaching and learning already exist.	Currently, we do not know enough about the brain from neuroscience to inform education.
Control	The real question is not what neuroscience can do for education, but rather what education can do for neuroscience.	If education relinquishes control over decisions to neuroscience, it will never regain its independence.
Payoffs	Some prefer to think in terms of physical systems rather than conceptual constructs.	In the past, neuroscience research findings have often been turned into neuromyths.

From "Scientific and pragmatic challenges for bridging education and neuroscience," *Educational Researcher, 37*(3), 140–152.

Attempts to relate what happens at a synaptic, cellular level to children's behavior and classroom practices, according to Bruer, were still considered a "bridge too far" when he wrote his 1977 article. Nevertheless, as we've noted throughout this chapter, advances in technology since the late 1990s have greatly increased our knowledge of how the brain works, including how it processes complex forms of learning most relevant to education. As a result, a growing number of researchers and practitioners are proposing programs and guidelines for enhancing student learning based on neuroscience research (e.g., Blakemore & Frith, 2005; Caine, Caine, McClintic, & Klimek, 2009; Jensen, 2000). More than a decade after Bruer's initial reprisal, Varma, McCandliss, and Schwartz (2008) suggest that it is time to revisit the question: should neuroscience research be used to guide educational practice?

To help educators decide whether recent research in neuroscience should guide practice, Varma, McCandliss, and Schwartz (2008) identify scientific and pragmatic opportunities and concerns regarding connecting neuroscience and education, summarized in Table 3.1.

Clearly, we must interpret the results of neuroscience research with caution. Relating research at a cellular level to human learning and behavior can be tenuous. However, there is little doubt that neuroscience will continue to increase our understanding of human cognition. Advances in neuroimaging technology and neuroscience research have already revolutionized medicine and surgery. To disregard the areas of neuroscience that could lead to significant insights into how and why people learn is, to say the least, shortsighted.

Conclusion

As a teaching tool for the 21st century, video games may provide an effective medium for facilitating learning, thus promoting positive changes in students' performance and brain function. In this chapter, we characterized our current understanding of how we learn from a neurobiological perspective and related specific attributes of gameplay to neuroscience research on repetition, attention, and emotions to provide a physiological rationale for playing games in schools. Although game-based learning is clearly supported by our current understanding of cognitive processing and motor skills, many questions of practical and theoretical importance remain. On a practical level, to promote the effective use of video games for training and education, we need to determine what qualities a game should provide to develop targeted skills and to ensure no compromise of performance in other areas of cognition and emotion on the individual and social levels. On a theoretical level, game-based learning research combined with new imaging techniques is opening a fascinating window into the amazing capabilities of the brain and, in turn, behavior to be reshaped by experience. Understanding the mechanisms that unleash such widespread applicability is one of the many challenges facing this field.

References

Atkinson, T. (2008). Second life for educators: Myths and realities. *TechTrends, 52*(5), 26–29.

Bailey, D. H., & Geary, D. C. (2009). Hominid brain evolution. *Human Nature, 20*(1), 67–79.

Bear, M. F., Connors, B. W., & Paradiso, M. A. (2007). *Neuroscience. Exploring the brain.* Philadelphia, PA: Lippincott Williams & Wilkins.

Becker, S. (2005). A computational principle for hippocampal learning and neurogenesis. *Hippocampus, 15*(6), 722–738.

Blakemore, S. J., & Frith, U. (2005). *The learning brain: Lessons for education.* Oxford, UK: Blackwell.

Bruer, J. T. (1997). Education and the brain: A bridge too far. *Educational Researcher, 26*, 4–16.

Cahill L., Gorski, L., & Le, K. (2003). Enhanced human memory consolidation with post-learning stress: Interaction with the degree of arousal at encoding. *Learning & Memory, 10*(4), 270–274.

Caine, R. N., Caine, G., McClintic, C., & Klimek, K. (2009). *12 Brain/Mind learning principles in action: Developing executive functions of the human brain* (2nd ed.). Thousand Oaks, CA: Corwin Press.

Carnegie Task Force. (1996). *Yes of promise: A comprehensive learning strategy for America's children.* New York, NY: Carnegie Corporation of New York.

Casey, B. J., Giedd, J. N., & Thomas, K. M. (2000). Structural and functional brain development and its relation to cognitive development. *Biological Psychology, 54*, 241–257.

Castrén, E. (2005). Is mood chemistry? *Nature Reviews: Neuroscience, 6*(3), 241–246.

Colton, C. C. ([1820] 2004). Lacon or many things in a few words: Addressed to those who think. Whitefish, MT: Kessinger Publishing.

Dietrich, A. (2004). Neurocognitive mechanisms underlying the experience of flow. *Consciousness and Cognition, 13*(4), 746–761.

Driesen, N. R., Naftali, R. (1995). The influence of sex, age, and handedness on corpus callosum morphology: A meta-analysis. *Psychobiology, 23*(3), 240–247.

Eriksson, P. S., Perfilieva, E., Björk-Eriksson, T., Alborn, A. M., Nordborg, C., Peterson, D. A., et al. (1998). Neurogenesis in the adult human hippocampus. *Nature Medicine, 4*(11), 1313–1317.

Gee, J. P. (2007). *What video games have to teach us about learning and literacy.* Basingstoke, UK: Palgrave Macmillan.

Gentile, D., Anderson, C., Yukawa, S., Ihori, N., Saleem, M., Lim, K. M. (2009). The effects of prosocial video games on prosocial behaviors: International evidence from correlational, longitudinal, and experimental studies. *Personality and Social Psychology Bulletin, 35*(6), 752–763.

Giedd, J. N., Vaituzis, A. C., Hamburger, S. D., Lange, N. Rajapakse, J. C., Kayssen, D., et al. (1996). Quantitative MRI of the temporal lobe, amygdala and hippocampus in normal human development: Ages 4–18 years. *Journal of Comparative Neurology, 366*(2), 223–230.

Goswami, U. (2006). Neuroscience and education: From research to practice? *Nature Reviews: Neuroscience, 7*(5), 406–411.

Gould, E., Beylin, A., Tanapat, P., Reeves, A., & Shors, T. J. (1999, March). Learning enhances adult neurogenesis in the hippocampal formation. *Nature Reviews: Neuroscience, 2*(3), 260–265.

Hebb, D. O. (1949). *The organization of behavior.* New York, NY: Wiley.

Hemisphere. (2009). Retrieved August 31, 2009, from http://upload.wikimedia.org/wikipedia/commons/1/1a/Gray728.svg

James, W. (1890). *The principles of psychology.* New York, NY: Dover.

Jensen, E. (2000). *Brain-based learning.* San Diego, CA: The Brain Store.

Johnson, S. (2007). This is your brain on video games. From the Brain special issue, published online July 9, 2007. *Discover Science, Technology, and The Future.* Available at www.discovermagazine.com/2007/brain/video-games/

Jones, E. G., & Mendell, L. M. (1999). Assessing the decade of the brain. *Science, 284,* 739.

Kensinger, E. A., & Schacter, D. L. (2007). Remembering the specific visual details of presented objects: Neuroimaging evidence for effects of emotion. *Neuropsychologia, 45*(13), 2951–2962.

LeDoux, J. E. (2002). *Synaptic self: How our brains become who we are.* New York, NY: Viking.

Levitin, D. J. (2006). *This is your brain on music: The science of a human obsession.* New York, NY: Dutton.

McGowan, K. (2009). How much of your memory is true? *Discover Science, Technology, and the Future.* Special issue published online August 3, 2009. Retrieved November 24, 2009, from http://discovermagazine.com/2009/jul-aug/03-how-much-of-your-memory-is-true

Mirescu, C., Peters, J. D., Noiman, L., & Gould, E. (2006). Sleep deprivation inhibits adult neurogenesis in the hippocampus by elevating glucocorticoids. *Proceedings of the National Academy of Sciences of the United States of America, 103*(50), 19170–19175.

Nagy, R. (2008). This is your brain on video games. GameSpot Unions. Posted June 4, 2008, at www.gamespot.com/pages/unions/read_article.php?topic_id=26417848&union_id=16720.

Neuron. (2009). Complete neuron cell diagram. Retrieved August 31, 2009, from http://upload.wikimedia.org/wikipedia/commons/3/3e/Neurons_big1.jpg

Neurotransmitters. (2009). Retrieved August 31, 2009, from www.brainexplorer.org/neurological_control/Neurological_Neurotransmitters.shtml

Pessoa, L. (2008). On the relationship between emotion and cognition. *Nature Reviews: Neuroscience. 9*(2), 148.

Phelps, E. A. (2006). Emotion and cognition: Insights from studies of the human amygdala. *Annual Review of Psychology, 57,* 27.

Rizzolatti, G., & Sinigaglia, C. (2008). *Mirrors in the brain: How our minds share actions and emotions.* Oxford, UK: Oxford University Press.

Rosser, J. C., Jr., Lynch, P. J., Cuddihy, L., Gentile, D. A., Klonsky, J., & Merrell, R. (2007). The impact of video games on training surgeons in the 21st century. *Archives of Surgery, 142*(2), 181–186.

Sacktor, T. C., & Fenton, A. A. (2008). PKMzeta maintains spatial, instrumental, and classically conditioned long-term memories. *PLoS Biology, 6*(12), 2698–2706.

Squire, L. R., & Kandel, E. R. (2000). *Memory: From mind to molecules.* New York, NY: Scientific American Library.

Varma, S., McCandliss, B. D., & Schwartz, D. L. (2008). Scientific and pragmatic challenges for bridging education and neuroscience. *Educational Researcher, 37*(3), 140–152.

Zimmer, C. (2009). The brain: Stop paying attention: Zoning out is a crucial mental state. *Discover Science, Technology, and the Future.* Retrieved November 24, 2009, from http://discovermagazine.com/2009/jul-aug/15-brain-stop-paying-attention-zoning-out-crucial-mental-state

4

Playing Games and the NETS

J.V. Bolkan

ISTE'S RECENTLY UPDATED National Educational Technology Standards (NETS) for Students (NETS•S) and Teachers (NETS•T) implicitly demand a high degree of creativity, innovation, communication, and collaboration from both parties. The highly motivating potential of instructional gaming, combined with the imaginative guidance of a teacher, can not only engage students in the curriculum being targeted, but also touch on virtually every aspect of the NETS. Digital-age learning and teaching require relevant, student-centered activities and experiences. Professional educators will find computer gaming to be an excellent and exciting tool for encouraging their students to meet the NETS•S. Understanding computer gaming can also provide a framework for professional development to help teachers achieve the proficiencies outlined in the NETS•T.

Why play video games in schools? In the previous chapters, the authors identify a number of reasons that center on games' capabilities of engaging students and helping them develop basic and complex skills. In this chapter, I illustrate how gameplay and the development of basic and complex skills afforded by video games offer students and teachers fun, effective opportunities for meeting ISTE's NETS. The NETS for Students and Teachers almost seem to have been written with educational gaming in mind. With an emphasis on learning strategies rather than tool-specific tasks, the NETS identify key elements that make learning and teaching more effective when combined with technology.

We'll see how games map to the various standards and performance indicators for the NETS for Students (NETS•S) and for Teachers (NETS•T). Naturally, a huge part of fulfilling the NETS for Teachers is ensuring that students meet the NETS•S, yet because the NETS•T are more comprehensive than taking responsibility for students' achievements, we'll examine some of the ways playing video games in the classroom can fulfill several additional requirements for teachers.

Although connecting some of the NETS performance indicators to games is relatively easy and natural, it is important to note that alignment is highly dependent on sound teaching practices. Without effective teaching strategies and support before and after gameplay, even the best educational games will not be as effective as they could be. Likewise, simple two-dimensional (2-D) and even flawed games can be powerful tools and catalysts for higher-order learning with appropriate guidance from a creative teacher.

Aligning to the NETS•S

Virtually all games may be excellent vehicles for introducing and examining metacognition in students. Beginning with the simple question, "Is this game fun?" can lead directly into "How did or didn't the game engage you?" Even younger students quickly understand that certain game styles appeal to different personality types more than to others. Some students may be better at real-time strategy games, and other students may excel at puzzle-style games.

I'll examine each of the six NETS•S standards as they apply to gaming and point out specific indicators where applicable.

The NETS•S Standards and Indicators

The National Educational Technology Standards for Students (ISTE, 2007) are divided into six broad categories: creativity and innovation; communication and collaboration; research and information fluency; critical thinking, problem solving, and decision making; digital citizenship; and technology operations and concepts. Each category is described by four indicators. Standards within each category are to be introduced and reinforced by teachers and mastered by students. Teachers can use these standards as guidelines for planning technology-based activities that will help students achieve success in learning, communication, and life skills. The standards and indicators are listed on the following page.

Standard 1. Creativity and Innovation

Students demonstrate creative thinking, construct knowledge, and develop innovative products and processes using technology. Students:

a. apply existing knowledge to generate new ideas, products, or processes

b. create original works as a means of personal or group expression

c. use models and simulations to explore complex systems and issues

d. identify trends and forecast possibilities

Standard 2. Communication and Collaboration

Students use digital media and environments to communicate and work collaboratively, including at a distance, to support individual learning and contribute to the learning of others. Students:

a. interact, collaborate, and publish with peers, experts, or others employing a variety of digital environments and media

b. communicate information and ideas effectively to multiple audiences using a variety of media and formats

c. develop cultural understanding and global awareness by engaging with learners of other cultures

d. contribute to project teams to produce original works or solve problems

Standard 3. Research and Information Fluency

Students apply digital tools to gather, evaluate, and use information. Students:

a. plan strategies to guide inquiry

b. locate, organize, analyze, evaluate, synthesize, and ethically use information from a variety of sources and media

c. evaluate and select information sources and digital tools based on the appropriateness to specific tasks

d. process data and report results

Standard 4. Critical Thinking, Problem Solving, and Decision Making

Students use critical-thinking skills to plan and conduct research, manage projects, solve problems, and make informed decisions using appropriate digital tools and resources. Students:

a. identify and define authentic problems and significant questions for investigation

b. plan and manage activities to develop a solution or complete a project

    c.   collect and analyze data to identify solutions and make informed decisions

    d.   use multiple processes and diverse perspectives to explore alternative solutions

Standard 5. Digital Citizenship

Students understand human, cultural, and societal issues related to technology and practice legal and ethical behavior. Students:

    a.   advocate and practice the safe, legal, and responsible use of information and technology

    b.   exhibit a positive attitude toward using technology that supports collaboration, learning, and productivity

    c.   demonstrate personal responsibility for lifelong learning

    d.   exhibit leadership for digital citizenship

Standard 6. Technology Operations and Concepts

Students demonstrate a sound understanding of technology concepts, systems, and operations. Students:

    a.   understand and use technology systems

    b.   select and use applications effectively and productively

    c.   troubleshoot systems and applications

    d.   transfer current knowledge to the learning of new technologies

Standard 1. Creativity and Innovation

Although the standards are not officially ranked in importance, it is significant that students' and teachers' standards lead with *creativity*. The broad consensus of the many educators who helped craft and refine the ISTE NETS was that creativity, including the ability to construct knowledge from the vast information streams now available, is essential. It is important to note that although these skills are critical for the future success of today's students, the NETS clearly state that teachers, too, must model and demonstrate these skills today to teach effectively.

Students are expected to demonstrate creative thinking, construct knowledge, and develop innovative products and processes using technology. Teachers are encouraged to use their knowledge of subject matter, teaching, learning, and technology to present experiences that advance student learning, creativity, and innovation in both face-to-face and virtual environments. In addition, teachers are entrusted with the responsibility for inspiring their students.

Games are excellent vehicles for developing the student skills specified by the four Standard 1 performance indicators. For instance, NETS•S 1.a. requires students to apply existing knowledge to generate new ideas, products, or processes. At the heart of many games is a central puzzle or concept that must be mastered to succeed. As they become more accomplished, players will often find creative and innovative ways to succeed, based on strategies that have worked well in other games, earlier in that game, or in real-life situations. In the best games, the puzzles and models are realistic and authentic, providing information and knowledge that can easily be transferred to venues outside the game environment itself.

Indicator 1.b. requires students to create original works as a means of personal or group expression. Many games allow either customized character play or, increasingly, the ability to customize or build the game environment itself (e.g., The Sims, Spore, World of Warcraft, Second Life). Using models and identifying trends are integral to most forms of games. In fact, gaming can be the best method of introducing students to computer models and simulations, as well as of helping them gain skills in identifying trends and forecasting possibilities (1.c. and 1.d.).

Standard 2. Communication and Collaboration

Because gaming skills and experiences vary widely, teachers need strategies to help keep students from outpacing or being outpaced by their peers. When using games that keep a record of high scores and allow players to ascend to higher levels or offer other tangible rewards, teachers can assign students to work in groups, so that each group's players have various competencies and skill levels. Setting a goal of having every member of the group hit a benchmark can encourage group members to share strategies, as the most skilled become motivated to help struggling peers. A final activity might involve asking groups or individuals to report on the strategies they used to "beat" the game, as well as the group strategies they employed to ensure everyone in the group reached the goal.

More and more games are being designed with collaboration and communication as key elements of gameplay. Reinforcing the positive communication lessons inherent in these games is relatively straightforward. Even the more traditional single-user games, such as the simple Solitaire card game, often cited as isolating experiences, can, in the hands of a creative teacher, become wonderful opportunities to foster communication and collaboration among students (2.a.). Encouraging students to share their strategies with their peers can lead into a number of lessons. For example, even Solitaire offers players choices that affect the probability of winning.

Increasingly, games are being developed with multiplayer, communication, and networking features as central components. Although a large number of multiplayer games are still competition based, more and more are community oriented, and some even reward or require collaborative play. One of the most successful early examples of these newer generation games, World of Warcraft (WOW), is almost as renowned for the intricate, exhaustive discussions and planning sessions among online players before and after missions as it is for the actual gameplay. Again, these attributes can be used to align to Standards 2 and 5 when classroom groups play the game.

Interacting and collaborating (2.a.) are the bases for massively multiplayer online role-playing games (MMORPG), which include hundreds of free games, as well as commercial games, such as WOW and Guild Wars. Additionally, multiplayer online games of all types almost always include a chat feature that fosters communication among teams and adversaries (2.b.). Because many online games, particularly the online multiplayer games, are accessible worldwide, it is fairly easy to seek and find learners from other cultures (*2.c.*). Any team-based game lends itself naturally to indicator *2.d.*, contributing to project teams; interestingly, many single-player games such as Age of Empires, feature pseudo partners (often referred to as AI players) with whom the player must interact and teams the player must manage.

Standard 3. Research and Information Fluency

In examining Standard 3 and how it relates to gaming, it is important to stress that although the games themselves may not be the vehicles for achieving educational goals, they can be positive and powerful motivators. All but the most basic (or rarely played) games have a plethora of game resources available, such as a printed user's guide, online tutorials, hint guides, and even online "cheat" sites. Guiding students to these and requiring them to research and evaluate the various resources would help achieve the indicators 3.a.–3.d. These research and evaluation activities would also provide excellent openings to discuss areas of digital citizenship (see Standard 5), particularly indicators 5.a. and 5.b.

Most games do not explicitly involve significant research and information fluency tasks. Yet, almost all games may have aspects that lend themselves to auxiliary research projects. For instance, a simulation-based game, such as SimCity or Spore, can energize students to conduct research projects based on economics or biology. Despite their heavy emphasis on battle, games such as Call to Duty and WWII Aces can provide context, motivation, and detail for history lessons. WebQuests and other information-seeking applications are often structured as games, with skills in research and information fluency being the keys to success and mastery of the games.

Standard 4. Critical Thinking, Problem Solving, and Decision Making

Because results/scores are such an integral part of most games, students naturally reflect upon their performances. The motivational and competitive aspects of games encourage students to become introspective. Successful gamers are acutely aware of their strengths and weaknesses. In fact, many role-playing games are built around the central theme that different characters have a range of skills (such as strength, courage, agility, cunning, or charm) and skill levels. Players must choose which type of character they are to start, and then they must constantly make decisions about which attributes they want to develop and which weaknesses they must compensate for. The planning and management of character attributes can be a natural and powerful scaffold for engaging students in discussions in which they compare and contrast their "real" attributes with those they value when playing. Such critical-thinking, problem-solving, and decision-making activities are directly related to indicators 4.a.–d.

Standard 4 obviously lends itself to puzzle- , mystery- , and simulation-style games, but even less obvious "twitch-style" or "arcade" games almost always require players to choose strategies, seek and recognize patterns, and evaluate information. The more sophisticated games available offer multiple paths to victory; for instance, in many of the real-time strategy games, such as Civilization, StarCraft, and Age of Empires, players can choose to be aggressive and disrupt their opponents from the beginning, or they can choose to focus on defense, building and collecting resources to assemble an overwhelming force later in the game. Historical and quasi-historical games, such as Company of Heroes, lend themselves particularly well to students' experimenting with different problem-solving and decision-making strategies (4.d.).

Gameplay is also an excellent starting point for encouraging and promoting research based on the real-life events behind the game framework. Such research projects could involve content-based learning in communications/language arts, history, psychology, mathematics, science, sociology, and theater. Depending on how these projects are structured, they could help students achieve higher levels of proficiency related to many indicators for all six NETS•S.

Standard 5. Digital Citizenship

Gaming of all types inevitably touches on digital citizenship. Even teachers who do not play games of any type in the classroom are likely to have discussed the health, safety, and ethical issues surrounding students' use of digital technology. Because of the deeply engaging nature of games and the relatively repetitive control motions required by joysticks and other controllers, understanding the ergonomics and physical effects of prolonged gaming are extremely important.

Perhaps the greatest potential benefit of playing games is the positive attitudes it can foster toward information technology (5.b.). Although it is true that students need to understand that technology is not solely "fun and games," artificially limiting technology in the classroom to "serious" applications creates a disconnection between how they are likely to use technologies inside and outside the classroom. Under such disparate conditions, students are even less likely to pursue activities outside the classroom that mix education and entertainment. Connecting personal uses of technology to learning encourages and reinforces the concept of lifelong learning (5.c.).

Because of an unfortunately flourishing subculture in the gaming community that trades in hacked, illegally copied, or inappropriate games, discussions and lessons on the ethical use of materials and respect for intellectual property are natural fits with indicators 5.a., c., and d. Even legal, mainstream games can be quite controversial due to violence and other adult content or themes.

Much like sports, gaming offers numerous opportunities for character and ethical development. Similarly, as in sports participation, the effectiveness of these lessons is highly dependent on the coach/teacher.

Standard 6. Technology Operations and Concepts

Gaming, particularly computer-based gaming, has a long and strong history of motivating players to delve deeply into the platform and systems running their games (6.a.). From nearly obsessive tweaking of computer systems to achieve higher video frame rates during gameplay (called over-clocking) to in-depth discussions of the merits of one game console specification over another, students have become intensely interested in technology concepts related to video games.

At the most basic level, even young students quickly learn keyboard and mouse control when needed within a game environment. These skills are, in most cases, highly transferable to other computer applications. More advanced concepts come into play as students gain experience with games offering sophisticated, networked, multiplayer options; complex visual display settings; and compatibility issues. Essentially, configuring a game among multiple players on a network or through the Internet is a skill that transfers directly to nongame connectivity applications (6.d.).

Games are among the most technologically demanding applications for computers. As a result, troubleshooting and careful reading of recommended and minimum hardware and software specifications are valuable skills for serious gamers (6.c.).

A surprisingly large number of gamers become system-tweaking and over-clocking enthusiasts. These enthusiasts discuss such arcane technological concepts as RAM chip latency as a limiting factor in the performance of dedicated three-dimensional (3-D) graphics shader models. Math, engineering, and physics all become extremely relevant subjects for students looking for a way to get their ATI 2400XT graphics cards to deliver one more frame per second when they are in the middle of an Unreal Tournament. As any experienced teacher will attest, motivation, especially in math and sciences, is more than half the battle.

Aligning to the NETS•T

The NETS for Teachers (ISTE, 2008) organizes competencies into five major categories that, for the most part, mirror the NETS for Students. The standards and indicators are listed below.

Standard 1. Facilitate and Inspire Student Learning and Creativity

Teachers use their knowledge of subject matter, teaching and learning, and technology to facilitate experiences that advance student learning, creativity, and innovation in both face-to-face and virtual environments. Teachers:

   a.   promote, support, and model creative and innovative thinking and inventiveness;

   b.   engage students in exploring real-world issues and solving authentic problems using digital tools and resources;

   c.   promote student reflection using collaborative tools to reveal and clarify students' conceptual understanding and thinking, planning, and creative processes; and

   d.   model collaborative knowledge construction by engaging in learning with students, colleagues, and others in face-to-face and virtual environments.

Standard 2. Design and Develop Digital-Age Learning Experiences and Assessments

Teachers design, develop, and evaluate authentic learning experiences and assessments incorporating contemporary tools and resources to maximize content learning in context and to develop the knowledge, skills, and attitudes identified in the NETS•S. Teachers:

   a.   design or adapt relevant learning experiences that incorporate digital tools and resources to promote student learning and creativity;

b. develop technology-enriched learning environments that enable all students to pursue their individual curiosities and become active participants in setting their own educational goals, managing their own learning, and assessing their own progress;

c. customize and personalize learning activities to address students' diverse learning styles, working strategies, and abilities using digital tools and resources; and

d. provide students with multiple and varied formative and summative assessments aligned with content and technology standards and use resulting data to inform learning and teaching.

Standard 3. Model Digital-Age Work and Learning

Teachers exhibit knowledge, skills, and work processes representative of an innovative professional in a global and digital society. Teachers:

a. demonstrate fluency in technology systems and the transfer of current knowledge to new technologies and situations;

b. collaborate with students, peers, parents, and community members using digital tools and resources to support student success and innovation;

c. communicate relevant information and ideas effectively to students, parents, and peers using a variety of digital-age media and formats; and

d. model and facilitate effective use of current and emerging digital tools to locate, analyze, evaluate, and use information resources to support research and learning.

Standard 4. Promote and Model Digital Citizenship and Responsibility

Teachers understand local and global societal issues and responsibilities in an evolving digital culture and exhibit legal and ethical behavior in their professional practices. Teachers:

a. advocate, model, and teach safe, legal, and ethical use of digital information and technology, including respect for copyright, intellectual property, and the appropriate documentation of sources;

b. address the diverse needs of all learners by using learner-centered strategies and providing equitable access to appropriate digital tools and resources;

c. promote and model digital etiquette and responsible social interactions related to the use of technology and information; and

d. develop and model cultural understanding and global awareness by engaging with colleagues and students of other cultures using digital-age communication and collaboration tools.

Standard 5. Engage in Professional Growth and Leadership

Teachers continuously improve their professional practice, model lifelong learning, and exhibit leadership in their school and professional community by promoting and demonstrating the effective use of digital tools and resources. Teachers:

a. participate in local and global learning communities to explore creative applications of technology to improve student learning;

b. exhibit leadership by demonstrating a vision of technology infusion, participating in shared decision making and community building, and developing the leadership and technology skills of others;

c. evaluate and reflect on current research and professional practice on a regular basis to make effective use of existing and emerging digital tools and resources in support of student learning; and

d. contribute to the effectiveness, vitality, and self-renewal of the teaching profession and of their school and community

In the process of helping ensure that students meet the performance indicators of the NETS•S, teachers will naturally meet many of the NETS•T performance indicators. It is critical to understand that modeling effective technology use and learning does not necessarily mean a teacher must be versed in each game. In other words, a teacher does not need to win or even play video games to satisfy the modeling indicators—demonstrating how instructional games are played and showing the potential of games to foster learning are examples of creativity that certainly qualify (1.a.–d., and 3.a., 3.c., 3.d.).

It is critical that teachers avoid falling into the trap of relying on games alone to foster learning. Even the best educational games are little more than instructional tools, like a whiteboard, laptops, or pencil and paper. To be truly aligned with the NETS•T, a teacher must continually design, develop, and assess the students' digital learning experiences to create an effective learning environment (2.a.–d.).

Although it may not be possible always to have a selection of games suited for a variety of differing student learning styles on hand, teachers are accountable for customizing the learning and lessons associated with games to meet the unique needs of their students. Because such a huge range of game types are available, teachers can easily find games suitable for students with differing abilities, explicitly highlighting skills that otherwise might not be highly valued or recognized among their peers. For example, a simulation game centered on building alliances and community is likely to have a different set of "winning" students than a game based on quick reflexes and pattern recognition.

Conclusions

One of the core beliefs underlying the NETS is that technology can transform and improve both teaching and learning. Games can be easily integrated into the classroom to provide motivation that can help students and teachers meet ISTE's standards and the ultimate goal of improved learning opportunities for all students.

References

International Society for Technology in Education (ISTE). (2007). National educational technology standards for students (NETS•S). Eugene, OR: ISTE. Available at www.iste.org/Content/NavigationMenu/NETS/ForStudents/2007Standards/NETS_for_Students_2007.htm

International Society for Technology in Education (ISTE). (2008). National educational technology standards for teachers (NETS•T). Eugene, OR: ISTE. Available at www.iste.org/Content/NavigationMenu/NETS/ForTeachers/2008Standards/NETS_for_Teachers_2008.htm

Section II
Games in Subject Areas

5

Games for Science Education

Edward Dieterle

THE FIRST HALF OF THIS CHAPTER provides educators, researchers, and policy makers with recommendations, best practices, and examples of high-quality science video games. A growing number of science video games are interactive simulations that leverage the qualities of for-entertainment video games and are built in virtual worlds. At the intersection of virtual worlds and video games are immersive simulations capable of supporting (a) learning from multiple perspectives, (b) learning through the activities, cultures, and theories of a discipline, and (c) the positive transfer of what is known in one context or situation to novel contexts and situations. One such learning innovation that exhibits these characteristics is Harvard University's River City Project, which uses an interactive, game-like simulation based in a virtual world to teach middle school students to think and act like scientists. Using River City as case study, the second half of the chapter explores how such a video game can change (a) curricular content, (b) relationships among students and teachers, (c) assessment practices, and (d) the knowledge and skills of teachers. As a result of reading this chapter, those interested in science video games will gain a critical lens through which to examine and evaluate science video games objectively.

The purpose of science instruction is not only to enable students to do well in class, but also to prepare the upcoming generation to function in a democratic society, contribute to the future workforce, steward our planet and its natural resources, live more rewarding lives, and realize a high quality of life. Such goals are achievable when science is studied holistically as a *discipline* and an *enterprise* but undermined when taught as a disconnected collection of facts, vocabulary words, concepts, and skills. "Disciplines," as Gardner (1999) argues, "inhere in the ways of thinking, developed by their practitioners, that allow those practitioners to make sense of the world in quite specific and largely non-intuitive ways" (p. 155). Through extended, purposeful, and scaffolded engagement with the discipline of science and the social practices of scientists, students begin to become scientists with expert knowledge in one or more fields of science (National Research Council, 2007).

The scientific enterprise involves *research*, the systematic investigation of phenomena to establish facts and build knowledge, but it does not stop there. It also includes (a) *teaching*: imparting knowledge and skills from one generation to the next; (b) *journalism*: presenting facts and descriptions in print and online publications of events with impartial interpretation; and (c) *policy making*: developing a course of action, from the private citizen making informed voting decisions to government leaders passing responsible federal legislation (National Academy of Sciences, 2009; Olson & Labov, 2008). All students, not only those labeled "gifted and talented" or those with a longstanding history of prior academic success, must actively engage in research, teaching, journalism, and policy making. From their sustained and meaningful experiences they will then develop a deep understanding of science as a discipline and an enterprise and be better prepared to thrive in a democratic society and in a 21st-century, globally competitive workforce with a high quality of life.

For educators to facilitate thoughtful and authentic practice, leading students to a deep understanding of science as a discipline and an enterprise, students must be provided with clear and relevant information, informative and timely feedback, and a favorable combination of extrinsic and intrinsic motivators as they work individually and collaboratively (Dieterle & Murray, 2009; Perkins, 1992, 2009). Facilitating such authentic learning experiences in traditional classrooms is fraught with technical and cultural challenges and barriers. Examples of technical challenges include limited instructional time; costs and safety factors associated with acquiring, maintaining, and using scientific instruments; and costs and time-consuming procedures required to transport students out of the classroom to engage in fieldwork.

More difficult to surmount than technical challenges are those that are culturally founded, based in deep-seated beliefs and customs. What is known about how people learn, as an example, often runs counter to conventional wisdoms and traditional pedagogies prevalent in many of today's science classrooms. Although learning is understood by many educators as a social activity, shaped by physical and mental development, personal interests, and sociocultural influences, science classes are often characterized by teaching-by-telling, individual performance, unaided thinking (i.e., working without tools), and lessons based on abstract, symbolic, decontextualized representations. Students end up engaging only in traditional classroom activities—memorizing vocabulary words, reciting the steps of the scientific method, and completing cookbook-style laboratories Many students, as a result, fail to comprehend, fail to develop a curiosity about, or fail to develop a concern for the concepts, activities, and cultures common throughout the scientific community. Overcoming such school-based cultural barriers requires concurrently affecting content, relationships, assessments, and teacher knowledge (Cohen & Ball, 1999; National Research Council, 2001, 2005).

This chapter provides educators, researchers, and policy makers with recommendations, best practices, and examples of high-quality science video games. The focus of this chapter is on science video games used primarily in schools and readers are encouraged to review Squire and Patterson's (2009) paper on games and simulations in informal science education, prepared for the National Research Council, for a comprehensive analysis of science video games and their use outside of formal educational environments. Video games designed around topics of substance, as argued in this chapter, combine modern learning theories and advanced technologies to offer interesting opportunities for students and teachers to study science as a discipline and experience multiple aspects of the scientific enterprise through authentic scenarios. The next section begins with procedures on determining the strengths and limits of science video games as instructional tools, followed by an overview of the general state of science video games, and a summary of important video games relevant to science educators. Selecting and then providing students with access to a game on its own, however, is not sufficient to maximize their likelihood of comprehending the nature or meaning of the scientific enterprise. The remainder of the chapter discusses methods for overcoming various challenges to optimize conditions for learning in schools with video games. As a case study, Harvard University's River City Project (see http://muve.gse.harvard.edu/rivercityproject) illustrates how using a well-designed video game can affect, in positive, productive ways, the content of science classes, change relationships among students and teachers, alter the way assessment data are collected and used to influence teaching, and change the knowledge and skills of teachers.

When (and When Not) to Use Science Video Games in Instruction

When educators are deciding whether to integrate a video game into their practice or policy-makers are deciding on which games to advocate for, they should consider the game in relation to *instructional logistics* and *learning objectives* before investing scarce time and resources on the game. The following yes-and-no questions, based on general principles and procedures derived from experience and practice, should be considered holistically. When educators respond with "yes" to the following sets of questions on instructional logistics and learning objectives, they can feel confident about moving forward with the integration of the game in question.

Questions Related to Instructional Logistics

▶ Have I contacted my technology coordinator regarding the installation and running of the video game?

▶ Have I discussed with my technology coordinator the game I would like to use in relation to available hardware and network resources and to school and district policies?

▶ Do I have support from a technology coordinator or staff member who is willing to help me run the game?

▶ Do I know on which platforms (e.g., laptop or desktop computer, handheld computer, smart phone, tablet PC) the game will and will not run?

▶ Do the hardware and networks I have access to meet the minimum workstation requirements with regard to operating system (Windows XP, Vista, and/or 7; Mac OS X), RAM, hard drive space, Internet connectivity (bandwidth), and firewall settings?

▶ Do I know how many computers I will need to run the game properly? For example, do I know whether the game requires each student to use a computer individually or if multiple students can play a game on a single computer simultaneously?

▶ Do I understand the total financial costs associated with the game, realizing that some games are available free of charge, others are distributed freely as evaluation copies with additional fees associated with the full version of the game, and others are only available for a fee?

▶ Do I know where students will have access to the game: in the classroom, the library, a computer lab, at home, or a combination thereof? Is our technology coordinator able to ensure that licensing issues are covered so that students may play the game at home and/or install it on a personal computer?

▶ Do I understand the time costs involved with students playing the game for instructional purposes? Have I determined whether the game time is cost effective for me? Do I know how long it takes to complete the game? Have I determined how much time students will have access to the game during science class, before and after school, and outside of school? Do I know how much time I am willing to devote to coordinating playing the game inside and outside of classes?

▶ Do I have a sense of how much time it will take for most of the students to learn how to play the game? Do I know of game-savvy students whom I can ask to help classmates learn to play the game outside of class time?

▶ Have I assessed how I am going to learn to use the game for instructional purposes? Am I aware of support materials, if any, provided with the game? Some games provide extensive professional development opportunities and ongoing support, and others require the instructor to learn how to play the game and teach with it on their own. Do I understand the extent to which I need to learn how to play the game to use in my instruction?

Questions Related to Learning Objectives

▶ Do I understand the overall purpose of the game?

▶ Do I understand what my students should end up knowing, being skilled at, caring about, or being motivated to do after working through the game?

▶ Does the video game align with the intended learning objectives and standards I wish to address?

▶ Is the game developmentally appropriate for my students?

▶ Can the game provide experiences that existing classroom practices and activities cannot?

▶ Am I aware of empirical evidence that supports the effectiveness and/or impact of the game on student learning? (Note: very few learning innovations, whether they be textbooks or games, have bodies of evidence documenting effectiveness, so it should not be a surprise to find missing or limited evidence of the game's impact on learning.) Absent research to support this game's effectiveness, am I prepared to explain its curricular relevance to my students, their parents, and the principal?

▶ Do I understand the conditions and circumstances under which the video game, like all learning innovations, may benefit or hinder student learning?

Of all of the considerations, the final two questions about learning and science video games may be the most nuanced and challenging for educators to think through and answer fully. The research based on learning and science video games is growing, but there is much more to learn and study. Foster and Mishra's (2009) literature review and analysis of the claims of learning in video games suggest a general lack of authentic, situated research studies that consider the pedagogical strengths and limitations of different game genres and also the importance of acquiring disciplinary knowledge through games. Clark and colleagues (2009), on behalf of the National Research Council, prepared an analytic paper that discusses the categorization of different game genres, provides examples of science video games, and reviews the evidence of learning associated with playing such games. The evidence of learning from simulations and games that they present is based on research findings from specific tools used in well-defined ways with supporting curricula. They recommend for all educators who seek to integrate science simulations or video games into their instruction, that they, "apply and adapt the tools to the tasks, recognizing the theoretical framework from which a given tool, learning perspective, or analytical methodology has sprung while carefully adapting the tools to new goals and settings" (p. 53).

With or without a body of evidence supporting learning from a particular game, educators may believe that because most students are highly motivated to play video games outside school, they should integrate video games into their lessons whenever possible. Just because a student has the ability to play video games and enjoys playing games for entertainment purposes does not guarantee he or she will prefer to use a game-like interface for classroom activities. For example, Salaway, Caruso, and Nelson's (2007) longitudinal study of college students' use of information technology reveals that on average more than 3 in 4 (78%) college students play computer and video games online or offline. In contrast, just over half of college students in the same study (53%) like learning through programs that they can control such as video games and simulations. A reason for this difference is perhaps games and simulations used to teach content many tend to be drill and skill in nature and lack the compelling game play of commercial games. In the most recent installment of the study, Smith, Salaway, and Caruso (2009) report similar trends in learner preferences regarding programs that they can control. However, in this report they break out the question by gender, revealing that more males (about 3 in 5) than females (about 2 in 5) state that they like to learn this way.

Just as students vary, so do the video games teachers might use with their students. In general, there are entertainment games designed to amuse or entertain users, which are readily available off the shelf and which may or may not have educational value, and serious games that are designed primarily to teach something of substance. While off-the-shelf commercial video games often include concepts and activities that teachers want their students to learn and engage in, many suffer from dilution of substantive content by irrelevant information or inappropriate activities that teachers and students cannot remove or ignore (Kirriemuir & McFarlane, 2004). However, a growing number of projects based primarily at research universities and non-profit organizations have been exploring the strengths and limits of video games for teaching and learning science, but many of these games have gone largely unnoticed by most educators because of limited promotion and distribution and also the technical and cultural barriers discussed previously. The next section highlights high-quality video games educators might consider integrating into their instruction. The goal of this chapter is not to document all science video games; titles included herein are high quality and represent what is available.

Science Video Games

The term "video games" has been part of everyday speech since coin-operated machines entered eateries and arcades in the 1970s and has continued as consoles found their way into living rooms and handheld devices became constant mobile companions (Kent, 2001). Despite their place within the vernacular, scholars have struggled to define clearly what video games are and are not (see, for example, Juul, 2005; Newman, 2004; Provenzo, 1991). Confusion results, in part, from ambiguity of the terms "simulation," "virtual world," and "video game" and from treating them as synonyms. Although all three are computer programs run on computer systems, they each carry with them unique and defining qualities.

For the purposes of this chapter, a *simulation* is defined as a dynamic and testable representation of an activity, behavior, process, situation, or a combination thereof whose parameters can be manipulated and studied. Simulations used to acquire new knowledge, as Casti (1997) argues, are representative artificial worlds in which research questions from a range of fields and disciplines can be tested and analyzed.

> We can use these surrogates as laboratories for carrying out the experiments needed to be able to construct viable theories of complex physical, social, biological, and behaviorial processes. In many ways this leaves us in the same position that physicists were in at the time of Galileo. We now have an essential tool that can be used to create theories of complex systems, theories that will ultimately compare favorably with the theories of mechanical processes that Newton and his successors developed to describe particle systems. (p. 35)

Simulations, however, are only as accurate as the assumptions on which they are built. If a simulation is built on inaccurate or incomplete understandings of key factors or if those key factors are missing, then the simulation will generate representations that can lead to misconceptions, poor decisions, or both. Therefore, it is important for science educators to carefully and critically examine the underpinning theories and assumption on which each simulation is built before considering it for his or her classroom.

PhET Interactive Simulations, one example of high-quality science simulations, is an ongoing effort to provide an extensive suite of simulations to improve the way that biology, chemistry, earth science, and physics are taught and learned. The simulations include interactive tools that enable students to make connections between real life phenomena and the underlying science that explains such phenomena. In order to help students visually comprehend these concepts, PhET simulations animate what is invisible to the eye through the use of graphics and intuitive controls such as click-and-drag manipulation, sliders, and radio buttons. To further encourage quantitative exploration, the simulations also offer measurement instruments including rulers, stopwatches, voltmeters, and thermometers. As the user manipulates these interactive tools, responses are immediately animated thus effectively illustrating cause-and-effect relationships as well as representations such as motion of the objects, graphs, and number readouts.

All PhET simulations are freely available from the PhET website and are easy to use and incorporate into the classroom. They are written in Java and Flash, and can be run using a standard web browser as long as Flash and Java are installed. In 2009, over 8 million simulations were run from the website. There are also options to download individual simulations or the entire website for offline use.

The PhET team of scientists, software engineers, and science educators use a research-based approach—incorporating findings from prior research and their own testing—to update and enhance their simulations and better support student engagement with and understanding of scientific concepts. Educational effectiveness and usability of the simulations are tested and evaluated by analysis of student interviews and user studies of the simulations in a variety of settings, including lectures, group work, homework, and lab work. Table 5.1 (next page) summarizes additional details about PhET and other high-quality science simulations.

A *virtual world* is a graphical or text-based representation of a real or imagined world in which a participant may control a digital emissary (i.e., an avatar) to traverse cyber-landscapes and interact with and create digital artifacts individually or with others in three-dimensional space. For the purposes of this chapter, all virtual worlds are simulations and considered platforms on which simulations and games can be built instead of simulations or games themselves. For a more in depth review of virtual worlds, see Bartle's (2010) review of the history of virtual worlds and Chapter 17 of the present volume.

Educators and policy makers interested in existing virtual worlds should explore the *Virtual Worlds Almanac*, developed and supported by the Federation of American Scientists (2008), which includes detailed records on 161 unique virtual worlds. The project's mission is to support a free, comprehensive, up-to-date, and reliable repository of information about existing virtual worlds. For those interested in developing and creating in virtual worlds, four open-source platforms potentially valuable to educators include Open Cobalt (www.opencobalt.org), Open Wonderland (http://openwonderland.org), OpenSimulator (http://opensimulator.org), and Sirikata (www.sirikata.com). Four commercial platforms also of potential interest to educators include Active Worlds (www.activeworlds.com), Second Life (http://secondlife.com), Torque 3D (www.garagegames.com/products/torque-3d/), and Unity (http://unity3d.com).

TABLE 5.1 ▶ Representative, high-quality science simulations

TITLE AND DEVELOPER	GRADES	TOPICS/CONTENT FOCUS	URL
Biologica *Concord Consortium*	9–12	Hypermodels for teaching and understanding genetics	http://biologica.concord.org
ChemSense *SRI International*	9–12	Investigation, construction, and discussion of ideas in chemistry supported	http://chemsense.org
Dance of The Planets *ARC Science*	6–8 and 9–12	Real time animation of the solar system	www.arcscience.com/otherProducts/ danceOfThePlanets.html
MIT PDA Simulations (Big Fish-Little Fish; Live Long and Prosper) *MIT's Scheller Teacher Education Program*	6–8 and 9–12	Predatory prey systems; heredity and variation in organisms illustrated	http://education.mit.edu/pda
NetLogo *Northwestern University*	6–8 and 9–12	Programmable modeling environments; models in areas of biology, chemistry, computer science, earth science, mathematics, and physics	http://ccl.northwestern.edu/netlogo
PhET Interactive Simulations *University of Colorado*	3–5, 6–8, and 9–12	Simulations of physical phenomena in areas of biology, chemistry, earth science, mathematics, and physics	http://phet.colorado.edu/index.php
SimCalc *University of Massachusetts Dartmouth*	6–8	The mathematics of change and variation; many examples are science related	www.kaputcenter.umassd.edu/ projects/simcalc
StarLogo TNG *MIT's Scheller Teacher Education Program*	6–8 and 9–12	Programmable modeling environments; models in areas of biology, chemistry, computer science, earth science, mathematics, and physics	http://education.mit.edu/drupal/ starlogo-tng

A *video game* is "rule-based with a variable and quantifiable outcome, where different outcomes are assigned different values, the player exerts effort in order to influence the outcome, the player feels emotionally attached to the outcome, and the consequences of the activity are negotiable" (Juul, 2005, p. 36). As with virtual worlds, all video games are simulations. However, not all video games are built into virtual worlds. For example, the Mystery of the Sick Puppy is a high-quality science video game that does not exist within a virtual world. The game, developed at the Center for Computer Integrated Systems for Microscopy and Manipulation (CISMM) at the University of North Carolina at Chapel Hill with funding from the National Science Foundation (NSF), is available free to educators and students for use in instructional contexts from the CISMM (http://ced.ncsu.edu/nanoscale/materials.htm). To play the game, students use a simulated atomic force microscope to study the shape of an unknown virus, its DNA or RNA, and its size. They identify the virus and then diagnose and treat the sick puppy.

Science Pirates: The Curse of Brownbeard (www.sciencepirates.org), developed at New Mexico State University and sponsored by the U.S. Department of Agriculture, is a second high-quality science video game. This interactive game targets students in Grades 6–8 and teaches food safety knowledge through a series of scientific explorations. Science vocabulary—such as "hypothesis," "independent variable," and "dependent variable"—are embedded throughout the game in a conversational manner. The culminating activity includes designing and then running an experiment that reveals the importance of hand washing. In so doing, students learn how to articulate a research question and test their hypothesis under carefully controlled conditions. All factors that might affect the outcome of the experiment are made uniform except for the variable being tested. Students draw conclusions from analysis of their data and publish their findings, informed recommendations for hand washing behavior. Additional high-quality science video games are summarized in Table 5.2 by category.

Although there are instances of video games that are not virtual worlds (e.g., Mystery of the Sick Puppy) and virtual worlds that are not video games (e.g., MPK20, Sun's Virtual Workplace, which is built on the Project Wonderland Toolkit), some programs share qualities of video games and virtual worlds. The Minnesota Zoo and Eduweb's WolfQuest (www.wolfquest.org), with content support from the International Wolf Center, is one example of a high-quality science video game that exists in a virtual world. Supported by the NSF, WolfQuest is a wildlife simulation that models wolf behavior and the relations between wolves and their environment. It primarily targets users ages 9–15 in informal settings and, to a lesser extent, students enrolled in formal science classes. The game, available in Mac and PC formats, is free and available to all interested parties through the project's website. In single player mode, the player is a lone wolf looking for a mate as he or she interacts with computer-controlled wolves from other packs. Successful players find a mate, who then helps the player hunt with the pack. In multiplayer mode, users join a wolf pack of up to five other users on their quest to grow stronger and thrive. Through their experiences in the virtual world, users begin to understand wolf behavior and the multiple competing ecological demands associated with individual and pack survival. According to recent summative evaluation of WolfQuest, users report, among other things, knowledge gain and stronger emotional attachment to wolves (Schaller, Goldman, Spickelmier, Allison-Bunnell, & Koepfler, 2009). Additionally, users exhibit significant behavioral outcomes. For example, large percentages of users complete wolf-related activities after experiencing the simulation, such as seeking out further information about wolves on the Internet, in books, and on television.

TABLE 5.2 ▶ High-quality science video games by scientific category

TITLE AND DEVELOPER	GRADES	TOPICS/CONTENT FOCUS	URL
Astronomy games that address the study of celestial bodies and the universe as a whole			
Moonbase Alpha *NASA*	6–12	To promote and encourage interest in NASA's mission, which is to pioneer the future in space exploration, scientific discovery, and aeronautics research	www.nasa.gov/moonbasealpha/
Race to Mars *Discovery Channel*	6–12	Complete various missions on foot and with remote rovers to explore and investigate Mars	www.racetomars.ca/mars/game_home.jsp

(Continued)

TABLE 5.2 *(Continued)*

TITLE AND DEVELOPER	GRADES	TOPICS/CONTENT FOCUS	URL
Biology games that address the study of living organisms			
The Great Flu *Erasmus MC: University Medical Center Rotterdam*	6–12	Transmission and control of disease	www.thegreatflu.com
Immune Attack *Federation of American Scientists*	9–12	Human immunology	fas.org/immuneattack
Mystery of the Sick Puppy *CISMM at University of North Carolina Chapel Hill*	9–12	Identifying viruses with nanotechnology instruments	http://cismm.cs.unc.edu/downloads/?dl_cat=13
Plant Cells *Genomics Digital Lab*	9–12	Plant physiology and biochemistry	www.genomicsdigitallab.com
Science Pirates: The Curse of Brownbeard *New Mexico State University*	6–8	Food safety science	www.sciencepirates.org/classroom.html
Resilient Planet Game *National Geographic*	6–12	Interrelationships among aquatic species	www.jason.org/public/WhatIs/CurrORPIndex.aspx *(for curriculum sampler)*
River City *Harvard University*	6–8	Disease transmission	http://128.103.176.29/rivercityproject/
Chemistry games that address the study of matter, its properties, and reactions			
The Reconstructors *Rice University*	6–8	Pharmacology	http://reconstructors.rice.edu
Environmental science games that address the study of organisms and their interrelation with the environment			
ElectroCity *Genesis Energy*	6–8	Environmental consequences of energy choices	www.electrocity.co.nz
Quest Atlantis *Indiana University*	6–8	A range of quests promote different aspects of social and moral development	http://atlantis.crlt.indiana.edu
Spore *Electronic Arts*	6–12	Evolution and adaptation of organisms	www.spore.com
WolfQuest *Minnesota Zoo, Eduweb*	6–8	Wolf behavior and ecology	www.wolfquest.org
Physics games that address the study of energy, force, matter, motion, space, and time and relations among them			
Armadillo Run *Peter Stock*	6–12	Newtonian physics	www.armadillorun.com
Time Engineers *Software Kids*	6–12	Engineering	www.software-kids.com/html/time_engineers
Whyville *Numedeon*	6–9	Scientific literacy and socially responsible behavior	www.whyville.net

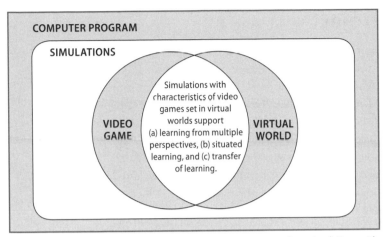

FIGURE 5.1 ▶ Intersecting points among computer programs where simulations with video game characteristics are set in virtual worlds

Figure 5.1 depicts the interrelation of computer programs, simulations, virtual worlds, and video games. At the point where virtual world and video games intersect, simulations are capable of supporting three interesting capabilities that have profound implications for teaching and learning (Dede, 2009a). First, users begin to make meaning of relevant and situation-specific activities, cultures, and theories by participating in physical and social contexts of the virtual world (for more information see Dieterle & Clarke, 2008). Second, users experience enhanced opportunities to transfer what is known in one context or situation to a novel context or situation in rich, positive, and powerful ways (for more information see Bossard, Kermarrec, Buche, & Tisseau, 2008; Mariano, Doolittle, & Hicks, 2009). Third, users learn from multiple perspectives. A user understands his or her assigned perspective by the visible aspects of objects and conditions in the virtual world, such as size, shape, and motion relative to the character being played and to other characters (for more information see Dede, Salzman, Loftin, & Ash, 2000; Dede, Salzman, Loftin, & Sprague, 1999). A user perceiving a virtual world through the first person perspective, the egocentric perspective, sees the world as if through goggles, which supports active participant experiences. A user perceiving a virtual world through the third person perspective, the exocentric perspective, sees the world as if a video camera were mounted just behind the avatar (i.e., the graphical embodiment of the user). This perspective supports learning as if from a distance or from the point of view of an observer.

The remainder of this chapter delves deeply into this space, where virtual worlds related to science video games intersect. The designers and developers of video games make design decisions based on such variables as *audience* (general versus targeted; formal education versus informal education); *game play* (individual versus multiplayer; online versus stand alone); and *purpose* (commercial versus research project). Thus, the findings from one game cannot be generalized to the collective. It is beyond the scope of this chapter to go deeply into the simulations and games listed in Table 5.1 and Table 5.2. However, the critical examination and evaluation of one high-quality game, River City, offers those interested in science video games a lens through which to examine and evaluate video games objectively. The following case study shows how this game changed curricular content, relationships among students and teachers, assessment practices, and the knowledge and skills of teachers.

The River City Project

In addition to being a simulation with video game-like qualities built on a virtual world, the River City Project was selected as a case study for further exploration because of its longevity, research focus, and extensive use by teachers and students in schools. As a research project, River City began in 2000 and continues. Three consecutive NSF grants and one Department of Education grant have funded the project and its rich research agenda. Extensive use of River City by students and teachers—more than 100 teachers and 5,500 students completed River City in academic year 2007–08, with similar numbers in academic year 2008–09—has resulted in data that has led to potentially transformative findings that extend and refine current theory and design models, research and assessment methods, and pedagogical practices.

Chris Dede, a professor at Harvard University, established the River City Project in the late 1990s when he was at George Mason University. The project, undertaken in response to the needs and demands of educators and students, translated policy directives into a practical research agenda. Working with science educators, Dede observed a common theme: many students fail to learn the complex thinking skills needed to carry out scientific investigations through traditional lessons and laboratory experiences.

This observation aligns with the findings of a report developed by the National Research Council (2000), which underscores the disconnect between how people learn and the traditional pedagogies prevalent in many of today's science classrooms:

> Students do not come to understand inquiry simply by learning words such as "hypothesis" and "inference" or by memorizing procedures such as "the steps of the scientific method." They must experience inquiry directly to gain a deep understanding of its characteristics. (p. 14)

The River City Project (RCP) is housed at Harvard University. The primary goal of the project is to develop and study the strengths and limits of a multiplayer video game for teaching scientific inquiry (defined as a systematic search for knowledge and understanding) and 21st-century skills (for example, creativity, innovation, critical thinking, problem solving, information technology skills, collaboration, and communication, including media literacy) to science students in the middle grades. Project researchers have investigated, among other things, motivation and usability of the River City interface (Ketelhut, Clarke, & Nelson, 2010; Ketelhut, Clarke, Nelson, & Dukas, 2008; Nelson, 2007); students' beliefs in their ability to do science and scientific investigations (Ketelhut, 2007; Nelson & Ketelhut, 2008); emerging research methodologies (Ketelhut, Dede, Clarke, Nelson, & Bowman, 2007; Nelson, Ketelhut, Clarke, Bowman, & Dede, 2005); media-based learning styles (Dede, Dieterle, Clarke, Ketelhut, & Nelson, 2007; Dieterle, 2009); and issues of "scale," that is, the challenges and opportunities of bringing River City to diverse schools, classrooms, and students across North America (Clarke & Dede, 2009a, 2009b).

In addition to studying River City itself as a learning innovation, researchers on the project have also studied the effects of participation in River City on student learning. In a recent study of 574 middle grade students who participated in the River City Project in academic year 2006–07, Dieterle (2009) reported a small to medium positive effect for science content understanding. In addition, he observed that, on average, students who (a) prefer creating and sharing artifacts through the Internet are well suited for learning about disease transmission and scientific problem solving skills in the project and (b) students who feel highly connected with the media, tools, and people they interact with for communication, expression, and problem solving in the project are more likely to believe they are able to complete activities common to practicing scientists. However, students who avoid the same activities or do not share the same predilections listed in (a) and (b) may not do as well in the River City Project.

The Content of River City

Using a multidisciplinary perspective, River City is designed around topics that are central to biological and epidemiological subject matter yet span the domains of biology, chemistry, earth science, ecology, and health/life sciences, as well as history. River City content derives from National Science Education Standards (National Research Council, 1996), National Educational Technology Standards for Students (International Society for Technology in Education, 2007), and 21st Century Skills (Partnership for 21st Century Skills, 2002). Implementation of River City includes a 17-hour, time-on-task curriculum and a pre-test, a post-test, and a research conference at the end of the project. Teachers are not expected to find extra time in the school year in order to implement River City. On the contrary, the River City curriculum is designed and intended to replace existing lessons that bedevil many students.

River City is a town besieged with problems stemming from three diseases—Escherichia coli, malaria, and tuberculosis—that simultaneously affect the health of its residents. Students have been commissioned by the mayor of River City to travel across time and distance to help the town understand why people are getting sick by investigating germ theory and disease transmission. The study of disease and disease transfer are two ideal subjects for study and investigation during the middle grades, in contrast with many other historically significant scientific discoveries that are more complex or abstract, such as continental drift and classical mechanics (American Association for the Advancement of Science, 1993). River City, based on authentic geographical, historical, and sociological conditions, is set in the late 1800s. Setting River City in the past was a design decision made early on by project researchers because even the least sophisticated person in the 21st century knows more about disease and disease transmission than the most sophisticated person living in the 19th century. As a result, all students have opportunities for success in River City, regardless of their prior knowledge or academic success. Furthermore, in traditional schooling, time is often held constant (60-minute periods, 6-hour schooldays, 180 school days per year) and learning is allowed to vary (some students earn As, while others earn Cs). Within River City, the amount of time allotted to complete activities within the curriculum varies, but all students put their understanding to work and demonstrate their mastery of disease transmission and experimental design by the end of the project.

Student–Content, Student–Student, and Student–Teacher Relationships in River City

Inquiry-based science is fundamental to the River City curriculum and accomplished by students actively completing four core experiences. First, River City students are engaged by scientifically oriented research questions that they develop as a team, which seek to help the town determine why residents are becoming sick. Students test these questions in a controlled experiment facilitated within the River City environment. Second, students give priority to evidence, which allows them to develop and evaluate explanations that address their research questions. Third, students formulate explanations from evidence that addresses their research questions in a report to the mayor. Fourth, students evaluate their conclusions and at the end of the project provide recommendations in light of alternative explanations, particularly those reflecting scientific understanding through a research conference, in which each team shares its findings with other teams.

When students actively participate in River City, they gain knowledge and skills in inquiry-based science and are supported and strengthened by the game's thoughtfully designed relationships—between students and the content they are engaging, among students working in teams, and between students and their teachers.

Student–Content Relationship in River City

Central to the River City Project is a multiuser virtual environment (MUVE). MUVEs are virtual spaces in which multiple users control digital representations of themselves to engage digital content and interact with fellow users to complete various kinds of tasks. Because River City is a networked application, students can access River City at any time during the project from any computer connected to the Internet with the River City simulation installed. The affordances of the River City MUVE, as depicted and described in Figure 5.2, allow users to (a) traverse the virtual world; (b) communicate with River City residents and teammates; (c) manipulate virtual instruments (e.g., a microscope); and (d) collect, manipulate, and analyze data.

Across their experiences in the River City Project, students work with a range of media (e.g., the Student Workspace, a synchronous chat tool, a virtual world, paper-based materials, and simulated tools) for varying purposes, which capitalize on the distributed and situated nature of learning. From a distributed perspective, cognitive processes—perception, learning, reasoning, and memory—are no longer confined within the head of an individual (Hutchins, 1995; Salomon, 1993). Instead, cognitive activity is viewed as distributed across internal human minds, tools and artifacts, groups of people, and space and time. Central to the situated perspective of cognition is the study of learning as a phenomenon that occurs in the course of participation in social contexts (Lave & Wenger, 1991). Knowing and understanding are entwined among the activities, concepts, and cultures in which they exist. For more information, see Dieterle and Clarke's (2008) discussion and analysis of how video games built in virtual worlds can be used to support situated and distributed learning and Ketelhut and colleagues' (2007) analysis of situated learning in River City.

The Virtual Space contains the three-dimensional world of River City, which students navigate and explore through control of their avatars (graphical embodiments of the players). The Virtual Space includes interactive residents (programmed characters that can perform a limited number of actions), objects, buildings, animals, and tools that carry information about River City. The "Chat Window" displays all dialogue between (a) a student and River City residents and (b) a student and his or her teammates. While in River City, students can see avatars of all other visitors (student players on their team and on other teams) and residents, but the interface is constrained so that students on different teams cannot communicate through text chatting. In addition, students on the same team cannot see the conversations their teammates have with residents.

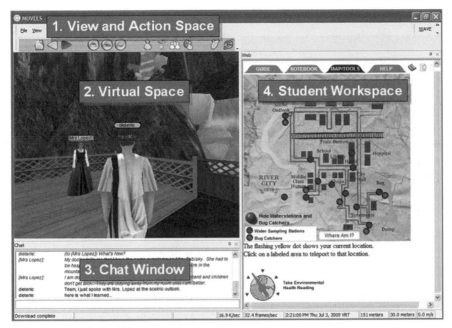

FIGURE 5.2 ▶ The River City multiuser virtual environment interface

The View and Action Space allows a student to change how things are viewed inside the simulation. Selecting different action icons, students can make their avatars spin, jump, or wave. Students' control over their avatars helps to support a feeling of "being there" when immersed inside a virtual environment (Winn, 2003). If students immersed within River City were asked, "Where are you?" they would likely describe their locations within River City and not in a science classroom interacting with a computer.

The Student Workspace provides and collects information through scaffolded learning activities built into the Guide and the Notebook, authentic scientific tools (e.g., bug catcher nets; microscopes), and an interactive map. Students use the Guide as their primary resource for navigating River City. The Guide scaffolds students through their River City experiences while inside the simulation. Students are prompted by the Guide to record ideas, observations, inferences, and reflections directly into the simulation via the Notebook. Notebook entries are searchable by season and world, date and location, and type of entry. The flexibility of the Notebook promotes key aspects of visualization, allowing students to (a) make meaning of large amounts of data through graphical representations and data charts, (b) perceive unanticipated and emergent properties of phenomena, (c) discern disparities in data quality when multiple datasets are compared site by side, and (d) formulate and test new and creative hypotheses (based on Ware, 2004).

The Map includes major buildings and areas in River City. Through the map, students can quickly and easily teleport to any part of the town, as well as access the environmental health meter (a general measure based on location and season), water sampling stations, and bug catching stations. The Microscope, which is used to measure water quality, and the Bug Sampling Station simulate scientific apparatuses from the late 1800s. Many teachers use this point in the curriculum as an opportunity to go more deeply into the cause and effect invention had on understanding disease.

The River City MUVE includes 10 sources for information that students use to determine why residents are becoming sick, each of which is described in Table 5.3. The multivariate problems that students study in River City are too complex for students to explore individually. Therefore, teams collectively seek, sort through, and synthesize experiences from multiple sources, rather than individually attempting to locate and absorb information from some single source.

Just as no single source of information will reveal definitively why residents are becoming sick, no single medium can support all of the communication requirements needed among students in River City. Whereas students spend approximately two-thirds of the 17-hour curriculum using a computer to access the River City MUVE and analyze data collected from the simulation, the rest of the time students work face-to-face, either with their team or as a whole class. Within their face-to-face team meetings, students are provided structured time to reflect on the activities they have completed and strategize next steps.

Participation in the River City Project involves students shifting their attention among different media and modes of communication, while learning the strengths and limits of each. For example, the team chat tool allows student teams to instant message with one another and with residents of River City synchronously. This tool is characterized by ideas moving rapidly between students but lacks many social cues, such as gestures and body language, and is not designed for extended responses. Therefore, it is not necessarily the best medium for all communications.

Student–Student Relationships in River City

As students progress through the River City Project, they advance through four different seasons chronologically and two different worlds as depicted in Figure 5.3. Progression through the project is characterized by increased levels of challenge, incremental growth of understanding, and ongoing opportunities for success, which Csíkszentmihályi (1990) describes as "optimal

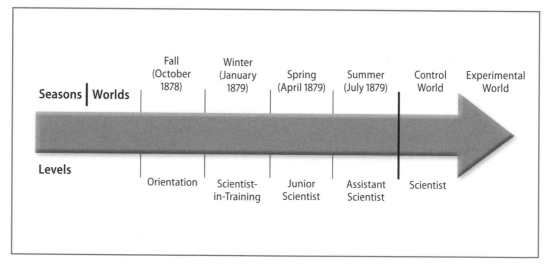

FIGURE 5.3 ▶ Six trips to River City. As students proceed through the various seasons, they advance in levels of experience on their way to becoming scientists.

TABLE 5.3 ▶ Informational sources available in the River City multiuser virtual environment by location and functionality

INFORMATION SOURCE	LOCATION	FUNCTIONALITY
Admissions Chart	Hospital	Lists dates and symptoms for admitted patients. Differences in patients' residency and symptoms help students to identify diseases.
Bug-Catchers	Scattered throughout River City. Near water sources.	Allow students to determine the mosquito density of different geographic areas over time. Areas near standing water in the summer, for example, have greater mosquito density than areas near rapidly moving water in the winter.
Clue Pictures	Scattered throughout River City. Found on walls of building.	Illustrate events of the 1880s. Information on Dr. Richards and Dr. Koch, for example, can be found by clicking on pictures on the walls of the University. These are authentic historical figures in science, and their research is portrayed accurately in River City.
Demographic Charts	Hospital	Contain population density information in River City by neighborhood.
Environmental Health Meter	Travels with student	A dynamic tool for measuring the general environmental health of an area. Areas near the dump, the tenements, and containing horse droppings are much less healthy than other areas.
Information Kiosks	Scattered throughout River City	Contain information relevant to a specific season and location, such as local weather and current events, like a sale on flush toilets.
Library Books	Library	Includes an online dictionary and "Introduction to Scientific Research." Students access the online dictionary by clicking on the dictionary at the main desk in the River City library when they are unsure of a word's meaning. In the book titled *Introduction to Scientific Research*, students can find more information on such topics as (a) an observation and an inference, (b) independent and dependent variables, and (c) control and experimental groups.
River City Residents	Scattered throughout River City	Can be interviewed to find out clues related to why residents are falling ill. Residents provide a single piece of information in each season and/or world, but that information varies between seasons and worlds.
Sights and Sounds of River City	Throughout River City	Vary from season to season and world to world. The intensity of coughing residents is greater in the tenements during winter-time. The leaves on trees, on the other hand, are rich and green in the spring and summer, multi-colored in fall, and absent in winter.
Water Sampling Stations	Scattered throughout River City. Near water sources.	In the microscope field, students observe two kinds of microbes, waterborne anthrax and *E. coli*. To analyze the water, students count the number of each microbe. Afterward they repeat the procedure until they have collected enough samples for their experimental purposes. Areas near the dump and bog during the warmer seasons have greater numbers of microbes than other areas and seasons.

flow." This situation allows students to experience the realities of doing science in a controlled learning environment that is intermediate in complexity between the real world, which can be overwhelming, and a "cookbook" lab, which is designed to be teacher- and student-proof.

Immersive experiences in River City evoke a sense of "being there" by stimulating a combination of the senses—the visual process of seeing what is on the screen, the auditory process of decoding sounds, and the kinesthetic process of moving a mouse and performing keystrokes—and higher-order cognitive processes, such as imagination, projection, and visualization. Engaged with authentic tasks in an immersive environment, as Dieterle and Clarke (2008) argue, students begin to become scientists as they learn the principles and concepts of science, acquire the reasoning and procedural skills of scientists, devise and carry out investigations that test their ideas, and understand why such investigations are uniquely powerful (National Research Council, 2000).

In addition to students working as researchers who systematically investigate disease and disease transmission in River City to establish facts and build knowledge, students experience the enterprise of science as teachers, journalists, and policy makers. As teachers, students impart knowledge and skills to each other while in small groups and as a whole class. As journalists, students present facts and descriptions of phenomena they have observed and studied with impartial interpretation through memos and reports. As policy makers, students develop a course of action that is presented to the mayor of River City, recommending to her how best to alleviate disease among residents.

During their first four trips to River City, students learn (a) the differences between observations and inferences, (b) how to use scientific tools, (c) specialized language used within the scientific community, (d) the scientific method, (e) how to articulate a testable research question, and (f) the steps for constructing and completing a controlled experiment. Students also experience multiple opportunities to (a) brainstorm, where failure is an expected part of learning, (b) engage multiple domains of knowledge, and (c) demonstrate, assess, and reflect on their understanding in order to improve performance. Each season involves a cycle of planning, doing, and reflecting. Planning requires students to think about the challenges they have chosen to investigate and to develop an action plan. Doing involves attacking the challenge head-on and coming up with (or failing to come up with) a solution. Reflecting includes monitoring progress, considering what has been done and how it might have been done differently, and proposing what should be done next.

By the end of summer (July 1879), teams of students have agreed on a research question and have described in detail their controlled experiment. On entering the control world, students complete the controlled portion of their experiment. If students have not yet mastered everything to a high level during earlier trips to River City, they are allowed to pull everything together during their visits to the control and experimental worlds.

Together, teams of students use their collective knowledge and understanding to formulate, enact, and interpret their controlled experiments to understand why residents are becoming sick. Each teammate does not need to become an expert in all aspects of the project as long as he or she understands who on the team can address specific problems. Not every student has to be the creative thinker, the fact gatherer/measurer who meticulously records data, and the astute observer of historical and social details. As the teams continue to work together, they have the potential to become what Bielaczyc and Collins (1999) define as a learning community, which is characterized as having (a) diversity of expertise among its members, who are valued for their contributions; (b) a shared objective of continually advancing the collective knowledge and skills; (c) an emphasis on learning how to learn individually and collectively; and (d) mechanisms for sharing what is learned.

Student–Teacher Relationships in River City

The student-teacher relationship in the popular children's TV series "The Magic School Bus" is characterized by Ms. Frizzle, the teacher who travels with her students to the Arctic, inside a human body, across the solar system, and within a cell. Along the way, she poses thoughtful questions to students and answers their questions as they arise. Together, the teacher and her students share the adventure, with the more knowledgeable teacher guiding the learning experience. In River City, this is not the case. The teacher does not travel back in time with the student; instead, he or she stays in the present time and walks around the classroom, offering guidance and support to students as they move through the curriculum.

During River City professional development, discussed in detail later, characters from the blockbuster movie "The Matrix" are used to compare and contrast the roles and responsibilities of teachers and students in River City. Students are likened to Neo, Trinity, and Morpheus, the heroes of the movie, who freely move between the real world and the virtual world. Inside the virtual world, students control how they look and can do things that are not possible in the real world (e.g., going back in time, teleporting, and flying). Teachers are likened to Tank and Doser, supporting characters, who communicate with Neo, Trinity, and Morpheus from the real world across interfaces and support them as they engage in a variety of activities. In fact, like Tank and Doser, teachers are unable to access the virtual world directly. Because teachers do not travel with students to River City, they can sincerely claim not to know why residents are becoming sick.

The student-teacher relationship in River City stems from the belief that given enough time, access, and motivation, almost everyone can learn just about anything to a great extent (e.g., Duckworth, 2001). Many learning innovations fall short on one or more of these dimensions and fail to maximize student learning. River City teachers are encouraged to give students time to practice with the ideas and procedures they are coming to understand. Instead of judging students' thinking as right or wrong, teachers help students confront inconsistencies in their "meaning making" or thinking (National Research Council, 2005). In contrast, when students are required to keep a sustained focus on traditional classroom learning activities, their motivation often wanes.

If a traditional classroom activity is too challenging, then students are quick to give up, dismissing the activity as "too hard." If a video game is not challenging, on the other hand, then players are quick to stop playing, dismissing the game as "too easy." Successful video games are marked by challenges that encourage extended engagement whereas, more often than not, success in school is characterized by quickly and efficiently providing the correct response or solution. While the game-like interface in River City evokes a strong sense of motivation, teachers are still responsible for making sure that ideas presented in the game, whether new or longstanding, are challenging and brought to a conscious level in students' minds (National Research Council, 2005).

River City teachers also serve as consensus builders among teams of students. Before student teams begin their controlled experiments, they must agree on a single, testable research question. Helping students reach consensus requires the teacher to facilitate opportunities for collaboration by (a) asking clarifying questions; (b) probing assumptions and goals; (c) openly offering and testing ideas; (d) welcoming, collecting, and synthesizing feedback; and (e) comparing, distilling, and synthesizing ideas (Perkins, 2003). To help teachers understand what students know (and what they do not know) a variety of tools that measure students' conceptions and misconceptions are part of the game and are explained in the River City professional development package.

Tools for Measuring What Students Know and Are Able to Do in River City

Limitations of traditional classroom practices make it impossible to monitor and track what every student is doing, leaving educators unsure of what students have (or have not) learned. Many assessments that are currently used to measure what students know are (a) set in a standardized format of multiple choice questions and brief constructed responses; (b) administered to test individual, unaided knowledge instead of team-based understandings; and (c) void of context, authenticity, or meaning to the students completing the assessment. Observing students' facial expressions, asking for shows of hands, and cold-calling individual students are haphazard ways of calibrating the learning taking place in a classroom, but they fail to capture the efforts of every student. River City students are given an opportunity for apprenticeship and reflection of their understanding through a variety of experiences that have been fully integrated into the River City storyline. Formative assessment data are collected through interactions with an investigative reporter and through memos to the mayor of River City. The primary summative assessment is a report to the mayor, summarizing the results and implications of students' controlled experiments in their teams. During teacher professional development, teachers are reminded that, unlike Andy Warhol's prediction that "In the future everyone will be famous for fifteen minutes," in River City, every student is anonymous for about 15 minutes while his or her keystrokes transfer from the student's computer to the River City database, where they are catalogued and attributed to the student.

By connecting the River City simulation to sophisticated databases, River City researchers can capture and record every keystroke students make within the simulation. These "log files" are processed and then e-mailed to teachers as summary reports within a 24-hour period, providing rich insights into student understanding.

Receiving log-file information in a daily report allows teachers to monitor student work throughout the project. Teachers can detect early on if students fall off task or need to review specific concepts immediately rather than waiting until the end of the project. This daily feedback also provides teachers with snapshots of student learning and work they can share with students, administrators, and parents. The continuous assessments of each student player, compiled in the game's daily summary progress reports, are tremendously useful to teachers. For example, post-implementation surveys of 51 participating teachers in academic year 2006–07 revealed that the majority of teachers appreciated receiving daily reports, and four in five (80%) believe that the embedded assessments and online notepad reports help them understand how students spend their time in River City (on task and making progress or off task) and what content they are struggling to understand (Dieterle, et al., 2008). As they study the reports of their students' progress, teachers become more effective at guiding students to answer their own questions during team and class discussions. With this explicit data on student progress, teachers can help individual students overcome their shortcomings immediately and can encourage and guide them to make challenging moves and pose pertinent hypotheses as they progress through the game.

Students regularly interact with Kent Brock, an investigative reporter who works for the town newspaper, during their trips to River City. Kent is symbolic of the *wise fool*—someone who asks obvious questions that bring about reflection and reexamination of beliefs or understandings. Students' exchanges with Kent allow for expression and performance of understanding through multiple representations. Instead of existing outside the River City storyline, Kent is considered a primary character within the town of River City. Kent interviews students to find out what they know and how they are making meaning of their experiences. As a good reporter, he is concerned with more than just the facts, asking students to explain, interpret, and apply what they are learning, as well as to empathize with residents and to engage in metacognition (thinking about one's own thinking) about their ideas (based on Wiggins & McTighe, 2005). In addition, Kent provides students with information to make sure they have interviewed important residents and accessed significant tools and artifacts found throughout the town of River City. Optional homework assignments ask students to review and edit articles written by Kent before they go to press at the *River City Telegraph*. Sprinkled throughout the articles are key ideas that students may have missed, as well as misconceptions that students are intended to correct.

Many people who are not professional writers report that they learned to write on the job, not in school (Anderson, 1985). Students in River City model workplace settings in which writing is an expected and valued form of communication. They learn by doing, completing increasingly complex tasks that put their understanding to work. Students demonstrate and deepen their understanding of the phenomena studied in River City by frequently writing about what they know and why they think they know it through "Time to Reflect" activities, memos to the mayor, and a report to the mayor.

The Knowledge and Skill of Teachers

By participating in the project, educators have opportunities to learn new methods of teaching, learning, and assessing; help others in the field of education understand the strengths and limits of the video-game interface for teaching and learning; and understand the process of high quality, rigorous research better themselves. Dede's (2009b) assessment of the context of learning and teaching with science video games, based on lessons learned from the River City Project and similar projects, argues that teachers effectively using such learning innovations in their classes can (a) use detailed knowledge of learners' intellectual and psychosocial characteristics to better assemble student teams, (b) alter their classroom instruction and support based on the feedback educational games and simulations provide, (c) better mainstream students with special needs, (d) prepare students to take full advantage of real world field trips, and (e) relate virtual experiences in science games and simulations to what is happening in the real world and in the lives of their students.

Before River City students travel across time and distance, teachers receive pre-implementation and ongoing professional development that allows them to work through the curriculum as learners and as instructors, connect their content and instructional expertise with the River City simulation and curriculum, measure their own understanding by reflecting on activities, and build confidence in themselves and the project. River City professional development focuses not only on the skills needed to implement the River City Project, but also on skills that teachers can use after the project is completed.

When working with large school districts or geographic areas with large numbers of interested teachers, the River City Project uses a "train the trainer" practice in which local trainers, trained by the research team, work with area teachers. In these instances, professional development takes place in two phases. In phase one, teachers work through an approximately eight-hour pre-session with their trainers. In phase two, teachers receive ongoing support from those trainers and have access to online resources while implementing River City with their students. Teachers working outside of trainer-based areas receive similar professional development and support by working directly with members of the River City research team through Elluminate, a user-friendly and intuitive web-collaboration tool.

The National Science Standards (National Research Council, 1996), along with other high-profile initiatives (American Association for the Advancement of Science, 1990, 1993), established the standards from which most states and districts developed their *intended curriculum*—the learning objectives and standards that define what is to be learned and in which sequence the material should be presented (National Research Council, 2003). "In theory," as Yogi Berra observed, "there is no difference between theory and practice; in practice, there is." Similarly, the intended curriculum once released into the dynamics of learning environments becomes an *enacted curriculum*, which may or may not align with the intended curriculum. The greatest attribute of science video games may not be in how they change the intended curriculum, but in how they change the enacted curriculum.

River City's student-centered curriculum involves orchestration among members of the research team and participating teachers and students, which can be understood through a music metaphor with the research team as composers, teachers as conductors, and students as musicians (see Figure 5.4). All three groups work in harmony to co-design learning experiences that are personalized to individual needs and preferences while adhering to the spirit of the curriculum.

At the end of each season, students first complete a "Time to Reflect" activity individually in the online notebook. Then they write a brief memo to the mayor, providing her with an update of the group's work to date. Students, as White and Frederiksen (1998) have shown, learn inquiry better when they regularly and explicitly are asked to think about, reflect on, and articulate their own thinking and understanding verbally and in writing. Students use sentence starters, such as the

TEACHER
Conductor who leads
the musical group

STUDENTS
Musicians who play
the musical instruments

RESEARCHER
Composer who
develops the score

FIGURE 5.4 ▶ A musical metaphor representing the roles of researcher, teacher, and students within the River City Project *(© 2006 Pedro Sánchez, GFDL + CCby2.5)*

ones that follow, to think about what they know and what they want to learn: "What I know about my problem so far is," "I wonder why," "I'm curious why there is," "I still have questions about," and "When I visit River City again I want to find out." Afterward, students synthesize their reflections into a memo to the mayor, providing her with a brief report of what they have done so far.

At the end of the project, after testing their team's hypothesis and analyzing data, all students communicate their findings to the mayor of River City, thereby demonstrating their understanding of scientific inquiry and disease transmission by independently writing evidence-based, scientific reports to the mayor. Their reports include explanations of why so many residents are becoming ill and recommendations for how to alleviate the problem by drawing on their River City experiences. As a result of this performance assessment, students demonstrate and deepen their understanding of this complex socio-scientific situation.

As composers, the research team has invested more than eight years developing and refining River City, blending empirical educational research with a theory-driven design of learning environments (Ketelhut, Clarke, & Nelson, 2010; Nelson, et al., 2005; Nelson, et al., 2007). Teachers, in turn, receive the curriculum and act as conductors, using their knowledge of the local culture and school setting to get the most out of their students. The teacher's role in River City is to guide students' performance through an immersive scientific inquiry experience. Teachers act as 21st-century experts who encourage students to solve problems rather than as sages who provide answers. Diversity of prior knowledge among students provides a wealth of experience and knowledge for teams to draw upon to engage the complexities River City provides. Just as musicians tend to specialize, not all students need to master every aspect of the project equally well. Instead, teammates can play off each other's strengths while they encourage each other to patch up their collective weaknesses as they learn new skills to produce the best team performance possible.

Conclusions

Thoughtfully designed video games implemented in science classrooms provide opportunities for students to understand the concepts, cultures, and practices of scientists and the scientific enterprise actively. Well-designed, game-based learning environments housed in virtual worlds, such as River City, have the potential to address unique and situation-specific needs of learners by concurrently providing clear information, opportunities for thoughtful practice, informative feedback, and a favorable combination of intrinsic and extrinsic motivators tailored to the individual learner, who works individually on some tasks and collaboratively on others. However, much more research is needed to measure and understand how people learn in science video games in and out of school and what knowledge and skills transfer from the game to the real world.

River City, as argued in this chapter, provides a rich example of how a video game can support learning science as a discipline and an enterprise by simultaneously enhancing content learning; student-content, student-student, and student-teacher relationships; the tools for measuring what students know and are able to do; and the knowledge and skills of teachers. Although every video game is unique, the presentation of River City as an informative case study should empower those interested in science video games with tools for examining and judging other potential learning innovations objectively.

Hardware, networking, and human-computer interaction innovations challenge the engineering and computer science disciplines (Abowd & Mynatt, 2000; Satyanarayanan, 2001). The popularity of Second Life and similar interfaces has lowered the learning curve required to develop in and experience video game-like environments for learning. Such environments, however, are merely containers into which content is poured. If the content is second-rate, the learning experience will likely be of inferior quality despite the fidelity of the medium in which it is presented. The primary implementation barriers for learning innovations are neither technical nor economic, but psychological, organizational, political, and cultural (Dede, 2001). The extent to which stakeholders overcome each of these barriers will determine the extent to which video games are adopted widely in classrooms.

Even with the widespread popularity of video games for entertainment purposes, they are rarely utilized by educators for substantive teaching and learning (Annetta, 2008). The goal of this chapter is to explore and potentially change this trend and empower educators, researchers, and policymakers with recommendations, best practices, and examples of high-quality science video games. Science video games are not a simple guaranteed solution, capable of automatically overcoming all of the challenges facing students and teachers of science. Rather, they are an alternative, potentially powerful medium through which to think and learn.

I would like to thank my colleagues from SRI International's Center for Technology in Learning, the members of the River City Research Team, Jody Clarke from the Virtual Assessments project at the Harvard Graduate School of Education, and Michelle Lucey-Roper from the U.S. Department of Engergy for their guidance, feedback, support, and wisdom.

References

Abowd, G. D., & Mynatt, E. D. (2000). Charting past, present, and future research in ubiquitous computing. *ACM Transactions on Computer-Human Interaction, 7*(1), 29–58.

American Association for the Advancement of Science. (1990). *Science for all Americans.* New York, NY: Oxford University Press.

American Association for the Advancement of Science. (1993). *Project 2061: Benchmarks for science literacy.* New York, NY: Oxford University Press.

Anderson, P. V. (1985). What survey research tells us about writing at work. In L. Odell & D. Goswami (Eds.), *Writing in nonacademic settings* (pp. 3–83). New York, NY: Guilford Press.

Annetta, L. A. (2008). Video games in education: Why they should be used and how they are being used. *Theory Into Practice, 47*(3), 229–239.

Bartle, R. A. (2010). From MUDs to MMORPGs: The history of virtual worlds. In J. Hunsinger, L. Klastrup, & M. Allen (Eds.), *International handbook of internet research* (pp. 23–39). New York, NY: Springer-Verlag.

Bielaczyc, K., & Collins, A. (1999). Learning communities in classrooms: A reconceptualization of educational practice. In C. M. Reigeluth (Ed.), *Instructional-design theories and models: A new paradigm of instructional theory* (Vol. 2, pp. 269–292). Mahwah, NJ: Lawrence Erlbaum.

Bossard, C., Kermarrec, G., Buche, C., & Tisseau, J. (2008). Transfer of learning in virtual environments: A new challenge? *Virtual Reality, 12*(3), 151–161.

Casti, J. L. (1997). *Would-be worlds: How simulation is changing the frontiers of science.* New York, NY: J. Wiley.

Clark, D., Nelson, B., Sengupta, P., & D'Angelo, C. (2009). Rethinking science learning through digital games and simulations: Genres, examples, and evidence. In National Research Council's (Eds.), *Learning science: Computer games, simulations, and education.* Available from www7.nationalacademies.org/bose/Clark_Gaming_CommissionedPaper.pdf

Clarke, J., & Dede, C. (2009a). Design for scalability: A case study of the River City curriculum. *Journal of Science Education and Technology, 18*(4), 353–365.

Clarke, J., & Dede, C. (2009b). Robust designs for scalability. In L. Moller, J. B. Huett, & D. M. Harvey (Eds.), *Learning and instructional technologies for the 21st century: Visions of the future* (pp. 27–48). New York, NY: Springer.

Cohen, D. K., & Ball, D. L. (1999). *Instruction, capacity, and improvement.* Philadelphia: Consortium for Policy Research in Education, University of Pennsylvania, Graduate School of Education.

Csíkszentmihályi, M. (1990). *Flow: The psychology of optimal experience.* New York, NY: Harper & Row.

Dede, C. (2001). *Creating research centers to enhance the effective use of learning technologies.* Retrieved from www.house.gov/science/research/may10/dede.htm
Paper submitted as part of testimony for "Classrooms as Laboratories: The Science of Learning Meets the Practice of Teaching." Hearing before the Subcommittee on Research, Committee on Science, U.S. House of Representatives, 107th Congress, First Session (May 10, 2001). Washington, DC: U.S. Government Printing Office.

Dede, C. (2009a). Immersive interfaces for engagement and learning. *Science, 323*(5910), 66–69.

Dede, C. (2009b). Learning context: Gaming, simulations, and science learning in the classroom. In National Research Council's (Eds.), *Learning science: Computer games, simulations, and education.* Available from www7.nationalacademies.org/bose/Dede_Gaming_CommissionedPaper.pdf

Dede, C., Dieterle, E., Clarke, J., Ketelhut, D. J., & Nelson, B. (2007). Media-based learning styles: Implications for distance education. In M. Moore (Ed.), *Handbook of distance education* (2nd ed., pp. 339–352). Mahwah, NJ: Lawrence Erlbaum.

Dede, C., Salzman, M., Loftin, B., & Ash, K. (2000). Using virtual reality technology to convey abstract scientific concepts. In M. Jacobson & R. B. Kozma (Eds.), *Learning the sciences of the 21st century: Research, design, and implementing advanced technology learning environments* (pp. 361–413). Mahwah, NJ: Lawrence Erlbaum.

Dede, C., Salzman, M., Loftin, B., & Sprague, D. (1999). Multisensory immersion as a modeling environment for learning complex scientific concepts. In W. Feurzeig & N. Roberts (Eds.), *Modeling and simulation in science and mathematics education* (pp. 282–319). New York, NY: Springer.

Dieterle, E. (2009). Neomillennial learning styles and River City. *Children, Youth and Environments, 19*(1), 245–278.

Dieterle, E., & Clarke, J. (2008). Multi-user virtual environments for teaching and learning. In M. Pagani (Ed.), *Encyclopedia of multimedia technology and networking* (2nd ed., Vol. 2, pp. 1033–1041). Hershey, PA: Idea Group, Inc.

Dieterle, E., Dede, C., Clarke, J., Dukas, G., Garduño, E., Ketelhut, D. J., et al. (2008, March). *Formative assessments integrated into a MUVE that provides real-time feedback for teachers on student learning.* Paper presented at the 2008 American Educational Research Association Conference, New York, NY.

Dieterle, E., & Murray, J. (2009). Realizing adaptive instruction (Ad-In): The convergence of learning, instruction, and assessment. In D. D. Schmorrow, I. V. Estabrooke & M. Grootjen (Eds.), *Foundations of augmented cognition: Neuroergonomics and operational neuroscience* (pp. 601–610). New York, NY: Springer.

Duckworth, E. R. (2001). *"Tell me more": Listening to learners explain.* New York, NY: Teachers College Press.

Federation of American Scientists. (2008). *Virtual worlds almanac.* Retrieved February 15, 2009, from http://vworld.fas.org

Foster, A. N., & Mishra, P. (2009). Games, claims, genres, and learning. In R. E. Ferdig (Ed.), *Handbook of research on effective electronic gaming in education* (Vol. 1, pp. 33–50). Hershey, PA: Information Science Reference.

Gardner, H. (1999). *The disciplined mind: What all students should understand.* New York, NY: Simon & Schuster.

Hutchins, E. (1995). *Cognition in the wild.* Cambridge, MA: MIT Press.

International Society for Technology in Education (ISTE). (2007). *National educational technology standards for students* (2nd ed.). Eugene, OR: Author.

Juul, J. (2005). *Half-real: Video games between real rules and fictional worlds*. Cambridge, MA: MIT Press.

Kent, S. L. (2001). *The ultimate history of video games: From Pong to Pokémon and beyond—the story behind the craze that touched our lives and changed the world*. Roseville, CA: Prima Pub.

Ketelhut, D. J. (2007). The impact of student self efficacy on scientific inquiry skills: An exploratory investigation in River City, a multi-user virtual environment. *Journal of Science Education and Technology, 16*(1), 99–111.

Ketelhut, D. J., Clarke, J., & Nelson, B. (2010). The development of River City, a multi-user virtual environment-based scientific inquiry curriculum: Historical and design evolutions. In M. Jacobson & P. Reimann (Eds.), *Designs for learning environments of the future: International learning sciences theory and research perspectives* (pp. 89–110). New York, NY: Springer-Verlag.

Ketelhut, D. J., Clarke, J., Nelson, B., & Dukas, G. (2008). Using multi-user virtual environments to simulate authentic scientific practice and enhance student engagement. In L. A. Annetta (Ed.), *Serious educational games: From theory to practice* (pp. 25–38). Rotterdam, Netherlands: Sense Press.

Ketelhut, D. J., Dede, C., Clarke, J., Nelson, B., & Bowman, C. (2007). Studying situated learning in a multi-user virtual environment. In E. Baker, J. Dickieson, W. Wulfeck, & H. O'Neil (Eds.), *Assessment of problem solving using simulations* (pp. 37–58). Mahwah, NJ: Lawrence Erlbaum.

Kirriemuir, J., & McFarlane, A. (2004). *Report 8: Literature review in games and learning*. Bristol, UK: NESTA Futurelab.

Lave, J., & Wenger, E. (1991). *Situated learning: Legitimate peripheral participation*. Cambridge, UK: Cambridge University Press.

Mariano, G. J., Doolittle, P. E., & Hicks, D. (2009). Fostering transfer in multimedia instructional environments. In R. Zheng (Ed.), *Cognitive effects of multimedia learning* (pp. 237–259). Hershey, PA: Information Science Reference.

National Academy of Sciences. (2009). *On being a scientist: A guide to responsible conduct in research* (3rd ed.). Washington, DC: National Academies Press.

National Research Council. (1996). *National science education standards: Observe, interact, change, learn*. Washington, DC: National Academies Press.

National Research Council. (2000). *Inquiry and the national science education standards: A guide for teaching and learning*. Washington, DC: National Academies Press.

National Research Council. (2001). *Knowing what students know: The science and design of educational assessment*. Washington, DC: National Academies Press.

National Research Council. (2003). *What is the influence of the National Science Education Standards?: Reviewing the evidence, a workshop summary*. Washington, DC: National Academies Press.

National Research Council. (2005). *How students learn: History, mathematics, and science in the classroom*. Washington, DC: National Academies Press.

Nelson, B. (2007). Exploring the use of individualized, reflective guidance in an educational multi-user virtual environment. *Journal of Science Education and Technology, 16*(1), 83–97.

Nelson, B., & Ketelhut, D. J. (2008). Exploring embedded guidance and self-efficacy in educational multi-user virtual environments. *International Journal of Computer-Supported Collaborative Learning, 3*(4), 413–427.

Nelson, B., Ketelhut, D. J., Clarke, J., Bowman, C., & Dede, C. (2005). Design-based research strategies for developing a scientific inquiry curriculum in a multi-user virtual environment. *Educational Technology, 45*(1), 21–27.

Nelson, B., Ketelhut, D. J., Clarke, J., Dieterle, E., Dede, C., & Erlandson, B. (2007). Robust design strategies for scaling educational innovations: The River City case study. In B. E. Shelton & D. A. Wiley (Eds.), *The educational design and use of computer simulation games* (pp. 224–246). Rotterdam, Netherlands: Sense Press.

Newman, J. (2004). *Video games*. London, UK: Routledge.

Olson, S., & Labov, J. B. (2008). *State science and technology policy advice: Issues, opportunities, and challenges. Summary of a National Convocation*. Washington, DC: National Academies Press.

Partnership for 21st Century Skills. (2002). *Learning for the 21st century: A report and mile guide for 21st century skills*. Washington, DC: Author.

Perkins, D. (1992). *Smart schools: Better thinking and learning for every child*. New York, NY: Free Press.

Perkins, D. (2003). *King Arthur's round table: How collaborative conversations create smart organizations*. New York, NY: Wiley.

Perkins, D. (2009). *Making learning whole: How seven principles of teaching can transform education*. San Francisco, CA: Jossey-Bass.

Provenzo, E. F. (1991). *Video kids: Making sense of Nintendo*. Cambridge, MA: Harvard University Press.

Salaway, G., Caruso, J. B., & Nelson, M. R. (2007). *The ECAR study of undergraduate students and information technology*. Boulder, CO: EDUCAUSE Center for Applied Research.

Salomon, G. (Ed.). (1993). *Distributed cognitions: Psychological and educational considerations*. Cambridge, UK: Cambridge University Press.

Satyanarayanan, M. (2001). Pervasive computing: Vision and challenges. *IEEE Personal Communications, 8*(4), 10–17.

Schaller, D. T., Goldman, K. H., Spickelmier, G., Allison-Bunnell, S., & Koepfler, J. (2009). Learning in the wild: What WolfQuest taught developers and game players. In J. Trant & D. Bearman (Eds.), *Museums and the Web 2009: Proceedings*. Toronto: Archives & Museum Informatics.

Smith, S. D., Salaway, G., & Caruso, J. B. (2009). *The ECAR study of undergraduate students and information technology, 2009*. Boulder, CO: EDUCAUSE Center for Applied Research.

Squire, K., & Patterson, N. (2009). Games and simulations in informal science education. In National Research Council's (Eds.), *Learning science: Computer games, simulations, and education*. Available from www7.nationalacademies.org/bose/Squire_Gaming_CommissionedPaper.pdf

Ware, C. (2004). *Information visualization: Perception for design* (2nd ed.). San Francisco, CA: Morgan Kaufman.

White, B. Y., & Frederiksen, J. R. (1998). Inquiry, modeling, and metacognition: Making science accessible to all students. *Cognition and Instruction, 16*(1), 3–118.

Wiggins, G. P., & McTighe, J. (2005). *Understanding by design* (expanded 2nd ed.). Alexandria, VA: Association for Supervision and Curriculum Development.

Winn, W. (2003). Learning in artificial environments: Embodiment, embeddedness and dynamic adaptation. *Technology, Instruction, Cognition and Learning, 1*(1), 87–114.

6

Games for Mathematics Education

Mansureh Kebritchi and Michael Hynes

THIS CHAPTER PROVIDES AN OVERVIEW of the design and use of digital mathematics video games in mathematics education in K–12 settings. The problem of low mathematics achievement and the need to improve mathematics education is discussed, based on major mathematics policy reports (National Commission on Excellence in Education, 1983; National Mathematics Advisory Panel, 2008). A survey of existing mathematics games along with an analysis of game-related empirical studies and literature reviews are provided. This analysis indicates that an increasing number of K–12 educators are integrating games in schools and that digital video games may be powerful learning tools that have positive effects on students' motivation and achievement. In addition, the analysis of existing games suggests that the pedagogical foundations and technical aspects of mathematics video games have improved in the last three decades. Finally, a number of barriers to using mathematics games are identified in the literature, such as curriculum integration, logistical and technical problems, and teachers' support and training issues. To address these barriers, nine guidelines for evaluating games' designs are offered to help educators understand the key factors that influence games' effectiveness as learning tools. And three integration guidelines are suggested to assist educators in planning curricula to determine when and how games can be incorporated into schools to improve students' learning.

Remember word problems?

> Train A left the station going east at an average speed of 35 mph, and Train B left another station on a parallel track traveling west at an average speed of 40 mph. If the two train stations are 300 miles apart, how far from each train station will the trains be when they meet?

Problems like these are still confounding students as they encounter Algebra I. As teachers we are also challenged, challenged with getting *all students* to understand basic algebraic concepts when we know that the success rate of many is dismally low. To help overcome such challenges for students and teachers, in this chapter we present the state of the art of digital video games to illustrate how they can be used to enhance mathematics education in K–12 settings.

The introductory word problem has other, more symbolic applications to this chapter. There are two other "trains" that have already left the station. First, there is the mathematics curriculum train. This train left its station as long ago as 1895 when the Committee of Fifteen gave their recommendations for changing the mathematics curriculum (National Council of Teachers of Mathematics, 1970). That train was powered by a small steam engine that left the station very slowly and had only a limited number of paths (tracks) to travel. This chapter will not look back to that little steam engine to examine the present state of mathematics. However, it will serve well to recall some of the events and publications of the latter half of the 20th century that set the course for where our mathematics curriculum is today.

There is another, modern "bullet" train that has left its station much more recently, and it seems to be traveling on many tracks at the same time. Also, the bullet train's engine seems to transform itself as technology progresses. Technology, in general, has a "half-life" that is very short, and technology-based games are an example of this phenomenon. Digital video games show amazing advances in graphics, story, and logic with the publication of each new version. Similar rapid changes are found in educational video games. Leung (2003) has said that rapidly changing technology also affects the useful life of any publication about technology, particularly games. While the authors accept this tenet about technology publications, the challenge to write a chapter that will have a relatively long "half-life" is accepted.

Challenges Facing Mathematics Education

History changed on October 4, 1957, when the Soviet Union successfully launched Sputnik I. The world's first artificial satellite was about the size of a beach ball (58 cm. or 22.8 inches in diameter), weighed only 83.6 kg. or 183.9 pounds, and took about 98 minutes to orbit the Earth on its elliptical path. That launch ushered in new political, military, technological, and scientific developments. While the Sputnik launch was a single event, it marked the start of the space age and the U.S.-U.S.S.R space race. (National Aeronautics and Space Administration, 2008, p. 1)

The successful launch of Sputnik was also the beginning of a fevered period of curriculum development in mathematics, a time when new teaching strategies were advocated by many research groups and when the federal government made a huge investment to improve the quality of mathematics teachers. This marked the beginning of the "new math" public phase in the United States. These efforts were made so improvements would be made in the human infrastructure in what has become known as the science, technology, engineering, and mathematics (STEM) profession. The new math movement was not an enduring success, to say the least. The lack of acceptance of the new ideas in mathematics teamed with poor economic conditions in the early 1970s, despite the Apollo program's success in landing men on the moon, led to some national introspection.

In 1981, Secretary of Education T. H. Bell created the National Commission on Excellence in Education. The Commission examined the quality of education in the United States and after 18 months concluded, "Our Nation is at risk; our once unchallenged preeminence in commerce, industry, science, and technological innovation is being overtaken by competitors throughout the world" (National Commission on Excellence in Education, 1983, p. 1).

The report was punctuated by statistics showing that schools were failing. Declining test scores were cited. For example, it was noted that there was more remedial mathematics being taught in colleges and universities. Gifted students were not performing to expectations in school. A long list of statistics painted a dismal picture of education in general and mathematics learning specifically. The Commission noted that these deficiencies were apparent in a time when technology was playing an ever-increasing role in society. Computers, laser technology, and robotics as well as a list of occupations that would be affected by technology were included. However, neither the development of video games nor the use of games in education had yet reached a point to warrant inclusion in the report, *A Nation at Risk: The Imperative for Educational Reform* (National Commission on Excellence in Education, 1983).

Approaches to Mathematics Education

In the 1980s, the mathematics education community was not ignoring the condition of education or the need to improve mathematics teaching and learning. The National Council of Teachers of Mathematics (NCTM) published *An Agenda for Action* (National Council of Teachers of Mathematics, 1980), launching an era of bold professional outreach by describing the shape that school mathematics programs should take (NCTM, 2008, p. i). The *Agenda for Action* outlined 10 recommendations for K–12 mathematics programs, focusing on the fundamental need of students to learn how to solve problems. The recommendation that was, perhaps, most important to this chapter was: "New curricular standards, programs and materials should be developed to encourage and challenge the development of promising mathematical students, regardless of gender, ethnicity, or socio-economic background" (NCTM, 1980).

This recommendation catalyzed the development of the *Curriculum and Evaluation Standards for School Mathematics*, published by NCTM in 1989, as well as the companion *Professional Standards for Teaching Mathematics* (NCTM, 1991) and the *Assessment Standards for School Mathematics* (NCTM, 1995). The 1989 Curriculum and Evaluation Standards were 11 years old at the turn of the century, and NCTM updated the earlier vision for mathematics teaching and learning by publishing the *Principles and Standards for School Mathematics* (PSSM) (NCTM, 2000). The PSSM included new underlying principles for teaching and learning school mathematics, and it clarified the earlier standards for each of the grade bands: K–2, 3–5, 6–8, and 9–12. The most recent curriculum and instruction document to be produced by NCTM is the *Curriculum Focal Points for Mathematics in Pre-kindergarten through Grade 8.* In this document, three curriculum focal points are identified and described for each grade level, PK–8, along with connections to guide integration of the focal points at that grade level and across grade levels to form a comprehensive mathematics curriculum. The purpose of identifying these grade-level curriculum focal points and connections is to enable students to learn the content in the context of a focused and cohesive curriculum that implements problem solving, reasoning, and critical thinking (NCTM, 2008).

With all the curriculum and instruction work completed by many NCTM committees, relatively little attention was paid to the role of technology, particularly, games. There was no mention of the use of digital video games to learn mathematical skills or concepts, let alone to develop problem solving, reasoning, and critical thinking skills.

More recently, NCTM released a new position statement about the use of technology in the learning and teaching of mathematics:

> Technology is an essential tool for learning mathematics in the 21st century, and all schools must ensure that all their students have access to technology. Effective teachers maximize the potential of technology to develop students' understanding, stimulate their interest, and increase their proficiency in mathematics. When technology is used strategically, it can provide access to mathematics for all students. (NCTM, 2008, p. 1)

While the clarifying paragraphs that follow this position statement do not explicitly mention the use of digital video games to teach mathematics concepts, skills, or problem solving, the following statement does not exclude the potential use of games:

> All schools and mathematics programs should provide students and teachers with access to instructional technology, including appropriate calculators, computers with mathematical software, Internet connectivity, handheld data-collection devices, and sensing probes. Curricula and courses of study should incorporate instructional technology in learning outcomes, lesson plans, and assessments of students' progress. (NCTM, 2008, p. 1)

The Math War

The first of several battles in the math war occurred with the new math movement about 30 years ago. New math succumbed to a call for the return to basics in the 1970s. During the difficult economic times of that period, the realization that globalization was happening rapidly and the emphasis on raising the threshold of achievement for the lowest students caused the public to advocate for abandoning all of the notions in the new curricula and, instead, to focus on basic skills testing in many states. The work of NCTM in the 1980s to revitalize the curriculum by creating national standards for school programs that were appropriate for helping all children learn mathematics began a new round of curriculum revision focused on school textbooks. Three large states with state textbook adoptions (California, Texas, and Florida) dictated the development of textbooks that conformed to the new mathematics standards, and each state began developing its own math standards aligned with those developed by NCTM.

Additionally, the National Science Foundation stepped into the picture and encouraged, with funding, the development of "exemplary curricula" for middle school mathematics. Once again, the back to basics folks became vocal, particularly in California, where the state mathematics standards were very controversial. The new math war pitched the back-to-basics side against what they termed "the new math" or "fuzzy math" or "whole math." Furthermore, the act of No Child Left Behind (NCLB) signed by President George W. Bush in 2001 required students to be proficient in reading and mathematics by 2013–2014 (No Child Left Behind, 2001). Such requirement directed teachers' focus toward back-to-basics and enforced coverage of a large amount of state-based curricula; leaving teachers with little time to incorporate alternative problem solving approaches. Thus, the math war continues. Should we have a focused and cohesive curriculum that implements problem solving, reasoning, and critical thinking (NCTM, 2008), or should we have a traditional curriculum with teacher presentation and organized practice?

National Mathematics Advisory Panel

To improve the teaching and learning of mathematics once more and to settle the math war, another national committee was instituted. In 2006 an executive order of former President George W. Bush created the National Mathematics Advisory Panel (2008). The Panel was charged to examine and summarize the scientific evidence related to the teaching and learning of mathematics, with a specific focus on preparation for and success in learning algebra. The final report of the Panel provided 45 recommendations, some of which are useful to the discussion at hand.

A key feature of the charge was the attention on research evidence. The Panel took this seriously and set a high standard for acceptable research. The general result was that little acceptable research was found to support particular practices in any aspect of teaching and learning mathematics. The final recommendations had a flavor of both the reform efforts in mathematics education and the "back to basics" movement. Each of the recommendations came only after a critical review of the research that supported each argument about the teaching and learning of mathematics.

An example of a recommendation that favors the reform movement includes the following rule:

> A focused, coherent progression of mathematics learning, with an emphasis on proficiency with key topics, should become the norm in elementary and middle school mathematics curricula. Any approach that continually revisits topics year after year without closure is to be avoided. (National Mathematics Advisory Panel, 2008, p. xvi)

Another recommendation acknowledges the existence of the math war and chastises both groups to some extent:

> To prepare students for algebra, the curriculum must simultaneously develop conceptual understanding, computational fluency, and problem solving skills. Debates regarding the relative importance of these aspects of mathematical

knowledge are misguided. These capabilities are mutually supportive, each facilitating learning of the others. Teachers should emphasize these interrelations; taken together, conceptual understanding of mathematical operations, fluent execution of procedures, and fast access to number combinations jointly support effective and efficient problem solving. (National Mathematics Advisory Panel, 2008, p. xix)

In the very next recommendation, the importance of practice is noted:

Computational proficiency with whole number operations is dependent on sufficient and appropriate practice to develop automatic recall of addition and related subtraction facts, and of multiplication and related division facts. It also requires fluency with the standard algorithms for addition, subtraction, multiplication, and division. Additionally it requires a solid understanding of core concepts, such as the commutative, distributive, and associative properties. Although the learning of concepts and algorithms reinforce one another, each is also dependent on different types of experiences, including practice. (National Mathematics Advisory Panel, 2008, p. xix)

In the 23rd recommendation, the bottom line for how mathematics should be taught is addressed according to research findings:

All-encompassing recommendations that instruction should be entirely "student centered" or "teacher directed" are not supported by research. If such recommendations exist, they should be rescinded. If they are being considered, they should be avoided. High-quality research does not support the exclusive use of either approach. (National Mathematics Advisory Panel, 2008, p. xxii)

The lack of high-quality research findings supporting either side of the math war means that it will continue. However, there is one caveat to the statement in recommendation 23. It relates to the use of explicit instruction with students who are struggling to learn mathematics:

Explicit instruction with students who have mathematical difficulties has shown consistently positive effects on performance with word problems and computation. Results are consistent for students with learning disabilities, as well as other students who perform in the lowest third of a typical class. ... (National Mathematics Advisory Panel, 2008, p. xxiii)

This finding does not mean that all of a student's mathematics instruction should be delivered in an explicit fashion. However, the Panel recommends that struggling students receive some explicit mathematics instruction regularly.

Note that even with this strong statement about explicit instruction, the Panel backed off on saying that this type of instruction is good for all students or all of the mathematics that a student is required to learn. Thus, in states conducting textbook selection exercises, we see that there are "calls" for both basal texts based on PSSM and on those listed in the original Focal Points report, as well as for "intervention texts" to provide specific instruction for struggling students. Thus, it appears that at least a consensus view of the best practices in mathematics teaching and learning is to provide all students with a mathematics program that not only provides students skills and concepts but also is rich with problem solving, reasoning, and critical thinking. Many students will thrive in mathematics classes such as these. However, some will struggle and will need more instructional time and, perhaps, another approach to learning mathematics to be successful.

The mathematics curriculum train is still chugging along. Occasionally, there are attempts to move the train to other tracks, but there is great resistance to doing so. Meanwhile, the digital video game "bullet train" is speeding along, but it has yet to link up with the mathematics curriculum train. It appears that few math education experts see the games train anywhere near the mathematics curriculum track. There are, however, some educators on the game train who have the mathematics train in their sights.

Why Mathematics Games?

In the last few years, instructional digital video games designed specifically for training or educational purposes have gained attention as a tool for facilitating learning across several sectors of society, including but not limited to the military, health care, and education. Continuing advances in technology, the increasing popularity of digital video games, and recent studies that underscore the potential of game-based learning (e.g., Federation of American Scientists, 2006; Egenfeldt-Nielsen, 2005; Mitchell & Savill-Smith, 2004) have renewed interest in the use of instructional games.

A number of factors have made instructional games attractive learning tools. The advancement of technology has made it possible to play games on simple platforms, such as mobile devices. This makes instructional games accessible to many people, including those who do not have personal computers (Mitchell & Savill-Smith, 2004). Instructional games may create a new learning culture, one that corresponds more closely with students' habits and interests (Prensky, 2001). More important, instructional games are thought to be effective tools for teaching difficult and complex procedures because they affect learners in the following ways: (a) use action instead of explanation, (b) create personal motivation and satisfaction, (c) accommodate multiple learning styles and skills, (d) reinforce mastery skills, and (e) provide interactive and decision-making contexts (Charles & McAlister, 2004; Holland, Jenkins, & Squire, 2003; Sheffield, 2005).

Our Assessment of Empirical and Non-Empirical Research Studies on Games' Learning Effects

The majority of the nine empirical studies we analyzed indicated that instructional mathematics video games improved students' achievement and motivation. We analyzed nine empirical studies that had been conducted on the effectiveness of mathematics games in K–12 settings. Table 6.1 summarizes the results of our analysis of the empirical studies, showing research variables, research methods, and results, that is, how well the games served as learning tools by assessing their effects on students' achievement and/or motivation.

TABLE 6.1 ▶ Results of nine empirical studies: The effects of instructional math video games on students' achievement and motivation

STUDY NO.	STUDY RESEARCHER/S	RESEARCH VARIABLE/S	RESEARCH METHOD/S	RESULTS OF FACILITATING LEARNING WITH GAMES
1.	Kebritchi (2008)	Achievement, Motivation	Mixed method, Experimental	Positive for achievement, Mixed for motivation
2.	Rosas et al. (2003)	Achievement, Motivation	Mixed method, Experimental	Positive for achievement and motivation
3.	Klawe (1998)	Achievement, Motivation	Qualitative	Positive for achievement and motivation
4.	Sedighian & Sedighian (1996)	Motivation	Qualitative	Positive for motivation
5.	Lopez-Moreto & Lopez (2007)	Motivation	Quantitative	Positive for motivation
6.	Ke & Grabowski (2007)	Achievement	Quantitative, Experimental	Positive for achievement
7.	Moreno (2002)	Achievement	Quantitative, Experimental	Positive for achievement
8.	Din & Caleo (2000)	Achievement	Quantitative, Experimental	Mixed, no improvement in achievement
9.	Laffey, Espinosa, Moore, & Lodree (2003)	Achievement	Quantitative, Experimental	Mixed due to method flaw

As Table 6.1 shows, five of seven empirical studies that examined the effects of instructional math video games on mathematics achievement found positive results: number 1, Kebritchi, 2008; number 2, Rosas et al., 2003; number 3, Klawe, 1998; number 6, Ke & Grabowski, 2007; and number 7, Moreno, 2002. Four of the five studies that investigated the effects of the games on students' motivation found positive effects: number 2, Rosas et al., 2003; number 3, Klawe, 1998; number 4, Sedighian & Sedighian, 1996; and number 5, Lopez-Moreto & Lopez, 2007. Thus, a majority of the empirical studies indicated that digital video games are effective learning tools in improving mathematics motivation and achievement.

In contrast, when we studied eight literature reviews that reported results of non-empirical studies, they indicated that instructional video games were sometimes but not always effective in improving students' learning. These reviews provided an overview of the general effects of the games on learning based on relatively large numbers of investigations. Of the total number of investigations of educational games conducted by each researcher or research team, some were math games. Table 6.2 summarizes the literature reviews that we analyzed along with the number of studies each one investigated and each one's conclusions on the overall effects of instructional video games on learning. Those overall effects applied to games related to various subject matter. When possible, we isolated data related to math games and report that data later in this chapter.

The inherent weakness of our comparative analysis of these eight literature reviews was examining different empirical studies with various methods, different games, and within different time periods. Therefore, our results had to be quite general. Having noted this caveat, perhaps the most convincing of the non-empirical reviews was number 1, conducted by Dempsey, Rasmussen, and Lucassen (1994) because they evaluated each of the video games according to the learning domains set out in Robert M. Gagné's taxonomy (1972; 1985). The more domains a game caused students to use, the more positively the researchers scored the game's effects in this study. Gagné's domains are "(1) motor skills, (2) verbal information, (3) intellectual skills, (4) cognitive strategies, and (5) attitudes" (Gagné, 1972, p. 90).

TABLE 6.2 ▶ Results of eight literature reviews on instructional games' effects on learning

LITERATURE REVIEW	NUMBER OF GAMES INVESTIGATED	RESULTS
1. Dempsey et al. (1994)	94	Positive Effects
2. Randel et al. (1992)	67	Mixed Effects
3. Hays (2005)	48	Mixed Effects
4. Vogel et al. (2006)	32	Positive Effects
5. VanSickle (1986)	26	Positive Effects
6. Emes (1997)	3	No Effects
7. Harris (2001)	2	No Effects
8. Mitchell & Savill-Smith (2004)	Unclear	Mixed Effects

As Table 6.2 shows, three of the eight literature reviews reported positive results: number 1, Dempsey et al., 1994; number 4, Vogel et al., 2006; and number 5, VanSickle, 1986. Review number 1, Dempsey et al., 1994, concluded that instructional video games required students to use skills encompassed by most of the learning domains in Gagné's taxonomy (1985), including problem solving, cognitive strategy, and attitudes toward the subject matter. Review number 4, Vogel et al., 2006, reported that interactive simulations and instructional video games were more effective than traditional classroom instruction in helping learners achieve cognitive gains. Review number 5, VanSickle 1986, found a slight improvement in students' learning and attitudes toward the subject matter as a result of playing the games instead of their teachers' use of traditional teaching methods.

In contrast, five of the eight literature reviews reported mixed results—number 2, Randel et al., 1992; number 3, Hays, 2005; and number 8, Mitchell & Savill-Smith, 2004—or no positive results—number 6, Emes, 1997; and number 7, Harris, 2001—on the effectiveness of instructional games.

Despite the literature reviews' mixed results, we concluded that instructional math video games can be effective mainstream as well as alternative learning tools for the following reasons:

▶ None of the literature reviews exclusively focused on mathematics instructional games in K–12 settings. However, mathematics games were included in all the literature reviews. Randel et al. (1992) concluded that the effects of instructional video games varied depending on the subjects; the games were more effective when learning objectives were explicit and precisely defined. There were indications that playing instructional games is more effective for student achievement in math, compared to other subjects. Students scored comparatively higher on math achievement tests after using mathematics games than they did on achievement tests for other subjects after using related instructional games. (Hays, 2005; Mitchell & Savill-Smith, 2004; Randel et al., 1992).

▶ The mixed results from three of the literature reviews might be due to improper ways some students used the games. For example, Mitchell and Savill-Smith (2004) found instructional games had both negative and positive effects on students' school performances. Frequent game playing at home that reduced students' available time to do homework was considered as a negative effect of the games. This issue should be addressed by students, who should use the games only after finishing their homework, and by parents, who need to monitor their children's time playing games. On the positive side, they reported that playing games made students ready for computer-oriented society and promoted spatial and cognitive skills.

▶ The mixed results might be due to methodological flaws in the empirical studies (Hays, 2005). One of the frequent problems is lack of control groups in the studies. Examining the effect of a treatment without comparison with a control group is problematic (Mitchell & Savill-Smith, 2004; Vogel et al., 2006).

As discussed earlier, a number of the major mathematics reports have discussed the need to improve American mathematics education over the last three decades (e.g., National Commission on Excellence in Education, 1983; National Mathematics Advisory Panel, 2008). Along the way, educational researchers and administrators have called for reforms (Ke & Grabowski, 2007). Specifically, the policy reports have recommended using problem solving, reasoning, and critical thinking as key features that improve students' mathematics understanding (National Mathematics Advisory Panel, 2008). Computer mathematics games can promote these critical skills (Charles & McAlister, 2004; Holland, Jenkins, & Squire, 2003; Sheffield, 2005).

As pointed out in our analysis of empirical studies, students who use computer games in K–12 settings have exhibited improved motivation to do mathematics and improved achievement in the subject. Thus, using mathematics games can be one of the ways to improve American mathematics education. The Federation of American Scientists (2006) agree that games can have positive effects on learning: "People acquire new knowledge and complex skills from game play, suggesting gaming could help address one of the nation's most pressing needs—strengthening our system of education and preparing workers for 21st century jobs" (p. 3).

A Survey of Existing Games for Mathematics Education

This section provides an overview of existing mathematics games. A list of mathematics games and resources for accessing them are provided. We have also reviewed the designs of particular mathematics games to share with educators the best ways to determine whether certain games will meet the needs of their students and fit well into their curricula.

Table 6.3 lists instructional mathematics video games for K–12 students. These games have been developed and made available since 1970. They also have been evaluated by a number of authors (e.g., Egenfeldt-Nielsen, 2005; Habgood, Ainsworth & Benford, 2005).

TABLE 6.3 ▶ Mathematics instructional games developed in the last three decades

MATHEMATICS GAME	YEAR	GENRE	STUDENT AUDIENCE
Darts-Plato project	1973	Problem solving	Elementary school
Basic Mathematics or Fun with Numbers	1977	Problem solving	Elementary school
The Electric Company: Math Fun	1979	Strategy	Elementary school
Harpoon	1981	Strategy	Elementary school
Sonar	1981	Strategy	Elementary school
Lemonade Stand	1985	Strategy	Elementary school
Mathematics Blaster	1986	Action-Adventure	Elementary/Middle school
Millie's Math House	1995	Strategy	PK–1
Super Tangram-EGEMS	1996	Puzzle	Middle school
Zoombinis-Logical Journey	1996	Puzzle	Elementary school
Phoenix Quest-EGEMS	1997	Puzzle	Middle school
Freddi Fish 5: The Case of the Creature of Coral Cove	2001	Strategy-Adventure	Elementary school
Mathematics Missions	2003	Strategy	K–2
Jumpstart Study Helper Math Booster	2003	Adventure	Elementary school
AquaMOOSE	2003	Strategy	High School
Interactive Instructors of Recreational Mathematics (IIRM)	2003	Strategy	High School
ASTRA EAGLE	2005	Strategy	Elementary school
Zombie Division	2005	Action-Adventure	Elementary school
DimensionM	2006	Action-Adventure	Middle–High school
Scratch	2007	Designing games	Middle–High school
Game Maker Academy	2008	Designing games	Middle–High school

To access more lists of mathematics computer games, consider searching the following helpful websites:

- ▶ Superkids (www.superkids.com)

- ▶ SpaceTime (www.spacetime.us/arcade/games.php)

- ▶ TEEM (www.teem.org.uk)

- ▶ Learning Village (www.learningvillage.com)

- ▶ World Village (www.worldvillage.com)

- ▶ GameZone's KidZone (www.gzkidzone.com)

- ▶ Discovery Education (School Resources, Review Corner: Best Educational Software) (http://school.discovery.com/parents/reviewcorner/software/)

- ▶ Children's Technology Review (http://childrenstech.com) Go to far right of homepage and scroll down to find interesting math-related topics. Subscribers to this review may access its large database of reviews of all types of games.

- ▶ Education World (www.educationworld.com/a_tech/archives/edurate.shtml) Look under "The Best K–12 Freeware" for numerous free educational software programs, including many games. Type "math games" in the search box at the top of the Archives page, and a wealth of games are listed, and many include lesson plans.

Review of Highlighted Mathematics Games

In this section, the design, interface, and application of a number of mathematics computer games that were subjects of the literature reviews listed in Table 6.2 are discussed in chronological order, starting with one of the earliest mathematics-oriented projects—the Plato project. Starting in 1973, the Plato project produced positive results for using instructional games for mathematics. These results fueled continued research and development in the field. One of the games created in the Plato project was a game called Darts that teaches fractions. The game was developed based on relating the fantasy of balloons and arrows to the skill of estimating fractions (Malone, 1981) (see Figure 6.1).

In 1981, two other instructional games, Harpoon and Sonar, were made based on the Darts game. They were intended to help students understand arithmetic in new ways related to everyday needs. Both Harpoon and Sonar proved successful in motivating and engaging players as they learned practical mathematics concepts (Levin, 1981).

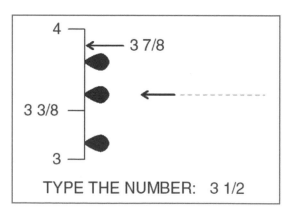

FIGURE 6.1 ▶ The screen layout of the Darts game

In the 1980s, the educational programming language Logo was popular for designing mathematics games. The basic approach was to teach mathematics by allowing learners to design math games (Egenfeldt-Nielsen, 2005). One of the early advocates of this approach was Yasmin B. Kafai (2001), who proposed the concept of students learning mathematics by constructing games themselves instead of teachers demonstrating games to teach (construction versus instruction). A number of studies indicated the effectiveness of this method in teaching mathematics (Kafai, 2001; Kafai & Resnick, 1996). This method of getting learners to design games has also been used and studied by other researchers (Kafai, Frank, Ching, & Shih, 1998). A number of more recent applications, including Scratch and Game Maker Academy, use the same approach, empowering student players to use their knowledge and creativity to design their own games (Myers, 2008).

The 1990s were highlighted by two successful research projects in mathematics-oriented games, Electronic Games for Education in Math and Science (E-GEMS) and Through the Glass Wall. The E-GEMS project, conducted by the University of British Columbia, made two mathematics games. The first game, Super Tangrams (ST), made in 1996, was designed to teach two-dimensional transformation geometry to sixth grade students. The game consisted of a series of puzzles that progressively became more difficult while providing a motivating, fun, and engaging learning environment (Sedighian & Sedighian, 1996). The second game in the E-GEMS project, Phoenix Quest, was created in 1997 as a game that would appeal to both girls and boys. Super Tangrams and Phoenix Quest (Figure 6.2) used the basic concept of puzzles with different approaches. Super Tangrams was activity oriented, and Phoenix Quest was story oriented.

A mixed-method study on how playing Super Tangrams affected the motivation of 50 students in Grades 6 and 7 was conducted over two years. The data were collected through observations, interviews, informal class discussions, and tests. The results indicated that the game had positive motivational effects because it provided students with meaningful learning, including goals, successes, challenges, and cognitive artifacts through interactivity and communication, as well as enjoyable associations through pleasure, attraction, and sensory stimuli, such as animation, sound effects, and background music (Sedighian & Sedighian, 1996).

To explore students' experiences of playing Phoenix Quest, a case study with six students and a large-scale study with 41 male and 57 female students in Grades 4, 5, and 6 were conducted. Both studies indicated that Phoenix Quest's approach of celebrating and challenging a female protagonist is important to engage the girls. In addition, the results revealed that the presence of a female protagonist did not discourage the boys, as they participated equally in the game, which involves cooperative play and group problem-solving (De Jean, Upitis, Koch, & Young, 1999). The researchers concluded that gender identification plays a key role in computer games, particularly that when girls' attention is attracted at first, their attention, enjoyment, and participation are likely to be sustained.

FIGURE 6.2 ▶ Phoenix Quest game

Results of another research project, Through the Glass Wall, suggest that using mathematics skills should be an integral part of playing instructional games to encourage mathematics-related reflection, thinking, and discussion. In addition, this project emphasized the importance of the narrative frame and gender-neutral approaches in designing games (Egenfeldt-Nielsen, 2005).

Three sets of qualitative studies were conducted on the games that were developed in the Through the Glass Wall Project. The studies focused on (a) the ways that children learn mathematics from computer games, (b) the characteristics of the games that support learning, and (c) the patterns of girls' and boys' game playing. Data were collected through interviews and observations in summer camps, after-school programs, and lab settings with elementary and middle school students. The researchers concluded that (a) engagement over time is necessary for strategic thinking and learning, and engagement can be achieved through communication, narrative connection, and puzzle connection; (b) the games that support learning should have mathematical potential, gender equity, and a game design leading to engagement; and (c) there was not a significant difference between the ways that girls and boys played the games (Rubin, Murray, O'Neil, & Ashley, 1997).

The 2000s were highlighted by the emergence of three-dimensional (3-D) instructional games, such as AquaMOOSE (Elliott & Bruckman, 2002) and Zombie Division (Habgood et al., 2005). Despite the popularity of these new games, other games with less complex interfaces were still used widely, such as a series of games similar to Nintendo's Game Boy games (Rosas et al., 2003), created by the Interactive Instructors of Recreational Mathematics (IIRM) (Lopez-Moreto & Lopez, 2007), and the web-based ASTRA EAGLE games (Ke & Grabowski, 2007).

AquaMOOSE (Figure 6.3) was designed to help students learn about the behavior of parametric equations. An underwater theme allows players to swim like fish in three directions. The design was based on constructivist philosophy, which advocates learning through students' own design and construction activities. In the AquaMOOSE environment, students use mathematics to design interesting graphical forms and create mathematical challenges and games to share with others (Elliott & Bruckman, 2002). The environment includes a number of games, such as the Ring game, in which students are presented with a set of rings and challenged to swim through as many rings as possible with one mathematics function.

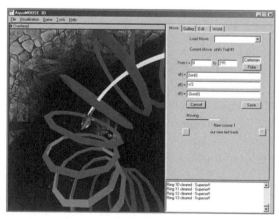

FIGURE 6.3 ▶ AquaMOOSE game

After 105 high school students played the AquaMOOSE game for six weeks, a formative evaluation asked them to suggest ways the game should be improved and to list their most and least favorite aspects of the game. The results indicated that the aesthetic qualities of the environment motivated students, but difficulties with usability posed problems. The aesthetic qualities students liked were the appealing 3-D graphics of the game's environment and features that allowed them to (a) explore various 3-D worlds provided in the environment, (b) edit the fish avatar in the game, and (c) observe the mathematics trails that they created. The usability problem referred to students' difficulties as they attempted to navigate in the environment.

Zombie Division (Figure 6.4) is an action-adventure game in which the players battle skeletons in hand-to-hand combat that requires players to use mathematical division skills (Habgood et al., 2005). The game was designed to create a flow experience for players as they learn to play with increasingly effective math skills. A flow experience is described as "Feelings of total concentration, distorted sense of time, and extension of self" (Habgood et al., 2005, p. 492, citing Csíkszentmihályi, 1988). In addition to flow, two additional guidelines were followed to enhance students' intrinsic motivation: the presentation of learning content in the most fun parts of the game and an external presentation of the content, such as a print-based quiz. The game's mathematical components are described, in part, as follows: "This action-adventure game is based around a combat mechanic in which the player must use different attacks to mathematically divide numbered skeletons in hand-to-hand combat. Each of the player's attacks has a different divisor, and the mathematical relationship between divisors is embodied in the structure of the player's attacks (e.g., using the sword once divides by two, twice divides by four, and three times divides by eight)" (Habgood et al., 2005, p. 495).

FIGURE 6.4 ▶ Zombie Division game

In 2007, two empirical studies compared one version of Zombie Division that was based on intrinsic motivation guidelines to a second version of Zombie Division developed based on opposing extrinsic motivation guidelines. The results of both studies indicated that the intrinsic game had significantly higher results in learning gains and motivation compared with the extrinsic game (Habgood, 2007).

Five basic games similar to Nintendo's Game Boy were developed to teach basic reading and mathematics skills to first and second graders (Rosas et al., 2003). The games were designed so that (a) students' attention was focused on playing and not on learning, (b) their content had increasingly higher levels of complexity that followed the school curriculum, and (c) progressive levels of difficulty, based on players' various learning paces, were presented, and feedback was provided based on players' performances. Each game has a story, a mission, and educational content for reading and mathematics. A sample of 1,274 first and second grade students from economically disadvantaged schools in Chile used these games in their classrooms. The results indicated that the games had positive effects on learners' motivation and classroom dynamics and, consequently, that they promoted learning within the classrooms.

The Interactive Instructors of Recreational Mathematics (IIRM) were developed as an alternative learning environment to motivate students' interest in mathematics. The environment integrates communication through instant messaging and chat rooms and allows students to customize the environment's content, layout, and appearance (Lopez-Moreto & Lopez, 2007). Mathematical concepts are presented in interactive, recreational ways integrated within the IIRM environment.

Research on IIRM was conducted with a total of 47 Mexican high school students. The participants were divided into three groups: 30 in group A, 6 in group B, and 11 in group C. Each group participated in a four-hour session developed in IIRM, and the students completed a Likert survey with 14 questions at the end of the session. Observations and interviews also were conducted. The results indicated that the use of the IIRM electronic environment positively affected these students' attitudes toward mathematics. Specifically, the use of collaboration and a multiplayer game promoted greater interaction among the players than they experienced in traditional math classes. The participants reported that the IIRM environment served as an aid in learning mathematics and a motivation tool.

ASTRA EAGLE consisted of a series of web-based computer games developed by the Centre for Advanced Technologies (Ke & Grabowski, 2007). The games were designed to reinforce academic standards for mathematics required by the Pennsylvania System of School Assessment (PSSA). The games, designed for fifth-grade students, were single-user strategy games that relied on thinking and problem solving (Crawford, 1984). These games contained a variety of problems, including measurement, comparing whole numbers, solving simple equations, and mapping x and y coordinates. Most problems were contextualized in real-life stories relevant to the students. For example, in a game called Up, Up, & Away, students traveled by balloons, and one of problems they faced was to estimate their balloons' traveling speeds. Each of the ASTRA EAGLE games had multiple levels. To move to higher levels, students needed to answer all the questions in their current level correctly. The more levels students conquered, the higher the scores they earned.

In an experimental study with 125 fifth-grade students, Ke and Grabowski (2007) used a cooperative learning technique known as Teams-Games-Tournament (TGT) to examine the effects of the games included in TGT on students' mathematics achievement and attitude. The participants' gender, socioeconomic status, and prior mathematics knowledge were used as moderating variables and covariates. The statistical test of Multivariate Analysis of Covariance (MANCOVA) indicated that game playing was more effective than drills in improving students' mathematics performance, and cooperative game playing was most effective for improving students' attitudes toward mathematics regardless of their individual differences of gender, socioeconomic status, and prior mathematics knowledge.

Trends and Issues in Mathematics Games in K–12 Settings

Our survey of existing math games revealed a number of trends and issues relevant to their use.

Edutainment and Modern Three-Dimensional Games

Major trends we noted during the last three decades, from the 1970s through the 2000s, are the evolution of pedagogical frameworks supporting the games and changes in the technical aspects of the games.

It appears that most of the early mathematics instructional games, such as Darts in the Plato project, focused on drill and practice of simple number operations and concepts. These games were easy to develop and improved students' mathematics fluency. However, drill and practice is only one of the many ways of learning mathematics (Klawe, 1998). The pedagogical frameworks of the games have evolved from drill and practice (e.g., Darts) to instruction and construction (see Kafai, 2001) to constructivism (e.g., AquaMOOSE), flow experience (e.g., Zombie Division), and collaborative community learning (e.g., IIRM).

A similar progressive trend can be seen in technical aspects of the games. As technology has advanced, mathematics games have become more complex in terms of graphic and interface design. Such progression can be noticed by comparing the simple interface of Darts with the two-dimensional (2-D) environments of Super Tangram and Phoenix Quest, and the 3-D environment of Zombie Division.

Along with the evolution of pedagogical and technical aspects of instructional games, edutainment games have been replaced with modern 3-D games. Edutainment refers to the games that were produced mainly in the 1980s and 1990s as combinations of entertainment and education.

However, edutainment was not very successful in integrating digital video games and education (Hirumi & Stapleton, 2008; Kirriemuir & McFarlane, 2004; Okan, 2003). Edutainment combined two worthy elements, but the result was less than the sum of its parts, failing to meet the standards of high-quality education or entertainment (Fabricatore, 2000). As the conceptual and technical aspects of the games evolved, modern 3-D games emerged as a new generation of instructional games. Modern instructional games are significantly different from edutainment, as they may use advanced 3-D graphics and interfaces, multiplayer options, high-speed telecommunication technologies, immersive 3-D environments, visual storytelling, and learner-centered and constructivist learning principles to engage learners and facilitate learning. Clearly, modern mathemathics video games can be justified as valuable learning tools.

Issues in Adopting and Using Mathematics Games in K–12 Settings

Mathematics computer games are not always designed for ease of use in classrooms. Teachers may need to plan for additional resources to support implementation of mathematics games in their classrooms. By identifying challenges teachers face when implementing games, it is our hope that game developers will understand these barriers and address them within their game support websites.

According to Kebritchi, Hirumi, Kappers, and Henry (2008), three basic categories of challenges are experienced by teachers and school media specialists who attempt to integrate instructional games into K–12 settings: (a) technical and logistical, (b) curriculum integration, and (c) teacher training. Table 6.4 summarizes the challenges that teachers need to prepare for before they integrate games into school settings. Perhaps the most important preparation teachers can make is to discuss their plans for using games with their school principal and curriculum coordinator to ensure that these administrators understand how the games fit curricular goals and what math (and others as applicable, such as reading and science) skills will be taught and strengthened by the games. Students also need to understand that game playing will help them become better at mathematics.

TABLE 6.4 ▶ Summary of challenges teachers may face when integrating games into classrooms (adapted from Kebritchi et al., 2008)

CHALLENGES	DETAILS
Curriculum Integration Challenges	• Unstructured lessons that do not go along with the curriculum • Clear presentation of what students are learning • Ease of implementation/integration • Gender and cultural biases • Use with students with disabilities • Learner assessment methods • Cost effectiveness (student achievement versus time playing)
Technical and Logistical Challenges	• Working with preexisting systems • Authentic use of communication tools • Ease of use • Technical support • Scheduling problems • Not enough chairs/computers • Broken or inadequate computers • Time constraints for teachers to implement and students to use games
Teacher Training Challenges	• Need to address individual teacher practices and methods • Lack of training in computer software and classroom management • Variance in technical ability • Teacher support teaching from prior experiences • Monitoring of students' appropriate use of the games

Guidelines for Design and Integration of Mathematics Games in K–12 Settings

To overcome the barriers of game adoption, a number of important game design and integration issues in K–12 settings are provided in this section.

Design Guidelines

The analysis of educational mathematics games revealed nine factors influencing the effectiveness of mathematics games in school settings. These factors can serve as guidelines for teachers to evaluate the most effective game designs and to decide how they can be used to enhance mathematics education.

1. **Motivation.** Game designers frequently stressed factors that related motivation to learning effectiveness of the games. (Elliott & Bruckman, 2002; Habgood et al., 2005; Lopez-Moreto & Lopez, 2007; Malone, 1981; Rosas et al., 2003; Sedighian & Sedighian, 1996). For example, Sedighian and Sedighian (1996) noted the following factors for increasing motivation in the games: (a) situating mathematics learning in the games, (b) providing a set of goals to achieve, (c) providing a balanced number of challenges so that students get excited but not overwhelmed, (d) making games' cognitive artifacts effective by incorporating two factors of interactivity and communication, (e) associating learning with pleasant memories, (f) providing a learning environment that allows students to experience the joy of learning, and (g) providing sensory stimuli by including attractive graphics and animation.

2. **Instructional strategy.** As discussed at the beginning of this chapter, problem solving and critical thinking are considered as the key skills required for the reformation of mathematics education (National Mathematics Advisory Panel, 2008). Thus, instructional strategies, such as constructivist learning environments (Jonassen, 1999), collaborative problem solving (Nelson, 1999), and Landamatics instructional design (Landa, 1999), that facilitate problem solving and critical thinking should be designed into mathematics games.

3. **Curriculum.** One of the greatest challenges facing those attempting to integrate educational mathematics games into classes is the alignment of the game with the school curriculum (Rosas et al., 2003; Squire et al., 2005). Using the principles and standards of the National Council of Teachers of Mathematics (2000) for developing mathematics games has been suggested as a guide for addressing this issue (Lopez-Moreto & Lopez, 2007). The NCTM principles were developed based on the mathematics curriculum used across the nation and should be shared with game designers to make them aware of current curriculum issues.

4. **Gender neutral.** The games should be attractive to both genders. Including story and narrative frameworks was suggested as one of the ways to make the games female- and male-friendly (Egenfeldt-Nielsen, 2005; Klawe, 1998). Female students are more interested in complex, rich stories that engage them in the games. Simple stories may not be enough to attract female students. For example, a recent mathematics game starts by explaining that there are a number of weather stations on an island, and the players need to locate the weather stations. According to teachers, this type of simple story may not motivate female students to participate in the games (Kebritchi, 2009).

5. **Feedback and scaffolding.** Providing elaborate feedback and scaffolding is necessary for facilitating learning and increasing games' effectiveness (Cameron & Dwyer, 2005; Klawe, 1998). When game players make mistakes in solving the game's mathematics problems, the game should explain how to solve the problems or provide sufficient scaffolding for learners to come up with their own solutions.

6. **Verbal and written reflection.** Mathematics-related reflection, thinking, and discussion were suggested as critical factors in improving the effectiveness of mathematics games (Egenfeldt-Nielsen, 2005). After solving mathematics problems, players should be encouraged to reflect on the process by discussing or writing about it.

In addition, producing verbal and written discourse in a purposeful, authentic context rather than in an instructional context may be a highly effective way for stimulating mathematics reflection for learners (Waywood, 1992). Players should be given opportunities in the games to discuss or write about the applications of mathematics concepts in their daily lives that are addressed in the games.

7. **Game genre**. A genre pattern that emerged from our findings indicates that the early mathematics games in the 1970s and 1980s can be categorized primarily as puzzle games, followed by strategy games in the 1990s and adventure games in the 2000s (see Table 6.3). However, all games have not followed this pattern. It is notable that instructional action games that incorporated educational materials into fast-paced environments and forced the players to respond quickly to continual challenges offered little time for reflection and were more appropriate for building skill fluency (i.e., speed and accuracy at exercising a skill) than for acquiring new and complex concepts (Baker, Habgood, Ainsworth, & Corbett, 2009).

8. **Balance between content and game.** To maintain the educational value of the game, the actual mechanics of play must always remain secondary to the instructional process (Habgood et al., 2005). The play should not be so intensive that it distracts players from learning the subject at hand. In addition, play components should guide the game players toward learning the subject. For example, if there is a shooting part in the game, aiming and firing should somehow help rather than distract players from learning the topic.

9. **Visual effects and usability.** The aesthetic qualities of the environment motivate students, whereas difficulties with usability pose problems (Elliott & Bruckman, 2002; Kiili, 2005; Shaffer, 1997). Aesthetic qualities refer to visual and graphic aspects of the games. For example, in AquaMOOSE, game players suggested that the three-dimensional graphics and the opportunities to observe visual trails of the mathematics problems being solved motivated them to participate in the game. Usability refers to the components of the game that help the game players control and play the game. For example, in AquaMOOSE, players reported navigation problems that they said discouraged them from participating in the game.

Integration Guidelines

A review of the literature by Kebritchi (2008) revealed three factors that could influence students' learning during mathematics game play that educators should consider in planning and integrating game-based learning into curricula:

1. Time and purpose of game implementation. To facilitate integration, game publishers should inform teachers of the following: (a) when the game should be used in the classroom and (b) whether the game is designed to teach skill acquisition or to provide practice opportunities for previously learned skills (Van Etten & Watson, 1976). A comprehensive training program should be offered by the game developer to instruct teachers and students in how to play the game before it is used in school settings (Kebritchi, 2008).

2. Transfer. Educators are often uncertain as to whether the skills learned from games will transfer to other learning contexts and real-life situations (Egenfeldt-Nielsen, 2005; Kebritchi, 2008; Klawe & Phillips, 1995; Shaffer, 2006). To address such uncertainties, teachers should be presented with the results of empirical studies that demonstrate student achievement and transfer of skills from game play in schools. In addition, school and district administrators should be informed about the potential benefits of using the mathematics games, so they consider playing games an effective use of class time (Kebritchi, 2008). Teachers need to understand that parents often question administrators about the relevance of game playing in classes. Teachers can help administrators anticipate these concerns by giving them a clear list of each game's subject matter objectives, linking them to the district's curriculum goals.

3. Logistics. Logistical issues, such as providing time and available computers for students to play the games, need to be addressed to ensure that games will be employed effectively in the classroom. School computer lab staff should be informed of all required software and hardware to play the games and involved in the planning process whenever possible. Time and resources should also be allocated for teacher training on how to help students play and how best to manage the use of games.

To address implementation, outcome, and logistical issues, game publishers are encouraged to create websites with game-related information, guidelines, and activities. For example, a website may contain online training for teachers and students on how to use the games, technical support, and online discussion forums for teachers to exchange their game experiences. An extensive treatment of the design and development of such supporting websites is provided by Kebritchi et al. (2008).

Conclusion

This chapter provides an overview of the design and use of digital video games in mathematics education. The problems of low student achievement and the need to improve mathematics education have been frequently discussed in mathematics policy reports (e.g., National Commission on Excellence in Education, 1983; National Mathematics Advisory Panel, 2008). However, the use of digital video games is not directly addressed by these reports.

Nevertheless, the "bullet train" carrying numerous well-designed instructional games is speeding along in search of connections between core mathematics curriculum and these modern digital video games. It appears that an increasing number of K–12 educators are integrating the games into schools, and a number of researchers suggest that the digital video games can be powerful learning tools with positive effects on students' motivation and achievement.

We conclude that pedagogical foundations and technical aspects of mathematics games have evolved significantly in the last three decades. Digital games have changed from edutainment with basic instructional strategies and simple graphics to modern computer games with learner-centered instructional strategies and immersive 3-D environments. Furthermore, mathematics games have been designed for various mathematics subjects, including but not limited to basic arithmetic, parametric equations, geometry, pre-algebra, and algebra.

In addition, a number of barriers to using mathematics games have been identified in the literature, such as curriculum integration, logistical and technical problems, and teachers' support and training issues (Kebritchi et al., 2008). To address these barriers, guidelines should be established that (a) address the use of appropriate instructional strategies in the design of games, such as experiential learning, situated learning, and constructivism-based approaches to teaching and learning (Kebritchi & Hirumi, 2008); (b) promote the design of games according to national mathematics principles and standards (NCTM, 2008); and (c) include game components and features such as gender-neutral themes, feedback, and clear learning objectives aligned with the national and state curricula (Kebritchi, in press). Specific integration guidelines include recommendations for addressing technical issues and informing educators about the appropriate time, intended purposes, and desired outcomes of using the games (Kebritchi et al., 2008).

Finally, there appears to be a dearth of empirical studies on the design and adoption of mathematics computer games. Only nine empirical studies were found with focuses on the achievement and motivational effects of the games. No study was found that focused on factors affecting the adoption of mathematics games. To provide better understanding for game developers and educators on the design and use of modern mathematics games, further large-scale studies should examine factors affecting the adoption and use of math games not only from teachers' and curriculum experts' perspectives, but also from students' and school administrators' perspectives. Much work must still be done so that the instructional games train and the mathematics curriculum train can actually meet to form a unified approach that motivates students to learn content in the context of a focused, cohesive curriculum that implements problem solving, reasoning, and critical thinking (National Council of Teachers of Mathematics, 2008).

References

Baker, de, R. S. J., Habgood, M. P. J., Ainsworth, S. E., & Corbett, A. T. (2009, July). Modeling the acquisition of fluent skill in educational action games. In C. Conati, K. McCoy, & G. Paliouras (Eds.), *User modeling 2007.* 11th Annual Conference, UM 2007, Corfu, Greece, July 25–29, 2007. LNCS (*Lecture Notes in Computer Science*), vol. 4511 (pp. 17–26). Berlin/Heidelberg, Germany: Springer. Conference article retrieved on July 11, 2007, from www.psychology.nottingham.ac.uk/staff/lpzrsb/BHAC2006UMFinal.pdf

Betz. J. A. (1995). Computer games: Increases learning in an interactive multidisciplinary environment. *Journal of Educational Technology Systems, 24*, 195–205.

Cameron, B., & Dwyer, F. (2005). The effects of online gaming, cognition and feedback type in facilitating delayed achievement of different learning objectives. *Journal of Interactive Learning Research, 16*(3), 243–258.

Charles, D., & McAlister, M. (2004). Integrating ideas about invisible playgrounds from play theory into online educational digital games. In M. Rauterberg (Ed.), LNCS (*Lecture Notes in Computer Science*), vol. 3166 (pp. 598–601). Berlin/Heidelberg, Germany: Springer.

Crawford, C. (1984). *The art of computer game design*. Berkeley, CA: McGraw-Hill.

Csíkszentmihályi, M. (1988). The flow experience and human psychology. In M. Csíkszentmihályi & I. S. Csíkszentmihályi (Eds.), *Optimal experience* (pp. 15–35). Cambridge, UK: Cambridge University Press.

De Jean, J., Upitis, R., Koch, C., & Young, J. (1999). The story of Phoenix Quest: How girls respond to a prototype language and mathematics computer game. *Gender and Education, 11*(2), 207–223.

Dempsey, J. V., Rasmussen, K., & Lucassen, B. (1994, February). Instructional gaming: Implications for instructional technology. Paper presented at the Annual Meeting of the Association for Educational Communications and Technology, Nashville, TN.

Din, F. S., & Caleo, J. (2000, February). Playing computer games versus better learning. Paper presented at the Eastern Educational Research Association. Clearwater, FL.

Egenfeldt-Nielsen, S. (2005). *Beyond edutainment: Exploring the educational potential of computer games*. Unpublished doctoral dissertation, IT-University of Copenhagen, Denmark. Retrieved July 11, 2010, from www.egenfeldt.eu/egenfeldt.pdf

Elliott, J., & Bruckman, A. (2002, June). Design of a 3D interactive math learning environment. *Proceedings of the conference on designing interactive systems: Processes, practices, methods, and techniques (DIS 2002)*. London, UK: Association for Computing Machinery (ACM). Retrieved July 7, 2007, from www.cc.gatech.edu/elc/aquamoose/pubs/amdis2002.pdf

Emes, C. E. (1997). Is Mr Pac Man eating our children? A review of the impact of video games on children. *Canadian Journal of Psychiatry, 42*(4), 409–414.

Fabricatore, C. (2000, October). *Learning and videogames: An unexploited synergy*. Paper presented at the International Conference of the Association for Educational Communications and Technology, Denver, CO. Retrieved June 1, 2004, from www.learndev.org/dl/FabricatoreAECT2000.pdf

Federation of American Scientists. (2006). *Summit on educational games 2006: Harnessing the power of video games for learning*. Retrieved January 30, 2007, from http://fas.org/gamesummit/

Gagné, R. M. (1972). Chapter 3: Domains of learning. Interchange 3. In *Conditions of learning*. Ontario, Canada: Ontario Institute for Studies in Education. The online pdf is an article by the author summarizing his ideas, written after the second edition of *Conditions of Learning* was published and reprinted by permission of Kluwer Academic Publishers. The ideas in the article were originally presented in a presidential address to the American Educational Research Association (n.d.). Available at www.ibstpi.org/Products/pdf/chapter_3.pdf

Gagné, R. M., (1985). *The Conditions of Learning and Theory of Instruction*. New York, NY: CBS College Publishing.

Habgood, M. P. J. (2005, June). *Zombie division: Intrinsic integration in digital learning games*. Paper presented at the 2005 workshop on human centred technology, Brighton, UK.

Habgood, M. P. J. (2007). *Zombie division: The effective integration of digital games and learning content*. Doctoral dissertation, University of Nottingham, UK. Available at http://zombiedivision.co.uk

Habgood, M. P. J., Ainsworth, S. E., & Benford, S. (2005). Endogenous fantasy and learning in digital games. *Simulation & Gaming, 36*(4), 483–498.

Harris, J. (2001). *The effects of computer games on young children—A review of the research.* RDS Occasional Paper No. 72. London, UK: Research, Development and Statistics Directorate, Communications Development Unit, Home Office.

Hays, R. T. (2005). The effectiveness of instructional games: A literature review and discussion. Naval Air Warfare Center Training Systems Division, Orlando, FL, November (Accession No. ADA441935). Retrieved October 7, 2007, from http://stinet.dtic.mil/oai/oai?&verb= getRecord&metadataPrefix=html&identifier=ADA441935

Hirumi, A., & Stapleton, C. (2008). Integrating fundamental ID tasks with game development processes to optimize game-based learning. In C. T. Miller (Ed.), *Games: Their purpose and potential in education* (pp. 127–162). New York, NY: Springer Publishing.

Holland, W., Jenkins, H., & Squire, K. (2003). Theory by design. In B. Perron, & M. Wolf (Eds.), *Video game theory reader* (pp. 25–46). New York, NY: Routledge.

Jonassen, D. (1999). Designing constructivist learning environments. In C. M. Reigeluth (Ed.), *Instructional-design theories and models: A new paradigm of instructional theory* (pp. 215–239). Mahwah, NJ: Lawrence Erlbaum.

Kafai, Y. B. (2001). *The educational potential of electronic games: From games-to-teach to games-to-learn.* Retrieved July 12, 2010, from http://culturalpolicy.uchicago.edu/papers/2001-video-games/ kafai.html

Kafai, Y., & Resnick, M. (Eds.). (1996). *Constructionism in practice: Designing, thinking, and learning in a digital world.* Mahwah, NJ: Lawrence Erlbaum.

Kafai, Y. B., Frank, M. L., Ching, C. C., & Shih, J. C. (1998). Game design as an interactive learning environment for fostering students' and teachers' mathematical inquiry. *International Journal of Computers for Mathematical Learning, 3*, 149–184.

Ke, F., & Grabowski, B. (2007). Gameplaying for mathematics learning: Cooperative or not? *British Journal of Educational Technology, 38*(2), 249–259.

Kebritchi, M. (2008). *Effects of a computer game on mathematics achievement and class motivation: An experimental study.* Unpublished doctoral dissertation, University of Central Florida, Orlando, FL.

Kebritchi, M. (2009). Factors affecting teachers' adoption of educational computer games: A case study. *British Journal of Educational Technology, 41*(2), 256–270.

Kebritchi, M., & Hirumi, A. (2008). Examining the pedagogical foundations of modern educational computer games to inform research and practice. *Computers & Education, 51*(4), 1729–1743.

Kebritchi, M., Hirumi, A., Kappers, W., & Henry, R. (2008). Analysis of the supporting websites for the use of instructional games in K–12 settings. *British Journal of Educational Technology, 40*(4), 733–754.

Kiili, K. (2005). Content creation challenges and flow experience in educational games: The IT-Emperor case. *The Internet and Higher Education, 8*(3), 183–198.

Kirriemuir, J., & McFarlane, A. (2004). *Literature review in games and learning.* Report 8 in Futurelab Series (March). Retrieved February 27, 2010, from www.futurelab.org.uk/resources/publications-reports-articles/literature-reviews/Literature-Review378

Klawe, M. M. (1998). *When does the use of computer games and other interactive multimedia software help students learn mathematics?* Unpublished manuscript. Retrieved July 17, 2007, from www.cs.ubc.ca/nest/egems/reports/NCTM.doc

Klawe, M., & Phillips, E. (1995). A classroom study: Electronic games engage children as researchers. In J. L. Schnase & E. L. Cunnius (Eds.), *Proceedings of CSCL '95: The first international conference on computer support for collaborative learning* (pp. 209–213). Mahwah, NJ: Lawrence Erlbaum.

Laffey, J. M., Espinosa, L., Moore, J., & Lodree, A. (2003). Supporting learning and behavior of at-risk young children: Computers in urban education. *Journal of Research on Technology in Education, 35*(4), 423–440.

Landa, L. N. (1999). Landamatics instructional design theory and methodology for teaching general methods of thinking. In C. M. Reigeluth (Ed.), *Instructional-design theories and models: A new paradigm of instructional theory* (pp. 341–369). Mahwah, NJ: Lawrence Erlbaum.

Leung, F. K. S. (2003). Introduction: Responses in mathematics education to technological developments. In A. J. Bishop, J. Kilpatrick, M. A. Clements, & C. Keitel. *Second international handbook of mathematics education.* London, UK: Kluwer Academic Publishers.

Levin, J. A. (1981). Estimation techniques for arithmetic: Everyday mathematics and mathematics instruction. *Educational Studies in Mathematics, 12*(4), 421–434.

Lopez-Moreto, G., & Lopez, G. (2007). Computer support for learning mathematics: A learning environment based on recreational learning objects. *Computers & Education, 48*(4), 618–641.

Malone, T. (1981). Toward a theory of intrinsically motivating instruction. *Cognitive Science, 5*(4), 333–369.

Mishra, P., & Koehler, M. J. (2006). Technological pedagogical content knowledge: A framework for teacher knowledge. *Teachers College Record, 108*(6), 1017–1054.

Mitchell, A., & Savill-Smith, C. (2004). *The use of computer and video games for learning: A review of the literature.* London, UK: Learning Skills and Development Agency. Retrieved July 23, 2007, from www.m-learning.org/archive/docs/The use of computer and video games for learning.pdf

Moreno, R. (2002). Who learns best with multiple representations? Cognitive theory implications for individual differences in multimedia learning. Paper presented at World Conference on Educational Multimedia, Hypermedia, & Telecommunications. Denver, CO. Available in *ED-MEDIA 2002 Proceedings* (pp. 1380–1385). Charlottesville, VA: AACE Press.

Myers, B. (2008). Minds at play. *American Libraries, 39*(5), 54–57.

National Aeronautics and Space Administration (NASA). (2008). Sputnik and the dawn of the space age. NASA main page multimedia interactive feature on 50th anniversary of the space age. Retrieved June 12, 2008, from http://history.nasa.gov/sputnik/

National Commission on Excellence in Education. (1983). Introduction. *A nation at risk: The imperative for educational reform.* Retrieved May 27, 2008, from www.ed.gov/pubs/NatAtRisk/intro.html

National Council of Teachers of Mathematics (NCTM). (1970). *History of mathematics education in the United States and Canada: 32nd yearbook.* Reston, VA: Author.

National Council of Teachers of Mathematics (NCTM). (1980). *An agenda for action: Recommendations for school mathematics of the 1980s.* Reston, VA: NCTM. Available at www.nctm.org/standards/content.aspx?id=17278

National Council of Teachers of Mathematics (NCTM). (1989). *Curriculum and evaluation standards.* Reston, VA: Author.

National Council of Teachers of Mathematics (NCTM). (1991). *Professional teaching standards for school mathematics.* Reston, VA: Author.

National Council of Teachers of Mathematics (NCTM). (1995). *Assessment standards for school mathematics.* Reston, VA: Author.

National Council of Teachers of Mathematics (NCTM). (2000). *Principles and standards for school mathematics.* Reston, VA: Author.

National Council of Teachers of Mathematics (NCTM). (2008). *The role of technology in the teaching and learning of mathematics.* Retrieved February 28, 2010, from www.nctm.org/about/content.aspx?id=14233

National Mathematics Advisory Panel. (2008). *Foundations for success: The final report of the national mathematics advisory panel.* (March). Washington, DC: U.S. Department of Education. On this website, under Features, select Final Report: www2.ed.gov/about/bdscomm/list/mathpanel/index.html

Nelson, L. M. (1999). Collaborative problem solving. In C. M. Reigeluth (Ed.), *Instructional-design theories and models: A new paradigm of instructional theory* (pp. 241–267). Mahwah, NJ: Lawrence Erlbaum.

Niess, M. L. (2005). Preparing teachers to teach science and mathematics with technology: Developing a technological content knowledge. *Teaching and Teacher Education, 21*, 509–523.

Niess, M. L. (2008). Knowledge needed for teaching with technologies—Call it TPACK. *AMTE Connections, 17*(2), 9–10. Available under Past Newsletters link: www.amte.net/publications/amte-connections

Okan, Z. (2003). Edutainment: Is learning at risk? *British Journal of Educational Technology, 34*(3), 255–264.

Prensky, M. (2001). *Digital game-based learning.* New York, NY: McGraw-Hill.

Quinn, C. N. (1994). Designing educational computer games. In K. Beattie, C. McNaught, & and S. Wills (Eds.), *Interactive multimedia in university education: Designing for change in teaching and learning* (pp. 45–57). Amsterdam: Elsevier Science BV.

Randel, J. M., Morris, B. A., Wetzel, C. D., & Whitehill, B. V. (1992). The effectiveness of games for educational purposes: A review of recent research. *Simulation and Gaming, 23*(3), 261–276.

Rosas, R., Nussbaum, M., Cumsille, P., Marianov, V., Correa, M., Flores, P., et al. (2003). Beyond Nintendo: Design and assessment of educational video games for first and second grade students. *Computers & Education, 40*(1), 71–24. Retrieved July 14, 2006, from http://search.ebscohost.com/login.aspx?direct=true&db=aph&AN=8575034&site=ehost-live

Rubin, A., Murray, M., O'Neil, K., & Ashley, J. (1997, April). What kind of educational computer games would girls like? AERA presentation. Retrieved August 26, 2008, from http://mathequity.terc.edu/gw/html/MITpaper.html

Sedighian, K., & Sedighian, A. (1996, October). Can educational computer games help educators learn about the psychology of learning mathematics in children? In E. Jakubowski, et al. (Eds.), *Proceedings of the Eighteenth Annual Meeting of the North American Chapter of the International Group for the Psychology of Mathematics Education* (Vol. 2, pp. 573–578), in Panama City, FL. Available at www.eric.ed.gov/ED400178

Shaffer, D. W. (1997). Learning mathematics through design: The anatomy of Escher's world. *Journal of Mathematical Behavior, 16*(2), 95–112.

Shaffer, D. W. (2006). Epistemic frames for epistemic games. *Computers & Education, 46*, 223–234.

Sheffield, B. (2005). What games have to teach us: An interview with James Paul Gee. *Game Developer, 12*(10), 4–9. An abstract of the interview is available, and the digital issue of the magazine may be purchased at www.gdmag.com/archive/nov05.htm

Shulman, L. S. (1986). Those who understand: Knowledge growth in teaching. *Educational Researcher, 15*(2), 4–14. (This paper was delivered to the American Educational Research Association [AERA] as Shulman's presidential address).

Shulman, L. S. (198, February 7). Knowledge and teaching: Foundations of the new reform. *Harvard Educational Review, 57,* 1–22.

Squire, K., Giovanetto, L., Devane, B., & Durga, S. (2005). From users to designers: Building a self-organizing game-based learning environment. *TechTrends. Linking Research & Practice to Improve Learning, 49*(5), 34–74.

Van Etten, C., & Watson, B. (1976). Programs, materials, and techniques. *Journal of Learning Disabilities, 9*(9), 541–550.

VanSickle, R. L. (1986). A quantitative review of research on instructional simulation gaming: A twenty-year perspective. *Theory and Research in Social Education, 14*(3), 245–264.

Vogel, J. J., Vogel, D. S., Cannon-Bowers, J., Bowers, C. A., Muse, K., & Wright, M. (2006). Computer gaming and interactive simulations for learning: A meta-analysis. *Journal of Educational Computing Research, 34*(3), 229–243.

Waywood, A. (1992). Journal writing and learning mathematics. *For the Learning of Mathematics, 12*(2), 34–43.

7

Games for Language Arts Education

Melinda Stevison and Jeffrey Kaplan

COMBINING THE THEORETICAL with the practical, this chapter devotes considerable attention to how video games can introduce, augment, and reinforce the development of English language arts skills and understandings. Topics discussed include (a) challenges facing the study and practice of English language arts education; (b) standards advocated by leading authorities in the study of language and literacy, including the National Council of Teachers of English; (c) the practical use of video games to improve language and literary skills; (d) research on the use of interactive video games to augment language and literacy instruction; (e) select video games designed to improve language and literacy skills and understandings; and (f) implications for further study.

Undoubtedly, the teaching of English language arts in the 21st century is remarkably different from any time in human history. Prior to the advent of educational technology tools, English language arts primarily involved skill-and-drill instruction and the reading and analysis of great literary works. Teachers frequently taught in a straightforward, teacher-centered approach that relied on disseminating information in a "chalk and talk" model. With blackboards behind them, teachers faced rows of students who listened and took notes as teachers lectured. Students were required to spell and define lists of vocabulary words and to learn grammar, punctuation, and writing skills. Teachers assigned readings from textbooks and led class discussions on the literature.

Twenty-first century students are infinitely more cognizant of the outside world than students were until the early 1990s, when computers and the Internet started to shape communication and began to be used in K–12 education. Young people today are aware of how the intersection of language and technology can make even the most mundane activity seem intriguing. Children and adolescents know that at the click of a mouse they can enter new realms of language and story that go far beyond traditional classroom fill-in-the-blank and multiple-choice exercises. Young people are technologically savvy and capable of exploring the uses of language in ways that allow style and content to build upon themselves in their depth and complexity. Technology has truly transformed the world of classroom instruction.

If teachers are not using computers, students know it. No longer can teachers answer students' questions with "I don't know," and "because I said so." Instead, teachers and students can turn to the World Wide Web together to locate answers to the most arcane questions. From grammar construction to profound ideas, the web provides a plethora of living, updated responses and understandings. Most children and teenagers are adept at locating information on the Internet and enjoy using a wide variety of digital devices. Witnessing young people's technological proficiency, teachers and parents may be fascinated and frustrated—fascinated because students can learn things beyond their ken and frustrated because young people often have difficulty discerning fact from fiction. The web comprises a treasure trove of information: some true, some false, some valuable, and some treacherous. Yet, the web has become an endless resource for human engagement, lifelong learning, and entertainment.

Thus, we devote this chapter to the latest trends and issues, instructional materials, and implications and considerations for playing games in the English language arts classroom. We survey a number of existing computer games designed to assist in English language arts instruction in elementary and secondary classrooms and discuss how playing games can enhance classroom learning and help teachers incorporate some of the most useful techniques for conveying curricular content that current research on English language arts education has to offer. Combining the theoretical with the practical, this chapter explains how teachers can integrate game playing into classes and how best to direct students individually as they reinforce and augment their language arts understandings.

Challenges Facing Language Arts Education

As in most academic disciplines, there is a definitive ideological split in what is considered the best approach toward learning and understanding English language arts. Traditional teachers regard students as empty wells, and these teachers pour their knowledge out, hoping that students' brains will absorb everything they need to know. In traditional classrooms, teachers disseminate information with little or no input from students. Teachers assign work; students complete work; teachers check work; teachers assign grades. The traditional building blocks of learning begin and end with the teacher, as students take in information and respond in a manner that is fitting to the classroom structure. Everything originates with the teacher and ends with the teacher. This top-down approach is known as teacher-directed instruction.

Non-traditional educators believe that students should direct, for the most part, their own learning as they make choices and decisions about the issues and concerns that interest them the most. This bottom-up approach is known as student-centered instruction. In many school districts, these two educational philosophies compete in the larger arena of curriculum decision making and student assessment. Holding different convictions, teachers clash over how best to teach students and what they need to know. In non-traditional classrooms, teachers maintain control over the skills that students are expected to master, but these teachers are willing to accede some degree of control over the process to their students. Teachers recognize that young people desire a certain degree of autonomy and choice so they can reconcile their desires and understandings into a recognizable whole. These teachers know that the best way for students to learn is through trial and error; thus, they try to provide students with as many choices and options as possible to demonstrate their understandings and proficiencies within a reasonable framework of control.

The split in educational philosophies between traditional and non-traditional teachers is not new. As they mature, young people desire to break free from their parents to explore the world on their own terms. What makes the philosophical argument more relevant today is the degree to which the conflict between choice and control permeates our educational system.

With the ascendance of high-stakes testing, educational administrators, teachers, and students are feeling more and more pressure to accommodate their teaching and learning to the demands of rigorous state examinations. "Teaching for" or "to pass" the state examination becomes the number-one priority in most, if not all, public schools throughout the country because real money follows schools rated highly in the number of students who successfully pass state examinations in reading, writing, and mathematics. Again, as pressure mounts, schools that fail to achieve successful pass rates do not earn monetary rewards, suffer the shame of public humiliation, and are forced to remediate the students who hindered their school's success.

What this means for English language arts teachers is that there is little room for innovative teaching—at least for the teaching that inspires individual choices and autonomy. Teachers are reluctant to try anything innovative if they are worried about how their students will fare on traditional pencil and paper tests. For many teachers, playing video games may seem out of the question as they ask themselves, "What does this have to do with helping my students succeed on state exams containing multiple-choice questions over content dictated by a highly defined state and county curriculum?" Researchers who interviewed teachers about the possibility of using commercial video games in their classes said, "For many we spoke with, the idea of learning is related only to schoolwork, the content of the curriculum, and particularly those specific materials that have traditionally been present in the classroom: books, paper, pencils, textbooks, and so on" (Licasa, Mendez, & Martinez, 2008, p. 341).

National Council of Teachers of English

Professional organizations, politicians, and parents recognize the dilemma that many elementary and secondary classroom instructors face as they try to decide what and how to teach. For example, the National Council of Teachers of English (NCTE), the professional umbrella organization for all teachers of English and language arts in U.S. elementary and secondary schools, supports open and engaging classroom instruction. In document after document, NCTE cites its support for teachers who promote problem solving and student-centered, inquiry-based classroom practices. Moreover, NCTE recognizes the primary role that technology plays in such instruction (NCTE, 2006).

Language arts, as defined by NCTE, is a subject matter that includes several interrelated learning domains, including vocabulary, reading fluency, comprehension, composition, and literary analysis. Because of the interrelatedness of each of these specific areas, increased proficiency in one area typically leads to higher proficiency in one or more of the other areas. For example, problems students have with reading comprehension are often related to problems in vocabulary and reading fluency. Thus, providing learning tools that help students in one domain are likely lead to success in another. This interdependency characterizes most teaching in English language arts as well as in other subject matter (NCTE, 2006).

Researchers who study English language arts instruction have found that (a) reading, writing, listening, and speaking are learned by doing, not principally by studying abstractions or completing exercises; (b) language growth is bound with the broader dimensions of human growth and development; (c) language teaching begins at the student's individual developmental level and moves him or her as far as possible; (d) the study of English language arts should broaden the range of discourse that students can employ both as users (e.g., listeners and readers) and as creators (e.g., speakers and writers); (e) the study of English language arts is naturally interdisciplinary; (f) a balanced English language arts curriculum looks at both the needs of individual students and the aims of an English language arts curriculum; and (g) the teaching and learning of language can be a natural, pleasurable, and invigorating experience (Beers, 2003; NCTE, 2006).

In its guidelines for preparing teachers of English language arts, NCTE advocates a holistic approach. These guidelines say that good teaching begins by helping students learn through problem solving and critical thinking, not by breaking learning into isolated bits of instruction. Smart instruction offers students opportunities to engage in real-world activities that prompt creative and reflective analysis (NCTE, 2006). When students are involved in projects that apply to real life, they will learn or become more proficient at the skills needed to accomplish the projects' goals. For example, as students produce a newsletter they send to another class in their school or to one halfway around the world, they will sharpen their reading and writing skills.

Naturally, NCTE acknowledges the critical role that technology plays in holistic instruction. The very nature of technology embraces a more involved learning style that requires students to make real choices in a digital arena. Moreover, technology allows students to enter new worlds where they can make choices and control aspects of the virtual environment within highly idealized settings. Technology provides English language arts teachers with safe, exciting environments that inform and amuse their eager, tech-savvy learners.

To support its advocacy of technology in the classroom, NCTE has issued several position statements, most notably, The National Standards for Language Arts, cosponsored by the International Reading Association (IRA). The national standards cover 12 particular skills and competencies that are vital to a complete understanding of reading and language arts. Although the standards are presented as separate items in a list, they are interrelated (IRA & NCTE, 1996).

In this well-reasoned document, the IRA and NCTE define technology as one of the primary cornerstones of English language arts instruction. Specifically, standard number eight reads, "Students use a variety of technological and informational resources (e.g., libraries, databases, computer networks, videos) to gather and synthesize information and to create and communicate knowledge" (IRA & NCTE, 1996, p. 3).

NCTE has also issued its support of the National Educational Technology Standards for Teachers as defined by the International Society for Technology in Education (ISTE). The document covers six distinct domains (also noted by Bolkan in Chapter 4, this volume) that are vital to integrating technology in the classroom. Of particular importance is Standard 2, which mentions the NETS•S (National Educational Technology Standards for Students):

2. Design and Develop Digital-Age Learning Experiences and Assessments

Teachers design, develop, and evaluate authentic learning experiences and assessment incorporating contemporary tools and resources to maximize content learning in context and to develop the knowledge, skills, and attitudes identified in the NETS•S. (ISTE, 2008, p. 1)

The NCTE standards and the ISTE standards advocate the use of print and non-print texts. Both standards recognize the need for the learner to understand both mediums and how each is interdependent on the other. By incorporating the Internet for reading and gathering information, for example, students can use technology as a tool for recognizing the significance of non-print media. Similarly, technology can assist students in developing a greater understanding of text by exposing them to a variety of resource materials.

Classroom teachers can choose from a wide variety of technological resources. The next section will delve into the details about one such resource, digital video games, exploring their feasibility for use in the language arts classroom and noting their benefits and drawbacks.

Playing Video Games in the English Language Arts Classroom

Even in the U.S.'s most impoverished educational systems, teachers find that many students are becoming increasingly technologically savvy. These students know that there exists a universe beyond the classroom door that beckons to them, offering connections and realizations greater than anything ordinary teachers can reveal. From e-mailing to podcasting and from instant messaging to videoconferencing, young people are generally well aware of how language construction and self-development can be enriched instantaneously by the exchange of ideas and visions across the web.

One way for teachers to meet students halfway in addressing their high-tech interests is to consider the use of digital video games as a teaching tool. Using digital video games as part of classroom instruction provides students with an avenue of self-instruction and, ultimately, self-expression that for many is already familiar. Teachers who use instructional video games are permitting the use of a universe that allows students to become more engaged, active, and involved than through typical classroom activities. Pen and paper and hand raising are replaced by engagement in learning in cyberspace and imaginative universes.

Thus, the use of video games in English language arts classrooms may satisfy a number of learning objectives. Most notably, students experience a *sense of autonomy*. They work actively alone or in groups to solve problems presented in the games. Unlike workbook exercises, the games require more than filling in blanks or selecting correct answers; they ask players to make active choices in simulated settings.

Using video games provides students with the *notion of self-control*. Not only do students get to make real choices in real time, they also learn to curb their impulses and to decide what and what not to do. Their freedom of choice comes with an implicit responsibility to define their learning on their own terms, making decisions as they see fit and in their own time.

Using video games provides students with *accessibility* that they might have never experienced in a public setting. With the web at their beck and call, they can reach far beyond their immediate surroundings, extending their learning beyond the classroom and their homes.

Using video games provides students with *critical thinking* activities as they engage in higher orders of skill development. By making real choices in real settings, they see firsthand the direct results of their simulated decision-making skills, and they recognize intuitively the consequences of their judgments. In a safe and protected environment, they develop the requisite building blocks for becoming thinking and productive adults.

Using video games provides students with *reinforcement of skills and concepts* within an engaging and exciting environment. No longer is learning relegated to skill and drill; instead, it becomes a multilayered platform of insights and discoveries. Learning is transformed into a colorful playing field of interesting choices and dilemmas. Students play the games within a safe arena, learning as they are doing, reinforcing concepts that are often learned indirectly as they become increasingly enraptured by their video gameplay.

Using video games provides students with *exposure to technology* and practice on skills that are becoming increasingly vital as we move through the 21st century. Years ago, computers were reserved for mathematicians working on complex formulas. Today, computers are nearly as essential as breathing. We use them to conduct everyday activities—paying bills, making appointments, and checking financial records—and to help us accomplish the most sophisticated functions—writing, researching, and analyzing—and all within a few strokes of the keyboard. As students need to understand technology to survive in the modern world, teachers should provide them with every opportunity to become more proficient technology users.

Using video games provides students with *interactivity*. Often it is said that this type of technology use is isolating. Bearing down on the keyboard and becoming lost in one's own universe is some adults' stereotypical vision of what young people experience when playing video games. Yet, what games often do is the opposite. While participating in multiplayer games, young people are interacting constantly with each other across cyberspace through real-time text, voice over IP (VoIP), and asynchronous message boards.

Using video games provides students with *cooperative learning skills*. Having students work in partnerships or in small groups with a computer-based activity as a guide allows young people to work collaboratively and in cohorts with synchronized goals and objectives. Multiplayer games are conducive to teamwork. Players often take advantage of multiplayer modes to form permanent groups where they can share information and develop complementary strategies and characters that work cooperatively.

Using video games provides students and teachers with *opportunities for differentiation*. Digital video games, especially with their use of multimedia, are particularly conducive to students' different learning styles. A game's use of three-dimensional (3-D) graphics, animations, sounds, and video along with various types of controllers can address the needs of visual, auditory, and kinesthetic learners simultaneously. Additionally, some instructional games target specific academic levels, allowing teachers to employ differentiated learning to meet various students' needs, from remediation to acceleration.

Using video games provides students with opportunities *to archive and return to their learning*. Video games can save information that is often impossible to record and store through traditional means. This leads to several advantages, most notably, tracking students' progress, returning to previous assignments, and providing repeated instruction of needed or favorite lessons.

Using video games also provides students with *engaging and exciting activities*. Schooling becomes much more than rote and repetition or skill-and-drill activities. Instead, by the power of technology and imagination, young people can become immersed in gamesmanship that ignites not only their desire to be amused, but also their inimitable thirst for learning. Video games can satisfy both hungers and often far exceed expectations. But what do research and the literature say about the educational applications of video games?

Research and Literature on Playing Digital Video Games

Research indicates that games can be useful as they have shown positive affective potential for remediating struggling high school readers. Adolescents in literacy classrooms tend to learn best when they are engaged and feel high levels of self-efficacy (Alvermann, 2002). They need material that motivates them, and they need to spend significant time practicing their skills (Bruning, Schraw, Norby, & Royce, 2004). They need to work with material they find personally relevant, which sometimes means leaving the realm of traditional print literacy to explore their communicative and expressive skills via media and technology (Alvermann, 2002; Schmar-Dobler, 2003). They need to learn to apply strategies to their reading, analyzing where their comprehension skills break down and choosing a method for solving their problem (Alvermann, 2002; NICHHD, 2000).

Many of these ingredients for effective adolescent literacy education are mirrored in digital gameplay. Video games attract many adolescents and motivate them to spend hours playing, practicing, and strategizing. A wealth of information that discusses these and other positive aspects of video games is available in the academic literature. In his thoughtful and accessible book, *Digital Game-Based Learning*, Prensky (2001) lists the attractive features of gameplay:

1. Games are a form of fun. That gives us enjoyment and pleasure.

2. Games are a form of play. That gives us intense and passionate enjoyment.

3. Games have rules. That gives us structure.

4. Games have goals. That gives us motivation.

5. Games are interactive. That gives us doing.

6. Games have outcomes and feedback. That gives us learning.

7. Games are adaptive. That gives us flow.

8. Games have win states. That gives us ego gratification.

9. Games have conflict/competition/challenge/opposition. That gives us adrenaline.

10. Games have problem solving. That sparks our creativity.

11. Games have interaction. That gives us social groups.

12. Games have representation and story. That gives us emotion. (p. 160)

All of these features come together to create an engaging experience for the gamer and support our earlier propositions regarding the use of video games for language arts education. Prensky (2001) connects these characteristics with K–12 education by advocating a learner-centered approach over traditional, content-centered curriculum. The foundation of his argument is that school children of the current generation have experienced changes in their cognitive processes and the physical structures of their brains due to their constant exposure to digital media. These changes have created a demarcation between so-called digital immigrants, those born before about 1970 and raised before personal computing and modern media technology were prevalent, and digital natives, those born after 1970 who grew up surrounded by computers, video games, and modern television programming (see also Prensky's Chapter 1, this volume).

Prensky's claim is based largely on anecdotal evidence rather than empirical data, but it does appear that whether the cause is physiological, psychological, or sociological or various combinations of these causes, adolescent digital natives have grown up to expect the type of information input they know from MTV, movies, and digital games. As a result, they quickly disengage when presented with traditional print- and lecture-based instruction. Learners' preferences are often overlooked in these materials, but many educators and policy makers blame the students when they are not engaged by such forms of instruction (Prensky, 2001).

This view is certainly shared by researchers in the field of English language arts education, who find that many schools fail to offer students alternatives to a teacher-centered, highly structured curriculum, in spite of research that shows students need access to educational methods and resources that capture their interests and offer them empowerment in the learning process (Alvermann, 2002; Phelps, 2005).

In looking for curricular innovations to address this problem, many authors agree that games are effective at engaging those who play them and capable of creating an ideal learning experience. Csíkszentmihályi (1990) discusses an optimal state of consciousness he calls the "flow" state. When experiencing flow, one exists in a state of happiness, concentration, and productivity that makes it possible to shut out external surroundings and to be completely caught up in a given task. The activity becomes intrinsically rewarding, done for its own sake. Although educators and parents would be delighted to see students in this state of mind about their academic work, few current curricular practices are designed to foster it. Prensky (2001) argues that use of digital games designed for education would evoke this flow state, motivating students to spend hours at play voluntarily, thereby also mastering the subject matter presented in the games.

In his seminal publication on the subject of motivation and learning, Malone (1981) agrees that learning is more successful when it is intrinsically motivated and even states that external rewards can damage learners' intrinsic motivation. He lists characteristics of educational experiences that stimulate intrinsic motivation: challenge, fantasy, and the arousal and satisfaction of curiosity. These characteristics are arguably part of the best video games. Unfortunately, most video games designed specifically for use in classrooms are the drill-and-practice variety (Prensky, 2001). These types of games require students to rely on extrinsic motivation as a reason for playing them because they are not designed to be enjoyed for their entertainment value. They do little to benefit students affectively.

The Becta report (2001) concurs that the right kind of video gameplay can be intrinsically motivating. It emphasizes that motivation happens when people are continually challenged by an activity while realizing regular degrees of success in the process. Gee's research (2003) adds that most best-selling video games are long, complicated, and challenging to figure out, yet players spend hours working to master them. This happens without force and without "dumbing down" the game to make it easier. In fact, people pay money for these experiences. He states that game designers have stumbled upon successful learning principles, which are being researched and studied in academic circles.

Gee (2004) also asserts that the modern essentialist school climate is failing U.S. students, in spite of the fact that the United States spends nearly $50 billion per year on education. He proposes the use of video games as an innovative reform solution. Gee discusses the "regime of competence principle" in cognitive science, which refers to being close to the outer edges of one's cognitive abilities but not quite beyond them. This leads to a compelling combination of frustration and enjoyment. Video games provide both experiences by cycling through mastery of one level of difficulty to the next level of challenge.

Pillay (2003) agrees that the structural skills and cognitive processes used in playing video games are also very beneficial in academic settings. Kirriemuir (2002) claims that video games help players develop complex and nonlinear strategic skills and that they provide a safe virtual environment where players can experiment and indulge their curiosity. Klawe's research (1994) indicates that video games can improve girls' confidence in learning math and science and can help lower the dropout rate among boys. Dempsey, Rasmussen, and Lucassen (1994) claim that video games promote self-esteem among players.

Video games seem to have great potential for creating enjoyable learning experiences with lasting, positive results. Certainly, some of the same benefits shown to accompany video gameplay are those that help define effective English language arts education. For example, Alvermann (2002) identifies certain affective components of ideal reading curricula. These include recognition of multiple literacies to include skills beyond reading (i.e., media and technology literacies relevant and important to teens), enhancement of students' sense of competence and interest, and use of students' everyday language and literacy skills as a foundation to build upon. Alvermann also discusses the culture-as-disability perspective for viewing struggling adolescent readers. Those who subscribe to this perspective believe that students need more than just the widely approved skills instruction found in most public schools; they need curricular alternatives that include what they find relevant and interesting.

Video games could be one such alternative, particularly when they are adapted for use in classes to improve students' literacy. Unfortunately, misconceptions and negative stereotypes about video games present a persistent problem for educators who would like to make games an attractive option for mainstream teachers and other educational stakeholders. In light of the growing body of research that extols the benefits of digital gameplay, one might wonder why negative images endure. Some still see video games as harmful to children, contributing to violent tendencies and aggression. This has been difficult to prove. Published studies on video games and aggression in youth behavior showed mixed results, from an increase in aggression to a calming effect to no obvious effect at all (Emes, 1997). And although data is limited, Emes found no evidence suggesting children are psychologically or emotionally harmed by frequent video gameplay. There is even some empirical evidence indicating that video gameplay assists adolescents' moral development (Sherer, 1994, as cited in Emes, 1997).

Other research, though, has indicated that video games might possess certain detrimental qualities. For example, there may be negative effects associated with prolonged use of certain types of video games (Mitchell & Savill-Smith, 2004). The same qualities that make them attractive and engaging can make them addictive to certain personalities with extended, uncontrolled use. Obviously, long-term studies are needed to gather more evidence on this issue.

Additionally, some think that games' engaging characteristics are problematic instead of beneficial because they distract students from more scholarly activities. Walsh (2002) argues that children today cannot read because they're not practicing reading; instead, they watch TV and play video games, two sources of "instant gratification." Reading, on the other hand, is a skill that requires regular practice and several years to master. Prensky (2001) and Gee (2003) might counter that this formula for success in reading also describes what it takes to accomplish success with complex video games and that for many children the video games are more engaging.

In spite of a few potential drawbacks, instructional video games' positive potential for improving achievement seems to validate exploring their use in English language arts instruction. Particularly useful could be further research to investigate how video games can be used to help the most disengaged students become more involved in learning, particularly in reading. It is important to keep in mind, however, that no existing research directly evaluates the use of educational video games with adolescent English language arts instruction.

Challenges to Gameplay in Language Arts Classrooms

It is easy to see why there is a debate about the use of digital video games in school classrooms. Video games seem to encourage learning experiences that are enjoyable and highly desirable. In contrast, some educators have concerns about the practicality of making such a seemingly drastic curricular change, especially in light of the lack of scientific data showing video games' potential for increased academic achievement. Many issues surround the use of video games in the classroom, not the least of which is consideration of what it might take for an educational game to be adopted as part of the curriculum. This may be particularly true in language arts classrooms, which are subject to increased scrutiny as the pressure to achieve learning gains continues to mount (Barksdale-Ladd & Thomas, 2000).

For instructional video games to be accepted as regular parts of the curriculum, educators and policy makers would need to know that the games are designed in alignment with state or national language arts curriculum standards. They would also want evidence that their use could lead to an increase in state-mandated accountability test scores. As existing video games are designed mostly for entertainment, new educational video games will need to be designed or existing ones modified to include instructional content capable of producing measurable learning gains.

The need for well-designed instructional games is a stumbling block for their widespread adoption in schools. Good video games are expensive. Companies spend millions in research, development, and marketing to produce compelling, entertaining games and have access to the finest design talent in the world (Prensky, 2001). Such resources simply do not exist in education. While educators do have access to rudimentary game development tools, allowing them to produce activities such as crossword puzzles, they do not have the resources to create sophisticated games capable of being aligned with curriculum standards and the unique needs of students in each class. Until the creation of educational video games becomes as lucrative to game design companies as designs of the purely entertaining variety, educational games will continue to be relatively scarce and mediocre. This is discussed further in the next section of this chapter.

Access to computers and other game technology can pose problems as well. Not every language arts classroom is equipped with computers, and while textbooks are priority items when schools plan their budgets, video games are unlikely to be given similar consideration unless research can show their effectiveness. Additionally, many schools would not be able to afford the technology or the games themselves even if educators, parents, and other community stakeholders could be convinced of their value.

Students may respond to video game use in classes with varied levels of acceptance. Different people have different learning preferences, and video games may not be equally engaging and motivating for all. The exploration of video game preferences among different student population subgroups is outside the scope of this review; however, educators who want to use video games in their classrooms may be able to locate studies of particular subgroups of students who would be likely to benefit from the games.

Likewise, teachers' attitudes toward video games will undoubtedly play a large role in determining whether video games are widely used in classrooms. Several authors agree that it is impossible to ensure productive educational experiences with video games without teacher involvement and commitment (Becta, 2001; Kirriemuir, 2002; Prensky, 2001; Squire, 2004). The same authors also agree that video games should be one part of an overall instructional strategy. Just as there are no "one size fits all" approaches to effective reading literacy instruction, there is no research to support the educational use of video games as a sole method of teaching any academic subject.

Kirriemuir and McFarlane (2003) elaborate on aspects of video games that reportedly make them difficult for educators to use. Learning to use video games and creating lesson plans around them are time consuming for teachers. Teachers surveyed as part of this research reported that they tried implementing video games within their curriculums and generally were not able or willing to spend enough time on preparation to ensure effective instructional experiences. Squire (2004) also mentions that this is a problem and says time constraints are an issue for students, too. Games that are complex enough to be rewarding take many hours to learn and play. Kirriemuir and McFarlane (2003) note that games not designed specifically for educational use contain some irrelevant and distracting content, which sometimes influences student outcomes in unintended ways.

High-tech cheating is another possible downside of video games and other instructional technology, especially if that technology is used for purposes of evaluation or measurement (Yan & Choi, 2002). Students do learn how to cheat when outcomes are measured. Educators need to consider this and prepare for potential problems, just as they do for other instructional methods.

Different subject matter may also make a difference in the effectiveness of video game learning experiences. Randel, Morris, Wetzel, and Whitehill (1992) examined empirical data from studies conducted on digital and non-digital instructional games between 1984 and 1991. Subject matter seemed to be the biggest determinant of whether games were appropriate for educational use. Math, physics, and language arts were deemed to be the best subjects for game-based instruction because of their specific, rule-based objectives.

The fact that games studied in language arts settings were determined to be effective seems promising for considering their use with reading instruction. The games Randel and colleagues (1992) studied were generally the drill-and-practice variety, however, teaching vocabulary, spelling, and grammar by rote. Because older drill-and-practice-style games were studied, results were more easily quantified than would be possible on more modern video games like Civilization III. It is worth remembering, though, that productive gameplay seems to depend heavily on context. Subject matter would thus be a large factor, indicating that it is difficult to generalize success or failure of games from one academic subject to another.

Just as some research points to the challenges inherent in playing video games in formal education, other research shows that they can offer viable, intriguing, and largely untapped possibilities for addressing modern educational problems, similar to those found in adolescent literacy instruction. Before video games can be accepted widely in English language arts classrooms, however, it seems that considerable research and development are needed to make them practical for large numbers of teachers to use.

Digital Video Games for English Language Arts Education

Video games cater to a large and diverse population. Naturally, young people make up a large portion of this diverse group, and they have varying levels of reading ability and interest. While it has been indicated in previous parts of this chapter that digital video games may be useful for reaching and motivating students of diverse backgrounds and abilities, teachers' options are somewhat limited. Far more drill-and-practice-type games are available for use in language arts classrooms than the more advanced and engaging variety of games advocated by Prensky and Gee. In fact, no sophisticated games have been designed with advanced story lines that fulfill the standards requirement for teaching high-level problem-solving skills in language arts. Although these types of games exist either as stand-alone products for use in other content areas (e.g., Tabula Digita's Dimension M for use in math classes) or as commercial, off-the-shelf (COTS) products that can be adapted for educational use (e.g., Civilization III for use in world history classes), the creation or adaptation of sophisticated games for language arts apparently has been much more difficult.

Again, there are a variety of reasons for this. The most engaging games are also the most expensive and come with the steepest learning curves. Schools may not have the resources to invest in them, and teachers may not have time to teach students how to play them. Drill-and-practice games are easier to use and faster to learn. It is also easier to quantify the benefits of using them. As they provide practice for basic skills and rules, it is easy to test their effectiveness. Assessing the critical thinking and problem-solving skills required by more sophisticated games, like those discussed by Prensky and Gee, is much harder. This is particularly problematic for teachers of adolescents. While skill-based games may be more appropriate for younger students than games employing more advanced or mature story lines, many adolescents are accustomed to playing sophisticated interactive games, like Medal of Honor and Tomb Raider, at home and with friends. Accomplished players of these popular commercial games may become quickly bored by the "plain vanilla" simplicity and story lines of instructional games deemed appropriate for all ages.

As drill-and-practice games make up the vast majority of options for English language arts teachers wanting to use digital video games in their classrooms, a sample of them will be described. Following this, there will be a discussion of alternatives for teachers who would like to reach beyond games that enable practice of basic skills.

Drill-and-Practice Games: Prekindergarten and Early Elementary

Game Goo (www.earobics.com/gamegoo/gooey.html). This website offers attractive flash games to drill young students in basic concepts, such as recognition of upper and lower case letters of the alphabet, vowel and consonant combinations, matching initial and final sounds in spoken words, and spelling of easy spoken words. It is free and is designed for single players. See Chapter 13 for more information on this type of web-based digital video drill-game.

Leap into Nursery Rhymes (by Leap into Learning, Inc., for Windows XP/NT, Mac OS 9). This video game for very young children introduces classic nursery rhymes while developing phonemic awareness. Phonemic awareness is the ability to hear sounds in words. A video game such as this is one vehicle for helping children hear what they are learning to pronounce.

K9.5 The Tail-Wag Tour (by Lightspan for Playstation). This game is for young learners and is designed to help improve reading and language arts skills. The players help five characters, Ella, Gershywn, Maxine, Riff, and Theo, get ready for a musical concert while learning about parts of speech. Dogs are a central feature of this program, hence, the title.

Drill-and-Practice Games: Late Elementary and Up

Furious Frogs (www.arcademicskillbuilders.com). Select the Language Arts tab on the menu bar. This web-based flash game lets players' frogs slurp up flies by matching antonyms, synonyms, and homonyms. Furious Frogs can be played as a single-player or multiplayer game. It is free, requires no downloads, and is simple to play. This website features several other easy, entertaining games in the language arts domain, allowing students to practice fundamental skills. See Chapter 13 for more information on this type of web-based digital video drill-game.

Spelling Challenges and More (by Crave Entertainment for Nintendo DS). This digital video game allows players to practice their spelling by choosing from 11 different interactive word games. Players can select the word that is misspelled, the one that is correct, unscramble words, and spell the word as it flashes by. All games have time limits, and players try to beat either their own or others' times by racking up high scores. Players can also enter their ages, and the game will identify the player's skill level by age. This game is appropriate for all ages.

Bookworm Deluxe (by Mumbo Jumbo for PC, Windows 98/2000/XP). This digital video game has players create new words to feed a hungry bookworm. At first glance, this looks like a children's game with a very simple premise. Players string letters together to build new words and eliminate those tiles from the board that are unnecessary. The catch is that the tiles are on fire; if they sink to the bottom of the screen, the game is over.

Two modes of play are available—the untimed classic game and the action game. The untimed classic game allows a leisurely approach to building new words, whereas the action game requires speed and agility before the flaming letters ignite the surrounding tiles and end the game. There are many variations of this game, providing players with different levels of ability opportunities to succeed while building their vocabularies.

School House Rock Grammar Rock (Riverside Interactive Learning for Windows 95/3.x). A favorite memory from the late 1970s, young people can gain confidence in their writing and speaking as they learn to use parts of speech—nouns, pronouns, verbs, adverbs, adjectives, prepositions, etc.—to complete interactive games. Music from the popular Grammar Rock videos is interspersed to entice a new generation of young learners.

Free Rice (www.freerice.com). A vocabulary activity with a humanitarian bent, Free Rice promises that for each word whose meaning the players choose correctly, 20 grams of rice are donated to the United Nations World Food Program. This activity is also available in a format that enables grammar practice.

Beyond Drill-and-Practice

While numerous drill-and-practice games are available for language arts teachers who want to harness the benefits of digital game technology in their classrooms, there are fewer choices that move beyond repetitive practice of fundamental skills. Examples of games that require higher-level skills are introduced and described in this section.

Rock & Write (www.rockandwrite.com). While this is not a digital video game, it is web-based technology that teachers of adolescents may find appealing for use in the English language arts classroom. This website offers teens a place to write song lyrics and receive feedback and tips. It advertises that young people "will learn the essence of songwriting, lyric basics, and various genres and styles; they will hear from an award winning creative director on how to tap into their creative energy and take their talent to the next level; and they will hear from songwriters on how they brought their ideas to life in song with tips and techniques." It also lists the fundamental skills exercised: "How to get your ideas, thoughts, and words on paper; turning words into lyrics; choosing the right genre and style; and protecting your creative work." While the site emphasizes writing for the music industry, a teacher could use this as an exercise in creative writing and poetry with a hook that may appeal to students who enjoy music and are not interested in more traditional lessons.

Homemade PowerPoint Games. These are somewhat outside the realm of digital video games but may have potential for infusing curriculum with some of the benefits and appeal associated with video gameplay, while allowing for much greater creativity and constructionism than possible with drill-and-practice games. The premise of such games is that students can work together to create a story line and other features of their own game; then they use Microsoft PowerPoint to produce it. This allows them the benefits of learning content well enough to present it creatively in the design and development of a game, whether the game is played by other students in their own classroom or by younger students in a different developmental stage. It is not difficult to see how creation of homemade PowerPoint games could serve a remedial purpose in the language arts classroom (e.g., older students practicing basic reading or grammar skills while creating a game for younger students, rendering the remediation more socially acceptable). It is also easy to envision PowerPoint games serving an enrichment purpose (e.g., advanced students exercising their creativity and language arts skills in a manner more entertaining than simply writing essays). For a more detailed description of homemade PowerPoint games, see Chapter 14.

Commercial Off-the-Shelf (COTS) Games. Not all games used for educational purposes were designed to be educational. The fact that COTS games like Medal of Honor were designed to be sophisticated forms of entertainment can be a real advantage to teachers with the patience and persistence to use them in the classroom. While such games are increasingly being tied back to curricular standards in content areas like social studies, history, and geography for use with adolescent students, it is difficult to find COTS games that apply to language arts. Traditional forms of print-oriented literacy are not often stressed in these advanced games, in which unwritten narrative and nonverbal visual stimulation take precedence. Reading skills are not often employed in this type of gameplay, nor are grammatical principles. One way a language arts teacher might consider using a COTS game would be in the exercise of creative writing skills; e.g., students could play a game like Civilization III and enjoy its nonverbal action. They could then use their gameplay experience to write a story from their avatar's perspective. For a more thorough discussion of the use of COTS games in K–12 education, including the many benefits and challenges associated with this use, see Chapter 12.

Conspiracy Code: Mindbender (www.360ed.com/products/). While the above activities and games move beyond the simplicity of the drill-and-skill genre, all are either educational activities without the elements of high-tech gameplay found in digital video games, or they are digital video games designed primarily for entertainment and adaptable to some degree for educational purposes. It is particularly difficult to find language arts games that are truly dual-purpose, simultaneously educational and possessing the "wow" factor inherent in the best digital video games. Although these do exist in other content areas (see Tabula Digita's Dimension M for mathematics [www.dimensionu.com/math/], for example), they have been lacking from language arts.

With that being said, a game currently under development by 360Ed, a leading educational game company, has the potential to fill the gap. Mindbender is being developed cooperatively by 360Ed and Florida Virtual School, an accredited, online public K–12 school, as an entire course for high school intensive reading. Mindbender is designed to be "an interactive 3-D adventure," with the following plot line and features:

> Students play as secret agents Eddie Flash and Libby Whitetree on a mission to save futuristic Coverton City—and maybe even the world—from the forces of Conspiracy Incorporated, a secret society that's begun corrupting citizens and computers alike through sinister subliminal messages. To stop them, Eddie and Libby must find, examine, and interpret captivating clues, all the while using an eclectic set of abilities to overcome enemy agents and well-meaning security forces. Each piece of clue content they encounter is aligned with state and national reading standards and incorporates scaffolding and comprehension strategies. Working through Eddie and Libby, students are assessed across the course with a wide variety of sophisticated assignments, all seamlessly integrated

into the gameplay setting and designed to promote New Literacies while testing higher-order thinking skills. Culminating mission assessments, scaffolding clue assignments, teacher reviews, logbook checks, and more all serve to verify each student's understanding of the course content, ensuring their work is both varied and authentic. (M. Laurence, personal communication, October 7, 2009)

In summary, it has traditionally been easier for English language arts teachers to use drill-and-practice games within the classroom than any of the more sophisticated digital video games that students—especially teens—find so attractive. Drill-and-practice games are often simpler for students to learn and have more of an educational "feel" to them that makes them acceptable to parents, administrators, and other community stakeholders. Drill-and-practice games are useful for teaching rules and skills where automaticity is desired, and packaging such rote performance in a game-like wrapping does make it more palatable for students. In order to go beyond these simpler levels of cognition, however, teachers must use their ingenuity to adapt the technology and games that are currently available. COTS games are often extremely difficult to adapt for teaching language arts because they do not involve many aspects of traditional, print-based literacy. Because of the narrow range of options available for teachers wanting to bring digital video gameplay into their language arts classrooms, further study is recommended. The next section of this chapter elaborates on these recommendations.

Implications for Further Gameplay Study

Although much literature now exists on the *potential* educational applications of video games, a relatively small number of studies quantify the kinds of achievement results required by administrators and policy makers. Many opportunities await exploration. With only a few exceptions, much of the quantitative research seems to have been done on subjects other than language arts and on people outside the high school age group. Samples of both early and recent quantitative studies of this type are highlighted in this section.

One early quantitative study conducted on the use of instructional games by a population of adolescent students (Thomas, Cahill, & Santilli, 1997), describes how the New York State Department of Health developed an interactive, time-travel adventure game called Life Challenge as a tool to enhance adolescents' self-efficacy in HIV/AIDS prevention programs. The authors' data showed that the subjects made learning gains, took game tasks of negotiation seriously, and improved their self-efficacy test scores.

In another early study, Bosworth (1994) investigated the use of computer games and simulations to teach health topics to adolescents. An interesting point in this work was that the importance of games in this instruction was greater for younger adolescents than older ones. Therefore, it might be important to conduct further research on whether the age of the student has major, direct bearing on the success of different types of digital video game–based instruction.

In a more recent study, Squire, Barnett, Grant, and Higginbotham (2004) explored the use of a digital simulation game called Supercharged! to teach electromagnetic concepts in a middle school science class. They conducted both quantitative and qualitative research, and found that students in the experimental group using Supercharged! earned higher post-test scores and relied more on experiential learning than those in the control group, whose post-test scores were lower and whose learning experience consisted primarily of rote memorization. And while there was a statistically significant difference in learning gains between the experimental and control groups, there was not a statistically significant effect due to gender.

Papastergiou (2009) studied the effectiveness of the use of a computer game to learn computer memory concepts. The author randomly assigned a sample of high school computer science students to either an experimental group using the instructional computer game, or to a control group using a computer application lacking a game component. The data indicated that the students assigned to the experimental computer game group saw increases in both learning gains and motivation as compared to the students in the non-game control group. Furthermore, analysis showed that gender made no significant difference in the levels of learning effectiveness and motivation experienced by students; boys and girls alike achieved equally positive outcomes using the computer game.

These results from research both by Papastergiou (2009) and Squire et al. (2004) bring up an interesting point of potential further study: it may be worthwhile to conduct additional research on gender roles and the use of instructional digital games, particularly exploring how gender preference for digital games or gender-related learning outcomes from them vary across age groups and content areas. Although these two studies found no real differences between genders, it may be that different educational settings or learner demographics could result in different outcomes.

Regarding use of digital games across content areas, it is notable that both of the previously mentioned studies examined the use of digital games in science and technology classrooms. It could be that certain content areas lend themselves more readily to the use of instructional digital games. There seems, then, to be a need for more research on use of video games across different subject matter settings.

The study by Randel et al. (1992) that was mentioned in an earlier section of this chapter recommends such research and also suggests that data need to be collected on use of games for remediating students who struggle with traditional instructional methods. This would certainly apply to the problem at the center of this review: teachers seeking unique reading remediation techniques simply do not have enough information that validates higher student achievement levels in language arts content areas after they use instructional games. If research were to generate this type of data, widespread adoption of video games as important parts of curricula could potentially be justified.

Unique solutions to this dilemma are beginning to present themselves. Shaffer, Squire, Halverson, and Gee (2005) discuss epistemic frames, which are learning communities of "situated understandings, effective social practices, powerful identities, shared values, and ways of thinking" (p. 108). Typical epistemic frames might include the medical community training doctors or the legal community training lawyers. Computers could be used to set up simulations of epistemic frames or epistemic games so that students could learn biology by "working" as geneticists. This seems to be a research topic worth pursuing, especially in language arts contexts. Students could become editors for fashion or sports magazines, for example, learning reading and writing skills as they simulate an interesting career activity.

It would also seem worthwhile to conduct further research on the impact that social and cultural contexts have on academic use of digital gameplay. Steinkuehler (2004) says that learning experiences through gameplay are so heavily contingent on the context in which they are used that it is very difficult to prescribe effective practices. Teachers need solid advice or instructions on how to employ games in certain pedagogical contexts; clearly, more research needs to be done before such recommendations can be made.

Research methods also need to be addressed. According to Williams (2005), video game research has reflected two dominant approaches: social scientists who study the effects of video games on users and humanists who seek to understand meanings and contexts of games. These two camps have different goals and methodologies, that is, quantitative, measurable results for social scientists versus qualitative, abstract data for humanists, which leads to a lack of collaboration. Williams (2005) states that social scientists and humanists need to bridge this gap and come to an understanding of each other so that opportunities for growth in the field are not lost.

Steinkuehler, Black, and Clinton (2005) agree that methodology needs further consolidation in this field but also point out that researchers need to consider a wider variety of methodological options. They further posit that educational researchers are investigating an ever-widening realm of topics on the use of digital technology in education, yet they often limit themselves to a narrow range of quantitative methodologies. Indeed, it would seem that both quantitative and qualitative research would be useful for explaining phenomena surrounding the use of video games for instruction. Obtaining and measuring quantitative results of instructional video game use continues to be difficult, especially when affective outcomes are considered. Wider use of qualitative research like Squire's (2004) could be beneficial for evaluating the affective results of video game use and would provide a needed supplement to quantitative data.

In Conclusion

As we discussed in this chapter and others have noted throughout this book, it certainly appears that digital video games possess characteristics that lend themselves to productive use in educational settings. It is also clear that widespread use of video games will require educators to re-evaluate their classroom procedures and may require greater time commitments for instruction and instructional planning. A modern standardized curriculum is arguably easier and safer to implement and rests on a research base that is relatively larger and more substantial than a curriculum that includes instructional video game use.

While video games are flourishing in the commercial sphere among children and adolescents, they are still in their infancy as successful applications within educational contexts. This is certainly true in the field of English language arts and literacy instruction. Clearly, educational video games remain controversial and somewhat challenging to implement, yet we may be closer to employing video games as part of innovative, student-centered language arts curricula.

Many of our students are learning from games in their free time, even as some fail to make adequate progress in academic subjects such as language arts. It behooves the educational community to become involved and to contribute research-based information on what and how today's students are learning. Video games can be used constructively or destructively. The challenge is to find ways to harness their constructive power, particularly as we try to re-connect with our most challenged digital native learners.

References

Alberti, J. (2008). The game of reading and writing: How video games reframe our understanding of literacy. *Computers and Composition, 25*(3), 258.

Alvermann, D. E. (2002). Effective literacy instruction for adolescents. *Journal of Literacy Research, 34,* 189–208. Retrieved November 9, 2007, from www.coe.uga.edu/lle/faculty/alvermann/effective2.pdf

Annetta, L. A. (2008). Video games in education: Why they should be used and how they are being used. *Theory into Practice, 47,* 229–239.

Atkinson, K. M. (2005). What should we do?: Computational representation of persuasive argument in practical reasoning. PhD thesis, Department of Computer Science. Liverpool, UK: University of Liverpool. Available (under 2005) at www.csc.liv.ac.uk/~katie/publications.html

Baek, Y. K. (2008). What hinders teachers in using computer and video games in the classroom? Exploring factors inhibiting the uptake of computer and video games. *CyberPsychology and Behavior, 11*(6), 665–671.

Barksdale-Ladd, M. A., & Thomas, K. F. (2000). What's at stake in high-stakes testing: Teachers and parents speak out. *Journal of Teacher Education, 51*(5), 384–397.

Barrell, B. R. C., & Hammett, R. F. (2004). *Teaching English today: Advocating change in the secondary curriculum.* New York, NY: Teachers College Press.

Becta (2001). *Computer games in education project: Report.* Retrieved November 11, 2007, from http://research.becta.org.uk/index.php?section=rh&rid=13595 and *Computer games in education project: Aspects.* Available at http://research.becta.org.uk/index.php?section=rh&&catcode=&rid=13588

Beers, K. (2003). *When kids can't read—what teachers can do: A guide for teachers, 6–12.* Portsmouth, NH: Heinemann.

Bosworth, K. (1994). Computer games and simulations as tools to reach and engage adolescents in health promotion activities. *Computers in Human Services, 11*(1), 109–119.

Bruce, B. C., & Levin, J. A. (2003). Roles for new technologies in language arts: Inquiry, communication, construction, and expression. In J. Flood, D. Lapp, J. R. Squire, & J. R. Jensen (Eds.), *Handbook of research on teaching the English language arts,* 2nd ed. (pp. 649–657). Mahwah, NJ: Lawrence Erlbaum. Retrieved July 7, 2010, from www.ideals.illinois.edu/bitstream/handle/2142/13422/roles_new_technologies_language_arts.pdf?sequence=2

Bruning, R. H., Schraw, G. J., Norby, M. M., & Royce, R. R. (2004). *Cognitive psychology and instruction.* Upper Saddle River, NJ: Pearson Prentice Hall.

Bryant, T. (2008). From age of empires to zork: Using games in the classroom. Posted on Academic Commons July 12, 2008. Retrieved December 10, 2008, from www.academiccommons.org/commons/essay/gamesinclassroom/

Bus, A. G., & Neuman, S. B. (Eds.). (2009). *Multimedia and literacy development: Improving achievement for young learners*. New York, NY: Routledge.

Charsky, D., & Mims, C. (2008). Integrating commercial off-the-shelf video games into school curriculums. *TechTrends, 52*(5), 38–44.

Clem, F. A., & Simpson, E. (2008). Enriched learning with video simulation games. *Connect Magazine, 21*(4), 4–8.

Cooper, H. (2003). Editorial. *Psychological Bulletin, 129*(1), 3–9.

Corbit, M. (2005). Moving into cyberspace: Game worlds for learning. *Knowledge Quest, 34*(1), 18–22.

Csíkszentmihályi, M. (1990). *Flow, the psychology of optimal experience*. New York, NY: Harper & Row.

Cunningham, J. W. (2001). Essay book reviews: The national reading panel report. *Reading Research Quarterly, 36*(3), 326–335. Retrieved November 9, 2007, from JSTOR database at www.reading.org/Publish.aspx?page=/publications/journals/rrq/v36/i3/abstracts/rrq-36-3-cunningham.html&mode=redirect

Debolt, D. (2008). How video games can help in the classroom and the world. *Chronicle of Higher Education, 55*(9), 11.

Dempsey, J. V., Rasmussen, K., & Lucassen B. (1994, February). Instructional gaming: Implications for instructional technology. Paper presented at the Annual Meeting of the Association for Educational Communications and Technology, Nashville, TN.

DimensionM. (n.d.). Electronic games for education in math and science. Retrieved November 11, 2007, from www.dimensionu.com/educator/home/?Section=dimM

Education Arcade, The. (n.d.). About the education arcade. Retrieved November 11, 2007, from http://educationarcade.org

EGEMS. (2002). Electronic games for education in math and science. Retrieved November 11, 2007, from www.cs.ubc.ca/nest/egems/projects.html

Emes, C. E. (1997). Is Mr Pac Man eating our children? A review of the effect of video games on children. *Canadian Journal of Psychiatry, 42*(4), 409–414. Retrieved November 11, 2007, from https://ww1.cpa-apc.org/Publications/Archives/PDF/1997/May/EMES.pdf

Garen, E. M. (2001). Beyond the smoke and mirrors: A critique of the national reading panel report on phonics. *Phi Delta Kappan, 82*(7, March), 500–506. Retrieved November 9, 2007, from EBSCOHost database (5281360).

Garen, E. M. (2005). Murder your darlings: A scientific response to the voice of evidence in reading research. *Phi Delta Kappan, 86*(6), 438. Retrieved November 9, 2007, from Gale Group database.

Gee, J. P. (2003). Games, not school, are teaching kids to think. *Wired, 11*(5).

Gee, J. P. (2004). *Situated language and learning: A critique of traditional schooling*. New York, NY: Routledge.

Gee, J. P. (2007). *What video games have to teach us about learning and literacy* (2nd ed.). New York, NY: Palgrave, Macmillan.

International Reading Association (IRA) and National Council of Teachers of English (NCTE). (1996). *Standards for the English language arts*. Newark, DE: IRA, & Urbana, IL: NCTE. Available at www.ncte.org/standards

International Society for Technology in Education (ISTE). (2007). *National educational technology standards for students* (NETS•S). Available at www.iste.org/Content/NavigationMenu/NETS/ForStudents/NETS_for_Students.htm

International Society for Technology in Education (ISTE). (2008). *National educational technology standards for teachers* (NETS•T). Available at www.iste.org/Content/NavigationMenu/NETS/ForTeachers/2008Standards/NETS_for_Teachers_2008.htm

Jones, S. (2003). Let the games begin: Gaming technology and entertainment among college students. *Pew Internet & American Life Project*. Retrieved March 2, 2009, from www.pewinternet.org/~/media/Files/Reports/2003/PIP_College_Gaming_Reporta.pdf

Kiili, K. (2005). Digital game-based learning: Towards an experiential gaming model. *The Internet and Higher Education, 8*(2),13–24. Available at www.savie.ca/SAGE/Articles/940_300027-KIILI-2005.pdf

Kirriemuir, J. (2002, April). The relevance of video games and gaming consoles to the higher and further education learning experience. *Techwatch Report* TSW 02.01. Retrieved July 7, 2010, from www.jisc.ac.uk/uploaded_documents/tsw_02-01.rtf

Kirriemuir, J., & McFarlane, A. (2003). Use of computer and video games in the classroom. Retrieved March 4, 2009, from www.slideshare.net/silversprite/use-of-computer-and-video-games-in-the-classroom

Klawe, M. M. (1994). The educational potential of electronic games and the E-GEMS Project (p. 611). In T. Ottman & I. Tomek (Eds.). *Proceedings of ED-MEDIA 94—World conference on educational multimedia and hypermedia*. Charlottesville, VA: Association for the Advancement of Computing in Education. Paper prepared for the panel, Can electronic games make a positive contribution to the learning of mathematics and science in the intermediate classroom? M. M. Klawe, chair; J. Lawry; K. Inkpen; K. Sedighian; R. Upitis (pp. 611–615). Association for the Advancement of Computing in Education, Vancouver, BC, June 1994. (ERIC Document Reproduction Service No. ED388210)

Krashen, S. (2001). More smoke and mirrors: A critique of the national reading panel (NRP) report on "fluency." *Phi Delta Kappan, 83*(2), 118. Retrieved November 9, 2007, from www.sdkrashen.com/articles/smoke/smoke.pdf

Krashen, S. (2005). Is in-school free reading good for children? Why the national reading panel is (still) wrong. *Phi Delta Kappan, 86*(6), 444. Retrieved November 9, 2007, from Gale Group database. Pre-publication article available at www.sdkrashen.com/articles/in-school%20FVR/index.html

Leung, W. M. (2003). The shift from a traditional to a digital classroom—Hong Kong kindergartens. *Childhood Education, 80*(1), 12–17. This article is in the 2003 annual theme issue of *Childhood Education* that focused on educational technology, Sudha Swaminathan and Nicola Yelland (guest eds.). Available to members of Questia; see www.questia.com/PM.qst?a=o&d=5002562804

Licasa, P., Mendez, L., & Martinez, R. (2008). Bringing commercial games into the classroom. *Computers and Composition, 25*(3), 341–358.

Lister, G. (2007). Play video games; they're educational. *American School Board Journal, 194*(1), 45.

Malone, T. W. (1981). Toward a theory of intrinsically motivating instruction. *Cognitive Science, 4,* 333–369.

Martin, J., & Ewing, R. (2008). Power-up! Using digital gaming techniques to enhance library instruction. *Internet Reference Services Quarterly, 13*(2/3), 209–225.

McCombs, J. S., Kirby, S. N., Barney, H., Darilek, H., & Magee, S. (2005). *Achieving state and national literacy goals, a long uphill road: A report to Carnegie Corporation of New York.* Santa Monica, CA: Rand Education. The pdf is available on the Carnegie website under tabs for year: "2005" and document type: "report to the corporation"; http://carnegie.org/publications/search-publications/

Mitchell, A., & Savill-Smith, C. (2004). *The use of computers and video games for learning: A review of the literature.* London, UK: Learning and Skills Development Agency. Retrieved March 1, 2009, from www.lsnlearning.org.uk/search/Resource-32183.aspx

Myers, J., & Beach, R. (2004). Constructing critical literacy practices through technology tools and inquiry. *Contemporary Issues in Technology and Teacher Education, 4*(3). Retrieved September 21, 2009, from www.citejournal.org/vol4/iss3/languagearts/article1.cfm

National Assessment of Educational Progress (NAEP). (2005). National trends in reading achievement: Trend in twelfth-grade NAEP reading achievement-level results 1992–2005. The nation's report card. Washington, DC: U.S. Department of Education. Retrieved November 11, 2007, from http://nationsreportcard.gov/reading_math_grade12_2005/s0203.asp

National Assessment of Educational Progress. (2007a). How the governing board guides the assessment. Washington, DC: U.S. Department of Education. Retrieved November 11, 2007, from http://nces.ed.gov/nationsreportcard/about/nagb/nagb_naep.asp

National Assessment of Educational Progress. (2007b). Trend in eighth-grade NAEP reading achievement-level performance. Washington, DC: U.S. Department of Education. Retrieved November 11, 2007, from http://nationsreportcard.gov/reading_2007/; under the heading at left for "Reading," select tab for "overall results" and then "achievement level"; above the chart, select "grade 8."

National Council of Teachers of English Standing Committee on Teacher Preparation and Certification. (2006). *Guidelines for the preparation of teachers of English language arts.* Urbana, IL: National Council of Teachers of English. Available at www1.ncte.org/store/books/standards/126639.htm

National Institute of Child Health and Human Development (NICHHD). (2000). *Report of the national reading panel. Teaching children to read: An evidence-based assessment of the scientific research literature on reading and its implications for reading instruction: Reports of the subgroups.* (NIH Publication No. 00–4754). Washington, DC: U.S. Government Printing Office. Retrieved November 9, 2007, from www.nichd.nih.gov/publications/nrp/report.cfm

Noddings, N. (Ed.). (2005). *Educating citizens for global awareness.* New York, NY: Teachers College Press.

O'Brien, D. (2001). "At-risk" adolescents: Redefining competence through the multiliteracies of intermediality, visual arts, and representation. *Reading Online, 4*(11). Available at www.readingonline.org/newliteracies/obrien/

Panitz, T. (1996). A definition of collaborative vs cooperative learning. Deliberations. (A website based in the Centre for Academic Professional Development at London Metropolitan University.) Retrieved November 6, 2007, from www.londonmet.ac.uk/deliberations/collaborative-learning/panitz-paper.cfm

Papastergiou, M. (2009). Digital game-based learning in high school computer science education: Impact on educational effectiveness and student motivation. *Computers and Education, 52*(1), 1–12.

Phelps, S. (2005). *Ten years of research on adolescent literacy, 1994–2004: A review.* Naperville, IL: Learning Point Associates. Retrieved November 7, 2007, from www.eric.ed.gov/ (ERIC Document Reproduction Service No. ED489531)

Pillay, H. (2003). An investigation of cognitive processes engaged in by recreational computer game players: Implications for skills of the future. *Journal of Research on Technology in Education, 34*(3), 336–350.

Pope, C. A., & Golub, J. N. (2000). Preparing tomorrow's English language arts teachers today: Principles and practices for infusing technology. *Contemporary Issues in Technology and Teacher Education, 1*(1). Retrieved October, 8, 2005, from www.citejournal.org/vol1/iss1/currentissues/english/article1.htm

Prensky, M. (2001). *Digital game-based learning.* New York, NY: McGraw Hill.

Prensky, M. (2008). The role of technology in teaching and the classroom. *Educational Technology,* (November–December). Retrieved February 8, 2009, from www.marcprensky.com/writing/default.asp

Quest Atlantis. (n.d.). Retrieved July 7, 2010, from http://atlantis.crlt.indiana.edu/site/view/Educators

Ranalli, J. (2008). Learning English with The Sims: Exploiting authentic computer simulation games for L2 learning. *Computer Assisted Language Learning, 21*(5), 441–455.

Randel, J. M., Morris, B. A., Wetzel, C. D., & Whitehill, B. V. (1992). The effectiveness of games for educational purposes: A review of recent research. *Simulation and Gaming, 23*(3), 261–276.

Ravenscroft, A. (n.d.). A tool for synchronous collaborative argumentation. From *AcademicTalk* website and the Distributed e-Learning Programme of the JISC (www.jisc.ac.uk/programme_edistributed.html). Retrieved November 11, 2007, from www.londonmet.ac.uk/ltri/research/projects/at.htm

Ravenscroft, A., & Matheson, M. P. (2006). Digital games and learning in cyberspace: A dialogical approach. *E-Learning, 3*(1), 37–50.

River City Project, The. (n.d.). Retrieved November 6, 2007, from http://muve.gse.harvard.edu/rivercityproject/

Schmar-Dobler, E. (2003). Reading on the Internet: The link between literacy and technology. *Journal of Adolescent and Adult Literacy, 47*(1), 80–85. Retrieved November 13, 2007, from EBSCOHost database (10956419).

SciFair (2007). SciCentr/SciFair programs 2007–2008. Retrieved November 11, 2007, from www.scicentr.org/Activities/Programs/

Serious Games Initiative. (n.d.). About the serious games initiative: The emergence of a serious games industry. Retrieved November 11, 2007, from www.seriousgames.org/about2.html

Shaffer, D. W., Squire, K. R., Halverson, R., & Gee, J. P. (2005). Video games and the future of learning. *Phi Delta Kappan, 87*(2), 105–111.

Sherer, M. (1994). The effect of computerized simulation games on the moral development of youth in distress. *Computers in Human Services, 11*, 81–95.

Sheridan, D. M., & Hart-Davidson, W. (2008). Just for fun: Writing and literacy learning as forms of play. *Computers & Composition, 25*(3), 258–269.

Sigafoos, J., & Green, V. A. (Eds.). (2007). Technology and teaching. New York, NY: Nova Science Publishers, Inc.

Smagorinsky, P., Cook, L. S., & Reed, P. M. (2005). The construction of meaning and identity in the composition and reading of an architectural text. *Reading Research Quarterly, 40*(1), 70–88. Retrieved November 8, 2007, from www.reading.org/General/Publications/Journals/RRQ/ ArchivesRRQ.aspx; at year 2005, select Vol. 40, no. 1.

Squire, K. (2004). *Replaying history: Learning world history through playing Civilization III.* Bloomington, IN: Indiana University.

Squire, K. (2004). Video games in education. Retrieved March 2, 2009, from www.educationarcade. org/gtt/pubs/IJIS.doc

Squire, K., Barnett, M., Grant, J. M., & Higginbotham, T. (2004). Electromagnetism supercharged!: Learning physics with digital simulation games. *Proceedings of the 6th International Conference on Learning Sciences.* International Society of the Learning Sciences: Santa Monica, CA.

Stahl, N. A. (2006). Strategic reading and learning, theory to practice: An interview with Michele Simpson and Sherrie Nist. *Journal of Developmental Education, 29*(3), 20–27. Retrieved November 13, 2007, from EBSCOHost database (20182433).

Steinkuehler, C. A. (2004). Learning in massively multiplayer online games. In Y. B. Kafai, W. A. Sandoval, N. Enyedy, A. S. Nixon, & F. Herrera (Eds.), *Proceedings of the sixth international conference of the learning sciences* (pp. 521–528). Mahwah, NJ: Lawrence Erlbaum.

Steinkuehler, C. A., Black, R. W., & Clinton, K. A. (2005). Researching literacy as tool, place, and way of being. *Reading Research Quarterly, 40*(1), 7–12.

Swenson, J., Rozema, R., Young, C. A., McGrail, E., & Whitin, P. (2005). Beliefs about technology and the preparation of English teachers: Beginning the conversation. *Contemporary Issues in Technology and Teacher Education, 5*(3/4). Retrieved April 2, 2006, from www.citejournal.org/ vol5/iss3/languagearts/article1.cfm

Szeuanni, M. (2008). Immersed in video games: Media education and ethical participation. *Screen Education, 50*, 44–49.

Tabula Digita. (n.d.). Retrieved November 11, 2007, from www.dimensionu.com

Tchudi, S., & Grossman, P. L. (n.d.). English education—Teaching of, preparation of teachers. Retrieved January 9, 2009, from http://education.stateuniversity.com/pages/1958/English-Education.html

Thomas, R., Cahill, J., & Santilli, L. (1997). Using an interactive computer game to increase skill and self-efficacy regarding safer sex negotiation: Field test results. *Health Education & Behavior, 24*(1), 71–86. Abstract available at http://heb.sagepub.com/content/vol24/issue1/; pdf retrieval requires a subscription to *Health Education & Behavior Online*.

Trotter, A. (2004). That's edutainment. *Teacher Magazine, 16*(2), 15.

Trotter, A. (2004). Digital games bring entertainment into learning realm. *Education Week, 23*(44), 8.

Vygotsky, L. (1962). *Thought and language*. Cambridge, MA: Harvard University Press.

Walsh, D. (2002). Why couch potatoes can't read. *Principal, 81*, 46.

Williams, D. (2005). Bridging the methodological divide in game research. *Simulation & Gaming, 36*(4), 447–463.

Yan, J. J. & Choi, H. J. (2002). Security issues in online games. *The Electronic Library, 20*(2), 125–133. Retrieved July 6, 2010, from http://cust.educ.ubc.ca/Wstudents/TSED2/TechEmotion/VideoGames/games%20copy.pdf

Young, C. A., & Bush, J. (2004). Teaching the English language arts with technology: A critical approach and pedagogical framework. *Contemporary Issues in Technology and Teacher Education, 4*(1). Retrieved from www.citejournal.org/vol4/iss1/languagearts/article1.cfm

8

Games for Social Studies Education

William R. Watson

AS A FORM OF POPULAR ENTERTAINMENT, digital video games have reached an all-time high in popularity, becoming a regular part of many students' lives. Games have become so pervasive that some are referring to the current generation as the "gamer generation" (Beck & Wade, 2004). Digital video games are also gaining an increased advocacy for their adaptation for educational purposes. This chapter addresses the appropriateness of video games for social studies and citizenship education and identifies available games, tying them to national standards for social studies and citizenship education.

An increasing number of practitioners and researchers are advocating digital computer and video games (also referred to simply as video games) as a promising form of instruction that can engage students and strengthen skills important in the current information age (Aldrich, 2004; Foreman, Gee, Herz, Hinrichs, Prensky, & Sawyer, 2004; Prensky, 2001; Quinn, 2005). In fact, the Federation of American Scientists (2006) has called for increased federal funding for educational game research, identifying games as well suited to educating students for today's knowledge economy.

Apart from being well suited for today's learners, video games have also become an extremely popular form of mainstream entertainment. Video game software sales reached a record $10.3 billion in the United States in 2002 and maintained their strong showing with $10 billion in sales in 2003 (NPD Group, 2004), exceeding the $9.1 billion in 2002 box office sales for the U.S./Canada movie industry (*Theatrical Market Statistics: 2009*, 2009). The growth of video games shows no sign of stopping, as total video game hardware and software sales increased 43% from 2006 to 2007, resulting in total revenues of nearly $18 billion and breaking records for the third consecutive year (NPD Group, 2008).

With their widespread popularity, video games also have a strong impact on the players themselves, altering the very ways in which they play and learn, creating a "gamer generation" (Beck & Wade, 2004) or "digital natives" (Prensky, 2005), who multitask, like to discover things for themselves through trial and error, and crave engagement and interactivity. Given such issues as the popularity of video games and their impact on players, proponents of educational video games believe they offer a viable alternative form of instruction to traditional, teacher-centric learning activities.

Despite growing recommendations for increased use of educational video games, quality studies on the effectiveness of educational games for raising students' achievement levels are scarce (Fletcher & Tobias, 2006). Along with limited available research, established guidelines for how to implement educational video games in classrooms and into curriculums are lacking. In reviewing the current research on educational games, I noted a number of researchers' conclusions that learning via gameplay in schools is not likely to be effective without additional instructional support and sound implementation strategies (Leemkuil, de Jong, de Hoog, & Christopher, 2003; O'Neil, Wainess, & Baker, 2005; Wolfe, 1997). Thus, there is a great need for additional research on real-world applications of educational video games in different contexts, including K–12 schools. In addition, the initial use of games could be daunting due to current conditions in schools, where class time limits, high stakes testing, lack of teacher familiarity with video games, and limited funds for purchasing games often exist.

In this chapter, I examine traditional approaches to social studies education and refer to readily available games that can be used for civic education. Today's students demand engaging instruction and disengage when they do not receive it (Prensky, 2005; Beck & Wade, 2004). Citizenship education is a pressing need in the United States, and video games hold great potential for reshaping citizenship education to meet the needs of today's students as global citizens more comprehensively.

Citizenship is perceived as a key goal of K–12 education, and I argue that educational video games are a strong fit for meeting the needs of social studies education. This chapter is organized into six sections. In the first section, I present an overview of the current state of social studies education and the push for citizenship education. I also discuss the appropriateness of using video games for social studies education and address the issue of national and state standards. In the second section, available commercial off-the-shelf (COTS) video games that can be used for social studies education are reviewed. In the third section, available educational games are reviewed, and in the fourth, available political games. The fifth section takes a brief look at the development of an educational game for social studies education and the implementation of an educational game in a high school history classroom. In the sixth section, I discuss lessons learned, provide guidelines for choosing and implementing appropriate games, and tie them to existing standards.

Social Studies and Citizenship Education

In this section, I offer an overview on the current status of social studies, including the sometimes controversial viewpoint that its primary goal should be citizenship education. Then I argue that video games are appropriate for use in social studies. I conclude with a discussion of social studies standards and how they relate to video games.

Social Studies in the Information Age: The Current State of the Field

In the United States, social studies education has a history of conflict among opposing camps seeking to control or influence its direction (Evans, 2004). Evans notes, "What began as a struggle among interest groups gradually evolved into a war against progressive social studies that has strongly influenced the current and future direction of the curriculum" (p. 176). In Evans and Passe (2007), Leming describes the two primary types of social studies education as progressive social studies, which promotes citizenship, and traditional social studies, which seeks "to transmit cultural knowledge and our civic heritage through a focus on subject matter and teacher-directed instruction" (p. 252).

Citizenship education is one of the most frequently stated goals of education (Parker, 1996) and a goal noted as increasingly important in the United States and in other countries worldwide. In his review of civic engagement, Galston (2007) notes that Americans under age 30 pay less attention to current events than their elders or those their age did two to three decades ago; the percentage of eligible voters aged 18–25 who voted in the presidential election dropped from 52% in 1972 to 37% in 2000, though the percentage has started to rise since then. And in general, whether evaluating "civic beliefs or civic behavior, there have been marked declines in the qualities and characteristics that we associate with successful democratic government," particularly among young adults (p. 639).

Furthermore, civic knowledge is extremely important in developing effective citizens. Galston (2007) found that civic knowledge (a) helps citizens understand their interests as individuals and group members; (b) increases the consistency of views on issues; (c) alters citizens' viewpoints on specific public issues, even when the civic knowledge is general; (d) lessens isolation from public life and feelings of generalized mistrust; (e) promotes support for democratic values; and

(f) promotes political participation. Galston's final point is that (g) without a basic level of civic knowledge, especially concerning political processes or institutions, citizens have difficulty understanding political events or integrating new information into their existing conceptual framework.

There is a growing body of research that suggests civic education can be effective if taught in a certain way. One comprehensive study showed that a "classroom environment that encourages respectful discussions of civic and political issues fosters both civic knowledge and engagement" (Galston, 2007, p. 639). The primary reason for traditional civic education's failure was its focus on teaching facts to passive students who memorized material they often considered irrelevant to their lives.

The call to move away from traditional civic education and focus on generating critical discussion and debate is echoed in Selwyn's (2007) review of information and computer technology (ICT) in civic education in the United Kingdom. He notes that there is a significant lack of research on using technology to teach civic education and that the implementation of ICT in civic education has often failed to produce significant results, as it is often little more than a repackaging of traditional instructional approaches that encourage students to remain passive. He calls for a move beyond passive memorization of facts to the use of software that engenders dialogue. He states, "At the heart of increasing the effectiveness of citizenship education in schools is making politics itself more engaging to young people" (Selwyn, 2007, p. 5).

Social Studies progressives are calling for re-envisioning the goals of citizenship education due to the increasingly pluralistic nature of the United States and the world. To understand how they can function as participating citizens in increasingly complex societies (as opposed to being passive consumers), students need to be challenged with new methods of learning (Banks, 2001; Kerr, 1999; Parker, 1996). Some of the recommendations for civic education reform fit particularly well with the reasons for utilizing educational video games.

The Appropriateness of Digital Video Games for Citizenship Education

In its recommendations for policy makers, the Education Commission of the States calls for "Making citizenship education experience grounded in knowledge and explicitly designed to engage students" (Torney-Purta & Vermeer, 2004, p. 5). The Education Commission of the States is a nonprofit, nationwide organization that helps state leaders shape education policy. Torney-Purta is senior advisor and Vermeer is project manager for the National Center for Learning and Citizenship, part of the Education Commission of the States. The two authors conducted the research and wrote the report, *Developing Citizenship Competencies from Kindergarten through Grade 12: A Background Paper for Policy Makers and Educators*, funded by the Carnegie Corporation of New York, for the Education Commission of the States.

One of the great promises of educational video games is their ability to engage students. The Federation of American Scientists (2006) highlights games' potential for motivation and encouraging time on task as chief reasons why they are well suited for education.

In identifying elements of engaged learning, Dickey details how games support each of the following elements:

- ▶ Focused goals

- ▶ Challenging tasks

- ▶ Clear and compelling standards

- ▶ Protection from adverse consequences for initial failures

- ▶ Affirmation of performance

- ▶ Affiliation with others

- ▶ Novelty and variety

- ▶ Choice

- ▶ Authenticity (Dickey, 2005, p. 70, citing Jones et al., and Schlechty)

Games represent a means for students to move away from passive learning to make choices, explore options, take on roles, and participate in realistic representations of real-world dilemmas and challenges.

If the promise of engagement is one reason video games are well suited to citizenship education, the possibility of transporting students to different environments and situations and allowing them to take on different roles and viewpoints via the games' simulations is another strength. The Education Commission of the States also notes that schools help to foster civic education when they are able to help students "express their views in media forms that are attractive and familiar to them" and "link knowledge gained in an abstract form to more concrete everyday situations in which it might be used" (Torney-Purta & Vermeer, 2004, p. 7). The popularity of video games among today's students has already been noted, so it is clear how allowing students to learn through their favorite media would be favorable. Furthermore, students are able to express their views and take on different roles through typical gameplay, experimenting with different identities and attempting to solve global conflicts.

Banks (2001) says that educators need to move away from the assimilationist notions of past civic education to help students develop clear, well-thought-out identification with both their nation-state and their cultural community. He also notes the need for students to develop "clarified global identifications and deep understandings of their roles in the world community" (Banks, 2001, p. 8). Games are an excellent fit for meeting these needs and reaching these goals because students play from differing viewpoints and immerse themselves in unfamiliar cultures or nations, face new and relevant problems, and learn to recognize and understand important conceptual linkages. The Federation of American Scientists (2006) also recommends games for education due to their strength in "contextual bridging (i.e., closing the gap between what is learned in theory and its use)" (p. 5). Games offer a means for students to become engaged with civic education, sparking further learning outside the game, and they hold promise for helping students to develop higher-level understandings of theory by allowing them to experience the theory through varied contexts.

Educational video games are gaining widespread support as a new form of instruction in schools, and the recognized benefits they offer are well suited to the needs of civic education. Furthermore, perhaps more than in any other subject area, video games have a history of being used for civic education. The rest of this chapter will illustrate how instructors and researchers do not need to wait to begin using video games for civic education—a wealth of available resources are available, including COTS video games and excellent online educational games; additionally, new educational video games are being designed and developed every year. In the next section, I review available COTS games currently used for civic education. Before the review, the issue of alignment with national and state standards will be addressed.

Games and Standards: Navigating the Maze of National and State Standards

The current era of standards and high-stakes testing has drawn a great deal of criticism for the ways it has limited educational content and instructional methods. Research shows that elementary schools are cutting social studies classes because federal testing does not call for them, students are learning only low-cognition facts in preparation for tests, and teachers and administrators are narrowing curricula to teach to the tests (Vogler & Virtue, 2007). Despite these criticisms, many teachers find themselves in environments that stress standards and testing and feel compelled to emphasize preparation for the tests. In my conversations with social studies teachers, I have learned that the narrowing curriculum is one of their greatest concerns when they consider adopting video games in their classrooms. This issue is discussed further toward the end of this chapter, as I relay the experiences of a high school teacher who utilizes an educational game in his history classroom.

In the meantime, for teachers in today's educational environment, there is an emphasis on tying all curricula to established standards. The next three sections of this chapter provide reviews of available games for social studies teachers. Ideally, the descriptions of the games in the reviews would identify standards for each teacher; however, with no commonly used national standards for social studies, it is beyond the scope of this chapter to identify standards for each state. Instead, the games will be tied to the curriculum standards provided by the National Council for the Social Studies (NCSS) Task Force (NCSS, 1994), titled *Expectations of Excellence: Curriculum Standards for Social Studies*. The standards are divided into 10 thematic strands: (a) culture; (b) time, continuity, and change; (c) people, places, and environment; (d) individual development and identity; (e) individuals, groups, and institutions; (f) power, authority, and governance; (g) production, distribution, and consumption; (h) science, technology, and society; (i) global connections; and (j) civic ideals and practice. Referring to these thematic strands, teachers will see how they tie a given game to their state standards. In a later section of this chapter, I offer advice for teachers seeking to do the same with local standards.

Matching curricula to various standards can be a complex task. The NCSS describes its standards as strongly interrelated and holistic and recommends that local education planners be guided by its 10 strands to define their own standards. The NCSS also advises local educators to seek additional guidance from "detailed content from standards developed for history, geography, civics, economics, and other fields" (NCSS, 1994, p. 15).

While research shows that the pressures of standards and high-stakes testing often drive teachers away from the learner-centered approaches to teaching social studies that have been increasingly recommended (Vogler & Virtue, 2007), members of the "noble profession" continue to seek to engage their students and spark a love of learning. Video games are a strong instructional option not only for engaging students, but also for promoting critical thinking, position taking, and problem solving. In the next three sections, I identify numerous games that are available to social studies teachers for use in and outside their classrooms.

Using COTS Games for Social Studies Education

Educators are using a number of commercial off-the-shelf (COTS) games as one effective method for teaching social studies. While other available games might have potential for use in social studies classrooms, Table 8.1 lists primary games known to have been adapted to teach social studies. Each game is described, including its appropriate grade levels, related NCSS standards, and cost. Grade levels are based on content ratings by the Entertainment Software Rating Board (ESRB) and the complexity of gameplay, not on the grade level when a specific topic is covered. The NCSS Standards referenced can be found on pages 196–202. Following Table 8.1, I present a quick summary of available research on the instructional application of the described games.

TABLE 8.1 ► Commercial (COTS) entertainment video games for teaching social studies

GAME SUMMARY	GRADE LEVELS (advisories)	NCSS STANDARDS (see pp. 196–202)	COST (per copy)	CURRICULAR SUPPORT
Civilization Civilization is a turn-based strategy game series; Civilization III, IV, and V are played on the computer, and Civilization Revolution is for console platforms, including the Xbox 360, PS3, and Nintendo's DS. Civilization allows players to establish, develop, and govern a nation over centuries to create a simulated history of that nation. Players determine where to establish cities; what cultural, scientific, and technological advancements to pursue; what forms of government to govern with; and when to declare war or sign treaties or trade agreements.	7–12 (violence)	**Middle Grades** I-a. b. d.; II-b. c. f.; III-a. e. h.; IV-h; VI-f. g.; VII-a.; VIII-a.; IX-a. b.; X-g **High School** I-a. b. g. h.; II-b. c. f.; III-a. e. h.; IV-h.; VI-e.; VII-a.; VIII-a.; IX-a. b.; X-g.	Civ III–$10 Civ IV–$30 Civ V–$50 CivRevolution: $60; DS is $30	No, but educators' discussion forum available on website: fireaxis.com/educators
Caesar IV Caesar IV is a city-building game in ancient Rome, where players manage the city, setting policies to encourage its growth and success.	5–12 (violence, alcohol use)	**Middle Grades & High School** I-a.; III-a.; IV-h.; VI-b. c. d.; VII-a. b. d.	$20	No
CivCity: Rome CivCity: Rome is a city-building game set in ancient Rome. It includes a "Citypedia" that shares historical facts about life in Rome.	5–12 (mild violence, alcohol references)	**Middle Grades & High School** I-a.; III-a.; IV-h.; VI-b. c. d.; VII-a. b. d.	$10	No

(Continued)

TABLE 8.1 *(Continued)*

GAME SUMMARY	GRADE LEVELS *(advisories)*	NCSS STANDARDS *(see pp. 196–202)*	COST *(per copy)*	CURRICULAR SUPPORT
Europa Universalis III Europa Universalis is a real-time strategy game that takes place in Europe between 1453 and 1789, the Napoleonic era. Players can choose to begin the game at any date in this time span and lead their nations through trade, exploration, diplomacy, and war.	7–12 *(mild violence, alcohol & tobacco references)*	**Middle Grades** I-a. b. d.; II-b. c. f.; III-a. e. h.; IV-h.; VI-f. g.; VII-a.; VIII-a.; IX-a. b.; X-g. **High School** I-a. b. g. h.; II-b. c. f.; III-a. e. h.; IV-h.; VI-e.; VII-a.; VIII-a.; IX-a. b.; X-g.	$20	No
SimCity 4 SimCity is a simulation game series allowing players to be the mayor and to design and build a city, dealing with population growth, pollution, commercial and residential zoning, quality of life, and so forth. It is largely responsible for the explosion of simulation games for entertainment and is a frequent model for educational simulation games as well as other city-building games. SimCity 4 is the latest version of the game, with the exception of SimCity Societies, a recent release that changes the game's focus from city management toward citizen values of different societal types.	5–12	**Middle Grades & High School** III-e. h. j.; VI-c.; VII-a. c. d. h.	$20	No
Railroad Tycoon Railroad Tycoon 3 and its sequel Sid Meier's Railroad! are business simulation games where the player builds a railroad company by laying track, building trains, managing the train schedule, and shipping goods. Railroad! also supports the player's competition against historical "rail barons."	5–12 *(alcohol references)*	**Middle Grades & High School** VII-a. c. d. h.	Tycoon 3: $20 Railroad!: $40 original Railroad Tycoon: free for download at 2kgames.com/railroads	No
Rise of Nations Rise of Nations is very similar to the Civilization series but with a stronger focus on warfare. It is a real-time strategy game where players can choose any of 18 societies to control at any time in history.	7–12 *(blood & gore, violence)*	**Middle Grades & High School** II-b. c.; III-a.; VII-a.; VIII-a.; IX-b.	$25	No
Age of Empires III Age of Empires III is a real-time strategy game similar to Rise of Nations, but with a focus on the European colonization of North America in the years 1500–1850. Players can choose to play eight different colonizing nations as well as a native American tribe after making a treaty.	7–12 *(blood & violence)*	**Middle Grades & High School** II-b. c.; III-a.; VII-a.; VIII-a.; IX-b.	$30	No

TABLE 8.1 *(Continued)*

GAME SUMMARY	GRADE LEVELS *(advisories)*	NCSS STANDARDS *(see pp. 196–202)*	COST *(per copy)*	CURRICULAR SUPPORT
Birth of America 1 and 2 Birth of America is a turn-based strategy game with 10 modules covering the French and Indian War and the American War for Independence. Players play one of two sides in each module, trying to achieve military and political victory. Each module also contains specific historical events. Birth of America 2 focuses solely on the War for Independence with a turn replay feature and updated graphics and rules.	5–12	**Middle Grades & High School** II-a. b. c. d. e. f.; III-a.; VI-b. c.; IX-b.; X-a. b. d. h. j.	$17.85 (download) $30 (shipped)	No
Victoria: An Empire Under the Sun / Victoria II Victoria is a real-time strategy game that takes place during the Victorian era (1836–1920). Players run a nation, seeking to generate enough victory points from prestige, industry, and military to win the game. Players manage their country, dealing with the economy and the social and political changes of industrialization.	7–12	**Middle Grades & High School** II-b. c. e. f.; III-a.; VI-b. c. f. g.; VII-a VIII-a. c.; IX-b. c.	$9 (Victoria) $40 (Victoria II)	No

Several COTS games described above have been applied and researched in classrooms. Squire (2004) conducted a study in which he implemented Civilization III in a U.S. high school for teaching world history. The study found that students played the game in very different ways and that their discussions on game strategies and gameplay experiences resulted in developing alternative approaches to the game. While students did not necessarily increase their knowledge of specific learning concepts, they did discuss the impact of these concepts on their gameplay experience, using broader conceptual terms. Squire concludes that student responses to their gameplay experiences can lead to strong learning opportunities.

Egenfeldt-Nielsen (2005) conducted a study using Europa Universalis II with 72 Danish high school students to support learning in a history course. The study found that students sometimes struggled to recognize connections between their gameplay experience and history, due to a lack of established understanding of history as well as struggles with understanding the game itself. The study concludes that most participants in the study gained experience through the game that offered potential for increased understanding; however, he notes that students often did not make the connection between gameplay and learning. Egenfeldt-Nielsen concludes that games in classrooms need to be directed by specific educational goals and guidance to maximize learning. This concept will be discussed further in the conclusion of this chapter.

While the use of COTS games for civic education has a history stretching back decades, instructors interested in utilizing games in their civics/social studies classrooms need not be limited by the availability of COTS games, as they can be a challenge to adapt for educational purposes because they were originally designed for entertainment. These games do provide immersive gameplay and impressive graphics but can also require greater technical requirements to run, more class time to play, and can be more expensive than games designed for educational purposes. The next section will detail available serious games; many are free to play, and all were developed for educational or other "serious" purposes.

Using Educational Games for Social Studies Education

Educational games are digital video games designed for educational purposes, as opposed to games created solely for entertainment. As educational games often are not expected to produce revenues equivalent with those of entertainment games, they often have much smaller budgets available for development. With smaller budgets and smaller development teams, educational games often struggle to match the advanced technology present in the latest COTS games. However, the lack of cutting-edge graphics does not mean a game cannot be successful in being engaging and effectively communicating its message.

Salen and Zimmerman (2004) label the focus on cutting-edge technology in games as "the immersive fallacy" (p. 450), which is "the belief that the pleasure of a media experience is the ability of that experience to sensually transport a player into an illusory reality" (p. 458). They argue that the immersive fallacy ignores the "metacommunicative nature of play" (p. 458), meaning that players are aware of the frame of a game as separate from their reality. To put it another way, the audience attending the production of a play realizes that what they are watching is not real, and often the production may not look remotely realistic, such as the barren sets of Thornton Wilder's play, *Our Town*; however, this does not prevent the audience from being effectively engaged with and immersed in the context of the play. In much the same way, games that lack realistic or sensational graphics can still engage players effectively.

Likely the most well-known educational game is The Oregon Trail, which was created in the 1980s and allows players to assume the roles of American pioneers traveling along the Oregon Trail to the West in the mid-1800s. The fifth edition of The Oregon Trail is available. While the game was highly popular and used in many classrooms, including social studies classes when I was a grade school student, as is the case with many games, no literature exists to evaluate the learning impact of the game. That being said, whole generations of students look back fondly on this game as a highlight of their elementary history classes.

Educational games have seen substantial growth in the last decade, and a number of games, many of them free, are now available for teachers or researchers wishing to use video games for civic education. As most of these games were developed fairly recently, no research regarding their use for education could be found for this chapter; however, they hold promise and were developed with a focus on more than just entertainment for their players. A brief overview of these games is listed in Table 8.2, including the web address to access to play, purchase, or find more information about the game, including appropriate grade levels, applicable standards, cost, and whether curriculum support is available.

TABLE 8.2 ▶ Serious games for teaching social studies

GAME SUMMARY	GRADE LEVELS	NCSS STANDARDS (see pp. 197–202)	COST (per copy)	CURRICULAR SUPPORT
The Oregon Trail *broderbund.com* The Oregon Trail (fifth edition) has the player take the role of a pioneer traveling west across the United States on the Oregon Trail. The player makes choices on purchases, locates food, and deals with obstacles on the trail.	3–9	**Early Grades** II-a. b.; III-a.; VII-a. b. g **Middle Grades** II-a. b.; III-a.; VII-a.	$20	No
Where in the World/USA Is Carmen Sandiego? *broderbund.com* Where in the World and Where in the USA Is Carmen Sandiego? are two well-known games for teaching about geography and history. Players seek to catch the criminal, Carmen Sandiego, as they chase her across the USA or the world, learning facts about the locations they visit.	3–6	**Early Grades & Middle Grades** II-b.; III-a.	$10	No
Discover Babylon *fas.org/babylon* Discover Babylon, created by the Federation of American Scientists, is a multiplayer game that puts players in a museum, learning about Mesopotamia by interacting with artifacts and asking questions of characters in the game.	3–9		free	Limited, website notes that educator's guide is coming soon.
Quest Atlantis *questatlantis.org* Quest Atlantis is aimed at students aged 9–16 and was developed by educational researchers. Students interact with each other in an online, immersive environment, similar to massive, multiplayer, online role-playing games (MMORPGs). Players complete various educational quests, such as conducting environmental research and researching other cultures.	3–9	**Early Grades & Middle Grades** I-a. c. e.; III-k.; IV-h.; VIII-e.	Free; requires an application for schools to show administrator and teacher support for the project.	Yes, built-in assessments and online teacher toolkits are provided.
Food Force *food-force.com* Food Force was developed for the United Nations' World Food Programme. It is free to play and provides teacher resources. Players in the game distribute food and try to help a struggling, fictitious country become self-sufficient, while learning about hunger and the UN's World Food Programme.	3–9	**Early Grades & Middle Grades** III-j.; V-g.; VII-b. g.; VIII-a.; IX-b. f.	Free	Yes, website provides numerous resources and recommendations for creating lesson plans.
Virtual History *knowledgematters.com/products/vhe/* (Ancient Egypt) *knowledgematters.com/products/vhsa/tour* (Settling America) Virtual History is available in two packages: Ancient Egypt and Settling America. In these games, players make decisions regarding the growth of a village in ancient Egypt or in pioneer America. Players are assessed with questions and quizzes throughout the game and given feedback, based on their decisions as they grow food, build buildings, and deal with the challenges of nature.	5–8	**Early Grades & Middle Grades** I-a.; II-b.; III-a. f. h.; VII-a. b.; VIII-a.	V-User = $195 Lab License = $395 Site License = $595	Yes, activities and matching standards for each state are provided on website.

(Continued)

TABLE 8.2 *(Continued)*

GAME SUMMARY	GRADE LEVELS	NCSS STANDARDS *(see pp. 197–202)*	COST *(per copy)*	CURRICULAR SUPPORT
Real Lives *educationalsimulations.com* Real Lives is a simulation game of a person's life. Based on statistical information, the user plays an assigned role; he or she will be born in a given country and have his or her life determined by the simulation's calculations and the role player's own decisions, such as what job to take, whether or not to marry or have children, what investments to make, etc. The person being simulated is scored on his/her health, happiness, wealth, and other factors.	4–12	**All Grade Levels** **I**-a. b. d.; **III**-a. j.; **IV**-c. e.; **VII**-a. b. g.; **VIII**-a.; **IX**-b. d. f.	1 download = $29 1 user/CD = $39 6 users/CDs = $199 30 users/CDs = $899 Site License = $1 per enrolled student in the school	No
3rd World Farmer *3rdworldfarmer.com* 3rd World Farmer is an online game in which players control a family of farmers, choosing what crops to plant, what livestock to raise, and how to spend money. Weather, political upheaval, and other events show the challenges of poverty faced by those in the third world and the difficulties of rising out of poverty.	3–12	**All Grade Levels** **III**-f. j.; **VII**-a. b.; **VIII**-a.; **IX**-b.	Free	No
Outbreak at Watersedge *mclph.umn.edu/watersedge* Outbreak at Watersedge is a mystery game where the player takes on the role of a public health specialist. It is foremost a game for introducing the field of public health as a potential career, but does introduce the terminology and role of public health officials, and therefore could be useful in starting discussions on the role of government.	9–12	**High School** **VI**-b. c.	Free. Also available on CD by calling 612-626-4515.	Yes, website includes a brief description of objectives and appropriate use of game; also provides a free download of Adobe Flashplayer 10 (needed to play the game).
People Power: The game of civil resistance *peoplepowergame.com* People Power is a simulation game that puts the player in the role of managing a nonviolent conflict, trying to overthrow dictators and corrupt governments using nonviolent strategies. This game is by the makers of A Force More Powerful (AFMP), a similar earlier game no longer available for purchase.	9–12	**High School** **V**-f.; **VI**-a. b. c. d. f. g. h.; **IX**-b. f.; **X**-d. e. g. h. i. j.	$10	Not currently; however, AFMP website has links to lesson plans, book, as well as additional resources that may help.
Ayiti: The Cost of Life *ayiti.newzcrew.org/ayitiunicef/* Ayiti: The Cost of Life was developed by the Global Kids initiative, which encourages urban public school students to reflect on their roles in the world and to develop leadership skills. The game asks the player to pick a strategy from the categories of health, education, happiness, and money (employment) to help manage an impoverished family in Haiti. Players must balance earning enough money for the family to survive while trying to educate them and lead them out of poverty.	4–12	**Early Grades** **IX**-d. f. **Middle Grades & High School** **IX**-d. f. g.	Free	Yes, lesson plans for using the game are available on the website.

TABLE 8.2 *(Continued)*

GAME SUMMARY	GRADE LEVELS	NCSS STANDARDS *(see pp. 197–202)*	COST *(per copy)*	CURRICULAR SUPPORT
Global Conflicts: Palestine *globalconflicts.eu* Global Conflicts: Palestine has the player taking on the role of a reporter in the Middle East. It allows the player to experience real-life stories of the conflict in the Middle East. Students are encouraged to write a news article after playing and to post it for the online community. An excellent video explaining the educational concepts behind this series is at www.youtube.com/tch?v=gRV0B5dOHME&NR=1 Global Conflicts also has the following versions available: Latin America, Child Soldiers (Uganda), Sweatshops (Bangladesh), and Peacemaker (Israeli-Palestinian conflict)	7–12	**Middle Grades & High School** II-a.b.c.e.f.; IV-e.f.g.; VI-f.h.; IX-a.b.f.	$20 Cost is higher for educational version with teaching materials.	Yes, teacher resources are on its website.
Making History *making-history.com* Making History is a World War II turn-based strategy game allowing for customizable win goals and teacher modifications of gameplay. In it, players can play against each other or the computer in setting policy, creating treaties, and planning military strategy.	9–12	**High School** II-b. c.; III-a.; VII-h.; VIII-a.; IX-b.	Single download = $39.95 Educator copy plus 5 licences = $199.95	Yes, teaching materials are available with the educational version.
Darfur Is Dying *darfurisdying.com* Darfur Is Dying is an activist game that seeks to educate people about the genocide in Darfur. Players control the members of a refugee family in Darfur, seeking to avoid rebel bandits in order to gather water for the camp. Players try to grow food, get medicine, and rebuild destroyed buildings while surviving as long as possible among the attacking rebels. The game is free to play and provides additional resources for those interested in Darfur-related activism.	3–12	**All Grade Levels** III-j.; V-g.; VII-b. g.; VIII-a.; IX-b. f.	Free	No
Freedom Force '56 *freedomfighter56.com* Freedom Force '56 (FF '56) is more like an interactive comic book than a video game. It seeks to educate players about the Hungarian Revolution of 1956, albeit with a very pro-revolutionary stance. There are mini-games available within the narrative, as players take on the roles of several revolutionaries.	7–12	**Middle Grades & High School** II-e.; IX-b.	$29.95	No, although a supporting nonfiction book with interviews of those who escaped and survived the 1956 revolution and a graphic novel, *The Hungarian Freedom Fighters of 1956*, are available.
Whyville *whyville.net* Whyville is an online, multiplayer virtual world with available mini-games focusing on art history, science, journalism, civics, and economics.	5–8	**Middle Grades** II-c.; III-a.	Free.	No

Using Political Games for Social Studies Education

Simulations of political organizations have been in use since before the creation of the United Nations (UN), and more than 400,000 students participate worldwide in the Model UN simulation each year (UNA-USA, 2004). In simulations such as Model UN, students prepare position papers, put forth resolutions, conduct debates, and adhere to established rules of procedure as they represent a country at conferences. In doing so, students take on the roles of real-life UN representatives and have the opportunity to experience firsthand how the UN operates.

A number of political video games and simulations are available that deal specifically with democratic and governmental issues. These games, a mixture of COTS games and free online games, allow players to take part in electoral and governmental simulations. Due to the number of games available on political issues, reviews of available games that are useful tools for teaching and learning in social studies classes are listed in the next section.

History Lessons: Perspectives on the Effective Use of Video Games

This section provides a brief look at two ongoing studies to provide current perspectives on the use of video games for teaching social studies. The first study communicates the perspectives of a high school teacher and his students on the use of Making History, an educational game for teaching World War II history. The second study presents the perspectives of game developers who are designing National Pastime, an educational game for teaching about the internment experience of Japanese-Americans during World War II.

Making History: Teacher and Student Perspectives on Using an Educational Game

Described in Table 8.2, Making History is an educational game developed by Muzzy Lane for teaching about World War II. In this section, I describe the perspectives of a teacher and students using Making History in a high school classroom.

The school is a small, rural high school in the Midwest. The social studies teacher has been utilizing Making History in his unit on World War II for several years. He initially agreed to be a beta-tester for the company and has continued using the game after seeing how engaged his students were when playing it.

To capture teacher and student experiences playing the game, we observed and video recorded classes before, during, and after the game was used. The teacher stated that his biggest reason for using the game was how engaged the students became. In observing the teacher in action, he seemed to be very skilled, firing questions to his students at a rapid pace rather than lecturing to them. Despite the teacher's approach, some students were clearly disengaged in the regular classroom: heads were down on desks and eyes were unfocused.

TABLE 8.3 ▶ Political games for teaching social studies

GAME SUMMARY	GRADE LEVELS	NCSS STANDARDS (see Appendix)	COST (per copy)	CURRICULAR SUPPORT
Democracy 2 *positech.co.uk/democracy2/* Democracy 2 is a political simulation, turn-based strategy game allowing players to adjust policy variables, for example, to set taxes and educational spending.	7–12	Middle Grades & High School V-e.; VI-a. b. e. f.; X-a.f.g.	$22.95	No
President Forever 2008 + Primaries *theoryspark.com/political_games/president_forever/info/* President Forever is a presidential election simulation game with data from presidential and primary elections from 1980 to 2008, with additional releases planned for the future, such as the California gubernatorial race in 2010, which will be available to download by purchasers for free. Players campaign, run ads, and set policy positions in an attempt to be elected.	7–12	Middle Grades & High School V-e.; VI-a. b. e. f.; X-a. f. g.	Single license—$19.95 Site licenses: # users/cost 5 users/$65 10 users/$120 25 users/$275 50 users/$500 100 users/$870	No
Senate Seeker *senateseeker.com* Senate Seeker is a free, weekly web-based game, requiring weekly voting as players represent political parties and seek votes, using forum discussions.	7–12	Middle Grades & High School V-e.; VI-a. b. e. f.; X-a. d. f. g. i.	Free	No
The ReDistricting Game *redistrictinggame.org* The ReDistricting Game is a political game that focuses on helping the player to understand gerrymandering, redrawing voter district maps to gain a political advantage.	7–12	Middle Grades & High School VI-b. f.; X-f.	Free	No
Particracy *classic.particracy.net* Particracy is a free, web-based game where players create political parties in a fictional nation, propose legislation, and vote on bills to garner votes and set policy.	7–12	Middle Grades & High School V-e.; VI-a. b. e. f.; X-a. d. f. g. i.	Free	No
NationStates *nationstates.net* NationStates is a web-based, somewhat cynical yet realistic political game created by Max Barry, author of the novel *Jennifer Government*. Players create a fictitious nation and answer a short questionnaire to determine the ideologies of that nation. Each day the player is asked to decide on a policy issue, and the nation evolves based on the player's responses. Players can also join international debates on the website forums.	7–12	Middle Grades & High School V-e.; VI-a. b. e. f.; X-a. d. f. g. i.	Free	No
The Oval Office The Oval Office is a political simulation where players play the President of the United States and can choose over 80 different policy changes, take polls to determine public opinion, balance the budget, and deal with special interest groups.	7–12	Middle Grades & High School V-e.; VI-a. b. e. f.; X-a. f. g.	$8.65	No

The atmosphere of the classroom when the game was being played was drastically different, with a tumult of noise as students chattered to each other about what strategies they should use in the game. After his first experiences, the teacher settled on the following method for using the game: students were divided into teams, each team controlling a country, and the team members were rotated during gameplay so that each had a turn at using the computer to control the team's actions. The different student teams played against each other, playing through the time period just before World War (WW) II broke out.

The teacher noted that he always used the module before WWII broke out with his students because it focused heavily on the treaties among the different countries and the causes for the war, which were the learning objectives he wanted the students to reach, rather than focusing solely on the warfare itself. That being said, he noted how his classes almost always went to war earlier than actually happened in history, but he felt this was an important learning opportunity for them, as students playing the role of Germany, for example, would often find themselves quickly defeated if they rushed off to war before they had developed enough resources to carry out their offenses.

"Teachable moments" was a term frequently used by the teacher in his description of teaching with the game. He noted that many teachers might feel that using the game would mean less work for them, but actually, he was required to be much more active when teaching with the game, as he circled the room, asking students questions and stopping gameplay to highlight these "teachable moments" and tie back in what was going on in the game with what actually happened.

The students universally preferred gameplay over traditional instruction. While many had reservations about stating that they would want to play video games in all subjects at school, noting that it might not be appropriate for some subjects, they were universal in enjoying the gameplay experience and felt that they better understood the World War II unit because they were more attentive to it. They noted how they discussed strategy in groups at lunch and outside of class, and none of the students found the game too difficult to play or understand.

One clear lesson from this experience was that technical challenges have to be overcome when using games in the classroom. First, as Making History was played as a multiplayer game, the classes had to move into a computer lab, which created scheduling challenges. Second, despite the fact that the teacher had taught with the game for several years, technical problems (before they were straightened out) wasted the first day of gameplay for the early classes. He noted that there always seemed to be technical problems no matter how much time and effort he and the lab manager spent in preparation.

The most visible conclusions we made from observing the use of Making History in the classroom was how active the classroom was when playing the game. Students were excited, and the teacher was racing around the room the entire class period, answering questions and posing his own, as well as stopping the entire class to point out important issues. After finishing play, the class had a debriefing session, talking about strategies the countries tried, how they differed from history, and what conclusions could be drawn. Students noted their own engagement, pointing out how some of their peers usually slept during class but were actively involved when the video game was used.

It should be noted that this study focused on capturing the experience of the teacher and students in using the game, not on evaluating their learning. That being said, the students and the teacher pointed out that the students were more likely to learn if they were engaged and attentive, which was the case when the game was used.

National Pastime: Designer Perspectives on the Creation of an Educational Game

National Pastime is an educational game being designed to teach high school students about the internment of Japanese-Americans in the United States during World War II. In this section, I offer a brief overview of the initial experience of designing National Pastime. First, I present a brief overview of the design process, followed by challenges faced during the process and lessons learned from the experience.

I completed the initial design of the game with a team of four graduate students enrolled in one of my courses. I previously developed a design process, the Games for Activating Thematic Engagement (GATE) model (Watson, 2007), which provided the guidelines for the design process. The design process began with defining learning objectives based on the topic of internment. We reviewed a great deal of the literature on the internment experience and sought to represent the experience in the game. Social studies standards were also immediately identified to ensure that they were reflected in the learning objectives.

We highlighted specific internment experiences we uncovered in the literature to inform the game's atmosphere and narrative. We also conducted interviews with several middle school and high school social studies teachers to identify challenges they faced in implementing a game in their classroom. Consistently, lack of time was the universal challenge the teachers raised. Under pressure to cover more content in less time, the teachers were consistent in their concern about not being able to devote more than a class period or two to the game.

An example was one teacher who covered the entire history of the United States in one semester. The majority of the teachers interviewed did not teach about the internment of Japanese-Americans, with one teacher spending "about five minutes" on it during his World War II unit. All stated the relevance of the game to current events but again cited the lack of time and the amount of content they were required to cover. Because of this, an important decision made in the game was to divide the games into "chapters," which would allow teachers control over how much of the narrative their students would play through, while allowing flexibility for a much longer gameplay experience for students who might play the game outside the classroom environment.

Another concern of teachers was the technological requirements the game would have. While the initial design did not focus on development, teachers' concerns were noted, and strong recommendations were recorded to develop the game using technology that would be readily available for schools, such as a web browser-based game.

Two high school students who had completed a unit on the internment were interviewed and asked (a) what they felt they had learned about the internment; (b) what, if any, relevance they saw in regard to the internment and current events or their own lives; (c) their preferences in video games; and (d) what specific aspects of video games engaged them. Neither student had retained much from the unit on the internment and could only provide the barest summary of the internment. Neither student could describe why the history of the internment was relevant to current events. The relevance of the internment history as well as history in general to the students was highlighted by the teachers interviewed as a primary goal they would have for the game. They wanted to develop an appreciation of history in their students and a realization of its relevance, and in interviewing the students, it was clear that this was currently lacking for them.

Because of these interviews, the design decision was made to create distinct bridges between the internment history and the attitudes and actions of the U.S. government following the September 11, 2001, attacks. We decided that the game would open with a game character looking at news of the terrorist attacks before flashing back to the attack on Pearl Harbor as a means to connect current events to the historical events of the internment.

The design moved forward to creating a narrative for the game, implementation guidelines for teachers to use the game in different ways and in different environments, as well as a scoring system to provide assessment and feedback within the game. Gameplay examples of successful commercial video games were discussed as models for engagement, along with the comments of the students interviewed and what aspects of certain games engaged them, such as the ability to customize their characters and have control over where they went and what they did.

We created and tested a paper prototype of a single chapter of the game to generate feedback on the initial design. Reflecting on the experience, we noted several design challenges, including the lack of gaming experience of several members of our team, who would struggle with understanding when other team members used commercial games as examples. The non-gamers on the team noted that gamers used an entirely different language in meetings, and the non-gamers initially struggled to understand due to their lack of gaming experience. These non-gamers felt much more comfortable as they played more games themselves to get a firmer grasp on the gamer vocabulary.

Other challenges faced were the issue of wanting to represent history accurately while ensuring the game was appropriate for students to play. For example, gambling was an important part of the internment experience; however, at one point, it was realized how strong a role gambling played in the game, and it was decided that this could be a problem for teachers and students' parents.

Ultimately, the game is undergoing revisions on its design based on the initial experience and the testing of the prototype. The design process calls for frequent iterations of testing and revision, and design team members commented that looking back, they would have benefited from conducting even earlier and more frequent testing. The challenges of designing an immersive gameplay experience that can promote critical thinking and problem-solving while ensuring the flexibility today's teachers need to be able to incorporate games into packed curricula and hectic schedules were strong lessons learned.

Lessons Learned

In this final section before the conclusion, I discuss lessons learned from reviewing the available games for teaching social studies and conducting two studies to capture the experience of designing and using video games to teach social studies. I begin with guidelines for choosing an appropriate game, followed by guidelines for implementing a game effectively, and conclude with guidelines for tying games to standards.

Guidelines for Choosing an Appropriate Game

In reviewing games for this chapter, a number of guidelines arose for choosing appropriate games, whether they are educational games or COTS games. The following guidelines are important to consider before choosing a game for educational use.

Be familiar with the game. While the teacher in the Making History study had never had any parents or students complain about his use of the game in the classroom, when he first started using the game, he actually thought it might happen. A teacher does not want to be unaware of any questionable content that might be in a game that parents or students might find objectionable. Furthermore, the teacher found the lack of any realistic violence an important factor in using Making History. While waging war is represented in the game, it is done in an abstract manner, which was important for him. While he found each year that his students were all able to understand and play the game with relative ease, it was important for him to know how to play the game because he needed to assess what he could expect from gameplay to identify opportunities for "teachable moments" and to best plan for how to use the game.

Identify learning objectives. It is important to know what learning is desired from the game. In the Making History study, having a game that depicted the outbreak of the war was extremely important to the teacher, as it matched his learning objectives for his larger curriculum. If the game only depicted the war itself, it would be much less useful in meeting his desired learning objectives. Furthermore, he had found that his students seemed to have a better grasp of world geography after playing the game, a learning outcome he had not expected. It is important to know what learning is desired from a game and then to determine whether a particular game can help meet those learning objectives or not.

Consider cost, time, and technical requirements. It is very important to consider how much a game will cost, how much time is required to play it, and whether or not available computers can support the game. Issues, such as how often a game allows players to save or how much minimum time the game requires to be meaningfully played, are important to understand to determine whether a game is appropriate for the specific learning environment. Furthermore, technical challenges will likely arise, and it is important to assess what available support exists to overcome such challenges.

Consider how the game will be used. Some limitations, such as time, can be creatively overcome by having students play games outside the classroom at home or in school labs. However, also consider whether students will play on teams or if it is also important for the game to provide single-player experiences. Plan how the game will be implemented, and create lesson plans beforehand to guide its use. Remember that not all aspects of a game have to be used for it to be effective.

Consider what standards the game can be tied to. It can be important to identify appropriate standards to link with the game. It is possible that some could see the use of video games for education as frivolous, and it is important in the current climate to tie the game to standards to identify its learning goals and how it fits into a district's existing curriculum.

Guidelines for Implementing a Game Effectively

Plan ahead. It is important to create a plan for how the game will be used. Research suggests the need to support gameplay with sound instructional strategies for learning to be effective (Leemkuil, de Jong, de Hoog, & Christopher, 2003; O'Neil, Wainess, & Baker, 2005; Wolfe, 1997), so it is important to have a plan for debriefing and connecting the gameplay experience to broader lessons. Also, technology is challenging, and it is important to be prepared to address these challenges as they arise.

Promote active learning. Games are being promoted for learning because of how they engage and require action on the part of the learners. However, it is important that the game is not the only place where learners are required to think and act. Try to create an environment in the curricular activities surrounding the game that also requires action and engagement on the part of the learners. Look at what games do well to engage: choice, interactivity, self-expression, problem solving, feedback, and trial and error. Structure an environment for assignments tied to the game or surrounding debriefing and learning from the game that includes similar features. Do not tell students what they learned but require them to demonstrate what they have learned by problem solving and being creative.

Plan for student interaction and reflection. Video games can be frenetic in their pacing; thus, it is important that students have the opportunity to reflect on their choices and game outcomes. Consider having students work in pairs or groups when playing a game. Plan for how the debriefing of the gameplay experience will be facilitated and supported.

Assess the game and its implementation. Much can be learned by evaluating the implementation of a game. Assess what the students learned from the game and how the implementation of the game worked or could be improved. Commit to improving the students' experience with the game by evaluating its implementation after each use.

Guidelines for Tying Games to National and State Standards

Consider not just the game but how it will be used. Identifying standards a game may meet can be a challenge because learning may not be effective in a game without additional sound instructional strategies supporting the gameplay experience. By only focusing on what objectives are clearly embedded in the game, the opportunity for teaching additional standards through activities surrounding the game may be lost. As mentioned in the guidelines for choosing a game, become familiar with the game, identify appropriate learning objectives for it, plan how the game will be used, and combine these to identify appropriate standards to be met by gameplay.

Identify "teachable moments" where learning may occur. A point really stressed by the teacher in the Making History study was how student errors, inaccurate conceptual understanding, and disconnects with actual history were actually prime opportunities for learning to occur. Plan for and be alert for "teachable moments" that arise during gameplay to hit on the target standards.

Establish or join a professional learning community. Some games have established online communities for educators using the game, and some games offer their own communities to support educators. Consider joining or establishing a community to share strategies for game use, identifying appropriate standards, and meeting them. Collaborate with fellow educators and practitioners.

Conclusion

Citizenship education, often a fundamental aspect of public education, is gaining recognition for its importance. With low voter turnout, an increasingly pluralistic society, and citizens who are passive in allowing their government to make choices for them, it is vital that today's students not only learn about the rights and responsibilities of being citizens, but also become engaged and encouraged to be active citizens.

Digital video games are being increasingly highlighted for their power to engage. With COTS and educational games available, many of them for free, the time is now for citizenship educators to utilize video games to educate and engage their students.

While video games hold great potential for citizenship education, it is important that citizenship teachers reflect on how best to utilize the games in their classrooms. My own experience in school, playing *Oregon Trail* in the 1980s, involved being asked to play the game during a class period and nothing else. With no discussion or reflection on the gameplay experience, little else was gained from the experience other than the knowledge that people died of dysentery and the experience that digital deer and rabbits are fun to shoot. The games should be used to foster discussion and debates, allowing students to solve problems actively and reflect on their experiences and what lessons can be learned.

Just as citizenship teachers are asking their students to learn to be active citizens and to reflect on their roles in society and responsibility to be informed, it is important that the teachers themselves are active and reflective in their incorporation of video games into the existing curriculum. Students should not only be asked to play the games, but also to reflect on their gameplay experiences, discuss what meanings can be drawn from those experiences, and actively participate in their own learning.

Video games offer great potential for engaging learners. In this chapter, I have noted and discussed a wide variety of video games available for citizenship education. The next steps are for teachers to implement the games, share their experiences with others, and create communities to support and improve the application of games for citizenship education.

References

Aldrich, C. (2004). *Simulations and the future of learning: An innovative (and perhaps revolutionary) approach to e-learning.* San Francisco, CA: Pfeiffer.

Banks, J. A. (2001). Citizenship education and diversity: Implications for teacher education. *Journal of Teacher Education, 52*(1), 5–16.

Beck, J. C., & Wade, M. (2004). *Got game: How the gamer generation is reshaping business forever.* Boston, MA: Harvard Business School Press.

Dickey, M. D. (2005). Engaging by design: How engagement strategies in popular computer and video games can inform instructional design. *ETR&D, 53*(2), 67–83.

Egenfeldt-Nielsen, S. (2005). Beyond edutainment: Exploring the educational potential of computer games. Unpublished dissertation, IT University of Copenhagen, Copenhagen, Denmark. Retrieved February 21, 2006, from http://web.archive.org/web/*/www.itu.dk/people/sen/egenfeldt.pdf

Evans, R. W. (2004). *The social studies wars: What should we teach the children?* New York, NY: Teachers College Press.

Evans, R. W., & Passe, J. (2007). Dare we make peace: A dialogue on the social studies wars. *The Social Studies, 98*(6), 251–256.

Federation of American Scientists. (2006). Summit on educational games: Harnessing the power of video games for learning. Washington, DC: Federation of American Scientists. Retrieved June 24, 2007, from www.fas.org/gamesummit/Resources/Summit%20on%20Educational%20Games.pdf

Fletcher, J. D., & Tobias, S. (2006, February). *Using computer games and simulations for instruction: A research review.* Paper presented at the Society for Applied Learning Technology Meeting, New Learning Technologies, Orlando, FL. A CD of the proceedings may be ordered from www.salt.org

Foreman, J., Gee, J. P., Herz, J. C., Hinrichs, R., Prensky, M., & Sawyer, B. (2004). Game-based learning: How to delight and instruct in the 21st century. *EDUCAUSE Review, 39*(5), 50–66.

Galston, W. A. (2007). Civic knowledge, civic education, and civic engagement: A summary of recent research. *International Journal of Public Administration, 30*(6), 623–642.

Jones, B., Valdez, G., Norakowski, J., & Rasmussen, C. (1994). Designing learning and technology for educational reform. *North Central Regional Educational Laboratory.* [Online]. Available: www.ncrtec .org/capacity/profile/profwww.htm

Kerr, D. (1999). Changing the political culture: The advisory group on education for citizenship and the teaching of democracy in schools. *Oxford Review of Education, 25*(1 & 2), 275–284.

Leemkuil, H., de Jong, T., de Hoog, R., & Christopher, N. (2003). KM Quest: A collaborative Internet-based simulation game. *Simulation & Gaming, 34,* 89–111.

National Council for the Social Studies (NCSS) Task Force. (1994). *Expectations of excellence: Curriculum standards for social studies.* Washington, DC: National Council for the Social Studies.

NPD Group. (2004). The NPD Group reports annual 2003 U.S. video game industry driven by console software sales, January 26. Available at www.npd.com/press/relcascs/press_040126a.htm

NPD Group. (2008). 2007 U.S. video game and PC game sales exceed $18.8 billion marking third consecutive year of record-breaking sales, January 31. Retrieved April 25, 2008, from www.npd.com/press/releases/press_080131b.html

O'Neil, H. F., Wainess, R., & Baker, E. L. (2005). Classification of learning outcomes: Evidence from the computer games literature. *The Curriculum Journal, 16*(4), 455–474.

Parker, W. C. (1996). "Advanced" ideas about democracy: Toward a pluralistic conception of citizen education. *Teachers College Record, 98*(1), 104–125.

Prensky, M. (2001). *Digital game-based learning.* New York, NY: McGraw-Hill.

Prensky, M. (2005). *Don't bother me Mom—I'm learning!* St. Paul, MN: Paragon House.

Quinn, C. N. (2005). *Engaging learning: Designing e-learning simulation games.* San Francisco, CA: Pfeiffer.

Salen, K., & Zimmerman, E. (2004). *Rules of play: Game design fundamentals.* Cambridge, MA: MIT Press.

Schlechty, P. C. (1997). Inventing better schools: An action plan for educational reform. San Francisco, CA: Jossey-Bass.

Selwyn, N. (2007). *Citizenship, technology and learning—A review of recent literature.* London, UK: Futurelab.

Squire, K. D. (2004). Replaying history: Learning world history through playing Civilization III. Unpublished doctoral dissertation, Indiana University, Bloomington, IN. Retrieved April 1, 2006, from http://website.education.wisc.edu/kdsquire/dissertation.html

Theatrical Market Statistics: 2009. (2009). Motion Picture Association of America. Retrieved July 16, 2010, from www.mpaa.org/Resources/091af5d6-faf7-4f58-9a8e-405466c1c5e5.pdf

Torney-Purta, J., & Vermeer, S. (2004). *Developing citizenship competencies from kindergarten through grade 12: A background paper for policy makers and educators,* April (5135.pdf). Denver, CO: National Center for Learning and Citizenship, Education Commission of the States. Available at www.ecs.org/html/ProjectsPartners/nclc/NCLC_Publications.asp

United Nations Association of the United States of America (UNA-USA). (2004). *Model UN frequently asked questions and answers.* Retrieved October 21, 2008, from www.unausa.org/modelunfaq

Vogler, K. E., & Virtue, D. C. (2007). "Just the facts, ma'am": Teaching social studies in the era of standards and high-stakes testing. *The Social Studies, 98*(2), 54–58.

Watson, W. R. (2007). *Formative research on an instructional design theory for educational video games.* Unpublished dissertation, Department of Instructional Systems Technology, Indiana University, Bloomington, IN. Available at www.indiana.edu/.../formative_resrch_isd-theory_edvideogames.pdf

Wolfe, J. (1997). The effectiveness of business games in strategic management course work. *Simulation & Gaming, 28,* 360–376.

NCSS Curriculum Standards for Social Studies

(This is an abridged list of the standards. Please see www.socialstudies.org to obtain a complete list of standards.)

I. Culture

Social studies programs should include experiences that provide for the study of culture and cultural diversity, so that the learner can:

Early Grades

a. explore and describe similarities and differences in the ways groups, societies, and cultures address similar human needs and concerns;

b. give examples of how experiences may be interpreted differently by people from diverse cultural perspectives and frames of reference;

c. describe ways in which language, stories, folktales, music, and artistic creations serve as expressions of culture and influence behavior of people living in a particular culture;

d. compare ways in which people from different cultures think about and deal with their physical environment and social conditions;

e. give examples and describe the importance of cultural unity and diversity within and across groups.

Middle Grades

a. Compare similarities and differences in the ways groups, societies, and cultures meet human needs and concerns;

b. Explain how information and experiences may be interpreted by people from diverse cultural perspectives and frames of reference;

c. Explain and give examples of how language, literature, the arts, architecture, other artifacts, traditions, beliefs, values, and behaviors contribute to the development and transmission of culture;

d. Explain why individuals and groups respond differently to their physical and social environments and/or changes to them on the basis of shared assumptions, values, and beliefs;

e. Articulate the implications of cultural diversity, as well as cohesion, within and across groups.

High School

a. Analyze and explain the ways groups, societies, and cultures address human needs and concerns;

b. Predict how data and experiences may be interpreted by people from diverse cultural perspectives and frames of reference;

d. Compare and analyze societal patterns for preserving and transmitting culture while adapting to environmental or social change;

g. construct reasoned judgments about specific cultural responses to persistent human issues;

h. explain and apply ideas, theories, and modes of inquiry drawn from anthropology and sociology in the examination of persistent issues and social problems.

II. Time, Continuity, & Change

Social studies programs should include experiences that provide for the study of the ways human beings view themselves in and over time, so that the learner can:

Early Grades

a. demonstrate an understanding that different people may describe the same event or situation in diverse ways, citing reasons for the differences in views;

b.   demonstrate an ability to use correctly vocabulary associated with time such as past, present, future, and long ago; read and construct simple timelines; identify examples of change; and recognize examples of cause and effect relationships.

Middle Grades

a.   Demonstrate an understanding that different scholars may describe the same event or situation in different ways but must provide reasons or evidence for their views;

b.   Identify and use key concepts such as chronology, causality, change, conflict, and complexity to explain, analyze, and show connections among patterns of historical change and continuity;

c.   Identify and describe selected historical periods and patterns of change within and across cultures, such as the rise of civilizations, the development of transportation systems, the growth and breakdown of colonial systems, and others;

e.   Develop critical sensitivities such as empathy and skepticism regarding attitudes, values, and behaviors of people in different historical contexts;

f.   Use knowledge of facts and concepts drawn from history, along with methods of historical inquiry, to inform decision-making about and action-taking on public issues.

High School

a.   Demonstrate that historical knowledge and the concept of time are socially influenced constructions that lead historians to be selective in the questions they seek to answer and the evidence they use;

b.   Apply key concepts such as time, chronology, causality, change, conflict, and complexity to explain, analyze, and show connections among patterns of historical change and continuity;

c.   Identify and describe significant historical periods and patterns of change within and across cultures, such as the development of ancient cultures and civilizations, the rise of nation-states, and social, economic, and political revolutions;

e.   Investigate, interpret, and analyze multiple historical and contemporary viewpoints within and across cultures related to important events, recurring dilemmas, and persistent issues, while employing empathy, skepticism, and critical judgement;

f.   Apply ideas, theories, and modes of historical inquiry to analyze historical and contemporary developments, and to inform and evaluate actions concerning public policy issues.

III.   People, Places, & Environments

Social studies programs should include experiences that provide for the study of people, places, and environments, so that the learner can:

Early Grades

a.   construct and use mental maps of locales, regions, and the world that demonstrate understanding of relative location, direction, size, and shape;

f.   describe and speculate about physical system changes, such as seasons, climate and weather, and the water cycle;

j.   observe and speculate about social and economic effects of environmental changes and crises resulting from phenomena such as floods, storms, and drought;

k.   consider existing uses and propose and evaluate alternative uses of resources and land in home, school, community, the region, and beyond.

Middle Grades

a.   Elaborate mental maps of locales, regions, and the world that demonstrate understanding of relative location, direction, size, and shape;

    e.   Locate and describe varying landforms and geographic features, such as mountains, plateaus, islands, rain forests, deserts, and oceans, and explain their relationships within the ecosystem;

    f.   describe physical system changes such as seasons, climate and weather, and the water cycle and identify geographic patterns associated with them;

    h.   examine, interpret, and analyze physical and cultural patterns and their interactions, such as land use, settlement patterns, cultural transmission of customs and ideas, and ecosystem changes;

    j.   observe and speculate about social and economic effects of environmental changes and crises resulting from phenomena such as floods, storms, and drought;

    k.   propose, compare, and evaluate alternative uses of land and resources in communities, regions, nations, and the world.

High School

    a.   Refine mental maps of locales, regions, and the world that demonstrate understanding of relative location, direction, size, and shape;

    e.   describe, differentiate, and explain the relationships among various regional and global patterns of geographic phenomena such as landforms, soils, climate, vegetations, natural resources, and population;

    f.   use knowledge of physical system changes such as seasons, climate and weather, and the water cycle to explain geographic phenomena;

    h.   examine, interpret, and analyze physical and cultural patterns and their interactions, such as land use, settlement patterns, cultural transmission of customs and ideas, and ecosystem changes;

    j.   analyze and evaluate social and economic effects of environmental changes and crises resulting from phenomena such as floods, storms, and drought.

IV. Individual Development & Identity

Social studies programs should include experiences that provide for the study of individual development and identity, so that the learner can:

Early Grades

    c.   describe the unique features of one's nuclear and extended families;

    e.   identify and describe ways family, groups, and community influence the individual's daily life and personal choices;

    h.   work independently and cooperatively to accomplish goals.

Middle Grades

    c.   describe the ways family, gender, ethnicity, nationality, and institutional affiliations contribute to personal identity;

    e.   identify and describe ways regional, ethnic, and national cultures influence individuals' daily lives;

    f.   identify and describe the influence of perception, attitudes, values, and beliefs on personal identity;

    g.   identify and interpret examples of stereotyping, conformity, and altruism;

    h.   work independently and cooperatively to accomplish goals.

High School

    c.   describe the ways family, religion, gender, ethnicity, nationality, socioeconomic status, and other group and cultural influences contribute to the development of a sense of self;

    e.   examine the interactions of ethnic, national, or cultural influences in specific situations or events;

    f.   analyze the role of perceptions, attitudes, values, and beliefs in the development of personal identity;

g. compare and evaluate the impact of stereotyping, conformity, acts of altruism, and other behaviors on individuals and groups;

h. work independently and cooperatively within groups and institutions to accomplish goals.

V. Individuals, Groups, & Institutions

Social studies programs should Include experiences that provide for the study of interactions among individuals, groups, and institutions, so that the learner can:

Early Grades

g. show how groups and institutions work to meet individual needs and promote the common good, and identify examples of where they fail to do so.

Middle Grades

e. identify and describe examples of tensions between belief systems and government policies and laws;

g. apply knowledge of how groups and institutions work to meet individual needs and promote the common good.

High School

e. describe and examine belief systems basic to specific traditions and laws in contemporary and historical movements;

f. evaluate the role of institutions in furthering both continuity and change.

VI. Power, Authority, & Governance

Social studies programs should include experiences that provide for the study of how people create and change structures of power, authority, and governance, so that the learner can:

Early Grades

b. explain the purpose of government;

c. give examples of how government does or does not provide for the needs and wants of people, establish order and security, and manage conflict.

Middle Grades

a. Examine persistent issues involving the rights, roles, and status of the individual in relation to the general welfare;

b. Describe the purpose of government and how its powers are acquired, used, and justified;

c. Analyze and explain ideas and governmental mechanisms to meet needs and wants of citizens, regulate territory, manage conflict, and establish order and security;

d. Describe the ways nations and organizations respond to forces of unity and diversity affecting order and security;

e. Identify and describe the basic features of the political system in the United States, and identify representative leaders from various levels and branches of government;

f. Explain conditions, actions, and motivations that contribute to conflict and cooperation within and among nations;

g. Describe and analyze the role of technology in communications, transportation, information-processing, weapons development, or other areas as it contributes to or helps resolve conflicts;

h. Explain and apply concepts such as power, role, status, justice, and influence to the examination of persistent issues and social problems.

High School

a. Examine persistent issues involving the rights, roles, and status of the individual in relation to the general welfare;

b. Explain the purpose of government and analyze how its powers are acquired, used, and justified;

c. Analyze and explain ideas and mechanisms to meet needs and wants of citizens, regulate territory, manage conflict, establish order and security, and balance competing conceptions of a just society;

d. Compare and analyze the ways nations and organizations respond to conflicts between forces of unity and forces of diversity;

e. Compare different political systems (their ideologies, structure, institutions, processes, and political cultures) with that of the United States, and identify representative political leaders from selected historical and contemporary settings;

f. Analyze and evaluate conditions, actions, and motivations that contribute to conflict and cooperation within and among nations;

g. Evaluate the role of technology in communications, transportation, information-processing, weapons development, or other areas as it contributes to or helps resolve conflicts;

h. Explain and apply ideas, theories, and modes of inquiry drawn from political science to the examination of persistent issues and social problems.

VII. Production, Distribution, & Consumption

Social studies programs should include experiences that provide for the study of how people organize for the production, distribution, and consumption of goods and services, so that the learner can:

Early Grades

a. give examples that show how scarcity and choice govern our economic decisions;

b. distinguish between needs and wants;

g. explain and demonstrate the role of money in everyday life;

h. describe the relationship of price to supply and demand.

Middle Grades

a. Give and explain examples of ways that economic systems structure choices about how goods and services are to be produced and distributed;

b. Describe the role that supply and demand, prices, incentives, and profits play in determining what is produced and distributed in a competitive market system;

c. Explain the difference between private and public goods and services;

d. Describe a range of examples of the various institutions that make up economic systems such as households, business firms, banks, government agencies, labor unions, and corporations;

g. Differentiate among various forms of exchange and money;

h. Compare basic economic systems according to who determines what is produced, distributed, and consumed.

High School

a. Explain how the scarcity of productive resources (human, capital, technological, and natural) requires the development of economic systems to make decisions about how goods and services are to be produced and distributed;

b. Analyze the role that supply and demand, prices, incentives, and profits play in determining what is produced and distributed in a competitive market system;

    c.   Consider the costs and benefits to society of allocating goods and services through private and public sectors;

    d.   Describe relationships among the various economic institutions that comprise economic systems such as households, business firms, banks, government agencies, labor unions, and corporations;

    g.   Compare basic economic systems according to how rules and procedures deal with demand, supply, prices, the role of government, banks, labor and labor unions, savings and investments, and capital;

    h.   Apply economic concepts and reasoning when evaluating historical and contemporary social developments and issues.

VIII. Science, Technology, & Society

Social studies programs should include experiences that provide for the study of relationships among science, technology, and society, so that the learner can:

Early Grades

    a.   identify and describe examples in which science and technology have changed the lives of people, such as in homemaking, childcare, work, transportation, and communication;

    e.   suggest ways to monitor science and technology in order to protect the physical environmental, individual rights, and the common good.

Middle Grades

    a.   Examine and describe the influence of culture on scientific and technological choices and advancement, such as in transportation, medicine, and warfare;

    e.   Seek reasonable and ethical solutions to problems that arise when scientific advancements and social norms or values come into conflict.

High School:

    a.   Identify and describe both current and historical examples of the interaction and interdependence of science, technology, and society in a variety of cultural settings.

IX. Global Connections

Social studies programs should include experiences that provide for the study of global connections and independence, so that the learner can:

Early Grades

    b.   give examples of conflict, cooperation, and interdependence among individuals, groups, and nations;

    d.   explore causes, consequences, and possible solutions to persistent, contemporary, and emerging global issues, such as pollution and endangered species;

    f.   investigate concerns, issues, standards, and conflicts related to universal human rights, such as the treatment of children, religious groups, and effects of war.

Middle Grades

    a.   Describe instances in which language, art, music, belief systems, and other cultural elements can facilitate global understanding or cause misunderstanding;

    b.   Analyze examples of conflict, cooperation, and interdependence among groups, societies, and nations;

    d.   Explore the causes, consequences, and possible solutions to persistent, contemporary, and emerging global issues, such as health, security, resource allocation, economic development, and environmental quality;

    f.   Demonstrate understanding of concerns, standards, issues, and conflicts related to universal human rights;

    g.   Identify and describe the roles of international and multinational organizations.

High School

a. Explain how language, art, music, belief systems, and other cultural elements can facilitate global understanding or cause misunderstanding;

b. Explain conditions and motivations that contribute to conflict, cooperation, and interdependence among groups, societies, and nations;

d. Analyze the causes, consequences, and possible solutions to persistent, contemporary, and emerging global issues, such as health, security, resources allocation, economic development, and environmental quality;

f. Analyze or formulate policy statements demonstrating an understanding of concerns, standards, issues, and conflicts related to universal human rights;

g. Describe and evaluate the role of international and multinational organizations in the global arena.

X. Civic Ideals & Practices

Social studies programs should include experiences that provide for the study of the ideals, principles, and practices of citizenship in a democratic republic, so that the learner can:

Middle Grades

a. Examine the origins and continuing influence of key ideals of the democratic republican form of government, such as individual human dignity, liberty, justice, equality, and the rule of law;

d. Practice forms of civic discussion and participation consistent with the ideals of citizens in a democratic republic;

f. Identify and explain the roles of formal and informal political actors in influencing and shaping public policy and decision-making;

g. Analyze the influence of diverse forms of public opinion on the development of public policy and decision-making;

i. Explain the relationship between policy statements and action plans used to address issues of public concern.

High School

a. Explain the origins and interpret the continuing influence of key ideals of the democratic republican form of government, such as individual human dignity, liberty, justice, equality, and the rule of law;

d. Practice forms of civic discussion and participation consistent with the ideals of citizens in a democratic republic;

e. Analyze and evaluate the influence of various forms of citizen action on public policy;

f. Analyze a variety of public policies and issues from the perspective of formal and informal political actors;

g. Evaluate the effectiveness of public opinion in influencing and shaping public policy development and decision-making;

h. Evaluate the degree to which public policies and citizen behaviors reflect or foster the stated ideals of a democratic republican form of government;

i. Construct a policy statement and an action plan to achieve one or more goals related to an issue of public concern;

j. Participate in activities to strengthen the "common good," based upon careful evaluation of possible options for citizen action.

9

Exergames for Health and Fitness

Joe W. Burden Jr.

TO FACILITATE DECLINING STUDENT ATTITUDES and motivation toward physical activity, it is important for physical educators and physical activity practitioners to be cognizant of cutting-edge technologies related to human movement—exergames. Exergames, video games that incorporate interactive exercise, have emerged as one of the most popular forms of entertainment today. Research indicates that exergames are effective in increasing individuals' health and fitness in a number of clinical settings (American Council on Exercise, 2008; Lanningham, Foster, McGrady, et al., 2009). Several national organizations and associations have endorsed exergames as an effective form of moderate to vigorous exercise and physical activity (American Council on Exercise & Anders, 2007; ACE, 2008; American College of Sports Medicine, 2009; International Sports Sciences Association, 2007; National Association for Sport and Physical Education, 2009). This chapter addresses the appropriateness of exergames for inclusion in K–12 physical education settings, provides pedagogical strategies for implementing exergames, identifies a variety of research findings related to exergames, discusses limitations of using exergames, and aligns exergames to national standards for physical education.

Achievement toward 2010 national health objectives for physical education appears stagnant. The Centers for Disease Control and Prevention (CDC, 2004) reported that in 2003, just over half of all high school students (55.7%) were enrolled in a physical education class, less than half (39.2%) were physically active during physical education classes, and only 28.4% were attending a physical education class on a daily basis. The CDC also found that the overall percentage of K–12 students physically involved in daily physical education classes decreased from 42% in 1991 to 28% in 2003. According to a CDC research report published two years later, *The School Health Policies and Programs Study* (CDC, 2006), little to no improvement in the percentage of students participating in physical education had been made. In fact, throughout the United States, only 4% of elementary schools, 8% of middle schools, and 2% of high schools provided daily physical education for all grades for the entire school year, and 22% of K–12 schools did not require students to take any physical education. The National Association for Sport and Physical Education (NASPE, 2007) found a similar pattern of less emphasis on physical education in public schools.

Since its inception in 1987, NASPE has published a *Shape of the Nation Report* that reveals the current status of each state's physical education programs every five years, including time requirements, exemptions/waivers and substitution, standards, class size, curriculum and pedagogical structure, student evaluations, physical education teacher certification, state support of National Board Certification in physical education, state physical education coordinator, and body mass index collection (NASPE & AHA, 2006). In 2006, NASPE along with the American Heart Association (AHA) found that most U.S. K–12 schools failed to provide their students with sufficient physical education (NASPE & AHA, 2006; Trickey, 2006). More specifically, the *Shape of the Nation Report* indicated that no U.S. K–12 schools require students to undergo a physical education assessment to fulfill graduation requirements, about 70% of K–12 schools mandate physical education for elementary and middle school students, and nearly one-fourth of K–12 schools permit physical education requirements to be obtained via online courses (NASPE & AHA, 2006).

Like many health and physical education practitioners and professionals, the researchers who compiled the data for the *Shape of the Nation Report* also came to the conclusion that the passing of the No Child Left Behind Act (NCLB, 2001) stagnated the development of students' personal health and physical fitness by de-emphasizing health education and physical education as a core academic subject, focusing more time in curricula on what the NCLB Act identifies as core academic subjects, such as English, reading and language arts, mathematics, science, foreign languages, civics and government, economics, arts, history, and geography (NASPE & AHA, 2006; Trickey, 2006).

Proposing the FIT Kids Act

As a result of the repudiation of physical education initiatives in the NCLB Act of 2001, health, fitness, sport, physical activity, and physical education practitioners and professionals, as well as related professional associations and organizations, have endorsed the Fitness Integrated with Teaching (FIT) Kids Act (AHA, 2009; AHA, 2010; NASPE, 2007). Introduced in the House of Representatives by Ron Kind (D-WI), Zach Wamp (R-TN), and Jay Inslee (D-WA) and in the

Senate by Senator Tom Harkin (D-IA), the FIT Kids Act proposes to amend the NCLB Act so that physical education is part of the standard curricula along with education on staying healthy through diet and exercise by (a) holding K–12 schools accountable for providing adequate physical activity/class time as nationally recommended by NASPE and AHA (2006), (b) appropriately assessing physical education curricula and adding quality to the reporting of these assessments, (c) facilitating professional development opportunities for any educators who administer physical activity in K–12 settings, and (d) providing funding for research that counters the rise of childhood obesity through health and physical activity (NASPE, 2009, p. 1).

The repudiation of physical education and physical activity in national curricular reforms also alarmed several professional athletes who claim physical education is instrumental in the personal development of today's youth. In fact, in March 2009, seven National Football League players marched to Capitol Hill in support of the passage of the FIT Kids Act (*USA Today*, 2009). Though the act has yet to pass through Congress, proactive efforts of this nature can help ensure that K–12 students engage in meaningful physical education and physical activity, with the hope that these experiences will encourage lifelong engagement in healthy lifestyles and behaviors.

Implications of Technology for Physical Activity and Health

A growing body of literature suggests that modern technology has stagnated human movement and is a contributing factor to childhood declines in physical activity and rises in obesity (e.g., Papastergiou, 2009; Stattler, Signer, & Suter, 2004). As Hansen and Witherspoon (2007) assert:

> Technological changes in society have proven to be an enjoyable and satisfying lifestyle upgrade to which our youth have become accustomed. Televisions, computers, iPods, and video games have taken over the lives of many youth, leaving little room for finding fun in fitness. (p. 24)

Scholars argue that stationary video gaming and television watching are part of a sedentary lifestyle that contributes to obesity and physical inactivity (Hansen & Witherspoon, 2007; Stattler, Signer, & Suter, 2004). For example, a study by Cessna, Raudenbush, Reed, and Hunker (2007) found that playing video games distracts children from paying attention to how much food they eat; the study concluded that video game playing could lead to underestimating food consumption. Stattler, Signer, and Suter (2004) reported that video game usage nearly doubles the risk for obesity by each hour per day the games are played. Similarly, an abundance of literature points to the correlation of television watching and obesity. In 2006, a study published in the *International Journal of Obesity* (Hancox & Poulton, 2006) indicates that time spent watching television is a strong predictor of childhood body mass index and obesity in children. Research also reveals that reducing television watching and stationary video game playing to two hours per day could lead to reductions in childhood obesity (Elsevier Health Sciences, 2008).

Childhood Obesity: On the Rise

How can the decline of quality physical education and physical activity in K–12 schools be correlated with the current rise in childhood obesity? First, several health and fitness organizations and professionals have associated the rising obesity epidemic to decreasing levels of physical activity experienced by American youth in K–12 schools (Bassett, 2008; CDC, 2006b; Levi, Vinter, Richardson, St. Laurent, & Segal, 2009). Second, statistics tell us that since 1980, childhood obesity rates in the United States have more than tripled (Bassett, 2008; CDC, 2007; Levi, Vinter, Richardson, St. Laurent, & Segal, 2009). According to a report sponsored by the Trust for America's Health and funded by a grant from the Robert Wood Johnson Foundation, *F as in Fat: How Obesity Policies Are Failing in America 2009*, 30% of children are obese in 30 U.S. states (Levi, Vinter, Richardson, St. Laurent, & Segal, 2009). Third, this report advocates a National Strategy to Combat Obesity, which includes collaboration among state, federal, and local governments to provide healthy drinks and foods to students at schools, accessibility of healthy foods in communities, and increasing the frequency, intensity, and duration of physical activity for students in schools. Declines in quality physical education programming within U.S. K–12 schools may limit children and adolescents' opportunities to become educated about and engaged in physical activity and physical fitness, which, in turn, may result in limiting students' knowledge about living healthy and fit lifestyles. This trend could lead to ill-prepared students who make unhealthy nutrition choices and lack regular engagement in physical fitness activities because they were never encouraged to value healthy nutrition and fitness. These factors are likely to contribute to rises in childhood obesity.

Declining Behaviors, Attitudes, and Motivation toward Physical Activity

Declines in physical activity among youth start in late elementary school and continue throughout high school and young adulthood (USDHHS, 2008; Ward, Saunders, Felton, Williams, Epping, & Pate, 2006). In fact, research indicates that the sharpest declines in physical activity occur between the ages of 13–18 (Sallis, 2000). A longitudinal study that monitored 1,032 children from the year 2000, when all of them were 9 years old, to 2006, when they were 15, found that this group's moderate to vigorous physical activity declined significantly between the ages of 9 and 15 (Nader, Bradley, Houts, McRitchie, & O'Brien, 2008).

Similar drastic declines in physical activity were highlighted in the 2005 Youth Risk Behavior Surveillance survey, which indicated that 64.2% of the high school students surveyed neither met the current recommended levels of physical activity nor engaged in physical activities that increased their cardiorespiratory rates for at least 60 minutes a day for five or more of the seven days preceding the survey (CDC, 2006b). A study conducted several years before the YRBSS monitored physical activity in 10-year-old to 16-year-old students by utilizing motion detectors rather than traditional, self-reported measures and also found that these children and adolescents only spent an average of 12.6 minutes per day engaged in vigorous physical activity, compared with the recommended 30 minutes a day (Strauss, Rodzilsky, Burack, & Colin, 2001).

Another research study concluded that declines in physical activity often result because students are not extrinsically motivated to participate in physical education classes (Ntoumanis, Pensgaard, Martin, & Pipe, 2004). Researchers Subramaniam and Silverman (2007) noted that students' affective attitudes toward physical education decline with age and grade. In fact, their study suggests that students' declining positive affective attitudes toward physical education more than likely result from repetitive physical education curricular structures and activities, which can lead to boredom and disengagement from most physical activity. For example, the CDC (2006a) reported that the percentage of K–12 schools where students failed physical education and needed to retake the subject increased between 2000 and 2006. A study by Ntoumanis (2005) revealed that students who opted out of taking physical education classes often reported less positive motivational experiences in those classes compared to those of the previous school year. Ntoumanis called for educators to promote students' self-determined motivation toward physical education by offering stimulating, positive experiences that enhance the physical activities taught in classes.

Lack of Technologically Prepared Physical Educators

Under Title II, part D, Enhancing Education through Technology, of the NCLB Act (2001), physical education was neglected as a core subject. This leads us to question how well prepared K–12 physical educators are to engage students in physical activities through the use of technology. In an era when some government-based educational initiatives and K–12 curricula de-emphasize the importance of physical activity, do not provide adequate resources for physical education, and do not require accountability for ensuring students' physical fitness and health development in public schools, technology is seen as a tool that could have significant positive impacts on children's health and fitness.

According to a qualitative study by Russell (2007), K–12 physical educators lacked hands-on experience and knowledge related to nine specific exergames, and when asked about using exergames in their classes, the teachers rated the games with low perceived value. Exergames can be defined as electronic games infused with exercise that create an interactive form of physical activity (Lieberman, 2006). Papastergiou (2009) asserts that despite the recent influx and popularity of exergames for recreation at home, to implement exergames in K–12 settings effectively it is important that physical educators be trained in how to operate them and how to teach their students to use them prior to introducing the games into classes. Becker (2007) says that teachers need to be trained effectively to implement interactive exergames so that they feel comfortable enough to utilize these technologies:

> Still, with few exceptions, teachers are not using games in their classrooms for anything other than rewards given after the "real" work is done. Although interest seems high, there are significant genuine barriers to adoption, which include a lack of resources (time and equipment) as well as a lack of understanding of how to use games. In other words, there is interest in using games, but there is also uncertainty. (p. 479)

In many instances, teachers do not understand how to apply the cutting-edge technologies to make learning more engaging, effective, or efficient. Many lack the skills and knowledge necessary to integrate technology effectively into their pedagogical practices (Becker, 2007; Sprague, 2004). Thus, it is important to prepare in-service and novice physical educators properly and to demonstrate how they can use a variety of learning and interactive technologies to increase students' engagement in physical activities.

Implementing Interactive Technologies to Enhance Student-Engaged Learning

Declines in quality K–12 physical education time, rising childhood obesity, greater percentages of K–12 students failing physical education, and the influx of modern technology (video games, computers, and televisions) that stagnate physical activity suggest that physical educators need more effective solutions to guide students in K–12 schools to place a higher value on the importance of physical activity. One solution could be for physical educators to educate themselves on the use of innovative instructional technologies and, in turn, encourage their students to "get up and get moving." In school districts where innovative instructional technologies are implemented, they may stimulate students' motivation and interest toward physical activity. As schools have reduced or eliminated physical education programs, many students have become intrigued with technological innovations and less engaged in physical activities. For example, digital video games engage a high percentage of American youth. Hansen and Witherspoon (2007) found that "83% of American children between the ages of 8 and 18 have one or more video game consoles, such as: Sony PlayStation, Microsoft Xbox, and Nintendo" (p. 24). Furthermore, in 2008, Americans spent a total of $22.9 billion for a variety of video game hardware, software, and accessories, a 19% increase from the previous year (Entertainment Merchants Association, 2009).

In an effort to counter declines in physical activity and the rising obesity epidemic among youth in America, the National Association for Sport and Physical Education (2009) released a position statement advocating that health, physical activity, and physical education professionals devise strategies to improve implementation of appropriate instructional technologies to connect students to meaningful, valuable, and enjoyable forms of human movement in schools.

To accomplish the goals listed above by NASPE, physical educators could infuse digital game-based learning (DGBL) into their pedagogy to increase student enjoyment and interest toward physical activity. DGBL has been identified as an instructional method that facilitates student learning. More video games with educational content are being designed with practical goals of engaging learners through increased motivation and psychological states of engagement during the activity (Prensky, 2001; Van Eck, 2006). DGBL is a learner-centered approach to education based on principles from constructivist theory (Becker, 2007; Prensky, 2001, 2005).

In Chapter 1 of this book, Prensky notes that games are strongly associated with the terms *fun* and *play*, and that playing video games gives one an increased sense of enjoyment and intense engagement. Prensky classifies today's generation of students as digital natives, noting that digital natives learn to process information differently due to their technological upbringing. Prensky implies that digital natives may not respond well to traditional forms of education because those practices do not connect them to what they would identify as meaningful or real-life experiences. Prensky also identifies today's teachers as "digital immigrants" because they need to find innovative methods to reach digital natives, who have always been exposed to and engaged with technology. Van Eck (2006) furthers this perspective by asserting that one of the factors for the widespread interest in games as learning tools is because of today's youth:

> Today's "Net Generation," or "digital natives," have become disengaged with traditional instruction. They require multiple streams of information, prefer inductive reasoning, want frequent and quick interactions with content, and have exceptional visual literacy skills, characteristics that are all matched well with DGBL. (p. 17)

After reviewing DGBL literature, I determined that there are three methods for integrating games into the learning process: (a) students create games from scratch, (b) educators and/or developers produce educational games from scratch that teach students, or (c) educators integrate commercial off-the-shelf (COTS) games into the classroom. Van Eck (2006) explains the third approach, integrating COTS games into the classroom, as taking existing games, which were not necessarily developed as learning games, and utilizing them in the classroom as learning tools. Chapters 10 and 12 in this book also delineate processes for repurposing COTS games and effectively integrating them to facilitate student learning. Adapting COTS games for use in schools is probably the most cost effective of the three approaches. Research conducted from this approach notes several possible benefits of utilizing COTS games, such as exergames, as an interactive measure to facilitate a variety of physical fitness activities (International Sports Sciences Association, 2007).

This chapter's overall goal is to inform physical educators and other health and fitness professionals about methods for implementing COTS games into their teaching and physical fitness training practices to increase students' interest and engagement in physical fitness and physical activity in K–12 settings. More specifically, the chapter addresses COTS games classified as exergames and details the origins and benefits of these games. The rest of this chapter includes (a) an explanation of how exergames are used, (b) short descriptions of various exergames on the market along with a summary of research identifying the benefits associated with each game, and (c) strategies for educators to use COTS exergames to meet national standards and objectives set forth by the National Association for Sport and Physical Education (NASPE, 2004).

Hey, What *Are* Exergames?

Bogost (2005) defines exergames as video games that require physical input devices and combine exercise and play. In addition, Lieberman (2006) identifies exergames or exertainment as interactive video games for participants to engage in dance, aerobics, kickboxing, martial arts, sport skills, or other forms of physical activity. Many exergames are readily accessible COTS games that can be purchased from most discount stores, toy stores, and many online sources.

Recently, schools have begun incorporating exergames into physical education to motivate students to engage in physical activity. The recent wave of popularity surrounding exergames has been noted by many national health, medical, and fitness organizations that have begun endorsing research regarding their use for facilitating physical activity among children, adolescents, and adults of all ages (Figure 9.1). In fact, in January 2009, the Robert Wood Johnson Foundation continued to provide $2 million in grant funding to institutions that facilitate and strengthen research on development and use of digital interactive games to improve health and fitness (RWJF, 2009) (*see www.healthgamesresearch.org*). Another interesting development along these lines occurred in January 2007, when the University of South Florida became the first university to open an interactive fitness research lab for children, called the XRKade Fitness Lab, to study how exergaming increases children's fitness levels and social and cognitive development, and how it may benefit students with special needs (Wade, 2007). As the USF fitness lab's results become available, perhaps in the future physical educators will have a plethora of interactive games to motivate students and enhance learning in their classes.

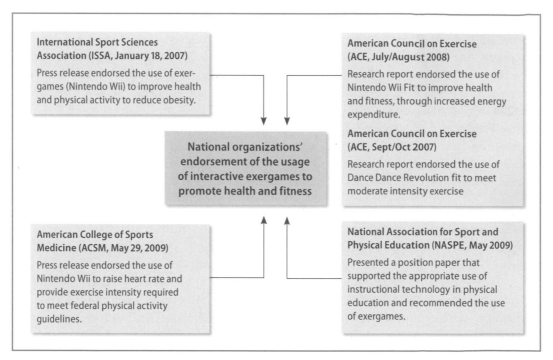

FIGURE 9.1   ▶   National Organizations'/Associations' Endorsements of Exergames

A wide variety of COTS exergames are available, but the best-selling, most popular, and most researched exergames are Dance Dance Revolution (DDR) and Nintendo's Wii Fit and Wii Sports. Table 9.1 provides a brief overview of exergames that educators may use to improve the physical health and fitness of your students.

Table 9.1 includes (a) the website link of the exergame, (b) the technology used to play the exergame, (c) a description of the exergame concept and fitness achieved, and (d) cost of the exergame. I hope this chart will be a useful resource for teachers seeking various types of exergames that could become teaching and coaching tools. Some of the games would also appeal to colleagues for before- and after-school workouts at times when students are not using them.

TABLE 9.1 ▶ Various COTS exergames appropriate for use in physical education classes

EXERGAME	TECHNOLOGY INVOLVED	HOW TO PLAY AND FITNESS ACHIEVED	AGE GROUP	COST
Dance Dance Revolution *ddronlinecommunity.com*	Game is made in an arcade version and for video game consoles such as Sony PlayStation, Nintendo Wii, Nintendo GameCube, and PCs. Game requires a dance pad with arrows facing forward, backward, left, and right.	Players can choose from several modes and difficulty levels within each mode. Arrows scroll from the bottom of the screen to the top, and the player must step on the corresponding arrow when it reaches the static bar at the top of the screen.	Games are available for all age groups	$39.99–$69.99 for game with 1 dance pad
Wii Sports *us.wii.com/wiisports*	Wii console uses sensor attached to television and wireless controls to sense movement made by player.	Players can choose from baseball, golf, boxing, tennis, and bowling and use Wii remote to mimic actions used when playing in real life. Game also has fitness and training features to measure speed, stamina, and strength.	All ages	$249.99 for Wii console and game
Wii Fit *nintendo.com/games/ detail/hoiNtus4JvlcPt-P8LQPyud4Kyy393oep* **Wii Fit Plus** *www.nintendo.com/wiifit*	Game comes with balance board that can measure movement, weight, and center of balance.	Player can choose from four training modes (yoga, balance games, strength training, and aerobics). Game can chart BMI, exercise time, and body control.	All ages	$90 for Wii Fit game and balance board; $20 to add Plus game to original Wii Fit; prices vary for entire Plus package.
Gamercize Pro-Sport *gamercize.net*	Made for Xbox 360, PlayStation 3, and Nintendo Wii. Power stepper or endurance cycle attaches to console and is compatible with all games.	Player selects exercise level and then must keep moving on apparatus in order for game to work. If player stops moving, the game will pause.	All ages	$259.00
Lightspace Play Floor *lightspacecorp.com/ products/lightspaceplay/*	Floor is made up of 16"x16" tiles to fit a 10' space. Game comes with a game cabinet to choose games. Floor can detect location, movement, and density.	Floor can light up different colors, patterns, and images. Games can involve stomping on shapes, running from dodgeballs, and jogging in place.	All ages	$22,995
Kinect *xbox.com/en-us/kinect/ games.htm*	Made for Xbox. System will connect to Xbox system. Camera and sound system detect movement and voice commands. Body acts as the controller.	Movement by user causes image on screen to move.	All ages	Xbox 360 Arcade $200; Xbox Elite, $300
Skywall *theskywall.com*	Motorized climbing wall. User can set the pegs to determine difficulty level. Has 10 speeds, 13 incline levels, and 5 preset programs.	The wall is in constant motion so the user must keep moving up the wall to stay off the ground. No need for safety equipment as user is never more than a few feet off the ground.	All ages	$11,500–$14,000 depending on size

(Continued)

TABLE 9.1 *(Continued)*

EXERGAME	TECHNOLOGY INVOLVED	HOW TO PLAY AND FITNESS ACHIEVED	AGE GROUP	COST
XaviXPORT System *xavix.com*	Console connects to television. Each application comes with wireless controllers that mimic real life motion.	Examples of applications include baseball, tennis, bowling, bass fishing, golf, and power boxing. Control game using real life motions. Also available are ZaviX Wellness and Health, Step Sensor, and Jackie Chan Studio Fitness.	All ages	$79.99 for XaviXPORT System and $49.99–$59.99 for applications
Gyroxus Exergaming Chair *gyroxus.com*	Made for XBox 360, PlayStation 3, and Windows. Uses hand-held controller and a motion system chair to control games.	Motion of chair creates a simulator experience so the user is not just sitting still. Compatible with all games.	12 years and older	$249.99
EyeToy *www.eyetoy.com*	Made for PlayStation 2 and 3. Small USB camera sits on top of television and connects to console. Places user's image in video game.	Game is controlled by the movements of the user. Examples of game types include martial arts, sports (football and golf), parachuting, personal trainer, and dancing games.	Various games for all age groups, PK–older adults	$39.99 for camera $29.99–$49.99 for games
GameBike Game Pad *gamebike.com* **GameCoach** *gamebike.com/ gamecoach.php*	Exercise bicycle can plug into PlayStation, Xbox, or Gamecube console. GameCoach combines high-tech computer gaming, using GameBike and GamePad, with traditional equipment found in most PE programs.	Bicycle requires user to pedal and uses steering mechanism to allow user to navigate terrain. GameBike and GamePad provide the aerobic exercise of a bike or dance pad. Kids who are good at GamePad might not be good at any other sport. GameCoach provides lessons for classes as well as training techniques for coaching.	Comes in small and large for 3'11"–6'7"	$400 Teachers may request more info via website.
PC GamerBike *pcgamerbike.com*	Available in mini bike or recumbent bike. Plugs into PC USB Port. Compatible with all PC games but works best with racing games or games players control themselves.	Use pedals to control the game. Pedal forward to move forward or backward to move in reverse. Players become game characters: cars, boats, bicycles, etc.	All ages	$209 for Mini Bike
Makoto Sports Arena *makoto-usa.com/new/ main/makotoYouth.html*	Machine has 3 posts placed in a triangle. Each post has 10 targets that light up and make sounds. In addition to aerobic exercise, the game may benefit those with learning disabilities, ADD/ADHD, and autism. Can be played solo or in teams.	Target lights up, and the player/s must find the post and the lit target and hit or kick it. The next target is randomly activated. Player/s accumulate points depending on speed and hitting the correct targets.	All ages	$7,395
EA Sports Active *easportsactive.com* More workouts and personal trainer are also available.	Compatible with Nintendo Wii system. Game comes with leg strap and resistance band to increase workout. Also compatible with Wii Balance Board.	Game has 25 different games and exercise activities to get user moving. Additional versions geared for fitness workouts and working out with a personal trainer.	All ages	$40–$60

What Does Research Say about the Benefits of Exergames?

Research has shown that even playing sedentary video games (with little to no physical activity involved) increases several cardiorespiratory functions, such as cardiovascular rate, blood pressure, and VO_2 max (oxygen consumption), to levels consistent with light-intensity exercise (Wang & Perry, 2006). In contrast, research on exergames indicates that children burn at least four times as many calories per minute while engaging in active games than they do when playing seated, sedentary video games (Mellecker & McManus, 2008). Research also reveals that exergaming leads to higher positive affective attitudes toward exercise adherence (Rhodes, Warburton, & Coble, 2008; Warburton, Bredin, Horita, et al., 2007) and affords players an array of physiological benefits (noted in Tables 9.2, 9.3, & 9.4). For example, Warburton et al. (2009) found that engaging in exerbiking led to higher metabolic requirements at submaximal constant workloads than traditional cycling.

The following discussion provides a brief overview of research related to three of the best-selling COTS exergames on the market: Wii, Dance Dance Revolution, and EyeToy. In addition, a brief overview of several other popular exergames, including EyeToy and Exerbikes, is given along with research findings related to these games (Table 9.4).

Nintendo Wii

The Nintendo Wii was designed in 2000 to revolutionize the home gaming console industry. By late 2006, the Nintendo Wii was one of the hottest games in America, and when stores failed to supply enough for the holidays, many people resorted to paying overwhelming prices for them online at eBay and other online sites (Goldsborough, 2008). In January and February 2009, Nintendo's Wii Fit sold 6 million units and was the top-selling video game in the United States (Painter, 2009). The wave of popularity surrounding Nintendo's Wii Fit and Wii Sports has led several scholars and health and fitness organizations to research the utility of Nintendo Wii as a tool to help promote health and physical fitness. Table 9.2 lists research projects that measured the effects of playing Nintendo Wii on children's, adolescents', and young adults' health and fitness.

FIGURE 9.2 ▶ Wii Fit exergames help promote physical fitness.

TABLE 9.2 ▶ Wii Fit and Wii Sports research findings

EXERGAME	AUTHORS, YEAR	RESEARCH SUBJECTS/ OBJECTIVE	KEY STUDY FINDINGS
Wii Fit **Wii Sports** (tennis, baseball, golf, bowling, & boxing) **Dance Dance Revolution (DDR)**	Graf, Pratt, Hester, & Short (2009)	23 subjects (14 boys and 9 girls, ages 10–13) To compare children's energy expenditure when playing Wii Fit, Wii Sports, and DDR versus treadmill walking	• High rates of energy expenditure, heart rate, and perceived exertion were indicated from playing Wii boxing and DDR level 2. • Energy expenditure during exergaming is comparable to moderate-intensity walking.
Wii Sports (tennis, baseball, golf, bowling, & boxing)	Porcari, Schmidt, Foster, & Anders (2008)	16 subjects (8 men and 8 women, ages 20–29) To discover the physiological effects of playing Wii Sports	• Playing Wii Sports can burn from 3.1 to 7.2 calories per minute. • Playing Wii Sports increases heart rate, maximum oxygen intake, perceived exertion, and burning of calories.
Wii Sports (tennis, baseball, golf, bowling, & boxing)	Graves, Stratton, Ridgers, & Cable (2007)	11 subjects (6 boys and 5 girls, ages 13–15) To compare energy expenditure of adolescents when playing sedentary games versus exergames	• Playing Wii bowling, tennis, and boxing expended more energy than playing sedentary games. • Playing exergames uses significantly more energy than playing sedentary video games but not as much energy as playing the sport itself.

Konami's Dance Dance Revolution

In 1999, Konami released Dance Dance Revolution (DDR) in the United States. Because of the exergame's initial popularity, Konami's volume of sales increased, and high demands resulted in a DDR scarcity in North America (Tran, 2000). DDR became so popular in Norway that it has been registered as an official sport in that country (Twist, 2004). DDR has also reached widespread popularity among youth in the United States, and several states have implemented DDR in physical education classes as a means to increase physical activity among children and adolescents in K–12 settings. In fact, a 2007 article in the *New York Times* (Schiesel, 2007) said that as a result of a partnership among West Virginia's Department of Education, its Public Employees Insurance Agency, and West Virginia University, West Virginia committed to installing DDR in all 765 of its

FIGURE 9.3 ▶ A child playing Dance Dance Revolution

public schools. More than 1,500 other schools across the country are planning to implement DDR into their physical education curricula by the end of the decade. A study by Yang and Foley (2008) comparing children's exercise intensity between engaging in DDR and the Sony EyeToy found that children spent more time engaged in moderate to vigorous physical activity (MVPA) while playing DDR compared to playing the exergame EyeToy. Table 9.3 provides examples of research on the effects of playing DDR on children's and young adults', older adult women's, experienced and inexperienced DDR players', and overweight and non-overweight individuals' health and fitness.

TABLE 9.3 ▶ Dance Dance Revolution (DDR) research findings

EXERGAME	AUTHORS, YEAR	RESEARCH SUBJECTS/ OBJECTIVE	KEY STUDY FINDINGS
Dance Dance Revolution	American Council on Exercise (ACE & Anders, 2007)	24 subjects (12 males and 12 females, ages 12 to 25) To assess the efficacy of DDR by evaluating subjects' perceived exertion, energy expenditure, and oxygen uptake	• All subjects showed increases in exercise intensity when engaged in difficult modes of DDR. • Older participants burned more calories when engaged in DDR.
Dance Dance Revolution	Inzitari, Greenlee, Hess, Subashan, and Studenski (2009)	40 subjects (40 sedentary, postmenopausal women) To elicit perceived advantages and disadvantages of using DDR to exercise	• Overall, DDR was viewed as appealing. The most frequently perceived advantages: "It's fun" and "Improves coordination." Disadvantages were "long learning process" and "cost."
Dance Dance Revolution	Sell, Lillie, and Taylor (2008)	19 subjects (12 experienced and 7 inexperienced DDR players) To assess maximal oxygen uptake during a 30-minute gaming session in experienced versus inexperienced DDR players	• Participants with greater DDR playing experience can work at higher intensity levels, reported higher enjoyment, and had higher caloric expenditures than inexperienced DDR players.
Dance Dance Revolution	Unnithan, Houser, and Fernhall (2006)	22 subjects (12 non-overweight and 10 overweight, ages 11–17) To assess DDR effects on energy expenditure, energy cost, and cardiorespiratory fitness in relation to ACSM recommendations	• Overweight participants who participated in DDR had higher energy expenditures than non-overweight participants. • Participants in DDR met the minimum heart rate ACSM recommendations, but VO_2 max was not met for ACSM recommendations.

Sony EyeToy

The Sony EyeToy was invented by astronautical and aeronautical engineer Richard Marx as a mini-camera that attaches to the Sony PlayStation 2 and transfers an individual's image and physiological movements back into the screen, creating a virtual game environment (Lieberman, 2006; Robischon, 2003). The EyeToy utilizes a full-vision camera lens that captures the player's entire body in order to detect all of its physical movements (Lieberman, 2006). The EyeToy gives

FIGURE 9.4 ▶ The Sony EyeToy creates a virtual game environment.

players opportunities to engage in a variety of exercises and workouts, such as martial arts activities, in which players jab, punch, and kick images of falling objects, or a 12-week fitness program coached by a virtual trainer (Lieberman, 2006). Earlier research investigated the practicality of EyeToy usage by individuals in clinical settings (Brooks & Petersson, 2005; Rand, Kizony, & Weiss, 2004). Rand, Kizony, and Weiss (2004) investigated the ease of use and enjoyment of the games in healthy young adults, healthy older adults, and adult stroke patients. In the study's results, all three groups reported that utilizing the EyeToy game was not difficult, they enjoyed the games, and they wanted to engage in EyeToy again in the future. In addition, participants in Brooks and Petersson's (2005) study reported similar perceived enjoyment, as 61% of the children said that engaging in EyeToy games was fun.

Traditionally, peripheral devices for video game consoles did not sell well, but the Sony EyeToy sold over 1 million cameras within the first six months of its initial July 2003 release in Britain (Robischon, 2003). By the end of 2003, Sony EyeToy had sold over 2 million units in Europe and 400,000 units in the United States (Pham, 2004), and as of November 2008, EyeToy has sold 10.5 million units internationally (Kim, 2008). Table 9.4 provides exemplars of research on the effects of the Sony EyeToy on children's and young adults' health and fitness.

TABLE 9.4 ▶ Sony EyeToy research findings

EXERGAME	AUTHORS, YEAR	RESEARCH SUBJECTS/ OBJECTIVE	KEY STUDY FINDINGS
EyeToy	Ni Mhurchu, Maddison, Jiang, Jull, Prapavessis, and Rodgers (2008)	22 subjects (22 children, 40% girls and 60% boys) To assess the effects of exergames (EyeToy) on children's physical activity levels	• The average time spent on all physical activities was greater among the exergaming group than the control group (no intervention). • Suggested that playing exergames on a regular basis can have positive effects on children's overall physical activity.
Exerbike	Russell & Newton (2008)	168 university students (78 males, 90 females; mean age 21.51 years) To examine short-term psychological effects of mood while subjects engaged in interactive exerbiking game	• Exerbiking led to immediate affective benefits compared with sedentary games' affective effects.

As the research indicates, COTS exergames have proved to be beneficial tools for encouraging children's and adolescents' health and fitness by providing fun and entertaining interactive physical activities. Now that some of the benefits associated with COTS exergames have been shown, the next section of this chapter discusses strategies for implementing the games in physical education curricula and aligning the games with the highest standards for the subject matter.

Aligning Exergames with the National Physical Education Standards

The contributors to Section III of this book offer teachers suggestions for implementing COTS games into their classes. Other experts, such as Deubel (2006), assert that when implementing and selecting appropriate digital games for their students, teachers should consider (a) students' ages, characteristics, gender, competitive nature, and previous gaming experiences; (b) the games' target age levels and whether the games comply with the standards-based accountability movement; (c) whether the games can accommodate students with special needs; (d) whether the games are inclusive and respectful to the racial and gender diversity of students; (e) the number of participants who can play or be involved in the game at once; and (f) whether the role of the teacher should be passive observer or active participant. Furthermore, Deubel offers several rules to ensure that digital game-based learning (DGBL) is implemented effectively: (a) the games should keep students' learning and engagement at high levels; (b) rules and goals should be established along with aspects of the game; (c) teachers should select nonviolent games that strengthen students' planning and problem-solving skills and that apply to the curriculum; (d) teachers should make the learning outcomes of the game clear and provide immediate feedback regarding students' development of skills in the game; and (e) students should interact with other students as they discuss the game and plan strategies, as well as play interactive roles with other students within the game itself.

A plethora of websites are available that K–12 educators can access to learn how to use DGBL effectively; several examples of these are listed in Table 9.5.

TABLE 9.5 ▶ Recommended websites for better understanding of DGBL

K–12 GAMES RESOURCES	
www.gamesparentsteachers.com	www.gameeducationnetwork.com
www.socialimpactgames.com	www.p21.org/route21
www.lostgarden.com	http://tonyforster.blogspot.com
www.pixelearning.com	http://brainmeld.org
www.assistivegaming.com	http://education.qld.gov.au/learningplace
www.educationarcade.org	www.atari.com/genre/kids
www.phunland.com/wiki/Home	http://gamesthatwork.com/ Select tab "for learning."

To provide another example of how educators may integrate the use of COTS games, the next section describes how Hirumi's (Chapter 10, this volume) five-step approach may be used to integrate exergames effectively into physical education.

Applying Steps to Integrate Exergames into Physical Education

In Chapter 10 of this book, Hirumi recommends five steps for integrating digital gameplay into the classroom: (1) selecting a grounded instructional strategy based on specified objectives, learner characteristics, context, and epistemological beliefs; (2) playing games and determining their suitability and instructional purpose (in other words, is gameplay appropriate, and what instructional events are addressed by the game?); (3) operationalizing instructional strategy by describing how each event will be applied and noting when the game should be played; (4) addressing technical and logistical issues (e.g., scheduling student access to computers and game); and (5) pilot testing gameplay and formatively evaluating instructional materials. I encourage physical educators to follow Hirumi's five-step approach to implement exergames effectively into their classrooms.

Step 1. When addressing Hirumi's first step, physical educators should select a grounded instructional strategy to integrate gameplay and facilitate achievement based on specified objectives, learner characteristics, context, and epistemological beliefs. This first step involves physical educators selecting an appropriate pedagogical approach/strategy as a foundation for ensuring that learning outcomes are achieved throughout the gameplay process. In Chapter 10, Hirumi provides numerous teacher-directed and learner-centered pedagogical approaches that physical educators could adopt to align learning outcomes with the gameplay process effectively.

Step 2. To address Hirumi's second step, physical educators should play the games themselves to determine their suitability and instructional purposes. According to this phase, physical educators should select games that are directly correlated with and meet specific curriculum needs. Prior to selecting an exergame for inclusion, physical educators must first determine current curriculum needs and/or desired learner outcomes and determine how specific games may fill those needs.

There are several factors physical educators must address to determine whether an exergame is suitable for implementation in K–12 educational settings. For instance, Hirumi stresses several key factors, such as determining whether you, your school, and your students have the required resources: computer hardware/software, funding to purchase the necessary equipment and exergames to be implemented, appropriate technological competence and skills to engage efficiently in the exergame, and required space and resources to accommodate the implementation of the exergame in the K–12 school setting. Point blank, if physical educators and their schools lack the appropriate resources for providing and using the exergame, it becomes worthless to invest time on aligning exergames to instructional practices and structured learning outcomes, as their implementation may not be systemically possible.

Consistent with Hirumi's ideology in Step 2, Van Eck (2006) also notes that implementing digital games involves aligning the game with curricular content. This is probably the most challenging phase of implementing COTS exergames for physical educators. As Van Eck asserts:

Educators recognize this as the biggest limitation of COTS games in DGBL. Any game designed to be engaging will tend to privilege that aspect over accuracy and completeness of content. So when we evaluate these games, we have to ask ourselves several questions. What is covered in the game? A game may take a breadth or a depth approach to the topic. . . . One of the biggest misconceptions among educators is that if a game is missing content or has inaccurate content, it cannot be used responsibly with DGBL. (p. 24)

From Van Eck's perspective, it is important that physical educators find methods (design activities) to infuse the necessary content into games so that students will learn the appropriate skills while playing them. Teachers can devise pre and post content knowledge quizzes for students to take before and after engaging in the games. By doing this, they can show how the games are relevant to curricular learning outcomes and objectives.

Step 3. To address Hirumi's third step, physical educators should operationalize each event of their selected instructional strategy, addressing methods for how and when students will engage in the exergames and identifying all instructional pre/post gameplay procedures. Hirumi recommends that teachers align their instructional gameplay activities with the instructional procedures that were selected to guide the learning outcomes. For instance, the instructional approach (teacher-directed or learner centered) selected should be aligned with activities related to each of the instructional procedures.

Step 4. Specifically, physical educators should evaluate any technical and logistics concerns as they relate to the use of exergames in the curriculum. Hirumi recommends that teachers address five technical and logistical issues (1) identifying when and where students are to access the game; (2) collaborating with your school's administrators and technology support staff to request and prepare resources needed for the game's inclusion in the classroom, library, and/or computer lab; (3) collaborating with your school's administrators and technology support staff to ensure proper policies and procedures are in place to regulate and monitor gameplay and access to the games; (4) accessing student data and tracking aspects related to evaluating students' gameplay; and (5) developing instructional methods that enhance and facilitate the effective use of gameplay in school settings. As stated in Hirumi's Step 4, addressing technical and logistics issues will ensure a smooth transition for incorporating digital game-based learning into physical education settings.

Step 5. The last step of Hirumi's approach is the teacher's evaluation, through pilot testing, formative evaluation, and/or research, of whether the exergame was a good fit with the curriculum and whether the students' learning was worth the work and resources invested into implementing the exergame. By this point, the teacher will have decided upon clear goals and objectives for playing the exergame. Physical educators should gather data during and after gameplay to determine whether the goals and objectives were reached and to identify areas for improvement. Van Eck (2006) suggests that ongoing, written evaluation will help teachers ensure that games are integrated well into tightly structured curricula and that they meet learning objectives at the same time.

Aligning Exergames to meet NASPE National Physical Education Standards

It is important to select games that are aligned with and directly supportive of the achievement of specified curricular outcomes. In this chapter, various types of exergames and identified health and fitness outcomes associated with participation in these games are discussed. The next section discusses ideas for how physical educators can utilize various exergames to meet the national physical education curricula standards set forth by the National Association for Sport and Physical Education (NASPE, 2004). Table 9.6 provides an overview of (a) the NASPE national physical education standards, (b) suggestions of appropriate exergames to achieve these standards, and (c) how teachers can align the exergames to comply with NASPE national standards for K–12 physical education.

TABLE 9.6 ▶ Aligning exergames to NASPE standards

NASPE STANDARDS	EXAMPLES OF APPROPRIATE EXERGAMES	EXERGAME ALIGNMENT WITH NASPE STANDARDS
1. Demonstrates competency in motor skills and movement patterns needed to perform a variety of physical activities.	Wii Fit and Wii Sports Dance Dance Revolution	These exergames align with Standard 1 as they emphasize fundamental motor skills (running, jumping) and specialized motor skills (executing a dance step, etc.).
2. Demonstrates understanding of movement concepts, principles, strategies, and tactics as they apply to the learning and performance of physical activities.	Wii Fit and Wii Sports	Wii Fit accommodates students' learning about aspects of physical fitness and provides assessment feedback. Wii Sports facilitates students' basic grasp of specialized skills (e.g., baseball, bowling, etc.).
3. Participates regularly in physical activity.	All exergames listed in Table 9.1	As long as students are actively engaging in daily physical activity, it does not matter which exergame is emphasized for learning. Students may be encouraged to play any exergames they value and enjoy. Students' interests in exergames will vary.
4. Achieves and maintains a health-enhancing level of physical fitness.	Exerbikes Dance Dance Revolution EyeToy Wii Fit, Wii Sports	All of these exergames have proved effective in clinical settings for facilitating and enhancing aspects of individuals' health and fitness (see Tables 9.2, 9.3, and 9.4).
5. Exhibits responsible personal and social behavior that respects self and others in physical activity settings.	Wii Sports	Wii Sports allow students to participate responsibly with each other as these games offer multiplayer settings.
6. Values physical activity for health, enjoyment, challenge, self-expression, and/or social interaction.	All exergames listed in Table 9.1	Playing any of the exergames in Table 9.1 could stimulate students' enjoyment of physical activity, leading to their placing high value on good health and physical activities as outlets for positive self-expression, personal challenge, and social interaction.

National Standards for Physical Education © NASPE National Association for Sport and Physical Education

When aligning exergames with NASPE standards, educators need to be sure to implement exergames at the appropriate fundamental levels. The objectives and levels of difficulty for selected exergames in physical education should be learner appropriate for age and grade level and free of any limitations that could impair the incorporation of these games into K–12 settings.

Limitations of Exergames in Physical Education

As physical educators begin to implement exergames into the curricula, they should be cognizant of the games' potential limitations. Table 9.7 details four specific limitations that educators may be confronted with when attempting to implement exergames into their pedagogical practices.

TABLE 9.7 ▶ Limitations of exergames

LIMITATION NUMBER	LIMITATION	DESCRIPTION OF LIMITATION
1	Lack of learner appropriateness	Many COTS exergames are not designed with educational intents or purposes of facilitating learning outcomes (Van Eck, 2006).
2	Safety/Liability	Concerns have been raised regarding injuries resulting from participation in specific exergames and the lack of appropriate guidance/instructions regarding associated risks of exergames.
3	Lack of effective teacher training for game-based learning	As reported by Russell (2007), many teachers lack the appropriate knowledge, competence, and experience for utilizing exergames. Few teacher training and professional development programs exist to help teachers understand how to adapt and use exergames for optimal student achievement.
4	Lack of effective exergame instructional models for physical educators	Insufficient instructional models specifically designed for implementing exergames into physical education curricula exist.

Limitation 1. When selecting exergames, teachers should not necessarily do so with various games' popularity in mind but for their relevance to learning outcomes. Teachers need to be aware that while exergames are popular, many games lack fundamental relevance to achieving health and physical education objectives and lack specific objectives within their design that meet curriculum objectives.

Limitation 2. When implementing exergames, physical educators must evaluate and implement rules, procedures, and protocols regarding the safe usage of the exergames. Due to exergames involving physical movement, teachers must consider the potential physical detriments associated with improper use and overuse of these games. Some researchers question the physical safety of participants engaging in exergames. For instance, Warren (2006) identifies injuries that can result from participating in Wii that are similar to typical sports injuries, including what some classify as "Wii elbow":

> The new console has been wildly successful, selling out at stores and winning high marks from critics and game buffs. But as players spend more time with the Wii, some are noticing that hours waving the game's controller around can add up to fairly intense exertion—resulting in aches and pains common in more familiar forms of exercise. They're reporting aching backs, sore shoulders—even something some have dubbed "Wii elbow." (p. 1)

A number of Wii-related injuries have resulted despite some Wii games' providing a warning every 15 minutes for participants to take a break (British Chiropractic Association, 2006; Warren, 2006). Nintendo has taken Wii-related injuries seriously, as the company includes a detailed safety manual in each game's package, which notes that people are capable of causing bizarre injuries to themselves and others when playing Wii (Bivings Group, 2006; British Chiropractic Association, 2006). Thus, it is extremely important that teachers closely monitor students whenever they are utilizing Wii or any other exergames in school settings. The British Chiropractic Association (2006) offers several recommendations and warm up activities to prepare for engagement in Wii. From an administrative perspective, it would be wise for school districts to make sure that their limited liability insurance covers exergame injuries. In addition, teachers should be cognizant of liability issues regarding direct supervision when students engage in exergames, thus being careful not to leave this responsibility to a substitute or pre-service teacher without their supervision of the exergame activities.

Limitation 3. As noted earlier in this chapter, Russell (2007) reported that many physical educators lack specific knowledge of how to utilize exergames' technologies in K–12 schools. In many instances, physical educators may want to implement exergames to facilitate learning outcomes, but they may be reluctant to try them because they do not understand how to use the technology.

Limitation 4. The final and perhaps most important limitation of incorporating exergames into K–12 physical education settings is the lack of relevant curricular models to guide implementation of exergames. One of the primary purposes of this chapter is to increase physical educators' understandings of pedagogical approaches to games that can facilitate health and physical fitness. Further educational research to develop curricular models to help physical educators who are interested in utilizing DGBL in physical education settings is needed.

Conclusion

Exergames are very popular among today's youth and now represent a significant part of the video game industry. Research studies have identified a plethora of physical benefits that can accrue to people of all ages from playing interactive exergames. As a result, a growing number of international and national fitness and health-related organizations are endorsing the use of exergames to help children and adolescents meet recommended exercise and physical activity requirements. With the omission of health and physical education as academic core areas in the No Child Left Behind Act (2001), schools have allocated less time and fewer resources for physical activity within their curricula (NASPE & AHA, 2006; Trickey, 2006). It seems that our government is sending contradictory messages, claiming in its report *Healthy People 2010* (USDHHS, 2000) that one of our country's goals is to improve citizens' health through regular engagement in physical activity but failing to include in the NCLB Act the initiatives, objectives, policies, and accountability that would require improvement of students' health and physical fitness in K–12 schools.

Since the implementation of the NCLB Act (NCLB, 2001), there have been marked efforts to better prepare teachers to utilize and implement technology to enhance student learning. For instance, the act's Title II, part D, Enhancing Education through Technology, lists specific objectives for technology implementations to enhance students' academic achievement in elementary and secondary schools. Despite the exclusion of health and physical education in the NCLB Act, all K–12 health and physical education teachers should expose their students to the most recent technologies, just as the NCLB Act advocates for core academic subjects. Physical educators should also consider incorporating digital game-based learning, including the use of exergames, into their classes as a methodology shown to be effective in addressing students' decline in positive attitudes, values, and behaviors toward traditional forms of physical activity in schools.

As noted by Van Eck (2006), problems teachers face when they start to use COTS exergames are (1) ensuring that the games cover the required content related to learning outcomes and then (2) aligning the games with curricular goals. Physical education is often taught along with health education, which covers issues related to health, nutrition, and wellness. As physical education and health education teachers evaluate exergames such as DDR and Nintendo Wii, they will see that these games provide feedback related to students' fitness, such as body mass index, calories burned, and length of activity. However, these games are not designed to include interactive feedback relative to amount and types of food consumed and how nutrition impacts overall health and fitness. I agree with Van Eck (2006), who noted the need for further DGBL research to provide "practical guidance for how (when, with whom, and under what conditions) games can be integrated into the learning process to maximize their learning potential" (p. 18). Physical educators also need to explore how information on health and nutrition can be integrated into exergames to encourage students to improve their lifestyle choices and, in so doing, meet the 2010 national health objectives for physical education.

References

American College of Sports Medicine (ACSM). (2009, May). Interactive video games help meet exercise recommendations. American College of Sports Medicine's 56th Annual Meeting, Seattle (May 29). Retrieved August 15, 2009, from www.acsm.org/AM/Template.cfm?Section=ACSM_News_Releases&CONTENTID=12880&TEMPLATE=/CM/ContentDisplay.cfm

American Council on Exercise (ACE). (2008). ACE announces study findings on fitness benefits of Nintendo Wii. (July 22). Retrieved from www.acefitness.org/pressroom/433/ace-announces-study-findings-on-fitness-benefits

American Council on Exercise (ACE), & Anders, M. (2007). Human joysticks: Could a videogame be the secret to making our kids more fit and less fat? *Fitness Matters, 13*(5, September/October), 7–9. Anders' article summarizes ACE-sponsored research conducted by Porcari, J. P., & Norlin, A. Available at www.acefitness.org/cp/pdfs/FitnessMatters/Sept07.pdf

American Heart Association (AHA). (2009). FIT Kids Act—Bill description. Retrieved October 17, 2009, from www.americanheart.org/presenter.jhtml?identifier=3049246

American Heart Association (AHA). (2010). FIT Kids Act—Bill summary (S. 634/H.R. 1585). Retrieved from www.americanheart.org/presenter.jhtml?identifier=3049245

Bassett, D. R. Jr. (2008). Physical activity of Canadian and American children: A focus on youth in Amish, Mennonite, and modern cultures. *Applied Physiology, Nutrition & Metabolism, 33*(4), 831–835.

Becker, K. (2007). Digital game based learning once removed: Teaching teachers. *British Journal of Educational Technology, 38*(3), 478–488.

Bivings Group, The. (2006, December 4). Wii injury report. Posted by the Bivings Group staff in gaming. Available at www.bivingsreport.com/2006/wii-injury-report/

Bogost, I. (2005). The rhetoric of exergaming. The Georgia Institute of Technology. Available at www.exergamefitness.com/pdf/The Rhetoric of Exergaming.pdf

British Chiropractic Association (2006, December 19). The Wii warm up: The British Chiropractic Association advises how to avoid Wii-injuries this yuletide. Retrieved January 11, 2010 from www.chiropractic-uk.co.uk/gfx/uploads/textbox/Press releases/0244104a Wii Warm Up.pdf

Brooks, A., & Petersson, E. (2005). Play therapy utilizing the Sony EyeToy. In Slater, M. (ed.) *Proc. of the Eighth International Workshop on Presence*, 303–314. Retrieved September 25, 2009 from www.temple.edu/ispr/prev_conferences/proceedings/2005/Brooks and Petersson.pdf

Brown, D. (2006). Playing to win: Video games and the fight against obesity. *Journal of the American Dietetic Association, 106*(2), 188–189.

Centers for Disease Control and Prevention (CDC). (2004). Participation in high school physical education—United States, 1991–2003. *Morbidity and Mortality Weekly Report, 53*(36), 844–847.

Centers for Disease Control and Prevention (CDC). (2006a). The school health policies and programs study (SHPPS). Available at www.cdc.gov/healthyYouth/shpps/index.htm

Centers for Disease Control (CDC). (2006b). Youth risk behavior surveillance survey—United States, 2005. Retrieved October 5 from www.cdc.gov/mmwr/PDF/SS/SS5505.pdf

Centers for Disease Control and Prevention (CDC). (2007). School wellness policies: Legislator policy brief. (May). Available via "quick view" tab at www.healthystates.csg.org/NR/rdonlyres/C87EB28D-B2F6-4399-B1BD-BC5617940019/0/SchoolWellnessPoliciesFINAL.pdf

Cessna, T., Raudenbush, B., Reed, A., & Hunker, R. (2007). Effects of video game play on snacking behavior. *Appetite, 49*(1, July), 282. Retrieved March 26, 2010, from www.addebook.com/biomed/html/medcine/appetite-volume-49-issue-01-july-2007-2_22006.html

Deubel, P. (2006, January 1). Game on! *T.H.E. Journal.* [Electronic version]. Retrieved September 22, 2009, from www.thejournal.com/articles/17788/

Eaton D. K., Kann L., Kinchen S., Ross, J., Hawkins, J., Harris, W. A., et al. Youth risk behavior surveillance—United States, 2005. *Morbidity and Mortality Weekly Report, 55*(5), 1–108.

Elsevier Health Sciences. (2008). Limit TV, video games, to two hours a day to reduce childhood obesity, study suggests. *Science Daily* (April 16). (Article summarizes Laurson, K. R., Eisenmann, J. C., Welk, G. J., Wickel, E. E., Gentile, D. A., & Walsh, D. A. Combined influence of physical activity and screen time recommendations on childhood overweight. *The Journal of Pediatrics, 153*(2), 209–214). Retrieved August 27, 2009, from www.sciencedaily.com/releases/2008/04/080416081631.htm

Entertainment Merchants Association. (2009). *EMA's 2009 annual report.* Available at www.entmerch.org/annual_reports.html

Goldsborough, L. (2008). The history of the Nintendo Wii. (August 21). Available at www.articlesbase.com/card-games-articles/the-history-of-the-nintendo-wii-531108.html

Graf, D., Pratt, L., Hester, C., & Short, K. (2009). Playing active video games increases energy expenditure in children. *Journal of Pediatrics, 124*(2), 534–540.

Graves, L., Stratton, G., Ridgers, N., & Cable, N. (2007). Energy expenditure in adolescents' playing new generation computer games. *British Medical Journal, 335*, 1282–1284. doi:10.1136/bmj.39415.632951.80

Hancox, R. J., & Poulton, R. (2006). Watching television is associated with childhood obesity: But is it clinically important? *International Journal of Obesity, 30*, 171–175.

Hansen, M., & Witherspoon, L. (2007). Exergaming: The key to fun fitness! *ClubSolutions magazine.* Retrieved October 10, 2009, from www.coedu.usf.edu/main/departments/physed/labs/documents/XRKPublications.html

International Sports Sciences Association (ISSA). (2007). Video games may offer health benefits, experts suggest. (January 18). Retrieved October 21, 2009, from www.issaonline.com/press-room/01-18-07.cfm

Inzitari, M., Greenlee, A., Hess, R., Subashan, P., & Studenski, S. (2009). Attitudes of Postmenopausal women toward interactive video dance for exercise. *Journal of Women's Health, 18*(8), 1239–1243.

Kim, T. (2008). In-depth: Eye to eye—The history of EyeToy. *Gamasutra.* (November 6). Retrieved November 15, 2008, from www.gamasutra.com/php-bin/news_index.php?story=20975

Lanningham, L., Foster, R., McGrady, S., Jensen, T., Mitre, N., & Levine, J. (2009). Activity-promoting video games and increased energy expenditure. *Journal of Pediatrics, 54*(6), 819–823.

Levi, J., Vinter, S., Richardson, L., St. Laurent, R., & Segal, L. M. (2009). *F as in fat: How obesity policies are failing in America 2009.* (July). Report sponsored by Trust for America's Health & Robert Wood Johnson Foundation. Available at http://healthyamericans.org/reports/obesity2009/Obesity2009Report.pdf

Lieberman, D. A. (2006). Dance games and other exergames: What the research says. Available at www.comm.ucsb.edu/faculty/lieberman/exergames.htm

Mellecker, R., & McManus, A. (2008). Energy expenditure and ardiovascular responses to seated and active gaming in children. *Archives of Pediatric Adolescent Medicine. 162*(9), 886–891.

Mohr, R. (2009). Exergaming inspires kids of all ages to get fit. Retrieved at http://magazine.angieslist.com/Articles/2009/August/NATIONAL/exergaming-inspires-fitness.aspx

Nader, P., Bradley, R., Houts, R., McRitchie, S., & O'Brien, M. (2008). Moderate to vigorous physical activity from ages 9 to 15 years. *The Journal of the American Medical Association, 300*(3), 295–305.

National Association for Sport and Physical Education (NASPE). (2004). *Moving into the future: National standards for physical education.* (2nd ed.). Reston, VA: NASPE.

National Association for Sport and Physical Education (NASPE). (2007). *No time to lose in physical education class.* Available at www.aahperd.org/naspe/template.cfm?template=pr07_1106.htm

National Association for Sport and Physical Education (NASPE). (2009). *Appropriate use of instructional technology in physical education.* (Position statement). Reston, VA: NASPE. Retrieved from www.aahperd.org/naspe/standards/loader.cfm?csModule=security/getfile&pageid=36901

National Association for Sport and Physical Education (NASPE) & American Heart Association (AHA). (2006). 2006 Shape of the nation report: Status of physical education in the USA. Reston, VA: National Association for Sport and Physical Education.

National Association for Sport and Physical Education (NASPE) & American Heart Association (AHA). (2010). 2010 Shape of the nation report: Status of physical education in the USA. Reston, VA: National Association for Sport and Physical Education. Retrieved January 10, 2010, from www.aahperd.org/naspe/publications/upload/Shape-of-the-Nation-2010-Final.pdf

Ni Mhurchu, C. Maddison, R., Jiang, Y., Jull, A., Prapavessis, H., & Rodgers, A. (2008). Couch potatoes to jumping beans: A pilot study of the effect of active video games on physical activity in children. *International Journal of Behavioral Nutrition and Physical Activity, 5*(8, February 7). Available at www.ijbnpa.org/content/5/1/8

No Child Left Behind (NCLB) Act. (2001, January 8). Public Law 107–110, 115 Stat. 1425–2094. 107th Congress. Congressional Record, Vol. 147 (2001). Available at www.gpo.gov/fdsys/pkg/PLAW-107publ110/content-detail.html

Ntoumanis, N. (2005). A prospective study of participation in optional school physical education using a self-determination theory framework. *Journal of Educational Psychology, 97*(3), 444–453.

Ntoumanis, N., Pensgaard, A., Martin, C., & Pipe, K. (2004). An ideographic analysis of amotivation in compulsory school physical education. *Journal of Sport & Exercise Psychology, 26*, 197–214.

Painter, K. (2009). Your health: Can games like 'Wii Fit' really work it? *USA Today.* (March 29). Retrieved at www.usatoday.com/news/health/painter/2009-03-29-your-health_N.htm

Papastergiou, M. (2009). Exploring the potential of computer and video games for health and physical education: A literature review. *Computers and Education, 53*, 603–622.

Pham, A. (2004). EyeToy Springs From One Man's Vision. *Los Angeles Times.* (January 18). Available at http://articles.latimes.com/2004/jan/18/business/fi-eyetoy18

Porcari, J. P., Schmidt, K., & Foster, C. & Anders, M. (2008 July/August). As good as the real thing? *Fitness Matters*, 7–9. San Diego, CA. American Council on Exercise. Retrieved Oct 15, 2009, from www.acefitness.org/getfit/studies/WiiStudy.pdf

Prensky, M. (2001). *Digital game-based learning.* New York, NY: McGraw-Hill.

Prensky, M. (2005). *Don't bother me Mom—I'm learning!* St. Paul, MN: Paragon House.

Ramsay, R. (2008). GameSpot editors' review: Wii Fit (Wii) review. Available at http://reviews.cnet. com/wii-games/wii-fit-wii/4505–9993_7–32513029.html

Rand, D., Kizony, R., & Weiss, P. L. (2004, September). Virtual reality rehabilitation for all: Vivid GX versus Sony PlayStation II EyeToy. In *Proceedings of the 5th International Conference on Disability, Virtual Reality and Associated Technologies*. Oxford, UK.

Rhodes, R, Warburton, D., Coble, J. (2008). Effect of interactive video bikes on exercise adherence and social cognitive expectancies in young men: A pilot study. *Annals of Behavioral Medicine, 35*, S62.

Robert Wood Johnson Foundation (RWJF). (2009). Discovering how video games can motivate healthy behaviors: More than $2 million awarded to 12 research teams across U.S. Retrieved October 17, 2009, from www.healthgamesresearch.org/sites/default/files/052908NPO%20%28Press% 20Release%29.pdf

Robischon, N. (2003, November 13). Smile, gamers: You're in the picture. *New York Times*. Available at www.nytimes.com/2003/11/13/technology/smile-gamers-you-re-in-the-picture.html

Russell, W. (2007). Physical educators' perceptions and attitudes toward interactive video game technology within the physical education curriculum. *Missouri Journal of Health, Physical Education, Recreation and Dance, 17*, 76–89.

Russell, W. D., & Newton, M. (2008). Short-term psychological effects of interactive video game technology exercise on mood and attention. *Educational Technology & Society, 11*(2), 294–308.

Sallis, J. F. (2000). Age-related decline in physical activity: A synthesis of human and animal studies. *Medicine and Science in Sports and Exercise, 32*, 1598–1600. (Introduction to a series of articles in a symposium section)

Schiesel, S. (2007, April 30). P.E. classes turn to video game that works legs. *New York Times*. Available at www.nytimes.com/2007/04/30/health/30exer.html

Sell, K., Lillie, T., & Taylor, J. (2008). Energy expenditure during physically interactive video game playing in male college students with different playing experience. *Journal of American College Health, 56*(5), 505–511.

Sprague, D. (2004). Technology and teacher education: Are we talking to ourselves? *Contemporary Issues in Technology and Teacher Education, 3*(4), 353–361.

Stattler, N., Signer, T., & Suter, P. (2004). Electronic games and environmental factors associated with childhood obesity in Switzerland. *Obesity Research, 12*, 896–903.

Strauss, R., Rodzilsky, D., Burack, G., & Colin, M. (2001). Psychosocial correlates of physical activity in healthy children. *Archives of Pediatric Adolescent Medicine, 155*(8), 897–902.

Subramaniam, P. R., & Silverman, S. (2007). Middle school students' attitudes toward physical education. *Teaching and Teacher Education, 23*, 602–611.

Tran, Khanh T. L. (2000, August 16). In the latest arcade craze, players demonstrate their fancy footwork. *Wall Street Journal*. Available at www.ddrfreak.com/newpress/WallStreetJournal.htm

Trickey, H. (2006, August 24). No child left out of the dodgeball game? *USA Today*. Retrieved October 10, 2009, from www.nytimes.com/2007/04/30/health/30exer.html

Twist, J. (2004, February, 3). Playing games on the dance floor. *BBC News.* Available at http://news.bbc.co.uk/2/hi/technology/3437819.stm

Unnithan, V., Houser, W., & Fernhall, B. (2006). Evaluation of the energy cost of playing a dance simulation video game in overweight and non-overweight children and adolescents. *International Journal of Sports Medicine, 27,* 804–809.

USA Today. (2009, March 20). *NFL Players call for improved physical education.* Posted on Daily Health Blog, USA Today, citing Associated Press, 2009. Available at www.usatoday.com/news/ health/2009–03–20-nfl-fitness

U.S. Department of Health and Human Services (USDHHS). (2000). *Healthy people 2010: Understanding and improving health and objectives for improving health* (2nd ed.). (Volumes I & II). Washington, DC: USDHHS. Available at www.healthypeople.gov/Publications/

U.S. Department of Health and Human Services (USDHHS). (2008). *Children's physical activity drops from age 9 to 15.* (July 15). Available at www.nih.gov/news/health/jul2008/nichd-15.htm

Van Eck, R. (2006). Digital game-based learning: It's not just the digital natives who are restless. *EDUCAUSE Review* (March/April). Available at www.educause.edu/ir/library/pdf/erm0620.pdf

Wade, L. (2007, January 3). Interactive fitness lab for children opens at USF; researchers may help combat childhood obesity. *USF News.* Available at http://usfweb3.usf.edu/absolutenm/ templates/?a=89&z=10

Wang, X., & Perry, A. (2006). Metabolic and physiologic responses to video game play in 7- to 10-year-old boys. *Archives of Pediatric Adolescent Medicine, 160*(4), 411–415.

Warburton, D., Bredin, S. S., Horita, L. T., Zbogar, D., Scott, J. M., Esch, B. T., et al. (2007). The health benefits of interactive video game exercise. *Applied Physiology Nutrition Metabolism, 32*(4), 655–663.

Warburton, D., Saranky, D., Johnson, M., Rhodes, R., Whitford, W., Esch, B., et al. (2009). Metabolic requirements of interactive video game cycling. *Medicine & Science in Sports & Exercise, 41*(4), 920–926.

Ward, D., Saunders, R., Felton, G., Williams, E., Epping, E., & Pate, R. (2006). Implementation of a school environment intervention to increase physical activity in high school girls. *Health Education Research, 21*(6), 896–910.

Warren, J. (2006, November 25). A Wii workout: When videogames hurt. *Wall Street Journal.* p. 1.

Yang, S. P., & Foley, J. T. (2008). Comparison of MVPA while playing DDR and EyeToy. *Research Quarterly for Exercise and Sport, 79*(1, Supplement), A-17.

Section III

Planning to Play Games

10

Integrating Games and Facilitating Game-Based Learning

Atsusi "2c" Hirumi

VIDEO GAMES DIFFER GREATLY in scope and nature. In addition, the relationship between gameplay and the achievement of curricular objectives may not always be readily apparent. To effectively integrate games into primary and secondary classes educators must see how specific games fit in with their instruction and facilitate important instructional events before and/or after gameplay. The first part of this chapter relates the basic structure and function of classroom instruction to the structure and function of games to illustrate different ways games may be applied in educational settings to facilitate learning. The second part of the chapter presents five steps for integrating instructional video games into classes, based on both teacher-directed and student-centered instructional strategies, to facilitate game-based learning.

ll video games are not created equally. Some games immerse players in elaborate, three-dimensional (3-D) environments that simulate laboratories, battles, cities, and planes, challenging players to think logically and make strategic decisions, based on multiple inputs, as they progress through different levels of gameplay. Other relatively simple (frame) games assess learners' abilities to recall facts or complete simple math computations by presenting players with conventional multiple-choice, true-false, fill-in-the-blank, and matching type questions in a format like a game show such as *Jeopardy!* or *Deal or No Deal*. Some may be viewed as action-adventure games, while others may be classified as first-person shooter games, role-playing games (RPG), or massive, multiplayer, online role-playing games (MMORPG). With such diversity, how do teachers select games and integrate gameplay with coursework, applying what we know about teaching and learning, to enhance student achievement and motivation?

In this chapter, I present a "grounded" approach for integrating digital video games with classroom instruction to facilitate learning in educational settings. The approach is grounded in that key pedagogical decisions (e.g., what to do before and after gameplay) are based on research and theories on human learning and instructional design. The chapter is divided into two major parts. In the first part, I relate the structure and function of games to the structure and function of classroom instruction to illustrate different ways games may be applied within a lesson or a course. In the second part, I posit five steps for selecting and integrating games, applying both teacher-directed and student-centered instructional strategies to facilitate game-based learning in educational settings. Examples are provided throughout the chapter to illustrate further the application of the grounded approach.

Relating Structure and Function

To effectively facilitate game-based learning in K–12 classes, it's important to see how games may be played and integrated at different levels of instruction and to relate these levels to how educators organize courses in terms of structure and function. Typically, training and educational programs are composed of courses that are divided into instructional units or modules. Depending on scope, an instructional unit may be equivalent to a "lesson" or may be further broken down into two or more lessons. Lessons, in turn, may be viewed as a series of instructional events. Figure 10.1 illustrates how a course may be divided into instructional units, and how instructional units may be divided into lessons, and how lessons may be viewed as a series of instructional events. Of course, the specific number of events, lessons, and units contained in a course will vary by course. As depicted in Figure 10.1, a course may consist of two to X number of units. A unit may consist of one lesson or may be broken down into two or more lessons, and each lesson may consist of a varying number of instructional events depending on the strategy that is used to guide the design and sequencing of events.

To integrate gameplay into courses, let's consider how a new game may be designed or an existing game may be applied at various levels:

> **Level I (Event Level).** Game played to address one or more instructional events within a lesson or across lessons;

Level II (Lesson Level). Game played to complete one or more instructional lessons;

Level III (Unit/Module Level). Game played to complete one or more instructional units, across lessons within the unit/module;

Level IV (Course Level). Game played as an entire course, including all lessons and units; and

Level V (Program Level). Game played as an instructional program of study made up of two or more courses.

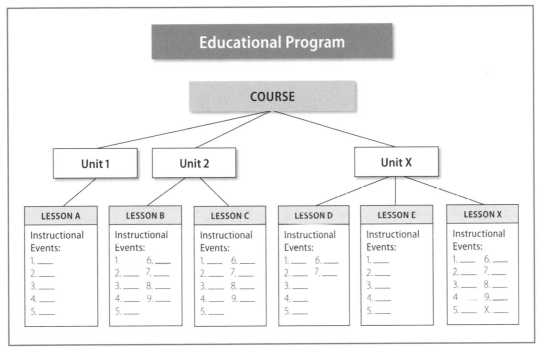

FIGURE 10.1 ▶ Educational course divided into events, lessons, and units

At the Event Level (Level I), a new educational video game may be designed or an existing video game may be integrated to facilitate one or more instructional events within an instructional lesson or across lessons. For example, a relatively simple drill and practice or frame-game may be designed or an existing game may be played to help students recall factual content or to promote their active involvement and discussion (Dempsey, Lucassen, Haynes, & Casey, 1996; Blake and Goodman, 1999). A similar game may also be played at Level I to address the same events across lessons. At the Lesson Level (Level II), a game may be played in place of an instructional lesson or multiple lessons, addressing all of the key events and activities associated with the lesson or lessons. At the Unit Level (Level III), a game may be played to complete one or more, but not all, instructional units contained in a course, addressing all of the events and activities including in the unit or units. At the Course Level (Level IV), one game may be played as an entire course of instruction, incorporating all units, lessons, and events associated with the course. It is also conceivable that a game may be designed or an existing game may be played at a Program Level

(Level V) where completion of the game would satisfy the requirements specified for two or more courses associated with a certificate, degree, or training program. However, the likelihood of such a large-scale game being developed or played at Level V seems remote, at least at this time.

To further illustrate the five levels of gameplay, let's consider the relationship between course structure and grounded instructional strategies. A grounded instructional strategy consists of a set of instructional events that are designed and sequenced based on learning or instructional theories and research. In other words, the strategy is grounded in research and theory. To see how video games may be integrated with instruction, let's look at two examples: one applying what may be considered as a traditional teacher-directed instructional strategy, Gagné's Nine Events of Instruction, and the other applying what may be viewed as a student-centered instructional strategy, the 5E instructional model.

Gagné's (1974, 1977) Nine Events of Instruction are grounded in cognitive information processing (CIP) theories of human learning. Each of Gagné's nine events is associated with and designed to facilitate a specific step in the cognitive information processing theory of learning and should be addressed to facilitate achievement of the objectives specified for an instructional lesson or unit. The following are Gagné's Nine Events of Instruction:

1. Gaining learners' attention

2. Informing learners of objectives

3. Recalling prior knowledge

4. Presenting stimulus (Content information)

5. Providing learning guidance

6. Eliciting performance

7. Providing feedback

8. Assessing performance

9. Enhancing retention and transfer

Gagné's instructional strategy is considered "teacher-directed" because the instructor takes primary responsibility for specifying objectives; selecting, organizing, and delivering the content information; defining student assessment methods and criteria; and otherwise directing the learning process to ensure that students retain the content learned as they transfer and apply it toward accomplishing meaningful work or research.

The relationship between course structure (i.e., event, lesson, unit, course, program) and instructional function, based on application of a grounded instructional strategy, is important for understanding the design and integration of games. Applying Gagné's nine events, for example, we can see that a game may be played at Level I to present stimulus, elicit performance, and/or assess performance (in other words, a subset of events within an instructional lesson or lessons). At Level II, gameplay would address all nine of Gagné's events to facilitate achievement of objectives specified for a lesson or lessons. At Level III, a game would be played to complete an entire unit or several units within a course that may, in turn, consist of multiple lessons. At level IV, a game would be played to fulfill the requirements associated with an entire course, addressing all of the instructional events specified for the units and lessons contained in the course. At Level V, the game would transcend multiple courses and either be played as a part of or form an entire program of study.

Now, consider another example of how a grounded approach can be used to design and integrate video games into instruction. Let's say you decide to apply the 5E instructional model to promote inquiry-based learning (BSCS, 2005). The 5E model calls for the instructor to design and facilitate five types of instructional events within an instructional lesson or unit, including:

1. **E**ngage learners in problem or topic;

2. Learners **E**xplore key skills, concepts, and content information;

3. Learners **E**xplain what they have learned from their exploration;

4. **E**laborate key concepts and skills with learners by filling in gaps, correcting misconceptions, and otherwise clarifying and adding to what was learned; and

5. **E**valuate learners' skills and knowledge, including learners' self-assessment.

Like the first example, at the Event Level, a new game may be designed or an existing game may be played to facilitate one or more instructional events within a lesson or lessons. For instance, a relatively simple game show (e.g., *Jeopardy!*) may be played to evaluate learners' acquisition of key concepts and verbal information. Or an adventure game may be used to engage learners and facilitate the exploration of key concepts, principles, and/or procedures, leaving the instructor to work with students to explain, elaborate, and evaluate what was learned from gameplay outside of the game environment. At the Lesson Level, a game would address all five events (i.e., engage, explore, explain, elaborate, and evaluate) contained in one or more lessons within a course. At the Unit Level, a game may be played in place of one or more, but not all, units in a course; in other words, the game would address all five events related to the 5E model multiple times. At the Course Level, a game would be played to address all of the events, lessons, and units contained in a course. And at Program Level IV, a game may cover all courses associated with a certificate, degree, or training program.

The two examples of instructional strategies illustrate how the grounded approach may be applied within the structure of a traditional, teacher-directed approach to teaching and learning, as well as within a relatively modern, learner-centered approach. In the first example, based on the application of Gagné's Nine Events of Instruction, the teacher informs students of learning objectives, organizes and presents content information, and directs the instructional process. (Note that some games are designed to tell students what they will be learning as they play the game.) In the second example of a learner-centered approach, based on the 5E instructional model, the teacher (and sometimes the game itself) may introduce one or more learning events, and then the students take more responsibility for and have more control over the learning process.

The two examples also depict the varying roles the teacher may take during instruction to guide and monitor game-based learning. In the first example, applying Gagné's Nine Events of Instruction, the teacher may do something at the beginning of a class to gain learners' attention, informing them of objectives and helping them to recall prior knowledge. The teacher may then ask learners to play a game that presents content information, provides learning guidance, elicits performance, and provides feedback. After gameplay, the teacher may step in to assess learners' performance and enhance retention and transfer. In the second example, applying the 5E instructional model, the teacher may use a game to engage students' interest and to encourage them to explore key skills, concepts, and questions and to design a research inquiry. After gameplay, the teacher may ask learners to explain what they learned from gameplay and then work with students to elaborate on explanations of how this knowledge can be applied to real-world situations. The instructor may then use different tools and techniques to evaluate student achievement, possibly asking students to assess how well the game delivered its objectives.

In the first part of this chapter, I related the structure and function of courses to the structure and function of games to distinguish five levels of gameplay, noting how (a) courses may be broken down into instructional units, lessons, and events; (b) grounded instructional strategies consist of a set of instructional events; (c) grounded strategies may be applied to a course; and (d) games may be played as a course, unit, lesson, and/or event. Two examples of how games may be applied at varying levels were presented, based on a traditional, teacher-directed strategy and on a more modern, learner-centered strategy for teaching and learning. In the second part of the chapter, I detail five steps for integrating games to facilitate learning in classroom settings based on grounded instructional strategies.

Five Steps for Integrating Gameplay

For teachers who are just beginning to use video games to enhance learning, the process for integrating gameplay into the curriculum may be easier to understand and apply by initially breaking it down into five relatively simple steps. As teachers increase their knowledge of games and gain experience playing and integrating games for educational purposes, these steps can be transformed into a set of guidelines that may be applied concurrently or in different combinations and sequences, depending on the context.

> **Step 1.** Select a grounded instructional strategy, based on specified objectives, learners' characteristics, classroom context, and epistemological beliefs.
>
> **Step 2.** Play games and determine their suitability and instructional purpose. (Is gameplay appropriate? What instructional events are addressed by the game?)
>
> **Step 3.** Operationalize instructional strategy by describing how each event will be applied and noting when a game should be played.

Step 4. Address technical and logistical issues (e.g., scheduling student access to computers and game).

Step 5. Pilot test gameplay and formatively evaluate instructional materials.

Step 1. Select a Grounded Instructional Strategy

I believe the selection and application of an appropriate instructional strategy is important for stimulating learning in general and essential for facilitating game-based learning. An instructional strategy consists of a comprehensive set of instructional events and activities necessary to help students achieve a specified set of objectives. This strategy guides the design and sequencing of events included in a lesson or unit. The strategy, whether it is teacher directed or learner centered, determines the nature of the learning environment. For game-based learning, the application of instructional strategy helps ensure that vital instructional events before and after gameplay are included to support learning in a lesson or unit; support which has been shown to be just as important as playing the game itself to facilitate learning.

Table 10.1 outlines a number of instructional strategies grounded in educational research and learning theories published over the past 10 to 15 years. The strategies range from traditional, teacher-directed methods to more learner-centered approaches to teaching and learning.

For teachers, selection of an appropriate strategy requires thinking about the desired learning outcomes and key contextual factors, as well as their personal values and beliefs about teaching and learning. Selecting an instructional strategy may also push teachers to step out of their comfort zones, possibly experimenting with a different strategy, one never experienced as students or as educators.

A fundamental instructional design principle is that the nature of the desired learning outcome(s) should drive the instructional design process. For instance, the specific technique used to analyze an instructional situation should be based on targeted learning outcomes (Jonassen, Tessmer, & Hannum, 1999). Similarly, learner assessment methods should be determined by the nature of specified objectives (Berge, 2002; Hirumi, 2002a). The same principle applies to the selection of a grounded instructional strategy.

For example, for instruction on the use of a new photocopying machine, a direct instructional strategy (e.g., Joyce, Weil, & Showers, 1992) may be most effective and efficient. When a problem has basically one correct answer and/or one correct method for deriving the answer, learners may not need to interact with others to derive meaning and construct knowledge through social discourse. In the case of the photocopying machine, the instruction may direct learners to push Button A, then Button B, and if something goes wrong, to check Buttons C and D. In contrast, if the desired learning outcome requires higher-order thinking and if more than one correct answer or more than one method for deriving the correct answer exists, then a student-centered approach that encourages learners to interact with experts and other learners to interpret and apply targeted skills and knowledge may be appropriate.

TABLE 10.1 ▶ Primary instructional events associated with grounded instructional strategies

LEARNER-CENTERED APPROACHES		
BSCS 5E Model *(Bybee, 2002; BSCS, 2005)* 1. Engage 2. Explore 3. Explain 4. Elaborate 5. Evaluate	**WebQuest** *(Dodge, 2007)* 1. Introduction 2. Task 3. Process 4. Resources 5. Evaluation 6. Conclusion	**Constructivist Learning** *(Jonassen, 1999)* 1. Select problem 2. Provide related cases 3. Provide information 4. Provide cognitive tools 5. Provide conversation tools 6. Provide social support
Learning by Doing *(Schank, Berman, & Macpherson, 1999)* 1. Define goals 2. Set mission 3. Present cover story 4. Establish roles 5. Operate scenarios 6. Provide resources 7. Provide feedback	**Collaborative Problem-Solving** *(Nelson, 1999)* 1. Build readiness 2. Form and norm groups 3. Determine preliminary problem 4. Define and assign roles 5. Engage in problem-solving 6. Finalize solution 7. Synthesize and reflect 8. Assess products and processes 9. Provide closure	**Eight Events of Student-Centered Learning** *(Hirumi, 2002b, 1996, 1998)* 1. Set learning challenge 2. Negotiate goals and objectives 3. Negotiate learning strategy 4. Construct knowledge 5. Negotiate performance criteria 6. Assess learning 7. Provide feedback (steps 1–6) 8. Communicate results
Case-Based Reasoning *(Aamodt & Plaza, 1994)* 1. Present new case/problem 2. Retrieve similar cases 3. Reuse information 4. Revise proposed solution 5. Retain useful experiences	**Simulation Model** *(Joyce, Weil, & Showers, 1992)* 1. Orientation 2. Participant training 3. Simulation operations 4. Participant debriefing 5. Appraise and redesign the simulation	**Interplay Strategy** *(Stapleton & Hirumi, in press)* 1. Expose 2. Inquire 3. Discover 4. Create 5. Experiment 6. Share
TEACHER-DIRECTED APPROACHES		
Nine Events of Instruction *(Gagné, 1974, 1977)* 1. Gain attention 2. Inform learner of objective(s) 3. Recall prior knowledge 4. Present stimulus materials 5. Provide learning guidance 6. Elicit performance 7. Provide feedback 8. Assess performance 9. Enhance retention and transfer	**Direct Instruction** *(Joyce, Weil, & Showers, 1992)* 1. Orientation 2. Presentation 3. Structured practice 4. Guided practice 5. Independent practice	**Elements of Lesson Design** *(Hunter, 1990)* 1. Anticipatory set 2. Objective and purpose 3. Input 4. Modeling 5. Check for understanding 6. Guided practice 7. Independent practice 8. Closure

Contextual factors, such as learner characteristics and the number and nature of learning sites, also affect the selection of an instructional strategy. In some situations, learners may have greatly varying prior knowledge of the subject matter. For example, it is not uncommon for some students to begin an introductory computer course with considerable computer experience, while others may start with few or no computer skills. In such cases, a learner-centered approach that allows students to negotiate their own learning objectives, strategies, and assessments based on their particular needs and interests can be useful (see Hirumi, 2002b). Whenever it is important for students to work at their own varied paces, a self-instructional strategy benefits the students and the teacher. Self-instructional materials that guide students to monitor and regulate their own learning, with few learner-instructor interactions, can be more appropriate than a collaborative approach that requires a high number of planned learner-learner and/or learner-instructor interactions.

In selecting an appropriate strategy, it is also important for educators to take into account their educational philosophies and epistemological beliefs. If you believe that people derive meaning and construct knowledge through social interactions, then a constructivist instructional strategy that includes some form of collaboration among your students may best support your beliefs and values. Similarly, if you believe people learn best by "doing," then an experiential approach may resonate with your educational philosophy.

Selecting an appropriate instructional strategy is neither simple, nor straightforward. The desired learning goals and objectives need to be considered above all, yet concerns for the learner, the context of the classroom, and the instructor's fundamental beliefs about teaching and learning also mediate the selection process. Perhaps even stronger influences are time and expertise. With insufficient time or training, educators often revert to what they know best; that is, teacher-directed methods and materials. To select an appropriate instructional strategy, the instructor and/or designer must have the time and skills necessary to analyze several important variables and to develop a good understanding of alternative strategies. They must also have the confidence, desire, and opportunity to apply alternative instructional strategies within the context of their jobs.

Step 2. Play Games and Determine Their Suitability and Instructional Purpose

After selecting a grounded instructional strategy, teachers should play and select games for potential use in their classes by determining (a) the suitability of gameplay in general and of specific games in particular, and (b) the instructional nature and purpose(s) of each of the selected games.

How can teachers determine whether playing games in general is suitable for their classes? How can they decide whether particular games fit their students' needs or are engaging? And how can the selected games meet the course's instructional objectives? In Chapter 5, Dieterle identified a series of logistical and instructional questions to help teachers determine whether games can and should be played to facilitate student learning in their classes. I also encourage teachers to answer the questions he poses regarding instructional logistics and learning objectives to help decide whether and when to play games in classes. In an analysis of websites designed to support the use of instructional games, Kebritchi, Hirumi, Kappers, and Henry (2008) noted key technical and logistical issues that must be addressed before playing games in schools, including compatibility with preexisting systems; the availability of necessary hardware, software, and technical support; and time/scheduling. Furthermore, as Hays notes in Chapter 11, studies with a wide range of learners in a variety of training and educational settings show that students can learn from playing games if appropriate games are used and properly integrated with instruction.

Now that we have covered the preliminary issues for teachers to consider before deciding to incorporate gameplaying into their classes, I am going to address each of you in a more personal manner. Assuming that you have considered key technical and logistical issues and have found that your students, classroom, and support system are suited for gameplay and that you know or have learned how to integrate games with instruction properly (as discussed in this chapter and throughout Section III of this book), how do you find appropriate games for your class?

Section II (Chapters 5–9) of this book identified a number of games that may be appropriate for math, science, social studies, language arts, and physical education. In those chapters, as well as in Chapter 11, the authors further stress the importance of selecting games that match students' skills and knowledge and present them with an appropriate level of challenge. We also know that the contents of the game should be current, accurate, and free of bias and that the game should support the achievement of specified instructional objectives. So, let's say you have played several games and have found one or more that may be appropriate for your class, then what? To integrate gameplay, it is also essential to understand the game's instructional nature and determine its purpose(s) within the context of your course, unit, and/or lesson.

What types of instructional events are facilitated by the game, or what role will it play within particular lesson(s) or unit(s)? In other words, what specific instructional purpose(s) will the game serve during a lesson, unit, or course? Is the game best suited to engage learners and capture their attention at the beginning of a lesson or unit? Does the game present relevant scenarios or simulations that students may operate to test hypotheses, identify trends and issues, or gain insights on how a system functions? Does the game teach new skills and content, or is it better suited to reinforce and give students opportunities to practice recently learned skills? Does the game include appropriate learner assessments and feedback?

Answering the aforementioned questions and determining the instructional nature and purposes of the selected games will help you decide how and when gameplay fits with your instructional strategy. You will also know what you must do before and after gameplay to facilitate learning. Note the instructional purposes of your game; that is, when and why you are going to integrate the game within your lesson, unit, or course, and go to Step 3.

Step 3. Operationalize Instructional Strategy

Operationalize each event of your selected instructional strategy, noting when and how games should be played and what additional instructional events must be addressed before and after gameplay. To complete Step 3, list the instructional events associated with your selected instructional strategy in one column and then describe how you plan to facilitate each event in a second column. Step 3 is best illustrated through a couple of examples.

Example 1—Integrating a Math Game with Hunter's Elements of Lesson Design

For this example, let's say a math teacher has been applying Hunter's (1990) elements of lesson design and wants to integrate gameplay with her pre-algebra class to enhance student motivation and achievement.

For Step 1, the teacher decides to keep using Hunter's elements of lesson design throughout most of her course because (a) she believes that a teacher-directed approach is the most efficient and effective way of achieving course objectives, given the nature of the objectives, which are applying basic math formulas and relatively simple math concepts, (b) it suits the number of students and classes, five classes with approximately 30 students per class, and (c) Hunter's elements are familiar and appear similar to how she has been teaching the class for the past three years.

For Step 2, the teacher finds that Tabula Digita publishes a set of single and multiplayer pre-algebra math games (DimensionM) that addresses many of the topics covered in her course. She plays the games and finds out that they play just like a modern video game, with 3-D immersive graphics, game worlds, and characters she thinks students will really like. She sees that the games provide a lot of good practice for applying many of the pre-algebra concepts she covers in class, but she realizes that the games do not actually teach the concepts. She notes that the games' primary instructional purposes would be for practice, reinforcement, and self-assessment.

Table 10.2 depicts the two-column table recommended earlier for operationalizing the instructional strategy selected during Step 1. It presents an example of how a teacher may apply an instructional strategy for a lesson on adding and subtracting integers that integrates the use of a math video game. Column 1 lists the key events associated with Hunter's elements of lesson design. Column 2 provides a short description of how the instructor plans to teach each event.

TABLE 10.2 ▶ An example of how a teacher would apply Hunter's elements for a lesson on adding and subtracting integers that integrates the use of a math video game

EVENTS	DESCRIPTIONS OF TEACHER'S ACTIONS
Anticipatory set	Gain attention by informing students they will be playing a video game for this lesson and others if this trial works out well. Note that to successfully complete one of the missions in the game, students must know how to add and subtract integers. Stimulate students' recall of prior knowledge by reviewing definitions and examples of related terms and concepts, such as integers, negative numbers, positive numbers, and opposite of numbers.
Objectives and purpose	Inform students that they will be expanding their understanding of integers by distinguishing negative and positive numbers and learning how to add and subtract integers. Have students identify and discuss real-life applications of integers and operations on these numbers, like temperature, acceleration, sports, finances, and altitude.
Input	Explain basic concepts by providing examples that combine saving and debts. Illustrate how the examples are similar to adding positive and negative numbers.
Modeling	Go over several additional situations involving positive and negative numbers as addends in a mathematical sentence. Also use number lines to represent the relationship between the addends using arrows and integers. Use examples such as calculating change in temperature, acceleration, and/or altitude.
Check for understanding	Distribute a handout and ask students to complete problems alone. Give students time to complete problems and then review them with class.

(Continued)

TABLE 10.2 ▶ *(Continued)*

EVENTS	DESCRIPTIONS OF TEACHER'S ACTIONS
Guided practice	Present problems and work through their answers together. Review the differences between each question and how positive and negative numbers affect the outcome of the total. Relate examples to the number line to give students a better understanding of the concept of positive and negative integers.
Independent practice	Have students go to the computer lab and complete Mission 09 of the Single Player Pre-Algebra Game. Explain to students that in the game the government is planning to use a satellite laser to erase the mistakes they made on Xeno Island, and the students' mission is to get to the Communication Center and cut off the satellite link by adding and subtracting integers. Ensure they know how to access and start the game. Considering printing and giving each student a short handout listing steps for accessing the game and getting to Mission 09. Be sure to tell students that they must complete the mission to earn credit. If they don't have time to complete it today, they can complete it by accessing the game from home or going to the lab later in the day or sometime tomorrow.
Closure	Ask students to write what they have learned about integers. Have students write any questions they may have. Also ask students to write down what, if anything, they would like to do differently the next time they play a game as a part of class.

As Table 10.2 indicates, it is important for the teacher to teach a number of important instructional events before and after students play the game because simply playing the game will not ensure that students will achieve the specified objectives. The teacher must (1) prepare for and facilitate events to gain students' attention and help them recall prior knowledge (anticipatory set), (2) inform students of the learning objectives and illustrate the importance of achieving the objectives, (3) teach and model application of the targeted math concepts, and (4) check for understanding and give some guided practice—all before playing the game! Additionally, the teacher must spend some time to explain how gameplay relates to the lesson, ensure students know how to access the game, and communicate expectations for playing the game. After gameplay, the teacher must also provide closure to enhance retention and reinforce knowledge and skills.

The next example illustrates how a game may be integrated with a learner-centered instructional strategy.

Example 2—Integrating a Science Game with the 5E Instructional Model

For Example 2, let's say a high school science teacher wants to integrate gameplay into his classes to enhance student learning. He decides to apply the 5E instructional model for an instructional unit on immunology. The teacher believes that a learner-centered, inquiry-oriented approach may be an effective way to achieve specified lesson objectives. He has heard that the 5E model is based on the natural inquiry process of children and problem-solving among adults.

Surfing the web, using the keywords "immunology" and "video game," the teacher discovers that the Federation of American Scientists (FAS) has published a game called Immune Attack (2008). He downloads the game, which is free for educational purposes, plays the game, and finds that it actually consists of five separate but interrelated games about different aspects of immunology. He is excited and relieved to see that FAS has published a teacher's guide, a game guide, and a technical support manual with FAQs for the game, and provides a mechanism for reporting problems.

Like Table 10.2, Table 10.3 illustrates how the teacher plans to apply the instructional strategy selected in Step 1 of the game integration process for an instructional unit on immunology. Column 1 lists the five key E words associated with the 5E instructional model, and Column 2 provides a short description of how the teacher plans to facilitate each event. Suggestions for engaging (Event 1) and elaborating on students' explanations (Event 4) were derived from a sample lesson plan posted by FAS (2008).

As Table 10.3 indicates, it is important for teachers to begin the unit or lesson and set up gameplay by asking students a series of questions. In this particular example, the questions are asked to get them to recall prior knowledge, to focus their attention, and to engage them as interested learners. The teacher then gives students time to play the selected game and explore its contents, ensuring they know why they are playing the game and what is expected of them.

TABLE 10.3 ▶ An example of how a teacher would apply the 5E instructional model for a unit on immunology, integrating the use of a science video game

EVENT	DESCRIPTION OF TEACHER'S FACILITATION
1. Engage	Engage students by saying they will be playing a video game to learn about the human immune system. Present and ask students to answer a series of questions to recall prior knowledge and focus their attention: • What is an infection? • How do our bodies fight infections? • What are bacteria? • How do medical doctors fight bacteria? • What may happen to you if your body cannot fight bacteria and infections?
2. Explore	Have students go to the computer lab and play Game 1 in Immune Attack. Inform students that the purpose of playing Game 1 is to learn about the process of transmigration. Tell them they will be asked to explain what they learned about transmigration after playing the game, and suggest that they take notes on the process as they play.
3. Explain	Ask students to explain the process of transmigration of monocytes. Ask them to write down their explanations and either e-mail their answers or submit hard copy at the beginning of the next class session.
4. Elaborate	Review students' explanations. Determine whether they identified five key concepts, including (a) monocytes flow in the blood vessels, (b) selectins help monocytes slow down, (c) ICAMs help monocytes to stop, (d) ICAMs help monocytes to move through the blood vessels' walls and into connective tissues, and (e) once a monocyte has entered the connective tissue, it is known as a macrophage. If students fail to identify some concepts, ask them leading questions (e.g., What do ICAMS do during the process?). If students fail to identify two or more concepts, ask them to replay Game 1 and to submit a revised explanation. Other key concepts related to transmigration covered by Game 1 include (a) What are leukocytes (white blood cells)? (b) What is a macrophage, and what does it do? (c) Macrophages can travel to a site of infection, and (d) Leukocytes can move from the blood stream into the tissue. Consider giving credit to students who include these concepts in their explanations as well as asking students to elaborate further if they do not include these concepts in their explanations.
5. Evaluate	Distribute and ask students to complete a regular paper-based test on the topic. Also ask students to write down what, if anything, they would like to do differently the next time they play a game as a part of class.

Event 3 in the 5E instructional model represents a significant departure from traditional, teacher-directed instructional methods. Rather than having the teacher lecture and explain key principles, concepts, and facts to students, the students are to explain what they learned from playing the selected game and exploring its contents. Student-generated explanations provide valuable insights into what they have learned, what they have not learned, and what misconceptions they may have about what they have learned. The teacher then uses this information to fill in any gaps in students' learning and correct misconceptions by asking them to elaborate on their explanations as described for Event 4 in Table 10.3, for example. Finally, the teacher evaluates students' learning and their reactions to the instructional unit/lesson to assess their achievement and progress, as well as the effectiveness and appeal of gameplay as a tool to convey the instructional unit/lesson.

Together, the two examples illustrate how teachers may operationalize their selected instructional strategy and integrate gameplay with their instruction. The examples also show how games may be played in the contexts of what may be considered a traditional, teacher-directed approach and a more student-centered approach to teaching and learning. Now that you have a basic plan for playing and integrating the use of games in your class, it's time to address technical and logistical issues to help ensure that all goes as planned.

Step 4. Address Technical and Logistical Issues

In Step 2 (Play Games and Determine Their Suitability), you considered a series of technical and logistical issues to determine whether gameplay in general and specific games in particular are suitable for your class. In short, you selected potential games for use in your class by determining whether you, your school, and/or students have the (a) hardware, software (e.g., operating system), and network infrastructure necessary to access and play the games; (b) money necessary to acquire the game(s); (c) basic technical skills to learn how to play the game(s) readily; and (d) time to play the game and resources necessary to provide sufficient access to the game(s). Now it's time to address the technical and logistical issues.

First, you must determine when and where students are to access the game(s). Are students to access the game at the beginning, at the end, or throughout an instructional unit? Are students to access the game in class, in computer labs, at home, and/or at community centers, such as in nearby libraries? Are students to access the game individually, in pairs, and/or in small groups? How much time do students need to play the game(s)? The answers to these questions will help you establish a schedule and, if necessary, a rotation for students to access the game(s).

Second, work with your school's administrators, technology coordinator, and technology support staff to acquire and set up the game(s) for use in class, library, and/or computer lab(s). If you plan to provide access to games in community centers, such as a local library, also be sure to contact the person in charge of the computers to ensure that the facility has the means and desire to provide access to the selected game(s). Make sure the school's tech support staff know when students are to access the games and how to contact technical support for the games' publisher to troubleshoot problems and maintain the games. Also, ensure that students know how to download the game(s) (if necessary) and what to do if they have problems setting up, accessing, or playing the games, particularly if they are expected to play at home. Consider writing out instructions for the school's tech staff as well as for your students and posting them on your own website or the school's website for easy access. Giving students a printed handout to take home is another option.

Third, work with your school's administrators, technology coordinator, technology support staff, and community center representative (if necessary) to ensure proper policies and procedures are in place to regulate and monitor gameplay and access to the games. Make sure the policies and procedures are properly documented and communicated to your students and their caregivers.

Fourth, make sure you know how to access your students' data so that you can monitor their gameplay. Many games record when and how long students access the game. Many also keep records of students' scores. If your unit or lesson requires students to complete certain missions, puzzles, and/or other activities within the game, make sure you know how to access and record relevant student data.

Finally, acquire and/or develop the instructional materials necessary to support, properly integrate, and facilitate the use of games in your class. In Step 3, you operationalized your instructional strategy and determined what instructional events must be addressed before, during, and after gameplay. Review your instructional strategy and either acquire or develop the materials that are necessary to facilitate each instructional event.

You should now be ready to play games in class to enhance student learning and motivation. However, before you actually implement your unit or lessons, I encourage you to run a pilot test of the game and your instructional materials with a group of students who represent the various academic and technological ability levels of your target learner population.

Step 5. Pilot Test Gameplay and Formatively Evaluate Instructional Materials

If students do not achieve specified instructional objectives or simply do not like the instruction built into playing video games, teachers often blame the students, and students typically blame the teacher. The fact is, neither the students nor the teacher may be to blame; rather, gameplay may not go as well as everyone originally thought it would, or the instructional materials used before, during and/or after gameplay may be the reasons why students did not learn or did not enjoy their experience. To ensure the effectiveness of gameplay before you actually use the game in class, you should pilot test each game and formatively evaluate the instructional materials.

No matter how often you have played a game with classes in the past or how much fun you think students will have playing the game, students are likely to differ in terms of their abilities to use the game and their gameplay preferences. Before you spend valuable class time playing the game, it's always a good idea to test the game with a few students who represent your learner population first. Take notes as they play the game and ask the following questions at the end of each test session: Are students readily able to learn how to play the game? How much time did it take before they felt comfortable playing the game? How much time did it take for students to complete targeted portions of the game? Is additional training necessary for some or all students?

Did they enjoy playing the game? The answers to each of these questions are important to verify the feasibility of integrating the game with instruction.

I encourage you to formatively evaluate the instructional materials you plan to use before, during, and/or after gameplay. Formative evaluation occurs prior to actual instructional delivery to ensure the effectiveness and efficiency of the instruction (Dick, Carey, & Carey, 2005). Specifically, the instructional materials should be tested with representative members of the target learner population for (a) clarity—is the message or what is being presented clear to individual learners? (b) impact—what is the impact of the instruction on various individuals' attitudes and achievement of the objectives and goals? and (c) feasibility—how feasible is the planned instruction given the available time and resources?

Summary

Like the use of other emerging technologies, the proper integration of games requires planning and the possible development of supporting instructional materials. In this chapter, I have presented a grounded approach to integrating instructional video games with instruction and facilitating game-based learning. In the first part, I analyzed the structure and function of classroom instruction and related them to the structure and function of games to illustrate how games may be applied at five levels, including Event Level I—as an instructional event or events; Lesson Level II—as an instructional lesson; Unit Level III—as an instructional unit or module, played across lessons; Course Level IV—as an instructional course, across all lessons and units; or Program Level V—as a program of study made up of two or more courses. Then, in the second part of the chapter, I presented five steps for integrating instructional video games with instruction based on teacher-directed and student-centered instructional strategies.

Similar to the other approaches for integrating games posited in Section III of this book, I also stress the importance of providing instructional support and facilitating key instructional events before and after gameplay to optimize game-based learning. Unlike the other approaches, I recommend selection and use of a grounded instructional strategy to determine when and how games are played and to ensure students experience all of the instructional events necessary to optimize game-based learning before, during, and after gameplay. This is not to say that the other approaches to integrating games are not as valid; rather, I provide an alternative approach to integrating games with instruction for teachers to consider.

While playing games in schools may not motivate all students or ensure that all of them achieve high academic standards, I do believe games offer a valuable addition to our arsenal of tools and techniques for enhancing individual and group learning, particularly as we compete with cell phones, entertaining video games, and the Internet for our students' time and attention. So, go ahead, play some games, and have some fun; you may find that you enjoy teaching with games as much as your students enjoy learning with them.

References

Aamodt, A., & Plaza, E. (1994). Case-based reasoning: Foundational issues, methodological variations, and systems approaches. *Artificial Intelligence Communications, 7*(1), 39–59. Retrieved April 8, 2010, from www.gaia.fdi.ucm.es/people/pedro/aad/Aamodt_Plaza94.pdf

Berge, Z. (2002). Active, interactive and reflective elearning. *Quarterly Review of Distance Education, 3*(2), 181–190.

Blake, J., & Goodman, J. (1999). Computer-based learning: Games as an instructional strategy. *The Association of Black Nursing Faculty Journal, 10*(2), 43–46.

BSCS Center for Professional Development. (2005). *Learning theory and the BSCS 5E instructional model.* Colorado Springs, CO: BSCS Center for Professional Development. Published for the NSTA Professional Development Institute's National Convention, Dallas, TX, March 31, 2005. Retrieved April 6, 2010, from http://iisme.5ecommunity.org/members/aliciab/images/5-E%20 Instructional%20Model.pdf

Bybee, R. W. (2002). Scientific inquiry, student learning, and the science curriculum. In R. W. Bybee (Ed.), *Learning science and the science of learning* (pp. 25–36). Arlington, VA: NSTA Press.

Dempsey, J. V., Lucassen, B. A., Haynes, L. L., & Casey, M. S. (1996). *Instructional applications of computer games.* New York: Annual Meeting of the American Educational Research Association. (ERIC Document Reproduction Service No. ED 394 500)

Dick, W., Carey, L., & Carey, J. O. (2005). *The systematic design of instruction* (6th ed.). Boston: Allyn & Bacon.

Dodge, B. (1998). *Webquest.Org.* Retrieved July 14, 2010, from http:///webquest.org

Federation of American Scientists (FAS). (2008). *Immune attack* general lesson plan, version 3.0, for Grades 9–12, covering immune system, disease, and infection. Available at http://fas.org/ immuneattack/wp-content/uploads/2008/05/ia-lesson-plan-v30.pdf

Gagné, R. M. (1974). *Principles of instructional design.* New York, NY: Holt, Rinehart, and Winston.

Gagné, R. M. (1977). *The conditions of learning* (3rd ed.). New York, NY: Holt, Rinehart, and Winston.

Hirumi, A. (1996, February). *Student-centered, technology-rich learning environments: A cognitive-constructivist approach.* Presentation at the Association for Educational Communication and Technology Conference, Indianapolis.

Hirumi, A. (1998, March). *The systematic design of student-centered, technology-rich learning environments.* Guest presentation given at the first Education Graduate Students and Academic Staff Regional Meeting, Guadalajara, Mexico.

Hirumi, A. (2002a). A framework for analyzing, designing and sequencing planned e-learning interactions. *Quarterly Review of Distance Education, 3*(2), 141–160.

Hirumi, A. (2002b). Student-centered, technology-rich learning environments (SCenTRLE): Operationalizing constructivist approaches to teaching and learning. *Journal of Technology and Teacher Education, 10*(4), 497–537.

Hunter, M. (1990). Lesson design helps achieve the goals of science instruction. *Educational Leadership, 48*(4), 79–81.

Jonassen, D. (1999). Designing constructivist learning environments. In C. M. Reigeluth (Ed.), *Instructional-design theories and models: A new paradigm of instructional theory. Volume II.* (pp. 215–239). Mahwah, NJ: Lawrence Erlbaum.

Jonassen, D. H., Tessmer, M., & Hannum, W. H. (1999). *Task analysis methods for instructional design.* Mahwah, NJ: Lawrence Erlbaum.

Joyce, B., Weil, M., & Showers, B. (1992). *Models of teaching* (4th ed.). Boston, MA: Allyn & Bacon.

Kebritchi, M., Hirumi, A., Kappers, W., & Henry, R. (2008). Analysis of the supporting websites for the use of instructional games in K–12 settings. *British Journal of Educational Technology, 40*(4), 733–754. Available from www3.interscience.wiley.com/journal/122455207/issue

Nelson, L. (1999). Collaborative problem-solving. In C. M. Reigeluth (Ed.), *Instructional-design theories and models: A new paradigm of instructional theory. Volume II.* (pp. 241–267). Mahwah, NJ: Lawrence Erlbaum.

Schank, R. C., Berman, T. R., & Macpherson, K. A. (1999). Learning by doing. In C. M. Reigeluth (Ed.), *Instructional-design theories and models: A new paradigm of instructional theory. Volume II.* (pp. 161–179). Mahwah, NJ: Lawrence Erlbaum.

Stapleton, C., & Hirumi, A. (in press). Interplay instructional strategy: Engaging learners with interactive entertainment conventions. In M. Shaughnessy & S. Veronikas (Eds.), *Implications for online instruction.* Hauppauge, NY: Nova Science Publishers.

11

Making Games More Effective in the Classroom

Robert T. Hays

WHO DOESN'T WANT TO IMPROVE EDUCATION and better serve our students? Some claim that using games and game-based technologies in the classroom will help us reach this goal. They assume that all games are instructionally effective and may be the preferred approach. However, before we accept this assumption, it is important to realize that the research on instructional games is mixed and that there is a great deal of confusion about games and how to use them. This chapter begins with a brief summary of the claims made about instructional games and some of the confusions about games. This is followed by a brief overview of the research on the instructional benefits of games and what we know about how to use games most effectively. Finally, a set of guidelines, based on research, is presented to help instructors effectively use games in the classroom. The guidelines are organized in four sections: (a) planning to use a game; (b) selecting a game; (c) using a game in the classroom, and (d) evaluating a game's effectiveness. The guidelines are supplemented with a series of evaluation scales that can also help instructors make decisions about selecting and using instructional games.

You've probably heard many people say that games can revolutionize education. They claim that using games in the classroom will motivate students and help them learn better. These kinds of claims have been made for many years, but many educators still have questions about when and how to use games effectively in the classroom.

In 1981, Greenblat surveyed and summarized evidence for six claims about the instructional benefits of games. Her data are summarized later in this chapter (see Table 11.1). The claims stated that using games could:

1. Increase the motivation and interest of learners

2. Improve learning

3. Change later coursework

4. Improve learners' attitudes about the subject matter

5. Improve learners' general affect toward learning

6. Support changes in classroom structure and relations

Although some data show that some games result in learning, other data indicate less positive results. Some games have been shown to be detrimental to learning while others provided no more benefits than other forms of instruction. The empirical evidence has also concluded that games can increase both positive and negative attitudes toward the subject matter. As with any instructional tool, the characteristics of the game and how it is used are the prime determinants of learners' attitudes about the game and its instructional effectiveness (Hays, 2006, 2008). Although games have large potential to be effective instructional tools, teachers need guidance to help them realize this potential.

This chapter provides guidelines that can help teachers get the most instructional benefits from the use of games in their classrooms. It begins with a discussion of important terms used in the literature on games. A brief overview of research on the effectiveness of instructional games follows, concluding with a reexamination of Greenblat's (1981) claims. A comparison of claims to available empirical evidence provides a snapshot of our progress in understanding the instructional effectiveness of games over the last 25 years. Next, guidelines based on the empirical data for selecting and using instructional games are presented. The chapter concludes with evaluation scales that can supplement the guidelines to help teachers use instructional games more effectively.

The Importance of Understanding the Definitions of Terms

Sometimes one can't tell whether a research effort actually studied a game. Even if the researchers used a game, it is difficult to determine its specific characteristics and how it was used. One of the many reasons for the lack of clarity in the literature on instructional games is confusion on the use of various terms in the literature on games (Greenblat & Duke, 1981; Hays, 2005, 2006; Rieber,

1996; Thomas, Cahill, & Santilli, 1997). The terms "model," "simulation," "game," and "simulation-game" are often used interchangeably in the same article. Confusion about these terms may lead to incorrect decisions about how to combine games with instructional approaches effectively in the classroom. The following sections include definitions of some of these important terms and discussions of different types of games.

Models and Simulations

Two terms that are often confused are model and simulation. As the U.S. Department of Defense (DoD) is one of the largest users of models and simulations, its definitions of these terms can help us understand their applications in instructional games. A *model* is defined as "a physical, mathematical, or otherwise logical representation of a system, entity, phenomenon, or process" (DoD, 1997, p. 138). Models represent selected aspects of the real world for specific purposes. They do not represent all aspects of any real-world phenomenon. If a model represented all these aspects, it would not be a model—it would be the real thing. Models serve as the foundation for dynamic simulations by providing the rules and the data that allow a simulation to function in a specific way to meet a specific purpose. A *simulation* is "a method for implementing a model over time" (DoD, 1997, p. 160). So, any simulation is based on and controlled by its underlying model. The model defines the characteristics of the simulation, and the simulation "runs" the model dynamically. Are all simulations also games? We examine this question in the next section.

Game

After reviewing many definitions of games (Hays 2005, 2006), I settled on the following definition: *A game is an artificially constructed, competitive activity with a specific goal, a set of rules and constraints that is located in a specific context.*

Let's look more closely at the four important parts of this definition.

1. A game is *artificially constructed*. A game is not real. Rather, it is a representation of reality. Therefore, a simulation is based on a model of reality, and we can say that *all games are simulations*. However, we must also say that *not all simulations are games*. It is vital that instructors understand the model upon which a game is based. Are your instructional objectives realistically supported by the characteristics of the model underlying the game? Here are a couple of simple examples. First, if simulated people are part of the game, they should move realistically; they should not be able to run at 40 mph. Second, if communications are part of the game, they should be realistic—one should have to use a communications device to communicate with distant players.

2. A game is a *competitive activity*. Only when a simulation includes competition can we call it a game. This competition can be against other players, against oneself, or against criteria set by the game.

3. A game has a *specific goal* established by its *rules and constraints*. Both teachers and learners must understand these rules and constraints. Furthermore, they must understand how similar the game's rules are to the real-world constraints of the knowledge or skills to be learned.

4. A game is *located in a specific context*. This means that each game must be designed, bought, and/or modified to meet the teacher's specific instructional goals. As discussed below, a simulation can be turned into a game if it is used competitively with a set of rules and constraints.

Instructional Game

Not all games are instructional games. An *instructional game* is specifically designed or modified to meet instructional objectives. An instructional game meets these objectives by including rules, constraints, and activities that closely replicate the constraints of the real-world knowledge and skills that are being taught. An instructional game must be incorporated into an instructional program in a manner that ensures that learners understand the instructional objectives of the game and receive detailed feedback about their performance and how their game performance supported the instructional objectives of the course. In most cases, an instructional game should be considered an instructional aid or tool rather than a method of stand-alone instruction. In some situations an instructional game must be used in a stand-alone mode (e.g., distance or distributed instruction). In these cases, the game must be designed to include all of the instructional capabilities that are otherwise provided by the teacher because the game itself is standing in as the instructor.

Types of Games

Many types of games can be used for instructional purposes, and games can be classified in many different ways. It is important that you appreciate the differences among game types so that you can choose the gaming approach that most closely meets your instructional goals. The following sections provide definitions of different types of games. Remember, a specific game often is a combination of several different game types.

Simulation-Based Games

All simulations are not games, but all games are simulations. Some games can even be based on existing simulations, for example, personal computer (PC) flight simulations. These are often called simulation-based games. Sometimes, the goal of a simulation-based game is to challenge the player to master the simulation, that is, to learn to take off, land, or use the simulated instruments. However, by the definition above, the simulation is not a game unless it includes game-like activities, such as specific goals, rules and constraints, competition, and so on. If the rules and algorithms that govern the simulation are realistic, in that they match the constraints and requirements of the task in the real word, it may be possible to use it as an instructional game. This will only be the case if the simulation-based game is incorporated into an instructional program that fully explains any differences between the real-world constraints and the characteristics of the simulation.

Individual or Group Games

Some games are designed to be played by a single individual, competing against the game or against a skill standard that allows the player to compete against himself or herself. Other games are designed to be played by groups of people competing against each other as individuals or teams. Even team games may require individual instruction before the learners are ready to interact with a group or as a team.

Games of Skill or Games of Chance

Some games are based on skill, such as board games, card games, mathematical games, and word games; others are based on chance, like dice games, casino games, and bingo. There is not a clear distinction between these types because chance games may also require certain skills, for example, knowing when to fold one's cards in poker or to hold in blackjack. Certain skill games may also incorporate randomly generated events as part of their scenarios, such as the effects of different market forces in an economics game.

Computer-Based or Live Games

When thinking of games, many people first think of computer-based video games. Although video games are very popular, many games involve live individuals, for example, sports and business games. When a live game has been converted to a video game, like video basketball or football, it is important to determine whether it retains the rules and conditions that apply in the real world.

Off-the-Shelf or Tailored Games

Many games can be purchased from computer stores or from the Internet. These are called commercial off-the-shelf (COTS) games. If you choose to use a COTS game, you must determine if it includes the appropriate task characteristics, constraints, and level of realism to support your instructional objectives. In most cases, a COTS game will include some realistic events, but it may also include unrealistic characteristics. If the game characteristics are unrealistic, playing the game may result in students learning the wrong things or learning to do things the wrong way. Alternatively, some games may be bought from a commercial source and then tailored for a specific need. These tailored games are targeted more narrowly than COTS games, but they still must be assessed to determine whether they include the appropriate task characteristics and constraints.

Hybrid Games

Most games are combinations of various elements from different game types. For example, a game used to teach urban planning may incorporate COTS simulations of various types of urban events, like the construction of large buildings and the resulting changes in traffic patterns during and after construction. These simulations could involve generation of events based on some form of random number generator. The game might also use tailored role-playing scenarios allowing live individuals to interact with the simulations.

Uses of Instructional Games

We can also classify instructional games by the type of learning task. Remember, like the above types of games, the following game classifications are not mutually exclusive.

Skills and Procedures Training Games

Sometimes we need to teach students how to perform specific skills, such as how to interpret a poem, how to distinguish a well-supported argument from a spurious argument, or how to organize information to support a decision, and procedures, for example, how to set up a volt meter, how to fix or operate a piece of equipment, or how to drive a vehicle.

Action Games

Action games require the learner to react to specific situations and engage in real-time actions, for example, first-person shooter games or multiplayer racing games. This type of game is very popular, and many people regard action games as the preferred gaming approach. Some instructional games incorporate action as a reward after a learner masters a segment of content. Unfortunately, some students may take shortcuts through the content to get to the action portions of the game.

Role-Playing Games

In role-playing games, students participate in a scenario that requires them to learn and practice specific activities required to reach a desired goal. These games can help students gain an appreciation for the different roles required in most real-world tasks. For example, they can learn the different issues that must be considered by a supervisor compared with those the members of a work team need to know.

Strategy Games

In strategy games, students participate in scenarios that require them to learn and practice information analysis, information synthesis, planning, and other strategy skills. Elements of strategy games are found in many other types of games. For example, in action games, players need to develop various strategies to complete segments of the game. These strategy elements are also often found in role-playing games.

The above summaries show that different types of games can be used as instructional tools. How instructionally effective are these games? The next section gives a brief overview of some of the empirical research that has attempted to answer this question.

Overview of Research on the Effectiveness of Instructional Games

Instructional games have been used for a wide variety of tasks with learners of different ages. Past reviews have found that the majority of articles on instructional games are opinions about whether to use games and about the potential of games to provide effective instruction (e.g., Dempsey et al., 1993–94). Far fewer articles provide empirical data from research that has investigated the instructional effectiveness of games. This section begins with a summary of the empirical data on instructional games. It is followed by a comparison of the data Greenblat (1981) used to support the claims about games with more recent data. This comparison provides a snapshot of what we have learned about the effectiveness of instructional games since 1981.

Summary of Empirical Evidence on Instructional Games

I conducted a review of more than 270 documents from the literature on games (Hays, 2005, 2006). Of these, only 48 provided empirical data on the instructional effectiveness of games. The review included discussions on the results of general review articles and results reported in articles on the effectiveness of specific games. For details on any of the articles, please see the original reviews (Hays, 2005, 2006) or the original articles.

Several observations can be derived from the literature review. First, the empirical research on instructional games examined their effects for a *wide range of age groups.* Twelve of the studies examined the learning effects of games with elementary school children and two with high school students. Eleven studies used instructional games with college students. Six studies examined game effects on military learners, and the remainder of the studies evaluated games for adults working in various industries. The results of any given research effort must be evaluated in a restricted manner. We should be very cautious when we attempt to generalize the results of a study conducted with one age group to try to apply those results to another age group.

The empirical research also includes studies that examined the instructional effectiveness of games for *many different tasks.* These tasks ranged from basic mathematics principles to complex decision-making tasks in business and marketing and from general reasoning tasks to specific repair tasks. To interpret instructional effectiveness from such a wide range of data, we must also take care when generalizing from one instructional task to tasks in another domain.

The empirical research *does not make a compelling case for games as the preferred instructional method.* In most cases, the research shows no instructional advantage of games over other instructional approaches (such as lectures). In several cases, games were shown to provide effective learning but were not compared to other instructional methods. The research does not allow us to conclude that games are more effective than other well-designed instructional activities.

Too much of the empirical research on instructional games contains *methodological problems,* for example, experimental confounds, that make it difficult to draw conclusions about the effectiveness of the games. Experimental confounds can occur when researchers allow their own biases to affect their estimation of causal effects and/or when events that happened prior to and during the experiment could affect the subjects' performances and, thus, make a difference in the study's conclusions. Researchers need to ensure that they understand experimental design and apply sound decisions when designing and reporting their research. In addition, editors of educational journals need to filter out studies that do not follow sound experimental design procedures.

A Reexamination of the Claims

Greenblat (1981) summarized evidence in support of six categories of claims about the efficacy of games used for instructional purposes. We can use the same categories of claims to help us summarize the research on the instructional uses of games since that time. By comparing the evidence presented by Greenblat in 1981 to the results of later research, we can draw some conclusions about the progress that has been made over the last 25 years in our understanding of the effectiveness of games for instructional purposes. Table 11.1 summarizes the evidence then and now.

Comparing the evidence on the instructional effectiveness of games that were available in 1981 to the results of research through 2005 shows that many questions that need to be answered about when and how to use games remained unanswered. The first claim, that games improve the motivation and interest of learners, is still weakly supported. Little additional evidence has been gathered beyond a few studies that use self-reports or time-on-task to show that games are motivational. Unfortunately, there is little evidence that these measures of motivation are related to improved task performance. Games do motivate players to play the game. This can be beneficial if the game is designed to target and meet instructional objectives. Otherwise, learners may spend their time learning to be successful at the game without receiving instructional benefits from these experiences.

The second claim, that games enhance cognitive learning, continues to be supported. The research shows that people can learn from games. However, the research does not indicate that games are superior to other instructional methods in all cases. Like any instructional activity, games should be chosen because they provide learners with interactive experiences that help them meet instructional objectives.

The third and sixth claims were not supported. No additional evidence was found that games change later course work. This effect may occur, but no research was found to support this claim. This may be because it is difficult to track learners from one class to another and document this effect. Likewise, no evidence was found for the sixth claim, that the use of games changes the classroom structure and relations. This does not mean that instructors who use games in their courses do not change their classroom structure or that game players do not change how they relate to other learners. Some anecdotal evidence indicates that these changes do occur, but no empirical evidence was found.

Finally, the fourth and fifth claims, that games change learners' feelings (affect) about the learning domain and learning in general, has mixed support. Two studies (Bredemeier et al., 1982; Williams, 1980) provide some support for the utility of games to change learners' attitudes toward subject matter (claim four). Both of these studies also indicate that a game is more effective when it is used in the appropriate context. No empirical research was found that supports the claim that games can change learners' attitudes about learning in general (claim five).

TABLE 11.1 ► Evidence in support of the claims: Then and now

CATEGORIES OF CLAIMS	ORIGINAL EVIDENCE (PRIOR TO 1981)	LATER EVIDENCE (1981–2005)
1. Motivation & interest	*Strongest support.* A great deal of anecdotal reports. Only one study (Robinson et al., 1966) used several indicators of motivation to show simulations generated greater interest than other modes of teaching.	*Little additional evidence.* A few studies found that learners indicated that they enjoyed games and spent more time playing (Dorn, 1989; Koran & McLaughlin, 1990; Malouf, 1988; Pange, 2003; Wishart, 1990). However, only a *weak connection* between this and improved performance was shown (e.g., Wellington & Faria, 1996).
2. Cognitive learning	Some *weak* empirical evidence favoring games (e.g., Alger, 1963; Boocock, 1967; Feldt, 1966). Some showing no differences (e.g., Anderson, 1970).	*Similar pattern.* Some studies show that games are effective for some learning tasks but do not show them superior to other instructional approaches (e.g., Renaud & Stolovitch, 1988; Serrano & Anderson, 2004; White, 1984; Wishart, 1990; Wood & Stewart, 1987). Some evidence that *games can be detrimental to learning if they do not include instructional support* (Caftori, 1994; Leutner, 1993; Rieber & Noah, 1997; Rowe, 2001). Games have been shown to be *more effective if they are followed by a debriefing* session that highlights the importance of the game experiences in terms of instructional objectives (Crookall, 1992; Lederman, 1992).
3. Changes in later course work	None found	None found
4. Affective learning of subject matter	*Mixed* results. Some anecdotal evidence (Boocock & Coleman, 1966; Goldhamer & Speier, 1959). Empirical evidence shows increases in both positive and negative attitudes (Boocock, 1967).	Two studies provide some additional support. There are indications that a game is more effective if used in the appropriate context (Bredemeir, Berstein, & Oxman, 1982; Williams, 1980).
5. General affective learning	Almost none (Boocock, 1967).	None found
6. Changes in classroom structure & relations	None found	None found

In summary, there are several general problems with instructional game research that make it difficult to draw firm conclusions (Hays, 2005, 2006), including the following:

▶ There are many published articles, but most only offer opinions about the "potential" of games. There are few empirical studies.

▶ There is considerable confusion in the use of terms. When is a simulation a game? Are all competitive activities games? It is often difficult to determine whether the instructional activity was actually a game.

▶ There are many methodological flaws in empirical game research, such as poor experimental designs that lack controls for or exclusion of possible confounding variables, for example, events that occurred prior to and during the evaluation that could have affected research conclusions.

▶ Some of the research is biased by the evaluators' interest in "proving" the effectiveness of their games, that is, some of the studies were conducted by individuals who had developed a game and wanted it to work.

▶ Too much of the research uses no control group who experienced an alternate form of instruction to compare the control group's learning to the game players' learning.

▶ Most published articles do not provide clear, detailed descriptions of the game itself, of the characteristics that made it a game.

To Game or Not to Game?

So, the research on the use of instructional games is mixed. How do we know whether to use a game? It appears that games can be of instructional value if they are well designed and targeted to meet specific instructional objectives (as discussed in Chapters 1–4 in Section I, "Why Play Games?"). Unfortunately, many program managers and game developers do not appreciate the importance of instructional design. They often assume that the game itself provides the necessary instruction.

Squire (2005) conducted case studies of three companies that develop game-based learning products and says, "It is worth noting that *none* of the featured companies started in instructional design … . [T]hey come from business strategy, marketing, and the games industry" (p. 13, my emphasis). Although each company used interdisciplinary design teams to create their instructional games, none of the teams included instructional designers. The teams usually consisted of (a) graphic artists, (b) program managers, and (c) programmers. Commenting on the absence of instructional designers, Squire stated, "Most game-based learning approaches do not employ that particular category of expert whatsoever" (p. 35). In most cases, the game designers fulfilled the role of instructional designers. It appears that the "instructional gaming" industry does not value the skills of instructional designers.

This is not a new phenomenon. Greenblat (1981) observed that the teaching enterprise is undervalued in our society. Technological issues involved in game development seem better able to catch people's interest, while the development of instructional objectives and logical programs of instruction seems to be boring. The data on instructional effectiveness of games (e.g., Parchman et al., 2000; Randel et al., 1992; Wolfe, 1997) indicate that the role of the instructor and the way a game is incorporated into an instructional program are major factors in whether a game will contribute to successful learning. Nevertheless, it is not clear that current game-development teams understand the principles of instructional design. At this time, instructors need to work together to share ways to tailor COTS games for effective classroom use. Several chapters in this book contain information on specific instructional games that K–12 teachers have found useful.

Instructors need to understand the specific characteristics of the game, including the game's setting, players' roles and activities, rules, level of difficulty, and other considerations listed by Hirumi in Chapter 10, and make sure that the characteristics of the game overlap with their specific instructional objectives. This overlap must be consciously structured on the basis of a thorough analysis of the reasons for the instruction and the instructional objectives to be met.

The guidelines discussed in the next section will also help instructors in these and other activities that will enhance the effectiveness of the games they choose to use in their classrooms.

Guidelines for Selecting and Using Instructional Games

The literature on instructional games supports the following guidelines to help ensure that the use of a game will provide effective instruction in the classroom. The guidelines assume a basic understanding of the instructional systems development (ISD) process. ISD is a controlled process for designing and developing instructional systems and evaluating their effectiveness (see Branson, Rayner, Cox, Furman, King, & Hannum, 1975; Hays, 2006). Following the basic ISD process, the guidelines are organized in four sections: (a) Planning for including a game, (b) selecting a game, (c) using a game, and (d) evaluating a game. Table 11.2 lists the guidelines. This is followed by brief discussions of each guideline.

TABLE 11.2 ▶ Guidelines for selecting and using instructional games

SECTIONS	GUIDELINES
Section 1. *Planning for gameplay*	**1.1** Document instructional objective(s)
	1.1.1 Review existing documentation of instructional objectives
	1.1.2 Develop new instructional objectives
	1.2 Review current instruction
	1.2.1 Review current instructional materials and approaches
	1.2.2 Document the deficiencies in current instruction
Section 2. *Selecting a game*	**2.1** Review the events in the game
	2.1.1 Determine whether game events appropriately match learners' skills and challenges
	2.2 Review the requirements of the game
	2.3 Develop introductory materials for the game
Section 3. *Using a game*	**3.1** Insert the game into your program of instruction
	3.2 Deliver an introduction to the game
	3.2.1 Explain how to play the game
	3.2.2 Explain how game events support instructional objectives
	3.3 Measure performance
	3.4 Deliver detailed performance feedback
Section 4. *Evaluating the game's effectiveness*	**4.1** Determine whether average performance of learners has improved
	4.2 Determine whether the instructional program is more efficient

Section 1. Planning for Gameplay

The first group of guidelines addresses activities that need to be completed before deciding to use a game or a game-based approach. Some of the guidelines include sub-guidelines to help you conduct more detailed activities if you choose to do so. Thinking through this process to discern how the game will meet the learning objectives you've selected will help you incorporate it more effectively. As you review your files of past lesson plans and notes, you may find that you already have most of the material mentioned in the guidelines.

Guideline 1.1. Document Instructional Objective(s)

The first activity is to understand and document the nature and requirements of each item of information or task to be learned. This is accomplished by first documenting your instructional objective(s). A complete instructional objective contains three main parts. First, it contains a description of an *observable action* in terms of performance or behavior. The *action* or behavior states what a learner will do to demonstrate that he or she has learned what is required. It must include an action verb such as "*type* a letter" or "*select* a menu option." Each objective should cover only one behavior and should include *only one verb*. If multiple behaviors or complicated behaviors are required, the objective should be broken down into *enabling objectives* that support the *main objective*.

The second part of an instructional objective includes at least one *measurable criterion* (standard) that states the level of acceptable performance in terms of quantity, quality, time, or other measures. The standard of performance answers questions such as "How many?" "How fast?" or "How well?" For example, how many correct answers did the student provide on a quiz? How fast did the student complete a series of exercises? How well did a student present an argument defending his or her position on a historical issue? A single instructional objective can contain more than one measurable criterion depending on the complexity of the task. However, as Clark (1995) cautioned, one should not fall into the trap of using only a time constraint because it is easier than finding another measure of performance. A time limit should only be used when it is required under normal working conditions.

The third part of an instructional objective includes the actual *condition(s)* under which the task will be observed. In addition, this portion of an instructional objective identifies the tools, procedures, materials, aids, or facilities to be used in performing the task. It is often expressed with a phrase, such as "without reference to the textbook," "using a notebook and a pen or pencil," or "using a calculator, paper, and pencil."

Guideline 1.1.1. Review existing documentation of instructional objectives. If the instructional objectives have been documented in existing documents, such as class syllabi, department plans, task analyses, handbooks, and task lists, you should review these documents to ensure that they contain complete descriptions of each instructional objective in terms of actions, conditions, and standards.

Guideline 1.1.2. Develop new instructional objectives. If the learning task is not fully described in existing documentation or if the instructional requirements have changed, new instructional objectives need to be written. These objectives should include descriptions of actions, conditions, and standards. If this is a new task, you may need to review the existing instruction for similar tasks.

Guideline 1.2. Review Current Instruction

Before you decide to use an instructional game, you need to understand how instruction is currently conducted. Review current instructional materials and collect inputs from other instructors.

Guideline 1.2.1. Review current instructional materials and approaches. Unless the instruction is for a totally new task, some form of instruction probably exists. You need to understand this current instruction if you are to improve it by adding gaming technologies. The current instructional materials, such as books, slides, animations, and simulations, should be reviewed to determine their effectiveness. Ask other teachers to tell you which instructional materials they find most effective for this learning objective.

Guideline 1.2.2. Document the deficiencies in the current instruction. If you are considering using a game for instruction, you may have identified a deficiency or deficiencies in the current instruction, or perhaps you think a game may make learning a particular set of facts or skills more enjoyable for your students. Reviewing the information under Guideline 1.2.1 may help to clarify the reason for using a game. By understanding current instructional deficiencies and needs, whether they are your own or arise from the curriculum, you will be able to forecast how a game may help to correct them. For example:

- ► A game could introduce new terms in a more realistic context.
- ► A game could allow the learners to practice new skills more efficiently than current instruction.
- ► A game could allow the learners to integrate knowledge and skills in realistic scenarios.
- ► A game could provide more efficient (i.e., faster) instruction.
- ► A game could give students feedback on their skill levels faster than current instruction to help them master each skill and advance to the next level.
- ► A game could provide individual incentives to master each skill, such as praise and a few moments of action play for fun.
- ► A game could provide a fresh approach for reviewing a particular set of facts or skills that students find difficult, making the learning less tedious and more enjoyable.

If you determine that a game cannot help correct identified instructional deficiency or cannot enhance current instruction, consider using an instructional approach other than a game.

Section 2. Selecting a Game

Before selecting any game for your classroom, completing the following activities will ensure that the gameplay fulfills instructional objectives. The most important activity is to understand the events that the learner will experience in the game and determine how closely these events match your instructional objectives. Understanding the events in the game will help determine whether an existing game can be used or whether you need to modify the existing game or develop a new game.

Guideline 2.1: Review the Events in the Game

Any game consists of a series of events that are governed by rules and constraints. In Section 1, you detailed the instructional objectives for your specific instructional task. It is important that the game you select meets as many of these instructional objectives as possible. The more overlap between instructional objectives and game activities, the greater the probability of effective instruction (Hays, 2005, 2006, 2008). This is illustrated in Figure 11.1. You can determine this overlap by understanding how closely your instructional objectives resemble and are supported by the events that occur in the game. If the specific game events are not a close match with the tasks, conditions, and standards as documented in your instructional objectives, the game may not be suitable or may need to be modified. However, you still may be able to use the game if you explain the differences to your students and help them narrow the gap between game events and instructional objectives. This is discussed in Guideline 3.2.2.

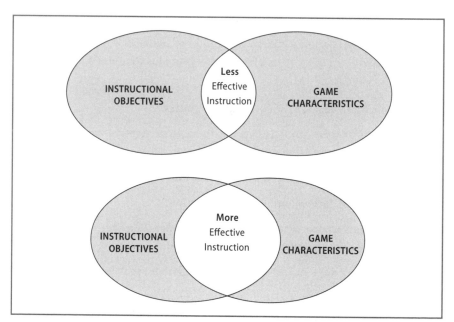

FIGURE 11.1 ▶ Instructional effectiveness as degree of overlap among instructional objectives and game characteristics

Guideline 2.1.1. Determine whether game events match learners' skills and challenges. Malone and Lepper (1987) developed a framework for designing intrinsically motivating instructional environments, and I slightly modified their framework to focus on instructional games (Hays, 2006). One of the most important motivational design recommendations is to ensure that the game provides an appropriate level of challenge for the learner. What does "appropriate level" mean? Csíkszentmihályi (1990) provides a way to judge appropriate level of challenge in his concept of "flow." He spent many years studying why people engage in various activities, including learning, playing music, and creating works of art, and why they find them enjoyable. He labeled the feeling of peak enjoyment as "flow" and documented the components that combine to produce this experience. The process of flow is shown in Figure 11.2. The two main variables of the flow experience are challenges and skills. These are shown on the axes of the figure. One may experience flow when the task offers little challenge and one's skills are not well developed (A1). As one develops higher skill levels, the task will become boring because it no longer provides a challenge (A2). On the other hand, one may experience anxiety if the task is too difficult (A3). If, however, one gradually develops higher skill levels as the task becomes more difficult (A4), it is possible to maintain the flow experience. The goal of an instructional game is to keep the learner in the flow channel by increasing the challenge levels of the game as the learner's skills improve.

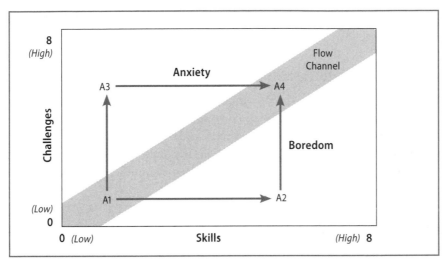

FIGURE 11.2 ▶ The process of "flow"

Guideline 2.2. Review the Requirements of the Game

Before your students can play any game, they must understand the rules and constraints of the game so they can function successfully in the game world. This may require them to learn various skills that are game-specific. Almost as important as the incorporation of realistic task requirements in the game is the elimination of as many unrealistic game requirements as possible. If learners are required to spend too much intellectual energy on learning and performing game activities that are not related to your instructional objectives, they will not be able to focus their attention on instructionally relevant game activities. Any game requirements that are not directly relevant to instructional objectives need to be recognized and explained to the learners both before they play the game and during their performance review session after playing the game (see Guidelines 3.2 and 3.4).

Guideline 2.3. Develop Introductory Materials for the Game

After you have selected an instructional game, you need to decide how you will use it in your classroom. Your first activity should be to develop the materials to introduce your students to the game. The characteristics and requirements of the game will determine the requirements of these introductory materials. The introductory materials should help students focus on the events of the game that support the class's instructional objectives. The introductory materials should also provide cues and aids to help learners complete game-specific activities quickly and easily so they can get on with the instructional purposes of the game.

Section 3: Using a Game

How you use a game is as important as the characteristics of the game itself (Hays, 2005, 2006, 2008). Plan how to use the game as a tool that supports the goals of your district's curriculum and your course's or class's objectives. In very few cases can one effectively use a game to provide stand-alone instruction. In any case, the game needs to be embedded into the instructional program so students are taught the necessary prerequisite knowledge and skills that will make the game a meaningful learning tool.

Guideline 3.1. Insert the Game into Your Program of Instruction

Have a clear plan for how the game will be used in your program of instruction. For example, decide at which point the game will be used and how many game sessions will be required. You might decide to conduct a series of game sessions with teacher and student feedback and discussions between sessions. You may want to use the game for both instruction and assessment. These decisions must be made prior to using the game so that learners can obtain the most instructional benefits from their gaming experiences.

Guideline 3.2. Deliver an Introduction to the Game

Allowing learners to engage in game activities (events) is the purpose of an instructional game. It is important that learners focus on the game events rather than wasting time and energy on learning how to play the game or on activities that do not support their instructional objectives. Your introduction should be based on the plans and materials developed under Guideline 2.3.

Guideline 3.2.1. Explain how to play the game. The introduction to the game should supply the learners with all of the information and assistance necessary for them to begin playing the game. Tell them not to worry about trying to figure out game-specific skills at this time; reassure them that the game will explain these skills and will give them time to practice and that you will help them if they need it while they play the game. Their focus should be on their experiences during important game events.

Guideline 3.2.2. Explain how game events support instructional objectives. In order to use a game as an instructional tool effectively, learners must understand why they are playing the game and how gameplay supports the class's instructional objectives. This should also be explained during the introduction to the game and repeated during the feedback session (see Guideline 3.4). The teacher could begin the feedback session by asking the students to explain why they have been playing the game.

Guideline 3.3. Measure Performance

The only way to determine whether students have learned new knowledge or skills is to measure their performance (Hays, 2006). After playing the game, students should be able to perform better, using the knowledge and skills learned in the game. Measure their performance using either existing performance measures, like tests or evaluation activities, or newly developed performance measures, such as evaluation game sessions. If their performances have not improved, the learners probably need additional instruction or game sessions, or you may need to change how you use the game.

Guideline 3.4. Deliver Detailed Performance Feedback

After engaging in game activities, learners need to receive detailed feedback that explains how well they performed in the game or other assessments and how the events and activities in the game supported their learning objectives. Some instructional video games keep track of each player's performance and provide teachers with the details.

Section 4: Evaluating the Game's Effectiveness

Just as the teacher evaluates the performances of learners who play the game (Guideline 3.3), he or she also needs to evaluate the effectiveness of the game itself. The effectiveness of the game can be determined in two ways: improved student performance and improved instructional efficiency.

Guideline 4.1. Determine Whether Average Performance of Learners Has Improved

If an instructional game is effective, the average performance of learners should show improvement. Records of performance obtained during the use of the game should be tabulated, and average performance improvements should be documented. If the average performance of learners has decreased, you should stop using this game and use an alternate instructional approach, or consult the technology coordinator and other teachers to see whether they know of other, more efficacious games. If the average student performance is the same as it is with other instructional approaches and students report generally positive experiences, you may decide to continue using the game and to adjust aspects of it until it improves the efficiency of your instructional program.

Guideline 4.2. Determine Whether the Instructional Program Is More Efficient

If the average performance of your students has improved or remained the same, an instructional game may still be the preferred instructional method because it has improved the efficiency of your instructional program. You can determine whether this is the case by comparing the efficiency of your instructional program including the game with your previous instructional approach. You will already have collected some data from your previous instructional approach (Guideline 1.2). Two of the measures of efficiency you might use are (a) time spent to complete this student learning objective, and (b) the number of learners who completed the learning objective in a given time period.

Instructional Game Evaluation Scales

In 2008, I presented a method to evaluate the instructional quality of computer-delivered courseware (Hays, 2008). The method used rating scales to address instructional features and user interface issues. I adapted some of the scales to evaluate the instructional quality of games. These scales can be used to supplement the guidelines presented in the previous section.

The game evaluation scales are presented below. It is important to assign ratings from the perspective of the students. For example, the first scale asks if the instructional goals are clearly stated. You should find out whether your students understand the instructional goals—not whether you or other instructional experts understand the goals.

The scales can be used during game development or instructional program delivery. During early conceptual development, the scales help focus designers on important issues that will increase the probability that the game will be instructionally effective. At later development stages, the scales should focus on specific game characteristics that can be improved prior to final delivery. After the game has been developed, the scales should be used to help incorporate the game into an instructional program and evaluate its effectiveness. The scales are divided into three sections: (a) instructional issues (b) technical issues, and (c) playability issues.

Instructional Issues

Instructional scales 1–7 directly address the instructional design and use of games.

1. Instructional goals are clearly stated

1	2	3	4	5
No instructional goals (or objectives) are stated.	*Some* instructional goals include *very general* statements (e.g., do not include statements about actions, conditions, and standards).	*Some* instructional goals include *general statements* about actions, conditions, and standards.	*Most* instructional goals include *specific statements* about actions, conditions, and standards.	*All* instructional goals include *specific statements* about actions, conditions and standards.

Rating scale 1 helps determine whether the instructional goals (or objectives) of the game are understood and communicated to the learners. At the early development stage, the scale should be used to ensure that developers fully understand and document the instructional goals of the game. Once a game has been developed and is being inserted into a program of instruction, the instructional goals will guide how the game will be used. At this stage, the scale can be used to determine how well these instructional goals are communicated to learners prior to any interaction with the game.

2. Instructions are included on how to play the game

1	2	3	4	5
Has *no* gameplay instructions.	Has *general* gameplay instructions.	Has *somewhat specific* gameplay instructions.	Has *specific* gameplay instructions.	Has *very specific* gameplay instructions.

Always remember that the purpose of the game is to provide task-relevant instruction, not to be played only for enjoyment. Although some game enthusiasts may enjoy learning to play the game, this is not an efficient use of instructional time. Data have demonstrated that games are more instructionally effective if they include guidance about how to play the game (Hays, 2005). Such guidance allows the learners to focus their energy on the game's instructional content activities rather than on figuring out the rules of the game.

3. Game activities support instructional goals (or objectives)

1	2	3	4	5
No game activities support instructional goals.	*Few* game activities support instructional goals.	*Some* game activities support instructional goals.	*Most* game activities support instructional goals.	*All* game activities support instructional goals.

A game can include many different activities. The instructional effectiveness of a game will be enhanced to the extent that game activities overlap with the instructional goals of the game (Hays, 2006). For example, ask yourself some of these questions:

▶ Do learners have to spend too much time learning the rules of the game rather than benefiting from its instructional information?

▶ Is the majority of the playing time focused on instructional information and exercises?

▶ Does the game reward successful completion of instructionally relevant activities?

▶ Do the game activities gradually increase in difficulty as learners master instructionally relevant knowledge and skills?

4. Game activities are realistic (conform to real-world conditions)

1	2	3	4	5
Almost all game activities are *very different* from real-world conditions. Differences are *not explained* to learners.	*Some* game activities are *different* from real-world conditions. Differences are *not explained* to learners.	*Few* activities are *different* from real-world conditions, and differences *are explained* to learners.	*Most* activities are *realistic* (conform to real-world conditions), and differences *are explained* to learners.	*Almost all* activities *are realistic* (conform to real-world conditions), and differences *are explained* to learners.

The goal of instruction is to help learners improve the knowledge and skills that will allow them to successfully perform the same or similar tasks in the real world. Like any instructional tool (e.g., simulations, case studies), a game should provide realistic activities that conform to real-world conditions. If game activities are not realistic, game experiences may result in negative transfer to the work environment. In this case, learners may need to relearn or unlearn these activities when they perform the task at work.

5. Game activities increase in difficulty as learners' performances improve

1	2	3	4	5
All game activities have a *constant level of difficulty*.	*A few* of the game activities *increase in difficulty* as learners' improve their performances.	*About half* of the game activities *increase in difficulty* as learners improve their performances.	*Most* game activities *increase in difficulty* as learners improve their performances.	*All* game activities *increase in difficulty* as learners improve their performances.

The importance of matching the difficulty of game activities with learner skills was discussed in Guideline 2.1.1. The balance between the challenge of game activities and learners' skills is an important factor in motivating the learner (Keller, 1983) and in helping them maintain a state of "flow" (Csíkszentmihályi, 1990). Keller's ARCS (attention, relevance, confidence, and satisfaction) model of motivation (Keller, 1979, 1983, 1987) explains how challenging activities with relevance to subject matter help to gain and maintain learners' attention; it also emphasizes how important it is to maintain learners' confidence, that is, their perceived likelihood of success during instruction, leading to satisfaction with the gameplay. (We have already discussed the importance of a game's relevance to the curriculum.) All of these goals can be achieved if the difficulty level of game activities increases as learners demonstrate improved knowledge and skills.

6. Game includes assessments of learners' actions

1	2	3	4	5
Has *no assessments* of game activities.	Has a *few assessments* game activities.	Has *assessments* of *about half* of game activities.	Has *assessments* of *most* game activities.	Has *assessments* of *all* game activities.

A game will be more effective if it includes assessments and summaries of learners' actions. During the debriefing session, these assessments should be used by the instructor to explain how the learners' performances met or failed to meet instructional goals. Learners can benefit from mistakes made during the game if they can understand the implications of the mistakes and are given opportunities to correct them (see scale 7).

7. Game provides feedback on learners' actions

1	2	3	4	5
No feedback provided.	*Very general feedback* provided on *overall result* of game.	*General feedback* provided on *some learner actions.*	*General feedback* provided on *all learner actions.*	*Specific feedback* provided on *all learner actions.*

Related to the above scale, the results of the learners' performance assessments need to be communicated to all students. Ideally, the instructor will communicate this feedback during an after-action-review (AAR) session, also called a game debriefing. Some feedback can be provided during the game to allow students to learn from their mistakes and correct their actions. If a game is used without an instructor, the quality of the feedback needs to be even higher.

Technical Issues

Technical scales 8–12 address how the game is presented to learners in terms of its technical quality.

8. Game graphics are clear and sharp

1	2	3	4	5
None of the graphics are clear and sharp.	*Few* of the graphics are clear and sharp.	*Some* of the graphics are clear and sharp.	*Most* of the graphics are clear and sharp.	*All* of the graphics are clear and sharp.

The graphics used in computer games can range from very simple line drawings, through cartoon-like representations, to photo-realistic representations. Depending on the instructional goals of the game, the graphics should be clearly presented. For example, if the instructional goal is to help students learn to read and interpret a map, the graphics need to depict the boundaries, elevations, and wording clearly. However, if the instructional goal is to teach students to locate and name the 50 states on a map of the United States, the clarity of the graphics showing elevations will not have to be as high as the clarity of the boundaries and wording. In all cases, supporting graphics and text should be clear and sharp.

9. Game audio is clear and sharp

1	2	3	4	5
None of the audio is clear and sharp.	*Little* of the audio is clear and sharp.	*Some* of the audio is clear and sharp.	*Most* of the audio is clear and sharp.	*All* of the audio is clear and sharp.

Some tasks require the learner to hear and understand certain sounds, such as musical tones or animals' cries. The audio should provide the necessary clarity to support task performance. Audioverbal instructions are frequently used to direct gameplay and provide feedback during gameplay. All sounds generated by the game should always be clear and sharp.

10. Game video is clear and sharp

1	2	3	4	5
None of the video is clear and sharp.	*Little* of the video is clear and sharp.	*Some* of the video is clear and sharp.	*Most* of the video is clear and sharp.	*All* of the video is clear and sharp.

Games may incorporate video clips showing real task activities or guidance from experts. In all cases these videos should be clear and sharp so that learners can see all of the necessary details that support instructional goals.

11. There are no sensory conflicts in the game

1	2	3	4	5
Different/conflicting information is *always* presented simultaneously in two or more modalities.	Different/conflicting information is *often* presented simultaneously in two or more modalities.	Different/conflicting information is *sometimes* presented simultaneously in two or more modalities.	Different/conflicting information is *seldom* presented simultaneously in two or more modalities.	Different/conflicting information is *never* presented simultaneously in two or more modalities.

Learners use all of their senses during gameplay. Paivio's dual coding theory (Clark & Paivio, 1991; Paivio, 1990) maintains that learning can be improved if information is transmitted in multiple sensory modes, for example, using visual representations while the same information is presented auditorily . However, this only improves learning if the information transmitted in the different sensory modes is mutually supportive, that is, if the content is exactly the same in all modes and if the material presented in each mode complements the information presented by the others. In contrast, if conflicting information is presented in the different sensory modes, it will likely result in sensory conflict and reduce the instructional effectiveness of the game (Gray & Wedderburn, 1960; Moreno & Mayer, 2000).

12. Game installation is easy or not required

1	2	3	4	5
Game requires *very difficult* installation.	Game requires *difficult* installation.	Game requires *somewhat easy* installation.	Game requires *easy* installation.	Game *does not* require installation, or installation is very easy.

Sometimes games must be installed on the learner's computer. Installation of the game should be avoided whenever possible. If this is necessary, the installation should be easy.

Playability Issues

Playability scales 13 and 14 address issues that affect the playability of the game, that is, how much learners enjoy playing the game.

13. Game screens are aesthetically pleasing

1	2	3	4	5
None of the game screens are aesthetically pleasing.	*Few* of the game screens are aesthetically pleasing.	*Some* of the game screens are aesthetically pleasing.	*Most* of the game screens are aesthetically pleasing.	*All* of the game screens are aesthetically pleasing.

A game will likely be more enjoyable if the screen displays are designed using accepted artistic principles, including using compatible colors and aesthetic shapes. For a discussion of the aesthetics of screen design, see Hays (2008).

14. Game activities are fun and engaging (attract and maintain learner attention)

1	2	3	4	5
None of the activities are engaging.	*Few* of the activities are engaging.	*Some* of the activities are engaging.	*Most* of the activities are engaging.	*All* of the activities are engaging.

Learners must engage with instructional activities and information if learning is to occur. One of the possible benefits of an instructional game is that it will be fun to play, thus engaging the learner with the activities that support instructional objectives. Csíkszentmihályi (1990) studied the factors that make an activity enjoyable. He found that people enjoy many different activities, including sports, other games like chess, dance, art, music, thinking, learning, and many others. He labeled this feeling of enjoyment "flow" (see Guideline 2.1.1). There are many ways to motivate learners and help them achieve and maintain the flow experience. Malone and Lepper (1987) categorized recommendations for motivating individuals in any instructional environment into four categories: challenge, fantasy, curiosity, and instructional quality. I modified their general recommendations to focus on instructional games (Hays, 2006). Table 11.3 shows these design recommendations. Many of the recommendations overlap with several of the previous evaluation scales (e.g., Scale 3 on game activities, Scale 5 on difficulty level, and Scale 7 on feedback). This is because the components of any instructional approach overlap and interact with one another. For this reason, Table 11.3 can be used as an additional, stand-alone set of recommendations.

TABLE 11.3 ▶ Design recommendations for instructional games

DESIGN CATEGORY	RECOMMENDATIONS
Challenge	**A. Goal** The game should have a clear goal. The goal should be consistent with the instructional objective. Performance feedback should be provided about how close the learner is to achieving the goal.
	B. Uncertain outcome The outcome of reaching the goal should be uncertain. The learner should have to exert effort to achieve the goal. If the subject matter is complex, the game should include multiple levels of difficulty or complexity. Sub-goals should help the learner successfully complete enabling learning objectives.
	C. Competition A game can be made more challenging by introducing competition. Competition can be against a live opponent, against a computer-controlled opponent, or against a criterion score. Achieving a criterion score can be one of the factors that allows a learner to advance to higher levels of difficulty. Game scores should be clearly related to the achievement of learning objectives (e.g., not just how many shots are fired accurately or how many opponents are defeated).
Fantasy	**A. Emotional appeal** The fantasy should embody emotional appeal for the learners. Not everyone reacts positively to shooting weapons or to complex interpersonal situations.
	B. Fantasy metaphor The metaphor used in the fantasy should embody physical or other characteristics that the learner already understands.
Curiosity	**A. Optimal level of complexity** The game should provide an optimal level of informational complexity to meet the learners' needs. The level of complexity should increase as learners gain higher levels of expertise.
	B. Incorporation of interesting media The game should use interesting audio and visual effects to enhance the fantasy and emphasize instructional content. The game can incorporate elements of randomness to avoid boredom for the learner.

TABLE 11.3 *(Continued)*

DESIGN CATEGORY	RECOMMENDATIONS
Instructional Quality	**A. Logical instructional structure** The game should capitalize on the learner's desire to have logical (well-formed) knowledge structures. Elements of the game should build on and reinforce each other to help build the learner's knowledge structures. Learners should easily be able to see when their knowledge structures are incomplete. Feedback during the game should be used to help learners complete their knowledge structures. **B. Incorporation into the larger instructional program** The game should not stand alone. Rather, it should be part of a larger instructional program. There should be clear instructions on how to play the game so learners do not waste time and can quickly begin interacting with instructional content. Debriefing and feedback should be provided after the game to help learners understand how the experiences in the game supported the learning objectives.

References

Alger, C. F. (1963). Use of the *Inter-Nation Simulation* in undergraduate teaching. In H. Guetzkow, C. F. Alger, R. A. Brody, R. C. Noel, & R. C. Snyder (Eds.). *Simulation in international relations: Developments for research and teaching* (pp. 150–189). Englewood Cliffs, NJ: Prentice-Hall.

Anderson, C. F. (1970). An experiment on behavioral learning in a consumer credit game. *Simulation and Games, 6*(March), 43–54.

Boocock, S. S. (1967). Life career game. *Personnel and Guidance Journal, 46*(December), 328–334.

Boocock, S. S., & Coleman, J. S. (1966). Games with simulated environments in learning. *Sociology of Education, 39*(Summer), 215–236.

Branson, R. K., Rayner, G. T., Cox, J. L., Furman, J. P., King, F. J., & Hannum, W. H. (1975). Interservice procedures for instructional systems development (5 vols.) (TRADOC Pam 350–30 and NAVEDTR 106A). Ft. Monroe, VA: U.S. Army Training and Doctrine Command.

Bredemeier, M. E., Bernstein, G., & Oxman, W. (1982). *Ba Fa Ba Fa* and dogmatism/ethnocentrism: A study of attitude change through simulation-gaming. *Simulation & Gaming, 13*(4), 413–436.

Caftori, N. (1994). Educational effectiveness of computer software. Technical horizons in Education. *(T.H.E.) Journal, 22*(1), 62–65.

Clark, D. (1995). Instructional system design (ADDIE)—Design chapter 3. In Big dog & little dog's performance juxtaposition. Retrieved June 23, 2003, and April 13, 2010, from www.nwlink.com/~donclark/hrd/sat.html

Clark, J. M., & Paivio, A. (1991). Dual-coding theory and education. *Educational Psychology Review, 3*(3), 149–210.

Crookall, D. (1992). Editorial: Debriefing. *Simulation & Gaming, 23*(2), 141–142.

Csíkszentmihályi, M. (1990). *Flow: The psychology of optimal experience.* New York, NY: Harper & Row.

Dempsey, J. V., Lucassen, B., Gilley, W., & Rasmussen, K. (1993–1994). Since Malone's theory of intrinsically motivating instruction: What's the score in the gaming literature? *Journal of Educational Technology Systems, 22*(2), 173–183.

DoD (U.S. Department of Defense). (1997). *DoD modeling and simulation (M&S) glossary* (DoD 5000.59-M). Alexandria, VA: Defense Modeling and Simulation Office. Available at www.scribd.com/doc/1469016/US-Air-Force-Abbreviation-and-Acronym-Dictionary

Dorn, D. S. (1989). Simulation games: One more tool on the pedagogical shelf. *Teaching Sociology, 17*(1), 1–18.

Feldt, A. (1966). Operational gaming in planning education. *Journal of the American Institute of Planners, 32*(January), 17–23.

Goldhamer, H., & Speier, H. (1959). Some observations on political gaming. *World Politics, 12* (October), 71–83.

Gray, J. A., & Wedderburn, A. A. I. (1960). Grouping strategies with simultaneous stimuli. *Quarterly Journal of Experimental Psychology, 12*, 180–184.

Greenblat, C. S. (1981). Teaching with simulation games: A review of claims and evidence. In C. S. Greenblat & R. D. Duke (Eds.), *Principles and practices of gaming-simulation* (pp. 139–153). Beverly Hills, CA: Sage Publications.

Greenblat, C. S., & Duke, R. D. (Eds.). (1981). *Principles and practices of gaming-simulation.* Beverly Hills, CA: Sage Publications.

Hays, R. T. (2005). *The effectiveness of instructional games: A literature review and discussion* (Technical Report 2005–004). Orlando, FL: Naval Air Warfare Center Training Systems Division. (Defense Technical Information Center No. ADA 441 935)

Hays, R. T. (2006). *The science of learning: A systems theory perspective.* Boca Raton, FL: BrownWalker Press.

Hays, R. T. (2008). *Quality instruction: Building and evaluating computer-delivered courseware.* Boca Raton, FL: Universal Publishers.

Keller, J. M. (1979). Motivation and instructional design: A theoretical perspective. *Journal of Instructional Development, 2*(4), 26–34.

Keller, J. M. (1983). Motivational design of instruction. In C. M. Reigeluth (Ed.), *Instructional-design theories and models: An overview of their current status* (pp. 383–434). Mahwah, NJ: Lawrence Erlbaum.

Keller, J. M. (1987). Development and use of the ARCS model of motivational design. *Journal of Instructional Development, 10*(3), 2–10.

Koran, L. J., & McLaughlin, T. F. (1990). Games or drill: Increasing the multiplication skills of students. *Journal of Instructional Psychology, 17*(4), 222–230.

Lederman, L. C. (1992). Debriefing: Toward a systematic assessment of theory and practice. *Simulation & Gaming, 23*(2), 145–160.

Leutner, D. (1993). Guided discovery learning with computer-based simulation games: Effects of adaptive and non-adaptive instructional support. *Learning and Instruction, 3,* 113–132.

Malone, T. W., & Lepper, M. R. (1987). Making learning fun: A taxonomy of intrinsic motivation for learning. In R. E. Snow & M. J. Farr (Eds.), *Aptitude, learning and instruction: Vol. 3: Conative and affective process analyses* (pp. 223–253). Mahwah, NJ: Lawrence Erlbaum.

Malouf, D. B. (1988). The effect of instructional computer games on continuing student motivation. *The Journal of Special Education, 21*(4), 27–38.

Moreno, R., & Mayer, R. E. (2000). A coherence effect in multimedia learning: The case for minimizing irrelevant sounds in the design of multimedia instructional messages. *Journal of Educational Psychology, 92*(1), 117–125.

Paivio, A. (1990). *Mental representations: A dual-coding approach.* New York, NY: Oxford University Press.

Pange, J. (2003). Teaching probabilities and statistics to preschool children. *Information Technology in Childhood Education Annual, 2003*(1), 163–172.

Parchman, S. W., Ellis, J. A., Christinaz, D., & Vogel, M. (2000). An evaluation of three computer-based instructional strategies in basic electricity and electronics training. *Military Psychology, 12*(1), 73–87.

Randel, J. M., Morris, B. A., Wetzel, C. D., & Whitehill, B. V. (1992). The effectiveness of games for educational purposes: A review of recent research. *Simulation & Gaming, 23*(3), 261–276.

Renaud, L., & Stolovitch, H. (1988). Simulation gaming: An effective strategy for creating appropriate traffic safety behaviors in five-year-old children. *Simulation & Games, 19*(3), 328–345.

Rieber, L. P. (1996). Seriously considering play: Designing interactive learning environments based on the blending of microworlds, simulations, and games. *Educational Technology Research and Development, 44*(2), 43–58.

Rieber, L. P., & Noah, D. (1997). Effect of gaming and visual metaphors on reflective cognition within computer-based simulations. Paper presented at the 1997 American Educational Research Association conference in Chicago. Retrieved September 9, 2005, from http://it.coe.uga.edu/ lrieber/gaming-simulation/rieber-gaming-simulation.pdf

Robinson, J. A., Anderson, L. F., Hermann, M. G., & Snyder, R. C. (1966). Teaching with Inter-Nation Simulation and case studies. *American Political Science Review, 60*(March), 53–64.

Rowe, J. C. (2001). An experiment in the use of games in the teaching of mental arithmetic. *Philosophy of Mathematics Education Journal, 14.* Retrieved August 1, 2005, from people.exeter.ac.uk/ PErnest/pome14/rowe.htm

Serrano, E. L., & Anderson, J. E. (2004). The evaluation of food pyramid games, a bilingual computer nutrition education program for Latino youth. *Journal of Family and Consumer Sciences Education, 22*(1), 1–16. Retrieved August 3, 2005, from www.natefacs.org/JFCSE/v22no1/ v22no1Serrano.pdf

Squire, K. (2005). *Game-based learning: Present and future state of the field.* Masie Center e-Learning Consortium, February. Retrieved August 8, 2005, from www.masie.com/xlearn/Game-Based_Learning.pdf

Thomas, R., Cahill, J., & Santilli, L. (1997). Using an interactive computer game to increase skill and self-efficacy regarding safer sex. *Health Education and Behavior, 24*(1), 71–86.

Wellington, W. J., & Faria, A. J. (1996). Team cohesion, player attitude, and performance expectations in simulation. *Simulation & Gaming, 27*(1), 23–40.

White, B. Y. (1984). Designing computer games to help physics students understand Newton's laws of motion. *Cognition and Instruction, 1*(1), 69–108.

Williams, R. H. (1980). Attitude change and simulation games: The ability of a simulation game to change attitudes when structured in accordance with either the cognitive dissonance or incentive models of attitude change. *Simulation & Games, 11*(2), 177–196.

Wishart, J. (1990). Cognitive factors related to user involvement with computers and their effects upon learning from an educational computer game. *Computers and Education, 15*(1–3), 145–150.

Wolfe, J. (1997). The effectiveness of business games in strategic management course work. (Special Issue: Teaching Strategic Management). *Simulation & Gaming, 28*(4), 360–376.

Wood, L. E., & Stewart, P. W. (1987). Improvement of practical reasoning skills with a computer game. *Journal of Computer-Based Instruction, 14*(2), 49–53.

12

Repurposing COTS Games

Yadi Ziaeehezarjeribi, Ingrid Graves,
and James Gentry

IN THIS CHAPTER, WE PROPOSE a framework for repurposing commercial off-the-shelf (COTS) games for enhancing learning in PK–12 settings. With the physical infrastructure of computer technology in place, simulations and games are becoming a viable source for educational and personal development to engage learners individually and in groups. However, educators typically do not have the time, resources, or expertise to develop original video games. Repurposing COTS games is presented in this chapter as a relatively low-cost solution for realizing the potential of video games for enhancing learning. First, we explain the basic principles and rationale for the use of games and simulations, based on research about the new generation of "players," our students, who are accustomed to dynamic learning. Next, we propose critical elements for repurposing games, followed by a step-by-step procedure for integrating games that address these elements into the classroom setting. Finally, we list COTS games that may be used to enhance learning in PK–12 settings, along with direct connections to national standards in content areas and examples of how to repurpose the games.

Educational and entertainment technologies, such as simulations, video games, digital books, tablet computers, e-learning, game consoles, and wireless and mobile computing are now providing teachers with creative tools for enhancing student-centered learning in the classroom. Now that the use of computers in schools is no longer a novelty (Bichelmeyer & Molenda, 2006), teachers are beginning to see the potential for commercially designed games as powerful tools to support classroom instruction. In this chapter, we will discuss some effects video games have had on PK–12 education and suggest methods for educators to enhance lesson plans through the use of commercial off-the-shelf (COTS) games.

Renewed Interest in Using Video Games in Education to Enhance Learning

With increased support for and use of multimedia technology in classrooms, many educators are echoing the sentiments of Albers, Vasquez, and Harste (2008):

> As educators, we must commit ourselves to learning the communication practices that our students use every day. … While all communication is multimodal, too often we ELA (English Language Arts) literacy teachers have a disproportionate reverence for the printed word, which keeps us from fully exploring the significance of other modes of meaningful expression. (p. 11)

While we share this reverence for traditional literacy practices, increased access to high-quality interactive media, such as video games and simulations, provides teachers with highly engaging tools to support instruction.

While Rosas et al. (2003), among others cited throughout this book, have demonstrated an instructional link between modified COTS games and increased student achievement, we would like to point out the substantial cost of modifying or developing an educational game for use in the classroom. According to the Federation of American Scientists (FAS) (2006), there is a need to find an easy way to "create learning games and simulations quickly, and at low cost" (p. 23). The solution to this need for low-cost learning games may be found in already popular COTS video games. By using popular COTS video games to support traditional instructional practices, teachers can learn to design lessons that connect the compelling nature of learning in video games to learning in the classroom setting.

In this chapter, we provide a framework for using existing COTS video games. First, we identify seven critical conditions for integrating video games in the classroom. Second, we posit a systematic process to assist teachers as they repurpose existing video games for education instead of entertainment in the classroom. Third, we describe three "missions" for playing popular COTS games in the classroom to enhance student learning. As video games are repurposed for instructional settings, classroom teachers are able to both support and check for understanding of subject matter, and provide cognitive bridges to classroom learning, before, during, and after game play. The three missions are intended only to provide teachers with ideas for integration. We are not endorsing one game over another, and we do not pretend the video games under consideration would be appropriate for all settings.

Critical Conditions for Integrating Games

When considering games to integrate into the classroom, we chose to use Cambourne's (1988) learning model to frame the discussion around "new literacies" in schools (Albers, et al., 2008; Barab, Sadler, Heiselt, Hickey, & Zuiker, 2007; Gee, 2003). We have also included recommendations from the FAS (2006) that support the National Education Technology Standards for Students (NETS•S) (ISTE, 2007). Based on this research, we have determined seven critical instructional conditions for choosing and playing COTS games in the classroom.

Condition 1. Opportunities for Applicable Learning

According to Cambourne (1988), young learners need to be immersed in an environment that contains "worthwhile, authentic learning tasks" (cited in Yellin, Blake, & Devries, 2008, p. 9). Games that provide opportunities for students to apply newly acquired knowledge may enable students to generalize what they have learned across contexts. Students should be allowed to practice all skills with the assistance of immediate feedback often found in video games. When students realize that the skills they are acquiring help them in practical ways, they value learning in school more highly. For instance, Squire (2008) notes that to be literate in the gaming medium means to be able to identify "tangible actions on screen and in real spaces" (p. 646). In other words, students remain focused on play if they are able to see that they are advancing through the game. These tangible goals must also include an environment that allows players to participate fully in the outcomes of the game.

Condition 2. Full Participation

Video games should allow students to interact, design, and become full participants in their environment, instead of being passive voyeurs (Yellin, et al., 2008). For instance, a student should be able to appreciate historical events from the perspectives of multiple actors, identify geography, create maps, and multiply fractions or use algebra for practical reasons using realistic scenarios. When students use a video game, they take responsibility for committing themselves to learn the knowledge needed to play the game. Gameplay requires students to make the decision to take responsibility for their own learning by choosing to spend the required time and energy to engage in challenging learning assignments. With a carefully selected video game, students become internally motivated to learn relevant content. Barab et al. (2007) note that when playing a video game, many students are more than willing to invest time toward learning. Students who participate fully in educational games will find opportunities to practice their skills in various contexts.

Condition 3. Multiple Avenues for Learning

According to Cambourne (1988), classrooms should include numerous and varied opportunities to learn a new skill or content area concept. Similarly, video games should provide for multiple entry points, that is, games should allow players to start as beginners as well as at various levels of expertise in using the game, based on students' varied levels of knowledge and ability. With the incorporation of multiple outcomes, students learn to solve problems based on their unique knowledge and to understand concepts such as cause and effect. For example, if a farmer over-fertilizes a field, plant, animal, and human inhabitants of environments downstream will be affected. Students should have opportunities to apply different solutions to a problem to see the outcome of their actions. Additionally, Hays (2005) notes that video games should be used to support learning but not as stand-alone instruction. While a video game should provide students with multiple avenues for learning, it must also draw students into a deeply developed story. As Cambourne's (1988) learning model illustrates, players expect interesting learning to include fresh ways of presenting instruction or information so that it holds their attention for longer than a few minutes.

Condition 4. Compelling Story Line

Video games should contain compelling story lines with fully developed characters and entertaining conditions for learning that match or exceed the media available to the student. As with popular novels, video games must allow students to identify with a character or characters in the story. For many students, hiding behind the mask of an avatar, that is, an alternate personification like an animal or inanimate object or a human character's identity within a game, provides opportunities to make mistakes that are risk free. According to students, the frustration of making mistakes is less intense in a game than in the traditional classroom setting (Ziaeehezarjeribi, Worrell, & Graves, 2008). For example, when we interviewed students for our research, they explained that when they make mistakes in the game, "no one is going to make fun of you." Players learn that making mistakes is simply an avenue for active learning. Several players also pointed out that the use of an avatar or an alternative identity found in first-person shooter games or simulations allows them to be willing to take greater risks than they would if they were playing as themselves. As an alternative to traditional learning or classroom environments, "mistakes" made in a game become a natural component of play. In many games, when players do not make wise choices or perform poorly, they are allowed another "life" or may regain their "health" or return to a previously established "safe port" to remain in the game. If a student fails a mission, the commander does not send a note home to parents; instead, he simply asks the player to try again or offers motivation for the person to remain engaged, using the language of the game (e.g., "OK, soldier, try that again."). Many students enjoy the fact that well-made video games provide different experiences each time they are played. Many of the newer video games provide multiple story lines with the same characters. In many cases, these multiple story lines encourage critical thinking, inquiry, and discovery.

Condition 5. Propel Students toward Inquiry and Discovery

Video games should help students understand what they have learned based on experience. Students should be allowed opportunities to become "experts" in a discipline by engaging with realistic contexts that facilitate inquiry and exploration (Kebritchi & Hirumi, 2008). Strategically placed video gaming in the classroom helps students to estimate their best learning at assessment time. Squire and Jenkins (2003) note that, "because each student has a somewhat different play experience, each brings something vital to the class discussion. Because those play experiences intersect each other, the game provides a common framework for discussion" (p. 17). Along with alternative methods of inquiry and discovery, students have also demonstrated the need for appropriate levels of challenge.

Condition 6. Provide Appropriate Levels of Challenge

Video games should be differentiated so that students perform and interact on the "edge of ability" (Steinkuehler & Chmiel, 2006) and stay engaged for extended periods of time without feeling bored by repetitive tasks. The most powerful application of games for learning is their capability of presenting challenges that match each student's current level of ability. Using students' choices and curiosity as motivators to take risks to engage again and again in challenging learning tasks, games support increased learning. As students master the skills of the game, they have varied experiences related to the concept/s being taught. Learning during gameplay on the edge of ability should also have practical applications to traditional learning environments.

Condition 7. Support Students' General Learning

Video games should improve the learning of all students, especially those who struggle to perform well when teachers use direct instruction or those who simply need more practice in order to learn a concept. As instructional video games are a relatively new medium, administrators may not support their use in the classroom if they cannot provide observable gains in student achievement (Stein, 2004). Moreover, video games should help students connect understanding across disciplines. For instance, Brock Dubbels was an eighth grade English teacher and graduate student in curriculum and instruction when a television reporter visited one of his classes in 2006. At that time Dubbels had been using video games to teach literary elements to urban students in Minneapolis for more than five years (DeRusha, 2006). In a video clip, Dubbels describes how pleased he was when one of his students explained his experience after playing Sonic the Hedgehog, saying, "It's much like the Odyssey; Sonic has to get home just like Odysseus." Additionally, Dubbels tells how he uses action video games as a tool together with reading books and writing to teach literature: "We're affecting point of view and the writer's purpose for the audience." As the interview with this middle school teacher clearly demonstrates, effectively integrating games into the classroom requires an understanding of more than just the game.

Systematic Process for Integrating Games

We have found that successful integration of games into schools is heavily dependent on financial, parental, technical, and administrator support because many people still see video games as a form of leisure activity (Bichelmeyer & Molenda, 2006). With that in mind, the following recommendations should help teachers as they learn to repurpose COTS games for the classroom.

Step 1. Evaluate the Learning Environment

As one begins the process of repurposing video games, the first step is to select games that bring together learning that occurs in the school, the community, the game, and the students' learning styles (Figure 12.1). We would suggest that the educator first determine if students in your class or courses like to play video games, if the school culture is conducive to the use of video games, if the community supports the use of video games, and, most important, if the content of the games being considered is appropriate for your school.

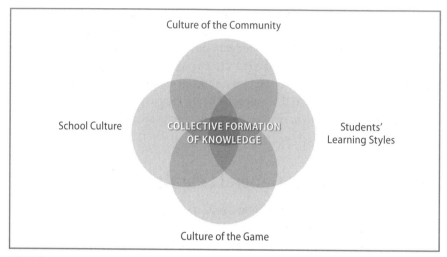

Culture of the Community

School Culture

COLLECTIVE FORMATION OF KNOWLEDGE

Students' Learning Styles

Culture of the Game

FIGURE 12.1 ▶ Factors to consider as teachers repurpose games

Teachers should survey students to find those who are already actively engaged in playing video games at home and to determine the "gaming" skills students have (Goldman, Cole, & Syer, 1999). Until the basic skills of the game are learned, your students will not be able to engage in connecting the game to classroom content. Many new players must spend time learning keystrokes on desk top computers or the functions of a gaming console that supports games such as Xbox, Wii, GameBoy, GameCube, PlayStation2, and others. Teachers should speak with students' parents to determine what types of video games they find acceptable for their children to play at home and at school. For instance, some communities are hesitant to use video games that contain the types of violent content found in Call of Duty or Medal of Honor (see Table 12.1 for rating system) or simulations that do not reflect factual content, for example, Spore has received mixed reviews from the science community because of its unrealistic portrayal of evolution (Bohannon, 2008).

Step 2. Selecting a Game

When selecting a video game to integrate into the curriculum, teachers must apply similar criteria to video games that they use for other media and reading material; consider using the seven critical conditions for integrating games. As one student gamer stated in an interview for our study, "When the story line is lame, you get really bored, and you don't want to spend any time with it" (Ziaeehezarjeribi et al., 2008). Careful repurposing involves rating the game, playing the game, and deciding whether connections can be made between components of the video game and national curriculum standards.

Repurposing involves more than just choosing a "sweet" game that is currently popular. The Entertainment Software Rating Board (ESRB, 2006) has created a simple rating system for video games (Table 12.1) similar to the one used by the movie industry, with the ratings of "EC" for early childhood, suitable for children ages 3 and older; "E" for everyone; "E10+" for children ages 10 and older; "T" for teens 13 and older; and "M" for mature audiences. Games rated EC may also be appropriate for use with special needs populations. We do not recommend using a game rated above E for any school contexts below ninth grade. Secondary school students are developmentally capable of engaging with T-rated video games but only after parent and teacher review of content. For example, Medal of Honor: Allied Assault and Call of Duty contain contextual violence that simulates World War II battles.

TABLE 12.1 ▶ Rating system for video games (ESRB, 2006)

ESRB RATING SYMBOLS AND CONTENT DESCRIPTORS	
EC (Early Childhood)	Titles rated **EC (Early Childhood)** have content that may be suitable for ages 3 and older. Contains no material that parents would find inappropriate.
E (Everyone)	Titles rated **E (Everyone)** have content that may be suitable for ages 6 and older. Titles in this category may contain minimal cartoon, fantasy or mild violence and/or infrequent use of mild language [profanity].
E10+ (Everyone 10 and older)	Titles rated **E10+ (Everyone 10 and older)** have content that may be suitable for ages 10 and older. Titles in this category may contain more cartoon, fantasy or mild violence, mild language and/or minimal suggestive themes.
T (Teen)	Titles rated **T (Teen)** have content that may be suitable for ages 13 and older. Titles in this category may contain violence, suggestive themes, crude humor, minimal blood, simulated gambling, and/or infrequent use of strong language.

Step 3. Play the Game

According to Charsky and Mims (2008), a teacher's understanding of a game is important for understanding how skills in the game can connect to those found in the school's curriculum. They also note the importance of the teacher's experience with the actual game to support students as they begin to play the game. For Step 3, we recommend that you (a) read the video game manual, (b) read online reviews about the game, (c) ask for feedback from students who play the game at home, and (d) play the game yourself.

Step 4. Connect Curriculum Standards to the Game

Caine and Caine (1997) note that many learners "do not automatically extract all the potential meaning" found in the activities they experience. We believe teachers should include activities that help students engage in "active processing" of information as they engage with learning activities. Active processing leads to deep understanding of content and includes the use of critical thinking to summarize, synthesize, problem-solve, and draw conclusions. As Caine and Caine (1997) claim, "active processing involves frequent questioning and expansion of student thinking, as well as an articulation of facts, concepts, and details" (p. 122). Additionally, Jenson (2005) talks about how important novel experiences are to learning because they "create stronger opportunity for new learning and pathways in the brain" (p. 120). In order to help design unique experiences connected to classroom learning, we have included a quick reference guide and three examples of "missions" that connect gameplay to the national standards. These titles are not all-inclusive and are not intended to endorse one product over another; they are simply games that were popular with students in the classrooms and labs where we conducted our research study (Ziaeehezarjeribi et al., 2008).

Please note that we purposefully excluded video games with a rating above Teen for secondary education and only used games with an Everyone rating for Grades 5 through 9. We do not recommend using a Teen-rated game in elementary settings because of their propensity for violence.

The National Standards Alignment Table (Table 12.2) was developed after we purposefully played the video games and spent time identifying content-specific skills that align with national standards for students from the following professional organizations: the National Council of Teachers of English and the International Reading Association (NCTE & IRA, 1996); the National Council of Teachers of Mathematics (NCTM, 2000); the National Science Teachers Association (NSTA, 2008); the National Council for the Social Studies (NCSS, 1994); and the National Association of Sports and Physical Education (Corbin, Pangrazi, & Le Masurier, 2004).

In Table 12.2, the first column lists names of games and their ESRB ratings. In the columns to the right of each game are specific national curriculum standards that we have determined hold the potential for building cognitive skills in each content area. For example, using Call of Duty in a world history class can provide background knowledge for English as a second language students who are struggling readers.

TABLE 12.2 ▶ National standards alignment of COTS games and simulations

NAME OF GAME AND GAME'S RATING	NCTE & IRA (LANGUAGE ARTS)	NCTM (MATH)	NSTA (SCIENCE)	NCSS (SOCIAL STUDIES)	NASPE (PHYSICAL EDUCATION)
High School (9th–12th grades)					
Civilization III and IV [TEEN T ESRB]	**Standard 6.** Students apply knowledge of language structure, language conventions, media techniques, figurative language, and genre to create, critique, and discuss print and nonprint text.			II. Time, community, and change III. People, places, and environments IV. Power, authority, and governance	

TABLE 12.2 (Continued)

NAME OF GAME AND GAME'S RATING	NCTE & IRA (LANGUAGE ARTS)	NCTM (MATH)	NSTA (SCIENCE)	NCSS (SOCIAL STUDIES)	NASPE (PHYSICAL EDUCATION)
Medal of Honor (TEEN T ESRB)	**Standard 8.** Students use a variety of technological and information resources (e.g., libraries, databases, computer networks, video) to gather and synthesize information and to create and communicate knowledge.			II. Time, community, and change III. People, places, and environments IV. Power, authority, and governance	
Call of Duty (TEEN T ESRB)	**Standard 12.** Students use spoken, written, and visual language to accomplish their own purposes (e.g., for learning, enjoyment, persuasion, and the exchange of information).			II. Time, community, and change III. People, places, and environments IV. Power, authority, and governance	
Making History: The Calm and the Storm (TEEN T ESRB)				II. Time, community, and change III. People, places, and environments IV. Power, authority, and governance	
Never Winter Nights (TEEN T ESRB)	**Standard 6.** Students apply knowledge of language structure, language conventions (e.g., spelling and punctuation), media techniques, figurative language, and genre to create, critique, and discuss print and nonprint texts. **Standard 11.** Students participate as knowledgeable, reflective, creative, and critical members of a variety of literacy communities.			II. Time, community, and change VI. Power, authority and governance VII. Science, technology, and society	

(Continued)

TABLE 12.2 *(Continued)*

NAME OF GAME AND GAME'S RATING	NCTE & IRA (LANGUAGE ARTS)	NCTM (MATH)	NSTA (SCIENCE)	NCSS (SOCIAL STUDIES)	NASPE (PHYSICAL EDUCATION)
Middle School (6th–8th grades)					
Dance Dance Revolution [E]					**Standard 2.** Demonstrates understanding of movement concepts, principles, strategies, and tactics as they apply to the learning and performance of physical activities. **Standard 6.** Values physical activity for health, enjoyment, challenge, self-expression, and/or social interaction.
Nancy Drew [E]	**Standard 6.** Students apply knowledge of language structure, language conventions, (e.g., spelling and punctuation), media techniques, figurative language, and genre to create, critique, and discuss print and nonprint text.				
SimCity [E]	**Standard 1.** Students read a wide range of print and nonprint texts to build an understanding of texts, of themselves, and of the cultures of the United States and the world; to acquire new information; to respond to the needs and demands of society and the workplace; and for personal fulfillment. Among these texts are fiction and nonfiction, classic and contemporary works.			III. People, places, and environments VII. Production, distribution, and consumption X. Civic ideals and practices	

TABLE 12.2 *(Continued)*

NAME OF GAME AND GAME'S RATING	NCTE & IRA (LANGUAGE ARTS)	NCTM (MATH)	NSTA (SCIENCE)	NCSS (SOCIAL STUDIES)	NASPE (PHYSICAL EDUCATION)
Spore			Populations and ecosystems Diversity and adaptations of organisms Life science	II. Time, community, and change III. People, places, and environments IV. Power, authority, and governance	
Elementary (4th–5th grades)					
Lemony Snicket's A Series of Unfortunate Events	Reading Listening skills Sequencing		Inventions Scientific inquiry		
Zelda Magora's Mask	Reading fluency Riddles Metaphors Symbolism Inquiry Critical stance	Money Free trade	Worlds Life science	III. People, places, and environments; map skills and legends X. Civic ideals and practices; social justice	
Zoo Tycoon		Numbers and operations		VII. Production, distribution, and consumption	
Elementary (PK–3rd grade)					
Little Bill Thinks Big		Numbers and operations			
Clifford the Big Red Dog Reading	Basic reading and writing Cognition				
Charlotte's Web: Word Rescue	Basic decoding and spelling				
Harvest Moon: A Wonderful Life Mission		Numbers and operations Geometry and measurement	Basic life science, gardening		

Step 5. Communicate with Your Administration

We have found that concerns arise when discussing the use of games in schools. Administrators, including principals, counselors, and curriculum directors, have asked us to show how video games can be used to meet state and national standards for content areas. As mentioned earlier, research that demonstrates gaming's direct impact on learning achievement as specified by state or national content standards is scarce. This may predispose curriculum leaders to maintain a "let's wait and see attitude" concerning the use of video games by their teachers. Additionally, some communities may be faced with concerns regarding the use of games by young people for any purpose, whether educational or recreational (Wartella & Jennings, 2000). These concerns are especially important as students are exposed to violent and/or sexual content embedded in popular entertainment products like video games (Haninger & Thompson, 2004; Kutner, Olson, Warner, & Hertzog, 2008). Noting educators' and parents' valid concerns about playing video games in classrooms, when planning to repurpose COTS video games, teachers should provide their administrators with a clear plan for implementation, including a proposed technology contract (provided at the end of this chapter).

Step 6. Talk to your Technology Support Staff

Before you move beyond planning, talk to the technology support staff to make sure the school's system meets the video game's requirements. You will need to have written specifications ready to show the technology support staff. For instance, Medal of Honor (EA Games, 2007) requires the following:

▶ Windows XP, Windows Me, Windows 98, or Windows 95 (Windows 2000 and Windows NT are not supported.)

▶ 450 MHz Intel Pentium II or 500 MHz AMD Athlon processor

▶ 128 MB RAM

▶ 8x CD/DVD drive

▶ 135 MB free hard disk space (additional space required for Windows swap-file, DirectX 8.0 installation, and GameSpy installation).

▶ 16 MB OpenGL capable video card using an Nvidia GeForce3, Nvidia GeForce2, Nvidia GeForce 256, Nvidia Riva TNT2, and Nvidia Riva TNT

▶ ATI Radeon, ATI Rage 128 Pro, ATI Rage 128, PowerVR3 Kyro II or PowerVR, Kyro chipset with OpenGL, and DirectX 8.0 compatible driver

▶ DirectX 8.0 compatible sound card

▶ Keyboard

▶ Mouse

Depending on your school system's regulations, you may need special permission to install a new game on your computers. If the video game has an online component, make sure the school does not have a firewall that will exclude gameplay. The next step involves engaging with the community.

Step 7. Communicate with Parents and Caregivers

Curriculum leaders who would like to consider the repurposing of video games to supplement instruction may be able to deflect criticism of game use by asking teachers first to prepare a clear plan that connects the proposed activity to curriculum standards. With this plan in place, formal meetings between parents and teachers can begin. When parents are given respect and choice, their fears and concerns about technology use in their children's educational experience may be minimized. Because many schools now block Internet sites, using sophisticated filtering/monitoring software to make questionable material inaccessible to students, most online simulations or games may not be available to them.

We would like to caution schools that censorship concerns may still arise regardless of how they choose to implement video games. To avoid policy implementation problems, which tend to arise when technologies with multimedia components like video gaming are used, acceptable use contracts may be used as an effective way to share the benefits and risks of multimedia technology use. Many school districts have adopted their own acceptable use policies (AUPs) for technology and Internet access. Administrators make sure that parents are given copies of the policy. Districts also post these policies on their official websites so that parents and students can access them easily. We have included a sample technology policy contract and parent notification letter at the end of this chapter (see pp. 305–306). Teachers should always provide alternative learning activities for students who choose not to play a video game. When implemented correctly, school policies may be used to assist gaming innovation in the classroom rather than prohibit its use.

Video Gaming "Missions"

Choosing a game that supports the curriculum presents one challenge—purposefully integrating that game into your class or courses is another. The following missions are designed to illustrate how a video game can be meaningfully integrated into a content-area activity. An overarching theme for each of the missions is given along with the national standards for students that can be strengthened by playing the game.

Lesson Plan

High School Mission

OVERARCHING THEME: World War II

GAME: Medal of Honor: Heroes 2 *(EA Games, 2007)*

National Council for the Social Studies (NCSS) Curriculum Standards

II.   Time, Community, and Change

III.   People, Places, and Environments

IV.   Individual Development and Identity

X.   Civic Ideals and Practices

National Council of Teachers of English (NCTE) and International Reading Association (IRA) Curriculum Standards

1.   Students read a wide range of print and nonprint text to build an understanding of texts, of themselves, and of the cultures of the United States and the world; to acquire new information; to respond to the needs and demands of society and the workplace; and for personal fulfillment.

4.   Students adjust their use of spoken, written, and visual language.

6.   Students apply knowledge of language structure, language conventions, media techniques, figurative language, and genre to create, critique, and discuss print and nonprint text.

11.   Students participate as knowledgeable, reflective, creative, and critical members of a variety of literacy communities.

Practical Application

Introduce this activity as a way for students to become active participants in the history of World War II. By becoming a soldier at the invasion of Normandy, students will begin to comprehend the enormous impact and resources needed to engage in an allied offensive. While students read about the invasion of Normandy in their history books, break them into pairs. At the beginning of each "mission," student teams are asked to read a memo from the Office of Strategic Services (OSS), predecessor of the Central Intelligence Agency (CIA). This memo and other messages are located at the beginning of each section of the Medal of Honor: Heroes 2 game. Explain to the students that they should choose the level that best matches the time they have already spent playing this (not any other) game. Level green is for beginners, level veteran for those with some experience with this game, and level hero for those who have advanced experience with this game. We recommend that all students begin playing the game at level green to accomplish the complete mission of this lesson. First ask students to read their missions all the way through. After they begin to play the game, the teacher should pause the game to collect information for their mission/s, outlined in the next section, Possibilities for Assessment.

Possibilities for Assessment

▶ After playing Medal of Honor for several class sessions, students break up into pairs and write a report to the commander in the same memo style as the one at the beginning of the game, using data gained from missions, such as the number of casualties and the problems encountered along the way. (Notes on this are in the arcade option.) The report to the commander must include a map of the battlefield (the teacher can provide a blank map if needed) in order to retrieve fallen members. (Soldiers never leave a brother or sister behind.) The map must include the name of the objective (found in the game), a legend, latitude and longitude (soldiers must be able to return to the site using these coordinates), compass rose, and a risk assessment, including projected casualties, wounded, and resources needed.

▶ Math connection: Students create a table that shows the number of casualties incurred in support of the report to commander.

▶ Prior to gameplay, the teacher asks students how military units are structured to assess their current knowledge. Students who understand the military are asked to prepare a 5-minute presentation for the next class session to give their classmates sufficient background information to understand the game and to play their roles realistically. Students gather in commands, groups of three–four students, and assume the role of the supreme commander of the unit and collaborate to create a plan of action. Each group presents its action plan to the teacher and the rest of the class for feedback. Students then construct a memo to be sent to field commanders, encouraging them to keep the faith with their troops and to prepare a path for the allied expeditionary force to obtain a foothold on a particular beach.

▶ Possible writing prompt (instructions to students): Based on your textbook reading and playing Medal of Honor, what are three objectives your commanders must consider before the allied assault? Use your prewriting strategies by getting together in groups of four; brainstorm ideas by building a concept map on a large sheet of paper (newspaper end rolls are great for this) that explains and answers these questions: Which allies need to be contacted prior to the mission? How will you do this? Do you need to find an interpreter? Does anyone in your unit understand French, German, Italian, or Spanish? Who are your allies? After discussion and recording this information in a group, present this to the rest of your class and ask them to give you feedback. Classmates should help each group to include all of the information needed. If there are any questions from classmates, make sure you answer these in your final written presentation to the class.

For Further Thought

▶ The teacher may require students with limited video gaming experience to play the "training portion" of any game you choose before the entire class starts playing the game. This will familiarize nongamers with game components and actions. While the control functions in video games on a PC platform are much different from those on an Xbox or Wii, students easily adapt to new platforms when given the opportunity. Students who are experienced gamers may be asked to sit with less experienced students to help train them until they feel comfortable with terminology and control functions.

▶ This game can be used during a six-week World War II unit. To benefit from the full effects of gameplay, students may appreciate the opportunity to engage in playing the game for long stretches of time, such as 2–4 hours. The teacher can apply this same pattern to other historically accurate video games related to wars. They all have command structures, communications systems, transportation, conquests, decision making involving causes and effects, era-specific armor for protection, and objectives specific to the conflict.

▶ An extension activity would be to ask students to write a play enacting an armistice or surrender. Ask students to assign roles for the meeting and to create or find artifacts, such as the armistice agreement, props, and costumes representative of the era and the leaders.

Lesson Plan

Middle School Mission

OVERARCHING THEME: Creature Feature—Creating and
Presenting a Story

GAME: Spore *(EA Games, 2008)*

National Council of Teachers of English (NCTE) and International Reading Association (IRA) Curriculum Standards

3. Students apply a wide range of strategies to comprehend, interpret, evaluate, and appreciate texts. They draw on their prior experience, their interactions with other readers and writers, their knowledge of word meaning and of other texts, their word identification strategies, and their understanding of textual features (e.g., sound-letter correspondence, sentence structure, context, graphics).

4. Students adjust their use of spoken, written, and visual language (e.g., conventions, style, vocabulary) to communicate effectively with a variety of audiences and for different purposes.

5. Students employ a wide range of strategies as they write and use different writing process elements appropriately to communicate with different audiences for a variety of purposes.

6. Students apply knowledge of language structure, language conventions (e.g., spelling and punctuation), media techniques, figurative language, and genre to create, critique, and discuss print and nonprint texts.

7. Students conduct research on issues and interests by generating ideas and questions and by posing problems. They gather, evaluate, and synthesize data from a variety of sources (e.g., print and nonprint texts, artifacts, people) to communicate their discoveries in ways that suit their purpose and audience.

8. Students use a variety of technological and information resources (e.g., libraries, databases, computer networks, video) to gather and synthesize information and to create and communicate knowledge.

9. Students develop an understanding of and respect for diversity in language use, patterns, and dialects across cultures, ethnic groups, geographic regions, and social roles.

10. Students whose first language is not English make use of their first language to develop competency in the English language arts and to develop understanding of content across the curriculum.

11. Students participate as knowledgeable, reflective, creative, and critical members of a variety of literacy communities.

National Science Teachers Association

Life Science

TESOL Standards (*TESOL, 1997*)

Goal 2. To use English to achieve academically in all content areas

Standard 1. Students will use English to interact in the classroom.

Standard 2. Students will use English to obtain, process, construct, and provide subject-matter information in spoken and written form.

Standard 3. Students will use appropriate learning strategies to construct and apply academic knowledge.

Description

Spore is a game with many different levels of engagement. The cell level provides an imaginative way to talk about and engage with science at the cellular level. The cell's characteristics determine what sort of creature it will develop into; at the creature level, each student's creature will meet other creatures from neutral and predatory animal species. When creatures' brains evolve to accommodate more complex abilities, they advance to the tribal level. Members of tribes use tools and interact with other players socially. At the civilization level, game players engage on a global level with civilizations. The tools associated with the civilization level of Spore allow students to create cities and vehicles. Students learn to engage in strategies based on economics and politics between groups. The last level in Spore is the space level, which is much more complex and enables players to create worlds and their associated civilizations. While Spore is intended only to mimic the real world (NPR, 2008), the game offers many scenarios that can spark students' interests in life science and ecosystems. As they play, students will enhance their knowledge and practice scientific vocabulary. According to William Wright (NPR, 2008), creator of the game, "There is nothing more interactive than making a universe come to life." The game acts as a "player's imagination amplifier" through the use of creative tools.

Practical Application

This mission is intended to support students for whom English is not a first or heritage language and/or for students who need additional support in using vocabulary embedded in a life science unit. Before beginning this mission, the teacher should become familiar with the "create function" of Spore. Before beginning this mission, make sure computers have one of the following: Microsoft PowerPoint, Movie Maker, Photo Story 3 (PC), iMovie (Mac). Students begin this mission by breaking off into small groups. Each group should be asked to have several life science textbooks available for easy reference to parts of animals. Before gameplay, either the teacher creates a set of cards with the names of animals that will be discussed, or the teacher gets the students to make the cards. The teacher could write the names of the animals on the board, give each group a card and a marker, and ask the groups to make specific animal cards. The teacher explains that students in their small groups will soon write a story together about one of these animals. Begin a discussion with the entire class using a Smart Board or a data projector with the Spore game running. The teacher selects a card from the following creature cards (Figure 12.2):

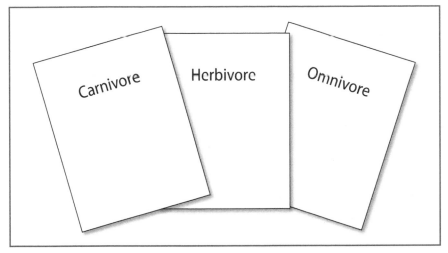

FIGURE 12.2 ► Creature cards for activity

Modeling the creative process. The teacher should first launch the COTS game Spore and select the creature game identified with an animal paw. Using the Spore video game, the teacher asks the class to help design the creature that has just been selected. The teacher needs to use the vocabulary found in the life science textbook. A terrestrial animal can be drawn with the creature editor function. Use questioning routines such as the following:

- What does *omnivore* mean?

- Name a(n) _____ in the real world.

- What are at least three characteristics that make that animal a(n) _____?

- How will my creature move?

- What does my creature need in order to eat?

- What type of mouth does my creature need as a(n) _____?

- What type of (skin, scales, feathers, etc.) does my creature need?

- What type of digestive system does my creature need?

- In what environment does my creature live?

Remember, these are only suggestions of how to guide an interactive lesson around life science vocabulary.

Now move the students into groups and hand out the enclosed plan (Figure 12.3). Explain that each group is in charge of its own plan, and the teacher will walk around the room to help with any questions. Before helping students, ask them if they have read, followed, and checked off the instructions.

Creature Feature: Story of a Creature

Our Plan

Group members' names here:

_____

☐ Select one creature card from the creature card stack.

☐ Write the name of the animal you picked here: _____

☐ Go to your life science textbook and make a list of all of your animal's characteristics here (Remember to use the words in your textbook): _____
_____

☐ Make a drawing of the animal you will be creating and studying.

☐ Label all of the parts. Use the scientific names from your textbook to label your creature.

☐ Check with your teacher to make sure all of your characteristics (descriptions) are accurate.

☐ Using what you have learned from reading about your creature, make a plan for a problem the creature faces. The carnivore may have trouble finding prey or a mate, etc.

☐ Write a story line for the story of your creature here. (What happens first, second, etc?)

FIRST	SECOND	THIRD

☐ Now that you have a plan for the story about your creature, you may go to the computer and open the game Spore.

☐ With your group, draw the creature from your group plan by selecting the paw icon on the left-hand side of the screen. Then use the draw functions in Creature Creator.

☐ Using the photo icon, take at least 10 different photos of your creature in different poses for your story. We will be using these photos to support your story later. Save these photos to your school file.

☐ As a group, lay the photos in the order you believe would help tell the story you would like to tell about your creature. After you have fully discussed the story line and refined your ideas, begin to write your story using scientific words.

☐ As a group, read the story out loud to determine if there are any ideas or sentences that need to be edited. Use spell check or the dictionary to check for spelling.

☐ After your first and second drafts, ask your teacher to check your spelling and grammar.

☐ Next, you will cut and paste your photos to a slide show program so you can read the story to the class. You may use Photo Story 3, Windows Movie Maker, or Microsoft PowerPoint.

☐ Practice reading your story out loud using the slide show you have created.

☐ After you have permission from your teacher, present your story to the whole class.

FIGURE 12.3 ▶   Group guidelines for creature feature

Possibilities for Assessment

As students work in groups, listen to them as they discuss their organizational plans. Check to see if groups need support with comprehension and vocabulary. Check to make sure students are supporting each other through this process. The teacher may use any phase of this process to check for comprehension, sequencing, cause and effect, and effective use of English. The framework found in the checklist is important to allow students a degree of autonomy and choice. This activity should evoke discussions in English using scientific vocabulary in context.

For Further Thought

▶ How do you plan to grade this activity? There are multiple subcomponents within this activity. Perhaps participation grades can be given during the process. The presentations and writing products should be included in the grading process.

▶ An extension activity that works well is to collect the photos of each group's creature and place them on a three-column poster to help support comprehension of herbivore, carnivore, and omnivore.

▶ Hold a contest to see which one of the creatures is designed the best, based on the way the creature functions. Students can hold a "Best of Show" contest using their own criteria.

▶ Based on the drawings students have created, which creature is the fastest? Which is the slowest? Students should write their findings in a journal.

▶ A Venn diagram can be used to compare and contrast various categories.

▶ This activity has unlimited possibilities but could be limited by students' varying abilities to use technology. Do you need to use the computer lab before beginning this activity? Do you need to teach the applications first?

Lesson Plan

■ ■ ■ Elementary School Mission ■ ■ ■

OVERARCHING THEME: Role Playing in Modern Children's Literature, Characterization

GAME: Lemony Snicket's A Series of Unfortunate Events
(Adrenium Games, 2004)

National Council for the Social Studies (NCSS) Curriculum Standards

II. Time, Continuity, and Change

III. People, Places, and Environments

National Council of Teachers of English (NCTE) and International Reading Association (IRA) Curriculum Standards

1. Students read a wide range of print and nonprint texts to build an understanding of texts, of themselves, and of the cultures of the United States and the world; to acquire new information; to respond to the needs and demands of society and the workplace; and for personal fulfillment. Among these texts are fiction and nonfiction, classic and contemporary work.

2. Students read a wide range of literature from many periods and many genres to build an understanding of the many dimensions (e.g., philosophical, ethical, aesthetic) of human experience.

3. Students apply a wide range of strategies to comprehend, interpret, evaluate, and appreciate texts. They draw on their prior experience, their interactions with other readers and writers, their knowledge of word meaning and of other texts., their word identification strategies, and their understanding of textual features (e.g., context and graphics).

6. Students apply knowledge of language conventions.

ISTE National Education Technology Standards for Students

3. Students apply digital tools to gather, evaluate, and use information. Students plan strategies to guide inquiry; locate, organize, analyze, evaluate, synthesize, and ethically use information from a variety of sources and media; process data; and report results.

National Science Teachers Association (NSTA) Curriculum Standards

Science as Inquiry

Practical Application

Students read one of the *Lemony Snicket's A Series of Unfortunate Events* books. Before, during, and after reading, students play the Lemony Snicket's A Series of Unfortunate Events video game and use copies of this progress chart (Figure 12.4). In groups of two, students answer questions as they explore and construct inventions throughout the game. The goal of this mission is to determine the reasons why inventors engage in scientific inquiry. This mission is especially important for students learning English as a new language or students who need to build background knowledge for improved reading comprehension. Ask students to use their progress charts to answer questions during the game.

PROGRESS CHART		
Name of Invention	Draw and describe the device. Write the number of pieces in this invention.	What problem was this invention designed to solve?
Brilliant Bopper		
Fruit Flinger		
Baby Booster		
Steady Stilts		
Math connection: What are the average number of pieces for all of your inventions? You can do this by first adding all of the pieces together and then dividing that number by the total number of inventions (4).		
TOTAL:		

FIGURE 12.4 ▶ Progress chart

Possibilities for Assessment

▶ Students use their progress charts to write a short paragraph to explain which one of the inventions in Lemony Snicket is their favorite or the most practical in the real world. Students must be able to explain the steps they took to make this decision. Make sure students write the problem the invention was intended to solve in their charts.

► Divide the class into groups of three or four and brainstorm ideas of famous inventors. Take at least one week to research famous inventors on the Internet or in the library. Students should record important information from at least five to six famous inventions or inventors. After students have gathered this information, the group has a discussion about which one of the inventors the group would like to present to the rest of the class. For many students, working in a social group helps to add meaning to their learning. For many poor readers, learning is enhanced if they have an opportunity to talk to their friends about what they have read. Alternatively, teachers can use this as a way to ask students to study for an end of unit exam.

► Students return to the class with notes from research and then determine how to create a "live action" game or skit that teaches other class members the timeline of how the inventor moved from coming up with an idea to the final product. For instance, students can design characters that will "zap" deadly viruses and demonstrate how an inventor might have used "homogenizing" technology to create safer milk products. The group is then responsible for collaborating to write the research paper to accompany the game. This begins by determining the format (outline) and preparing a rough draft. Students should be allowed to go through the writing cycle (prewriting, drafting, revision, editing, publishing).

► As a class, brainstorm problems within the students' community that need solving. Pose the question: Is there an invention that has the potential to solve the problem? In groups, design a mock invention and ask students to present their solutions in the form of a commercial. As the teacher moves through this activity, determine areas where you can use Lemony Snickets as a metaphor for understanding the need to solve problems.

For Further Thought

As you consider whether the use of games in your classroom is practical, remember to check with other teachers and the technology coordinator or lab teacher in your school community before implementing video games into your classroom. Ask your colleagues the following questions and find out whether and how they have used video games in their classes.

► Are students in your school's classrooms already actively engaged in video gaming? If so, you may not need to spend much time teaching students to play the game. If students are not familiar with the use of technology, the teacher will need to invest several instructional periods teaching students to negotiate a game.

► Do you need to coordinate this with your computer lab teacher? This teacher may be willing to support this activity as a way to meet state and national technology standards.

► How do you propose to grade the activities that emerge from these activities? You may want to give participation points during the activity and a grade for the final product.

Conclusion

Consider for a moment that children between the ages of 8 and 13 are now directly involved in the selection and purchase of video games. Youth drive the video game market. Video game developers, who know their customers, are willing to innovate in order to remain a viable industry. In response to gamer demands for more realistic environments, TN Games has begun to market its "3rd Space" Gaming Vest (Santo, 2007), which can be used by a player to become fully immersed in a game by allowing a player to "feel" the impact of actions. For instance, a player can now feel the G-forces of flying a jet. British Petroleum and Electronic Arts (Businesswire.com, 2007) are now in collaboration to build software that explicitly teaches "environmental awareness about low-carbon power." Video games are no longer simply a form of leisure; they drive innovation. Video games have become an integral part of many sectors of the globe. While engaged with video games, players are willing to undertake difficult tasks, such as mastering foreign languages, simply to meet the game's objectives.

To remain viable as an institution, education may need to pay more attention to the video gaming industry. Educators who wish to capture the hearts and minds of their students should treat them more like the gaming industry treats its customers. Imagine a ninth grade student picking up an iPod in homeroom class with the math assignment for the day that has been specifically tailored to the individual student's ability level. It contains a 2- to 5-minute streaming video introduction of the day's lesson, an interface activity/game that allows the student to apply the day's information practically, including formative feedback, followed by a summative assessment (summary of student abilities) that is remotely downloaded instantly into the teacher's grade book. Each consecutive assignment includes more complex applications of the course's academic content that can include using multiple computer programs. We contend that this type of learning environment or "classroom" can be supported by software presently available to the general public.

The future of teaching and learning belongs to children who have already impacted the manner in which schools deliver information, from curriculum standards in technology to high-stakes testing. We believe there is a great potential for the next generation of video games to become fully integrated into PK–12 classrooms.

References

Adrenium Games. (2004). *Lemony Snicket's A series of unfortunate events.* Los Angeles: Activision Publishing, Inc.

Albers, P., Vasquez, V., & Harste, J. (2008). A classroom with a view: Teachers, multimodality, and new literacies. *Talking Points, 19*(2), 3–13.

Barab, S., Sadler, T., Heiselt, C., Hickey, D., & Zuiker, S. (2007). Relating narrative, inquiry, and inscriptions: Supporting consequential play. *Journal of Science Education and Technology, 16*(1), 59–82.

Bichelmeyer, B., & Molenda, M. (2006). *Issues and trends in instructional technology: Gradual growth atop tectonic shifts.* Unpublished manuscript, Indiana University, Bloomington, IN.

Bohannon, J. (2008). Flunking Spore. *Science, 322*(5901), 531. Retrieved November 15, 2008, from www.sciencemag.org/cgi/content/full/322/5901/531b

Businesswire.com. (2007, October 10). EA and BP collaborate to include climate education in SimCity societies. Retrieved October 12, 2007, from www.businesswire.com

Caine, R., & Caine, G. (1997). *Education on the edge of possibility.* Alexandria, VA: Association for Supervision and Curriculum Development.

Cambourne, B. (1988). *The whole story: Natural learning and the acquisition of literacy in the classroom.* Auckland, New Zealand: Ashton Scholastic.

Charsky, D., & Mims, C. (2008). Integrating commercial off-the-shelf video games into school curriculums. *TechTrends, 52*(5), 38–52.

Corbin, C. B., Pangrazi, R. P., & Le Masurier, G. C. (2004). *Physical activity for children: A statement of guidelines for children ages 5–12* (2nd ed.). Reston, VA: National Association of Sports and Physical Education (NASPE) Publications. Retrieved November 11, 2008, from www.aahperd.org/naspe/template.cfm?template=publications-nationalstandards.html

DeRusha, J. (2006, June 12). Teacher uses video games in English class. WCCO-TV website. Retrieved June 20, 2008, from http://wcco.com/video/?id=17627@wcco.dayport.com

EA Games. (2007). *Medal of honor: Heroes 2.* Redwood Shores, CA: Electronic Arts.

EA Games. (2008). *Spore.* Redwood Shores, CA: Electronic Arts.

Entertainment Software Rating Board (ESRB). (2006). *Game rating and descriptor guide.* Retrieved November 15, 2008, from www.esrb.org/ratings/ratings_guide.jsp

Federation of American Scientists (FAS). (2006). *Summit on educational games: Harnessing the power of video games for learning.* Retrieved January 15, 2008, from www.fas.org/gamesummit/Resources/Summit%20on%20Educational%20Games.pdf

Gee, J. (2003). *What video games have to teach us about learning and literacy.* New York, NY: Palgrave MacMillan.

Goldman, S., Cole, K., and Syer, C. (1999, July). The technology/content dilemma. Paper presented at the Secretary's Conference on Educational Technology–1999, Washington, DC. Retrieved November 16, 2008, from www2.ed.gov/rschstat/eval/tech/techconf99/whitepapers/paper4.html

Greenemeier, L. (2007, October 25). Video game vest simulates sensation of being capped: Video game maker TN Games delivers a vest filled with sensors that promises to give fans a more authentic experience. *Scientific American.* Retrieved June 14, 2010, from www.scientificamerican.com/article.cfm?id=video-game-vest-simulates

Haninger, K., & Thompson, K. (2004). Content ratings of teen-rated video games. *Journal of the American Medical Association, 291*(7), 856–865.

Hays, R. T. (2005). *The effectiveness of instructional games: A literature review and discussion* (Technical Report 2005–004). Orlando, FL: Naval Air Warfare Center Training Systems Division. (Defense Technical Information Center No. ADA 441 935)

Infinity Ward. (2005). *Call of duty.* Santa Monica, CA: Activision Publishing, Inc.

International Society for Technology in Education (ISTE). (2007). *National education technology standards for students* (NETS•S). Retrieved October 29, 2008, from www.iste.org/Content/ NavigationMenu/NETS/ForStudents/2007Standards/NETS_for_Students_2007_Standards.pdf

Jenson, E. (2005). *Teaching with the brain in mind.* (2nd ed.). Alexandria, VA: Association for Supervision and Curriculum Development.

Kebritchi, M., & Hirumi, A. (2008). Examining the pedagogical foundations of modern educational computer games. *Computers & Education, 51,* 1729–1743.

Kutner, L., Olson, C., Warner, D., & Hertzog, S. (2008) Parents' and sons' perspectives on video game play: A qualitative study. *Journal of Adolescent Research, 23*(1). 76–96.

National Council for the Social Studies (NCSS). (1994). *Curriculum standards for the social studies: Expectations of excellence (Bulletin 89).* Washington, DC: NCSS.

National Council of Teachers of English (NCTE) & International Reading Association (IRA). (1996). Standards for the English language arts. Newark, DE: IRA; Urbana, IL: NCTE. Retrieved April 24, 2008, from www.ncte.org/library/NCTEFiles/Resources/Books/Sample/StandardsDoc.pdf

National Council of Teachers of Mathematics (NCTM). (2000). *Principles and standards for school mathematics: An overview.* Retrieved November 15, 2008, from http://standards.nctm.org

National Public Radio (NPR). (2008, September 12). Spore: Does evolution really happen like that? Talk of the Nation. Evolutionary biologist Richard Prum discusses the science behind Spore with its creator, Will Wright. Retrieved September 12, 2008, from www.npr.org/templates/story/story. php?storyId=94563046

National Science Teachers Association (NSTA). (2008). National Science Education Standards. Retrieved June 14, 2010, from www.nsta.org/publications/nses.aspx

Rosas, R., Nussbaum, M., Cumsille, P., Marianov, V., Correa, M., Flores, P., et al. (2003). Beyond *Nintendo*: Design and assessment of educational video games for first and second grade students. *Computers & Education, 40,* 71–94.

Santo, M. (2007, October 20). *3rd Space* vest lets you feel blows in video games. *RealTechNews.* Retrieved June 21, 2008, from www.realtechnews.com/posts/498

Squire, K. (2008). Video-game literacy: A literacy of expertise. In J. Coiro, M. Knobel, C. Lankshear, & D. Leu (Eds.), *Handbook of research on new literacies* (pp. 635–669). Mahwah, NJ: Lawrence Erlbaum.

Squire, K., & Jenkins, H. (2003). Harnessing the power of games in education. *InSight, 3*(8), 7–33.

Stein, S. (2004). *The culture of education policy.* New York, NY: Teachers College Press.

Steinkuehler, C., & Chmiel, M. (2006). Fostering scientific habits of mind in the context of online play. *Proceedings of the 7th international conference of the learning sciences* (ICLS 2006), Bloomington, IN, 723–729.

Teachers of English to Speakers of Other Languages (TESOL). (1997). *ESL standards for pre-K–12 students.* Retrieved January 1, 2009, from www.tesol.org/s_tesol/seccss.asp?CID=113&DID=1583

Wartella, E., & Jennings, N. (2000). Children and computers: New technology—old concerns. *Children and Computer Technology, 10*(2), 31–43.

Yellin, D., Blake, M. E., & Devries, B. A. (2008). *Integrating the language arts* (4th ed.). Scottsdale, AZ: Holcomb Hathaway.

Ziaeehezarjeribi, Y., Worrell, P., & Graves, I. (2008). Effective application of computer game technology K–12. In E. Simsonson (Ed.), *31st annual proceedings: Selected research and development papers presented at the annual convention of the Association for Educational Communications and Technology*, Orlando, FL, section 2, 405–410. (ERIC Document Reproduction Service No. ED504371)

Technology, Internet, Gaming, and Simulation Consent Form

My child, _____,
(printed name of student)

has my permission to access the Internet at school, including the use of instructional software, local files, and teacher-led activities. Yes _____ No _____

(Writing your initials beside "No" above means that your child will not be able to access educational resources and resources on the Internet at school.)

I give permission for my child to be limited to using only those Internet sites approved by the teacher that are filtered by the school's technology coordinator, including access to Internet video/computer games and store-bought computer games and simulations. Yes _____ No _____

(Writing your initials beside "Yes" above means that your child will be able to play video/computer games to meet educational goals. A note will be sent to you before games are used in the classroom with the game's title, rating (if there is one), and the educational goals or objectives to be reached using the video/computer game. Writing your initials beside "No" above means that your child will not be allowed to engage in learning activities and experiences using video/computer games to meet educational goals.)

I understand that access to technology at school is a privilege designed only for educational purposes. If my child violates any of these policies, he or she will lose access to technology, the Internet, and video/computer gaming experiences. Violations will result in disciplinary action and/or appropriate legal action initiated against my child. I also understand that this consent document remains in effect until such time my child leaves this school or I modify the permissions in writing.

Parent/Guardian Name Printed:

_____

Parent/Guardian Signature:

_____ Date _____

(For more information about online safety, please read the U.S. Department of Justice's online publication, Parent's Guide to Children's Online Safety, at www.justice.gov/criminal/ceos/onlinesafety.html)

Student Technology Contract

I _____ agree to follow instructions on the use of
(printed name of student)

video games and the Internet from my teacher. I also promise to follow the rules established in my school's Technology, Internet, and Gaming Access Policy and the Children's Internet Protection Act of 2000.

Student's Signature _____ Date _____

Video/Simulation/Gaming Permission Note

Date _____

Dear _____ ,
                  (printed first and last name of parent/s)

Our class will be using a game titled _____

on this day/s: _____ .

The game is rated for (teacher has checked the rating):

☐	**EC**	Early Childhood (PK–age 9)
☐	**E+10**	10+ (ages 10 and older)
☐	**E**	Everyone
☐	**T**	Teen (ages 13 and older)

Educational goals or objectives for this activity include (Teacher has listed the learning goals): _____

_____

Your child will be provided with an alternative activity if this game is not acceptable to you. Please feel free to preview the game in our computer lab on any of the following days: _____

at these times: _____

The alternative activity will include:

_____
               (list the alternative activities the teacher will provide for the student)

Thank you for your continued partnership in the success of our school.

Sincerely,

_____
               (name of teacher)

_____
               (contact Information: e-mail address, telephone number/s)

13

Web-Based Drill-Games

Peter J. Fadde

THIS CHAPTER COVERS A SUBSET of digital video games that combines the proven instructional strategy of drill and practice with arcade-style gameplay to facilitate learning. Although drill-and-practice games have been around for many years in CD format, there are now many more available—often at no cost—on the Internet. The challenge for teachers lies in finding games that not only fit curricular objectives but also are instructionally sound and engaging for students. This chapter helps teachers locate appropriate drill-and-practice games, evaluate them in terms of drill structure and gameplay, and integrate them into regular classroom activities.

This chapter covers a small but important subset of digital video games that combines the structure of drill and practice with the playfulness of games to produce relatively simple games (henceforth referred to as drill-games) that are engaging while maintaining the focus and instructional efficiency of drills. Drill-games have been around as a form of "edutainment" since the 1970s and are often derided as "drill-and-kill" (Egenfeldt-Nielsen, 2007). However, two recent technology developments may change educators' impressions of drill-games.

First, many excellent drill-games, now available for free on the Internet, provide variety and accessibility beyond classic edutainment games, such as the Math Blaster! series, that traditionally were distributed on CDs through school or district media centers. Second, the development of Flash animation allows developers to create games that look better and play better than older games.

Websites such as Game Goo (www.earobics.com/gamegoo/gooey.html) and Arcademic Skill Builders (www.arcademicskillbuilders.com) offer free access to visually enticing Flash games that also have high learning value. While not as "Flashy," many older drill-games also combine learning and fun. The quantity and quality of drill-games that are accessible and searchable on the Internet should lead educators to reconsider making edutaining drill-games part of their schools' curricula.

Definition and Value of Drill-Games

Drills use the key elements of repetition, immediate feedback, and progressive difficulty to build fluency, especially in basic math and language skills (Alessi & Trollip, 2001). The value of drill-and-practice learning in math is emphasized in *Foundations for Success: The Final Report of the Mathematics Advisory Panel* (U.S. Department of Education, 2008), which states, "For all content areas, practice allows students to achieve automaticity of basic skills—the fast, accurate, and effortless processing of content information—which frees up working memory for more complex aspects of problem solving" (p. 30).

Although drill-and-practice is well established as an effective instructional method, students—especially young ones—sometimes need to be enticed into drill-based learning by adding gameplay. Gameplay not only invites students to try a drill-game but also provides incentives for them to persist. As with most games, drill-games are driven by players competing—against themselves, other students, the computer, the clock, or a standard of some type (Newby, Stepich, Lehman, & Russell, 2000). Stapleton and Hirumi (2010) make an important point: Though a game may be about winning, losing also needs to be fun so that players are encouraged to try again.

Beyond making drills more palatable, gameplay can also help students develop and strengthen essential mental skills, such as concentration, memory, spatial awareness, hand-eye coordination, and problem solving (Bottino, Ferlino, Ott, & Tavella, 2007). However, "developing students' mental skills through gameplay" has not become a learning objective in typical K–12 curricula. In spite of the many positive aspects of using educational games in schools, the use of purely entertaining video games, like Tetris, as part of formal classroom activities has not been justified yet, though a creative geometry teacher might be able to use it as a teaching tool. When drill-games are combined with traditional teacher-led activities to accomplish the primary curricular objectives of teaching basic skills, the mental skills development associated with playing digital video games can provide valuable secondary learning. For teachers who want to explore incorporating digital video games into their classrooms, drill-games are a natural starting point.

The availability and potential benefits of effective instructional drill-games suggest that students and teachers will receive significant educational value when these games are integrated into classroom instruction. However, teachers need to proceed with a degree of caution because the combination of drill structure and gameplay that can work together to create enticing and effective instruction can also work against each other to produce drill-games that are neither fun nor effective. The key to successful incorporation of drill-games into classes is to evaluate the quality and appropriateness for your students and your particular learning activities, which is the focus of this chapter. Of course, you need to find appropriate drill-games first. The next section covers locating digital video drill-games in the vast, sometimes confusing, realm of the Internet.

Locating Drill-Games

You can search the web using terms such as "math drill games" and find a haphazard array of drills without gameplay, games without drill structure, and perhaps a few actual drill-games. A more efficient approach is to visit teacher-produced or teacher-oriented portals—websites that collect and categorize links to a variety of resources for teachers, most of which reside on other websites.

Portals for Instructional Games

Portals such as Teachers First (www.teachersfirst. com/index.cfm) and Teachers' Domain (www. teachersdomain.org) collect links to online resources for teachers—including lesson plans, worksheets, flash cards, and digital video games, which may include quiz-games, puzzle-games, and simulation-games in addition to drill-games. Resources are usually categorized by type, by content area, and by grade level. Some portals are specific to content areas, for instance, Reading Comprehension Connection (www. readingcomprehensionconnection.com), and Syvum (www.syvum.com), which is oriented to foreign-language learning and math and science homework help. Syvum charges a membership fee and offers a "Complete Solution for Teachers" with interactive learning materials in reading, math, and foreign languages.

TIP

When exploring portals, be sure to take notes and bookmark favorite URLs on your browser. A better approach is to use a social bookmarking program, like Delicious, so that you and your colleagues can access the bookmarks from any Internet-connected computer. Bookmarking programs also let you and other teachers add comments to posted URLs.

FIGURE 13.1 ▶ WWILD search results for Grades 3–6 math games

Although educator portals provide access to valuable resources, be aware that many portals are vehicles for advertising and promotion. Portals are also limited in that they typically do not provide reviews or recommendations of the resources they collect.

A handful of educator portals focus on games, including drill-games, and provide evaluations that are contributed by educators who use the portal. A good starting place to look for digital video drill-games is the World Wide Interactive Learning (WWILD) site (http://it.coe.uga.edu/wwild/), created in 1999 by Lloyd Rieber (1996), an early advocate of simple digital video games for learning. The WWILD website, depicted in Figure 13.1, continues to be maintained by the University of Georgia and features a searchable database with more than 1,000 profiles of interactive modules, many of which are drill-games.

Teachers are invited to use the database to find interactive modules and to become WWILD Team members and contribute reviews. Profiles of interactive modules include author name, subject area, module format (including "game"), subject area, grade level, and a brief description.

An advantage of WWILD's format is that all listed games are recommended by the educators who posted them. A drawback to WWILD's reliance on member-posted reviews is that the list of titles is not as comprehensive or current as some non-reviewing portals. For comprehensiveness, teachers are well served by exploring the Gamequarium (http://gamequarium.org) portal, developed by a teacher who started the site as a graduate course project and has maintained it since. Gamequarium does not provide recommendations or reviews of titles but does present a large and varied collection of teacher resources that include digital video drill-games. The portal organizes links to off-site digital resources according to subject area and grade level.

Another noncommercial resource for drill-games is the portal Multimedia Educational Resource for Learning and Online Teaching (http://merlot.org). MERLOT complements WWILD, which favors simple educational games appropriate for elementary grades. MERLOT collects links to many multimedia learning activities, most of which are designed for secondary and higher education use. Activities catalogued on MERLOT are organized by subject and can be sorted by material type, which does not include "games" as a category but does include "drill-and-practice." Educators post all multimedia resources profiled on MERLOT, and many profiles include evaluations and comments.

Single-Organization Game Websites

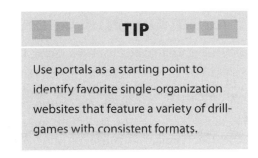

While portals provide links to resources from a variety of websites, single-organization websites contain games that are produced by a single organization or company. Many single-organization websites feature games of varying types that have a consistent look and format and address a variety of content areas and grade levels including drill-games. When teachers use games in class that have familiar rules, goals, and interface controls, then teachers and students need to invest less time in getting up and running with a new game. Some notable single-organization websites that produce and distribute digital video drill-games are profiled in the Single-Entity Drill-Game Websites supplement (see page 326).

The following scenario illustrates a teacher using a portal to locate a digital video drill-game. The scenario will be continued in later sections of this chapter on evaluating and integrating drill-games.

Scenario

Chris Fitch has decided to use a math drill-game to help her fifth grade students gain confidence for year-end standardized testing. She goes to the WWILD website to see if she can find an appropriate drill-game. She joins the WWILD team by registering and does a search of the database for subject area = mathematics, intended audience = 3–6, module format = Game. The search turns up 42 hits. One called Batter's Up Baseball (www.prongo.com) catches her eye. She often talks about baseball with her students and thinks that a baseball theme will get their attention. Here is WWILD's description of the game:

> The game provides questions about multiplication and addition. The player can choose the difficulty level of each question by choosing a single (easy), a double (medium), or a home run (difficult). For each correct answer, players are moved around the bases. An incorrect answer results in a strike. Three strikes—You're Out. You can change your level and play again.

Chris checks comments posted by other WWILD members. One comment notes that the game is, "a decent drill with a little game context," and another comment notes that it is very challenging to do the home run-level problems without scratch paper. Chris decides that Batter's Up Baseball may work for her instructional purpose.

Chris then proceeds to evaluate the game—a process that is described in the next section and then illustrated in the continuing teacher scenario.

Evaluating Drill-Games

Evaluating drill-games requires looking at a number of dimensions, including drill structure and gameplay. In addition to working as a drill and as a game, a digital video drill-game must also work as interactive multimedia. Multimedia design, then, joins drill structure and gameplay as fundamental dimensions of drill-games. Multimedia design involves appropriate use of animation, sound, and color to gain students' attention without distracting or confusing them. Multimedia design also includes intuitiveness and friendliness of the user interface that directly affects how the computer program communicates with the user (e.g., on-screen control buttons being consistently placed and directions being readable by the intended users).

Multimedia design, drill structure, and gameplay are key dimensions of the Drill-Game Evaluation Form (Figure 13.3) used by teachers and instructional technology graduate students in the Collaboratory for Interactive Learning Research (CILR) to profile drill-games (see the Drill-Game Reviews supplement [page 328] for sample profiles). The CILR acts as an online gathering of resources and research activities being pursued by faculty and graduate students in Southern Illinois University's Instructional Technology and Instructional Design programs (http://idt. siu.edu/cilr/research-projects/). Each dimension of the drill-game evaluation form is delineated below the sample form (Figure 13.3). A fourth dimension of drill-game evaluation, use recommendations, appears at the bottom of the form and is discussed in the Integrate section of this chapter.

Drill-Game Evaluation Form

The CILR Drill-Game Evaluation Form depicted in Figure 13.3 was filled out by a teacher-evaluator for the drill-game Word Frog (Figure 13.2).

Although you may not always conduct as detailed an evaluation of all drill-games that you are considering as this one, the CILR form identifies key factors for evaluating drill-games.

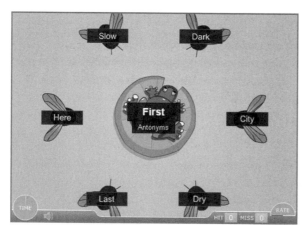

FIGURE 13.2 ▶ Word Frog screen

Title/Source/URL. The title of the drill-game is given separately from the URL of the website where the game is found. This is because some drill-games are available from multiple websites. It is worth searching the web for different locations of the same game. Different sites may have newer versions of a game. Different sites also have different amounts or types of advertising—which often comes with free online access.

The source of the drill-game refers to the producer of the game rather than the website on which it appears. Single-organization websites, such as Arcademic Skill Builders (profiled in the Single-Entity Drill-Game Websites supplement, page 326), are preferred because they usually have the most recent version of a game that they produce and also because they are less likely to have intrusive or inappropriate advertising. Another benefit of using drill-games produced by a single company or organization is that the games often have consistent drill structures and styles of gameplay, so that teachers and students learn what to expect and spend less time figuring out how to play. For example, Word Frog's gameplay is almost identical to Arcademic Skill Builder's math drill-game Meteor Multiplication.

DRILL-GAME EVALUATION FORM

Title/Source/URL: Word Frog (Arcademic Skill Builders)
www.arcademicskillbuilders.com/games/frog/frog.html

Content Area/Grade Level/Learning Objectives. Language arts. Elementary grades. Builds fluency in recognizing antonyms, synonyms, and homonyms. Develops visual searching and manual coordination.

Description. Target-shooting arcade-style game. The frog in the middle of the pond uses its tongue to "zap" flies. A target word is superimposed on the frog with other words on the approaching flies. You spin the frog to aim and zap the correct synonym, antonym, or homonym.

Multimedia Design. High quality Flash animation and sound. Score and directions easy to see and read. Controls easy to use for age level but may be hard for kids with some disabilities.

Drill Structure. Time element creates urgency but not panic. Rewards going faster but not a lot of punishment for mistakes. Nine levels with each type of word relationship. Lots of repetition with feedback and progressive difficulty. Solid as a drill.

Gameplay. Fun, well paced intuitive play. The player uses arrow keys to aim the frog at flies (words) as they approach and the space bar to "zap" them. Physically and mentally active.

Use Recommendations. Stands up to repeated use. Good for home use or in computer lab.

FIGURE 13.3 ▶ CILR Drill-game evaluation form for Word Frog

Content Area/Grade Level/Learning Objectives. Write the content area, grade level, and learning objective(s) addressed by the game. Although most drill-games are intended for mathematics or language arts (including foreign languages), digital video games for science, history, social studies, and other areas can also be found. Two especially good sources for drill-games in different content areas are BBC: Learning (www.bbc.uk.org) and Quia (www.quia.com) (see Single-Entity Drill-Game Websites supplement, page 326).

The great majority of drill-games are intended for elementary grade levels. Some drills are designed for middle and high school (e.g., BBC: Learning) and even higher education (e.g., MERLOT and Syvum), but those intended for older students often consist of less gameplay. Portals and single-entity sites usually indicate the intended grade level for drill-games, but you should write the grade level that you think the drill-game is actually most appropriate for on the form.

Drill-games often address a single learning objective. For example, the Word Frog evaluator, depicted in Figure 13.3, wrote that the game: "Builds fluency in recognizing antonyms, synonyms, and homonyms." Along with writing the primary objective, you may also note secondary mental skills that are developed by playing the drill-game. For example, the Word Frog evaluator noted that it also: "Develops visual searching and manual coordination."

Description. A short description of the drill-game tells others what to expect from a game. For instance, the Word Frog evaluator wrote: "Target-shooting arcade-style game. The frog in the middle of the pond uses its tongue to 'zap' flies. A target word is superimposed on the frog with other words on the approaching flies. You spin the frog to aim and zap the correct synonym, antonym, or homonym." This description should not include detailed comments on multimedia design, drill structure, and gameplay as those dimensions have their own place on the CILR Drill-Game Evaluation Form.

Multimedia Design. Multimedia design includes the appropriate use of animation, video, graphics, sound, text, and colors. For example, the Word Frog evaluator wrote: "High quality Flash animation and sound. Score and directions easy to see and read." In a drill-game, the primary concern is that media elements appeal to students' sense of curiosity and imagination but do not distract them from primary learning objectives (Clark & Mayer, 2003). While Flash animation enlivens newer drill-games, older HTML-based drill-games may still attract students' attention with minimal media use (see Fun Brain in the supplement on page 327). Remember to base your judgment on what you think students will like rather than what you like.

Multimedia design also addresses user interface issues, such as the placement of on-screen control buttons and methods of inputting answers (Alessi & Trollip, 2001). Interface issues are revealed by observing students playing the game or by playing the game yourself while assuming the role of a student. Interface evaluation should start with what happens when you click on the game's URL. Questions to ask yourself include the following: Does a title screen or splash screen appear that tells you how you will benefit by playing the drill-game (i.e., objectives) and/or how to play the game (directions)? Can you figure out how to play right away, or do you have to play the game once or twice to figure it out? Do you need to refer to written directions to figure out the game, and, if so, are they readily accessible and easy to follow? You don't need to address all of these questions; just use them to point to any potential problems. For example, the Word Frog evaluator noted: "Controls easy to use for age level but may be hard for kids with some disabilities."

Drill Structure. Drills build students' fluency with already learned skills and knowledge through repetition, immediate feedback, and progressive difficulty. Drill-games embody repetition, feedback, and difficulty level within a drill structure that consists of a sequence of steps:

1. Create an item pool,
2. Present each item to the student,

3. Accept the student's input,

4. Judge the student's input and provide corrective feedback,

5. Queue missed items for re-presentation during the drill,

6. Conclude the drill and give summary feedback, and

7. Guide the student to repeat the drill or advance to a more difficult level based on the student's performance. (Alessi & Trollip, 2001)

Few drill-games fully execute all six drill structure steps described. However, the more steps that are included and the more fully the steps are executed, the more effective the drill should be.

First, the key question to ask regarding repetition is: Does repeated play of the drill-game present different items or sequences of items? That is, does the game employ *varied repetition*? Many free web-delivered games, especially those outside of math and language content areas, quiz students on facts and concepts using a limited set of items. Repeating the game gives the same questions, often in the same order. Although quiz games have learning value, they do not support the type of repeated use associated with effective drill-and-practice.

Second, along with varied repetition, drill structure also requires the *delivery of many items in a short time span*. Alessi and Trollip (2001) suggest that drills should take no more than 10 or 15 minutes to complete, in part because drills should involve intense concentration. One of the reasons that many drill-games adopt arcade-style formats is that the rapid-fire presentation of drill items as targets to shoot, zap, or blast does not slow down the pacing of the drill.

Third, *appropriate response time* is also an important aspect of drill structure. Drills usually involve a speed/accuracy tradeoff, and fluency is built by pushing the speed factor so that students' mental process becomes more of an association than a calculation (math) or a translation (foreign language). However, time pressure can also be frustrating, especially for very young students (Alessi & Trollip, 2001). Therefore, appropriate use of speed-based scoring is often a key aspect of evaluating drill-games. For example, the evaluator of Word Frog noted: "Time element creates urgency but not panic. Rewards going faster but not a lot of punishment for mistakes."

Fourth, *appropriate corrective feedback* is an essential element of drill structure. In Word Frog, feedback is provided by the fly/word either being swallowed for a correct answer or continuing to advance for an incorrect answer. A teacher playing Word Frog will notice that the drill-game does not give corrective feedback for missed items; rather, players shoot until they get the correct answer.

Whether corrective feedback is appropriate depends on the knowledge level of the students and the teacher's goals in using the drill-game. If a teacher is confident that students already know the synonyms and antonyms of most words and decides to have students play Word Frog to build fluency, then forgoing corrective feedback to maximize the number of items presented and to create consistent drill pacing is a good tradeoff. On the other hand, it is also important that students eventually answer every item presented in a drill correctly.

Fifth, the best drills are designed to cycle missed items back into the item queue to be presented again before the drill is completed, providing *systematic queuing schemes*. The most basic approach is flashcard-style queuing in which missed items are put at the back of the queue (Alessi & Trollip, 2001). Most online drill-games do not have systematic queuing schemes. However, as commercial education publishers are increasingly involved in producing and distributing drill-games, systematic queuing schemes should become more common.

> **TIP**
>
> Drills build mental fluency in the same way that weight lifting builds muscles, through massed repetition and progressive difficulty.

The sixth essential element of drill structure is *progressive difficulty*, designed for players to advance through more difficult levels of a drill-game as they meet the performance criteria for each successive level. Levels of difficulty can result from presenting increasingly difficult items, presenting more items of similar difficulty in the same time frame, or presenting the same number of items in less time. The teacher-evaluator of Word Frog noted that the drill-game has "Nine levels with each type of word relationship." The evaluator concluded the drill structure comment by writing: "Lots of repetition with feedback and progressive difficulty. Solid as a drill."

While teachers do not need to be experts on drill structure, it is important to recognize how the essential drill elements of (1) effective varied repetition, (2) delivery of many items in a short time span, (3) appropriate response time, (4) appropriate corrective feedback, (5) systematic queuing schemes, and (6) progressive difficulty work together to build fluency. Keeping these elements in mind, you can judge whether a particular drill-game is likely to produce the type of learning experience that you want for your students. To be an effective learning tool, a drill-game should have, at minimum, these three most essential basic elements: effective varied repetition, appropriate corrective feedback, and progressive difficulty.

Gameplay. The essential elements of interactive entertainment posited by Hirumi and Stapleton (2008) are play, story, and game. In this chapter, the elements of play, story, and game are considered together as making up the gameplay dimension of drill-games. In Word Frog, the play element consists of manipulating the left and right arrow keys to rotate the frog and hitting the space bar to zap the bugs. The play element gets the player physically involved by stimulating a response that leads to a reward that generates more stimulation, response, and reward in an on-going cycle. For example, the Word Frog evaluator wrote: "Fun, well-paced. Physically and mentally active." Teachers evaluating a drill-game intended for very young students or students with disabilities should try to play the game as a student would. Try playing the game opposite-handed, for example, with your left hand if you are right-handed, to check that the play element is appropriate.

Although usually associated with much more complex simulation-games, the power of story is at work in even a modest arcade-style game (Stapleton & Hirumi, 2010). In Word Frog, the story is that the frog needs to zap the approaching flies before they reach the frog. In the arcade-style game on which Word Frog is patterned, meteors must be blasted before they reach and assumedly blow up the planet. It's not clear what will happen to the frog if a fly makes it through, and in that way the story element of Word Frog is fairly weak.

The question to ask in evaluating the story element of gameplay is, "Does the story entice students initially to play and to persist through repeated rounds of the game?" Some drill-games have lengthy exposition before, during, or after the game. For example, Multiflyer (www.brainormous. com/online/loader_multiflyer.html) is a multiplication drill-game with an elaborate story. Gravitational fields of surrounding planets are causing problems with life-support systems throughout the player's homeland. The player is tasked with going to each planet to deliver a stabilizer that will counteract the problem. Solving multiplication problems provides the player's space ship with the required power to reach the next planet. Multiflyer also includes a multimedia tool to assist players in finding a multiplication answer that they don't know yet.

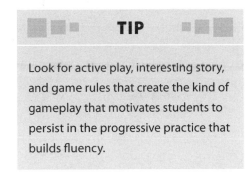

TIP

Look for active play, interesting story, and game rules that create the kind of gameplay that motivates students to persist in the progressive practice that builds fluency.

A teacher evaluating Multiflyer should note that the elaborate story might interfere with drill structure but that the game may provide just the right learning experience for students who don't yet know all the multiplication tables or who have an aversion to math.

The third element of gameplay is game—that is, the rules, tools, and goal(s) that govern the game. The rules governing Word Frog are obvious; you need to zap the flies before they reach the frog. Although the story aspect of what happens if a fly reaches the frog isn't clear, the game aspect is absolutely clear. If a fly reaches the frog, then that game round ends, and you will need to start over at the first level. You need to beat nine levels each of antonyms, synonyms, and homonyms ultimately to win the game of Word Frog. That game structure of Word Frog can result in students playing multiple rounds and practicing hundreds of synonyms, antonyms, and homonyms.

Use Recommendations. The final dimension on the CILR Drill-Game Evaluation Form refers to ways of using a drill-game as a classroom activity and is covered in more detail in the Integration section to follow. First, we return to the Locate/Evaluate/Integrate teacher scenario.

Scenario

Fifth-grade teacher Chris Fitch has located a digital video drill-game that she thinks may help students build fluency in basic math skills. Although the WWILD portal on which she found Batter's Up Baseball included a description of the game, Chris realizes that she needs to evaluate the game herself before turning over class time to playing it. Chris clicks on the provided URL link, and Batter's Up Baseball opens up to an introduction screen. The first thing she notices is that the screen has animated advertisements on it that might distract students. She decides to evaluate the game and then decide if it's worth tolerating the advertisements. Knowing that she will only see the game with fresh eyes the first time, Chris makes sure she has pad and pen ready, with a reminder note to look at multimedia design, drill structure, and gameplay. She puts on her favorite ball cap backward to help her remember to think like a fifth grader.

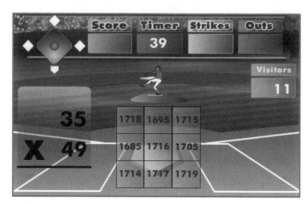

FIGURE 13.4 ▶ Batter's Up Baseball item screen (home run difficulty level)

Chris reads the directions: a strike for a wrong answer (get to try again), three strikes and you miss the problem, three outs and the game is over: Basic baseball rules. The game offers addition or multiplication mode; she chooses multiplication. The scoreboard appears showing that the other team (the computer) has scored 8 runs. So the game's story is that Chris will have to score more runs than the computer to win the game.

Batter's Up Baseball lets Chris choose whether to try to hit (solve) a single (easier, one-digit by one-digit problem), double (more difficult, two-digit by one-digit problem), or home run (most difficult, two-digit by two-digit problem). Great! The game entices students with a bigger reward for trying harder problems. After the player chooses the difficulty level, then the computer presents a multiplication problem along with a nine-cell grid showing answer choices. Chris applies a bit of baseball strategy, choosing to "hit" singles three times to load the bases. Then she goes for the Home Run. The computer displays a two-digit by two-digit multiplication problem. She reaches for her pen to work the problem, but then she thinks to test how it could challenge even her best math students to solve the problem using mental math. She makes a quick mental math calculation and … strike one! That's OK; she has two strikes to go. She tries again, and the game announcer intones, "It might be, it could be … Home Run!" Four runs go on the scoreboard for the home team. Cool!

Chris plays a while longer, trying numerous multiplication problems at all levels. She then takes off her ball cap to make some teacher notes about Batter's Up Baseball. The multimedia design includes modest but entertaining animation, graphics, and sound. The game announcer is funny and doesn't get old too quickly. The game control functions work consistently. She notes that once she started playing the game, she didn't notice the advertisements any more.

Chris then considers the drill structure of Batter's Up Baseball. The problems seem to be randomly generated, so it will stand up to repeated play. There's immediate feedback with "strike" or "hit," although the feedback is slower than it would be in a straight drill. Having players choose different levels of difficulty for each problem is an interesting and unusual feature. But what if some students do not choose to challenge themselves to try harder problems? Most drill-games force the player to higher levels of difficulty. Batter's

Up Baseball rewards players for trying more difficult problems, but does not force them to. Chris notes that if she decides to use Batter's Up in class, she needs to observe whether all of the students challenge themselves appropriately.

Chris notices that Batter's Up Baseball gives the player 45 seconds to answer single, double, or home run-level questions. "That's way too much time for math-facts level problems," Chris thinks. Students should also be able to answer both the one-digit by one-digit and the two-digit by one-digit problems in well under 45 seconds. Of course, Chris can't change the programming code of Batter's Up Baseball. But she can change the *rules* and the *rewards* when playing the game in class. If she takes the students to the computer lab so that they are playing the game individually then she can declare that the first inning is "singles only" and time the inning herself with a stopwatch. "Get as many runs as you can in two minutes. Remember, you have 3 'strikes' for each problem so go as fast as you can. When I call 'time' write down how many runs you scored on your score-card. Ready . . . go!" The 45-second-per-item issue doesn't come into play because the short *total* time provides incentive to answer items as quickly as possible. The 3-strike rule encourages students to push their speed/accuracy comfort zone.

Chris can then call the second inning as "doubles only," again instructing the students to get as many hits (correct questions) as possible in a designated time frame. Chris could also indicate on students' scorecards whether or not they are allowed to use scratch paper when "hitting doubles"—thereby creating differentiated practice depending on the students' level of multiplication ability. Within the same room, using the same drill-game, some of Chris's fifth-graders can be reviewing basic computational skills (multiplying on paper) while others who are ready can be challenged with mental math.

After trying several home run-level problems, Chris realizes that all students will need to write these two-digit by two-digit problems on scratch paper and perform long multipli-cation. Chris concludes that, for home-run level problems, 45 seconds is an appropriate time limit to write down the problem, perform long multiplication, then find and click the correct answer on the computer screen. But she may need to reconsider the 3-strike rule. With easier problems, Chris felt that the 3-strike rule in the game was appropriate because her goal was for students to increase fluency (speed) on problems that they could easily solve. With more complex, calculation type problems, Chris was more concerned with accuracy and didn't want to encourage guessing. Therefore, she decides to allow students only one "swing" per home-run problem.

Chris shows that she is thinking of a drill-game not as a stand-alone learning activity but rather as part of a learning system in which she plays a critical role. By adjusting the rules for playing the game, Chris has not only overcome deficiencies in the drill structure but she has also customized this simple drill-game into a sophisticated, differentiated learning platform. Overall, Chris concludes that, with her adjustments, the drill struc-ture of Batter's Up Baseball is sound with repetition, feedback, and progressive difficulty.

Looking at gameplay elements, Chris notices that the physical action is limited to clicking the mouse to choose the problem difficulty level (single, double, home run) and then choosing the answer, so the play element is limited, compared with the thumb-numbing action of the portable video games and cell phone games that kids play. The pace of play is also a bit slow, although Chris notes that real baseball is also slow. The story element is true to real baseball, with the opponent (computer) scoring in the top of the inning and the player trying to match or beat the score in the bottom of the inning. Chris concludes that students who like baseball should enjoy Batter's Up Baseball. But she's a little worried about the students, including some international students, who may not understand or like baseball. Chris cuts out some of the baseball aspect of the game by turning down the sound and focuses on just solving math problems. She finds that while the game isn't as much fun without the baseball connection, it is still challenging and should engage students' interest long enough to get some good math practice.

Chris concludes that, although Batter's Up Baseball has advertising on the site and some problems with the game's scoring rules, she can make the game work in a lot of different ways for her students and to meet the class's learning objectives. She likes the baseball theme and, more importantly, thinks that her students will like it. She also likes being able to have students each work on individual math learning needs—whether practicing multiplication tables, developing mental math, or doing long multiplication on paper to solve more difficult problems.

With these observations, Chris has moved beyond locating and evaluating a drill-game and on to integrating the drill-game into classroom use. Figure 13.5 shows Chris's Drill-Game Evaluation of Batter's Up Baseball, including use recommendations.

DRILL-GAME EVALUATION FORM

Title/Source/URL: Batter's Up Baseball (Prongo)
www.prongo.com/math

Content Area/Grade Level/Learning Objectives. Math addition and multiplication. Various grades. Practice of addition and multiplication facts, calculations, and mental math.

Description. Baseball theme playing against the computer. Player chooses easy (single), medium (double) or hard (home run) math problems to solve. Runs score like baseball.

Multimedia Design. Modest graphics but cool announcer audio and baseball sounds. Easy directions and controls. Has advertisements on game screen that may distract students.

Drill Structure. Automatic problem generation so can play repeatedly. Students choose difficulty level for each problem. First two levels of addition and multiplication can be mental math; home run-level requires long multiplication or addition on paper.

Gameplay. Realistic for baseball fans but fun even if students don't know baseball. Should keep interest for 10 or 15 minutes.

Use Recommendations. Can challenge students according to their abilities. Good for computer lab or for home use. Need to be sure students challenge themselves when choosing difficulty level of problems. Good to set time limit to make game more challenging. Suggest doing one problem level per "inning."

FIGURE 13.5 ▶ CILR drill-game evaluation form for Batter's Up Baseball

Integrating Drill-Games into Classes

This section addresses the teacher's role in integrating drill-games into classroom activities. Questions to consider include the following: What phase of instruction might a particular drill-game be used in? Can the game be used as an individual, small group, or whole class learning activity? What can I do to improve drill structure or gameplay?

What phase of instruction might a particular drill-game be used in?

According to Alessi and Trollip (2001), there are four basic phases of instruction: introduction, presentation, practice, and assessment. Drill-games are most commonly associated with the practice phase. However, drill-games can also be used in the introduction phase, especially as a pre-test to help teachers determine the beginning skill level of individual students and of the overall class. Teachers can then adjust their teaching based on students' pre-test scores or level attained in the drill-game. Playing a drill-game can also be used for students to demonstrate mastery of target skills during the assessment phase of instruction.

Sometimes the same drill-game can be used in different stages of instruction. For instance, you can have students play Word Frog at the introduction of a unit on figures of speech to see if they need more instruction in synonyms, antonyms, or homonyms. After teaching a lesson on synonyms, you can have students play Word Frog specifically to practice synonyms to a level of fluency. For a detailed discussion of instructional phases and when and how to integrate games based on various instructional strategies, I encourage you to read Hirumi's Chapter 10 in this book on a grounded approach to playing games.

By playing Word Frog yourself, you'll have an idea of what level of the game you can expect students to reach. Students who don't reach the target level in Word Frog can be encouraged or assigned to play the game more at home, in the media center, or wherever a web-linked computer is available until they do reach the target level.

Can the game be used as an individual, group, or whole-class activity?

Drills are generally designed for individualized, self-paced practice. Drill-games, on the other hand, can often be played by pairs of students, by small groups of students, or even by a whole class.

Individualized drill-game activities. Research dating back to the mid-1970s has consistently shown positive learning effects for computer-assisted instruction, mostly using the drill-and-practice method (Kulik & Kulik, 1991). Indeed, drill-based edutainment games have been accepted in classrooms for many years in the important yet ultimately limited role of remediation or enrichment for a few students (Squire, 2003). Drill-games can provide individualized practice to each student in a computer lab or classroom that has a computer for every student. The availability of drill-games on the Internet also increases the feasibility of teachers recommending or assigning drill-games as homework.

Two-player drill-game activities. An alternative approach for situations with less than one computer for every student is to have students play a drill-game in pairs—which not only extends computer resources but also introduces peer interaction. Some drill-games are actually designed with a two-player mode. Other drill-games, such as Word Frog, can be turned into multiplayer games by having students open multiple game windows on the same computer screen and then asking students to take turns playing a round of their own game. Indeed, Gee (2003) notes that one of the lessons educators can draw from how kids play video games is that kids typically learn to play a video game by watching other kids play the game. You can use your knowledge of students' abilities and personalities to put together pairs of students that are evenly matched so they will drive each other with competition or, alternatively, put together pairs in which a less accomplished student can learn from watching a more adept student play the game.

Small-group drill-game activities. Students can be broken up into groups of three or four working as a team at a single computer and competing against other small groups of students using another computer. Although progressive drill-games such as Word Frog are designed as single-player games, the game's nine levels of play—each of which takes only about a minute to play—allow students in a small group to take turns playing a level of the same game. Group playing of games can develop competition strategies, cooperation and teamwork, and conflict resolution.

When you set up a team competition, you are creating a whole new set of game rules—not the rules of Word Frog but the rules of the in-class contest. You can name captains and have them choose teams, playground style. Alternatively, you can assign students to create equivalent teams. You can allow players a few "tip chips" to use to get hints from the team captain or other team-mates if they get stuck on an item. The goal is to cultivate cooperation within each team and competition among the teams.

Whole-class drill-game activities. If you are working with one computer and a data projector, sometimes you can break a reasonably sized class into two large competing teams. For example, the classic language arts drill-game Chicktionary (http://kewlbox.com/Games/GameDetail. aspx?gameID=117) lends itself to large-group play. You can download Chicktionary (Figure 13.6) and play the game on the class computer/projector without needing an Internet connection. Divide the class into two teams and start a Chicktionary game. Alternate which team gets to form a new word from the letters in "eggs" that the chickens lay at the start of the game. Keep score on the board of the words that each team gets, giving more points as the game goes on and it gets more difficult to think of new words.

You can set the game rules of classroom Chicktionary to manipulate playing and learning conditions. For example, during a team's turn you can allow any student on the team to shout out a word, which you or a student game-master then types into the computer. Alternatively, you can increase the individual accountability of students by calling on team members individually—but not necessarily in a set order—to make the next Chicktionary word. If the students don't know whom you are going to call on, they all need to have a word ready. You can balance the challenge and frustration aspects of Chicktionary by selectively calling on students based on your knowledge of students' confidence and ability. When both teams get stuck on forming a word, the game is over. You can recognize the team with the most points on the board as the winner and reward the whole class if they combine to reach a target score in the Chicktionary game.

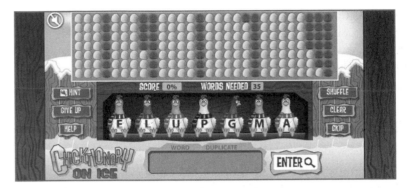

FIGURE 13.6 ▶ Chicktionary game screen

What can I do to improve the drill structure or gameplay of a drill-game?

In the course of evaluating a drill-game, you can often identify deficiencies in drill structure or gameplay. In many cases, however, you can overcome these deficiencies by changing or adding rules. For example, except for very young students, the building of fluency requires that students increase their speed as well as their accuracy in drills (Alessi & Trollip, 2001). Arcade-based games almost always have a speed element. Many other online drill-games, however, do not include a speed factor. You can enhance drill structure and gameplay by setting time limits for students to beat a level. You can then decrease the length of time to increase the level of difficulty.

As the teacher, you will be able to make adjustments in the classroom use of a drill-game when you have evaluated it thoroughly, including playing it through several times yourself, and when you understand the dimensions of drill structure and gameplay. When a drill-game is well designed and when a teacher integrates it thoughtfully and creatively into the curriculum, the game format can facilitate highly effective and engaging learning.

Let's return to Chris as she wraps up her evaluation of Batter's Up Baseball.

■·■·■

Scenario

Chris Fitch has located and positively evaluated the math drill-game Batter's Up Baseball and is now considering how she can use it with her class. One option is to use the game as a pre-test early in the school year. The students should have the basic multiplication tables down cold, but if any of them don't, then Chris wants to find out and make sure those students get up to speed. Using a computer for each student, Chris can give a multiplication facts pre-test by instructing the students that they may only hit "singles" and cannot get any strikes. She knows from playing Batter's Up Baseball that a student who knows his or her multiplication tables should easily be able to answer 10 problems correctly in 90 seconds of play. A couple of short, timed "innings" of Batter's Up should suffice as a painless pre-test.

To develop students' multiplication fluency beyond the basic tables, Chris can change the rules so that students hit only doubles. Some of these two-digit by one-digit multiplication problems are at the math facts level, while other problems involve fairly challenging mental math. Chris estimates students can comfortably complete 10 double-level problems in two-minute innings. Since this activity is intended to develop rather than test students' multiplication skills, Chris will have them complete numerous innings of doubles-only Batter's Up Baseball, perhaps over several sessions.

Chris also envisions having the students occasionally play Batter's Up in home run-only mode to practice long multiplication. The activity is similar to completing multiplication worksheets, but the gameplay adds interest, and the immediate feedback that the computer provides to students with every problem is superior to the delayed feedback they would receive on a graded worksheet. The game's instant feedback also saves Chris the time she would have spent grading worksheets.

Chris also starts thinking of how she can use Batter's Up Baseball in a more social learning context to take advantage of the single Internet-connected computer she has in her classroom. She envisions making multiple competing teams, each consisting of four students of varying ability. The students would play Batter's Up as designed (without her modifications), self-selecting to attempt singles, doubles, or home runs. The only house rule would be a time limit of five minutes to play a game. Having a limited time to score as many runs as possible should provide an incentive for the students to try more difficult home run-level problems. Team members would take turns "batting" on the classroom computer while the rest of the students complete workbook pages—and wait for their turn on the computer (if their workbook pages are done). Students could give their teams names and write their team scores on the board. If the students take to the game, Chris conceives of a Batter's Up Baseball league, where teams can challenge the team above them in the standings. Chris's efforts have led her to locate and evaluate a fun drill-game that has the potential to be integrated into a variety of learning activities throughout the school year.

Summary

After years of being criticized as "drill-and-kill" edutainment, drill-games—many of them available for free on the Internet—are rapidly increasing in quantity and quality. With the National Mathematics Advisory Panel (U.S. Department of Education, 2008) specifically emphasizing the need to develop fluency in essential math operations and with many years of research supporting the positive effects of drill-and-practice in multiple content areas, drills have an important place in classrooms. Combining drill structure with gameplay makes drill-games more enticing and keeps students playing—achieving the repetition that is necessary to build fluency.

The current generation of web-based drill-games features much higher quality animation than previous generations of edutainment, with the games produced and distributed by Arcademic Skill Builders representing the state-of-the-art arcade-style drill-games. Drill-games like Word Frog and the similarly formatted Meteor Multiplication have solid drill structures and are fun for students to play. Grand Prix Multiplication, also by Arcademic Skill Builders, brings digital video drill-games into the realm of multiplayer online gaming, as students can "race" online with other students in the class or with students who happen to be online anywhere in the world.

As large education companies, such as Houghton Mifflin (Fun Brain) and Pearson Education (Game Goo), become more involved in producing digital video drill-games, we can anticipate advances being made in the structures of drill-games as well as in the overall quality of gameplay. For example, look for more sophisticated queuing schemes to insure that students master all of the content or problems in a drill-game. You can also expect to see advances in tracking students' performance as they play drill-games, both to guide the students' individual development and to provide feedback to teachers and administrators on the effectiveness of a drill-game. At some point, the best multiplayer, online drill-games with the most complete student feedback and assessment tracking will be offered as commercial educational services available for purchase at the school or district level—and without advertisements. In the meantime, you and other teachers, parents, and students can easily access a wide variety of free and fun online drill-games.

The lasting appeal of drill-games is that they motivate students to practice and learn, while the drill dimension helps parents, teachers, and administrators embrace gameplay for instructional purposes. For teachers who want to explore integrating digital video games into their classrooms, drill-games can be a great place to start.

References

Alessi, S. M., & Trollip, S. (2001). *Multimedia for learning: Methods and development* (3rd ed.). Boston, MA: Allyn & Bacon.

Bottino, R. M., Ferlino, L., Ott, M., & Tavella, M. (2007). Developing strategic and reasoning abilities with computer games at primary school level. *Computers and Education, 49*(4), 1272–1286. doi:10.1016/j.compedu.2006.02.003

Clark, R. C., & Mayer, R. E. (2003). *e-learning and the science of instruction: Proven guidelines for consumers and designers of multimedia learning.* San Francisco, CA: Pfeiffer.

Egenfeldt-Nielsen, S. (2007). Third generation educational use of computer games. *Journal of Educational Multimedia and Hypermedia, 16*(3), 263–281.

Gee, J. P. (2003). *What video games have to teach us about learning and literacy.* New York, NY: Palgrave Macmillan.

Hirumi, A., & Stapleton, C. (2008). Applying pedagogy during game development to enhance game-based learning. In C. T. Miller (Ed.), *Games: Their purpose and potential in education* (pp. 127–162). New York, NY: Springer Publishing.

Kulik, C. C., & Kulik, J. A. (1991). Effectiveness of computer-based instruction: An updated analysis. *Computers in Human Behavior, 7*(1–2), 75–94.

Newby, T. J., Stepich, D. A., Lehman, J. D., & Russell, J. D. (2000). *Instructional technology for teaching and learning: Designing instruction, integrating computers, and using media.* (2nd ed.). Upper Saddle River, NJ: Prentice Hall.

Rieber, L. P. (1996). Seriously considering play: Designing interactive learning environments based on the blending of microworlds, simulations, and games. *Educational Technology Research & Development, 44*(2), 43–58.

Squire, K. (2003). Video games in education. *International Journal of Intelligent Simulations and Gaming, 2*(1), 49–62.

Stapleton, C. B., & Hirumi, A. (2010). Interplay instructional strategy: Engaging learners with interactive entertainment conventions. In M. Shaughnessy & S. Veronikas (Eds.), *Pedagogical implications for online instruction.* Cairo, Egypt: Hindawi Publishing Corporation.

U.S. Department of Education. (2008). *Foundations for success: The final report of the national mathematics advisory panel.* Retrieved October 12, 2008, from www.ed.gov/about/bdscomm/list/mathpanel/report/final-report.pdf

Single-Entity Drill-Game Websites

Game Goo

www.earobics.com/gamegoo/gooeyhome.html

This commercial site features Flash drill-games produced by a company called Earobics and hosted by the Houghton Mifflin Company. The games are free, and there are no banners or ads. The Flash games are consistent in approach and full of funny and funky Flash animation and sounds, many of which adults can also enjoy. The games have sound instructional designs. Game Goo has drill-games to help young learners practice language and reading skills, such as opposites, letter recognition, alphabetical order, capitalization, and fiction versus nonfiction. Games are organized into three levels of difficulty. Students can choose to view or skip the introduction and directions. These are state-of-the-art Flash drill-games for elementary and preschool learners.

BBC Learning: Schools

www.bbc.co.uk/schools

This non-commercial site, managed by the British Broadcasting Corporation (BBC), has a wide variety of drill-games and other activities for preschool through high school levels and covers essentially all content areas. Flash drill-games for elementary language skills are well executed—and listening to English spoken with a British accent is fun. This site is especially valuable as a source of multimedia activities for secondary students, as they are harder to find on the web. There are many multimedia activities to explore in addition to games, including a link to the BBC's home page, with access to international news; sports; feature stories on health, history, science, music, arts, recipes children can follow; and more. The biggest problem is that there is so much on the site that it can be confusing to use at first. Educational games and activities are of a consistently high quality, and the site has no pop-up advertising.

Fun Brain

www.funbrain.com/kidscenter.html

Fun Brain is a commercial site with ads. The site has numerous parts. Pearson Education runs the site and has added new activities and games, including drill-games. The classic Fun Brain games are also available. Drill-games, such as Math Baseball and Grammar Gorillas, are older and very basic graphically, but many have good drill structures. For instance, Spellaroo displays sentences and has players click on the misspelled word—developing the critical skill of recognizing misspelled words in context. The newer parts of the Fun Brain site are much flashier but not always as instructionally sound. Arcade and Math Arcade each feature 25 Flash mini-games, some with clear instructional objectives and some not. In the site's arcade areas, players are forced to play the games in order, and ads are embedded. Fortunately, the same games can be accessed individually and without ads (kidscenter page). The centerpiece of the new area of Fun Brain is an exploratory learning environment called Poptropica. Players are asked whether they are a girl or boy and how old they are (up to age 15). A game board appears that offers (for example, after signing in as a 15-year-old girl) 12 islands to choose from, each with a different game, such as mythology, spy, super power, reality TV, astro-knights, shark tooth, time tangled, and 24 carrot.

Arcademic Skill Builders

www.arcademicskillbuilders.com

This noncommercial site contains drill-games that incorporate features of arcade games into fun, online drill-games that are highly evolved by the site founder, a professor of special education at University of Kansas who has long history in developing educational video games going back to 1970s. The math and language arts drill-games are state-of-the-art Flash games with simple gameplay, good animation, and sound drill design. The online, multi-player Grand Prix game takes drill-games to a new level. All of the drill-games stand up to repeated play and emphasize players' development of fluency in basic skills.

Quia

www.quia.com/web

This noncommercial site offers templates to teachers for creating their own quiz games and various other multimedia activities. The quiz games are then organized by content area and type of multimedia activity (e.g., quiz, hangman, battleship, scavenger hunt, jumbled words) and are available to anybody using the Quia site. Because the games are "homemade" teachers should check them thoroughly before having students use them. The game templates work best with concept and definition content rather than the vocabulary or math content that both call for true drill-and-practice. Teachers who register for a modest fee can use the templates to make games and can also register their students so that students' participation and performances are recorded individually.

Drill-Game Reviews

Squanky, the Tooth Taker *(Game Goo)*
www.earobics.com/gamegoo/games/squanky/squanky.html

Content Area/Grade Level/Objectives. Language arts. Early elementary readers or pre-readers. Match a given word with its antonym. There is also a synonym game.

Description. The tooth taker leads the learner through the drill-game. Each of 10 kids asleep in a big bed is associated with a word. A trigger word appears out of a chest of drawers. The player clicks on the word/kid with the opposite meaning. If the answer is correct, positive feedback is given. If an incorrect answer is given, the learner is cued to try again. After three misses, the answer is given, and the game moves on—although the missed word will be re-presented later (queuing). After all words are matched, then the player is "rewarded" by moving the cursor to place teeth into empty spaces in a gaping mouth. Kids seem to get it.

Multimedia Design. The Flash animation and sounds are high quality and "ticklish." The voices are humorous. The interface controls are easy for a target learner to use. Words are highlighted and pronounced on mouse rollover.

Drill Structure. Good repetition; the game can be played repeatedly. Immediate and corrective feedback is provided. No progressive difficulty, though the Game Goo site has games categorized as beginner, intermediate, or advanced levels that learners self-select.

Gameplay. Good example of drill structure and gameplay working to amplify the value of both. The "pedagogical agent" (tooth taker) is silly and a bit obnoxious yet supportive. Pacing is appropriate. The game is fun and seems to connect with kids.

Use Recommendations. Could be used as a one-computer group activity.

Grand Prix Multiplication *(Arcademic Skill Builders)*
www.arcademicskillbuilders.com

Content Area/Grade Level/Learning Objectives. Math. Elementary grades. Practice multiplication facts and some calculations.

Description. Players race cars by answering multiplication questions. Players choose to race against the computer, classmates, or unseen people on the Internet.

Multimedia Design. Nice Flash animation and good race sounds.

Drill Structure. Rewards speed as well as accuracy. Doesn't punish mistakes too much—the car loses speed. Doesn't give correct answer if player gives wrong answer. Wrong answers with correct answer are shown on post-race report.

Gameplay. Great multiplayer gameplay. OK against computer but really fun against classmates or unseen online players. Game and drill well integrated. Stands up to repeated playing.

Use Recommendations. Great for learners who have more confidence in gameplaying ability than math ability. Can be used in a computer lab with up to four students in a race.

Ball Hogs *(Family Education Network)*

http://fen.com/studentactivities/BallHogs/BallHogs.html

Content Area/Grade Level/Learning Objectives. Language arts for elementary grades. The game says it goes up to Grade 6, but it's too easy for average sixth graders. Appropriate for Grades 1–4 and for remediation and ESL students through Grade 6. Practice synonyms and antonyms.

Description. Pig-like characters squat as ball boys/girls on either side of a tennis net. After the tennis ball goes back and forth over the net a few times, a target word appears on screen. Three other words rotate, one of which is the desired synonym or antonym of the target word. The player-pig and another player-pig or computer-generated pig compete to jump on the ball when the correct word appears. First to get three correct answers wins the round. A tournament includes multiple rounds with zany pig characters.

Multimedia Design. Simple but creative Flash animation and sounds.

Drill Structure. Good design to have consistent time for players to see the clue and anticipate what the answer might be. The player should be ready to jump fast if the expected word is revealed but also must be open to changing to another word if the expected word doesn't show up, a unique drill feature. Corrective feedback is not given. If the player jumps on the first answer word and it is incorrect, the other player gets the point. Sometimes a missed item repeats.

Gameplay. Different sort of game from arcade-style games. It is playful, especially in two-player mode. Unique format may not stand up to repeated play. Changing grade levels as an option doesn't seem to change the difficulty much.

Use Recommendations. Good for occasional use, especially in two-player mode. Rounds are short enough to allow multiple students to take turns on one computer.

Section IV

Additional Perspectives on Gameplay

14

Homemade PowerPoint Games

Michael Barbour, Gretchen Thomas,
Dawn Rauscher, and Lloyd Rieber

THERE HAS BEEN MUCH RECENT INTEREST in the use of computer and video games in the classroom. Unfortunately, this interest has often been met with resistance from the educational establishment. The resistance, coupled with technical and logistical barriers to the use of commercial off-the-shelf games in K–12 classrooms, suggests that the full potential of learning by playing games will likely not be realized anytime soon. Fortunately, there are alternatives. We propose having students design their own low-tech games using Microsoft PowerPoint. PowerPoint is a ubiquitous classroom tool that most teachers are comfortable using and can be used as a game creation tool. In this chapter we describe the concept of homemade PowerPoint games, provide a rationale for their use, and outline a five-day method for incorporating this form of design activity into your classroom.

ee (2007a, 2007b) argues that educators can learn a great deal about learning from how the best video games are designed. For example, in the best video games, players learn rules and procedures as they play, accessing vital information at the very moment when they need and are ready to use it. Successful video games also immerse players in an environment that promotes trial and error, permits more than one solution to a problem, and allows for failure without judgment. Just-in-time information, trial and error, multiple solutions, and failure-free settings are thought to be attributes of optimal learning environments—these are also the attributes of first-rate game environments.

There are many barriers preventing teachers from realizing the potential of games for enhancing learning, ranging from cost, necessary infrastructure, and perceived violence in current video games (Rice, 2006) to the current political climate in education (Squire, 2006). Even if we were able to overcome these barriers, teachers would still need to be trained in both the technology and the pedagogy of games for them to be integrated effectively into classrooms. And like many other technological innovations, well-designed professional development in technology does not necessarily lead to its adoption once the external supports to encourage adoption have been removed (Fishman, Marx, Blumenfeld, Krajcik, & Soloway, 2004; Fogleman, Fishman & Krajcik, 2006). Because of these realities, there is a need for a low-tech, nonthreatening alternative to incorporating video games in the classroom. In this chapter we propose the use of homemade PowerPoint games as such an alternative.

Of all the technology-based tools available in K–12 classrooms, Microsoft PowerPoint is likely to be found in almost every school in America—and most teachers feel confident in their ability to use PowerPoint. Unlike many of the other chapters in this book, we focus upon students not as game players but as designers of games. While there may be better game-design tools, we believe that harnessing teachers' and students' familiarity and comfort with PowerPoint is a practical way to bring game design into classrooms. In this chapter, we begin by describing our rationale for using a design activity, such as creating homemade PowerPoint games, in the classroom. After a description of what a homemade PowerPoint game looks like, we discuss our philosophical justification for why having students create homemade PowerPoint games can be an important learning tool. Finally, we outline a five-day process for creating homemade PowerPoint games.

Why Homemade PowerPoint Games?

To play games in class, students and teachers can either use educational games designed by others or design their own games. Research on whether playing games leads to learning focus on the use of games designed by people other than the teacher or student, and studies have yielded mixed results (Kirriemuir & McFarlane, 2004). Many of these studies compare achievement between students taught specific content using games and students taught the same content using traditional classroom instruction, usually lectures. In these studies few differences in learning are reported (Dempsey, Lucassen, Gilley, & Rasmussen, 1993–1994; Gredler, 2003; Randel, Morris, Wetzel, & Whitehill, 1992). This is also true when other innovative educational technologies are compared with traditional instruction (compare with Clark, 1983; Reeves, 2005; Russell, 1997).

The alternative approach to playing games in class focuses on what students learn from designing their own games. A good example of how students are able to learn from designing a game can be seen in the work of Kafai and her colleagues (Kafai, 1994, 1995; Kafai & Harel, 1991). Their research focused on how students' building of their own multimedia projects affected their motivation and learning. In these projects, elementary school students were tasked with designing an educational game for a younger audience (i.e., sixth graders designing for second graders). Results from one of their published studies showed how students used the design activity as an opportunity to engage in content-related discussions and found that students who designed games increased their own learning of key concepts (Kafai, Ching, & Marshall, 1997).

The original idea for homemade PowerPoint games came from our own experiences with elementary and middle school students, helping them to design and develop educational computer games (Rieber, Davis, Matzko, & Grant, 2001; Rieber, Luke, & Smith, 1998). In the initial project, called Project KID DESIGNER, students worked in teams to design the content, format, and mechanics of an educational game. Graduate students were assigned to each team and were responsible for completing the technical aspects of the game. The student team and the graduate students would meet regularly to discuss the game prototypes. Project KID DESIGNER showed that students were able to work effectively in groups to produce games that creatively embedded subject matter; however, the technology chosen was beyond the skill levels of most of the students and teachers involved in the project. We concluded that a relatively low-tech solution is necessary to realize the potential of games for enhancing learning in the classroom.

We propose using PowerPoint as a game design tool because it is a nearly ubiquitous program in classrooms and homes. PowerPoint is directly associated with technology integration, and teachers neither need special permission to use it nor report many problems using it. PowerPoint is a very robust and reliable application that is culturally accepted by teachers and is also commonplace in work environments outside of K–12 schools. Additionally, as teachers master PowerPoint as a presentation tool, it becomes relatively easy to coax them to use it in other ways (Rieber, Barbour, Thomas, & Rauscher, 2008).

Interestingly, some educators already employ PowerPoint games that use existing templates to mimic popular TV games (e.g., *Jeopardy!*) to promote learning. Unlike these examples, however, homemade PowerPoint games do not sugarcoat the memorization of factual content; instead, they aim to cultivate students' conceptual understandings. Students take ownership for their learning as they analyze content information and design the game.

Homemade PowerPoint Games: An Example

So, what does a homemade PowerPoint game look like? Like many good games, it starts with a good story. A good story provides the context for understanding the game's goals and relationships among its rules and educational content. Let's consider a homemade PowerPoint game titled By the Light of the Moon, designed by Tricia Williams when she was a preservice teacher education student at the University of Georgia. The game is intended for fourth graders on the topic of astronomy. (The game can be downloaded from this site: http://it.coe.uga.edu/wwild/pptgames/). As described on the website, here is the game's story:

> Hundreds of years ago, there was an evil wizard who was jealous of all the beautiful stars in the sky. So one day, he cast a spell that turned all of the stars into a dull ugly color. The only way to break the wizard's spell and make the stars bright and beautiful again is to collect 15 stars by answering 15 of the wizard's questions correctly. It is a dangerous task. The evil wizard will try to cast spells on you to slow you down or to stop you, so beware!

The game is played on a traditional game board, which the teacher or students can construct by printing out and taping together four PowerPoint slides (each slide is one-fourth of a scanned image of the game board, see Figure 14.1). Slides with game pieces and stars also need to be printed out ahead of time. Players choose a game piece and put it on the starting square. Stars are earned when questions are answered correctly.

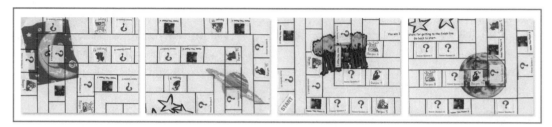

FIGURE 14.1 ▶ To create the game board used in the game By the Light of the Moon, these four PowerPoint slides are printed out and taped together.

Taking turns, each player rolls one of a pair of dice to progress on the game board. As players move, they land on one of four different kinds of squares: Danger, Name This Planet, Question, or a blank square. If a player lands on a blank square, that player's turn is up. A Danger square consists of a random event (e.g., a spell cast by the wizard) designed to add intrigue to the game, such as "A hail storm occurs and you must take shelter in a case for 3 days. Go back 2 spaces." If a player lands on a Name This Planet square, the player is asked to look at a PowerPoint slide showing a planet. The player must identify the planet by clicking on the correct answer in a multiple-choice format. The slide is programmed using PowerPoint's hyperlinking feature to link to the appropriate feedback if the player's answer is correct or incorrect. Similarly, the Question squares give the player an assortment of astronomy questions appropriate for fourth grade, again with PowerPoint controlling and managing the feedback.

As the example illustrates, PowerPoint is used in a variety of ways. First, the entire game is contained within one file, although several game elements, such as the game board, must be printed out prior to playing. The game's story, directions, and various questions are programmed into the PowerPoint file to facilitate gameplay, so the PowerPoint file needs to be up and running on a computer while the game is being played. In this example, PowerPoint is used to set up, access, and play the game.

In actuality, students can design games using whatever PowerPoint features and capabilities they want in whatever ways make sense for their games. Designers are limited only by their creativity. Some games are played solely on the computer, though most involve a mixture of traditional game board play with some game elements remaining on the computer. We have been impressed by students' creativity, even in the ways they set up their games. For example, one student designed the game pieces to stand up on the game board by suggesting in the directions that binder clips be found and used. The idea is that the game piece is held by the binder clip with the flat side of the binder clip pointing down, allowing the game piece to "stand up." Other games have called for string or yarn to be used as part of the game board. Of course, it is important for the designer to choose materials that can be found in a typical school classroom. A wonderful thing about the use of everyday materials is that the games can have an "arts and crafts" feel to their construction. These inexpensive, ordinary materials add accessible, creative touches to the otherwise high tech world of computer games (see Figure 14.2).

FIGURE 14.2 ▶ A screen snapshot of a homemade PowerPoint game in which the designer used everyday objects to enhance gameplay, such as binder clips to make it possible for game pieces to stand up

It is also important to notice how PowerPoint is used to replicate and distribute the game free of charge to anyone with an Internet connection. The game described above and many others can be downloaded from the homemade PowerPoint game section of the WWILD team website (http://it.coe.uga.edu/wwild/pptgames/), a free online educational resource maintained by the University of Georgia. The designers of the games on this site have all agreed to allow educators and students to modify their games in any way, similar to an open source programming philosophy. So, if a game uses a map of Georgia as the game board, a classroom in Eugene could substitute a map of Oregon. The modifiability of homemade PowerPoint games allows and encourages other teachers and students to create their own games, based on their own minor or major adaptations. As students learn how to modify existing games, they are encouraged to take the next step, to become game designers themselves. In short, we think that the real educational value begins when students begin designing their own original games. The thinking and creative processes involved in designing games take students to deeper levels of understanding and interpreting subject matter.

The Philosophical Justification for Homemade PowerPoint Games

Our conception of deeper understanding is based on the levels of historical understanding defined by Wineburg (2001). Wineburg developed a theory that students' historical understanding can be measured on a continuum from being heavily based on factual information to more sophisticated levels of understanding. At these higher levels, students are able to analyze and interpret historical events using original sources. Following Wineburg's model, a nondiscipline-specific version of student understanding would include the following four levels:

Level I is characterized by "just because" explanations given by students and is heavily based on factual representations.

Level II understanding is also superficial and is characterized by rational, logical thinking processes—students seeing facts as being like pieces of a puzzle that have to fit together.

Level III understanding begins to show a more sophisticated awareness of the role of interpretation and how different interpretations based on the same evidence can occur.

Level IV understanding is a mature level, characterized by students being able to analyze and interpret information using original contexts and sources.

We believe that homemade PowerPoint games can assist in moving students' understanding along this continuum, based upon three elements of homemade PowerPoint games: the act of constructing a game, the writing of the game's narrative or story, and the creation of questions or problems.

Constructionism

Master teachers continually ask themselves this fundamental question: "What do my students know about this [topic, lesson, unit, etc.]?" This is the essence of the teaching and learning process, a question that is constantly negotiated between the students and the teacher. The question, "What does it mean to know something?" is also the focus of one of the two principal branches of philosophy—epistemology. The other branch, ontology, centers on the question, "What does it mean 'to be'?"

Consider any subject matter or topic within it. Let's take the unit on electricity typically taught within middle school science. Teacher A, who has less experience, may be most interested in just getting through the unit in a timely fashion because to fall behind means risking not finishing the science curriculum in that academic year. Teacher B, a master teacher, is far less concerned about simply getting through the content. Instead, she or he is constantly wondering, "What are the students' understandings of the concepts and principles discussed so far?" Teacher A is quickly satisfied that a student "knows" about electricity if the student answers 18 of 20 questions right on the unit test.

Teacher B, in contrast, not only is dissatisfied with such a superficial measure of understanding but also is fascinated by why another student, who did much worse on the test, thought that answer D, "battery," was the answer to the question "What do you call the part that is used to complete an electric circuit?" The teacher is curious because this very same student spoke with incredible enthusiasm about how his dad had to "flip the breaker" to get the lights back on one night after installing a new window air conditioner. The student spoke about how he helped his dad out and specifically mentioned getting new batteries for the flashlight. This student was obviously motivated by the discussion and was trying to relate it to a personal experience. Teacher B is trying to piece together the student's thinking and is looking forward to speaking with the student tomorrow to "get inside his head" for an explanation. Teacher B is also looking forward to building on that student's knowledge and motivation and knows that whatever misconceptions the student might have can easily be remedied. Indeed, the philosophy here is always to build on a student's knowledge and understanding and never to think of the student's knowledge in simplistic terms of being right or wrong. Teacher B's desire to understand as fully as possible what this student actually knows is the essence of epistemology from a teacher's point of view. Of course, helping a student to know something at a deep and personal level requires much time and effort from the teacher and the student. So, Teacher B is often frustrated by the rapid sequence of the school's curriculum and wants to take the time to help students engage in, understand, and enjoy their learning, irrespective of the results shown on a superficial test.

The epistemology of constructivism has been strongly influenced by the work of Piaget, Vygotsky, and Dewey (Duffy & Cunningham, 1996). Indeed, Piaget identified himself as an epistemologist. Constructionism is an educational application of constructivism and, as the name suggests, uses the analogy of learning by constructing or building as aptly summarized by Papert (1991), one of the central architects of constructionism:

> Constructionism—the N word as opposed to the V word—shares constructivism's connotation of learning as "building knowledge structures" irrespective of the circumstances of the learning. It then adds the idea that this happens especially felicitously in a context where the learner is engaged in constructing a public entity, whether it's a sand castle on the beach or a theory of the universe. (p. 1)

In our earlier work with children as game designers, we explored their understanding of electricity through game design. The first step was to have the children write a story for the game, putting their newly gained science knowledge to some interesting or creative use. One notable example was called Haunted House; players found themselves in a haunted house late in the day, and the sun was going down. As it became darker outside, they had to find the necessary parts of an electric circuit (involving a light bulb). If players built the circuit before the sun finally set, they won the game and used the light to scare away the ghosts. However, if they ran out of time, darkness would descend on the house, and they would lose the game.

The act of building some external artifact, whether a story, a game, or a model, in which a person's knowledge "resides" is believed to be one of the best ways to promote deeper and more personal understanding. When students place artifacts they have created in a public sphere—in their classroom among classmates, on YouTube, or in a blog—they have to be ready to defend and explain their creations to others. To do so requires students first to have a "driving question" that motivated them to want to build their artifacts or inventions in the first place (Blumenfeld et al., 1991).

Writing the Narrative

The second reason we make the argument that homemade PowerPoint games can assist students' deeper understanding is based on the process that students undertake in the writing of their games' narratives or stories. Writing conventions, such as setting, plot, character development, and so on, are key elements of a strong narrative structure in good literature and in good games. Good games, like good stories, develop and balance these writing conventions to provoke the players' emotions and capture their interest. However, unlike a story, a game invites true participation because the end of the game largely depends on what the players do during the course of the game. According to Wolf (2001), games "involve the audience in a uniquely direct manner, making the *viewer* into a participant or *player* [emphasis in the original], by allowing the player to control (to some degree) a character" (p. 93). The story provides the player with motivation to affect the outcome of the narrative and, thus, the conclusion of the game.

The writing involved in the students' construction of homemade PowerPoint games, particularly the game narrative or the story slide, requires students to address many important details in a small space—as they have only a single slide to write on. This is a specific form of concise writing that is quite similar to a microtheme—a method of writing commonly used in the sciences. A microtheme is an essay that can fit on a 5- by 8-inch index card (Work, 1979). To write that much information in such a small space requires students to summarize information to include only the most essential details. Research into the use of microthemes has consistently shown that students who are able to write in a concise, highly structured way about a topic perform better in course assessments than students who did not complete such microthemes (e.g., Ambron, 1987; Collins, 2000; Kirkpatrick & Pittendrigh, 1984; Moore, 1993, 1994). In creating a homemade PowerPoint game, students have to write narratives that provide players with background information about the game, the basic context and setting of the game, and the motivational elements that they hope will entice players to play the game … all on a single PowerPoint slide.

Higher-Order Questions

The final element of designing homemade PowerPoint games that we believe assists in moving students deeper along the continuum of understanding is when they generate their own questions or problems. Within most homemade PowerPoint games, the questions provide the skills or challenges, which makes writing good questions essential. If the questions are too easy, players are not challenged to continue to play the game, and if the questions are too difficult, players cannot proceed. In either situation, players would stop playing the game out of boredom or frustration. Many researchers and gaming enthusiasts have discussed the levels of challenge and the uncertainty of the outcome as the primary variables that affect players' motivation to play and persist in playing games (e.g., Dempsey, Lucassen, Gilley, & Rasmussen, 1993–1994; Prensky, 2001; Ryan, Rigby & Przybylski, 2006). Therefore, it is important for students to provide the appropriate level/s of challenge when they design games.

One way that students can provide appropriate levels of challenge in their games is to write higher-order questions, based on the taxonomy of educational objectives (Bloom, 1956). The *Taxonomy of Educational Objectives*, more commonly called Bloom's taxonomy, presents educators with a holistic view of education, examining outcomes in the affective (emotional reaction), psychomotor (physical manipulation), and cognitive (thinking) domains. Homemade PowerPoint games tend to focus on cognitive learning outcomes, beginning with knowledge and progressing through comprehension, application, analysis, synthesis, and ending with evaluation. Higher-order skills, based upon Bloom's taxonomy, focus on the three final levels: analysis, synthesis, and evaluation.

It is important for students as game designers to write challenging questions—not only to motivate players but also to benefit from writing questions that require analysis, synthesis, and evaluation. Researchers have found that students who were able to write higher-order questions were able to process the original information better than students who reviewed the content using other methods (Rickards & DiVesta, 1974). Essentially, the skill required to synthesize information into a question, write a correct answer, and then construct three plausible incorrect responses demands better comprehension of the material than merely knowing the material well enough to answer simple questions about it. In fact, the benefits of student-generated questions have been well documented. In her review of 27 research studies from 1965 to 1982, Wong (1985) found that the research data consistently indicated that generating questions enhanced students' processing of the material.

We submit that students' understandings of most topics would be developed at deeper levels by designing their own homemade PowerPoint games, based on our research and first-hand experiences with constructionism. When students design games, they engage in narrative writing and question creation, both of which lead to deeper levels of understanding.

Now that we have described homemade PowerPoint games, provided an example of a game, and discussed our rationale for having students design their own games, we turn our attention to how teachers can prepare to use homemade PowerPoint games in their classrooms.

Creating Homemade Games: A Five-Day Professional Development Process

Creating your own homemade PowerPoint game is the first step toward teaching with learning games. In addition to creating action buttons and inserting clip art, game designers must write creative stories, develop challenging questions, and evaluate learners' needs. This section discusses a five-day process that we have used with our own students, who were preservice and in-service K–12 teachers, to teach them how to create their own homemade PowerPoint games. We have also used this same process, in a more limited way, directly with K–12 students. It is important to remember that in order for homemade PowerPoint games to be a constructionist activity, K–12 students must be involved in game development. As such, this model for learning how to create games can be adapted for student-centered homemade PowerPoint game creation with your own students.

Day One: Creating an Idea for a Game

Sharing Favorites. Students are introduced to homemade PowerPoint games by discussing games from childhood. They are asked to list their favorite games and to list the components of a "good game." Most students find common childhood game favorites, regardless of age difference. Sharing favorites sets a collaborative tone for the remainder of the project. Teachers and students work together to come up with a list of five necessary components for a good game—defining what "good" means. Common responses include element of strategy, appropriate levels of challenge, element of luck, various levels of play, and the opportunity for different age groups to play together.

Playing a Game. After discussing games, students play a sample game, such as The Traveling Georgia Artist—an elementary- and middle school-level social studies and mathematics homemade PowerPoint game. As play continues, students discuss their original list of necessary game components, refining them based on their experiences with homemade PowerPoint games. Students suggest improvements to The Traveling Georgia Artist and discuss what is realistic in terms of what can be created for educational purposes. Students are given the URL for the WWILD Team website so they may view other homemade PowerPoint games developed by previous students (http://it.coe.uga.edu/wwild/pptgames/).

Discussing Game Design. As a group, students are introduced to the idea of game design and constructionism through reading Rieber's (n.d.) article on homemade PowerPoint games (http://it.coe.uga.edu/wwild/pptgames/ppt-gamespaper.html). In addition, they discuss their own experiences, positive and negative, using educational games in K–12 settings. Students discuss the different levels of game design: from using an existing game, to teacher development of games, to K–12 students' own game development.

Outside of class, students are expected to review content standards in their subject areas to determine the targeted standards for their own game designs. Students take those targeted standards and begin to develop a story structure for their own games. For example, a student may identify a science standard related to the study of inertia and begin to develop a game based on a story about roller coaster design. Developing the story allows students to place a creative twist on the content standard by grabbing the attention of the intended audience, their peers.

Day Two: Creating a Game

Sharing Stories. Students begin class by sharing their story and game ideas with one another. As a class, students discuss how the various game ideas can address content standards. Students are reminded that their games will introduce and teach content prescribed in the standards and are encouraged to develop broad and engaging stories. Stories that begin with a sentence like "You are studying for a science quiz on Newton's laws of motion …" do not lend themselves to anything but a review game. A better example of a story for the same topic might begin, "You have been hired to design roller coasters for a theme park. You know a lot about Newton's laws of motion but will need to do research to find out how these laws impact ride design." Students work with one another to improve their stories by offering ideas that will place the players in real-world scenarios.

Working with the Template. Students are introduced to the technical aspects of the homemade PowerPoint games project by downloading the game template provided on the WWILD Team website (see Figure 14.3).

The course instructor assists students in navigating the template and directs them in how to make changes to the template. Students are shown how to create action buttons within PowerPoint to create the slides that will house their game's questions.

Writing Sample Questions. Outside of class, students are expected to begin entering their stories into the game template and to write three sample game questions that they plan to use. Students are encouraged to use resources available to them—such as textbooks and professional websites—to assist in question development.

FIGURE 14.3 ▶ A screen snapshot of the first slide of the homemade PowerPoint game template that students can download and use as they create their own games

Day Three: Writing Good Questions

Working with Bloom's Taxonomy. Students are introduced to the concept of different levels of questioning, based on Bloom's taxonomy. Students work in pairs to improve their three sample questions to ensure that the games will promote higher-order thinking skills rather than the basic recall of facts. Students are also encouraged to make sure questions relate back to the original story. Instead of, "What is the definition of inertia?" a game might ask, "Why will the riders on your roller coaster need to wear seatbelts?" This activity encourages students to write short-answer and open-ended questions instead of multiple choice questions.

Independent Work Time. After sharing improved questions with the class and viewing model questions from sample games downloaded from the WWILD Team website, students will use the remainder of this session to work on game design and development.

Day Four: Feedback and Final Work

Sharing Peer Feedback. Students will work in pairs to conduct formative peer reviews of their games. They need to give feedback on the strengths and weaknesses of each other's games and offer suggestions for improvement. Peers will look for a connection between the content standard addressed and the story idea, questions that require higher-level thinking, and an engaging game concept that will hold the interest of students in the targeted grade level. Students will review their original list of five components of a good game (see Day One) to determine whether student-designed games possess some or all of the components.

Creating a Game Board. Most games will require students to use the drawing tools in PowerPoint to create game boards. Some students may choose to draw boards and scan them into PowerPoint. Game boards help students to create engaging games. Boards allow students to develop games with a clear connection between the story and the game questions. A game about inertia might have a board that looks like a roller coaster—requiring game players to advance around the board, collecting parts of a roller coaster as questions are answered correctly. Students will use the remainder of this session to complete their game design and development work.

Day Five: Sharing Final Games

Game Presentations. Students will share their games with the class. Upon completion of game presentations, students will discuss the role of game design in K–12 teaching and learning: how do teacher-designed games promote critical thinking among students? How do student-designed games promote critical thinking among students? When/where are teacher- and student-designed games appropriate and most effective in educational settings? As a group, students will select exemplary games to be added to the WWILD Team website. (Note that our students are teachers; discussions with K–12 students will focus on what they learned from the design process.)

Conclusions

It has been our experience and the experience of other researchers that students are capable of designing compelling, curriculum-based games using PowerPoint. While more sophisticated tools are available for designing games, teachers may not have the time to learn them, or a school's administration may be unwilling to pay for and install them. Fortunately, PowerPoint offers students and teachers a tool that they may already be comfortable and confident in using. So far, most of the homemade PowerPoint games designed by students that have been submitted to the WWILD Team website resemble classical board games; they use PowerPoint as both a development and delivery tool, employing features of PowerPoint as parts of the gameplay itself (e.g., using the hyperlinking feature of PowerPoint to create and present random questions).

Our philosophical justification for having students create homemade PowerPoint games is based upon the belief that the skills necessary to construct a game narrative and the appropriate level of challenge through the writing of higher-order problems or questions will lead students to a deeper understanding of the curriculum. By turning the responsibility for learning over to the students, we have found that they are able to construct their own knowledge (based on content area standards) through the creative design activity. We believe that this method (constructionism) is a more powerful and effective way for students to learn than traditional methodologies based on teachers directing information toward passive students.

The five-day process we have outlined for creating homemade PowerPoint games can give educators a blueprint for adding game design to their curricula. Story writing is a core element of this design process, followed by a reflective and iterative design cycle that overtly considers Bloom's taxonomy and peer feedback to ensure the appropriate level/s of challenge. Designers continue the feedback loop during the development of their working prototype until the game is completed and they are ready to share the final products they have constructed. As our students are now preservice and in-service teachers, we note that some adaptations will need to be made to the five-day process when using this directly with K–12 students (e.g., the teacher may need to be more directly involved in the peer review stages, and the discussion on day five should be focused on students' sharing what they learned about their games' content and what they learned from the design process rather than the pedagogical value of the process). Also, presenting their games to the class may well take more than one day, as students will have fun demonstrating their games and telling their classmates how they improved upon their original ideas to create the final products. Another consideration, expressed well in several other chapters in this volume, is that the final step of asking students to reflect on what they have learned—in this instance, the depth of their learning of their games' content and what they learned from going through the design process—may be more effective as a separate day's class activity.

It is worth repeating that, unlike other authors in this volume, our view of games in education focus upon the students as game designers—not as game players. This view requires a shift in thinking about the traditional classroom: from students as receivers of knowledge to students as creators of new ways to learn that knowledge and to understand it at deeper levels; from the teacher as the individual who delivers the content to the individual who helps students as they create their own journeys. This shift in the dynamics of learning in the classroom can be a challenging one, which is why it is important to ensure that teachers are familiar with and comfortable using the tools required to accomplish the type of learning required by this game design activity. We believe that our concept of homemade PowerPoint games meets this challenge.

References

Ambron, J. (1987). Writing to improve learning in biology. *Journal of College Science Teaching, 16*(4), 263–266.

Bloom, B. S. (Ed.). (1956). *Taxonomy of educational objectives: The classification of educational goals. Handbook I: Cognitive domain.* New York, NY: Longman.

Blumenfeld, P. C., Soloway, E., Marx, R. W., Krajcik, J. S., Guzdial, M., & Palinscar, A. (1991). Motivating project-based learning: Sustaining the doing, supporting the learning. *Educational Psychologist, 26*(3–4), 369–398.

Clark, R. (1983). Reconsidering research on learning from media. *Review of Educational Research, 53*(4), 445–459.

Collins, M. A. J. (2000, April). Do microthemes improve student learning of biology? Paper presented at the annual National Science Teachers Association National Convention, Orlando, FL.

Dempsey, J., Lucassen, B., Gilley, W., & Rasmussen, K. (1993–1994). Since Malone's theory of intrinsically motivating instruction: What's the score in the gaming literature? *Journal of Educational Technology Systems, 22*(2), 173–183.

Duffy, T. M., & Cunningham, D. J. (1996). Constructivism: Implications for the design and delivery of instruction. In D. Jonassen (Ed.), *Handbook of research for educational communications and technology* (pp. 170–198). Washington, DC: Association for Educational Communications and Technology.

Fishman, B., Marx, R. W., Blumenfeld, P., Krajcik, J., & Soloway, E. (2004). Creating a framework for research on systematic technology innovations. *Journal of the Learning Sciences, 13*(1), 43–76.

Fogleman, J., Fishman, B., & Krajcik, J. (2006). Sustaining innovations through lead teacher learning: A learning sciences perspective on supporting professional development. *Teaching Education, 17*(2), 181–194.

Gee, J. P. (2007a). *Good video games and good learning: Collected essays on video games, learning and literacy.* New York, NY: Peter Lang Publishing, Inc.

Gee, J. P. (2007b). *What video games have to teach us about learning and literacy* (2nd ed.). New York, NY: Palgrave Macmillan.

Gredler, M. E. (2003).Games and simulations and their relationships to learning. In D. Jonassen (Ed.), *Handbook of research for educational communications and technology* (2nd ed., pp. 571–581). Mahwah, NJ: Lawrence Erlbaum.

Kafai, Y. (1994). Electronic play worlds: Children's construction of video games. In Y. Kafai & M. Resnick (Eds.), *Constructionism in practice: Rethinking the roles of technology in learning.* Mahwah, NJ: Lawrence Erlbaum.

Kafai, Y. (1995). *Minds in play: Computer game design as a context for children's learning.* Mahwah, NJ: Lawrence Erlbaum.

Kafai, Y., Ching, C., & Marshall, S. (1997). Children as designers of educational multimedia software. *Computers and Education, 29,* 117–126.

Kafai, Y., & Harel, I. (1991). Learning through design and teaching: Exploring social and collaborative aspects of constructionism. In I. Harel & S. Papert (Eds.), *Constructionism* (pp. 85–106). Norwood, NJ: Ablex.

Kirkpatrick, L. D., & Pittendrigh, A. S. (1984). A writing teacher in the physics classroom. *The Physics Teacher, 22*(3), 159–164.

Kirriemuir, J., & McFarlane, A. ([2004] 2006). Literature review in games and learning: A report for NESTA Futurelab. Bristol, UK: Futurelab. Available from www.futurelab.org.uk/resources/documents/lit_reviews/Games_Review.pdf

Moore, R. (1993). Does writing about science improve learning about science? *Journal of College Science Teaching, 22*(4), 212–217.

Moore, R. (1994). Writing to learn biology. *Journal of College Science Teaching, 23*(5), 289–295.

Papert, S. (1991). Situating constructionism. In I. Harel & S. Papert (Eds.), *Constructionism* (pp. 1–11). Norwood, NJ: Ablex.

Prensky, M. (2001). *Digital game-based learning.* New York, NY: McGraw-Hill.

Randel, J. M., Morris, B. A., Wetzel, C. D., & Whitehill, B. V. (1992). The effectiveness of games for educational purposes: A review of recent research. *Simulation and gaming, 23*(3), 261–276.

Reeves, T. C. (2005). No significant differences revisited: A historical perspective on the research informing contemporary online learning. In G. Kearsley (Ed.), *Online learning: Personal reflections on the transformation of education* (pp. 299–308). Englewood Cliffs, NJ: Educational Technology Publications.

Rice, J. W. (2006, April). New media resistance: Barriers to implementation of computer video games in the classroom. Paper presented at the American Educational Research Association Annual Meeting 2006, San Francisco, CA.

Rickards, J. P., & DiVesta, F. J. (1974). Type and frequency of questions in processing textual material. *Journal of Educational Psychology, 66*(3), 354–362.

Rieber, L. P. (n.d.). Homemade PowerPoint games: A constructionist alternative to WebQuests. Retrieved November 10, 2006, from http://it.coe.uga.edu/wwild/pptgames/ppt-gamespaper.html

Rieber, L. P., Barbour, M. K., Thomas, G. B., & Rauscher, D. (2008). Learning by designing games: homemade PowerPoint games. In C. Miller (Ed.), *Games: Purpose and potential in education* (pp. 23–42). New York, NY: Springer Publishing.

Rieber, L. P., Davis, J., Matzko, M., & Grant, M. (2001, April). Children as multimedia critics: Middle school students' motivation for and critical analysis of educational multimedia designed by other children. Paper presented at the annual meeting of the American Educational Research Association, Seattle, WA.

Rieber, L. P., Luke, N., & Smith, J. (1998). Project KID DESIGNER: Constructivism at work through play. *Meridian: A Middle School Computer Technologies Journal, 1*(1). Available at: www.ncsu.edu/meridian/jan98/index.html

Russell, T. L. (1997). *The "no significant difference" phenomenon as reported in 248 research reports, summaries, and papers.* (4th ed.). Raleigh, NC: North Carolina State University.

Ryan, R. M., Rigby, C. S., & Przybylski, A. (2006). The motivational pull of video games: A self-determination theory approach. *Motivation and Emotion, 30*(4), 344–360.

Squire, K. D. (2006). From content to context: Videogames as designed experience. *Educational Researcher, 35*(8), 19–29.

Williams, Tricia. (2003). *By the light of the moon.* A homemade PowerPoint game. Available at http://it.coe.uga.edu/wwild/pptgames/ and at http://it.coe.uga.edu/~lrieber/pptgames/space.ppt

Wineburg, S. (2001). *Historical thinking and other unnatural acts: Changing the future of teaching the past.* Philadelphia, PA: Temple University Press.

Wolf, M. J. P. (2001). Narrative in the video game. In M. J. P. Wolf (Ed.), *The medium of the video game* (pp. 93–112). Austin, TX: University of Texas Press.

Wong, B. Y. L. (1985). Self-questioning instructional research: A review. *Review of Educational Research, 55*(2), 227–268.

Work, J. C. (1979). Reducing three papers to ten: A method in literature courses. In G. Stanford (Ed.), *How to handle the paper load: Classroom practices in teaching English* (pp. 80–88). Urbana, IL: National Council of Teachers of English.

15

Educational Gameplay without Computers

Luca Botturi

WITH OR WITHOUT COMPUTERS, the essence of gameplay makes learning fun and natural. The integration of both digital and nondigital video games in prekindergarten through Grade 12 education can foster engagement and enhance learning, yet playing without computers is often more affordable in classroom settings and potentially more beneficial for young students. This chapter explores how you can create interactive and engaging game experiences for learning by using nondigital tools and objects. To understand at a basic level the language in which games are designed and how they work, I will first discuss some of the "nuts and bolts" of games. Then, some common types of games will be analyzed and illustrated with real examples to show how these nuts and bolts can be put to work in your classroom without the use of computers.

As I run through the metal sliding door, I notice I'm late: my companions are already starting the engines of their spaceships. I just manage to hop on Ed's ship and take control of the rear gun. It's actually difficult to do a good job when someone else steers the veering space ship while you are trying to aim. We manage to get into the Empire's ship—we now have to look for the shield generator and destroy it without being shot. Of course we coordinate with the rest of the Rebels: other teams are up to bomb the engines.

With my seven letters I can form the word "UNSTABLE" if I manage to find a free "A." There's one right there, but only if Kathy doesn't use it, or take some other nearby cell, blocking my plan. She's actually looking somewhere else, so I guess she will not bother me. If I can really do this, I can also get the extra points for using all my letters, and I'll take the lead.

The first paragraph is a transcript of a gameplay experience with the video game Star Wars Battlefront, in a situation that blends spaceflight simulation with strategy and first-person shooting. The second paragraph comes from a simple Scrabble session, rather close to the end of the game where a good move will make the difference between winning and losing. Both paragraphs emphasize challenge (aiming while steering, combining the highest number of letters), goal setting (destroy the generator, gain the lead in points), and facing opponents (characters shooting at you, other players)—and all of this generates tension, namely, the desire to perform well and win the game. Engagement is the personal commitment to respond to tension with the intent to solve it in a positive way. It is having the drive to play the game again to improve your chances of winning.

Video games are of interest to educators because they create situations in which learning occurs naturally in the pursuit of meaningful tasks; plus, they're fun! The power to create situations where learning appears effortless is the purview not only of video games but of gameplay in general. In other words, you do not necessarily need computer technology to enhance your PK–12 teaching with gameplay.

In the first part of this chapter, I will discuss three important concepts that describe gameplay and separate it from other activities. By doing so, I argue that the power of video games to enhance learning comes from gameplay, which is not dependent on the use of computers or game consoles. In the next part of the chapter, I will address the question, as a teacher, of how to rethink classroom activities and make them game-based. I will provide insights into the "nuts and bolts" of game design to explain how games work and how they are designed. In the final part of the chapter, I will demonstrate, using real-life examples, how the nuts and bolts of some well-known games can be employed in classrooms to generate enjoyable and powerful learning experiences through gameplay.

If you want to impress your friends with Spanish food, producing something that merely *looks* like paella is surely not enough. It should *look*, *taste* and *smell* like paella; in other words, it should *be* paella. To make the dish, you need to know the rather complex procedures required to cook it. Then, if you want to improve the recipe by adding a new type of local fish, for example, you need to understand the recipe in even greater depth, and know how Spanish cuisine works with various ingredients and blends flavors. In the same way, transferring game devices to teaching requires understanding games in a more in-depth way than the average observer or player. Presenting students with something that *looks like* a game (e.g., having points, levels, or competition) does not suffice—it may even spoil the class. If the game is not compelling, players will not be engaged, and nobody will want to play it or learn from it.

Gameplay and Learning

In this part of the chapter, I will pinpoint key elements about games and gameplay that hold true for both video games and for games in general. I propose that gameplay is different from other kinds of educational experiences, particularly those found in standard Western schools. The elements I identify will help readers understand some principles of game design, and provide practical guidance for examples that appear later in the chapter.

The Magic Circle

Picture a nonprofessional soccer team a couple of hours before their weekly match. Everybody is minding their own business: writing e-mails, taking care of the kids, washing the car, and so forth. After a while, they change into their uniforms, go to the soccer field, and start warming up; they talk to each other, greet their opponents, and do some exercises together. When the match begins, however, something changes: opponents are now someone to beat, players do not refrain from even hard physical contact, and they yell at each other. The *gameplay* generates a tension that changes players' relationships and behaviors for the limited time of the match.

Playing a game means to willingly enter a *magic circle* (Huizinga, 1955), a sort of different dimension where a new system of rules exists—namely, the rules of the game, which supersede the rules of normal life. For example, in normal life nobody yells when a ball hits a net, and nobody jumps in the mud to prevent it.

The magic circle is *tyrannical, totalitarian, egalitarian,* and *safe,* all at the same time.

▶ It is *tyrannical* in that it will require players' full attention: no other circle, or even events in real life, will easily distract a real player from playing.

▶ It is *totalitarian* in the sense that *all* of the game rules should be respected—not just some of them. Within the magic circle, it is a frustrating experience when a player says, "I was not aware of this rule!" They cannot dismiss the rule again if they want to continue to play.

▶ It is *egalitarian* because no matter their real-life situation, all players are just players when they enter the circle, and their ability in the game is the only thing that can make them better or worse.

▶ It is *safe* because consequences of wrong decisions are meant to remain enclosed within the circle, which disappears once the game is over (however, the consequences *on the player*—new knowledge or bad habits—may not disappear!).

Kids enter a magic circle whenever they get together and play with dolls or a game of basketball. Teenagers enter the circle when they connect over the Internet and play Guild Wars, and even adults enter it when they play cards or gamble in a casino. Each of these contexts activates a different mode of experience—namely, gameplay—an experience that requires constant learning at different levels:

▶ Learning the rules and the use of the toys/tools of the game, which means acquiring the full status of a player, or full citizenship, within the game's magic circle.

▶ Learning how to overcome challenges, beat competitors, and cope with unexpected situations. Such goals generate the tension and engagement of learning during gameplay, which is fun exactly because it is hard learning (Papert, 1998), while games with objectives that are too simple are boring.

▶ Learning to improve one's ability to play similar kinds of games.

Learning and Gameplay

Learning is actually the core of gameplay: it is what makes each game session unique, and why we continue to play a game we like for long periods of time. Gee (2003) claims that video games foster the development of skills, social relationships, and identity. I would argue that this is also true for nondigital games.

Gameplay is a natural mode of experience for young children (Sutton-Smith, 1979). Indeed, while children often have to learn how to learn in the way schools expect them to, they do not have to learn how to play—they just start playing! During their school career, they will of course also have to learn such skills as sitting still and taking notes, but why couldn't these skills be introduced initially through a game? Adults, on the other hand, have to be *willing* to enter the magic circle. Free choice is what turns a group of friends with a deck of cards into gameplay (Huizinga, 1955): a choice motivated by the desire to have fun.

Understanding the relationship between play and pleasure actually leads to a new way of looking at learning. When a little child takes her first steps, she giggles with joy. She is happy she can walk like her mother and her siblings do, and it is the same joy she will experience when she will utter her first words and, years later, when she will be able to ride a bike or drive a car. When we want to learn, learning itself is a pleasant experience, no matter how hard the process. Old Latin used a special phrase for describing pleasure: *gaudium de veritate*; that is, the pleasure of learning the truth. St. Augustine used the phrase to imply that true learning is a pleasure. True play implies learning, and should therefore be pleasant. The relationship between playing and learning is actually so tight that it is embedded into the very roots of many Western languages. In ancient Greek the word *skolé* was used to refer to both *school* and *playing* (Botturi & Loh, 2009). As George Bernard Shaw put it:

> A master in the art of living knows no sharp distinction between his work and his play, his labor and his leisure, his mind and his body, his education and his recreation. He hardly knows which is which. He simply pursues his vision of excellence through whatever he is doing and leaves others to determine whether he is working or playing. To himself he always seems to be doing both.
> (as cited in Cloke & Goldsmith, 1997, p. 61)

So why do children, teenagers, and adults often complain when it comes to attending class? What has made it so difficult for schools to enter the magic circle?

First and foremost, I believe gameplay is about free choice. Only those who decide to play a game on their own volition can have a full gameplay experience. Lack of free choice is the problem when a teacher forces a class to play a game that they do not like. We should observe and better understand the motivational keys that make children and teenagers willing to play a sport or choose to listen to a particular song. Indeed, we generally perceive school as the *job* of young people—something they *have* to do—and games as something fun and entertaining, something they *want* to do.

Second, gameplay is about control. Games give the players control over key variables and their own fate. Attending school is mandatory: the school moves in its own direction and by its own power, and students must try to keep pace. Playing a game means just the opposite: the players are the main force giving life to the game, and giving it the momentum it needs. Games create environments where I, the player, am the center of the action, sometimes with others: my teammates or opponents.

Free choice and player control are paramount in understanding gameplay. As Prensky (2006) advises, to make your teaching more gamelike and benefit from the learning power of games, you do not need high quality 3-D graphics or advanced computing skills. All you need is to create consistent and compelling magic circles that students will be willing to enter and in which they will gain full control over their own gameplay. In the following section, I present some useful tools to help you think of classroom activities in terms of game design.

Inside the Game: The "Nuts and Bolts" of Games

If you want to make your own wine, the first step is learning to critically taste wine, attentive to subtle differences in flavor. Once you can do that, you will be able to decide which kind of wine you want to make, and then learn about winemaking techniques. Sommeliers have actually developed a systematic technical vocabulary for describing the different nuances in taste that wine can have, and training programs to teach it. Similarly, if you want to start making your own games or begin playing games in your classroom, you should learn how to analyze games in a critically sophisticated manner. To do so, it's important to learn the words and concepts that game designers and game scholars use to describe games. Game designers and game scholars are those who are able to create consistent and compelling game circles that unleash the power of games to enhance learning.

In this part of the chapter, I deal with the following questions: How do experts describe games? How can I use such vocabulary for my classroom activities? How can I use game design ideas to shape my teaching? The elements we just discussed (magic circle, free choice, control) represent the hallmarks of the gameplay experience; here, I will try to zoom in and analyze what happens *within* the magic circle. The game design concepts discussed in this part will then inform the case studies presented in the final part of the chapter.

As with any design activity, from fashion design to architecture, game design will never fit into a recipe book: there is no definite set of rules for creating a fun and engaging game (Costikyan, 1994). Consequently, there is no scientifically sound process that can take some content and make it into an engaging game, or game-based classroom activity. Even when it is game-based, teaching remains an art, and teachers, like artists, get new ideas when they learn new techniques and styles. So, how can we try to uncover the inner gears that make a game fun to play, and unleash the power of games for engaging players and facilitating learning?

Think of a game as an instrument, such as a saxophone. To have music come out of a saxophone, there must be two elements: the materials that form the structure of the instrument, such as the metal, wood, and ivory parts that compose the brass body, keys, and mouthpiece; and the force applied to the parts, which results in music—the breath and finger pressure of the musician. All mechanical devices consist of these two main elements, *structure* and *force*, and the combination of the two produces an *effect* (which could be fed back to the system to activate another cycle). Metaphorically, we can say that games work the same way.

Structure: Rules and Toys

The structure of a game is determined by its mechanics, namely, its rules. Salen and Zimmermann (2004) identify types of games that emphasize different types of rules to create engagement. For example, in billiards, the ability to skillfully use the game's equipment (the cue stick) is the key to performance, just like in many other sports. Similarly, children's games using marbles, rubber bands, or hula hoops are based on mastering specific abilities, and can be labeled *ability games*; that is, games that require players to master one or more specific abilities in order to perform. Abilities can be physical, as in sports, or mental, as in Trivial Pursuit. But of course, winning at billiards requires more than ability: strategy plays a role, too. In fact, most team sports, such as basketball, soccer, or football, have strategic components as well.

At the other end of the continuum are strategy games, in which planning moves and confounding the opponent earn victory. The most famous examples are chess and the traditional Japanese game Go, both of which are pure strategy games: victory is exclusively dependent on one's ability to make effective moves at each turn, in attack and defense.

Other examples are Stratego or Risk, where the strategy is bound to important hidden information: Risk works because I do not know my opponents' goals; Stratego works because I have to guess where the various ranks are located. Stratego and Risk are strategy games that also contain many characteristics of information games. Such games work because they put players in a situation in which information is lacking and then require them to guess or discover it through their moves. Pure *information games* include Concentration (or Memory), in which players must locate pairs of cards that match, and Battleship (or Naval Battle), in which players must guess the location of the opponent's ships.

Another element that is crucial in the inner working of many games is chance: be it by rolling dice or dealing cards, chance is important in creating balance in the game structure. Some games use it as side ingredient, such as the rolling of dice in Trivial Pursuit or dealing a card in Pictionary. In others, such as poker or gambling games, it is the main structure of the game; these are called *chance games*.

The magic circle into which a game leads is a different world, and in that world we assume our distinct player identity: for example, a shy child can become a tough lacrosse player when wearing the mask; a difficult teenager can display a high degree of concentration when playing a video game. Some games leverage this transformation by creating gameplay from roles, letting players enjoy the pleasure of pretending to be somebody else and looking at things through different eyes. In these *role-playing games*, such as Dungeons and Dragons, the interaction between roles generates a narrative in which players are the main characters who can make decisions that change the plot.

In all games, part of the fun comes from playing with or against others, sharing the game circle with others and re-inventing our mutual relationships, and possibly generating trust. This is exactly what happens in noncompetitive sport matches, such as when some friends grab a ball and play soccer without really trying to beat each other. Some games, called *interaction games*, make the social dimension of gameplay their main mechanism. The interaction among the players becomes the center of the game, as in Mafia or charades. Table 15.1 summarizes the structural elements that can be used to design a game according to Salen & Zimmermann (2004).

TABLE 15.1 ▶ Structural game design elements

ELEMENT	FOCUS ON	EXAMPLE
Ability	Physical or mental ability	Sports (*pool, golf*) Trivial Pursuit
Strategy	Sequence of moves	Stratego Risk
Information	Discovering/guessing hidden information	Concentration Battleship
Role-playing	Playing a different character, generating the story	Dungeons and Dragons Magic
Chance	Luck	Gambling (*poker, roulette, etc.*)
Interaction	Relationship among the players	Mafia Charades

For the examples in Table 15.1, I used generic terms, such as *ability* or *strategy*, to define game categories. Actually, almost every game is a blend of the six elements: the generic terms indicate which one is the core of that game. For example, I stated that sports are ability games, but we all know that a football game depends also on the team (so it includes interaction), on strategy, and on chance. Poker is a classic game of chance, but a good poker player also develops a strategy in his bets, and is a skillful manager of the interactions around the table, especially when it comes to bluffing.

A good game designer is like a skillful tea master whose craft consists in blending the nuances of various elements to create an enjoyable balance. This is also what creates a game's compelling magic circle, a safe space in which to encourage having fun and learning through gameplay. Using games in the classroom requires no less awareness and craft than making blends of tea: the content to be learned should find its place in the game without disturbing the game's balance, or, even better, by defining a new balance altogether. Actually, we recognize—and students will recognize—unbalanced games right away. An experience common to many is that of nearing the end of the Trivial Pursuit board before one's competitors but losing the game nonetheless because you cannot roll the specific number on the dice that is needed to complete the game. The unbalance here resides in having chance decide the outcome in an ability game.

The game types I just presented are useful for understanding the structure of games. Teachers who familiarize themselves with these game types will find them helpful in deciding which game-based activities will work best for specific learning goals. If students should learn facts, an information game can be useful; if they have to learn to manage complex social situations, role-playing can be the right choice. I will discuss this again through the examples in the concluding part of this chapter.

Game rules formally express a game's structure. To make rules simpler, to reduce cognitive load, and in the end make a more enjoyable game, designers embed some rules into game boards, such as pegs, dice, cards, and so forth. For example, instead of using points to tally a score, Monopoly has money; Risk has a map and small tanks instead of rules that limit invasions from one place to another and a pen for counting forces on paper. Video games use computer images instead of game boards, cards, and game pieces—which means that they can implement incredibly complex rules without the player even realizing their existence. Also, they use computer graphics that can display images of unprecedented quality to create powerful, compelling stories. These differences in complexity make video games their own class of games, even from the point of view of game design and game structures.

Finally, game structures can be tight or loose, and everything in between. This is like the difference between a high-precision Swiss watch and a hand-carved wooden cuckoo clock. The Swiss watch would be a game in which rules must be strictly followed, such as chess or cribbage; these are well-defined games in which the primary choice players make is to step in the game circle. The cuckoo clock would be more free-form games, in which rules provide generic guidance and leave space for adaptation, such as children's make-believe games or Lego blocks. After entering this sort of game circle, players have to draw part of it by themselves to let the game start, and they can decide to change it while playing. Interestingly enough, video games usually do not allow player adaptation, unless they include adaptive features in their design (i.e., they can accept modifications, or *mods*).

Force: Tension and Release

Previously, I suggested that a game is like a saxophone. So far, we have explored the neck, the keys, and the mouthpiece of the instrument, but it will not play a sound unless a musician blows in it. Even the most perfect game generates no fun if there are not players to play it. So the key question for game designers and for teachers who wish to use game-based activities is: why should players spend their time playing my game?

Callois (2001), a French intellectual and sociologist, identified basic archetypes or dimensions of games across cultures, which he labeled using Greek words. His work identifies four main drives or *dynamics* (literally, Greek for "forces") that generate engagement in players.

The first dynamic is *agon* (competition), that is, the main drive of most sport games: beating the opponent, or being the best. During a competition, the perfect execution of the very same movements is the criteria for winning or losing. Competition is also a driving force of most board games, such as chess, cribbage, or Stratego.

A completely different driving force is at work when we play a game like Dungeons and Dragons or Mafia. Of course players are competing, but they are also playing out their roles as actors. Callois labeled these games *mimicry*, that is, make-believe. The dynamic is that of trying on a different pair of shoes and pretending to be somebody else for a while, acquiring a new identity as we enter the magic circle, whether as mother, boss, or superhero. While playing with identity is natural in children's games, role-playing games and simulations exploit the same dynamic, especially through game themes (science fiction or fantasy) and narratives (solving a mystery).

I mentioned chance as one of the structural elements of game design. Actually, the sense of being "in the hand of fate" and of betting everything on chance is in itself a kind of pleasure, so intense that it can be addictive. The dynamic of *alea*, or chance, is the thrill we experience when we roll the dice for the deciding move of the game—double six or we lose our last territory, the game, and our fame as unbeatable military strategist.

Finally, *ilinx*, or vertigo, is the dynamic of games that push players beyond the ordinary physical experience, possibly toward an alteration of the senses, resulting in players completely losing control. Examples are bungee jumping or parachuting, but also flight simulators and car races. Ilinx is a very strong dynamic, and the success of media-intensive video games surely is one of its expressions.

The first two dynamics (*agon* and *mimicry*) are inner forces of players: competing and acting. The last two (*alea* and *ilinx*) describe dynamics that "take possession" of players: pleasure consists in letting uncontrolled forces take control—of course, within a game's safe magic circle. As with structural elements, the four dynamics are not mutually exclusive. Pictionary, for example, blends *agon* and *alea* (the cards you draw), and Magic, *mimicry* and *alea*.

Why are the four dynamics useful? They describe what makes gameplay interesting to players, and of course, not all players are alike: different players enjoy different types of games. So the four dynamics provide guidelines for creating compelling and engaging games *for particular players*. Competition can be a good draw for some students, while *mimicry* can be more appealing to others, and so on.

Decision Making and Feedback

So far, I have described games as a structure made of rules, which is put in motion by players that follow a dynamic. But how do players move within the game? How is competition or chance developed during the game? The dynamic movement of a game develops during gameplay by increases and releases of tension through decisions.

Take Chinese checkers as an example: you win if you are the first to move all your marbles or pegs to other side of the board. It is a strategy game, and the main dynamic is competition, which creates a tension at the outset of the game: who will win? That tension is released by making moves, that is, by *making decisions* (Prensky, 2006): each decision puts the game into motion, and it can raise (you are blocked by an opponent) or lower (you bring a peg home) the tension.

Each decision/move should generate *feedback* that influences the following decisions/moves: the position of pegs on the board, the score, a card drawn, and so forth. In a good game, feedback comes after every move and stimulates the game tension accordingly, generating more energy to be released in the dynamic of the game (Betrus, 2005). Imagine a different way to play Chinese checkers, one that considers its nature as a mathematical game: "Take Chinese checkers, develop a strategy as a set of formal rules, then come back and I'll tell you how good your strategy is." It would probably not be a game anymore, because no feedback would sustain the tension, and very few people would be able to "play" it this way.

Decision making is the design device by which players gain control of the gameplay, as I discussed earlier in this chapter. Decision making is what distinguishes interactive from passive media (Squire & Jenkins, 2004), and what makes games unpredictable. The unpredictability of games can prevent some teachers from actually using them in class (see Chapter 2), yet there is no way around this: decision making and unpredictability are core features of gameplay (and of life in general!).

In this part, I explored some concepts from game design to provide insights into the nuts and bolts of games. Describing game structures, I mentioned six game types: ability, strategy, information, role-playing, chance, and interaction games. I also pointed out that rules can be embedded in game boards, cards, and pieces. Describing game forces, I presented four dynamics that generate gameplay: *agon, mimicry, alea,* and *ilinx.* I noted that these dynamics are unleashed into the game structure through decision making and are sustained by feedback. Understanding the concepts discussed in this part is necessary if one is to use games in class activities in a sensible way, without having content spoil the fun, or the games disturb the learning process.

Game Types and Their Uses in the Classroom

Now I will turn to the application of the elements of gameplay and of the game design concepts discussed earlier, applying them to real cases of both games and classroom activities. Using some common games and analyzing them as structure and force, I then pair each game with a game-based classroom activity. The challenge is twofold: on the one hand providing inspiring examples of game-based activities without computers; on the other, illustrating how game design principles can be applied to the benefit of classroom teaching.

For reasons of space, I will focus on three types of games: strategy, interaction, and role-playing games. To promote engagement, I will describe the games from my personal perspective, that is, from my particular gameplay style. I am a competitive player, so my descriptions might seem unfamiliar to people with a different playing style. The subject matter for classroom activities is incidental. While I chose communication and media as my field of expertise, the principles and method outlined are generic. Creative teachers will have no trouble in applying them to their domain.

Strategy Games and Problem Solving: The Design Challenge

I grew up in a large building with about a hundred apartments, and I used to play with a group of six or seven children of my age in the building's playground. When the snow made soccer impossible, we spent the afternoon playing board games, and when we were between the ages of 10 and 12, Risk was the main game we used to play.

I usually had luck in the territories I got from the cards. I liked black tanks the most, but I was not the only one, so these were often taken by my older playmates. The outset of the game was usually calm: first attacks, some invasions, a good balance was kept. Then somebody started to get aggressive and attack someone else's armies on any occasion. Sometimes I wondered if it was his objective or just his desire to be nasty. My strategies were naïve: I went straight to my goal. I remember being very surprised when an older mate tricked me into achieving his goal (destroying the green army) when I thought he was almost out of the game: he covered his moves with a side strategy and fooled the whole group! When I was the one being attacked, I usually resisted well, but then would come the inevitable shift in the weather: roll after roll I started getting 1, 2, and 3, and I lost all my armies. Once I did manage to resist, against all odds, a massive attack: while confined in Madagascar, I destroyed about 20 enemy tanks with my last 4 tanks. I had honor but no benefit, as another player took advantage of the situation and won the battle. We did not only play the game—we actually played out our parts: Communists in the East, Chinese and Japanese in the far East, Americans on the other side of the Atlantic. We fancied ourselves to be the people living in strangely named territories, whose actual existence we only realized after the downfall of the Soviet Union.

Risk is a strategy game that balances strategy, hidden information, and chance. Chance really comes in two forms: (a) at the start of the game each player is randomly assigned some territories and a secret goal, and (b) direct attacks of armies are decided by multiple dice rolls.

My personal account of Risk shows the forces that put the game into motion: earning a military victory (*agon*), as well as the risk of being in the hands of fate or luck in critical moments (*alea*). While I enjoy the former, I dislike the latter. As a group of players, we also used the game for *mimicry*, trying to talk with foreign accents as we attacked from different territories, or being nastier if we were in (to our childlike eyes) remote and hostile territories. But pure competition was what gave *me* the thrill of it.

Risk is a game with a rather steep learning curve. It stimulates strategic thinking, the ability to develop plans and disguise them, and also the ability to read opponents' moves to guess their strategy and possibly hinder it. Risk promotes intelligent resource management: how many armies can you afford to lose in a single turn? At any given moment, the decision depends on your plans, on your opponents' plans, and on chance, fostering complex thinking. Also, players can develop alliances, for example against the "world's strongest," or start direct open conflicts between two armies. Relational skills are also involved.

Now, let's move to the classroom. Can we learn something from Risk that can be used to improve class activities? I propose a strategy game for problem solving that could be played, with some adjustments, in all grades. For this example, let's take a 10th grade class. The class is given a scenario: three years from now when they are just out of school and start their first serious job. In that job, they work as interns at a small business that wants to launch a new bike model. The class is divided in groups of four or five students each, and their goal is to develop the best marketing campaign possible. The best group wins, according to the teacher's assessment against a set of criteria. The teacher serves here as "game master." Each group is given a set of actions they can decide to carry out, and each of these has a cost in terms of time, for example: (a) search the web for competitor products (three hours), (b) analyze the two best competitors (one day), (c) interview a sample of friends about the new product (two days).

For each group action, the teacher will mark the number of hours used and will hand out a piece of information. Of course, each group has a limited amount of game time at their disposal: the boss wants a proposal in 24 hours! Groups have to decide what strategy to take and how to invest their time.

Careful design of the game should contain both useful and misleading feedback, and even actions that lead to no information at all (such as, "Phone your old high-school teacher and ask"). Also, no single action should deliver all the necessary information for developing the campaign. Some actions may clearly indicate that other actions are highly desirable to take (even if it might be too late to carry them out!), or lead to extra actions not listed in the original selection (for example, the group who chooses the option for the interview with a more experienced colleague will find that he offers them a chance to look at an old but similar campaign; the group can then decide whether to spend additional time for reviewing it). For the game to succeed, it must be ensured that a group cannot perform all actions in the available time.

This kind of game should run for 1.5 or 2 hours, followed by a debriefing. It can work for almost any design problem, and games of a similar kind can be applied to all open or ill-defined problems.

The gameplay generates a very interesting dynamic both inside the groups and among groups. At first, groups start developing their own strategy—some take risks, some do not—but after a while, competition fires up and they start observing each other: Why are those in that group so happy? What have they found out? The teacher can support competition by providing cues, and then point out during the debriefing the different strategies that have been developed, and the different results they produced. Indeed, it is a great way to increase awareness of different learning styles.

Also, groups will start with as many different strategies as they have members, and they will have to negotiate to define a common group strategy. Some may never achieve a common strategy and will probably fail, while others will have conflicts for leadership—more interesting points to debrief.

Finally, the game can create opportunities for discussing the actual product being marketed: Is it made with some new material? What features does it have? To whom can it be marketed? How can potential buyers be reached? The basic concepts of a marketing campaign and of advertising can be discussed as solutions to a game, when they fit within a highly relevant and motivating experience.

The game just presented implements positive competition: teams can do nothing to stop opponents. You might want to introduce negative competition by including actions that can be performed only by one group, for example, taking a book from the library or interviewing an extremely busy person. Also, there can be actions that block others, like sending e-mails with false information, or hiding information. The game can be as complex as you wish—and it can all stay on a single sheet of paper that indicates the pairs: Action taken by the group (Cost) ↔ Information released.

Variations on such a simple rule set are potentially countless. Competition could be enhanced by providing more comparative feedback, such as a board that shows the time spent and the points (in terms of useful information) achieved by each group. Also, roles can be embedded into the game: One group member can be the official speaker, another can be the collector of all information, and so forth.

In my description of the design game, I used some game design concepts in describing the mechanics of the game (e.g., strategy game, information hiding, competition, roles). The gameplay elements presented in the first part of the chapter are useful in outlining the *setting* in which the game can be played. The conditions necessary to create a game's magic circle are:

Free Choice. Students should willingly decide to play. In a classroom setting this means motivating them to participate, stimulating their interest, and making sure that they like the roles they have chosen.

Player Control. Within the limits of the rules, students/players should have full control over the game. This means they should be allowed to do everything wrong, miss the right information, perform the wrong actions, and eventually lose. While this can be excruciating for a teacher to watch, it can at the same time generate a great opportunity for reflection and learning.

While I will not repeat these remarks later, they hold true for any game-based learning activity, as they represent the core features of a game-based environment.

Interaction Games and Relational Skills: The Colored Puzzle

I like interaction games for two reasons. First, they usually have simple rules; second, they are fun to play because people find themselves in strange situations and have to give their best to succeed. Although it looks like an ability game based on visual representation skills, Pictionary is in large part an interaction game. I realized this when I played it with a graphic artist: he really could use the pencil as it is meant to be used. His drawings were so clear that it was extremely easy to understand the hidden meaning. Unlike me, he did not make sounds or "act" while drawing—his sketches were enough. When he drew, his team was silent; there was no shouting to guess the right word because they were certain that in a few seconds they would have received a clear picture. At the other end of the table, another team was really in trouble: two long-time friends were having a lot of fun, but neither of them actually knew how to draw even the simplest forms. A cat looked like a horse, a hotel like a shack. After a while, this team found a strategy that led them to win the game: not drawing, but remembering together. Their common experience had offered a wealth of details that they tended to describe with the very same words; thus, it was not difficult for them to draw "laziness" or "vacation" by representing situations they had lived through together and connected to those terms. This is why Pictionary, like charades, is—or can be—an interaction game: except in those cases in which artists are among the players, the mechanic of the game is based not on drawing but on having your team getting the right word, and most players use drawings not to represent things, but to recall shared experiences. Also, the time-stress situation can bring out hidden personality facets.

The dynamic of the game is clearly competition: picture after picture, teams play against each other and against time. A sprinkle of chance, introduced through dealing the cards, makes it intriguing. Pictionary is a game that develops expressive and relational skills but goes beyond just improving visual communication. Time and stress management also come into play.

To move the concept of interaction games to the classroom, consider that interpersonal and team communications are like light: we cannot live without them, but we are not able to completely understand or define them. An effective strategy I use for making students aware of how communications work, and to show them how they can improve their personal skills, is to throw them into a weird situation and give them a chance to observe themselves and reflect on their behavior. The following is a simple game that can be used for Grades 10–12. In this example, a class of 18 students in the 11th grade were the players.

The game requires 12 identical sets of 6 shapes, cut out in plastic, wood, or other material. Each set should be of a different color, and the shapes should be unusual and as different as possible, as illustrated in Figure 15.1.

FIGURE 15.1 ▶ Puzzle with unusual shapes

At the outset of the game, the teacher tells the class that they will be divided in teams, and that each team will have to find the missing pieces of a puzzle. He will explain that there are identical sets of six shapes, and he can show one, but only briefly.

The class should be divided in three teams of six people, and all students should be blindfolded. Each team should be given four sets of shapes, from which the teacher will have removed three random shapes. The instructor will distribute three or four pieces to each student, so that all pieces are in the hands of students, except the three that were removed. Students can freely touch their shapes and talk to each other, but they cannot exchange shapes with each other, or look at the shapes. Students can also raise their hand and ask the color of a single piece, to which the instructor will answer. Their goal is figuring out the missing shapes, holding out a shape and saying something like, "We're missing this shape in blue." The first team to guess the three missing shapes wins.

During this simple game, teams will learn about communication through at least three important events that commonly occur:

1. Each team develops a language for describing the pieces. Some use geometrical references ("the convex shape"), some use metaphors ("the tree, the gun, the lion"), some describe the touch ("if you move your hand you feel an angle").

2. Each team finds a leader, or two competing leaders, or a leader and a sparring partner. Through communication, the team finds a structure that allows it to work together. It is interesting to identify secondary roles (e.g., those helping the leader) and emphasizing that real leaders do not always have the largest amount of talking time.

3. Each team develops a working strategy, then refines it, maybe drops it, and looks for a new one—but it will not reach the end without a systematic approach of some kind.

Competition lets the game run wild, as students hear other teams declaring their missing pieces and sees their chances of victory decrease. Actually, once a team finds a good and agreed-upon strategy, solving the puzzle is rather easy, so that a team can rapidly change the odds of the game.

As in all game-based activities, debriefing after gameplay is essential for learning. In the design game example, students reflected on their strategy, and the teacher provided opportunities for comparing strategies. The teacher's role in this example is that of a mirror: students should be able to "see" themselves in action and reflect on what they instinctively did within their team. Such self-observation will allow them to learn from themselves, and eventually improve their language, leadership, and cooperation skills. The teacher can prepare for the debriefing by taking notes and pictures during the game, or even recording part of the session. One or two students can serve as observers.

After the game, students typically do not talk about communication in general, or about someone else's problems, but about the silly metaphors their team used, about that girl that used that weird word "convex," or about the fact that with just a few words the shy guy actually suggested how to identify the missing pieces. Whether they won or lost, they always seem to want to understand why. The teacher's role during the debriefing is to pull players gently out of the magic circle and bring them back to their student life: to reflect on what happened in the game, and how it is analogous to what happens in many real-life situations. For example, learning the specific language of the workplace is one of the main tasks during the first months of any job, and learning to support a leader when you cannot lead is also a key skill, as is understanding that a leader is nothing if she has not gained trustworthy supporters. The game also fosters the development of reflective skills, an attitude of self-observation that is essential in all "soft skills," from communication to leadership, from negotiation to presentation—and which is a distinctive feature of all expert players, who always wonder, in the back of their minds, "How can I perform better the next time I play?"

The specific example I provided may have been based on colored shapes, but the key to harnessing the potential of interaction games in general lies in generating situations in which a challenge can be won only if effective relationships are established among the players.

Role-Playing Games and Language Learning

I mentioned Risk as the game that I played when I was 12 years old—a few years later, my friends and I discovered another game that kept us stuck in the magic circle even on sunny days when we could have played soccer: Dungeons and Dragons. In Dungeons and Dragons, players select characters from such mythical races as warriors, dwarves, wizards, and elves.

My first character was an elf, a creature I have always fancied. But the character that I managed to grow the most was a thief (whose score card I still have!). The thief's name was Iago, and he managed to get out of many adventures alive, protected only by leather armor. He also succeeded in learning different spells—not bad for a thief. Probably because of my ethical background, he was never really interested in stealing despite the fact that he was a thief. He just did not like the brute force of warriors or the sometimes incomprehensible power of wizards; he preferred to be smart and fast rather than strong and powerful. As the extensions of the game came out, Iago learned new spells, got new weapons, and founded a local guild. After a while he got wealthy enough to build a small house, close to the guild's seat, and he also got married. His adventure companions were an immensely powerful warrior played by our older friend, an elf (which had survived my own elf, and which I envied), a wizard, and some other characters.

While we all bought the original basic game set, we photocopied the extension books, and we had no money to buy anything else than the dice—no miniatures, and no ready-made adventures. Ours was a strongly oral game: the "dungeon master" (designated narrator) narrated the story, and players made decisions about where to go, what to say, and so on. During the time in which I served as dungeon master, I spent entire evenings drawing maps and preparing scenarios, or simply thinking about the new weapons I wanted for Iago.

Dungeons and Dragons was a milestone in fantasy role-playing games. The basic set has relatively simple rules; a book with different characters and creatures, to boost the imagination of the players; and a set of dice that spices up the gameplay with chance. The amazing power of engagement that Dungeons and Dragons has is that no adventure is like another, since each comes from the mind and words of the dungeon master, and from the choices of players. It is based on mimicry, blended with competition and chance.

Characters were a kind of virtual dolls for us: we looked after them, and we used them to try out possibilities. Some of the issues I thought about were: What kind of person will Iago be? Will he be nice? What if he gets a role in the guild? Will he have time for adventures? Or, on a different note: What happens if I betray my friends for money? What if I die for saving them from the red dragon? For a teenager, answering such questions means exploring a new realm, trying to figure out what he would do as an adult in that situation.

Role-playing is also a way to experiment with identity. While it might be difficult to talk to your parents about becoming a rock star, there is no reason why your character could not learn to play and sing as a bard. How would hard-working warriors relate to a rock star? Role-playing games let you have a virtual double within the game circle, an avatar that can try out new scenarios for you. It is an interesting feature in personal development and for working on creativity and imagination. But role-playing games offer much more for learning, as one cannot get into another's shoes without learning what he knows. I cannot be a wise wizard if I do not at least try to be wise and think before I act. I cannot be a fierce warrior if I'm not brave enough to be the first to attack even the most deadly foes.

The key to bringing role-playing into the classroom is in creating a compelling narrative. We know people through seeing them in action, and in the same way, characters actually only exist within a story. Embedding learning into narrative is widely used in primary education—how would that work for teenagers? Two elements of Dungeons and Dragons will be central to the effective use of role-playing games in the classroom:

1. Characters should be believable and likable (because only skillful actors can pretend to be somebody they dislike). Dungeons and Dragons achieves this by providing both strict rules for the creation of a character (a roll of the dice for abilities, types selected from a closed set) and large space for imagination. In the classroom, this could mean offering types, such as journalist, policeman, fashion designer, and then providing rules for customization.

2. Stories should be compelling, but competition can also motivate players. Really compelling stories often need a professional writer, but competition can also fire up players if the story is mediocre.

Keeping these two simple rules in mind, you can set up a number of role-playing sessions for language and culture learning for example. Let's take a class of advanced Italian for Grade 10. As a starting point, create a scenario: a small village in Tuscany. You can create locations by looking for pictures or drawings, and taking some simple notes.

Then build a simple plot around a central event: a theft would be classic, but also finding a person or secret place, or anything that is meaningful to your students. Going to a bar and getting a Coke, an example that appears in many second language books, is not really meaningful; getting a date with a nice girl is more meaningful; saving that girl from her brutal boyfriend without getting hurt is definitely meaningful. The plot should have a conflict to resolve (here is why the Coke alone is not really interesting), and should be articulated into the beginning, middle, and end of the story (for a very useful book about writing stories, please see McKee, 1997). To make the game interactive, you really need to have the interactions ready: setting the scene and defining the starting goal.

Finally, who are the characters in the plot? The girl, the boyfriend, the newcomer? Why not the girl's parents as well? They might have a forgotten love story from when they were teenagers. Some characters will be played by the players; others will be nonplaying characters and will be your puppets in the story.

With these materials (location, plot/introduction, character) you are ready to go. For each playing character in your story, be it per student or per team, you will need an introduction to the world of the game from her/his point of view. As in real life, each individual or team has a goal and different information. Then, you must prepare a map so the players can decide where and how to move. The map could also be partially hidden at the outset of the game, and be revealed step-by-step. Finally, you can have students create their characters. Have students read the introduction, then make choices. They will find themselves in situations in which they have to do something: explain ("What are you doing in my garden?"), negotiate ("I need that bike but I don't have enough money for a deposit"), be polite (Ask for directions to a policeman), and so on.

As the teacher, you can guide these situations, which can be also acted live on a stage. But most of all, you should prepare students by having them work out the geography, culture, history, and, of course, language: If a *carabiniere* arrives, what is he exactly? A policeman? A military person? Can he complain because my car is parked illegally? If I have to travel from A to B, what options do I have? How should I address an older lady? What should I expect for a Sunday lunch at a family's table?

A compelling narrative is a highly effective form of learning media. When the narrative structure contains space for our choices as a character, and when this is done interactively with other players, multiple possibilities are open for creative teaching that can employ role-playing for learning.

Conclusions

In this chapter, I started by noting the connection between playing and learning. I observed that pleasure is a fundamental experience in both gameplay and learning, and that learning is a natural part of gameplay. I discussed three important elements of gameplaying: the game magic circle, free choice, and control. I then presented key concepts from game design: structure (rule and game types) and force (the dynamics of gameplay). Finally, I provided three examples to illustrate how the elements of gameplay and game design concepts from well-known games can be transferred to class activities, focusing on strategy games, interaction games, and role-playing games.

This chapter presents a small sample of principles and lessons that can be learned from games. The main contribution I want to make is to identify where the fun comes from during play by observing the learning that occurs during the experience. The cornerstone of this method is simple—namely, playing! You would not feel comfortable teaching art-based sessions unless you took part in a session of that kind. In the same way, you will not be able to get real learning out of a game if you do not start playing.

As a school teacher, you do not need an Xbox or other expensive computers. All you need is to play the games you like and ask yourself: What is the structure and force of this game? Why do players play it? With the answers to these questions you will have the proper words and concepts to describe the design of the game, to understand it, and to play it in class.

In the search for effective teaching practices, technology often brings us back to tradition: distance learning reminds us of the importance of physical presence; multimedia reveals that nothing sensory is richer than real presence. In the same way, video games are pushing us toward the re-creation of a more natural teaching and learning environment, where learning is a pleasure because it exposes hearts and minds to truth in a form similar to our own lived experience: through a story, within an action, shared with fellow learners. The lessons we are learning come before computers, and go beyond them, and we can apply them nondigitally. Playing is not merely a distraction from learning, and pleasure is a great catalyst for learning. Learning, even at school, does not need to be unpleasant—even hard work can be fun, if the payoff is sufficient.

References

Betrus, A. K. (2005). *Motivational Game Elements*. Presentation at the AECT Convention. Orlando, FL.

Betrus, A. K., & Botturi, L. (2008, July). *Increasing player engagement without breaking your budget: Simple choices that make a big difference*. Presentation at Games + Learning + Society, Madison, WI.

Botturi, L., & Loh, C. S. (2009). Once upon a game: Rediscovering the roots of games in education. In C. T. Miller (Ed.), *Games: Purpose and potential in education* (pp. 1–22). New York, NY: Springer.

Callois, R. (2001). *Man, play, and games*. Champaign, IL: University of Illinois Press.

Cloke, K., & Goldsmith, J. (1997). *Thank God it's Monday: 14 values we need to humanize the way we work*. Toronto, Canada: Irwin Professional.

Costikyan, G. (1994). *I have no words & I must design*. Retrieved from www.costik.com/nowords.html (Originally published in *Interactive Fantasy, 2*)

Gee, J. P. (2003). *What video games have to teach us about learning and literacy*. New York, NY: Palgrave-MacMillan.

Huizinga, J. (1955). *Homo ludens: A study of the play element in culture*. Boston, MA: Beacon Press.

Jonassen, D. H., Peck, K. L., & Wilson, B. G. (1999) *Learning with technology*. Upper Saddle River, NJ: Merrill.

Koster, R. (2000). *Declaring the rights of players*. Retrieved from www.raphkoster.com/gaming/playerrights.shtml.

McKee, R. (1997). *Story, substance, structure, style, and the principles of screenwriting*. New York, NY: HarperCollins.

Papert, S. (1998). Does easy do it? Children, games, and learning. *Game Developer*, June 1998, p. 88. Available at www.papert.org/articles/Doeseasydoit.html

Parrish, P. (2008). Plotting a learning experience. In L. Botturi & T. Stubbs (Eds.), *Handbook of visual languages in instructional design: Theories and practices*. (pp. 91–111). Hershey, PA: Informing Science Reference.

Prensky, M. (2003). *Digital game-based learning*. St. Paul, MN: Paragon House.

Prensky, M. (2006). *Don't bother me Mom—I'm learning*. St. Paul, MN: Paragon House.

Salen, K., & Zimmerman, E. (2004). *Rules of play: Game design fundamentals*. Cambridge, MA: MIT Press.

Squire, K., & Jenkins, H. (2004). Harnessing the power of games in education. *Insight, 3*(1), 5–33.

Sutton-Smith, B. (1979). *Play and learning*. New York, NY: Gardner Press.

16

The Magic of Online Games

Rick Hall

ONLINE GAMES OFFER STUDENTS and educators unique challenges and benefits. In this chapter, we distinguish three types of online games (basic, multiplayer, and massively multiplayer) and discuss how they apply to educational purposes. We begin by defining several different genres of game mechanics, showing which are best suited to educational applications. This leads to a discussion of how the introduction of an online model can improve the benefits of games in terms of student engagement, collaboration, and teacher interaction, and can present a variety of logistical advantages. To provide perspective, we discuss how online components create complex challenges that single-player games need not face. Although the majority of these challenges are technical in nature, it is important to understand that there are also significant social and behavioral issues to consider. By using behavioral patterns observed in entertainment-based online games as a model, it is possible to predict the most significant of these challenges and plan around them to enhance learning in schools.

Games offer a number of benefits to education, but there are many different kinds of games, and each type offers different advantages and disadvantages. For our purposes, we will classify computer games into two broad categories: online and offline. Online games are superior in many respects to the offline variety. These advantages they provide include: superior immersion for students, more options for collaboration, the opportunity to monitor student progress, increased efficiency in teaching, the potential for enhanced teacher interaction, continuous content updating, and the chance to leverage existing online assets. The accumulation of these advantages creates a compelling case for the value of online educational games. However, there are a few caveats to online games, such as their expense, the complex infrastructures they require, the susceptibility of players online to the aberrant behavior of others, longer construction times, and risks in terms of Internet security. Since these problems are not usually difficult to mitigate, the benefits of online games tend to outweigh the difficulties.

To help teachers use games in schools to enhance learning, we first distinguish three types of online games (basic, multiplayer, and massively multiplayer) and discuss several different genres. We then detail advantages of online gaming to help teachers realize the benefits they provide, and also note several caveats to mitigate potential downfalls.

Online Options

Before discussing the plusses and minuses of online games in detail, we shall first seek to understand what basic forms these online games may take. To begin, we will turn to our three main categories of online games: basic online, multiplayer, and massively multiplayer online game (MMOG).

Basic Online

A basic online game is one that requires the player to have an Internet connection but in general does not directly involve the player in encounters with more than one other human at a time. Consider if one made an educational game out of chess. The player would encounter one opponent at a time, with no possibility of more than that. In fact, it might even be arranged that the player could play against a computer opponent that resides on a server. In this example, the player clearly requires the Internet connection, but otherwise, his or her contact with other people is nonexistent. Basic online games (sometimes referred to as head-to-head games) offer the weakest benefits of any kind of online game.

Multiplayer

A multiplayer game is one in which the player can encounter numerous opponents (or allies) at once. Typically, a multiplayer game will have a maximum of 64 simultaneous players. Players can be organized to act independently, such as with a trivia-style game, or in cooperation with other students on a "team." Gameplay sessions usually last from 30 minutes to an hour, with the playing field "resetting" at the end.

Massively Multiplayer Online Game (MMOG)

In a massively multiplayer online game (MMOG), a virtually unlimited number of players can coexist simultaneously. Often in very large MMOGs, thousands or even millions of players can roam about freely in the game world. Aside from the numbers, an MMOG is also distinguished from a multiplayer game in that MMOGs are almost always "persistent state worlds." This means that when a player logs off and comes back later, the world of the game has retained its state. For instance, if a player achieves a certain accomplishment during a game session, which might be reflected by an increase in level, property, or money, this accomplishment is retained no matter how often they log on and off. Additionally, other players may go on to achieve things, or even make changes to the world (such as adding houses, defeating certain opponents, and so forth) while everyone else is logged off. Thus, it is possible for things in the MMOG world to "evolve" whether any particular player is logged in or not. MMOGs are sometimes referred to as "virtual worlds," and it is easy to understand why. In many ways, they indeed seem to become worlds in themselves.

Game Genres

Aside from the scope of the game's online nature, there are additional properties by which games may be classified. Game developers often refer to a game's genre. The genre is a label that describes the game's main mechanic. Some mechanics are more appropriate for educational purposes than others. We believe that the most appropriate genres for educational purposes are: adventure games, simulations, role-playing games, and alternative-reality games (also known as ARGs). Games that fall into other genres might not be as useful for education since most of them focus on hand-eye coordination, with little time for thinking or processing. This less useful group would probably include things like first-person shooters, action games, and sports games (unless, of course, your educational goal is to teach learners how to shoot or play a sport). Before moving on to the next section, it will be helpful to provide short descriptions for the genres that might be useful in educational settings.

Adventure Games

Adventure games are generally very story-driven. They include lots of dialogue, memorable characters, and puzzle solving. Some popular adventure games are: Monkey Island, Day of the Tentacle, Grim Fandango, and the Indiana Jones series of games. Adventure games might be particularly well-suited to teach subjects like social studies or language arts.

Simulations

A simulation is a broad category of games that could include any behavioral model of a real world object or system. Simulations have been made for everything from physics to chemistry, military maneuvers, surgery, disaster management, economics, and political elections. Simulations are thought to have many practical applications for education.

Role-Playing Games

Role-playing games (known as RPGs) are similar to adventure games, except that they are less dependent on a specific, scripted story. In an RPG, the progression of the player's character is more important, and interaction with other players is generally far more common. An example of an RPG would be World of Warcraft. RPGs might be well-suited to almost any educational subject.

Alternative-Reality Games

Alternative-reality games (known as ARGs) are unique in that they take advantage of an array of communication mediums. An ARG often doesn't have a defined "character" wandering around a virtual world. Instead, the *player* is the main character, and the game takes place on websites, PDAs, and cell phones, through instant messaging, text messaging, and e-mail. Often utilizing contemporary conspiracy themes, ARGs might also present a mystery to be solved. The player may take on the role of an investigator, or agent, and attempt to find information about the mystery that is hidden throughout the Internet. Other players, agents, characters, or teachers could contact the student through any of the mediums just listed, at any time, whether or not they are currently sitting at the computer screen. The effect is almost always very immersive, as the player never really "stops playing." Like RPGs, ARGs are well suited to a variety of educational subjects.

Advantages of Online Games

With a better understanding of the online options that are available, we can now explore the effects that these games will have on the player and the advantages they afford teaching and learning, in terms of immersion, collaboration, monitoring, efficiency, interactivity/feedback, and content updating.

Immersion

One of the most fundamental effects of gameplay is known in game development circles as *immersion*. Essentially, this is the educational equivalent of *engagement*. It is a measure of how involved the student is in the game world or activities.

In the game development community, online games are believed to have much greater potential for immersion than single-player games. This belief comes mostly through anecdotal experience and is attributed to a few simple conditions: a sense of competition, greater realism, community, and what we might call *bragging rights*.

Sense of competition. At this stage in technology, no artificial intelligence (AI) has been developed that can provide the same level of diversity and unpredictability as a real human opponent. As a result, humans inherently provide more challenging and more interesting competition than computers do. Often, players engaging AI opponents are able to employ tricks that would be nonsensical against a human opponent but work exceptionally well to exploit a weakness in a computer's AI. Although players will invariably make use of these tricks to succeed, such moves don't actually provide a challenge. Once the "pattern" is learned, all subsequent conflict between the player and an AI opponent is rendered boring. Indeed, computer AI rarely ever "learns" from player tendencies, and will often make the same obvious mistake relentlessly. Human opponents, on the other hand, will employ a wide array of suboptimal techniques and strategies against each other. Thus, although they may not play to perfection, this is offset by the unpredictable nature of their moves. Additionally, once a "trick" is used against a human, it often won't work more than a few times. Players learn and adapt, unlike most AIs. Thus, when one plays against a human opponent, the adaptability and diversity of the techniques employed provide for a more interesting and challenging conflict. And as we might predict, this is more immersive, or engaging, thus holding players' attention more effectively.

Greater realism. Similar to the notion of conflict and competition, we can view the population of the computer world. When a virtual world is populated by computer-controlled characters (referred to as non-player characters [NPCs]), these characters are often so limited in their ability to interact that players quickly dismiss them as uninteresting. Any time a player hears an NPC utter a nonsensical reply to a question, or endlessly babble the same sentence over and over, it makes the player hyperaware that this character is not real. Upon reaching that realization, consciously or unconsciously, the player will view the NPC character as meaningless.

Conversely, when a world is populated by other human players, a more realistic form of interaction takes place. Each character has its own life and personality, and is therefore interesting. Whether the player likes or despises the other characters becomes secondary to the fact that they are "real," hence more interesting. Again, the presence of other humans, which in computer games can best be accomplished with the online medium, contributes in a positive way to make the world a more interesting place.

Community. A third benefit that contributes to the immersive quality of online games is the idea of community. While community is viewed as an educationally positive thing in its own right, it is also beneficial to the environment. Game developers have long realized that the impact of *peer pressure* can have lasting effect on an online game's success. While a single-player game can be played (or ignored) on a whim, often the presence of online friends and community provides incentive for a player to rejoin a game world more often. When you know your friend will be online Thursday night at 7:00, you're more likely to log into the game even if you wouldn't have otherwise. This continued, subtle pressure to log in and play keeps the game current and fresh in a player's mind. It reinforces the need to play more often, thus encouraging a player to devote more time to the game. And while more time in an educational game is probably a good thing in its own right, peer pressure additionally contributes to the immersion factor. The more exposure and familiarity a player has with a virtual world, the more it becomes almost like a second home. The presence of the community creates diversity and interest, often filling the gaps when the game experience itself is waning.

Bragging rights. Napoleon once said, "A soldier will fight long and hard for a bit of colored ribbon." It turns out that what is true of life-and-death struggles is equally true for game players. Players will jump through nearly any hoop, endure nearly any hardship, and go to ridiculous lengths to obtain any sort of unique distinction from their fellow players. Game developers refer to these achievements as *bragging rights*. Every MMOG ever developed contains rewards for players that allow them to differentiate themselves from other players. Whether this comes in the form of visual customizations, gameplay-enhancing gadgets, or chat room titles makes little difference. All that matters to players is that they are able to appear different from their fellow competitors. The differences they earn signify that they have accomplished something other players have not, and thus gives them bragging rights.

It is important to understand that the rewards players receive in MMOG would be considered meaningless in a single-player game. A player in a single-player game couldn't care less if their character has the title of "general." If the title doesn't offer some functional advantage, then it's nothing but fluff. However, in an online world, there is an *audience* of other players. Everyone can *see* the accomplishment, and this gives it value. Other players will often approach someone who has one of these differentiators and ask them how and where they obtained it. This provides the owner of the item with a sense of worth, and that is certainly a valuable contributor to the notion of immersion.

As we can see, the presence of other human beings in a game world contributes in several distinct ways to the level of immersion that the player feels. In a sense, we might view the difference between single-player and online games as similar to the difference between two dimensions and three. Single-player experiences, no matter how well crafted, are static and flat. After a relatively short period of time, they will become tedious. Conversely, an online game is rich in diversity. It is a living, breathing world that surrounds the player with a sense of community, belonging, and, in many cases, self worth.

Collaboration

Current educational thinking holds that collaboration between students is strongly beneficial to the learning process. Clearly, online games provide a solid avenue for collaborative activities. In a gaming sense, we can find many examples of in-game collaboration between players. Nearly all online games contain modes that allow for both competitive and cooperative play. Such game modes will allow players to combine forces to form groups that may contain as few as two cooperating players, or as many as several dozen, or even, in some cases, hundreds.

These groups can be either temporary or permanent in nature. Temporary groups, often known as *pick-up groups*, are usually small bands of players that get together for a brief period of time up to a few hours, to accomplish some goal that they could not otherwise accomplish on their own. MMOGs such as World of Warcraft have provided a plethora of different in-game tools that allow players to "advertise" for such temporary groups, organize a temporary hierarchy, communicate, and efficiently combine efforts.

More permanent groups, sometimes referred to as *guilds*, are also encouraged in online games. Again, MMOGS usually provide a wide array of tools that allow the formation of such groups, as well as offering options for customization and individualization.

In both instances we should recognize that the key to encouraging collaborative activity in an online game lies in the quality and quantity of tools that are provided to facilitate it. Successful online games have well developed, easy-to-use tools for creating groups, establishing structure and identity, communicating, and combining player efforts in the service of directed group experiences. Without an effective set of such tools, collaborative activities become extremely difficult.

Beyond in-game collaboration, however, there are other methods that groups of players commonly use to share knowledge and work together. Discussion boards are the most obvious example. When a player encounters a difficult challenge, it is quite helpful to have a discussion forum where they can appeal to other players for advice. In fact, conversations about overcoming obstacles are only a small part of the information exchanges that take place on most discussion boards. Players will use discussion boards to exchange strategies, help each other solve hardware problems or bugs that hamper game play, or discuss out-of-game issues. No matter what form the conversations take, discussion boards help to establish strong communities that give a player a sense that nothing in the game is ever impossible to overcome. Somewhere, someone always knows the answer, thus providing a *safety net* of sorts that increases the player's comfort level with the game.

Yet another interesting example of collaborative, shared knowledge occurs in the form of player created databases; THOTTBOT (www.thottbotcom) is a good example of this. At this site, a World of Warcraft player can look up the solutions to any quest in the game, locate any monster or NPC player, obtain maps of the world, receive advice on optimizing characters, and exchange strategies for nearly any challenge in the game. Amazingly, this database was created entirely by players, without any contribution whatsoever from Blizzard, the developer of World of Warcraft. It is a fascinating example of how the simple existence of other players will encourage tremendous collaborative efforts between very large collections of players.

Finally, we might also consider *fan art* as a form of collaborative activity. In most online communities, there exists a subgroup of players who feel the need to use the game world as a creative outlet. They create art and videos, write stories, and even compose music about the game and its fiction. This fan art is then distributed through websites and the discussion boards, serving as a further exchange of ideas and information.

Monitoring Student Progress

One glaring drawback of single-player games is that they do not allow teachers to monitor student progress. Without an Internet connection to a server, a teacher has almost no way of knowing whether students are progressing or encountering difficulties, or even how to provide them with feedback on their efforts. Unless the student is playing the game in the immediate physical proximity of the teacher, it will be an isolated experience.

Fortunately, this is an area where online games truly shine. It is easy, almost trivial, to include monitoring features in an online game. Through an Internet connection, large amounts of player data can be uploaded to a server where a teacher can monitor them at any time, viewing these data in the most useful formats.

While this might sound obvious at first, if we look a little deeper, we can understand the real power of online connectivity. Let's consider the example of a game that teaches intensive reading. Let's say that one of the features of the game is a little virtual finger that students control with their mouse. As they read, they slide the finger along under the words, much as they might do with their real hands when reading a book. What data can we collect from this?

Initially, we can measure simple reading speed. By measuring the velocity of the finger traveling across the page, we can find an exact measure of a student's reading speed. Moreover, as time goes on, these data can be collected to form a trend graph. Over the course of a semester, we can see how the student's reading speed is improving through the use of a very precise measurement. In fact, the data that can be collected with this simple technique will actually be more accurate than the observations a live teacher could produce with the student reading to them aloud.

Additionally, by watching where the virtual finger hesitates, moves backward, and so forth, teachers can identify the words students found difficult, or the places in the reading where they got lost and had to move backward. Again, it would be possible to collect trend data, and ultimately produce a catalogue of the kinds of words, phrases, and concepts that each student had difficulty with. Armed with these sorts of data, a good teacher could then adapt to students' individual needs and adjust the content or pace accordingly with the simple touch of a button.

Through the use of data-gathering tools, teachers will be able to better understand their students' exact study habits. They can know how often and how long each given study session is, how often a student must redo assessments before success, or whether they tend to study alone or in groups. Such data can provide teachers with aggregated, collective metrics that allow them to know when content should be adjusted because it is too easy or too hard. Even the students' notes could be perused, provided the students entered them into a game-world notebook.

As we can see, the possibility for quantifying students' study and learning habits is nearly unlimited. In fact, we can say with relative certainty that the quantity and quality of data that can be collected in a game environment will be in every way superior to what a live teacher could accomplish by hand. And in allotting such tedious data collection to a computer, the teacher will become freer to perform the important work of using that data to adapt to the exact needs of each individual student.

Efficiency

As we might imagine from the previous section, the ability to gather player data in the game can provide the added benefit of increasing the teacher's efficiency. Even if the teacher was able to gather the quantity and quality of data mentioned earlier, the process would be laborious and time consuming. It would be a far more efficient use of the teacher's time to let a computer gather these kinds of data, thus allowing the teacher to devote time to interpreting and using it.

There are several other ways that an online game can increase teacher efficiency. The four main ways we will discuss here are automation of assessments, course completion times, brick-and-mortar efficiencies, and uniformity of quality.

Automation of assessments. While the assessment of higher-order thinking skills, particularly when there may be multiple correct answers or multiple means of deriving the correct answer, will still probably require a teacher's evaluation skills, there are many relatively objective assessments that may take place within a typical course. Any conventional criterion-referenced test that contains multiple-choice, fill-in-the-blank, true/false, or matching questions can be handled entirely by automation. In allowing the game to administer pop quizzes and multiple-choice tests, teachers will free up a percentage of their time, thus enabling them to focus on assessing students' higher-order thinking skills, as well as handle a greater number of students.

Course completion times. As noted previously, the immersive qualities of games will tend to encourage students to devote a larger percentage of their time to the subject matter than they might if it was a traditional course. Many students have faster completion times when playing educational games. If students are able to get through the course material more quickly as a result, this will again allow for teachers to handle a larger number of students per academic year.

Brick-and-mortar efficiencies. In many smaller school districts, it is common to have a small number of students who desire to take fairly obscure courses, such as Latin. Given typical budgetary constraints, the smaller school districts often simply cannot afford to hire a full-time teacher to accommodate a handful of students. However, with an online course the students and teacher can be literally anywhere in the country. As a result, a few students from school A can be added to a few from school B, and a few more from school C, until a full class that warrants a full-time teacher can be filled. In this way, smaller school districts can pool resources with other schools, and offer the full breadth of courses even when only a small number of students want to take certain subjects.

Additionally, since online classes can offer the opportunity for students to take courses physically outside of the classroom, then the expense of brick-and-mortar classrooms themselves can be reduced. New physical classrooms need not be constructed when the classes are virtual.

Uniformity of quality. Another interesting benefit of online games is that they offer a consistent level of quality. Unlike in traditional classrooms, where the quality of the education is largely dependent on the skills of the individual teacher, educational games provide a very similar experience to every student. Since the game itself presents most of the information, facilitates collaborative activities, and handles conventional criterion-referenced assessments, and the game does not change from student to student, no matter how many students play it, then efficiency is created. Provided the game is of high quality, then every student who participates in it will be provided with the same high standards. The level of variation from one teacher to the next will be significantly mitigated.

Teacher Interaction and Feedback

Although the point is perhaps obvious, we would be remiss if we failed to mention that online games provide a channel for teachers to give direct feedback and engage in interaction with the students. There should be no assumption that educational games will completely replace teachers. Rather, they can act as the delivery platform for basic content and assessments, freeing teachers to actually teach instead of performing much of the menial tasks that come with brick-and-mortar schools.

If this is the case, then it is essential for teachers to be able to directly communicate with the students, whether en masse, in small groups, or individually. Online games provide a solid medium for these kinds of communication.

Simple, well-used technology currently allows teachers to deliver live lectures directly across broadband connections. While this in itself is useful, the usefulness is enhanced when we realize that these lectures can be easily captured and reviewed as often as desired on later dates.

By participating in text-based discussion boards, teachers can additionally field questions from the students outside of real time. A student could ask a question at any time, and a few hours later, when the teacher logs on, the question can be answered for all students to see.

In addition to this, some games are experimenting with options for teachers to participate directly in the game. For example, a teacher could adopt the persona of an in-game character and wander around the virtual world, participating in the storyline, acting as a mentor or an opponent, or monitoring student activities. If the teacher actually plays a character, the enhancement of the immersion factor also contributes to a more positive, productive experience.

Continuous Content Updating

One of the most valuable features of online games is their ability to be enhanced and updated. Because online games are accessed through an Internet connection, game developers are able to fix bugs that occur after the game launches, add new features at will, and update content whenever needed. Most teachers have experienced the impact of changing standards that necessitate corresponding changes to course content. In an online environment, these changes can take place seamlessly, without the need to print up new books or write new software. A simple online patch can keep the course current long after it was originally deployed.

The opportunities for enhancing content extend far beyond simple patches and updates, however. If we consider the World Wide Web, it is possible to view online educational games in a wholly new light. Consider the possibilities of leveraging existing Internet content, linking to it from inside the game. In this manner, an educational game can take advantage of a vast warehouse of information that resides in wikis, news and current events sites, technology sites, personal websites, and so on. By integrating these links into a game, it is possible to greatly expand the amount of information that is available to the student, without having to directly involve game developers.

The possibilities here are vast. As more and more developers create educational games, they will each contribute information to a general pool that can be accessed online. It is not inconceivable that a national school network would develop, one that assembles an enormous database of information on every subject imaginable and then shares it with the schools of the entire nation. By leveraging information across the Internet in this way, an entirely new level of education is possible.

Before leaving this topic, we should also visit a common concern among opponents of educational games. Some opponents worry that large collections of students all connected via the Internet will be in a position to cheat far more often and effectively. By trading reports and work across schools, it might be possible for students to "cut and paste" their way through a class.

Care should be taken before allowing this kind of argument to get out of control. In reality, nothing prevents students in a traditional classroom from engaging in such behavior. Any student with access to the Internet can already purchase or trade work with another student, and turn it in as their own. This problem already exists, and is not limited to educational games. The student can visit such sites as Termpapers.com and buy reports that cover nearly any subject at nearly any grade level.

The solution to this problem lies in the variety of anticheating sites that already exist as a resource for teachers. Sites like Glatt Plagiarism Services (www.plagiarism.com) and Turnitin (www.turnitin.com), and applications such as Mediaphor AG's Plagiarism-Finder were built to combat this exact phenomenon. An online educational game could (and should) include this as part of the teacher's toolbox. In fact, because students' work in an online game will already be in a digital format (a Word file, PDF, etc.), then is it actually easier for a teacher to check it against antiplagiarism sites than if it were in hard copy.

Caveats

To be fair, the use of games for educational purposes is not without its difficulties. While this chapter has expounded on the benefits of games as a vehicle for education, the challenges mentioned at the beginning of the chapter deserve some attention. Here are some brief summaries.

Expense

A well-made computer game that can compete with some of the more successful commercial entertainment properties is not necessarily cheap. Keep in mind that a typical modern computer game can require a budget of between $1 million and $5 million, and require 12 to 24 months to construct. Although it is possible to build cheaper games, the more corners that are cut, the more difficult it will be to compete for the player's attention.

Infrastructural Components

An online game in particular requires a considerable infrastructure behind it for support. Such infrastructural components will include login servers, patchers, databases, networking code, security, servers, and server-monitoring tools at a minimum. In many cases, there is just as much work and expense involved in providing the infrastructure as there is in building the game itself.

Aberrant Behavior

A side effect of the relative anonymity of Internet gaming is that players can sometimes descend into antisocial behavior. In commercial games especially, since the player is almost completely anonymous, there are few if any ramifications for bad behavior. There will almost always be a small percentage of players who seem to derive entertainment from ruining the experience of those around them. This can be partially compensated for in an educational situation by removing some of the anonymity, as well as through vigilant monitoring by authority figures.

Internet Predators

Especially in an educational situation, it will be of paramount importance to maintain high levels of security to prevent Internet predators from entering into the virtual learning environment.

Specialized Training

To operate in a virtual environment, teachers will need to be prepared with specialized training. Aside from simply understanding the technical operation of the system itself, teachers or authority figures must observe specific procedures for dealing with aberrant behavior online (which is different from aberrant behavior in a face-to-face situation), time management (remember that an online game operates 24/7, which is quite different from a school setting), and possibly some more specialized statistical analysis (so they can benefit from the numerous methods of gathering metrics and trend data).

Parting Thoughts

It seems clear that online computer games and education are well suited for each other. There are simply too many similarities between the two for this not to be the case. And aside from the similarities, there are also things that educators and game developers can learn from the other. Doubtless, if more computer game developers paid attention to proven educational practices, their games would be far more effective and improve in overall quality. Understanding teaching methods and how they operate on the brain of the game player would be valuable data for the game developer, even if the information is applied to purely entertainment-based products. Likewise, educators have just as much to learn from entertainers. The primary lesson here would be to pay special attention to the word "fun." Too often in this author's experience, educators are overly cautious about students "playing games" when they are supposed to be learning. Educators often fall much too easily into a pattern in which they want the benefit that games provide but are unwilling to allow the mechanism through which that benefit is created. Educators must remember that the first rule of teaching is to *engage the student*. If that is to be accomplished via a game, then the fun must be present.

Finally, if we raise our vantage point to a higher level, we should ask ourselves, How can teachers and students employ online games to achieve learning goals? To a degree, the answer to this question depends on our own unique definition of what those goals are. For some, the most useful outcome may be an improvement in the effectiveness of the time they spend teaching. Tedious tasks may be removed while powerful data can be collected that allows for individualized attention to each student. For others, the goal may be to inspire a more pervasive *desire to learn*. In real world educational environments, presentation of subject matter may often be dry and clinical, failing to interest all but the most dedicated, self-motivated students. However, when an online game combines a competitive, colorful, entertaining graphical world with the immersive social and collaborative components mentioned earlier, it may result in a place where the student *enjoys* going. When the students actually look forward to entering a learning environment, it's likely that their desire to learn will increase along the way, whether or not they realize it at the time.

17

Virtual Worlds

Tom Atkinson

Every role humans engage in, from social roles,
to political roles, to athletic roles, to business roles,
is in fact best understood in the context of games.

—Herbert Gintis (2005)

AS EDUCATORS TRANSFORM INSTRUCTION from real world to virtual world, an understanding of how real-life issues transfer to the immersive spaces of virtual life may be critical for effective learning. This chapter offers a framework for better understanding virtual worlds in the context of games by (a) identifying characteristics that distinguish virtual worlds from games; (b) examining aspects of teaching and learning with virtual worlds, which include developing instruction, learner engagement, and social behaviors; (c) addressing issues of real life, privacy, and security; and (d) exploring future directions into the Metaverse.

If you would only put a fraction of that time and energy into your schoolwork, you'd be an A+ student!

It is the universal cry of parents and teachers everywhere, fueled by the endless hours children spend mastering the intricacies of a video game. To the parent, video games represent an insidious archrival of homework and learning. But the child perceives something very different, something engaging enough to focus attention and imagination beyond reality. Meanwhile, teachers find themselves somewhere in the middle—often dismayed by commercially popular games with little, if any, educational value, and dissatisfied with instructional games that are often, at best, repetitive efforts at drill and practice that fail to use the potential of video games to engage learners.

If only there was an instructional game that captured the essence of the best kinds of learning and engaged students at the same time. Some educators believe they've found a solution that reduces absenteeism, increases concentration, enhances learning through constructivist pedagogy, builds skills required in the 21st-century world of high-tech society, and leaves students eager for more. Students, teachers, and administrators are beginning to discover that what appears to be a simple online immersive environment may be much more than just another video game. In Chapter 1, Prensky highlights this new view of learning by describing how the gamer generation is redefining the learning experience as a partnership with highly interactive and immersive encounters. While many good examples of immersive environments with manipulated objects, including animated characters, have proven effective for learning, recent trends in games that involve multiple users have transformed our approach for teaching online (Atkinson, Atkinson, & Smith, 2002).

As educators transform instruction from real world to virtual world, an understanding of how real-life issues transfer to the immersive spaces of virtual life may be critical for effective learning. This chapter offers a framework for better understanding virtual worlds in the context of games by (a) identifying characteristics that distinguish virtual worlds from games; (b) examining aspects of teaching and learning with virtual worlds, which include developing instruction, learner engagement, and social behaviors; (c) addressing issues of real life, privacy, and security; and (d) exploring future directions into the Metaverse.

Virtual World or Game?

In the early stages of game development, story-based textual narratives about civilizations and fantasy worlds popularized commercial game software for personal computers. Technological limitations meant that complex three-dimensional graphics were sacrificed in favor of speed of operation. As computer technology and performance improved, graphical images of mythical creatures and animated characters inhabited landscapes that fueled players' imagination. Navigating twisted mazes of passageways by typing instructions to go left, go right, or pick up and use objects, players became adventurers who overcame obstacles and completed structured tasks to achieve the goal and win the game (T. Atkinson, 2008a).

Early serious game developers required complex tools and programming knowledge to simulate the real world for instructional applications, which were often repetitive and uninspiring. Developments in wide area networking and broadband connectivity gave players online access to others with similar interests that unleashed social networking and attracted millions of players to multiuser virtual environments (MUVEs). Unlike specific goal-oriented games, MUVEs rely more on social interaction for task completion in an internally consistent fictional or fantasy-based realm. Multiplayer games led to simulated virtual reality environments like SimCity (pictured in Figure 17.1), where players experience virtual life in cyberspace (Smart, Cascio, & Paffendorf, 2007).

First released in 1989 and designed by Will Wright, SimCity is a construction simulation game (http://simcitysocieties.ea.com). The concept came from a game that allowed Wright to create his own maps. Originally based on real world cities, the game challenged the player, who acts as the mayor of the city, with goal-centered, timed scenarios that could be won or lost depending on performance.

FIGURE 17.1 ▶ Sample screen from construction simulation game SimCity

While in previous versions of SimCity the player is the mayor of a virtual city, a more recent version of the game includes social engineering. In this version, six "social energies," called societal values (i.e., productivity, prosperity, creativity, spirituality, authority, and knowledge), allow players to discover characteristics of the citizens in their city (see the SimCity Societies official site, http://simcity.ea.com/about.php). Spore, another game from the creator of SimCity, is perhaps the most creative concept in virtual-world games: it simulates the development of a species on a galactic scope as players develop a creature across many generations, from a single-cell organism emerging from the primordial soup to a complex multicellular organism that lives in advanced civilizations across the galaxy (www.spore.com/what).

So, when does a game become a virtual world? In its simplest form, a virtual world is similar to a three-dimensional (3-D) multiplayer game. Both applications simulate 3-D spaces with interactive objects that support collaboration and social networking. But, unlike most games, virtual worlds impose few overt goals and value structures, instead supporting a "sense of place" and providing open-ended options that allow users to create objects for economic gain and to interact in almost unlimited ways. This social presence is thought to make learning more of a human experience than it is in most other online environments. Additionally, participants in virtual worlds enhance their social presence and feelings of ownership by constructing spaces and personalizing their appearance as animated characters called avatars.

In an instructional virtual world, avatars typically investigate areas for learning activities instead of searching for treasures or scoring points. For example, rather than attacking others, an avatar in an instructional visual world might approach someone in a library to ask questions about available books or media. To enhance the illusion of a classroom, media support for visual worlds includes streaming audio and video for sound effects, music, movies, and voice, with proximal settings so those who are farther away sound softer. Although several languages can be automatically interpreted when participants encounter those who use foreign languages, students can attend areas in which the role-playing activities are geared specifically toward learning new languages. Virtual worlds provide educators with a platform rich in visual media and interactive capabilities; even a novice can use them to simulate activities that provide engaging gameplay for students. However, these same capabilities perpetuate the impression that virtual worlds are just like games, even when the focus is on instructional activities.

A sophisticated example of an instructional virtual world is the River City Project, created by educators from several universities and implemented by about 60 teachers for 4,000 students in the United States and Australia. It places students in a classroom where they collaborate in teams of three. Students direct avatars in a simulated American river town in the late 1800s. The town faces a health crisis, and students are challenged to discover why the residents of River City are getting sick and what can be done to help them. Students view archival photos from the Smithsonian Institution and gather data with virtual tools such as microscopes and bug catchers, then share their findings with teammates. Although the world is populated with several virtual characters, students interact with the avatars of classmates, including those from other schools, by communicating primarily through text chats (Dede, Clarke, Ketelhut, Nelson, & Bowman, 2005). For a more detailed description of this project, see Chapter 5.

Another early example of a virtual world, Project ScienceSpace, actually consists of three worlds: (a) NewtonWorld, in which students investigate kinematics and dynamics of one-dimensional motion; (b) MaxwellWorld, where they explore electrostatics; and (c) PaulingWorld, where they study molecular structures. Viewing the worlds requires a high-performance graphics workstation with two video output channels; a color, stereoscopic head-mounted display; a stereo sound system; a magnetic tracking system for the head and hands; a 3-D mouse and menu; and a haptic vest with touch sensors. The display shows 3-D objects and images with colored, shaded polygons and textures. NASA-developed software links objects with behaviors designed to immerse students in 3-D simulations using visual, auditory, and tactile senses (Project ScienceSpace, 2008).

One of the largest virtual worlds, Second Life (SL; pictured in Figure 17.2), supports an online community within a 3-D virtual world almost entirely built and owned by its residents, who explore, build, socialize, and participate in their own economy. Although the main SL grid is restricted to those of age 18 and older, Teen Second Life is designated for ages 13–17.

According to its creator, Linden Lab (2008), SL is inhabited by more than 15 million users, called residents, from around the globe, with an average of 45,000 residents concurrently inworld. Some believe this virtual world's success stems from the fact that its residents can earn real money by buying and selling digital assets in the form of virtual apparel, real estate properties, and objects to enhance functions. Others locate the popularity in SL's virtual economy, which runs on currency called Linden dollars ($L), and the Linden Scripting Language (LSL), an open source

FIGURE 17.2 ▶ Second Life (SL) is an open-ended virtual world developed by Linden Lab that allows residents to explore, socialize, and learn.

programming language that allows users to add features to the world. Some virtual worlds are designed specifically for children and youth. While many of these are spinoffs from commercial products (e.g., Barbie Girls, Build-a-Bear World, WebkinzWorld), others are developed with education in mind.

For example, Dizzywood, for ages 8–12, focuses on learning activities with story-themed missions that advance players to more challenging levels by rewarding achievement and persistence. Learners manipulate and alter avatars and virtual homes to promote creativity and expression in visual formats. The Dizzywood Explorer's Journal blog (www.dizzywood.com/blog/explorers) provides a forum for kids to contribute stories, comments, or ideas in written form. Dizzywood's story format helps students develop reading skills and new vocabulary as they progress through word games, puzzles, riddles, and other activities that promote critical thinking. Reed Union School District in Marin County, California, adopted Dizzywood to reinforce the schools' effort to build character (e.g., caring, citizenship, fairness, respect) and develop academic and cooperative skills. The YMCA of San Francisco also uses Dizzywood to help students learn new skills and develop confidence.

Another example of a virtual world for children is Disney's Club Penguin, designed for ages 7–14. Available in English, Portuguese, and French, it features a snowy imaginative world where the avatars are all penguins that chat, play games, participate in plays, care for virtual pets, and even decorate their own igloos and design new clothes. Although standard membership is free, priority access to certain areas, party events, and other features are only available to paid subscribers. To ensure a safe experience, members choose words and phrases from an approved list or enter words through filters that eliminate unapproved language or personal information. Additionally, inworld staff members assist visitors and monitor communications for misconduct. Club Penguin fosters reading skills, keyboarding, math concepts, money management, communication, cooperation, and creativity in a safe, interactive environment.

With over 20 years of research in education and cooperative learning, a group of Caltech scientists applied the Caltech Precollege Science Initiative (CAPSI) to develop learning models that feature hands-on, inquiry-based constructivist pedagogy that equates learning with engagement. To implement that pedagogy, they created the virtual world Whyville (www.whyville.net/smmk/nice), one of the first and most popular virtual worlds for children and teens. Partners in the project include the Getty Museum, NASA, the School Nutrition Association, and the Woods Hole Oceanographic Institution.

Named by the International Academy of Digital Arts and Sciences as one of the best virtual-world sites for youth, Whyville (pictured in Figure 17.3) targets middle school students for two reasons. First, students at this age, especially girls, sometimes lose interest in math and science. Second, the academic interests and future career decisions of students at this age may be influenced by outside activities and information. Whyville, a virtual city, provides opportunities for students to learn about everything from art history to zoology.

FIGURE 17.3 ▶ Whyville introduces a broad range of topics—from science and business to art and geography—that use gameplay and role-play to engage learners.

Virtual-world instruction often changes teachers' customary role: instead of providing answers, they become constructivists using an inquiry process to provide situated learning. In making this shift, teachers engage students in active learning by asking questions that facilitate problem solving rather than merely presenting definitions and facts. To accomplish this process, teachers should become familiar with how the world's creators organize and present content, as well as the world's capabilities and limitations. Using that knowledge, educators can then make informed decisions about how virtual-world activities can be used to meet curricular standards.

This process leads to the development of instructional objectives, facilitates the incorporation of virtual-world content into the curriculum, and provides effective methods of assessing what is learned. The next section identifies methods for promoting effective teaching and learning in virtual worlds.

Teaching and Learning in Virtual Worlds

Unlike educational video games that may already contain specific learning goals and objectives, a virtual-world teacher must often determine how curricular needs match the features within the virtual world and then craft problems that combine these needs with inworld activities. For example, some of the activities in Whyville simulate the motion of skaters to explain rotational axes and symmetry. Others require navigation of a hot air balloon to explore altitude and vector fields. One activity fosters design of a dance to apply vector arithmetic. A teacher could identify standards for math or science that coincide with the concepts and create instructional objectives to help structure the experience. As students interact with various aspects of the virtual world, they could apply critical thinking skills to suggest possible outcomes. After recording observations, they might discuss the results and construct a lab report with snapshots to highlight their experience. Sometimes such activities require the teacher to build structures in the virtual world and develop ways for students to report activities according to identified curricular goals. Even if resources are available inworld, teachers can still ask students to leave the virtual environment to perform certain activities, such as contributing to wikis, blogs, and so forth, which can be linked to inworld.

As students explore virtual worlds, teachers need to become skilled at facilitating discussions that create and sustain student-centered classroom inquiry, and assisting students as they learn to ask good questions and collaborate in teams. Decentralizing the role of the teacher may alter students' perceptions of their own role in the education process. An important benefit of using virtual worlds to deliver instruction is that students often learn how to learn. In traditional classrooms, where the teacher is considered the primary source of information, students sometimes learn to play along or tune out. Virtual worlds can create a safe and engaging zone where students can ask questions and explore ideas without fear of penalties (Blaisdell, 2006).

Thus, teaching and learning in virtual worlds may require a conceptual shift in thinking about how one teaches and how students learn. The following section identifies several considerations for developing effective instruction in virtual worlds, and presents specific resources that support educators. It further examines issues for engaging learners and recognizing social behaviors encountered in virtual-world environments.

Developing Instruction

Instructional activities in virtual worlds often include unfettered exploration by students. Just as learners choose how they appear in the game world, they are also free to roam and choose what to do. This approach can result in a variety of incidental learning. Some students may do things that result in increased knowledge or skills, while others wander aimlessly without achieving objectives or disengage when the activity becomes too challenging. A "hit-or-miss" approach may not contribute to effective teaching and learning in SL. Rather, educators need to be aware of ways to structure the environment so that it is engaging, but not daunting. In terms of instruction, teachers need to know how to help students maximize experiences that address specific curricular needs. In short, educators have to help students move from the role of virtual resident to that of virtual learner.

While no specific model for developing instruction in virtual worlds has become apparent, some educators seem to prefer a game-based learning approach with simulation and interactive features. Driscoll (2005) provides a foundation for designing effective instruction in virtual worlds that can be summarized as follows:

- ▶ Learning process engages through exploration and reflection.

- ▶ Learning is embedded in a 3-D environment where learners interact through role-play.

- ▶ Learning is proactive and collaborative where learners test and compare multiple perspectives.

- ▶ Learning simulates real life in an authentic context through real-world activities, behaviors, actions, and events.

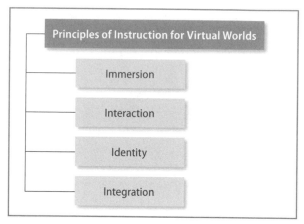

FIGURE 17.4 ▶ Principles of instruction for virtual worlds

Figure 17.4 illustrates how these conditions can be represented by four basic principles of instruction for virtual worlds: immersion, interaction, identity, and integration.

Immersion. Although using immersion to engage learners is nothing new, technology has redefined the process by which developers simulate the real world. Learners' attention is best focused when they are immersed in realistic environments that represent familiar places, such as the classroom pictured in Figure 17.5. When students have specific areas in which to interact and share ideas, they are encouraged to stay focused. Virtual worlds allow learners to enhance their presence by changing aspects such as camera position and orientation to provide other points of view. The concept of telepresence, the sense of being in a mediated environment rather than in the physical environment, has been studied since virtual reality began. Two dimensions contribute to telepresence: vividness and interactivity (Steuer, 1992).

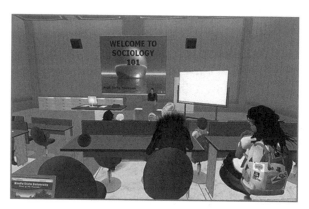

FIGURE 17.5 ▶ In virtual worlds, learners engage in authentic and familiar surroundings that simulate classroom environments.

Vividness describes the impact the environment has on our senses. Our brain records what we see, hear, taste, smell, and feel. The vividness of the experience is based on how many senses are used and the intensity or quality of their reception. Incorporating more senses intensifies the experience and may influence retention of learning. Thus, as educators make instructional decisions about how to incorporate virtual-world content, they should look for activities that stimulate the senses and structure learner experiences to illuminate them fully. Although virtual worlds typically offer only visual and auditory stimuli, educators can add textures, smells, and other physical aspects. For example, a teacher might provide evergreen scents, wool sweaters, and ice when exploring a simulation of an igloo in a polar region.

According to Dede (1995), students engage in deeper learning when inducing symbolic immersion that suspends disbelief by triggering semantic associations through content of the virtual environment. For example, reading a horror novel at midnight in a strange house may stimulate a mounting sense of fear even though one's physical being is unthreatened. As a result, the reader is more engaged in the story. Stimulating intellectual, emotional, and normative archetypes through virtual environments deepens one's experience by imposing a structure of associative mental models. For example, using journaling techniques by recording "machinimas" (animated videos) in virtual worlds may help capture and document the relevant qualities of the experience for reflection and analysis.

Interaction. Interaction describes our ability to control or change the form or content of the environment in real time measured by speed (real-time or delayed), range (number of attributes manipulated), and mapping (moving objects). Increased interaction correlates with engaging learners in instructional activities. To improve interaction in virtual worlds, educators should choose activities that permit the greatest range of learner control and use. For example, a teacher might choose an activity in which a student controls movements and alters objects rather than using a simple keystroke to respond to a prompt.

How we interact with virtual space is often defined by physical attributes. For example, during encounters in virtual worlds, students remain sensitive to subtle cues like eye contact, spatial proximity, and social behavior. When approached too closely, learners reposition their avatar, even though the space violation is merely an image on the screen. Apparently, in social contexts, our brains are not specialized to distinguish virtual experience from reality. Thus, the way a teacher arranges a virtual classroom to encourage interactions and avoid awkward behaviors may parallel decisions made for real-life classrooms (T. Atkinson, 2008c).

Virtual worlds inherently require human computer interaction, which in turn calls for system and usability evaluations, typically through measurement of human behavior, including aspects of perception, action, and task performance. Educators often rely on user feedback to determine if an interface is compatible with needs and preferences. Most evaluations can be completed quickly but vary with the size and complexity of the activity, the purpose of the review, the nature of the usability issues that arise in the review, and the competence of the reviewers. Usability problems are categorized using a numeric scale according to their estimated impact on user performance or acceptance. Perhaps the most popular method for evaluating a user interface is Nielsen's (1994) set of heuristics:

- ▶ Simple and natural dialogue
- ▶ Language friendly
- ▶ Low cognitive and memory requirements
- ▶ Consistent format and standards
- ▶ Visible status feedback
- ▶ Clearly marked exits
- ▶ Shortcuts and user controls
- ▶ Error messages and recovery
- ▶ Error prevention
- ▶ Help and documentation

A frequent criticism of heuristic methods of evaluation is that results are highly influenced by the knowledge of the reviewer. Although Nielsen's method provides a basis for evaluating common user interfaces, better criteria for defining specific features found in virtual-world applications are desperately needed.

Identity. Perhaps the most intriguing principle of instruction in virtual worlds is that they highlight how we see ourselves. Just as in the real world, appearance matters. At the click of a button, we can alter gender, age, attractiveness, and skin tone. But as we choose our avatars online, how do avatars change us?

It is not unusual for learners to literally experience the virtual world with a different identity. While some teachers insist that avatars' appearance conform to the same expectations that exist in a traditional classroom, others allow students to explore characters by assuming different identities. Although role-play can be a powerful aspect of learning in virtual worlds, lack of specific, published guidelines for the activity often leads to inappropriate behaviors or distractions.

Distinguishing the virtual and the real world can be confusing for students. Researchers have only recently begun to study the social dynamics of virtual worlds, but thus far it seems that experiences in virtual life mirror those in real life. Some people actually report forming closer and deeper relationships more easily and quickly in virtual worlds than in real life (Yee, 2007; Dooley, 2007).

Integration. As one of the least defined principles, integration is still evolving. For example, mobile technologies like cellular telephones integrate virtual worlds with the real world through audio, video, and text. Once again, some educators may find themselves bracing for the next wave as technologies merge to form new capabilities.

Developing instruction in most virtual worlds for children and youth (e.g., Dizzywood, Club Penguin) is much like integrating other technologies into classroom instruction. Once a teacher determines that the virtual world has relevant information and activities that meet specific curricular needs (e.g., skill or knowledge development, application, enhancement, or remediation), the teacher focuses attention on specific features that help students maximize their experience and achieve specific instructional goals. Teachers often feel comfortable in this role because the professional designers and managers of structured virtual worlds make the content and activities quite clear.

Some suggest that integrating virtual worlds with physical worlds will erode distinctions between the two and create new issues concerning identity, trust and reputation, social roles, rules, and interaction (Smart, Cascio, & Paffendorf, 2007). In essence, learners may become indistinguishable from teachers as learning communities become immersed and adapt to the integration of virtual and real worlds. The so-called classroom without walls may eventually become the classroom without boundaries that supports continuous learning on demand as we exchange skills for access, knowledge for acquisition, and experience for relationships.

Implementing the four instructional principles of immersion, interaction, identity, and integration in open-ended virtual worlds can be challenging and time consuming. Fortunately, there are many web and inworld resources that provide general guidelines and specific tools to help teachers be more productive. Most groups who host these resources recruit professional members with experience in simulation and game-based learning and invite educational institutions to participate in their organizations. Some of these resources provide a list of best practices for teaching and learning in virtual worlds and help sponsor conferences. The following section describes several key resources found in SL to assist educators in applying the four instructional principles for virtual-world development.

Instructional Resources

Among the largest developers in virtual worlds is the New Media Consortium (NMC), an international group of more than 250 colleges, universities, museums, corporations, and other learning-focused organizations dedicated to the exploration and use of new media and new technologies. In 2006, the NMC established a virtual campus in SL (pictured in Figure 17.6), which is chronicled by the *NMC Campus Observer blog*. The project's goal was to create an immersive 3-D environment in which higher education and museum professionals could interact, collaborate, and experiment, while exploring the boundaries of SL. The virtual campus provides prebuilt spaces for conducting research in social interaction that is supported by a variety of traditional media, including posters, slides, photographs, charts/graphs, videos, and web links (Johnson, 2009).

FIGURE 17.6 ▶ Located in Second Life, the New Media Consortium Virtual Campus provides space for researchers and students to conduct experiments in social interaction within virtual worlds.

Another major resource is SimTeach (www.simteach.com), which sponsors the Second Life for Educators (SLED) forum that shares research and web links for online communities through wikis and blogs. Their published guidelines contain frequently asked questions (FAQs) for getting started in virtual worlds, teaching and curriculum ideas, and technical details for participants. A list of schools, colleges and universities, professional organizations, libraries, and museums provides locations, lesson plans, best practices, and many other teaching resources. Many teachers find the most valuable and practical information about what works in the classroom are discussed in the teachers' lounge or other informal venues.

The International Society for Technology in Education (ISTE) created such a place at ISTE Island, where teachers can learn about SL at inworld socials and other special events, including their annual conference and exposition. ISTE's cadre of virtual volunteers offer greetings to newcomers, guided tours, information about best practices, opportunities to collaborate, and inworld broadcasts of interviews with leading experts (pictured in Figure 17.7). They host weekly networking socials and topical events, including a live television series broadcast (ISTE, 2009).

FIGURE 17.7 ▶ ISTE provides a venue for educators to network and learn from each other about real-life education opportunities and best practices in Second Life.

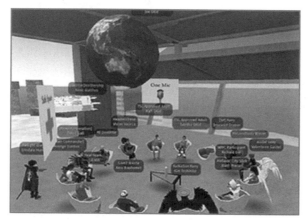

FIGURE 17.8 ▶ Global Kids sponsors global awareness events in Second Life. They provide handouts for teaching SL skills to students and teachers.

Another important resource, Global Kids, Inc. (pictured in Figure 17.8), recommends several simple ways for teachers to maximize their SL experience (Global Kids, 2007). First, teachers should link places and activities in regular, predictable locations. For example, always begin sessions in the same virtual location (e.g., classroom, clubhouse, gym, and auditorium) or consistently hold discussions on a scheduled arrangement. Just as teachers might have students do research or create presentations in the classroom, they can ask students to find and utilize the same resources (e.g., images, media, links, and podcasts) in SL. To bring real-world situations and problems into SL, teachers should use real-world artifacts (e.g., actual data, photographs, and video) to make learning more realistic and relevant.

Global Kids provides a Second Life curriculum that combines global literacy skills with SL strategies for students and teachers. Located at www.RezEd.org, the curriculum can be used to provide handouts that develop specific skills in SL, or to teach subjects such as science, filmmaking, or literature. The curriculum consists of nine sequential levels with modules containing 163 individual lesson plans described as missions. Teachers can adapt the materials for use in their classroom and share best practices with other professionals.

Engaging learners in virtual worlds opens pathways to a variety of unexpected social behaviors. This can be especially problematic when working with children and youth. Games have long been targeted among virtual reality products as a source for inappropriate behavior, so it comes as no surprise that social behaviors in virtual worlds are scrutinized under the same lens.

Social Behaviors

The ability to instantly communicate with millions by simply posting a message or interacting intimately with strangers in distant lands, or even right next door, has forever changed our view of the world and influenced our behavior. Until now, most social interactions on the web have been limited to text or perhaps video. Virtual worlds, however, provide us with opportunities to interact and communicate more intimately with others as anyone or anything we desire to be, and to do anything we want with few consequences. The freedoms that come with these kinds of social behavior can be both beneficial and damaging.

Unlike traditional games in which the developers establish rules of behavior and set limitations for interactions, the only limitation in open-ended virtual worlds is the imagination and skill of the residents. Although lack of structure and rules may lead to some improper behaviors, most residents appear courteous, open to conversation, and represent their real-life personas. Contrary to the many sensational tales describing disruptive behaviors in virtual worlds, most residents conform to real-life etiquette by regulating their behavior voluntarily, whether in response to peer pressure or from a fear of being ostracized from the community (Llewelyn, 2008).

Virtual worlds designed for children and youth often structure the environment to support appropriate social behaviors. For example, all of the avatars are penguins in Club Penguin, and Whyville limits avatar choices to floating heads. Club Penguin controls interactions with a safe chat feature, and Whyville uses language filters and reviews chat logs. Trained staff members monitor interactions, correct inappropriate behavior, and help residents find what they need.

Most virtual worlds provide report tools that users can use to notify managers about problems and encourage residents to be proactive in protecting themselves and setting boundaries for appropriate behavior. Although Teen Second Life provides a more open environment with fewer controls and limitations, it restricts membership to residents under the age of 18 to prevent adults from interacting with younger residents. Teachers and researchers can gain access to specific areas in Teen Second Life by submitting a request that includes a background check. Teens are warned when adults enter the area.

Of course, first impressions are just as important in virtual worlds as they are in real life. They frequently set the tone for the kinds of social behaviors that follow. Most residents in both adult and youth-oriented virtual worlds spend considerable time enhancing their appearance and behavior. An avatar is more often an expression of creativity and diversity than an accurate physical representation of the person. Although the majority of residents appear quite human, with many of the same features (e.g., eyeglasses, hair color, shape) found in the individuals they represent, participants tend to assume younger and shapelier physiques, possibly as a result of default settings that later become preferences. Some reports suggest that stereotyping may result from participants' practice of experimenting with identities by switching their avatar genders. In some cases, participants in virtual worlds may get to know people's real nature without judging their appearance first; the opposite is often true in real life.

Because virtual life provides a venue for the expression of both imagination and reality, some avatars imitate mythical creatures from legends, emulate modern cyber icons, or even switch genders. According to Winkler (2008), who interviewed a male resident posing as a female DJ, virtual worlds are full of creative avatars that depart from traditional roles of male and female, adult and child, and may even verge into the realm of creatures, animals, and cybernetics. Because it's possible to fly in some virtual worlds, avatars may actually have wings even though they are not needed to actually fly. As a result, some new residents' interactions and behavior may be influenced by their perceptions when encountering the strange shapes and behaviors of virtual-world creatures.

No matter how they appear, the vast majority of learners seem actively engaged in normal social behaviors and display the same personality traits and beliefs they possess in real life. They tend to explore, experiment, express, and validate the hidden complexities of their true selves, which are less subject to criticism and censure in virtual worlds. Some residents rely on anonymity and disguise to cloak their behavior and real identity. Although physical constraints such as body shape, gender, race, or age can have a profound effect on self-image and presentation in the real world (Collins & Kuczaj, 1991), these characteristics become interchangeable in virtual worlds. Anonymity in virtual environments may encourage exploring one's identity in the form of a self-constructed avatar (Huffaker & Calvert, 2005).

While some teachers allow students to assume unusual forms and multiple identities during instructional activities, many others set specific guidelines for avatars and prefer that they look the same throughout a course to promote recognition. Frequent changes of appearance during instructional activities may become distracting. To some extent, how students choose their appearance may have significant beneficial effects.

In fact, virtual worlds may function as a therapeutic tool for social behavior. Research indicates that those with few friends in real life actually feel happier in their virtual-world life (de Nood & Attema, 2006). Meeting in virtual space and interacting socially with others helps create a sense of community that keeps students engaged in learning. This seems especially true of international students. They overcome shyness during discourse and demonstrate less fear of speaking and interacting by channeling their feelings and ideas through the avatars. Students don't worry about dominating the discussion, interrupting others, or hesitating to respond when using the text chat feature (Lamont, 2007).

While social behavior varies in every virtual world, the development of effective social interactions and behavior is usually an explicit goal for virtual worlds developed for children and youth. For example, Global Kids encourages students to experiment with and learn from the development of their avatars through creative activities that include games, scavenger hunts, guest speakers, panel discussions, debates, role-plays, movie screenings, and presentations that are promoted on their social network in Teen Second Life. After developing scripts, sets, props, and costumes for their avatars, students capture animated videos, called "machinimas," to explore issues facing teens worldwide (Global Kids, 2007).

FIGURE 17.9 ▶ Dizzywood provides children with a safe learning environment that includes many activities and events.

Dizzywood (www.dizzywood.com) promotes good social behavior through encouraging collaborations among players to reach goals. Most activity takes place in the form of minigames and group events, such as growing a plant or tree, or finding a treasure in a rock pile. This requires students to learn how to communicate and work together cooperatively while developing their confidence. Dizzywood also holds virtual events (e.g., the Dizzywood elections) to provide opportunities for students to experience and see the results of practices that may often seem like abstractions (e.g., voter registration, campaigning). Players learn that their behavior inworld may have effects in the real world. For example, collaboration between Dizzywood and the Arbor Day Foundation resulted in the planting of trees in the real world after players planted virtual trees to rebuild a damaged forest in Dizzywood (pictured in Figure 17.9). Like Dizzywood, Club Penguin also provides a way for virtual-world residents to influence their real world by trading virtual coins for contributions to a philanthropic foundation.

Even though developing effective instruction that engages learners and fosters good social behavior seems feasible, many factors can derail such efforts. When implementing instruction in virtual worlds, we often face many of the same issues found in the real world. Gender bias, misperceptions, inappropriate behaviors, and loss of identity can become serious barriers when implementing virtual-world instruction. The next section identifies some of the complex issues that confront proponents of virtual worlds.

Implementation Issues

When it comes to implementing instruction in virtual worlds, accountability may be a prevailing issue, not only in terms of expense but also in ethics and social behavior. Like school principals who fear the consequences of a class field trip or unstructured use of the web, many educators feel it's safer to stay in the classroom and lock the doors. In reality, a virtual world is no more threatening than other activities that expose students to alternative venues; however, inappropriate behavior may not be as obvious or unavoidable as in the real world. Teachers can protect everyone by properly informing administrators and students about the activities and establishing procedures similar to methods that control access to the web. According to investigators, a strong interest in integrating these controls exists, but products still need development (Kemp & Livingstone, 2007).

Several issues remain about reliability, security, confidentiality, and exposure to inappropriate behaviors in virtual worlds, but no more so than what occurred during the introduction of the web into school systems. To mitigate these problems, schools often require students to sign agreements for the terms of service, but the responsibility for enforcement remains with the teacher. Some teachers make participation in virtual-world activities optional, especially for features that require expense, changing identities, and leaving secure areas. Before implementing virtual-world activities, teachers need to consider the effect of real-life issues in the virtual realm, and address concerns about the security and privacy of students.

Real Life

While many busy school teachers can't fathom the idea of taking on another set of commitments, especially imaginary ones, virtual worlds are quickly finding their way into the mainstream of education. With some 40 million people now involved worldwide, there is mounting concern that some participants are squandering, even damaging, their real lives by obsessing over their virtual ones. That's always been a concern with video games, but a field of study suggests that the boundary between virtual worlds and reality may be more porous than experts previously imagined (T. Atkinson, 2008c).

Nearly 40% of men and 53% of women who play online games said their relationships with virtual friends were equal to or better than those with their real-life friends (Yee, 2007). More than a quarter of gamers said the emotional highlight of the past week occurred in a virtual world. The study implies that the boundaries between the virtual world and the real world are becoming increasingly complicated. Researchers have only recently begun to study the social dynamics of virtual worlds. Some say they are astonished by how closely virtual relationships mirror real life (Dooley, 2007).

Teachers can help structure opportunities for students to safely explore different roles and situations and focus their observations in terms of the outcomes of their efforts. For example, a teacher could ask students to conduct an experiment in which they approach someone in the virtual world and stand at different distances from that individual. The teacher could have students predict what they think will occur and note their observations. Then, the teacher could ask students to compare their virtual experiences with those they have had in the real world.

"People respond to interactive technology on social and emotional levels much more than we ever thought," says Byron Reeves (quoted in Alter, 2007, "Weekends As 'Dutch'" section, para. 5), at Stanford University. "People feel bad when something bad happens to their avatar, and they feel quite good when something good happens." Just as teachers try to create positive learning experiences in real-life classrooms, they must also consider how to apply these techniques in virtual worlds. Because rules, morality, laws, and cultural imperatives may have no connection in virtual space to the constraints on a person in the real world, incentives and risks in virtual spaces may seem quite different than in real life. Mapping virtual-world incentives to those in the real world may be necessary to establish a connection with consequences and appropriate behaviors (Alter, 2007).

Even with incentives, neurological studies suggest students fully engaged in virtual worlds may have difficulty distinguishing between virtual and real-life situations. In a study (cited in Alter, 2007), subjects received fMRI scans as they played a simple computer game that moved colored discs to form a pattern. When told that they were playing with a person rather than a computer, participants showed increased activity in areas of the brain that govern social behavior. Since perception is reality, teachers must be aware of how they create academic realities and the perceptions they plan to invoke. This is another reason for teachers to be aware of the kinds of information and activities a virtual world contains: to prepare students appropriately for what they will experience. The younger the student, the more preparation is probably needed so that students are not surprised by the effects of virtual reality.

The issues that have emerged along with the popularity of virtual worlds are increasingly becoming global in scope. For example, Korea is facing significant social and economic problems because a large percentage of its population spends considerable time in virtual reality games. The Korean experience may foretell the future of other countries. Although many educators view virtual reality as an opportunity, the problems in Korea may suggest that teachers should integrate immersive experiences into real world education or risk losing learners' attention to far more compelling spaces in the virtual world (Castronova, 2005).

To further complicate the connection between real-life issues and the virtual world, many teachers, administrators, and parents feel threatened by the lack of controls present in virtual worlds, especially given that students in virtual space might reveal their identities (or those of others) or encounter harassing situations. With awareness as the first line of defense, teachers should be prepared to warn students about the perils awaiting them in virtual worlds.

Security

It is common perception that security in most virtual worlds is almost nonexistent. In fact, many of the virtual worlds prohibit the sharing of personal information or real-life locations beyond what appears in resident profiles; however, disclosing information without specific reference or making statements no reasonable person would believe (e.g., "Tom said, you're the greatest" or "Professor Tomsen is from Mars") are not considered violations.

As with most web applications, logon IDs and passwords protect access to accounts and specific areas in virtual worlds. The best advice for students is to avoid attachments or links and never give out personal information. Members are often tempted to share or accept virtual gifts from others, or to give information about their geographical locations. Unfortunately, gifts can contain program code that can spread malicious properties and cause malfunctions. And although revealing one's true identity in virtual classrooms is common and may seem unimportant, institutions often face legal consequences when student information is released to the public. In 2006, the real identities of nearly 650,000 members in Second Life were compromised when hackers gained access to computer servers at the Linden Lab headquarters.

Although most virtual worlds establish procedures for managing inworld construction and economy, they rely primarily on members to monitor and report disruptive or inappropriate behaviors. Like in real life, most behaviors are tolerated unless they are publicly displayed or illegal in the real world. When transgressions are verified, members are banned from specific areas or their logon IDs are terminated. However, it's often a simple process to rejoin under a new identity.

A persistent issue within virtual worlds is known as "griefing," which refers to harassment often perpetrated by inworld gangs. The marauders enter an area and mutate into obscene images to instigate a "grid attack" that leads to performance problems or disruption of service.

Acts such as harassing others, sharing their personal information, recording conversations, taking their picture, or simply eavesdropping without their knowledge or consent often violate policies in most educational settings. To avoid entanglement with these issues, participants usually post a clearly visible sign indicating their intent near certain activities (i.e., recording in progress). This practice may prevent researchers from secretly monitoring activities inworld but does not address the propriety of publishing or sharing such information and conversations in the real world, unless specific laws apply to the behavior (i.e., slander or personal identity information). Whatever the source or cause, inappropriate inworld behavior may discourage development and result in greater security, with residents virtually locked behind doors. When confronted with annoyances, most residents simply move to other locations. Unfortunately, that's not always possible during events or classes held at public venues, in which case the behavior is typically ignored or the person is pressured to leave. Most private areas like classrooms already require permission to enter the virtual space.

The proliferation of sensory and analysis tools that are either worn or embedded in the environment makes deception or abuse of others more difficult. Public misbehavior or duplicity becomes part of the public record, establishing a "mutually assured transparency" that is equivalent across social divisions, thus reducing the opportunities for abuses of power. Such transparency and reputation issues often occur in virtual communities where members experiment with social rules using anonymous identities. For some residents, gaining status, capabilities, and recognition that they cannot attain in the real world proves very alluring. Virtual worlds typically provide benefits based on skills, social networks, and personality, rather than on real-life achievements, reputation, or credentials.

For most virtual worlds, identity and age verification provides some security for students. However, this process may be ineffective in some cases, since requirements or enforcement is often weak and subject to inaccuracies. One possible solution is to privatize servers or rely on virtual worlds that allow the host to control membership and access. For example, Forterra offers the Online Interactive Virtual Environment, or OLIVE, which can be installed on private servers so a school can maintain full control of access and meet federal standards for protecting student identities. As an alternative to private servers, Teen Second Life (TSL) restricts access to learners under the age of 18 on public servers but provides limited access for researchers, teachers, or those who provide resources or services. Adult-owned spaces are isolated from the teen areas. With permission, teen residents can visit the adult areas in Teen Second Life but are automatically informed that there are adults present. Special permission can be obtained for students who become 18 and need to attend inworld activities during a school year.

So far, very few standards have been created to consistently address these issues among virtual worlds. However, businesses and institutions are working collaboratively to develop open standards for maintaining avatar security and ownership of digital assets when visiting multiple worlds. As interoperability and commercialization move into virtual worlds, the experimental and anonymous feel of social networks will likely diminish. Improved digital identity, reputation tracking, and real-world branding may convert the majority of virtual worlds into sites for the more mundane and restrictive varieties of relationships and identities.

Eventually, only the theme-based games and less popular social networks will remain havens for anonymous behavior and experimentation. As more institutions invest valuable resources to integrate curricula into virtual worlds, developers must ensure a safe, secure, and reliable environment for the future. The following section describes how some of these issues are being addressed.

Future Directions

As with most emerging technologies, virtual worlds may change before we can fully understand or adapt them for educational purposes. If the past provides a context for current applications, the rapid evolution of virtual worlds means that their future is not only significant but may actually form a critical part of the roadmap. This section describes recent developments in the management of learning in virtual worlds and two models that are redefining the virtual-world experience.

Learning Management

While many environments offer documented learning paths, social bookmarking, information repository, and class planning, most of these capabilities are still being developed for virtual worlds. SCORM-compliant formative and summative assessment tools that send data dynamically to learning-management systems would enable students to maintain their e-portfolios inworld.

FIGURE 17.10 ▶ Sloodle combines Moodle, an open source learning management system, and Second Life connectivity features to mirror online classrooms with inworld learning spaces and interactive objects.

As new applications add functionality for web users, mash-ups can expand virtual-world features. For example, Sloodle (pictured in Figure 17.10) combines Second Life and a web-based learning management system called Moodle to develop and share tools that support instruction in virtual worlds, making teaching easier. As a 2-D learning management system, Moodle is both open source and free to use, requiring only server space and some technical knowledge to install and administer. The software has been adopted by universities, schools, and commercial training companies worldwide. To create the Sloodle mash-up, a 2-D Moodle webpage links to a 3-D classroom in Second Life where tools (i.e., enrollment, registration, discussions, blogs, assignment drop-boxes, and quizzes) become interactive. Calendar information may be rendered as a wall display. Real Simple Syndication (RSS) feeds may appear as radios or teletype machines that automate transfer of instructional materials or recordings.

Some applications include objects for accessing blogs, chats, and quizzes. Most functions are available through the Sloodle heads-up display (HUD), which provides easy access to functions when worn by an avatar. Other tools are "rezzed" (created) when needed as 3-D objects that are accessible to all avatars. This means that the Sloodle environment becomes a classroom metaphor; in other words, teaching and learning tools are available to the class and to the students, but without the necessity of maintaining real-world classroom metaphors, and there are no limits caused by the 2-D interaction of Moodle (Kemp & Livingstone, 2007).

Emerging Models

A recent trend in computing services comes in the form of a "cloud." Cloud computing refers to the use of web-based services that are dynamically scalable to the needs of the user. For example, files could be stored on the web at a service called Box.Net instead of on a local drive. Many services have adopted the utility computing model (pay for what you use), others are billed on a subscription basis, and some are actually free (e.g., Google, Yahoo, Amazon). Cloud computing led to a proliferation of new applications on what is now referred to as Web 2.0, which can be described as a perceived second generation of web development and design intended to facilitate communication, secure information-sharing, interoperability, and collaboration. Web 2.0 concepts have led to the development and evolution of web-based communities, hosted services, and applications, such as social-networking sites, video-sharing sites, wikis, blogs, and folksonomies for classifying social tags (Haynie, 2009).

Collectively, Web 2.0 applications represent complex systems for managing multiple tasks. O'Driscoll (2008) refers to this collection as the iWeb, which consists of four vectors: immediate, intuitive, interactive, and immersive. He believes that as this 3-D, avatar-mediated space emerges, virtual worlds will combine these vectors into a singularity, a worldwide virtual platform that allows users to engage in what matters most to them.

The "immediate vector" identifies 2-D learning applications, sometimes referred to as flatland, that integrate with knowledge-sharing repositories where networked virtual spaces emerge. These spaces integrate synchronous sharing with asynchronous storage using products like SharePoint, Live Meeting, Blackboard, and Webex. The "intuitive vector" combines Web 2.0 technologies (blogs, wikis, podcasts, etc.) and social media sites like Facebook and MySpace that use tags to access information and interact with others about specific activities. Certainly, access is no panacea. For much of the world, the problem isn't the lack of information, but the inability to find the right information. Filters, metadata, tags, and search systems may be the most important infrastructure technology for virtual environments.

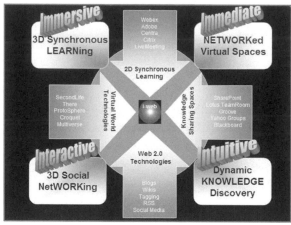

FIGURE 17.11 ▶ Diagram of iWeb singularity. (http://wadatripp.wordpress.com/2008/04/04/the-i-Web-singularity-redux)

As the web enters the next dimension, most of the social networking sites like Facebook and MySpace will replace web pages with web spaces to form O'Driscoll's "interactive vector." Likewise, in the "immersive vector," synchronous 2-D learning platforms will become 3-D as distance-learning systems like Webex, Centra, and Live Meeting integrate with virtual spaces, as illustrated in Figure 17.11.

As virtual worlds mature, many will merge with other instructional systems to boost productivity and usefulness. While some call this merged environment "the web 3-D," others refer to it as a "Metaverse" that combines an enhanced physical reality with a physically persistent virtual space. No single entity represents the Metaverse—rather, there are many ways in which virtualization of web 3-D tools and objects are embedded everywhere in the environment as persistent features in real life (Smart, Cascio, & Paffendorf, 2007). For example, medical training and monitoring devices may rely extensively on simulating activities and communicating patient data in hospitals, schools, and homes.

Although the World Wide Web is defined by a specific set of protocols and online applications, the term has become synonymous with being online. The idea of the Metaverse may play a similar role by referring to a particular set of technologies and how we redefine the online experience. Many instructional developers recognize the complexity and cost of using game-design techniques for instructional activities. As the Metaverse evolves, virtual worlds will offer sophisticated design spaces for rapid-prototyping of learning activities with built-in communication features that may, or may not, take the form of a game (T. Atkinson, 2009).

Early models identify at least four scenarios that define overlapping boundaries of the Metaverse: virtual worlds, mirror worlds, augmented reality, and lifelogging. Each scenario emphasizes different functions, types, or various technologies and applications placed on a continuum ranging from augmentation to simulation and intimate to externally focused, as depicted in Figure 17.12.

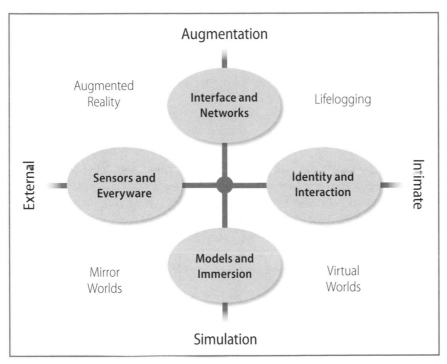

FIGURE 17.12 ▶ Components of the Metaverse (www.Metaverseroadmap.org/overview/03.html)

As predicted by proponents of the Metaverse model, the convergence of virtual worlds with physical world communities has created issues of identity, trust and reputation, social roles, rules, and interaction (Smart, Cascio, & Paffendorf, 2007). Sensors, networked devices, and intelligent materials link the mirror worlds and augmented reality components. Both depend on the deployment of multiple systems to monitor and influence properties of the physical world distinguished by the interface used to access data. While mirror worlds serve large-system monitoring and control, augmented reality systems function as mediators of personal interaction and point control, such as integration of mobile technologies like cellular telephones.

Lifelogging supported by augmented reality might function as an interface for experiencing an enhanced awareness of one's physical and social environment with sufficient network capacity to support continuous personal use. The most effective methods will likely include unobtrusive wearable or embedded devices with networked processing of tasks that support a consistent digital identity for seamless interaction between virtual and real environments. Development of a secure infrastructure across multiple platforms that identify personal attributes and connectivity will become more critical as the classroom expands to global proportions.

Future augmented reality and mirror worlds could offer context-aware versions of Google or Wikipedia available simply at a glance, while lifelogging and virtual worlds, being more intrinsically personal, could offer a more detailed understanding of one's own life and relationships. As systems expand to biographies, revealing personal trajectories and intimate glimpses into the lives and behaviors of ordinary individuals, organizations, and locations around the world, we may run the risk of building overly subjective appraisals of the world, relying too heavily on individual observations and insufficiently on considered, detached analysis (Smart, Cascio, & Paffendorf, 2007). In our concern to avoid becoming an Orwellian society that fears Big Brother, we may soon discover that everyone possesses the ability to access the information shadows of the Metaverse.

Conclusion

Various forms of multiplayer games, immersive environments, and social networks have existed for decades. The convergence of interactive entertainment, architectural concepts, instructional strategies, and web-design principles driven by brain-based research will become prominent in determining the effectiveness of virtual worlds. More recently, developments in large-group remote interaction, identity creation, and object design, particularly with regard to persistent qualities, should lay the groundwork for even more advanced interfaces and capabilities. Simulation of real world and augmented virtual realities requires a functional array of sensor technologies distributed widely and densely enough to provide both useful information and meaningful context. Power sources, networking protocols, and universal access for interoperability while maintaining proprietary control remain as unanswered questions.

Acceptance of virtual worlds requires a suspension of disbelief and a willingness to engage with 3-D information using a 2-D interface. While this may seem viable for certain types of work and entertainment, it's unclear whether such environments offer a sufficiently immersive experience to trigger the necessary economic and social changes that would make virtual worlds a clear choice for instructional systems. Since the only exposure to virtual worlds for the mainstream public may be an episode of *CSI* on television, students and especially teachers may be faced with defining boundaries for their existence in both virtual and real worlds until they merge into a cohesive Metaverse.

References

Alter, A. (2007, August 10). Is this man cheating on his wife? *The Wall Street Journal.* Retrieved from http://online.wsj.com

Atkinson, T. (2008a). Second Life for educators: Inside Linden Lab. *Springer Boston: TechTrends, 52*(2), 18–21.

Atkinson, T. (2008b). Second Life for educators: Inside Linden Lab. *Springer Boston: TechTrends, 52*(3), 16–18.

Atkinson, T. (2008c). Second Life for educators: Myths and realities. *Springer Boston: TechTrends, 52*(5), 26–29.

Atkinson, T. (2009). Virtual worlds at AECT 2008. *Springer Boston: TechTrends, 53*(1), 29–35.

Atkinson, T., Atkinson, R. H., & Smith, D. (2002). GOALS (Graduate online active learning strategies). *Journal of Computing Sciences in Colleges, 17*(3), 251–64.

Au, J. W. (2008, January 17). Second life events: Rik's picks for January 17–20 [Blog post]. Retrieved from http://nwn.blogs.com/nwn/2008/01/second-life-e-2.html

Bennett, J., & Peachey, A. (2007). Mashing the MUVE: A mashup model for collaborative learning in multi-user virtual environments. *Proceedings of the International Conference of Interactive Computer Aided Learning ICL2007: EPortofolio and Quality in e-Learning, September 26–28, 2007, Villach, Austria.*

Blaisdell, M. (2006, September 1). Educational gaming: All the right MUVEs. *T.H.E. Journal.* Retrieved from www.thejournal.com/articles/19173

Calvert, S. L. (2002). Identity construction on the Internet. In S. L. Calvert, A. B. Jordan, & R. R. Cocking (Eds.), *Children in the digital age: Influences of electronic media on development* (pp. 57–70). Westport, CT: Praeger.

Castronova, E. (2005). *Synthetic worlds: The business and culture of online games.* Chicago, IL: University of Chicago Press.

Collins, W. A., & Kuczaj, S. A. (1991). *Developmental psychology: Childhood and adolescence.* New York, NY: MacMillan.

Dawly, L. (2007). *Persistent social learning: An emergent ID model for virtual world design.* Symposium conducted online at http://breeze/boisestate.edu/persistence, November 2007.

Dede, C. (1995). The evolution of constructivist learning environments: Immersion in distributed, virtual worlds. *Educational Technology 35*(5), 46–52.

Dede, C., Clarke, J., Ketelhut, D. J., Nelson, B., & Bowman, C. V. (2005). *Fostering motivation, learning, and transfer in multi-user virtual environments.* Paper presented at the American Educational Research Association Conference, Montreal, Canada.

de Nood, D., & Attema, J. (2006). SL: The SL of virtual reality. *The Hague, EPN-Electronic Highway Platform, 1.* Retrieved from www.epn.net/interrealiteit/PN-REPORT-The_Second_Life_of_VR.pdf

Dooley, R. (2007). The neuroscience of Second Life [Blog post]. Retrieved from www.neurosciencemarketing.com/blog/articles/second-life-neuroscience.htm

Driscoll, M. P. (2005). *Psychology of learning for instruction* (3rd ed.). Boston, MA: Pearson Allyn & Bacon.

Gintis, H. (2005). *Moral sentiments and material interests: The foundations of cooperation in economic life* (4th ed.). Cambridge, MA: MIT Press.

Global Kids (2007). *Best practices in using virtual worlds for education.* Retrieved from http://olpglobalkids.org/pdfs/BestPractices.pdf

Haynie, Mark (2009). *Enterprise cloud services: Deriving business value from loud computing.* Micro Focus [White Paper]. Retrieved from http://cloudservices.microfocus.com/main/Namespaces/ MFECS/doc/MFECS-WP-deriving-business-value.pdf

Huffaker, D. A., & Calvert, S. L. (2005). Gender, identity, and language use in teenage blogs. *Journal of Computer-Mediated Communication, 10*(2), article 1. Retrieved from http://jcmc.indiana.edu/vol10/issue2/huffaker.html

ISTE (2009). *ISTE in Second Life.* Retrieved from www.iste.org/Content/NavigationMenu/ Membership/Member_Networking/ISTE_Second_Life.htm

Johnson, L. (2009). *About* [New Media Consortium]. Retrieved from http://sl.nmc.org/about/

Kemp, J., & Livingstone, D. (2007). *Putting a Second Life "metaverse" skin on learning management systems.* Sloodle [White Paper]. Retrieved from www.sloodle.com/whitepaper.pdf

Lamont, I. (2007, May 21). Harvard's virtual education experiment in Second Life [Blog post]. Retrieved from http://blogs.computerworld.com/node/5553

Levine, J. (2006, June 8). Second Life Library 20 [Blog post]. Retrieved from www.theshiftedlibrarian. com/archives/2006/06/08/second_life_library_20.html

Linden Lab. (2008). What is Second Life? Retrieved from http://secondlife.com/whatis/

Linden, Z. (2007). State of the virtual world—key metrics, January 2007 [Blog post containing link to the document Second Life Stats_200703.xls]. Retrieved from https://blogs.secondlife.com/ community/features/blog/2007/02/09/state-of-the-virtual-world-key-metrics-january-2007

Llewelyn, G. (2008, February 15). Sex, lies and reality. Retrieved July 25, 2008, from http://gwynethllewelyn.net/2008/02/15/sex-lies-and-reality/

Nielsen, J. (1994). Heuristic evaluation. In J. Nielsen and R. L. Mack (Eds.), *Usability inspection methods* (pp. 25-64). New York, NY: John Wiley & Sons.

Nino, T. (2008, January 1). Peering inside—looking back at 2007. Massively. Retrieved from www.massively.com/2008/01/01/peering-inside-looking-back-at-2007

O'Driscoll, T. (2008, April 4). The iWeb singularity redux [Blog post]. Retrieved from http://wadatripp.wordpress.com/2008/04/04/the-i-Web-singularity-redux

Prensky, M. (2006). *Don't bother me Mom—I'm learning.* St. Paul, MN: Paragon House.

Project ScienceSpace. (2008). *ScienceSpace's immersive virtual worlds.* Retrieved from www.virtual.gmu.edu/ss_worlds

Sanchez, J. (2007, November 5). Breaking the Second Life high learning curve [Blog post]. Retrieved from http://connect.educause.edu/blog/joesanchez/breakingthesecondlifehigh/ 45469?time=1216855830

Smart, J., Cascio, J., & Paffendorf, J., (2007). *Metaverse roadmap overview.* Retrieved from www.metaverseroadmap.org/overview/index.html

Steuer, J. (1992) Defining virtual reality: Dimensions determining telepresence. *Journal of Communication, 42*(4), 73–93.

Topher, C. (2008, February 16). Investigating the learning power of Second Life, February 16, 2008 [Blog post]. Retrieved from http://muveforward.blogspot.com/2008/02/investigating-learning-power-of-second.html

Winkler, F. (2008). Female Reflection of a Male DJ [Blog post]. Retrieved from http://dtpsl.wordpress.com/2008/03/12/female-reflection-of-a-male-dj/

Yee, N. (2007). Motivations of Play in Online Games. *Cyber Psychology and Behavior, 9,* 772–75.

Virtual-World Project

This sample project can be incorporated into classroom activities and adapted for grade level by changing the complexity of the tasks.

VIRTUAL-WORLD PROJECT ASSIGNMENT

Requirements

In this assignment you will work on a team to design and develop instruction for a virtual-world environment. The project should teach a topic that takes advantage of the features of the virtual world and address the following:

Teach something other than the mechanics of the virtual world set in the real world.

From a constructivist perspective, develop instruction that includes avatar appearance, object construction, buildings and furniture, participation among distant players, or scripted objects and behaviors.

Address educational benefits that outweigh the cognitive load required for participants to learn to use the SL interface. In other words, keep it simple!

Your design should be scalable but only develop one activity.

Project Types

Recommended project types include, but are not limited to, the following:

Role-play Simulations. Role-play has been an integral part of the learning process for decades. Simulate an existing role beyond what's possible in a face-to-face situation without losing the qualities of immediacy and emotional impact of face-to-face interactions.

Interactive Exhibits. Create a virtual exhibit that supports learner interaction beyond a simple web page with interaction based in Flash. Consider avatar-to-avatar interaction as part of the design.

Language Practice. To bring together language learners with native speakers of the target language, design an environment that allows interaction and feedback between learners as they practice speaking, listening, reading, and writing. Your design should include an environment stocked with topics to discuss.

WebQuests. Using an existing WebQuest, create a simulation for implementing it in the MUVE.

Historical Re-creations. Create an environment in which participants experience a different time and place. Include interactions, buildings, and clothing that simulate the period.

Documentation

Create a PowerPoint presentation to illustrate the following information:

- Project title
- Educational objectives
- Design and development time required
- A brief description of similar virtual worlds already in existence

Provide learner analysis with attributes.

Describe the rules, roles, props, and other digital assets.

Identify the design principles of motivation, emotion, and so forth and describe how they apply.

Provide captured images as a representative sampling of the project.

Optional: Create a machinima as a trailer for the project.

Virtual-World Activity Rubric

This sample rubric provides a structure for implementing virtual-world activities within a course of instruction. It is divided into sections for adapting to different skill levels—1, 2, and 3.

	LEVEL 1 *(5 points each)*	LEVEL 2 *(5 points each)*	LEVEL 3 *(5 points each)*
Beginning Activities	Read about a minimum of three VWs and provide a written description of each. Create an avatar. Locate inworld orientation activities. Identify navigation features. List your objects.	Construct a Venn diagram to compare and contrast general features of at least three VWs. Create an avatar and change at least three features. Complete VW orientation activities. Explain how navigation features work in your VW. Identify three avatar or object animations.	Complete a Venn diagram to compare and contrast instruction in at least three VWs in terms of relevance and preference. Create an avatar and change at least five features. Provide rationale for modifications. Complete VW orientation activities and explore environment. Demonstrate navigation features. Create an object.
Intermediate Activities	Provide a transcript of a chat with another avatar you met inworld. Find at least half the items in the scavenger hunt. Find a list of presentations or panel discussions. List the locations visited in the VW. Exchange three objects.	Provide a transcript and describe three avatars you met inworld. Find all items in the scavenger hunt. Attend a presentation or panel discussion. Locate and describe an instructional activity. Wear an animated object.	Collaborate with another avatar to create a role-play scenario. Create a scavenger hunt. Give a presentation or participate in a panel discussion. Develop an inworld instructional activity. Create an avatar animation.
Final Activity **Total = 100**	Take a test over VW concepts. *(50 points)*	Write a paper about your VW experience. *(50 points)*	Create a machinima of your VW activity. *(50 points)*

(Rubric created by R. H. Atkinson)

18

Educational Gaming: Where Is the Industry Going?

Matthew Laurence

COMBINING THE FIELDS OF GAMING and education is a concept that bristles with potential, yet attempts to do so have met with a tepid response, at best. Where are the games that teach? This chapter examines the shared history of gaming and education and attempts to answer the question of where their joint future lies. The inadequacies of "edutainment" and the misapplications of the simulation industry are detailed as part of an explanation for why educational games have yet to truly catch on. By reviewing trends in gaming and Internet education, an intriguing link is discovered, and the possibilities for their intersection beyond the boundaries of the classroom are examined. This chapter concludes by positing that the future of games rests not within the walls of our brick and mortar institutions but in the Internet at large, where a vast educational revolution is already underway. Games that teach fully accredited courses are coming, and their early adopters will be virtual schools and the digital natives that swell their ranks.

Where'd the future go? Wasn't it supposed to be jetpacks and lunar colonies ... or at least sentient computers and robot servants? Nowadays, most people aren't expecting those wonders to make an appearance in their lifetimes, and expectations for the future vary widely, ranging from the woefully bleak to the unbelievably optimistic. So just where *are* we heading, and when can we expect to arrive? Well, in a way, we're already there—and the new millennium has more potential than you might think. True, we haven't yet set a human footprint on Mars, but we've got portable gadgets that can play feature films, locate our homes by satellite, and call our friends. We dreamt big, but ended up getting really, *really* small.

Discussing *all* of our future technologies is, of course, beyond the scope of this chapter. Instead, I'm going to focus on the future of video games and education—how and in what ways these two disparate industries are converging, and what that means. However, all of the futuristic sci-fi chatter is not without a point; the joint future of entertainment and education has a great deal to do with the emerging technologies of the Information Age.

Before we get into that, there are a few things to discuss. First, try to rid yourself of preconceptions you may have concerning the term "video games." Applied to an industry at large, the term occupies a somewhat negative brain space—for many, it may imply frivolity, lack of structure, and general societal worthlessness.

Instead, I encourage you to think of video games as a form of "interactive entertainment"—an active technological change across a broad spectrum that can be integrated into the same brain space as education, training, medicine, and other more "acceptable" social institutions. Nobody will listen to you if you pitch a "video game that teaches open-heart surgery," but if you tell them that you're "combining interactive entertainment with the latest medical advances to create an open-heart surgical training simulation," you're in business. As mentioned by Hirumi in the introduction to this book, video games in and of themselves are viewed as a technology with a limited life span. The concepts behind interactive entertainment are thought to be what's truly important, and will transcend time.

Finally, it is important to note that our approach to examining the industries of interactive entertainment and education will be integrative, not all-inclusive. Both of these fields are simply enormous. In the former alone, a detailed analysis of its broad spectrum of platforms, content delivery formats, gameplay genres, and markets would fill far more than a single book—let alone a chapter. As such, when discussing these two important fields, I will focus primarily on their convergence: basically, how interactive entertainment has been—and will be—influenced by education, and vice versa.

There has been a great deal of interplay between entertainment and education in the past, and I hope to make it clear that their continued convergence is not only inevitable, but already well underway. The future—at least in terms of these two important industries—is a lot closer than you think.

A Brief Look at Where We've Been

To understand our future (and present), we need to have a clear picture of the past. For the video game industry, the past wasn't all that long ago. A relatively young field, it has penetrated an incredible array of markets in a brief time, to an extent greater than that of many entertainment media. For instance, at the time of this writing, the largest entertainment launch in history no longer belongs to a movie, television show, book, or musician—rather, it is for the video game Grand Theft Auto IV, which earned $310 million in its first 24 hours of release and more than $500 million in the first week. This beat out the previous record holder, the film *Pirates of the Caribbean: At World's End*, which had held the all-time entertainment launch record after grossing $404 million in six days (Offner, 2008). Of course, this is relevant only in an economic sense—the number of *people* who go to movies is still far greater, as a video game costs about six times as much as a movie ticket, on average.

So why is this bit of trivia interesting? Because when considering the disparate histories of film and gaming, the time frames of these achievements are starkly different. What filmmaking as an industry has achieved in 120 years, video games have surpassed—at least economically—in 50. Even more intriguing is that the "Golden Age of Hollywood"—a period of impressive growth in terms of genre exploration, technology, quality, and creativity covering a period of time from approximately 1930 to 1948—occurred approximately 50 years into the existence of the medium. Fifty years just happens to be the current age of the gaming industry.

It may seem as if I'm getting far afield with these comparisons between video games and films, but things become a little clearer once you bring education into the picture: education has always tried to take advantage of emerging media and technologies to support the goals of learning. When movies began to overcome their primary technical limitations (in terms of sound, color, cameras, and so on), broaden their reach, and gain societal acceptance on a grand scale, educators were quick to adopt the technology. Is it truly surprising that, concurrent with the Golden Age of the movie industry, educational films began to appear and audiovisual resources started playing an ever-greater role in the classroom?

Basically, what I'm trying to say is this: there is a strong precedent for educators making use of popular, socially accepted forms of entertainment and reverse-engineering them for the purpose of teaching their students, and video games are the next logical step in this cycle.

So just where *are* our educational games? Right now, students are playing games that let them do … well … pretty much *anything*, for good or ill. Why aren't they playing games that teach them a course in college? To understand why, we need to delve into the misbegotten field of … *edutainment*.

The catch here is that educators have already *tried* using games to bolster education, just as they did with video. For the past 15–20 years, computers have sat in the backs of classrooms, gathering dust, loaded with Carmen Sandiego, Oregon Trail, and similar edutainment titles. Why do games like these often fail to find lasting acceptance among educators and students alike? The problem is that the stance taken toward edutainment was similar to the stance taken with classroom use of film and video, which appears to be the reason why they failed.

In comparison to games, videos are easy to create—ridiculously easy. Once all the pieces are in place, a single episode of *Bill Nye the Science Guy* teaching the basics of outer space can take a handful of weeks to produce. A video game that teaches the same topic, on the other hand, can take upwards of one to two *years* to create. It *can*, however, teach the topic much more thoroughly than any single half-hour program. Games, you see, are *deep* but not *broad*, making them difficult to incorporate into a classroom lesson plan. Who's going to budget 15 hours of gameplay for each of their students on a *single topic* when they can just as easily teach it themselves in a few hours and maybe spend 26 minutes showing a relevant *Bill Nye* episode to seal the deal?

The depth of games (coupled with their development costs) is one of the reasons why edutainment has corroded, and why no better forms of gaming have appeared in the classroom—simply put, games *don't belong there*. It's the wrong format—the business model in terms of time invested, student learning, and tangible results is completely off. This isn't to say that edutainment developers haven't attempted to correct the issue, but their solution actually just made matters worse. They recognized the problem as one of scalability; a game that teaches third graders about space is worthless beyond that narrow scope, and easily replaced by a dedicated teacher. So they made their edutainment titles into templates—nearly identical software packages scaled to apply to multiple grade levels and subjects with only minor differences (those being primarily in terms of educational content, not actual gameplay or graphical assets), and bundled them into value-priced "suites" of products.

The side effect of the templated approach, however, is that any given portion of one of these scalable titles was undeniably … *cheap*. Taken on its own, one edutainment "course" simply didn't engage students or impress educators, and it certainly didn't convince anyone that it was a viable replacement for standardized schooling. In effect, these attempts to salvage edutainment actually alienated most people from the field. Gamers certainly view edutainment with derision, and if these are the people we're trying to engage, then that's a bad place to be.

So that's where things stand—and have stood for a surprisingly long time, considering the overarching pace of technological change. Games and education, separated by the very nature of the environment in which learning tends to take place. "But wait!" you may say. "What about simulations? NASA, the Armed Forces, medical organizations, and all sorts of other big, important institutions use simulations all the time! We can teach all sorts of things with simulations—why can't we teach our students, too? After all, I hear they're getting to be *really* advanced."

And they are. Simulations are doing an extremely impressive job of immersing professionals in real-world situations with little to no risk … but they're not exactly the solution to our problem. Simulations aren't made to teach students; the fundamental assumption behind them is that their users either *want* or *have* to use them, with no alternatives. "Serious business," if you will. Additionally, simulations *train* skills and abilities. Rote behavior, basic actions with simple variations, and the testing of knowledge retention are at the heart of simulation. Now, this focus on training *isn't* a bad thing (rather, it works quite well for the diverse fields that employ simulators), but when you consider using simulations as a blueprint for designing educational games for students, you betray a misunderstanding of the basic nature of simulation. Simulations reinforce: they grant experience, strengthen practical skills, and provide real-world training through an artificial environment.

They don't, strictly speaking, teach. Now, I'm not trying to bash simulations—my point here is that while they represent a *very* capable means of training practical skills in many professions and industries, they are not the future of education. Their design strategies should not be seen as the first steps down the path to an alternative means of educating our students. The essential aspect of *engagement* is something deeply interwoven into the methods behind interactive entertainment, and while edutainment may have failed, video games still have the potential to teach. It's all in how you approach it.

The Future of … Everything?

Let's set our sights forward a bit and get down to the meat of things. Up until now, we've been operating under somewhat contradictory assumptions. I keep saying, "Games can educate!" while providing examples of just how badly they've failed at this goal. In particular, I've tried to make it abundantly clear that they don't fit into a traditional curriculum—that trying to cram them into the classroom is an exercise in futility.

Well, I firmly believe that this is still true. However, I also feel that games truly can be a source of learning. How does one come to grips with such disparate viewpoints? Simple! Remove the classroom, substitute the game. *This* is where our industries are headed: games that teach entire courses on their own. It's not just wild speculation on my part, either—rather, it's practically inevitable.

Change is coming, and *fast*. On the fringes of education, this is obvious—you can point to online courses, universities, and degrees, as well as flashy educational animations, programs, and teacher dashboards as agents of that change. The fact that most students still go to physical schools should not color your perceptions. The pace of technology has already begun to influence education, and this effect will inevitably increase.

Now, there are a number of data points we need to traverse in quick succession if we are to support this "inevitability" statement, not to mention tie everything back into interactive entertainment:

▶   When adjusted for inflation, the per capita cost of traditional education has increased by 56.3% in the past 20 years, while performance has "improved only slightly" (LeFevre, 2008).

▶   As the number of students taught increases, the cost-effectiveness of online learning improves. Conversely, the cost of traditional education remains static (Bartley & Golek, 2004).

▶   The cost of computing power has been decreasing steadily in accordance with Moore's Law: a predicted doubling every two years of the number of transistors that can be inexpensively placed on integrated circuits (Moore, 1995).

▶   Distance-learning degrees are increasingly rated to be "as good as" a residential option—gaining up to 90% approval when the name of the institution is immediately recognizable to the employer (Philips, 2008).

▶ There are now online alternatives for elementary, secondary, undergraduate, and graduate school.

▶ The growth of online enrollment has been steadily increasing for years now, to the point where students taking at least one online course now represent almost 20 percent of *total* enrollments in higher education—almost 3.5 *million* students (Allen & Seaman, 2007).

Here is where gaming and education will meet, and where the future lies: not in the classroom, but on the Internet. Online learning isn't going away—in fact, it's steadily growing, and one of the many reasons for this is its cost-effectiveness. Simply put, ensuring that students have a seat in a virtual classroom is far less expensive than surrounding them with brick and mortar, especially when the initial startup costs are out of the way (Bartley & Golek, 2004). At the same time, remember that games are deep but not broad—they can cover one concept very well, but they run into trouble when trying to perform cursory reinforcement of a topic. As such, they are most cost-effective when dedicated to the presentation of a large subject, rather than merely strengthening certain elements of one.

Combine these two conclusions for cost-effective education and gaming, and what do we get? Games that teach fully accredited online courses, with teachers grading behind the scenes. "Edutainment," such as it is, *can't* be done correctly—not if you want to satisfy students and educators alike. It's really an all-or-nothing proposition when it comes to educational gaming, and attempting to compromise by making games that merely *reinforce* coursework will never engender widespread acceptance. Games *can* teach, but they have to be given the opportunity to do so … and the online market is the perfect place for that to happen. Granted, entertainment and "engagement" are extremely subjective concepts, so simply saying that the market is ready for the arrival of course-based gaming doesn't go far toward answering qualitative concerns. I'm not saying that every student will want to learn via this method, nor am I saying that all of these games will be excellent simply because "the time is right."

There will be poorly done attempts, and there will be polished ones—just as with any other creative medium. Inevitably, we will see atrocious games that neither teach nor entertain, just as we will see stellar masterpieces that engage students and get the material across smoothly and efficiently. My primary point has nothing to do with any of these subjective nuances. Rather, it is simply that the place where interactive entertainment and education will truly meet is in online courses.

Think about it—engagement and education, wrapped together in worlds as polished and immersive as anything a professional game developer can create. Assuming that it is created with the assistance of educators to magnify their efforts in the virtual world, software will be able to allow teachers to monitor student progress and grade/assign coursework invisibly through the game's interface.

The full implications don't end there, however—if technology has managed to permeate just about every facet of our lives, then where does that leave us when considering online education and course-based games? The merger of education and entertainment will pull the possibilities for learning outside the classroom and into our basic day-to-day lives. Brick and mortar will give way to fiber optics and social networking, and the transition is already underway. The full scope of this online expansion is simply not considered very often, primarily because all of these disparate pieces have yet to be integrated. Consider this, however: if you can reach the Internet and you can enjoy interactive entertainment anywhere and from just about any source, then shouldn't you be able to teach a classroom of students anywhere, too?

Now, don't reach for the pitchforks and tar just yet—I'm not trying to say this approach will be *better* than traditional schooling … merely that it will be available and pervasive, judging by the increasing popularity of online education and video games as an entertainment medium. The argument as to whether or not this change will lock our children indoors and turn the coming generation into sedentary hermits is not conclusive, though I will hasten to point out that the rise of gaming hasn't yet imperiled society in such a way.

Finally, these predictions are all well and good, but they don't directly address the human element. To be quite specific, they don't mention you, or the part you need to play in all this. This is no time to be passive: just because I say these things are inevitable doesn't mean we shouldn't help guide them along. The time to focus on shaping the entertainment–education merger is here and now. Sitting down and letting things happen means trusting that the emerging standard will be an effective teaching tool, and that kind of trust can be extremely dangerous. You can choose to hang back and watch it unfold, attempt to fight it with all your might, or take charge and help it integrate smoothly and efficiently. The thing is, it's going to happen—like it or not—but the possible benefits to be gleaned from it will be far greater (and arrive sooner!) if people choose a helpful and proactive stance.

Simply put, there are two sides to the equation, and both are equally important. Game-based courses can't be successful without the help of dedicated game developers *and* educators. We need designers who understand how to make games entertaining and engaging just as much as we need teachers who understand effective pedagogical techniques and how to structure and create courses. The future *is* here and now … as long as we are committed to attaining the level of cooperation and acceptance needed to make it happen.

Everybody's Got Issues

So where does this leave us? There certainly isn't a great proliferation of games that teach entire online courses right now. We barely have any—at least not ones that teach in an accredited and official capacity—so it's natural to be skeptical about their capability to fulfill the grand vision of the future I described earlier. This situation is probably compounded by a few key factors, a few of which I've already touched on. Here, then, is a laundry list of likely objections to this scenario, along with some additional counterpoints, clarifications, and advice for potential developers.

Game Developers Aren't Educators!

This is a subtle yet vastly important consideration—more often than not, the people who create games don't know how to teach students. It's just not a standard part of the development skill set, and as a result, educational gaming titles tend to either pay lip service to the pedagogical standards they're attempting to utilize (if any), or companies find an available educational approach *after* primary game design and development are complete and try to apply it retroactively so they can say they used *something*.

Note that the reverse is just as true—the considerations of educators in designing even something as high tech and interactive as an online course are far removed from the mindset of interactive entertainment. Simply put, neither group knows how to accomplish or duplicate the goals and abilities of the other (Hirumi & Stapleton, in press). This is a major concern for a future where games teach courses, and one of the key routes by which it could be derailed. Thankfully, it also has a clear and simple solution—when making a game that teaches, you need to make utterly and completely certain that you include the input and advice of both game developers and professional educators (Hirumi & Stapleton, 2008; Hirumi & Stapleton, in press).

Games Are Disliked By a LOT of People

And that's putting it mildly. No matter how often you ask someone to conjure up benign images of Mario, Pikachu, and terms like "interactive entertainment," they'll always have an image in the back of their heads of a digital hoodlum beating a prostitute to death with a golf club, and somebody's kid—maybe even their own—at the controls. As such, the video game industry has had a pall over its head for years now, and, well … that's to be expected. Games are still a very young form of entertainment, they're hard to understand if you're not "into" them, and they're very popular with our children. As such, they fall firmly into the "scary and new" category of diversions.

This means that while games may be vilified like crazy … that hatred isn't crazy at all. It's simple social psychology, and games are going to be assimilated soon enough, just like talking pictures, television, and rock 'n' roll. We can accept that a given movie might show terrible things and be unsafe for children *without* tarnishing the film industry as a whole, but *that was not always the case*. Every generation has had trouble understanding the cultural ideals and foci of its progeny. As an example, here is a surprisingly relevant excerpt from a recent report on attracting teens to libraries, describing how views on accomplishing this have changed over the years:

> [Margaret] Edwards expressed disapproval, however, of one NYPL branch where the librarians [in the mid-1930s] had enticed "juvenile delinquents" into the library with chess and board games. "This was the one activity I observed that I could not accept," she said. (Levine, 2008)

Oh, those hooligans and their board games. This is merely one example of the endlessly mutable cycle of cultural mores, and on that wheel of approval and dislike, video games are shifting through the paces of the latter category. This means that they will become an accepted part of our social entertainment tapestry in good time, and that we should be ready for this mass-scale shift in public opinion. Above all else, we should *not* let it cloud our judgment concerning how games and education can be combined.

Course-Based Games Are Untested

This is a big one. How can I safely say that games truly provide accredited coursework to students when we've never seen a single example of one doing so? Well, there are several defenses that can help support my claim. First, games as a whole aren't truly "untested." *Accredited coursework* through gameplay certainly hasn't been developed, but there is a wealth of research concerning the capacity for games to teach skills and improve performance. Studies and meta-analyses "have consistently found that games promote learning and/or reduce instructional time across multiple disciplines and ages" (Van Eck, 2006). Many studies have concluded that games are effective tools for teaching hard and complex procedures, and "could help address one of the nation's most pressing needs—strengthening our system of education and preparing workers for 21st century jobs" (Charles & McAlister, 2004; Federation of American Scientists, 2006; Holland, Jenkins, & Squire, 2002; Sheffield, 2005). The potential is essentially there.

In addition, it's unlikely that every course is going to be appropriate for presentation through a game—at least not yet. Quantitative efforts will probably be the easiest to translate. I doubt we'll be seeing a game-based *Philosophy of Mind* course in the near future, but any subject that features key facts and analyses should be fair game for assessing the student. The reason for this is that multiple-choice tests, essays, and similar forms of student performance are simple enough to replicate in a gaming environment. All we'll really need is to make sure we present the material to students in an engaging manner, and ensure that we have professional teachers working behind the scenes to grade their work—particularly any essays and assessments of higher-order thinking.

Conclusions Abound

So far, I've provided several assertions that, for some, must be old news. Vast arrays of research articles and book chapters have been produced concerning entertainment, education, and the panoply of possibilities for the intersection between the two. At the same time, my steadfast claim that gaming in the classroom is a flawed endeavor may have raised an eyebrow or two. If you take away anything from this chapter, however, I believe it should be this point: It's not about whether games *can* teach—it's *where* they teach that's important. The future of our industries is in the Internet, not the classroom. Consider the advancements made in digital worlds and distance learning over the last few years, and the sheer wealth of opportunities simply boggles the mind.

Assuming it's going to happen (and relatively soon), there are some key points to keep in mind for developers and educators alike. First of all, educators should not fear for their livelihood. Teachers' jobs aren't going anywhere, though the location they teach *from* might be in for a change. Assume that course-based gaming will become a viable substitution for brick-and-mortar classes. Such a shift will necessitate having a wealth of behind-the-scenes educators grading, monitoring, and helping students through the game interface.

This leads to another implication for game developers: Your games are going to require a *great deal* more development beyond what the student will see on the screen. You will also need to create a full-fledged network infrastructure and teacher dashboard on the backend to allow educators to view and affect the performance of their students. Basically, every course-based game you undertake will be serving two masters: the player and the instructor.

I've already mentioned several times just how important collaboration between educators and developers will be in the creation of a successful course-based game, but it bears reiteration one last time. Both sides *must* create common cause, and form an in-depth understanding of the processes they each go through to accomplish their goals. Educators need to know the strengths and limitations of the game development process, just as game designers need to appreciate the challenges and techniques behind implementing and reinforcing pedagogical practices and coursework.

It's all coming—and soon. The future of video games and education is around us, here and now, its potential just waiting to be tapped. No matter what you may think of video games right this moment, the simple truth is that they are changing at an incredible pace—to assume that they will forever remain little more than sources of entertainment is to hold fast to a premillennial perspective. Their integration into every facet of modern culture has occurred surprisingly smoothly and rapidly, all things considered. With this in mind, we must all plan accordingly; "interactive entertainment" will not just mean "games" for very long, and when that paradigm shifts, we need to be prepared to participate.

References

Allen, I. E., & Seaman, J. (2007). *Online nation: Five years of growth in online learning*. Needham, MA: Sloan Consortium.

Bartley, S. J., & Golek, J. H. (2004). Evaluating the cost effectiveness of online and face-to-face instruction. *Educational Technology & Society, 7*(4), 167–75.

Charles, D., & McAlister, M. (2004). Integrating ideas about invisible playgrounds from play theory into online educational digital games. In *Lecture Notes in Computer Science Series, Vol. 3166: Entertainment Computing—ICEC 2004* (pp. 598–601). Heidelberg, Germany: Springer Berlin. Retrieved from www.springerlink.com/content/qea4e988k00ugny9/

Federation of American Scientists (2006). *Harnessing the power of video games for learning*. (Summit on Educational Games, 2006). Retrieved from www.fas.org/gamesummit

Hirumi, A., & Stapleton, C. (2008). Integrating fundamental ID tasks with game development processes to optimize game-based learning. In C. Miller (Ed.), *Games: Their purpose and potential in education* (pp. 127–62). New York, NY: Springer.

Hirumi, A., & Stapleton, C. (in press). Climbing Jacob's ladder to optimize game-based learning. In M. Shaughnessy (Ed). *Pedagogical implications for online instruction*.

Holland, W., Jenkins, H., & Squire, K. (2002). Theory by design. In B. Perron and M. Wolf (Eds.), *Video game theory* (pp. 25–46). New York, NY: Routledge.

LeFevre, A. (2008). *Report card on American education: A state-by-state analysis, 1985–1986 to 2006–2007* (ALEC 2007 Edition). Washington, D.C.: American Legislative Exchange Council.

Levine, J. (2008). *Gaming and libraries update: Broadening the intersections.* Chicago, IL: American Library Association.

Moore, G. E. (1995). Lithography and the Future of Moore's Law. In Timothy Brunner (Ed.), *Optical/Laser Microlithography VIII: Proceedings of SPIE, 2440,* 2–17.

Offner, J. (2008, May). *'Grand Theft Auto' gets away with half a billion dollars.* Retrieved from www.ecommercetimes.com/story/62911.html

Phillips, V. (2008). *Are online degrees really as good as their campus counterparts?* Retrieved June 6, 2007, from www.geteducated.com/surveys/publicacct.asp

Sheffield, B. (2005, November). What games have to teach us: An interview with James Paul Gee. *Game Developer, 12*(10), 4–9.

Van Eck, R. (2006). Digital game-based learning: It's not just the digital natives who are restless. *EDUCAUSE Review, 41*(2), 16–30. Retrieved from http://net.educause.edu/ir/library/pdf/ERM0620.pdf

National Educational Technology Standards

National Educational Technology Standards for Students (NETS•S)

All K–12 students should be prepared to meet the following standards and performance indicators.

1. **Creativity and Innovation**

   Students demonstrate creative thinking, construct knowledge, and develop innovative products and processes using technology. Students:

   a. apply existing knowledge to generate new ideas, products, or processes

   b. create original works as a means of personal or group expression

   c. use models and simulations to explore complex systems and issues

   d. identify trends and forecast possibilities

2. **Communication and Collaboration**

   Students use digital media and environments to communicate and work collaboratively, including at a distance, to support individual learning and contribute to the learning of others. Students:

   a. interact, collaborate, and publish with peers, experts, or others employing a variety of digital environments and media

   b. communicate information and ideas effectively to multiple audiences using a variety of media and formats

   c. develop cultural understanding and global awareness by engaging with learners of other cultures

   d. contribute to project teams to produce original works or solve problems

3. Research and Information Fluency

Students apply digital tools to gather, evaluate, and use information. Students:

    a. plan strategies to guide inquiry

    b. locate, organize, analyze, evaluate, synthesize, and ethically use information from a variety of sources and media

    c. evaluate and select information sources and digital tools based on the appropriateness to specific tasks

    d. process data and report results

4. Critical Thinking, Problem Solving, and Decision Making

Students use critical-thinking skills to plan and conduct research, manage projects, solve problems, and make informed decisions using appropriate digital tools and resources. Students:

    a. identify and define authentic problems and significant questions for investigation

    b. plan and manage activities to develop a solution or complete a project

    c. collect and analyze data to identify solutions and make informed decisions

    d. use multiple processes and diverse perspectives to explore alternative solutions

5. Digital Citizenship

Students understand human, cultural, and societal issues related to technology and practice legal and ethical behavior. Students:

    a. advocate and practice the safe, legal, and responsible use of information and technology

    b. exhibit a positive attitude toward using technology that supports collaboration, learning, and productivity

    c. demonstrate personal responsibility for lifelong learning

    d. exhibit leadership for digital citizenship

6. Technology Operations and Concepts

Students demonstrate a sound understanding of technology concepts, systems, and operations. Students:

    a. understand and use technology systems

    b. select and use applications effectively and productively

    c. troubleshoot systems and applications

    d. transfer current knowledge to the learning of new technologies

National Educational Technology Standards for Teachers (NETS•T)

All classroom teachers should be prepared to meet the following standards and performance indicators.

1. **Facilitate and Inspire Student Learning and Creativity**

   Teachers use their knowledge of subject matter, teaching and learning, and technology to facilitate experiences that advance student learning, creativity, and innovation in both face-to-face and virtual environments. Teachers:

   a. promote, support, and model creative and innovative thinking and inventiveness

   b. engage students in exploring real-world issues and solving authentic problems using digital tools and resources

   c. promote student reflection using collaborative tools to reveal and clarify students' conceptual understanding and thinking, planning, and creative processes

   d. model collaborative knowledge construction by engaging in learning with students, colleagues, and others in face-to-face and virtual environments

2. **Design and Develop Digital-Age Learning Experiences and Assessments**

   Teachers design, develop, and evaluate authentic learning experiences and assessments incorporating contemporary tools and resources to maximize content learning in context and to develop the knowledge, skills, and attitudes identified in the NETS•S. Teachers:

   a. design or adapt relevant learning experiences that incorporate digital tools and resources to promote student learning and creativity

   b. develop technology-enriched learning environments that enable all students to pursue their individual curiosities and become active participants in setting their own educational goals, managing their own learning, and assessing their own progress

   c. customize and personalize learning activities to address students' diverse learning styles, working strategies, and abilities using digital tools and resources

   d. provide students with multiple and varied formative and summative assessments aligned with content and technology standards and use resulting data to inform learning and teaching

3. **Model Digital-Age Work and Learning**

   Teachers exhibit knowledge, skills, and work processes representative of an innovative professional in a global and digital society. Teachers:

   a. demonstrate fluency in technology systems and the transfer of current knowledge to new technologies and situations

   b. collaborate with students, peers, parents, and community members using digital tools and resources to support student success and innovation

   c. communicate relevant information and ideas effectively to students, parents, and peers using a variety of digital-age media and formats

   d. model and facilitate effective use of current and emerging digital tools to locate, analyze, evaluate, and use information resources to support research and learning

4. Promote and Model Digital Citizenship and Responsibility

Teachers understand local and global societal issues and responsibilities in an evolving digital culture and exhibit legal and ethical behavior in their professional practices. Teachers:

   a. advocate, model, and teach safe, legal, and ethical use of digital information and technology, including respect for copyright, intellectual property, and the appropriate documentation of sources

   b. address the diverse needs of all learners by using learner-centered strategies and providing equitable access to appropriate digital tools and resources

   c. promote and model digital etiquette and responsible social interactions related to the use of technology and information

   d. develop and model cultural understanding and global awareness by engaging with colleagues and students of other cultures using digital-age communication and collaboration tools

5. Engage in Professional Growth and Leadership

Teachers continuously improve their professional practice, model lifelong learning, and exhibit leadership in their school and professional community by promoting and demonstrating the effective use of digital tools and resources. Teachers:

   a. participate in local and global learning communities to explore creative applications of technology to improve student learning

   b. exhibit leadership by demonstrating a vision of technology infusion, participating in shared decision making and community building, and developing the leadership and technology skills of others

   c. evaluate and reflect on current research and professional practice on a regular basis to make effective use of existing and emerging digital tools and resources in support of student learning

   d. contribute to the effectiveness, vitality, and self-renewal of the teaching profession and of their school and community

Index

Connect Theory to Practice

ISTE journals help you make the connection.

- Stay on top of current trends and challenges in educational technology
- Apply specific, research-based applications
- Discover a forum for sharing research and developments

My professional growth is enhanced by access to outstanding educational technology innovators, leaders, and resources I find in ISTE's publications and website.

—Karen M. Ortiz
Technology Integration Coach
Member since 2000

Journal of Research on Technology in Education

ISTE's *Journal of Research on Technology in Education* (*JRTE*) features the most relevant ed tech research from around the globe. This peer-reviewed journal covers topics ranging from original research to theoretical positions and systems analysis. *JRTE*, highly respected for examining and exploring the future horizons of technology developments, is published quarterly. www.iste.org/JRTE

4 times a year	1 year	2 years	3 years
Nonmember	$155	$295	$430
Member	$54	$108	$162

Journal of Digital Learning in Teacher Education

The *Journal of Digital Learning in Teacher Education* (*JDLTE*) is a refereed journal published in partnership with ISTE's Special Interest Group for Teacher Educators (SIGTE). The journal provides a forum for sharing information among departments, schools, and colleges of education that are confronting the issues associated with providing computer and technology education for preservice and inservice teachers. *JDLTE*, formerly the *Journal of Computing in Teacher Education*), is published quarterly. www.iste.org/JDLTE

4 times a year	1 year	2 years	3 years
Nonmember	$122	$224	$325
Member	$32	$64	$96

To order, visit **www.iste.org/publications**

Related Titles from ISTE

Considerations on Technology and Teachers: The Best of *JRTE*

Edited by Lynne Schrum

ISTE Member Price $24.45
Nonmember Price $34.95

Research offers a way to start conversations that can affect educational reform. *Considerations on Technology and Teachers* is a collection of the best research articles from the *Journal of Research on Technology in Education* (*JRTE*) over the past five years. *JRTE* editor Lynne Schrum and the editorial review board chose these articles because they provide context about where we have been and how we should be moving forward, both in research and in practice. At the conclusion of each article, the original authors reflect on their study, examine the landscape since their research was published, and provide suggestions for further study.

Web 2.0: New Tools, New Schools

By Gwen Solomon and Lynne Schrum

ISTE Member Price $24.45
Nonmember Price $34.95

"A good read for those without any knowledge of Web 2.0 as well as experienced users."

— *District Administration*

Web 2.0: New Tools, New Schools provides a comprehensive overview of the emerging Web 2.0 technologies and their use in the classroom and in professional development. Topics include blogging as a natural tool for writing instruction, wikis and their role in project collaboration, podcasting as a useful means of presenting information and ideas, and Web 2.0 tools for professional development. Also included are a discussion about Web 2.0 safety and security issues and the future of the Web 2.0 movement. *Web 2.0: New Tools, New Schools* is essential reading for teachers, administrators, technology coordinators, and teacher educators.

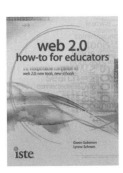

Web 2.0 How-To for Educators

By Gwen Solomon and Lynne Schrum

ISTE Member Price $24.45
Nonmember Price $34.95

In this companion book, the authors of the best-selling *Web 2.0: New Tools, New Schools* introduce you to more Web 2.0 tools and expertly lead you through classroom and professional applications that help improve student and teacher learning. The book explores the very best online collaborative tools available today (including blogs, wikis, and social networking) and Web 2.0 applications (Skype, Google Earth, Wordle, and more) that make a difference in education. Using a simple formula for each concept, the book describes what the tool is, when you should use it, why it is useful, who is using it, how you can use the tool, and where you can find additional resources. This book is a valuable resource for any educator wanting to integrate Web 2.0 technology.

NETS Booklets for students, teachers, and administrators

ISTE Member Price $9.05 each
Nonmember Price $12.95 each

ISTE pioneered the development of technology standards more than 10 years ago in a unique partnership with teachers and teacher educators, curriculum and education associations, government, business, and private foundations. The standards have been recently updated and released. These full-color booklets include the refreshed text of the NETS•S, NETS•T, and NETS•A as well as profiles, rubrics, scenarios, and performance indicators.

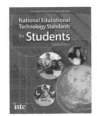  

The booklets are also available as a bundle for just $25.25 to ISTE members ($34.95 for nonmembers).

Find these books and more in the ISTE Store under Books & Courseware. **www.iste.org/bookstore**